The COMPLETE OPERAS of VERDI

The
COMPLETE
OPERAS *of*
VERDI

CHARLES OSBORNE

ALFRED A. KNOPF
New York   1979

THIS IS A BORZOI BOOK
PUBLISHED BY ALFRED A. KNOPF, INC.

Published January 22, 1970
Reprinted Once
Third Printing, August 1979

Library of Congress Catalog Card Number: 78-79352

Manufactured in the United States of America

To

MAX OLDAKER

"*Amici in vita e morte*"

(*La forza del destino*)

Contents

The COMPLETE OPERAS *of* VERDI

Introduction

I am an arrogant and impatient listener; but in the case of a few composers, a very few, when I hear a work I do not like I am convinced it is my own fault. Verdi is one of these composers.

Benjamin Britten[1]

THE COMPOSER TO whom Britten pays such graceful homage, whether in the above quotation or in his music, from the *Otello*-influenced *Peter Grimes* to the affectionate parody of Bottom's aria in *A Midsummer Night's Dream*, a composer in whom Bernard Shaw admired "the relevance of every bar of his mature scores to the dramatic situation", whose instrumentation, harmony and part-writing Stravinsky has been moved to praise, and whose operas are universally popular, has come a long way since those days only a generation or two ago when he and the whole of nineteenth-century Italian opera were considered to be beyond the musical pale. Verdian biography has come a long way, too. Today the facts of Verdi's life are reasonably well known. In addition to Frank Walker's *The Man Verdi*, a truly magnificent series of notes for an unwritten biography, there are other excellent lives including those by the conventional Carlo Gatti and the eccentric Vincent Sheean. But, since Francis Toye's pioneer work of forty years ago, there has not been in any language a full-length study of the operas themselves. That is why I have written this book.

Toye's *Verdi* was published at a time when it was still not considered musically respectable to enjoy or even seriously to consider the operas of Verdi. A revival of interest in Austria and Germany, due largely to the efforts of Franz Werfel, was just getting under way, but, even so, fewer than a third of the operas were generally available in performance. Toye understandably concentrated on proselytising for the later and greater works, in order to gain acceptance for which he tended, in my view, to underestimate, certainly to refrain from advancing the claims of, several very fine works among the earlier operas. To these earlier works he devoted proportionately little space and attention.

Although today Verdi is hardly in need of promotion, indeed

[1] *Opera*, February, 1951, p. 115.

precisely because what used to be thought of as his more obscure operas
are now not infrequently to be encountered in stage performance, I
have thought it useful to consider all the operas in some detail, in order
not only to trace Verdi's development throughout his incredibly long
and productive creative life, but also to explore the similarities as well
as the differences between the earlier and the later works. I have
also investigated the literary or theatrical sources of Verdi's libretti,
and something of the background to each opera. And not only the
operas: Verdi was predominantly a musical dramatist, but his *œuvre*
included choral works other than the Requiem, as well as more than
twenty songs and a String Quartet, all of which are included in this
survey.

In order to relate the works to the milieu from which they emerged,
I have embedded discussion of them into a biographical narrative. I
must emphasise, however, that my intention has been to concentrate
on the operas. In general, I have included only as much biography as
seemed necessary to place each work in its context. Although this is a
study of the operas Verdi wrote, rather than those he might have written
or intended to write, I found it impossible to restrain myself from discussing *Rocester*, an opera which, if it exists, is missing, and *Il re Lear*,
an opera which Verdi seriously considered composing at several times
throughout his career. A discussion of the *Rocester* problem will be
found in the chapter on *Oberto*, and an account of Verdi's attempts to
grapple with *Lear* is included in the chapter on *Ernani*.

To study an opera, particularly a Verdi opera, only in score is to
have no clear idea of its value as a piece of musical theatre. Forty, even
twenty years ago, it was not possible to have seen the majority of Verdi's
operas on the stage, but now the situation has changed: I did not begin
to write this study until I had seen every one of the operas staged in,
amongst other places, Milan, Vienna, Salzburg, Berlin, Leipzig, Rome,
Venice, New York, Melbourne, Moscow, Covent Garden, Glyndebourne, St Pancras and Parma.

Verdi's incredible achievement was that, over a period of nearly sixty
years, he led Italian opera from relative Donizettian innocence to
post-Wagnerian wisdom. And he conducted this humanising process
entirely alone. A born man of the theatre, he created an operatic
language in which the drama is carried by, yet gives form to, the
melody. In this he shows himself to be as much a revolutionary as
Wagner. He differs considerably, however, from his great German
contemporary (they were born in the same year) in his breadth of
sympathy and his artistic discretion and judgment. In the greatness of
his vision, Verdi's affinities are not with Wagner but with Mozart and
Shakespeare. With Mozart he also shares a melodic fecundity, with
Shakespeare a renaissance humanistic philosophy, and, with both, that

unsimulatable compassion for mankind which, though it may be felt by many, only the very greatest artists seem able instinctively and unconsciously to infuse into their creations. If Verdi's music contains an implicit message, it is Terence's "Humani nil a me alienum puto."

The sources I have consulted in writing this book will be readily discovered from the bibliography at the end of the volume, where full details will be found of any books mentioned in footnotes. Wherever I have wanted to be certain the reader understood the sense of quotations in a foreign language, I have added an English translation. But, in the case of titles, opening lines of arias and the like, I have refrained from doing so: the single translated phrase can, out of context, too easily sound absurd. I wish to thank my friend Michael Levey for much assistance with the interpretation or translation of Italian. I fear he may not thank *me* for freely acknowledging that the translation of several lines of doggerel on pages 123 and 124 is entirely his. Other translations from French, German and Italian are my own, except for the three letters taken from Walker. My thanks are also due to Mr Harold Rosenthal for information and Mr Kenneth Thomson for advice.

C. O.

I

Oberto, Conte di San Bonifacio

Dramatis personae:

Cuniza, sister of Ezzelino of Romano   (mezzo-soprano)
Riccardo, Count of Salinguerra   (tenor)
Oberto, Count of San Bonifacio   (bass)
Leonora, his daughter   (soprano)
Imelda, Cuniza's confidante   (mezzo-soprano)

LIBRETTO by Antonio Piazza and Temistocle Solera

TIME: 1228
PLACE: Ezzelino's castle, near Bassano

FIRST PERFORMED at La Scala, Milan, November 17, 1839, with
Antonietta Marini (Leonora); Maria Shaw (Cuniza); Marietta Sacchi
(Imelda); Lorenzo Salvi (Riccardo); Ignazio Marini (Oberto)

Oberto, Conte di San Bonifacio

I

GIUSEPPE VERDI WAS twenty-six years old when his opera *Oberto* was first performed at La Scala, Milan. The son of illiterate peasants who ran the local tavern and grocery store, he was born on October 10, 1813 in the village of Le Roncole, about three miles from the small town of Busseto in the Duchy of Parma. His beginnings were as humble as they could be, and his childhood, as he himself attested in later life, was hard. The countryside in which he grew up was continually being fought over by France and Austria: the united Kingdom of Italy did not then exist, and the various small kingdoms and dukedoms were at the mercy of the belligerent European powers. When Verdi was born, Parma was in the hands of the French, and so he was christened in French, Joseph Fortunin François. A year later, Russian forces chased the French out. The story of the peasant woman Luigia Verdi who had the intelligence to hide up in the belfry of the church with her infant son when a band of marauders swept through the town, plundering and killing, is found in all the biographies of the composer.

As a boy he was lonely and shy. He took early and naturally to music, was fascinated by the itinerant musicians he heard in Le Roncole, and by the church organ. Another often-repeated anecdote tells how, serving as an acolyte at mass, he became lost in the sound of the music, neglected some ritual act or other, and came to only when an over-emphatic nudge from the priest sent him reeling down the altar steps.

His father bought Giuseppe an old, broken-down spinet which a neighbour repaired for him, and on which the lad began to learn the rudiments of music. Verdi retained in later life a sentimental affection for this instrument, and never parted with it. He was given lessons by the organist of the village church: by the time he was twelve he himself had become the village organist. His father was sympathetic enough to realise that the boy now needed tuition of a higher standard than could be found in Le Roncole, and sent him to live in the nearby town of Busseto where he could learn music as part of the school curriculum. Busseto possessed a military band and an enthusiastic amateur Philharmonic Society, so the lad was able to hear a certain amount of music. Every Sunday, he walked to and from Le Roncole to play the organ in the village church.

At Busseto, Giuseppe attracted the interest of Antonio Barezzi, a successful merchant and amateur musician, president of the Philharmonic Society. The boy was badly in need of quasi-parental affection in Busseto, and soon became a close friend of the Barezzi family. Antonio Barezzi taught him to play several wind instruments, including the serpent; soon he became a lodger in Barezzi's house. Now in his early teens, he had already instinctively broken away from his own class, from his peasant origins; and although he was never ashamed of the class he came from, he accepted with an easy confidence the fact that he was different from his parents and the villagers in his concerns and his abilities. Music was his life. He was now having lessons from Ferdinando Provesi, head of the local music school and organist at the cathedral, to the annoyance of the priest Seletti who was Verdi's teacher at the grammar school. Seletti complained that Verdi was devoting too much of his energy to music, but in time it became obvious to him that the boy was destined for a musical career, and he ceased to be obstructive.

By the time he was fifteen, Verdi had begun to compose songs and orchestral pieces for performances by the Philharmonic Society or the town band. When a visiting opera company performed Rossini's *Il barbiere di Siviglia*, Verdi wrote a new overture for it, which was played with great success. His cantata, *I deliri di Saul*, composed at this time, was described by Barezzi as showing "a vivid imagination, a philosophical outlook and sound judgment in the arrangement of the instrumental parts". It received several performances in Busseto and the surrounding district, but it was never published. Verdi in later years took care to suppress all of his juvenilia.

After the sixteen-year-old youth had unsuccessfully applied for the post of organist at the nearby village of Soragna, his benefactor Barezzi began to realise that there was no real future for the boy locally, and that his talents were too rare to be allowed to stultify. He decided that Giuseppe should be sent to Milan to study at the Conservatorium. At his instigation, Giuseppe's father Carlo Verdi applied to the Monte di Pietà e d'Abbondanza, a charitable institution which offered grants towards the education of poor children. The application was successful, but provided only part of the money required to support the boy in Milan while he was a student. Barezzi himself advanced the remainder. So Verdi went to Milan and presented himself at the Conservatorium for examination and interview. The board of examiners rejected him: he was four years older than the official age-limit of fourteen, his piano technique was irregular or was of a kind not approved by the Conservatorium, and no doubt the boy was awkward and did not interview impressively. Nevertheless, although he was refused admission to the Conservatorium, he had impressed the Board whose private notes of the examination describe him as being exceptionally talented and showing promise of becoming a good composer. Politics were perhaps involved in the rejection. To the Milanese, a foreigner from Parma would not have especially commended himself. Whatever the cause, Verdi took the setback very hard. Years later, when the Conservatorium wanted to re-name itself after him, his only comment was: "They wouldn't have me young, they can't have me old."

One of the examiners, Alessandro Rollo, a conductor at La Scala, advised Verdi to study privately with Vincenzo Lavigna, La Scala's chief conductor and a first-rate teacher. Verdi accepted this advice, and studied in Milan under Lavigna for two years. He was a brilliant student, quickly mastered the intricacies of harmony, counterpoint and fugue, and began to compose works which he sent back to Busseto for performance. In Milan, he conducted at short notice a rehearsal of Haydn's *The Creation*, so successfully that he was invited to conduct the performance as well, a performance which had to be repeated twice, the second repeat being a command performance at the residence of the Austrian Governor.

As a consequence of this highly promising activity, the young Verdi received his first important commission: to write an opera for the Teatro Filodrammatico in Milan. The opera, *Rocester*, was not performed. It may not even have been completed. There is a possibility that it never existed, and that the opera on which the young composer began to work early in 1836, and which he claimed in mid-September to have almost finished, was the one eventually produced in 1839 at La Scala as his first, *Oberto*.

We are concerned in this study of Verdi's operas with those he wrote rather than those he might have written, but the *Rocester* problem is a teasing one and sufficiently interesting to be considered here. Writers on Verdi are divided on the subject. Gatti and Toye incline to the belief that *Rocester* was reworked into *Oberto*. Frank Walker leaves the question open, but favours the suggestion that there were two separate operas. The four-volume biography by Abbiati quotes a little-known letter of 1871 from Verdi to Emilio Seletti, the son of an old friend, in which he refers to *Oberto* being based on a libretto by Antonio Piazza, called *Lord Hamilton*.[1] Abbiati thinks *Lord Hamilton* had its title changed to *Rocester* before ending up as *Oberto*. This is possible. But the letters and reminiscences of Verdi in middle age are unreliable testimony. He is known to have remembered inaccurately such important and affecting events of his youth as the deaths of his first wife and two children. We must arrive at a decision about *Rocester* aided only by Verdi's letters of the time, and by the letters of others.

It is a fact that Verdi wrote an opera in 1836. As early as July 28, 1835, he had written to Pietro Massini, the Director of the Teatro Filodrammatico: ". . . by the time you return to Milan, I hope to

[1] Abbiati, Vol. I, p. 326. The letter is in the Museo Teatrale alla Scala, Milan.

have sketched out all the pieces."[1] He went on to ask for information about the types of voices available. The opera was completed in 1836. This, as well as being true, makes sense. Verdi may not have possessed the manic fecundity of Donizetti, but he certainly never took three or four years to write one of his early or middle-period operas. Toye's suggestion that the composer may have taken a long time over *Oberto* because he had not yet acquired "the fluency characteristic of his later years" simply does not ring psychologically true. Verdi in his youth wrote quickly and easily.

An opera, then, was completed by the autumn of 1836, and there was a possibility of its being performed at the theatre in Parma. In a letter to Massini of September 21, 1837, Verdi mentioned the opera by name: "It is not unlikely that I shall be able to put the opera *Rocester* on the stage at Parma this Carnival. . . . If Piazza wishes to alter the verses here and there, we are still in time, and I do indeed beg him to prolong the duet for the two women, to make it a more grandiose piece."[2] This letter is a significant piece of evidence: although there are two women in *Oberto*, as there are in most operas, they do not have a duet but merely a few lines of dialogue together in recitative. Is it likely that, having wanted a duet extended, the composer would instead delete it from his finished score?

Giuseppe Demaldè in his *Cenni biografici*[3] mentions that Verdi completed *Rocester* in the spring of 1838, and continues: "It seems, however, that the librettist objected to the verses and opposed a production on the grounds that in the autumn of 1839 *Oberto* was being produced at La Scala." Here is more evidence from a contemporary source. Demaldè was a friend of Verdi in his Busseto years, and was at one time the treasurer of the Monte di Pietà which had helped the young composer. His statement that the opera was completed in the spring of 1838 admittedly conflicts somewhat with Verdi's letter of the previous September asserting that the opera was virtually finished.

The conclusion most frequently arrived at by writers on Verdi that *Rocester* was merely an earlier draft of *Oberto* is not supported by the condition of the manuscript score of *Oberto* now in the Ricordi archives. Although, like many another Verdi score, it is an untidy and much worked-over manuscript with a great deal of alteration and substitution, there are no changes in the names of characters or in details of plot. It clearly began life as *Oberto*. If Verdi's letter of 1871, dragging in the red herring of *Lord Hamilton*, is to be considered at all, it ought surely to be read as confirmation that, if *Oberto* was based on an earlier work, it was certainly not *Rocester*. Until further evidence comes to light, it seems most likely that an opera called *Rocester* was written to a libretto by Piazza, remained unproduced, and is at present lost. *Oberto* is most

---

[1] Walker, *The Man Verdi*, p. 25.   [2] Walker; *The Man Verdi*, p. 26.
[3] Unpublished MS. in the possession of the Monte di Credito su Pegno, Busseto.

probably not a musical revision of an existing work, though its libretto may conceivably have been, as Verdi thought he remembered thirty-five years later in his letter to Seletti, "altered and added to by Solera, on the basis of a libretto entitled *Lord Hamilton* by Antonio Piazza".

The questions to be asked are:

(*a*) Could there be a connection between the names of Lord Hamilton and Rocester?

(*b*) Who or what was Rocester? Alas, not the character in Charlotte Brontë's *Jane Eyre* which was not published until 1847.

(*c*) Is there anything in the fact that Piazza, the librettist of *Oberto* (? and of *Lord Hamilton*), wrote a story ten years later which involved the composer Pergolesi and the daughter of a British ambassador? (On the basis of this, Frank Walker maintains that Piazza "appears to have had a predeliction for fantasies about the British aristocracy".)[1]

(*d*) Could Piazza's *Rocester* libretto have been a story of the licentious court of Charles II and the libertine poet and philosopher John Wilmot, second Earl of Rochester, who had been a student at the University of Padua? Rochester was said to have been the man on whom the character of the hero Dorimant in Etherege's play *Sir Fopling Flutter, or The Man of Mode* was based. Would Piazza, with his penchant for the English nobility, have known of him or of Etherege? Dr Johnson said that Rochester had "blazed out his youth and health in lavish voluptuousness". He *could* have made a Verdi hero.

(*e*) Did Verdi know a play called *Rochester*, by Antier and Nézel, which was first performed in Paris in 1829? It is said to have been a *réchauffé* of an earlier play, *La Jeunesse de Richelieu ou le Lovelace français*, and to be very similar to Dumas' *Kean*. Verdi was later to consider *Kean* as an operatic subject. In Paris, the actor Frédérick Lemaître played both Kean and Rochester.

(*f*) What are the three or four operas of Emanuele Muzio, Verdi's pupil and disciple like? Probably very much after Verdi. Would one of them offer a clue?

(*g*) Could some of the arias, duets and choruses by Verdi which were performed at concerts of the Busseto Philharmonic Society in 1837 and 1838, some programmes of which are to be found in the Civic Museum at Busseto, possibly have been excerpts from the by-then discarded opera, *Rocester*? This music was, presumbly, destroyed after Verdi's death, if not before.

To return from speculation to fact, in 1836 the twenty-three-year-old Verdi had married Margherita, the daughter of his benefactor Barezzi. He had returned to Busseto to apply for the post of cathedral

[1] *The Man Verdi*, p. 29.

organist, but the ecclesiastical authorities appointed another candidate. This almost caused civil war in Busseto, as the town divided itself into pro- and anti-Verdi factions. Finally, the post became Verdi's. By this time, however, he had written one or perhaps two operas, and he was yearning to be back in Milan.

II

Oberto was written in Busseto in the winter of 1837–8 to a libretto originally provided by the Milanese journalist Antonio Piazza. Massini was no longer the Director of the Filodrammatico, but he used his influence to persuade Bartolomeo Merelli, the impresario of La Scala, to produce the opera for a charity performance in the spring of 1839. A cast was chosen, and rehearsals commenced, but the illness of the tenor Napoleone Moriani led to the entire enterprise being abandoned. It was very largely due to the efforts of Giuseppina Strepponi, who was to have sung the leading soprano role, that Merelli agreed to schedule the opera for performance in the autumn season of the same year. Strepponi, a popular Milan soprano, was at this time Merelli's mistress. It is fascinating, and rather touching, that she should have been instrumental in getting Verdi's *Oberto* put on to the stage, for some years later she and he were to become lovers and to live together for twelve years before marrying and growing old together. She was still by his side at the first night of *Falstaff* fifty-four years after the première of *Oberto*. Verdi had, of course, frequently heard her sing in Milan, before the abortive rehearsals of *Oberto* began, and considered her an excellent artist. Unfortunately, when the performances of *Oberto* were postponed for several months, Strepponi was unable to take part in the eventual première. During those months Verdi made some alterations to his score, modifying the tessitura in places. He added one number, the quartet, the dramatic situation of which was suggested by Merelli, the actual words being provided by Temistocle Solera who had edited and revised Piazza's original draft before the composer had begun working on it, and who, as a good professional working librettist, no doubt expected to have to stand by during rehearsals to alter, to adapt and add when called on to do so.

Solera, who at this time was barely twenty, had already led an adventurous life. When his father had been imprisoned for political activities, he had been sent to school in Vienna. He ran away from school and did several odd jobs before being picked up by the police in Hungary. By 1838 he was back in Milan earning a precarious living as both poet and composer. His own opera, *Ildegonda*, was produced at La Scala some months after *Oberto*, but how much of the words and music he published was really his own is open to question. More than one charge of plagiarism has been proved against him.

The libretto of *Oberto* is not a particularly distinguished one. In fact, at moments it is downright silly. But before pouring scorn on the librettists who served Italian composers in the nineteenth century one ought to remember to relate their libretti to the spoken drama of the time. The plays which reached the stage are for the most part as foolish, inanely motivated, badly constructed and sloppily versified as the worst of the hastily put together libretti. Frequently, of course, they are written by the same men. It is only from a background of considerably improved conditions in the theatre nearly half a century later that a talent like Boito's is able to emerge. The Milanese theatrical and literary scene in the 1830s consisted largely of figures like Piazza and Solera. In an article on Verdi's librettists,[1] the American critic William Weaver supports this contention:

> The hit plays of Verdi's time—in the long theatrical gap between Alfieri and Pirandello—are unreadable: bombastic, long-winded, artificial, they seem librettos with the notes missing. Piave, Cammarano, Somma, the maligned librettists, were no worse than most of their now forgotten contemporaries, and even the great Manzoni, when he turned to the theatre and wrote *Adelchi*, created a fairly turgid piece (though it is officially regarded in Italy as a classic).

By the time *Oberto* was staged, Verdi had had his first taste of personal and domestic tragedy. His wife Margherita had produced two children, a girl, Virginia, in 1837, and a boy, Icilio, in 1838. A month after the boy was born, the girl died. Fifteen months later, a few weeks before the première of *Oberto*, the boy also died. In these same years, Verdi's first published works appeared: an album of six songs in 1838, and two songs and a trio with flute obbligato in 1839 (see pp. 454–6).

When *Oberto* finally reached the stage of La Scala, on November 17, 1839, the singers were Ignazio Marini (Oberto), Antonietta Marini (Leonora), Lorenzo Salvi (Riccardo), Maria Shaw, an English mezzosoprano (Cuniza) and Marietta Sacchi (Imelda). The opera was warmly received, was performed fourteen times during the autumn season, and was bought for publication by the firm of Ricordi whose fortunes were to become closely entwined with Verdi's for the remainder of the century. The Scala impresario, Merelli, immediately put Verdi under contract to compose three more operas over a period of two years, for production in Milan and Vienna. Critical reaction to *Oberto* was favourable, though the influence of Bellini was discerned, and there were complaints about the weakness of the libretto. On the whole, it was a real success for the composer and an encouragement for the future. Other Italian theatres asked for *Oberto*, and in the following two seasons it was performed in Turin, Genoa and Naples.

[1] In *High Fidelity*, October 1963.

III

Oberto, Conte di San Bonifacio is in two acts, which take place in Bassano at Ezzelino's castle and its surroundings. The time is given precisely as the year 1228. Ezzelino da Romano himself never appears. His sister Cuniza is engaged to be married to Riccardo, Count of Salinguerra, and in the opening scene of the opera a party of courtiers and servants has gathered in what the libretto calls "deliziosa cam- pagna" to meet Riccardo. The castle can be glimpsed in the distance. A chorus of welcome is sung, and Riccardo enters, expressing his joyful anticipation of nuptial bliss. The courtiers bear him off to the castle, and, when they have gone, Leonora enters. Her recitative and cavatina reveal that she has been seduced by Riccardo, and that she now seeks vengeance. She is almost Donna Elvira-like in the violence of her feelings and, as we shall discover, in the ambivalence of her attitude to the lover who has discarded her. Her father, Oberto, the exiled Count of Bonifacio who had disowned her, now appears upon the scene. He sings of his joy at being back in his own beloved country, and of his desire for vengeance on the man who has betrayed his daughter. He suddenly hears Leonora's voice bewailing the fact that the wedding of Riccardo and Cuniza is to be celebrated that evening. Leonora and he meet, and at first he will have nothing to do with her. "Take care," he says. "On my brow you see the marks of sorrow which have been imprinted there by your lewdness." ("Guardami! Sul mio ciglio vedi del duol le impronte, nell' impudica fronte sculto il terror ti sta.") She has disgraced the family honour, and she is no longer his child. But when she reveals to her father that she now desires only to be avenged on her ex-lover, and invokes the tears of her mother in heaven, he finally relents and blesses his daughter. Together they depart towards the castle.

The second scene takes place in a magnificent hall in Ezzelino's castle. The chorus, led by Imelda, Cuniza's confidante, sings its greetings to the happy couple. Cuniza dismisses them, and she and Riccardo sing of their love, though she is beset by a certain foreboding ("Questa gioia che il petto m'inonda è commista a un arcano timor") which he urges her to dispel in the brightness of the new day which dawns for them both. They go out together, and Imelda enters with Leonora who has asked to see Cuniza. Oberto, with a proper sense of dramatic effect, has adopted a less straight-forward approach. He remains concealed for the time being. Cuniza enters, and Leonora tells her story. Oberto suddenly reveals himself and joins his daughter in warning Cuniza against her betrothed who had sworn his undying love for Leonora, had seduced her and then disappeared. Cuniza is shocked and horrified. Sending Oberto into another room, she calls for Riccardo, and, in front of the assembled guests and courtiers, confronts him with Leonora. Again, at the appropriate moment, Oberto steps forward to confound Riccardo. A huge ensemble brings the act to an end.

The second act is also in two scenes, the first of which takes place in Cuniza's apartment in the castle. Imelda and her attendants commiserate with her, and Cuniza sings of her short-lived happiness. She decides that Riccardo must marry Leonora. The scene changes to a remote corner of the castle gardens where a chorus of cavaliers comments on the situation and then disperses. Oberto enters. He has challenged Riccardo and is awaiting his answer. Having risked death in returning to the land from which he was banished, he is determined on vengeance. The cavaliers return to inform him that he need no longer fear for his life. Cuniza has interceded for him with her brother, and he is now a welcome guest. He thanks the cavaliers, mentioning that presently he will pay his respects to Cuniza, but when they have departed he exclaims: "Salvo! Che importa? Vendetta io vo' " ("Saved? what does that matter? It's vengeance I want"), and reaffirms that his one desire is to spill Riccardo's blood.

Riccardo arrives, but is unwilling to fight a duel with so old a man. He is, however, roused to anger by Oberto's taunts of cowardice, "Vili all' armi, a donne eroi" ("Cowards with arms, heroes with women"). He draws his sword, but is restrained by the sudden appearance of Cuniza and Leonora. In a quartet, he expresses his shame, Leonora her love for him in spite of all that has happened, Cuniza her determination that he shall redeem himself, and Oberto his single-minded obsession with vengeance by bloodshed. Cuniza commands Riccardo to marry Leonora. Oberto, in an aside to him, tells him that unless he is an absolute coward he must merely pretend to accept. Riccardo accepts Oberto's challenge and offers his hand to Leonora. Oberto disappears into the woods to await Riccardo, while the others leave in an opposite direction. Again the cavaliers enter and give their views. A cry is heard from the woods, and they rush off to investigate. Riccardo enters, his sword in his hand. He has killed Oberto and now suffers the most bitter remorse. With the old man's dying groans still echoing in his ears, he prays for forgiveness, and sadly departs.

Cuniza and Imelda enter. Cuniza has had a presentiment that all is still not well, and when the courtiers enter to say they have found the body of Oberto in the woods, she cries, "Ah troppo veri, troppo veri miei presagi" ("My forebodings were too true"). Leonora appears, and her father's death is revealed to her. She cries to heaven to bring her release through death. A messenger arrives with a letter for Cuniza. Riccardo has fled from Italy for ever, and has bequeathed his possessions to Leonora, "come ai di del primo amore" ("as on the day of our first love"). The opera ends with Leonora in despair, and Cuniza, Imelda and the chorus imploring heaven to comfort her.

There is not a great deal one can say for Piazza's rather silly libretto. The verses are those of a hack; the plot, though simple to the point of simple-mindedness, is confusingly laid out and would have benefited from an introductory act showing the Leonora–Riccardo relationship which is all over by the time the curtain rises; and the most interesting dramatic situation is that of the quartet which was suggested by the theatre impresario and for which the words were provided by Solera. It is interesting, however, to note that elements in the characters, their relationships, and the story itself manage somehow to adumbrate themes and situations of which Verdi was to make recurring use in later years. These, as we shall see, are intricately bound up with his musical treatment of them.

IV

If there is little to be said for Piazza's contribution to *Oberto*, there is a great deal to be said for Verdi's. Earlier commentators have either ignored the first two operas, *Oberto* and *Un giorno di regno*, or glossed over them in a few lines. Even Toye devotes no more than two pages each to them, and the usually reliable Kobbé[1] dismisses *Oberto* in one sentence, describing it inaccurately as "a story of the struggle for power in northern Italy in the thirteenth century". *Un giorno di regno* is anything but an artistic failure, and *Oberto* possesses not only the vigour for which it is occasionally faintly praised, but also a Bellinian delicacy, and a wealth of enjoyable and tuneful melody much of which would not disgrace the pages of *Il trovatore*. And I assume that nowadays no eyebrows will be raised at the suggestion that *Il trovatore* is a work of genius.

It is obvious from the very first bars of the overture to *Oberto* that its composer is something out of the ordinary. The scoring, though not complex, is thoroughly assured: the old taunt that, until late in his career, Verdi did not know how to write for the orchestra is patently absurd. He knew exactly what sound he wanted the orchestra to make, and by his mid-twenties he knew how to get it, which is more than can be said for Chopin or even Schumann. As he grew older, what he wanted in the way of orchestral texture grew more complex, and his talent expanded at every step to meet his requirements. In the *Oberto* overture, the instrumental writing is excellent, and the melodic fluency which was never to desert Verdi asserts itself immediately. After the opening nine bars of chords with which the composer is merely expansively claiming the attention of his audience, the overture proper begins with a charming and graceful *andante mosso* in 3/4 time. The tune itself is simple, and Verdi has yet to acquire his wonderful ability to make emotional mountains out of thematic molehills. Nevertheless, the tone of voice is individual. It is not quite indolent enough to be Bellini. It could perhaps be said to owe something to Rossini, but it

---

[1] *Kobbé's Complete Opera Book* (1954 revised edition.)

could never be mistaken for that composer. The *andante* gives way to thirty-eight bars of conventional *allegro* bustle which is the bridge to a thirty-two bar section marked *un poco meno* and is, to modern ears, unmistakably Verdian. The final lively section of the overture bears a distinct similarity to the party music at the beginning of *La traviata*. Perhaps one should not refer to it as an overture: Verdi's term was *sinfonia*, the kind of one-movement symphony in three or four sections of which he had composed many examples during his Busseto days.

The opening chorus has little to commend it, though even here there are two moments when the mature voice of Verdi seems to break through. One occurs in the allegro section, at the words "scorran di guerra i turbini per l'itale città" [Ex. 1] whose tune could not have

Ex. 1

been written by an earlier composer. This is difficult to explain: on the page, admittedly, it looks as though it could be by either Bellini or Donizetti. When it is played and sung, however, the warmth of Verdi's personality sounds through it to anyone with even the slightest knowledge of the better-known operas from *Rigoletto* onwards.

Riccardo's first aria "Son fra voi" seems to me a rather perfunctory affair, though Toye thought it successful. Its tessitura is rather high, hovering about the top of the stave and reaching up to a B natural. The cabaletta is of no particular interest until its orchestral postlude which has been heard in the overture. Leonora's cavatina, "Sotto il paterno, tetto", is preceded by a long recitative whose opening phrases immediately proclaim her a forerunner of Verdi's more fully conceived Leonoras in *La forza del destino* and *Il trovatore*. She is decidedly of the same mould, a soprano spinto with a strong chest register. An impressive two-octave scale passage in the recitative takes her from A above the stave down to the A below middle C. Her recitative is not without interest, moving through *arioso* into a pleasantly graceful *andantino*. Its quality of gracefulness is preserved in the *allegro* cabaletta, a gentle piece which, though individual, has echoes of Bellini. As early as this, Verdi was bringing the Verdian soprano into being. The voices he wrote for at this stage of his career were, of course, voices trained to sing Bellini and Donizetti, and this can be heard in the melodies he wrote for them in *Oberto* and *Un giorno di regno*. But almost from the very beginning he added something of his own to the Bellinian cantilena. This first aria of Verdi's first soprano rôle would not have sounded unusual or strange to ears hearing it in 1839, but heard with the ears of today it has more in common with middle-period Verdi than with his predecessors.

Verdi had not attempted to forge any new paths in *Oberto*: he was content to take the operatic form as it existed and, at the beginnng of his career, simply to add his voice. Throughout his entire working life, in fact, although he broke important new ground, he never once did so merely to put into practice any theory of the musical drama. He had none. As he developed, he found the existing forms restrictive and he altered them to suit his own practical purposes. That in doing so he was taking an important step forward and forcing the art of Italian opera to accompany him is now an historical fact. At the time, he was simply a craftsman trying out something new. But in *Oberto* there is, formally, nothing new. What distinguishes *Oberto* from the other operas produced in Milan in 1839—from Mercadante's *Il bravo* or Donizetti's *Gianni di Parigi*, for instance—is the personality of its composer. Despite occasional echoes of Bellini and Donizetti in the score of *Oberto*, the music is original. This is no mere student work, even though the form is conventional: self-contained numbers, most of them introduced by accompanied recitative, a cabaletta to each aria, and an introductory chorus in each scene.

The scena which follows Leonora's aria, and in which Leonora and her father meet, is the first of Verdi's duets for father and daughter which were to culminate many years later in the magnificent series of duets for Rigoletto and Gilda. The father-daughter relationship recurs in many of Verdi's operas and seems always to have inspired really fine music. The tenderness of Oberto's love for his dishonoured daughter is not far beneath the surface of his anger. The situation adumbrated here in Piazza's libretto has elements in common with both *Rigoletto* (the dishonour) and *Simon Boccanegra* (the return of the lost daughter), and Verdi already rises nobly to them in an extended duet. After a recitative which is both concise and expressive, Oberto sings "Non ti basto il periglio", a great tune that would not be out of place in *Rigoletto* [Ex. 2]. In its progressions from one elegant melody to another, this duet also foreshadows the superb scene for Leonora and her spiritual father, Padre Guardiano, in *La forza del destino* which Verdi wrote more than twenty years later. In *Oberto* Leonora takes up her

Ex. 2

Non ti bastò il pe-ri-glio d'un pa-dre sven-tu- ra - to l'o-

-no - re hai tu mac-chia-to di sua ca-den-te e-tà, di su - a ca-den-te e-tà.

father's tune with the words "A una tradita e misera, dona un amplesso, o padre", and then, through the expressive *andante maestoso* of "Del tuo favor soccorimi" to the big moderato tune of "Un amplesso ricevi, o pentita" [Ex. 3], the great duet unfolds in the most glorious vocal

Ex. 3

Un am-ples-so ri - ce-vi, o pen-ti - - - ta; ti fia pe-gno al per-do-no pro-mes-so.

melody. Verdi was to make more expansive use of the orchestra in later years, to use it to say much that could not be sung, to suggest sub-conscious forces at work, or, more rarely, to make his own quasi-Brechtian comment on the dramatic situation; but he was never to lose his expressive vocal line, or to subjugate it to the orchestra. This is as true of *Falstaff* as it is of *Oberto*. The orchestra is used to superb dramatic effect, however, even in this *Oberto* duet. The means are simple, though by no means crude: to emphasise and clinch the reconciliation between Oberto and Leonora, before the final section of the duet which they begin together in thirds, the orchestra plays six chromatically ascending anticipatory chords which clear the air and prepare us for the C major ending of the scene more eloquently than, at that moment, any more elaborate writing could do.

The second scene opens with a brief chorus which does no more than serve its purpose, which is to indicate a festive mood. Of much greater interest is the duet which follows, for Cuniza and Riccardo. Cuniza is a dramatically colourless character, but an occasional phrase of hers points forward to the great mezzo-soprano roles that Verdi was to create. For the most part her tessitura hardly differs from that of Leonora. Nevertheless, the roles were sung by soprano and mezzo-soprano in the first production, and the sketchy characterisation is certainly helped by a difference in the colour of the two women's voices. The duet "Il pensier d'un amore felice" is melodically naïve in comparison with the Oberto–Leonora duet of the preceding scene, but it has a graceful, somewhat Bellinian quality, and a disarming freshness.

Leonora, Cuniza and Oberto confront one another in a terzetto which is no more than serviceable, though Oberto's *andantino*, after Cuniza has been told that the seducer is her betrothed, makes another of those leaps into middle-period Verdi which are sufficiently frequent in *Oberto* to distinguish it from those other early operas whose virtues, though distinct, are often somewhat crude. Disconcertingly, in some middle-period Verdi operas the situation is reversed: a page or two of hasty *Alzira*-like writing will obtrude into the composer's more highly refined style.

Oberto's first act finale is given distinct character by the lively and forceful opening lines for Leonora, and by an *andante mosso* of typically Verdian melancholy. The second act opens with another of those strangely ineffective choruses. The act finales demonstrate that, as early as his mid-twenties, Verdi could create superb ensembles, but he appears to have been daunted by Piazza's formal use of the chorus to open each scene with a verse or two of sententious comment. Cuniza's aria in this scene has a pleasantly individual cabaletta with, at the end, a splendid optional B natural.

The chorus of cavaliers which opens the last scene assures us that, in this life, misery and virtue are bedfellows. ("Son compagne in questa vita la sventura e la virtù".) Oberto's aria, as he waits for Riccardo to join him, is first-rate stuff of its kind: naïve, but direct in its communication of feeling. After its *andante* section, the cavaliers come on again to a few bars of delicious, absurd hustle-and-bustle music, and announce to Oberto that he is no longer exiled. They trip off to the same music, and Oberto, snarling for vengeance, launches into a brilliant *allegro marziale* cabaletta. Riccardo appears but, before they can fight, the two women enter. The ensuing quartet is one of the finest numbers in the opera, and Verdi himself in later years continued to think well of it. Like the more celebrated *Rigoletto* quartet, it is begun by the tenor, but its *adagio* tune is more spaciously phrased, more sinuous, than "Bella figlia dell'amore" [Ex. 4].

Ex. 4

Distinctly reminiscent of Bellini, it begins to sound more Verdian when taken up by the other voices and developed in ensemble. As in the *Rigoletto* quartet, the four characters each voice their own widely differing reactions to the situation. Solera's verses are simple and to the point. They also possess a dignity which is conspicuously absent from the libretto as a whole:

Riccardo

La vergogna ed il dispetto
ahi combattono il mio seno.
Il rimorso a quell' aspetto
lacerando il cor mi va.
Deh spalancati, o terreno,
e m'ascondi per pieta.

(Shame and annoyance struggle within my breast. Her stricken face brings
remorse to my heart. If only the earth
would open and in pity engulf me.)

Leonora

Egli è infame, è traditore,
ed ancora io l'amerai.
Ah, l'incendio d'un amore
chi mai spegnere potrà?
Ma la morte or sceglieri
altra speme il cor non ha.

(He is infamous, a traitor, and yet I
love him. Ah, who can ever extinguish
love's flame? But my heart has no
other hope now than death.)

Cuniza

Sciagurato! e tanto ardiva
mentre a me chiedea parola
e al rimorso il core apriva
d'un orribile viltà.
Infelice! ti consola,
al tuo seno ei tornerà.

(Wretch. To dare thus, while making
your suit to me. To my remorse, I
opened my heart to your vile cowardice. Unhappy Leonora, console yourself. He will return to you.)

Oberto

Ah, codardo! al brando
mio,
no, sfugire non potrai.
Pari al fulmine di Dio
te dovunque ei cogliera.
Nel tuo sangue laverai
fin de' padri la viltà.

(Ah, base creature, you cannot flee
from my wrath. Like a thunderbolt
from heaven it will strike wherever you
are, spilling your cowardly blood.)

In the *allegro* section of the quartet, Cuniza commands Riccardo
to return to Leonora, whose interpolated phrase, "Oh generosa", is
a minor stroke of genius easily overlooked because it is not emphasised
nor is the tempo modified for it. The concluding *allegro vivace*, begun
most excitingly by Leonora, tails off into a conventional ending. The
stagey chorus of cavaliers which follows is mercifully brief. As they rush
into the woods to trace the source of "qual rumor", Riccardo enters.
He has fought with and killed Oberto, rather in the manner of a Don
Giovanni *manqué*. Unlike Giovanni, he is bitterly ashamed and remorseful. In an agitated *andante mosso*, he expresses his despair, and prays to
heaven in a beautiful and all too short aria, "Ciel pietoso, ciel clemente".
Verdi has the taste not to follow this with a rousing cabaletta about
seeking death in a foreign clime, though I dare say there was something
of the kind in Piazza's draft libretto.

Cuniza's scene with the chorus, in which she learns of Oberto's death, is brusquely conventional, but the final number in the opera, a recitative, *andante* and *rondo* for Leonora and chorus, makes handsome amends. Here Leonora rises to the stature of her namesake in *Il trovatore*. The recitative and andante are most moving, and the chorus interjection in the *andante* is masterly. Sung by a Milanov, this could not fail to be affecting. At its conclusion, a messenger enters with Ricardo's note to Cuniza. "Un messagio a questa volta?" ("A message at this time?") asks the incredulous and offended chorus, as well it might. Riccardo's will and testament are made known to Leonora whose sombrely distraught cabaletta brings the opera to an end.

Oberto, then, has many splendours. But it adds up to no more than the sum of its parts. While later operas such as *La traviata*, *Un ballo in maschera* or *La forza del destino*, have a resonance that cannot be analysed into separate component parts, *Oberto*'s excellence exists on a lower level. That it *is* an excellent and immensely enjoyable work can, I think, no longer be denied. Writers on Verdi have, in the past, been willing to dismiss *Oberto* either because they did not know it or because they were more immediately concerned with pleading the cause of the greater operas to come. But Verdi's first produced opera is a valid musical experience in its own right, and not simply because the composer's humanity, his pessimism, his energy and his heart-lifting melodic gift are to be found in it in adumbration. His ability to characterise in musical terms, though already greater than Haydn's, was hardly awakened, and, although he seems to take to the stage like the proverbial duck to water, he has much to learn. *Oberto* is a concise piece of work: some of the other early operas, in fact, are so concise as to be almost brutish. Verdi was never to become garrulous, never to lose his glorious inability to be dull or long-winded. He was never to waste a note. *Oberto* worthily begins a career which moves inexorably through the nineteenth-century, though by no means in a straight line, towards *Falstaff*.

II

Un giorno di regno

Dramatis personae:

The Cavalier Belfiore, posing as Stanislao, King of Poland	(baritone)
Baron Kelbar	(buffo bass)
The Marchesa del Poggio, young widow, niece of the Baron	(soprano)
Giulietta, the Baron's daughter	(mezzo-soprano)
La Rocca, Treasurer of the States of Brittany	(buffo bass)
Edoardo, his nephew	(tenor)
Count Ivrea, Commandant of Brest	(tenor)
Delmonte, Belfiore's steward	(tenor)

LIBRETTO by Felice Romani

TIME: 1733
PLACE: Baron Kelbar's castle, near Brest

FIRST PERFORMED at La Scala, Milan, September 5, 1840, with Antonietta Marini (Marchesa); Luigia Abbadia (Giulietta); Lorenzo Salvi (Edoardo); Raffaele Ferlotti (Belfiore); Raffaele Scalese (Baron); Agostino Rovere (La Rocca); Giuseppe Vaschetti (Delmonte); Napoleone Marconi (Count Ivrea)

Un giorno di regno

I

FOR THE FIRST opera under the terms of their contract, Merelli recommended the librettist Gaetano Rossi to Verdi. Rossi, who had written the libretto for Rossini's *Semiramide* seventeen years earlier, produced a manuscript entitled *Il proscritto* (The Outlaw), but Verdi was not enthusiastic about it, and hesitated to begin work. Merelli, on his return from a visit to his Court Theatre in Vienna, told Verdi that, instead of an *opera seria*, he now needed a comic opera or *opera buffa* for the forthcoming autumn season in 1840. He offered Verdi several libretti, most of which had been set before by other composers. Verdi was not keen on any of them but finally chose the one he disliked least, *Il finto Stanislao* (The false Stanislaus) by Felice Romani, a successful playwright and the librettist of many operas including Rossini's *Il turco in Italia*, Bellini's *Il pirata*, *I Capuleti ed i Montecchi*, *La sonnambula* and *Norma*, and Donizetti's *Anna Bolena*, *L'elisir d'amore* and *Lucrezia Borgia*. Romani had originally written *Il finto Stanislao* for the prolific Bohemian composer Adalbert Gyrowetz, and the opera had been produced at La Scala in 1818. It had not been successful and, since over twenty years had elapsed, Romani was quite happy to see the libretto used again. Merelli appears not to have asked him to write something new for Verdi, although Romani was still actively involved in the libretto industry. It was decided to give his old libretto a new title, *Un giorno di regno* (which could be translated as "A One-day Reign" or "King for a Day", but not, as it appears in the English translation of a French book on Verdi, "A day of rain"!).

While he was unwillingly at work on *Un giorno di regno*, Verdi became ill and his wife Margherita nursed him. When after some weeks he recovered, she fell seriously ill, and died of encephalitis. She was twenty-seven years old, the same age as Verdi. He returned to Busseto in black despair, having asked Merelli to release him from his contract. But the impresario insisted on Verdi's finishing the opera, and from what one knows of Merelli's character it was probably a kindly and well-intended insistence. Verdi came back to Milan, to the house where Margherita had died, proceeded icily but steadily to write his comic opera, and proceeded just as steadily along the road to nervous collapse.

The first performance of *Un giorno di regno* at La Scala on September

5, 1840 was a failure. The audience was hostile, and there was much booing and hissing. The press was unfavourable. All other performances were cancelled, and Merelli hastily revived *Oberto*.[1] Verdi retreated further into himself and announced that he would never compose again. Nearly twenty years later, in a letter to Tito Ricordi, he referred to his second opera: "From that day to this," he wrote, "I have not seen *Un giorno di regno*. It may well be a poor opera, though many others no better have won applause. . . . I do not mean to blame the public, but I accept their criticism and scorn only so long as I do not have to be grateful for their applause."[2]

II

Romani's libretto is loosely based on an incident which occurred during the wars of the Polish Succession. The young Palatine of Poznan, Stanislaus Leszczynski, had been proclaimed King in 1704, but his right to the throne was contested by the Saxon monarch, Frederick Augustus. Defeated at the battle of Poltava in 1709, Stanislaus took refuge in France. His daughter married Louis XV and, when Frederick Augustus died in 1733, Louis supported the attempt of Stanislaus to claim the throne of Poland. At the instigation of Cardinal Fleury, it was decided that Stanislaus should travel to Poland in secret, accompanied only by an aide-de-camp. Arriving safely in Poland, Stanislaus revealed himself at a service in Warsaw cathedral, and was acclaimed as rightful King. Romani's libretto supposes a subterfuge resorted to in order to distract attention from the exact whereabouts of Stanislaus until he was safely in Warsaw.

In fact, the second reign of King Stanislaus lasted for only two years. He was defeated by the Saxons with the aid of Russian forces, and was deposed. He returned to France and was given the Duchy of Lorraine.

Un giorno di regno, a melodramma giocoso, is in two acts which take place in the castle of Baron Kelbar, near the town of Brest. Act I is divided into three scenes, the first of which is set in a gallery of the castle. A double wedding is to take place, and the servants and staff sing of their joy in the proceedings. The Baron's daughter Giulietta is being forced by her father to marry La Rocca, Treasurer of the States of Brittany, for his money, though she is in love with his nephew Edoardo. The Baron's niece, the Marchesa del Poggio, is to marry Count Ivrea, the Commandant of Brest. No one is forcing her to do so: she is acting out of spite, in the belief that the Cavalier Belfiore to whom she was engaged has deserted her. In reality, as we shall see, he

---

[1] One month later, the three principal singers of *Un giorno di regno*, Abbadia, Salvi and Scalese appeared again at La Scala in the first Italian performances of a more successful work, Donizetti's *La figlia del reggimento*.

[2] *Copialettere*, p. 557.

still loves her, but is engaged on a secret mission in which he must pose as Stanislao, King of Poland, in order to give the real king an opportunity of reaching Warsaw and gaining the favour of the Polish Diet or parliament.

After the Baron and the Treasurer have sung of their happiness in becoming related to each other through Giulietta's marriage, Belfiore's steward enters to announce the imminent arrival of Stanislao, King of Poland. The Cavalier Belfiore arrives, is greeted with due deference and courtesy, and is invited to stay for the double wedding. He asks who the brides are and, when he is told that one is the Marchesa del Poggio, he can scarcely conceal his surprise and dismay. Dismissing the Baron and the Treasurer from his presence, he immediately writes a note to the Court, wherever or whatever it may be, asking for permission to "abdicate" for fear he may lose his beloved.

Edoardo enters and asks to be allowed to accompany His Majesty to Poland. Life in Brest is pointless now that Giulietta is about to marry his uncle. Belfiore pretends to accept Edoardo as a member of his retinue. They leave the gallery together, and the Marchesa enters. She has seen and recognised Belfiore, realises that she still loves him and swears that, if he is unfaithful to her, she will renounce love forever.

The scene changes to a part of the castle garden where Giulietta sits grieving over her forthcoming marriage. A chorus of yokels and country girls presents her with fruit and flowers on this, the happiest day of her life, and audibly wonders why she is looking so mournful at such a time. Giulietta sings of her distaste for the old man she must marry, and longs for Edoardo to come and console her. The lads and lasses wander off. Edoardo enters, but has with him the Baron, the Treasurer and the supposed King. The Baron introduces his daughter to the King, who surprises the others by announcing that he has made Edoardo his First Lieutenant and ordering him to converse with his future aunt. Thus the young lovers are able to talk to each other in the presence of her father and his uncle. The king makes the two men sit so that they have their backs to Giulietta and Edoardo, spreads out a map in front of them, and forces them to discuss the military situation. The Marchesa enters. When her uncle the Baron introduces her to the King of Poland, she is disconcerted and wonders if she can have been mistaken in supposing him to be Belfiore. A sextet develops in which varying sentiments are expressed. The Baron and the Treasurer, both happy at the prospect of advancement by the King, depart with Belfiore, leaving the Marchesa with the young lovers, who call on her to help them. She can scarcely focus her attention on their problem, as her mind is completely occupied with Belfiore. Her apparent lack of interest in them depresses the young couple, but the situation is put right during a trio in which all three take heart at the fact that they are young and in love.

The third scene is set in the gallery where Belfiore, in an attempt to help Giulietta and Edoardo, offers the Treasurer a much finer match, the hand of the wealthy Polish Princess Ineska in marriage. His vanity and greed aroused, the Treasurer resolves not to proceed with his marriage to Giulietta. When the Baron enters with the wedding certificate, the Treasurer explains that he has changed his mind. Furious, the Baron challenges him to a duel. At the height of their quarrel, the Marchesa, Giulietta, Edoardo and the servants enter and add to the confusion and noise. Suddenly Belfiore appears, and they are all mortified at having allowed themselves to be discovered by royalty indulging in a vulgar and undignified row. The ensuing ensemble brings the first act to an end.

Act II opens in the gallery. The servants wonder why the wedding plans are not going forward and what has caused everyone at the castle to fall into a state of gloom. Edoardo enters and tells them of his desperate situation. Giulietta is still, he thinks, to marry the Treasurer. The servants depart and Belfiore enters with Giulietta and the Treasurer. Belfiore, as King, orders the Treasurer to hand over one of his castles and 5,000 scudi a year to his nephew Edoardo in order to make him a worthy suitor for Giulietta. The Treasurer agrees, and Belfiore and the young couple leave him alone to face the wrath of the Baron. After another of their comical arguments, the Baron and Treasurer rush off to fight.

The scene now changes to a ground floor vestibule leading to the garden. The Marchesa is still not sure whether the King is Belfiore. He enters and in a duet they continue their cat-and-mouse game. She feigns indifference. He is not yet able to reveal his identity to her, but is disturbed at her expressed intention to proceed with her marriage to Count Ivrea, Commandant of Brest. Her uncle informs her he has just heard from the Commandant, who is now on his way to the castle to claim his bride. The Marchesa professes to be happy at this news, but when Belfiore asks "What of your Cavalier?" she hints that if he were to arrive and ask her forgiveness, she would return to him. As Belfiore fails to take advantage of this, she reaffirms that she will marry Count Ivrea. The servants enter, announcing the Count's arrival, and the Marchesa goes out to meet him while Belfiore angrily stalks off in the opposite direction.

Giulietta and Edoardo enter. The Baron has finally consented to their marriage, but Edoardo is unhappy because he has, of course, promised to accompany the King to Poland. Giulietta promises to intercede for him with the King. The Baron now enters with Count Ivrea and the Marchesa, who announces that, if Belfiore has not appeared within the hour, the wedding will proceed. (No one appears to consider the Count's feelings.) Belfiore enters, still as the King, demanding that Count Ivrea accompany him immediately on a secret mission. These delaying tactics throw the party into confusion, but fortunately at this moment a courier arrives from the Court with an important letter for Belfiore. The King has arrived in Warsaw and has been acclaimed by the Diet, so Belfiore is allowed to abdicate. For his service, he is created Marshal. "But who *are* you?" asks the Baron. "Il Cavalier Belfior'," announces that gentleman as he takes the Marchesa in his arms, "and faithful to his first love." The opera ends in the happiness of the majority and the delight of the servants at the reinstatement of plans for a double wedding.

This is as silly a story as anyone ever concocted. It is in Romani's farcical vein, and has nothing of the gentler comedy of his *Sonnambula*. But it is no worse than many a libretto which was fed into the comic Donizetti computer to emerge decently solved in musical terms. Let us see what Verdi made of it.

III

The Overture or Sinfonia, a sprightly piece in the manner of Rossini, is quite pleasant in a fairly business-like way. Some of its themes are heard in the opera, notably in the final chorus. The boy from Busseto makes a more successful stab at metropolitan sophistication than he was to manage on one or two later occasions. The opening chorus and the duettino for the two buffo basses are both fast-moving and attractive pieces, while Belfiore's opening cavatina and stretta proclaim him to be a true forerunner of the real Verdi baritone. The florid nature of his pleasantly tuneful cavatina is Donizettian, but the manner in which the voice clings to the upper fifth of its range is, as we know today, distinctly Verdian. The vocal line continually rises to F and F sharp. There are baritone roles in Donizetti which could be, and are, sung by basses; if one goes back to the days of Mozart when no clear distinction was made between baritone and bass, one finds several roles whose tessitura is suitable to either, such as Figaro, the Count, Don Giovanni, Leporello, Guglielmo. By 1840, the in-between categories of baritone and mezzo-soprano were becoming more exactly defined, and it was Verdi more than any other composer who helped to define them. The Italian baritone of today with his brilliant top, and the dramatic mezzo as distinct from the Rossinian agile mezzo were coaxed into being by the kind of music Verdi wrote for them.

When the others have departed, Belfiore has a few bars of *recitativo secco*, or recitative accompanied only by an obbligato instrument, in which he decides to write to the Court asking to be released from his royal engagement. He then speaks the words of the letter as he writes it. *Un giorno di regno* is the only opera in which Verdi resorted to *recitativo secco*. Setting out large chunks of dialogue to pitched speech rhythms was not the kind of chore he would have been likely to enjoy: even in this opera he uses it sparingly, preferring to write the more expressive *recitativo stromentato* or accompanied recitative, using his normal orchestra.

Edoardo enters to place his useless life at the service of His Majesty. Verdi has written this role not for the *tenore spinto* of *Oberto* or of, one could almost say, Italian opera in general, but for a lyric *tenorino*. His opening recitative sets the style and gracefulness of all Edoardo's utterances. His duet with Belfiore is an absolutely charming piece, the end of whose first section recalls Figaro and Almaviva in the opening scene of *Il barbiere*, with the tenor singing a slow legato melody over the baritone's quick, staccato patter [Ex. 5]. The lively cabaletta in which

Ex. 5

Edoardo and Belfiore sing in thirds is less reminiscent of Rossini. By a stretch of the imagination it is possible to hear in it something of the *Don Carlo* friendship duet, though Bellini's "Suoni la tromba" in *I Puritani* comes more easily to mind. The scene ends with the Marchesa's recitative and aria. The *andante* is graceful and the cabaletta good-natured, the whole making an attractive scene for a lyric soprano with coloratura agility and a good trill.

In the second scene, after an inventively tuneful chorus we meet the unhappy Giulietta. Officially for mezzo-soprano, Giulietta's role can equally well be sung by another lyric soprano, of fuller voice than the Marchesa for contrast. The tessitura of her B flat *andantino* is high, and both in it and in the ensuing cabaletta she sustains top B flats. The *andantino* is charmingly Bellinian, and the cabaletta an engagingly dotty piece which sounds as though it has strayed from a Viennese operetta. When Belfiore, Edoardo, the Baron and the Treasurer enter, the quintet that follows, in which two people make love while three others discuss war, is one of the most attractive numbers in the score, love soaring beautifully above lowly intrigue. It is as though Pamina and Tamino had strayed into the café when Guglielmo, Ferrando and Don Alfonso were hatching the plot of *Così fan tutte* [Ex. 6].

Ex. 6

The sextet that follows the Marchesa's entrance is a lively piece of bustle, and the trio for her, Giulietta and Edoardo is particuarly appealing in its assurance and personality. The G major cabaletta, "Noi siamo amanti", looks embarrassingly simple on the page, but is gaily effective in performance. Buffo duets can be dreadful things, but the one Verdi has written here for the Baron and the Treasurer is

certainly as good as the average Donizetti example of the genre: its
melodic interest is by no means slight. The finale to the act develops
into a first-rate Verdian ensemble after Belfiore's haughty interruption
of the quarrelling. Scenes of public humiliation and conflicting interest
were always to excite Verdi's creative interest. One thinks of the ensembles in *La traviata*, *Un ballo in maschera* and *Otello*. Indeed, in the
present one, the Marchesa's top line is a clear adumbration of Verdi's
Ballo manner [Ex. 7]. The vivacious *allegro* conclusion has an accom-

Ex. 7

paniment figure already heard in the opening *allegro* of the Overture.

Act II begins with one of those choruses in which the servants
comment on their masters and discuss the ways of the household. A
more recent example can be found in Strauss's *Capriccio* when the
servants enthuse over the prospect of "ein Abend ohne Gäste". Donizetti included a chorus similar in dramatic content to Verdi's in his
Don Pasquale, which reached the stage only three years after *Un giorno
di regno*. It is quite possible that he and Giovanni Ruffini, the librettist
with whom he worked closely on *Don Pasquale*, took the idea from *Un
giorno di regno*. But the servants' chorus may have existed in Stefano
Pavesi's *Ser Marc' Antonio*, an opera which had its première at La Scala
in 1810 and from which Donizetti and Ruffini filched their plot, in
which case Romani's use of the device when he first wrote *Il finto
Stanislao* may well have stemmed from the same source.

After the servants have had their say, Edoardo enters and, addressing
them democratically as "amici cari", pours out his sorrows in a
beautiful aria which must be sheer delight for a real *bel canto* tenor
to sing. The idiom is that of Bellini, but already Verdi's personality
is becoming discernible. A cadenza takes the tenor up to a top C, one
of the top C's that Verdi actually wrote, unlike the more famous but
spurious ones that poke out of Manrico's "Di quella pira" in *Il trovatore*.
Edoardo's cabaletta, in a moderate tempo, makes an extremely graceful
appendage to the aria. The Baron and the Treasurer indulge in another
of their frenetic buffo duets: this one is high-spirited, tuneful and
immensely enjoyable in stage performance. It is followed by a duet of a
different kind, for the Marchesa and Belfiore, a gay and light-hearted
number which, like so much of this score, is quite irresistible, given
reasonably good singers. The Marchesa's aria, "Si mostri a chi l'adora",

is both melodically charming and delicately accompanied. It is preceded by seven bars of recitative, the last three of which are a kind of brief orchestral prelude to the *andante*. These three bars are so expressively chromatic that they could easily fit into one of the finest pages of *Otello*, which was still fifty years in the future. The soprano's effective range is cruelly tested by the aria which calls for an A below middle C as well as a top B. The cabaletta sung by the Marchesa on hearing that Count Ivrea has arrived combines determination with a pleasing individuality. The really enjoyable numbers in this opera strongly outweigh the very occasional deadwood. "Giurai sequirlo in campo", the duet for Giulietta and Edoardo is delicious. Giulietta should certainly be sung by a soprano in preference to a chesty mezzo who, in this music, would simply not know what to do with her chest, so to speak. Belfiore's announcement that Count Ivrea must accompany him on a secret mission precipitates an impressive slow septet which leads straight into the finale in which Belfiore is able to reveal his identity in a confident solo phrase, and regain his Marchesa. The brief final chorus utilises themes from the Overture.

It is surprising just how enjoyable Verdi's early comic opera is, when one considers his temperament and the circumstances of personal tragedy in which the work was written. Of course, at this stage of his career with only one other opera to his credit, he would have had no reason not to expect that, like Rossini and Donizetti, he was going to be called on to churn out tragic and comic pieces with equal facility, as required. The nature and strength of Verdi's genius forged a path for itself which was to differ radically from that trodden by his predecessors; but, had he been merely another talented and prolific composer, he would doubtless have gone on producing comic operas when the occasion required them. There is no reason to assume he would not, in time, have acquired a Donizettian flair for the genre. *Un giorno di regno*, his first and, until *Falstaff*, only comic opera, already rivals all but the best of Donizetti: it requires no special pleading to demonstrate that Verdi's dressing-up of Romani's unexceptionable libretto is, if not riotously funny, at least an opera of great charm and melodic facility. Verdi cleverly keeps his orchestration light by frequent use of the piccolo and, like Rossini, though by no means so inexorably, equates high spirits with liberal use of the percussion instruments. In later years, his mastery of the orchestra was to make the scoring of *Un giorno di regno* seem primitive. But the vocal writing had assurance and style, and still displays it.

Neither of Verdi's pre-*Nabucco* operas has been treated fairly by posterity. *Oberto* and *Un giorno di regno* are both worth reviving. *Oberto* points more clearly and directly to the paths Verdi was later to follow, while *Un giorno di regno* is a splendidly entertaining early example of his work in a genre which he was not to touch again for half a century. I can easily imagine it being successful under Glyndebourne or other small-scale conditions: an audience that finds pleasure in Rossini's *La pietra del paragone* would hardly be likely to turn its nose up at a well-cast *Giorno*.

III

Nabucco

Dramatis personae:

Nabucodonosor (Nabucco), King of Babylon	(baritone)
Ismaele, nephew of Sedecia, King of Jerusalem	(tenor)
Zaccaria, a Hebrew prophet	(bass)
Abigaille, slave, believed to be the eldest daughter of Nabucco	(soprano)
Fenena, daughter of Nabucco	(soprano)
High Priest of Baal	(bass)
Abdallo, old retainer of Nabucco	(tenor)
Anna, sister of Zaccaria	(soprano)

LIBRETTO by Temistocle Solera

TIME: 586 B.C.
PLACE: Jerusalem and Babylon

FIRST PERFORMED at La Scala, Milan, March 9, 1842, with Giuseppina Strepponi (Abigaille); Giovannina Bellinzaghi (Fenena); Teresa Ruggeri (Anna); Corrado Miraglia (Ismaele); Giorgio Ronconi (Nabucco); Prospero Derivis (Zaccaria); Napoleone Marconi (Abdallo); Gaetano Rossi (High Priest)

Nabucco

I

THROUGHOUT HIS LIFE Verdi was loath to talk about himself; he consistently refused requests from publishers and editors that he write his memoirs. In 1879, however, when the composer was sixty-six, his publisher and friend Giulio Ricordi[1] persuaded him to talk about his early years in Milan. A book about him was being written by Arthur Pougin and, although Verdi professed disinterest in the venture, he agreed that if it was to be published it ought to be as accurate as possible. He collaborated to the extent of dictating to Ricordi his recollections of his early years. Here is Verdi's account of the events leading to *Nabucco*:

Un giorno di regno failed to please. Certainly the music was partly to blame, but so, too, was the performance. With a mind tormented by my domestic tragedy, embittered by the failure of my work, I was convinced that I could find no consolation in music and decided never to compose again. I even wrote to Signor Pasetti asking him to persuade Merelli to release me from my contract.

Merelli sent for me and treated me like a capricious child. He would not allow me to be discouraged by the failure of one opera and so on. But I insisted, until finally he gave me the contract back, and said: "Listen, Verdi! I can't force you to compose. But my faith in you is undiminished. Who knows whether, one day, you may not decide to write again? In which case, if you give me two months' notice before the beginning of a season, I promise your opera shall be performed." I thanked him, but these words did not suffice to alter my decision, and I left.

I took rooms in Milan, in the Corsia de' Servi. I had lost heart, and no longer thought about music, but one winter evening as I was leaving the Galleria De Cristoforis, I ran into Merelli who was on his way to the theatre. It was snowing heavily. Taking me by the arm, he asked me to accompany him to his office at La Scala. On the way we talked, and he told me he was having difficulty over a new opera. He had commissioned Nicolai who was, however, dissatisfied with the libretto.

---

[1] Verdi dealt with three generations of Ricordis. When he signed his first contract, the head of the firm was its founder Giovanni Ricordi (1785–1853). He was succeeded by his son Tito (1811–88). Tito's son Giulio (1840–1912) entered the firm during Tito's lifetime.

"Just think," said Merelli, "a libretto by Solera! Stupendous! Magnificent! Extraordinary! Effective, grandiose dramatic situations and beautiful verses! But that pig-headed composer won't hear of it, and says it's a hopeless libretto. I've no idea where to find another one quickly."

"I can help you there," I replied. "You gave me the libretto for *Il proscritto*, but I haven't written a note of it. I put it at your disposal now."

"Oh, splendid. What luck!"

Talking like this, we had reached the theatre. Merelli called Bassi who was poet, stage manager, call-boy, librarian and so on, and asked him to look at once in the archives for a copy of *Il proscritto*. A copy was found. But meanwhile, Merelli picked up another manuscript and, showing it to me, exclaimed: "Look, here is Solera's libretto. Such a beautiful subject, and now it's turned down. Take it and read it."

"What on earth should I do with it? No, no, I don't want to read any librettos."

"Come on, it won't bite you. Read it and then bring it back to me." And he gave me the manuscript. It was written on large paper in big letters, as was customary then. I rolled it up, said goodbye to Merelli and went home.

On the way I felt a kind of indefinable uneasiness, a deep sadness, an anguish that filled my heart. When I got home, I threw the manuscript on the table with a violent gesture, and stood staring at it. It had fallen open, and without realising it I gazed at the page and read the line: "Va, pensiero, sull' ali dorate."

I glanced through the following verses and was deeply moved, particularly since they were almost a paraphrase of the Bible which I have always enjoyed reading.

I read one passage, then another. Then, resolute in my determination never to compose again, I forced myself to close the book and go to bed. But *Nabucco* kept running through my mind, and I couldn't sleep. I got up and read the libretto, not once but two or three times so that by morning I almost knew it by heart. Even so, I was determined to stick to my decision, and that day I returned to the theatre and handed the manuscript back to Merelli.

"Beautiful, isn't it?" he said.

"Very beautiful."

"Well then, set it to music."

"Certainly not. I wouldn't think of it."

"Set it to music! Set it to music!" And with that, he took the libretto, thrust it into my overcoat pocket, grabbed me by the shoulders and not only pushed me out of the room but locked the door in my face.

What was I to do? I went home with *Nabucco* in my pocket. One day a verse, the next day another, at one time a note, at another a phrase. Little by little the opera was written.

It was the autumn of 1841, and remembering Merelli's promise I went to see him, announced that *Nabucco* was written and could be performed in the next Carnival season.

Merelli declared himself ready to keep his word, but at the same time pointed out that it would be impossible to stage the opera in the forthcoming season, because the repertory, which included three new operas by famous composers, was already settled. To give a fourth opera by someone who was almost a beginner would be risky for everyone, and especially so for me. It would be better therefore to wait for the spring season, which was not yet filled. He assured me that decent artists would be engaged. But I refused. Either during the Carnival season, or not at all. And I had good reasons, knowing that it would not be possible to find better artists than Strepponi and Ronconi, whom I knew were under contract and on whom I was relying.

Merelli, although he wanted to oblige me, was not altogether wrong from the impresario's point of view. To give four new operas in the one season would be risky. But I still had good artistic reasons for opposing him. In the end, after accepting and then refusing, the Scala programme bills were posted—and *Nabucco* was not announced!

I was young and hot-blooded! I wrote Merelli a nasty letter, in which I poured out all my resentment. I confess that as soon as I had sent it I was remorseful, and feared I might have ruined everything.

Merelli sent for me, and when he saw me he exclaimed angrily: "Is this the way to write to a friend? Still, you're quite right. We'll give this *Nabucco*. But you must understand that I have heavy expenses in connection with the other three operas, so I can't afford new scenery or costumes for *Nabucco*. I will fit it out as best I can from whatever I have in the warehouse."

I agreed to everything, for I was anxious that the opera should be given. A new bill was issued on which I finally read: NABUCCO!

I remember an amusing scene I had with Solera a little earlier. In the third act he had written a love duet for Fenena and Ismaele. I didn't like it, as it held up the action and seemed to me to detract somewhat from the Biblical grandeur of the drama. One morning I said so to Solera. But he was loath to agree, not because he thought the comment unfair, but because it annoyed him to revise anything he had written. We argued about it, and both stood firm. He asked me what I wanted to replace the duet, and I suggested the prophecy of Zaccaria. He thought that wasn't a bad idea, and with a few ifs and buts said he'd think about it and then write it. That was no good to me, for I knew that a good many days would pass before Solera sat down to write a verse. So I locked the door, put the key in my pocket, and said half seriously and half flippantly: "You're not leaving here until you've written the prophecy. Here's the Bible, you have the words ready made."

Solera, who had a violent temper, didn't care for my joke. An angry look appeared in his eye, and I was nervous for a moment for the poet was certainly big enough to put an obstinate composer in his place. But suddenly he sat at the table, and in a quarter of an hour the prophecy was written.

Finally, at the end of February 1842, rehearsals began, and twelve days after the first piano rehearsal the opera was produced on March 9th, with Mesdames Strepponi and Bellinzaghi, and Messieurs Ronconi, Miraglia and Derivis in the cast.

With this opera it is fair to say my artistic career began. And in spite of the difficulties I had to contend with, *Nabucco* was born under a lucky star. For even the things that might have harmed the work turned to its advantage. I had written a furious letter to Merelli who could easily have sent the young maestro packing. But the opposite occurred. The refashioned costumes looked splendid. The old scenery, touched up by the painter Perroni, made an extraordinary impression. The first scene in the temple, for instance, produced such an effect that the audience applauded for ten minutes. At the dress rehearsal no one knew when or where the stage band was to come in. The conductor Tutsch was embarrassed. I pointed out a bar to him, and at the performance the band entered on the crescendo with such precision that the audience burst into applause.

But it does not always do to trust in lucky stars! Experience has taught me the truth of the proverb: "Fidarsi è bene, ma non fidarsi è meglio" ("To trust is good, but not to trust is better").[1]

Verdi does not exaggerate: the opera was an enormous success. Giuseppina Strepponi, the future Signora Verdi, was apparently not in her best voice as Abigaille. Nevertheless, on the first night there were scenes of wild enthusiasm after Act I, an enthusiasm which grew even more fevered as the performance progressed. Before the first night, it had been clear from the extraordinary excitement generated by the final rehearsals that *Nabucco* was destined to be a riotous popular success. The stage-hands, painters, dancers and hangers-on who crowded into the wings to listen were heard to exclaim at the novelty of the music. The audience at the première was sent into a state of delirium by the third act chorus, "Va, pensiero", and insisted on its being repeated. A law was in force in Milan, forbidding encores: they were too frequently turned into demonstrations against Austrian rule. And "Va, pensiero" was pretty inflammatory stuff. It was easy for the Milanese governed by Austrians to see themselves as Jews suffering under the Babylonian yoke; they made the connection, and made it vociferously. With this one chorus in an opera on a biblical subject, Verdi immediately and inadvertently became the composer of the Risorgimento, the movement towards a united and free Italy.

I say "inadvertently" because we have no reason to suppose that, when he wrote "Va, pensiero", Verdi had any intention other than to set the biblical story in Solera's verses to the best of his ability. But his sympathies were with the Italian nationalist liberal cause and, although in the series of "patriotic" operas that followed *Nabucco* he probably did not, with the exception of *La battaglia di Legnano*, deliberately set out to write music for the cause, he was by no means displeased at the association made by his audiences.

The title of the opera was really *Nabucodonosor*, but the use of the diminutive "Nabucco" caught on, and the opera is now known by that name. The year after its Milan première, it was staged in Vienna, and

[1] Arthur Pougin: *Giuseppe Verdi: Histoire Anecdotique*, pp. 60–8.

Donizetti, temporarily resident there, took an interest in its production which he helped to supervise. He was an enthusiastic admirer of the younger composer, and once wrote to Giuseppina Appiani that he had no doubts of Verdi's talents or of his "artistic destiny".[1]

In the years following its première, *Nabucco* was performed not only throughout Europe, but in North, Central and South America as well. In Milan it continued to be revived season after season. At its first revival in the autumn of 1842, only a few months after the initial eight performances, it was given fifty-seven times during the season, creating a new record. It ran into trouble in London where, by law, biblical subjects could not be portrayed on the stage, and was produced in 1846 at Her Majesty's Theatre as *Nino, re d'Assyria* with all the characters renamed and the exiled Hebrews turned into exiled Babylonians. Four years later it was given at Covent Garden, this time as *Anato*.

When *Nabucco* was produced in Paris in 1845, the French reacted to the noisiness of its great choruses with the following piece of doggerel:

> Vraiment l'affiche est dans son tort,
> En faux on devrait la poursuivre.
> Pourquoi nous annoncer Nabucodonos—or
> Quand c'est Nabucodonos—cuivre.

Francis Toye called this an "amusing (and, alas! untranslatable) epigram", so, naturally, I have translated it, even though the pun ("or"—"gold") is lost.

> Surely the poster is quite in the wrong;
> The lie that it tells is a whopper.
> The work's not Nabucodonòs—made of gold,
> but Nabucodonòs—made of copper.

The German composer Nicolai (1810–49)[2] for whom Solera's libretto was originally intended, never changed his opinion of it. In his diary, he wrote:

> Verdi is the Italian opera composer of today. He has set the libretto which I rejected, and made his fortune with it. But his operas are absolutely dreadful, and utterly degrading for Italy.[3]

Nicolai's feelings could hardly have been relieved when he himself suffered a dismal failure with *Il proscritto*, the libretto he accepted after Verdi had refused it!

---

[1] Guido Zavadini: *Donizetti: Vita, Musiche, Epistolario* (Bergamo, 1948), p. 735.

[2] Nicolai's best-known opera is *Die lustigen Weiber von Windsor*, based on the Shakespeare play, *The Merry Wives of Windsor*, from which Verdi was eventually to create *Falstaff*.

[3] *Otto Nicolais Tagebücher, nebst biographischen Ergänzungen von D. Schröder* (Leipzig, 1892), p. 130.

II

Solera's libretto was based on Old Testament references to the Babylonian emperor Nebuchadnezzar and his subjugation of Jerusalem. Though the character of Nebuchadnezzar (in Italian, Nabucodonosor) is historical, the other characters in the drama were invented by Solera. Or rather, it was supposed that they were: when the opera was staged in Paris it was discovered that Solera had taken his plot, or some part of it, from a French play produced at the Théâtre l'Ambigüe, and the playwright successfully claimed a royalty.[1] This was neither the first nor the last time in his career that Solera was to be accused of plagiarism. He passed off music by Antonio Bazzini as his own, and his libretto for Verdi's next opera *I Lombardi* was apparently lifted without acknowledgment from another source. He had, nevertheless, a gift for versification. The libretto of *Nabucco* is not without a certain distinction; Solera was responsible at least for the actual Italian words even if some of the plot's structure had been taken from a French play.

The opera is in four acts, each of which is headed by a sub-title and a brief quotation or paraphrase from the Book of Jeremiah, by way of preface. Act I is "Jerusalem", and its prefatory text is: "Thus saith the Lord: Behold I will give this city into the hands of the king of Babylon: he will burn it with fire."

The year is 586 B.C., the place the Temple of Solomon in Jerusalem. The Hebrews bewail their defeat by Nabucco, and call upon heaven to defend the holy Temple. Zaccaria, a Hebrew prophet, enters with a

---

[1] Five years after the première of *Nabucco*, when he was in Florence rehearsing *Macbeth*, Verdi made the acquaintance of a number of Florentine intellectuals, writers and artists, among them the Tuscan poet, and leading dramatist of the Risorgimento, Giovanni Batista Niccolini, who was then in his 60s. Discovering that Niccolini had nearly thirty years earlier written a play called *Nabucco*, I procured a copy, half-expecting to discover an unacknowledged source for Solera's *Nabucco*. But Niccolini's five-act play of 1819, more concerned to hint at parallels with Napoleon, has absolutely nothing in common with Solera's libretto. Its principal characters are Nabucco (an earlier emperor), his mother, Vasti; his wife, Amiti; his counsellor, Asfene; a High Priest called Mitrane; and a Satrap or Governor, Arsace. Nabucco (Napoleon), having returned from a Scythian expedition, finds himself opposed by an assembly of rulers. The High Priest Mitrane is a thinly disguised Pius VII. The play ends with the stage direction: "Appena Nabucco si è gettato nell' Eufrate, soprarrivano i nemici vittoriosi, e cade il sipario" ("Hardly has Nabucco flung himself into the Euphrates when his victorious enemies arrive, and the curtain falls").

Niccolini also wrote a play about the Sicilian Vespers, called *Giovanni da Procida* (1830). But, not surprisingly, it bears no resemblance to the patchwork hack libretto that Scribe provided for Verdi's *Les Vêpres siciliennes*. These two plays, like most of Niccolini's, were intended as patriotic propaganda and, as such, were apparently effective.

prisoner, Fenena, daughter of Nabucco, and exhorts the people to trust in God. Giving Fenena into the care of Ismaele, a young Hebrew officer and nephew of the king, he leads the crowd in a prayer invoking God's aid against the Babylonians. When Zaccaria and the crowd have departed, Ismaele and Fenena confess their love for each other. Ismaele had first met Fenena when he was Ambassador to Babylon and was being amorously pursued by her sister Abigaille. He had been imprisoned in Babylon, but had escaped with Fenena's aid. He now offers to allow her to escape but, before he can guide her to safety, Fenena's sister Abigaille suddenly enters, sword in hand, at the head of a band of Babylonian soldiers disguised as Hebrews. She has captured the Temple, but offers Ismaele his safety in return for his love, an offer which he contemptuously declines.

The Hebrews and Levite priests rush back into the Temple, followed by retreating soldiers who inform them that Nabucco is riding towards the Temple. Babylonian soldiers appear, and Nabucco enters the Temple on horseback. Zaccaria denounces him as a madman and warns him that he is in the house of God. "Di Dio che parli?" ("What's that about God?"), Nabucco asks, laughing. Zaccaria seizes Nabucco's younger daughter, Fenena, and raising a knife threatens to kill her if Nabucco continues to profane the Temple. Nabucco finds it expedient to dismount, and the several characters voice their feelings in ensemble. Nabucco orders the Hebrews to their knees. Zaccaria renews his threat to Fenena, but has the knife snatched from his hand by Ismaele. Nabucco orders his soldiers to plunder and burn the temple.

Act II is "L'empio" (The Wicked Man): ("Behold the whirlwind of the Lord goeth forth with fury; it shall fall upon the head of the wicked.") The act takes place in Nabucco's palace in Babylon. The Jews have been taken to Babylon as prisoners; Nabucco has appointed Fenena as Regent while he is away fighting again. In the first scene, in the royal apartments, Abigaille enters with a parchment she has found amongst Nabucco's belongings, proving that she is not his daughter but a slave girl whom he had adopted. She gives voice to her jealousy of Fenena and, recalling that once she was tender, warm-hearted and in love, vows that her fury now will descend upon all: upon Fenena, Nabucco, the entire kingdom, and even upon herself. The Babylonian High Priest enters to inform her that Fenena is setting the Hebrews free, and incites her to rebellion. He, the nobles and elders have already spread the rumour that the King has been killed in battle. Abigaille agrees to seize the throne, and looks forward to her so-called father and sister having to abase themselves before a humble slave.

The second scene takes place in a large hall in the palace. Zaccaria, accompanied by a Levite, enters carrying the Tables of the Law. He believes the Lord has appointed him to convert Fenena to the Jewish faith. After praying for guidance, he and the Levite go to Fenena's apartment. A crowd of Levites now assembles, wondering who can have summoned them to a meeting in these surroundings. Ismaele enters and attempts to address them, but they shun him in horror as a traitor accursed by God. Zaccaria now enters, accompanied by his sister Anna and Fenena. "Forgive him, brethren," cries Anna. "The maiden whose life he saved is now a Hebrew." A commotion is heard outside, and Abdallo, a loyal old retainer of Nabucco, rushes in and warns Fenena to flee. The king's death has been announced, and the people are calling for Abigaille. Abigaille enters, demanding that Fenena give up the crown. Fenena refuses. Suddenly, Nabucco enters with his soldiers and, seizing the crown from Fenena, places it upon his head, daring Abigaille to remove it. He rages against the Babylonians: their God has turned them into traitors, but from now on there is no other God than Nabucco himself. Zaccaria warns him that Jehovah will strike him down for his blasphemy, at which Nabucco orders that that he and the rest of the Jews be put to death. Fenena declares that, having embraced their faith, she will die with them. Nabucco repeats that he is God. A deafening thunderbolt is heard, and the crown is lifted from Nabucco's head by an unseen force, and dashed to the ground. It becomes clear from Nabucco's countenance that his reason is leaving him. Muttering of the phantoms that torment him, he collapses. "Heaven has punished the boaster," says Zaccaria. Seizing the fallen crown, Abigaille cries that nevertheless the splendour of Baal shall not wane.

Act III is entitled "La profezia" (The Prophecy). ("The wild beasts of the desert shall dwell in Babylon, together with owls; and hoopoes shall dwell therein.") It has two scenes, the first of which takes place in the Hanging Gardens of Babylon. Abigaille, seated upon the throne, is surrounded by her retinue. The High Priest is about to persuade her to sign Fenena's death sentence when a dishevelled and distraught Nabucco enters. Recognising his surroundings, he approaches the throne, is surprised to find it already occupied, and at first does not recognise Abigaille. She tells him she was merely custodian of the throne during his illness, and asks for his signature on the death sentence for all the Hebrew rebels. He is reluctant to sign: something, he is not sure what it is, is gnawing at his mind. But when Abigaille taunts him with being afraid of the Hebrews he snatches the parchment in a frenzy and signs it. He remembers Fenena, and asks of her. "She is a traitress and shall die," replies Abigaille, handing the order to guards, who immediately leave with it. Nabucco angrily informs Abigaille she is no daughter of his, but a slave. He searches in his garments for the document of proof, but Abigaille herself produces it and tears it into pieces. As Nabucco collapses in despair, a sound of trumpets is heard, signifying that the sentence of death to the Hebrews has been confirmed. Rousing himself, Nabucco calls for his guards but is scornfully informed by Abigaille that the guards are there simply to keep him prisoner. Nabucco begs for Fenena's life, but Abigaille is unmoved.

The second scene of Act III is set on the banks of the Euphrates where the Hebrews, in chains, are at enforced labour. They sing of their homeland, of the banks of the Jordan, of the city of Jerusalem. Zaccaria enters and chides them for lamenting. Soon, he tells them, the Lord will set them free, and the wrath of the Lion of Judah will fall upon Babylon. He rouses them to a more defiant mood.

Act IV is "L'idolo infranto" (The Broken Idol). ("Baal is confounded: his idols are broken in pieces".) In scene 1, Nabucco, still distracted, awakes from a nightmare to hear shouts outside. At first he thinks it is a call to arms against Zion, but soon realises that the crowd is calling Fenena's name. Going to the balcony, he sees her in chains being led to execution. He rushes to the doors, only to find them locked. Falling on his knees, he prays to the Hebrew God. He asks for forgiveness, promising that the Temple of Judah shall be restored if only God will clear his mind of its confusion. He feels his senses beginning to return to him. "True and omnipotent God," he cries, "henceforth I shall worship you forever." As he rushes again to one of the doors and attempts to force it open, his retainer Abdallo enters, accompanied by soldiers, and tries to dissuade the sick king from exposing himself to the distress of seeing his daughter put to death. Announcing that he is no longer ill, Nabucco demands his sword. Joyfully Abdallo gives it to him, and they go off to save Fenena.

Scene 2 is in the Hanging Gardens. The Babylonian High Priest stands by a sacrificial altar, while those condemned to die are brought in. Zaccaria comforts Fenena, telling her she will find peace in Heaven. A cry of "Long live Nabucco" is heard, and the King enters, sword in hand. He orders the idol of Baal to be destroyed, and the idol immediately shatters. All are confounded by this miracle. Nabucco commands that the Jews be released and that a new Temple be built to their God. He announces that Abigaille has taken poison, and asks Fenena to kneel with him in prayer. A dying and repentent Abigaille is carried in. She asks Nabucco to bless the union of Fenena and Ismaele, implores God to forgive her, and dies.

III

In style, the Overture to *Nabucco* is almost interchangeable with that of *Oberto*. Constructed mainly on themes to be heard in the opera, including the great chorus "Va, pensiero" (in 3/8 time, and much less effective than when heard chorally in the opera), it emphasises by its reliance on march rhythms the processional aspect of the work. Act I, "Gerusalemme", opens with a broadly planned chorus which, after its initial *allegro mosso*, settles into a more solemn tempo, deploying

with immense skill and maximum effectiveness its component forces of
Hebrews, Levites, and Hebrew virgins. The framework derives, no
doubt, from Rossini, but the authority with which it is filled in shows
an advance on the more naïve choral writing of Verdi's earlier two
operas. Zaccaria's *andante maestoso* cavatina, exhorting his people to
put their trust in God, has the authentic Verdian *slancio*. The composer's use of the chorus in unison with the soloist is sufficiently in-
frequent to be peculiarly affecting wherever it occurs. Zaccaria's
cabaletta is thematically of no great distinction, but the important
part played in it by the chorus is unusual and arresting. The following
recitative and trio are dominated by the personality of Abigaille, and
her fearsome vocal line. Her scornful "Prode guerrier" to Ismaele
begins on the B below middle C, and the recitative takes her to the B
two octaves above. In the more gentle trio, she twice rises to C. The
brief, urgent chorus whose theme is tossed from group to group as first
the women, then the Elders, the Levites and the soldiers come rushing in
to tell of the imminent approach of Nabucco, sounds meaningless and
somewhat threadbare when it is divorced from the stage action, but
Verdi's innate dramatic sense has led him to produce exactly the right
kind of hustle preparatory to Nabucco's entrance. The first act finale
begins with the brassy yet curiously playful Babylonian march, as
Nabucco and his forces draw nearer. Nabucco rides into the Temple
and, when rebuked by Zaccaria, opens the *andante* ensemble with
"Tremin gl'insani del mio furore". A hectically Rossinian presto section
of the ensemble brings the Act to a close.

Act II opens with a short scene consisting of Abigaille's recitative,
aria and cabaletta. The vigorous C major recitative, which contains a
startling two-octave leap from top C to middle C, leads by way of a
bridge passage for solo flute into the *andante* cavatina in G, "Anch'io
dischiuso un giorno", a most beautiful aria whose sinuous line and
elegant figuration recall Bellini's "Casta diva" [Ex. 8].

Ex. 8

chi   del perdu - to   in can - to............................ mi

tor - na un gior - - no sol?

Abigaille's war-like C major cabaletta is a really splendid piece of
musical invective and belligerence. The fact that it rises twice to top C
has encouraged sopranos to end it on that note as well, instead of the
written C an octave lower. The second scene of Act II opens with

Zaccaria's prayer, "Tu sul labbro", whose orchestral introduction shows the influence of Mozart and, more particularly, Haydn. Verdi was certainly familiar with several of their quartets, and he had only a few years earlier conducted *The Creation* in Milan. The sixteen bars of orchestral introduction to Zaccaria's prayer, a solemn tune for cellos with a prominent solo part, could as easily lead into the opening allegro of a Haydn quartet. The prayer itself is superbly, though quite simply scored. Its first twelve bars are accompanied only by a single bass line. Later, divided strings support the voice. This is most sensitive writing of the kind that one expects more readily to find in *Don Carlo* than in the operas of Verdi's earliest period. But it is useless to generalise about Verdi. The line from *Oberto* to *Falstaff* is by no means a straight and steady ascent: just as a few bars of *Otello* will appear to lapse into the manner of *Il corsaro*, so for a page or so *I due Foscari* or *Alzira* will suddenly leap into the future.

The quick march chorus of the Levites as they shun Ismaele with pious violence has already been heard in the Overture. It is followed by a scene for Anna, Zaccaria, Abdallo and Fenena in which Abigaille enters demanding the crown. The unexpected arrival of Nabucco leads into the second act finale, a canon quartet begun by Nabucco himself, and taken up by Abigaille, Ismaele and Fenena. Finally, the other characters and the chorus add their voices. Nabucco's defiant recitative culminates in his proclaiming himself God. When the thunderbolt robs him of his crown, the hushed and terrified murmur of the ensemble is followed by Nabucco's crazed, broken arioso, which veers in tempo between fast and slow, ending not with a bang but a whimper: a clear adumbration of Rigoletto's "Cortigiani, vil razza dannata". Abigaille seizes the crown triumphantly as the curtain falls.

Act III has a formal opening chorus in which the Assyrians sing the praises of their country, victorious in war and prosperous in peace. It, too, has already been heard in the Overture. A passage of recitative in which the High Priest presents the death sentence for Abigaille's approval only to be interrupted by the distraught entrance of Nabucco leads to the splendid duet for Nabucco and Abigaille. This is not the first of Verdi's father-daughter duets, as we have seen: there is an excellent example in *Oberto*, his first produced opera. But it certainly belongs in the great line of such duets which continues through *I due Foscari*, *Giovanna d'Arco*, *Luisa Miller*, *Rigoletto*, *La traviata*, *Simon Boccanegra*, *Aroldo*, *La forza del destino* and *Aida*. On this occasion, however, the usual family feeling is not in evidence.

In Act III, Scene 2, the captive Jews toiling by the banks of the Euphrates sing of their homeland. Verdi's great, largely unison chorus achieves its very moving effect by the simplest and sincerest of means. The same can be said of Solera's verses which, while hardly beautiful poetry, possess an affecting directness of diction which obviously touched Verdi. Solera did not always write with such biblical simplicity. These, as Verdi himself has told us, are the verses which caught his eye and his imagination when the manuscript fell open on his desk. It is easy to understand the feeling they aroused in him:

> Va, pensiero, sull' ali dorate;
> va, ti posa sui clivi, sui colli,
> ove olezzano tepide e molli
> L'aure dolci del suolo natal.
>
> Del Giordano le rive saluta,
> di Sionne le torri atterate;
> o mia patria sì bella e perduta,
> o membranza sì cara e fatal.
>
> Arpa d'òr de fatidici vati,
> perchè muta dal salice pendi?
> Le memorie nel petto raccendi,
> ci favella del tempo che fu.
>
> O simile di Solima ai fati
> traggi un suono di crudo lamento,
> o t'inspiri il Signore un concento
> che ne infonda al patire virtù.

(I have attempted a verse translation:

> Fly, o thought, on wings of gold,
> rest upon those hills, that sand
> where the air is soft and mild
> in my dearest native land.
>
> Greet the fallen towers of Zion
> and the Jordan's shimmering heat.
> O my country, fair and lost,
> O remembrance, fatal, sweet.
>
> Golden harp of ancient bards,
> hanging silent on the tree,
> stir my heart's fond memories now,
> sing of when our land was free.
>
> Solomon's sad fate recall
> in your deep lamenting song
> which I pray God to inspire:
> tragic, hopeful, patient, strong.)

How could the Milanese fail to respond to the pathos of "O mio patria sì bella e perduta, o membranza sì cara e fatal" and to Verdi's heartfelt setting of it, with its sudden crescendo at the beginning of the phrase? [Ex. 9.] From this moment on, until the unification of Italy

Ex. 9

Oh mia pa - tria si bel - la e per - du - ta! Oh mem -

bran - za si ca - ra e fa - tal!

nearly thirty years later, Verdi was to find himself continually in trouble with the censorhip, usually Austrian or papal.

By way of cabaletta to the moving appeal and patriotic nostaglia of "Va, pensiero", Zaccaria leads his people in a vigorous prophecy. The Lion of Judah will triumph and Babylon shall be destroyed. Zaccaria's vocal line ranges over two octaves from his low to his high F sharp. This is the section that Verdi forced Solera to write by locking him in until he had finished it. The librettist had, after "Va, pensiero", introduced a love scene between Fenena and Ismaele.

The first scene of Act IV in which, after asking Jehovah's pardon, Nabucco recovers his senses is a remarkable solo scene. The orchestral introduction cleverly conveys Nabucco's confused state of mind: passages of meaningless violence alternate with reminiscence of ceremonial pomp. After he calls despairingly, "Dio degli Ebrei, perdono", a stillness descends. Then solo cello and flute alternate for six bars in enveloping him in peace and resignation. He begins his prayer, "Dio di Giuda", to a tune which seems to have been common intellectual property in the first half of the nineteenth century. It forms part of Anna Bolena's mad scene in Donizetti's opera, and is also known as Bishop's "Home, Sweet Home" [Ex. 10]. The cabaletta in which,

Ex. 10

restored to sanity, Nabucco prepares to rescue Fenena is one which looks crude on the page but sounds exciting in performance.

The finale of the opera is somewhat perfunctory. Fenena's funeral march is effective in context, though her prayer, for all its simplicity, falls short of achieving real distinction. The unaccompanied choral hymn is dramatically just right. In future years Verdi hardly ever failed with dying music, especially music for dying sopranos, but Abigaille's last utterances do not have the individuality of Violetta's or Gilda's or of either of the later Leonoras. She enters to the sound of a solo oboe, and her call to heaven brings the more peaceful timbre of solo flute, to which she dies calmly and quietly. Zaccaria's abrupt cry to Nabucco that, in serving Jehovah, he will be King of Kings, ends the opera.

I cannot agree with Toye that *Nabucco* is the "most satisfactory of all the early Verdi operas": for me it is surpassed by *Macbeth*. Nevertheless, it is the first great peak one encounters amongst the early works. To Bellinian grace and Donizettian flair and enthusiasm Verdi has added freshness, vigour and, most important of all, emotional intensity. *Nabucco* is his earliest opera to hold its place in the repertoire; it is also his first in which the complete work can be said to possess a significance of its own, above and beyond the sum of its superb components. The choruses are splendid. They cover a wide range of expression, and really are the centre pieces of the entire work. *Nabucco* is a choral opera in the sense that Rossini's *Mosè in Egitto* is choral, but Verdi's characters are brought considerably closer to aesthetic life than Rossini's. It is in *Nabucco*, too, that we begin to perceive Verdi's interest in the expressive use of orchestral colour. How cleverly, for instance, he uses various combinations of woodwind to create that dark, melancholy sound which is so distinctive a feature of his mature orchestration. The opera is pervaded by a sense of exile and loss. Behind the ceremonial pomp, the marches and the choruses, there exist the yearning for home of the captive Jews and the tortured despair of the despotic and neurotic Nabucco. It is perhaps most of all in the individual characters that Verdi begins to define himself. Abigaille is a definite ancestor of Lady Macbeth, just as the more shadowy Nabucco is a sketch for Macbeth, a character equally dominated by a female relative. The martial and political aspects of relationships are predominant in *Nabucco*. The love interest is minimal and the tenor's role unimportant, though both love and tenor were, along with politics, to play larger parts in the operas of the next few years. Verdi's remark that his artistic career began with *Nabucco* is sound, although the immediate effect of its commercial success was to drive him to produce opera after opera with maniacal haste. He did not write each one within a few days as Donizetti was occasionally capable of doing; nevertheless, the operas of the "galley years" as he called them do contain pages where the speed in composition is apparent. Eventually Verdi was to raise the artistic stature of Italian opera to heights undreamed of by Rossini and Donizetti, though perhaps dreamed of by Bellini. But the struggle against prevailing conditions and contemporary tastes was to be a long one.

IV

I Lombardi alla prima crociata and *Jérusalem*

Dramatis personae:

Arvino, son of the Governor of Rhodes, Folco	(tenor)
Pagano, Arvino's brother	(bass)
Viclinda, Arvino's wife	(soprano)
Giselda, their daughter	(soprano)
Pirro, Pagano's steward	(bass)
The Prior of Milan	(tenor)
Acciano, tyrant of Antioch	(bass)
Sofia, his wife	(soprano)
Oronte, their son	(tenor)

The Count of Toulouse	(baritone)
Roger, his brother	(bass)
Hélène, the Count's daughter	(soprano)
Isaure, her companion	(soprano)
A soldier	(bass)
Papal Ambassador	(bass)
The Emir of Ramla	(bass)
Gaston, Viscount of Béarn	(tenor)
Raymond, Gaston's steward	(tenor)
The Emir's officer	(tenor)

LIBRETTO by Temistocle Solera, based on Tomasso Grossi's poem *I Lombardi alla prima crociata*

TIME: 1099
PLACE: Milan, Antioch, the country near Jerusalem

FIRST PERFORMED at La Scala, Milan, February 11, 1843, with Erminia Frezzolini (Giselda); Teresa Ruggeri (Viclinda); Carlo Guasco (Oronte); Napoleone Marconi (Arvino); Prospero Derivis (Pagano); Gaetano Rossi (Pirro); Giovanni Severi (Prior of Milan)

LIBRETTO by Alphonse Royer and Gustav Vaëz, based on Solera's *I Lombardi*

TIME: 1095–1099
PLACE: Toulouse, Palestine

FIRST PERFORMED at the Paris Opéra, November 26, 1847, with Julian Van Gelder (Hélène); Muller (Isaure); Gilbert Louis Duprez (Gaston); Charles Portheaut (Count of Toulouse); Alizard (Roger); Hippolyte Brémont (Papal Ambassador)

I Lombardi alla prima crociata and *Jérusalem*

I

IN THE NINE years between *Nabucco* (1842) and *Rigoletto* (1851), Verdi wrote at least one opera a year, and sometimes two. Looking back on this period later from the more comfortable situation of the wealthy composer who wrote only when he wanted to, and was able to devote to each composition as much time as he required, he referred to it as his years in the galley. His standard of achievement varied widely during these years; even within individual operas passages of superb invention alternate with scenes that are crudely and hastily concocted. In saying this, one might be describing the operas of Donizetti: the difference is that Verdi was almost incapable of writing a dull page. He brought to Italian opera of the eighteen-forties a nervous energy, a brooding romanticism and a rough vigour which succeeded one another with astonishing rapidity. Even at their silliest, the operas Verdi wrote during this decade have a fresh vitality that completely holds one's interest from beginning to end. Some of these operas, *Macbeth* and *Ernani* for instance, are indisputably works of genius; some, such as *Il corsaro* and *Alzira* are merely ordinary stuff shot through with Verdi's individuality and profuse melodic gift. All, on their different levels, are immensely enjoyable in performance. And many, of course, were at the time associated with the cause of a united and free Italy.

After the success of *Nabucco*, Merelli immediately asked Verdi for another opera, telling the composer he could name his own terms. Verdi consulted the singer Giuseppina Strepponi, who advised him to hold out for a decent but not an impossible fee, and suggested he ask for the same amount as Bellini had received eleven years earlier for *Norma*. Verdi took her advice and Merelli accepted his terms. Solera was again selected as librettist, and chose as his subject Tommaso Grossi's dramatic poem in fifteen parts, *I Lombardi alla prima crociata* (The Lombards at the First Crusade), which had been published in Milan in 1826. Within a few months the opera was ready. The Archbishop of Milan heard that it included a sacrilegious stage representation of the sacrament of baptism, and ordered the Chief of Police to ban its performance. The Chief of Police attempted to persuade Verdi to compromise, but the composer refused to discuss the matter. Solera and Merelli were both interviewed by the Chief of Police and they made it clear to him that they had no influence over their stubborn composer. Finally he agreed to allow the performance as long as the line "Ave Maria" was changed to "Salve Maria". On behalf of the composer, Merelli accepted this momentous alteration, and *I Lombardi* had its première at La Scala on February 11, 1843, before a keyed-up audience, many of whom had queued for several hours to obtain seats. The evening was a triumph, and the police rule of no encores was broken again and again. The Milanese decided from the very beginning of the opera that they were the Lombards, that the Holy Land they were defending was Italy, and that Saracens had a great deal in common with Austrians. When, in the last act, the Lombards were incited to battle with the words "La Santa Terra oggi nostra sarà" ("Today the Holy Land will be ours"), many of the audience spontaneously shouted "Si!" and there was an outburst of loud cheering. Again the twenty-nine-year-old Verdi, without consciously intending to, had identified with the aspirations of his audience, and had written music to stir their patriotic feelings, to rouse them to action, and to make the soothed breast savage.

II

Tommaso Grossi (1790–1853) was one of a group of Milanese romantic poets and playwrights who were followers of the writer and patriot, Manzoni. Though hardly a major poet, Grossi is still frequently to be encountered in anthologies of Italian verse, usually represented by his sentimental little poem "La rondinella". His long narrative verse epic, *I Lombardi alla prima crociata*, which he wrote between 1821 and 1826, was inspired by and is to some extent an imitation of the *Gerusalemme Liberata* of the sixteenth-century poet Torquato Tasso (1544–1595). It is also the work of someone who has read Scott's *Ivanhoe*. Grossi's poem recounts the adventures of a Lombard family in the first Crusade, and Solera based his libretto on part of Grossi's narrative, altering some but not all of the characters' names. Giselda, for instance, retains her name, but Grossi's Saladino becomes Solera's Oronte. Solera's libretto is in four acts, each act having its own sub-title, as in *Nabucco*. The time is the late eleventh century: since Jerusalem is captured at the end of the opera, we can pin it down to 1099.

The first act, "La vendetta" (The Revenge), takes place in Milan: Scene 1 is the Piazza di Sant' Ambrogio, where the citizens have gathered to welcome Pagano back from the exile to which years ago he had been sentenced. He and his brother Arvino had fallen in love with the same woman, Viclinda. Viclinda accepted Arvino and, on the way to their wedding, Pagano in a fit of jealousy had tried to kill his brother. For this he was banished. Now, repentant, he has returned home. From the church of Sant' Ambrogio in the square, Pagano, Arvino, Viclinda and Giselda, the daughter of Viclinda and Arvino, now emerge, preceded by the Prior of Milan. Before the crowd, the brothers Pagano and Arvino embrace. But Arvino feels a lingering uneasiness, as well he might, for Pagano almost immediately begins to plot with his henchman Pirro. The Prior announces that Arvino has been chosen to lead the Lombard Crusaders. The citizens acclaim Arvino, and all depart except Pagano and Pirro. From the church a chorus of nuns is heard praying for peace. "Vergini," cries Pagano, "il ciel per ora a vostre preci è chiuso" ("Virgins, heaven now is deaf to your prayers"). He is still tormented by his love for Viclinda, and plans to abduct her that night and to kill Arvino. Pirro assembles the band of ruffians Pagano has hired.

The scene changes to a gallery in the palace of Folco, the father of Arvino and Pagano, with whom Arvino and his family live. It is night. Viclinda asks Giselda to pray with her for Arvino's safety, but Arvino has a presentiment of more immediate danger than the Crusade, and orders his wife to take refuge in her room. Giselda and Viclinda kneel, and Giselda prays to the Virgin Mary. The women leave, and Pagano and Pirro enter stealthily. They extinguish the lights, and Pagano goes off towards Arvino's room. Pirro disappears in another direction to investigate a noise of sword-play. Pagano comes back and encounters Viclinda. He is about to carry her off by force when Arvino, Giselda and a number of servants enter with torches. Pagano is stupefied. He asks whose blood is on his sword, and is told it is his father's. Stricken with remorse, he tries to kill himself, but is restrained by Arvino's retainers. An ensemble in which all express their horror brings the act to an end.

Act II is entitled "L'uomo della caverna" (The Man in the Cave) and takes place at Antioch. The first scene is a hall in the palace of Acciano, the tyrant of Antioch. Acciano is seated on his throne, surrounded by ambassadors, soldiers and citizens. After invoking the wrath of Allah on the Crusaders, they all go off, and Acciano's wife Sofia enters with their son Oronte. Giselda has been captured by the Muslims, and Oronte has fallen in love with her. He asks his mother for news of Giselda, and is told that she thinks only of him, weeps, sighs and calls his name continually. Oronte confesses his love for Giselda, and says he is willing to embrace the Christian faith for her sake. This pleases his mother, who is secretly a Christian.

The scene changes to the entrance of a cave on a mountain-side, the home of a hermit greatly renowned as a holy man. He is, in fact, Pagano who, having repented of his sins, is attempting to expiate them. He anxiously awaits the arrival of the Crusaders, whom he will help to free the Holy Land. He sees someone approaching, wearing Muslim garments.

This turns out to be his former steward Pirro, who has become a Muslim. Full of remorse for his part in the murder of Pagano's father, he seeks the hermit's guidance. He confesses his identity, but Pagano does not reveal his. The distant sound of the approaching Crusaders delights Pagano, who tells Pirro that his sins will be pardoned if he guides the Crusaders into the city. As the Crusaders draw nearer, Pagano realises they are Lombards. Entering his cave with Pirro, he returns wearing a helmet and carrying a sword. Arvino, his brother, enters at the head of his troops. He has come to seek the Holy Man's aid in rescuing Giselda from her Muslim captors. The hermit assures him that Giselda will be saved, and that before nightfall the city will have fallen to the Lombards.

The third scene of Act II takes place in the women's quarters in Acciano's palace. Giselda, taunted by the other members of the harem, calls despairingly upon heaven to aid her. Suddenly there is a commotion outside: the Crusaders have attacked the palace. Sofia enters to inform Giselda that both Acciano and Oronte have been killed. The Crusaders rush in, led by Arvino and the Hermit, who points out Giselda to her father. Sofia identifies Arvino as the slayer of her husband and son and, when Arvino attempts to embrace his daughter, Giselda recoils from him in horror, crying that God cannot have willed this slaughter. Furious at her blasphemy, Arvino is about to raise his sword to her when he is restrained by the Hermit, who tells him that the poor girl has lost her reason.

Act III is entitled "La Conversione" (The Conversion). In the first scene, set in the Valley of Jehoshaphat, Jerusalem can be glimpsed in the far distance. After a chorus of pilgrims has passed on its way, Giselda enters, distraught and dishevelled. She encounters Oronte who is dressed in Lombard costume. He had only been wounded, and had managed to escape from the palace. Giselda and Oronte swear their love for each other. Hearing a sound from the nearby Lombard camp which spells danger for Oronte, they flee.

In the second scene Arvino, alone in his tent in the Lombard camp, invokes the wrath of heaven against his impious daughter. Soldiers enter to inform him that his brother Pagano has been seen in the vicinity of the camp. Not realising that Pagano is the Hermit, Arvino imagines he is lurking about to cause trouble, and swears vengeance upon his brother.

The last scene of Act III is a grotto, through an aperture of which the banks of the Jordan can be seen. Giselda and Oronte, who is dying of his wounds, have taken shelter in the grotto. When Giselda apostrophises God, calling him cruel, the Hermit suddenly appears and persuades her to desist from such blasphemy. He baptizes Orontes, who dies assuring Giselda that they will be reunited in heaven.

The last act, "Il santo sepolcro" (The Holy Sepulchre), opens in a cave in the hills outside Jerusalem. The sleeping Giselda experiences a vision in which a celestial choir leads her to Oronte, who tells her that the fountain of Siloam will gush forth in the desert, bringing water to the parched Crusaders. In the next scene, the Lombard camp near the sepulchre of Rachel, the Crusaders and pilgrims lament their fate, without water and surrounded by desert. Giselda, Arvino and the Hermit enter, announcing that the fountain of Siloam is miraculously flowing. The Lombards drink, are refreshed, and are led into battle by Arvino. The final scene takes place in Arvino's tent. The Hermit, who has been seriously wounded in the fighting, reveals his true identity to Giselda and Arvino. Arvino forgives him and, supporting the dying man, opens the tent door to reveal in the distance the Holy City of Jerusalem from whose towers the Cross of the Crusaders can be seen fluttering in the breeze.

Solera of course acknowledged Grossi's poem as the provenance of his libretto: it was so well known that he could hardly do otherwise. It seems, however, that he plagiarised a play on the same subject as well. Its author, Giulio Pullè, brought charges against him in March 1843, a mere few weeks after the première. In a city less tense than Milan must have been in 1843, such a muddled and perfunctory libretto would have been more strongly criticised. As it was, *I Lombardi* fulfilled a need of the time. The audience which a few months earlier identified with the Jews of the Old Testament now saw themselves as Lombard Crusaders whose sacred mission was to free Jerusalem from the infidels, or Milan from the Austrians. The libretto's idiocies were forgiven: its message was read clearly as an incitement to rebellion. Its crude directness and Verdi's unquenchable vitality ensured the success of the opera in Milan.

III

I Lombardi has no full-scale self-contained Overture: a brief orchestral *adagio*, some of whose *religioso* material will be encountered in altered form later in the opera, leads straight into the opening chorus, and immediately one is in the thick of the opera's merits and defects, for the chorus is rather silly, yet appealing; the section in which Pagano's attempted fratricide of years past is narrated is particularly jolly. After a page of recitative, Giselda launches a magnificent ensemble with her "T'assale un tremito". The characters voice their feelings of smug joy, of vague foreboding, of, in the case of Pagano and Pirro, bloody intent. Giselda's floridly decorated top line prepares us for the excellent coloratura writing elsewhere in this spinto role. After the Prior of Milan's announcement, a galloping *allegro vivace* introduces the Crusaders' March. Pagano's solo scene not only contains some very fine writing for the voice, but also in form and situation foreshadows the

Count's attempted abduction of Leonora in Act III of *Il trovatore*: first the chorus of nuns, then Pagano's love-crazed recitative, in which he actually sums himself up in a line: "Amor dovea renderla santa o rea". ("Love must become sacred or guilty".) He is a creature obsessed by love: in the first half of the opera he is without doubt *reo* because of this, but the same love makes him *santo* when he gets to the Holy Land. His aria, "Sciagurata, hai tu creduto", is particularly interesting. Under the determination, *con slancio*, of the vocal line, Verdi's orchestra comments on Pagano's troubled state of mind. The chorus of ruffians is very funny: it is the kind of thing satirized by Gilbert and Sullivan in "With cat-like tread". Their *piano* phrases are punctuated by *forte* chords from an orchestra apparently determined to warn of their presence. The nuns are heard briefly from within the church, and then Pagano and his villains plunge into a good rough piece of cabaletta.

The second scene opens with Giselda's very beautiful and delicately scored "Salve Maria" which, to my mind, is as fine a piece as Desdemona's "Ave Maria". The old ignorant jeer that, before *Aida*, Verdi wrote nothing but barrel organ tunes to skeletal accompaniments that merely marked the rhythm for the singer, was always absurdly misdirected. At his best the young Verdi wrote for his orchestra with the imagination and skill of a Berlioz, and with a mastery of effect gained by economical means. The first part of Giselda's exquisite prayer is harmonically interesting, and all of it is imaginatively scored, particularly the section where only flute and clarinet accompany the voice. The Leonora di Vargas-like melody into which the aria broadens, over tremolando chords, at "Vergine santa" is one of those tunes which Verdi was able miraculously to extract from a simple ascending or descending scale. ("Caro nome" is the most famous example, and the dying music of Leonora in *Il trovatore* perhaps the most beautiful.) [Ex. 11.]

Ex. 11

The First act finale, incorporating Pagano's inadvertent murder of his father, his bungled abduction of Viclinda and his banishment for the second time, contains some excellent pages, particularly in the first part of the ensemble "Mostro d'averno orribile", from which Pagano's sinuous cry of almost ecstatic shame and despair slithers its way up the stave [Ex. 12].

Ex. 12

The Rossinian *presto*, though less individual than the preceding ensemble, adequately performs its function of ending the Act quickly and dramatically.

The second act opens with a somewhat perfunctory chorus of ambassadors to Acciano's court in Antioch. But Oronte's cavatina, "La mia letizia infondere", is a graceful and rewarding aria for which Verdi wrote two alternative cabalettas. Both are effective, but the second, printed in Ricordi's vocal score as "cabaletta nuova", is the more individual of the two. The Hermit's recitative and *adagio* aria are not without interest, though his short scenes with Pirro and with Arvino are somewhat mechanically written. However, the phrase Arvino sings to the words, "Narran tutti in questi lochi, Dio si mostri alla tua fe", turns up a quarter of a century later in Walther's "Preislied" in Wagner's *Die Meistersinger*. The awful yet splendid March of the Lombards makes a reappearance. In the next scene, the Harem chorus is an extremely inane piece indeed. Mercifully, it is brief. The remainder of the scene, basically consisting of Giselda's aria and cabaletta, is really fine. The vocal range of the very attractive aria is extensive: high Cs, C sharps and Bs proliferate. The cabaletta is particularly remarkable in that it does not merely present a static situation, but carries the action forward. Giselda's cry that God has not willed this slaughter, "No, Dio nol vuole", ironically contrasts with the Hermit Pagano's earlier impassioned assertion that a heavenly voice had said to him, "Dio lo vuole". In Solera's libretto this juxtaposition was probably meant to be dramatically important. In the opera, Verdi somewhat obscures the point.

The Pilgrims' Chorus which opens Act III seems to me vacuous, though Toye found it expressive. The duet for Oronte and Giselda certainly is expressive, and its *andantino* section beginning at "Oh belle, a questa miseria" is particularly beautiful. It ends with Giselda's *fil di voce* on a high B flat [Ex. 13] in rehearsal for a similar moment in the

"Libera Me" of the Requiem [Ex. 115]. The duet's concluding *allegro*, however, is disappointingly unimaginative.

Act III, Scene 2, in Arvino's tent consists solely of a rather poor recitative, aria and truncated cabaletta for Arvino. But the following scene is superb. It opens with a long orchestral introduction containing

an important solo violin part which could easily be mistaken for the slow movement of a concerto by Spohr or Mendelssohn, a charming and tuneful *cantabile* [Ex. 14] which leads into a brilliant *allegro*. The solo violin continues to provide elaborate arpeggios during the trio for Giselda, Oronte and the Hermit, in the course of which Oronte is baptised, to thematic material which recalls the opera's prelude. This beautiful trio [Ex. 15], in particular its concluding *andantino*, is a worthy forerunner of the final trio in *La forza del destino*.

Ex. 15

In the last act the dramatic action degenerates into sheer lunacy, and the musical interest is intermittent. Oronte's spirit sings appropriately accompanied by harp, Giselda's aria is lively, but the fame of the chorus, "O Signore, dal tetto natio", seems to me unmerited. The piece is by no means unpleasing, but Solera's and Verdi's cynical attempt to cash in on the success of their "Va, pensiero" in *Nabucco* fails to come off. In *Nabucco* the situation was real and felt: in *I Lombardi* it appears contrived. The C major, predominantly unison chorus does not compel one's belief in it.

The fountain gushes forth, the Crusaders drink and, refreshed, rush off into battle to their by now familiar tune. The opera ends, like *Forza*, with a trio. The dying Hermit, now revealed as Pagano to his brother and his niece, is consoled by Giselda in one of Verdi's beautifully compassionate phrases [Ex. 16]:

Ex. 16

I Lombardi is fairly typical early Verdi. The composer's inspiration is nervous, fleeting, rarely sustained. Brilliant passages and scenes alternate with mechanical clap-trap. He is rarely dull, but he is some times brutish: this is the price he pays for the masculinity of his temperament compared with Bellini's feminine sensibility and Donizetti's curiously epicene quality. Verdi at this stage of his life certainly possessed the defects of his virtues, but equally certainly possessed those virtues in abundance. One of his Italian biographers, Gino Monaldi, wrote that in *I Lombardi* Verdi seemed "gloomy, agitated, coarse, careless. A curious nervousness takes possession of him. There are plenty of musical themes but they do not build up into a musical edifice. The score of *I Lombardi* is like a waterfall partially hidden by rocks and various obstacles, whose stream gushes forth at some points but is obscured at others, never flowing evenly and distinctly."[1]

This is fair comment. The finest pages of *I Lombardi* have that melodic beauty and creative energy which, by the time of *Il trovatore*, were to become Verdian characteristics. But much of the opera merely matches the crudity of Solera's historical imagination.

IV

Four years and six operas later, in the summer of 1847 when Verdi was in Paris on his way back to Italy after conducting the first performances of *I masnadieri* in London, the Paris Opéra approached him to write an opera for their autumn season. Verdi refused to undertake so important a commission in a few weeks, and instead agreed to adapt *I Lombardi* for performance in Paris. Solera's Italian libretto was refashioned in French by Gustav Vaëz and Alphonse Royer as *Jérusalem*, the Lombard Crusaders becoming French Crusaders from Toulouse. The plot was altered, but as much of the shape and the emotional curve as possible was retained. Until recently, *Jérusalem* had disappeared from the repertoire. Since, however, it is now occasionally performed, a synopsis of the French libretto may be useful:

Act I. The Palace of the Count of Toulouse. About to depart for the Crusades, the Count gives his daughter Hélène in marriage to Gaston Viscount of Béarn, with whom formerly he has quarrelled. The Count's brother Roger, himself in love with Hélène, decides to kill his rival Gaston, and engages a mercenary to do the job. The mercenary kills the Count of Toulouse by mistake, is pursued and captured, and when questioned hits on the idea of accusing Gaston of the crime. The Knights, who had in any case doubted the sincerity of Gaston's reconciliation with the Count, pronounce him accursed, and banish him. The guilty Roger is filled with remorse.

Act II, Scene 1. The Ramla Mountains, Palestine. Roger, now a hermit, kneels at the foot of a cross. For three years he has wandered in the desert, seeking to expiate his sin and asking heaven for pardon. He vows that he will die when he has captured the Holy Sepulchre from the Muslems. Gaston has also made his way to Palestine. Hélène, who has believed him dead, encounters his steward near the Crusaders' camp and is told that Gaston has been taken prisoner by the Emir of Ramla.

[1] *Verdi: 1839–1898.* Second edition, pp. 42–3.

Having never doubted his innocence, she resolves to see him. Pilgrims dying of thirst in the desert are saved by the arrival of the Crusaders. Roger goes to meet them and is stupefied at the sight of his brother, the Count of Toulouse, who had not, after all, been mortally wounded.

Act II, Scene 2. The Palace of the Emir of Ramla. The Emir is told that a Christian woman has been found in the town of Ramla. Hélène is brought in, and in order to discover her identity the Emir has her left alone with Gaston. Hélène suggests to Gaston a means of escape: they will take advantage of the tumult caused by the approach of the Crusaders. At the moment of escape, however, they are stopped by the Emir's guards.

Act III, Scene 1. The Harem gardens. The Crusaders have taken the town and most of the palace, but Hélène is being held by the Emir as a hostage. Gaston has been taken prisoner by the Crusaders and condemned to death for a crime he did not commit.

Act III, Scene 2. A public square in Ramla. Gaston, still protesting his innocence, is made to march in his own funeral procession. He is told that he will be executed under the walls of Jerusalem, having first been stripped of his honours and orders. Gaston implores his comrades to kill him without this dishonour, but his plea goes unanswered. A herald strips him of his armour, piece by piece, calling "This is the helmet" [the shield, the sword] "of a traitorous and disloyal knight." "You lie," Gaston cries in despair, as the knights shout cries of malediction and penitents lugubriously recite a Latin psalm.

Act IV, Scene 1. The Valley of Jehoshaphat. Preparing for combat, the Crusaders invoke God's aid. Roger, now venerated by the Crusaders as a Holy Man, is asked to bring consolation to the last moments of a knight condemned to death. When Hélène arrives to say farewell to her beloved, Roger thus finds himself alone with the woman for love of whom he has committed a crime and the man who is being punished for it, whom he is persuaded to bless. "I die without being allowed to fight the infidels," Gaston cries. "No," replies Roger, "take this sword and with it capture the Holy Sepulchre."

Act IV, Scene 2. The Count of Toulouse's tent. The battle is won. Among the knights who rush in with the captured Muslim standards is one who keeps his vizor down. "You, who were the first to raise our flag in the Holy City, what is your name?" asks the Count. "You have vilified it," replies Gaston. "Destroy this sword, and lead me to execution." "Stop," cries Roger who at that moment enters mortally wounded.

"Do not punish an innocent man for a crime committed by me, Roger, your brother. So that God may pardon me, give me your blessing before I die." The Count forgives him, and the dying man's last wish is granted: the flaps of the tent are turned back so that he can see the banner of the Crusaders flying in the breeze over Jerusalem.

The psychological development of this new plot, in so far as it can be said to develop at all, runs parallel with that of *I Lombardi*. Consequently, a great deal of the score of the earlier opera had merely to undergo minor revision, change of key, and rearrangement of order. Verdi wrote a new orchestral introduction, based on a theme from the trio, to replace the brief prelude of *I Lombardi*. It combines the opera's melancholy and martial aspects. The short scene between Gaston and Hélène is new. It is followed by Hélène's "Ave Maria" which is the "Salve Maria" of the earlier opera. The next number, a somewhat overwrought piece of orchestral scene-painting portraying the sunrise, is new. Verdi did this kind of thing with more sureness and delicacy years later in *Simon Boccanegra*. The chorus that follows is a version of *I Lombardi*'s opening chorus, while the succeeding sextet and chorus, "Je tremble, je tremble encore", is *I Lombardi*'s "T'assale, t'assale un tremito". The female chorus which precedes Roger's aria is taken over from the earlier work, and the aria, "Oh! dans l'ombre", is Pagano's "Sciagurata" with a different, though similar, cabaletta. The first-act finales utilise the same material.

The "Invocation" which opens Act II of *Jérusalem* turns out to be the Hermit's aria, and Hélène's Polonaise, "Quelle ivresse", is Giselda's "Non fu sogno!" from Act IV of *I Lombardi*. The Pilgrims' Chorus is, not surprisingly, "O Signore, dal tetto natio", but the Crusaders' March is new, and rather more stirring than that in the earlier work. The Crusaders' Chorus, also new, is a nondescript *maestoso* piece, with parts for a solo trio consisting of the Count, Roger and the Papal Legate. Gaston's aria, "Je veux encore entendre" is Oronte's "La mia letizia infondere", shorn of its cabaletta. The duet for Hélène and Gaston, which ends the Act, is the Act III duet from *I Lombardi*.

Act III of *Jérusalem* begins with the obligatory ballet. Its opening "choeur dansé" is the chorus of slaves from *I Lombardi*, but the four movements of pleasant and colourfully scored ballet music are, of course, newly composed. They consist of (i) pas de quatre; (ii) pas de deux; (iii) pas solo; (iv) pas d'ensemble. Hélène's aria, "Que m'importe la vie" is Giselda's "Se vano, se vano è il pregare", from Act II of *I Lombardi*. The Marche Funèbre, which moves from sombre dignity to high drama, is new, as is the entire scene of Gaston's disgrace, and his *andante mosso* aria, "O mes amis". The aria is routine, but the scene as a whole is interesting as well as being dramatically effective. The Herald's three-fold cry, "Ceci est le heaume [la targe, l'estoc] de ce traitre deloyal chevalier", with the ritual response of the knights, "Au traitre point de merci", anticipates the trial of Radames in *Aida*. Gaston's desperate cabaletta brings the scene to an end.

Act IV opens with the processional chorus from Act III of *I Lombardi*. The trio, also from Act III of the earlier opera, follows—but without its miniature violin concerto introduction. The splendidly colourful battle music is new; the finale of the opera, however, is a reworking for ensemble of the trio finale of *I Lombardi*.

Jérusalem was given a cool reception in Paris, but was revived, and apparently more enthusiastically received, in French provincial towns. It was later translated into Italian and produced in Milan in 1850 as *Gerusalemme*, though without success. There seems no compelling reason to perform *Jérusalem* today: it contains little music of interest that is not already in the original score, and it understandably lacks the impetus of the perhaps slightly cruder yet immensely more enjoyable *Lombardi*. As *Gerusalemme*, it was revived for the first time this century in 1963 at the Teatro Fenice, Venice.

V

Ernani

Dramatis personae:

Ernani, a bandit	(tenor)
Don Carlo, King of Spain	(baritone)
Don Ruy Gomez de Silva, grandee of Spain	(bass)
Elvira, his niece and his betrothed	(soprano)
Giovanna, her confidante	(soprano)
Don Riccardo, the King's steward	(tenor)
Jago, Silva's steward	(bass)

LIBRETTO by Francesco Maria Piave, based on the play *Hernani* by Victor Hugo

TIME: 1519
PLACE: Spain

FIRST PERFORMED at the Teatro la Fenice, Venice, March 9, 1844, with Sophie Loewe (Elvira); Carlo Guasco (Ernani); Antonio Superchi (Carlo); Antonio Selva (Silva)

Ernani

VERDI'S FIRST FOUR operas had had their premières at La Scala, Milan. Perhaps now he thought it time he wrote for another theatre and another city for, when Count Mocenigo, director of the Teatro La Fenice in Venice, offered to open his autumn season with *I Lombardi*, asking Verdi to conduct the opera and to write a new one for performance the following month, the composer immediately agreed in principle and began to discuss possible subjects and librettists. It was at this time that his thoughts first turned seriously to the possibility of setting a Shakespeare play. He considered turning *King Lear* into an opera. As this was a project which Verdi returned to, on and off, for the remainder of his life, and as *Lear* is certainly the most tantalising of any unwritten Verdi opera, it is worth pausing here to examine the reasons why, although he was so strongly attracted to the idea, Verdi never wrote his *Lear*.

His reason for not immediately proceeding with *Lear* in 1843 was a purely practical one. The role of King Lear would surely have been written for bass or baritone, and would in any case have called for a singer of exceptional attainment. The Fenice had no really first-rate bass or baritone, and, as Verdi at this time of his life preferred to examine the forces available and to write specifically for them, he decided to shelve *Lear* until he received a commission from a theatre with an appropriate singer for the title role.

In 1846, during negotiations with the English impresario Benjamin Lumley, who had asked him to write an opera for Her Majesty's Theatre, London, Verdi again considered *King Lear*. Lumley was able to offer, as Lear, the great French-Irish bass, Luigi Lablache who was then in his early fifties. Terms were, in fact, agreed between Verdi and Lumley for the composition of *King Lear*, on the understanding that the role of Lear would be written for Lablache. But, as Lumley puts it, "Signor Verdi's health gave way, he was unequal to the arduous task, and the opera itself was not forthcoming."[1] The following year, 1847, when Verdi had emerged from his six months of nervous prostration and was ready to fulfil his commission, the star attraction of Lumley's London season was Jenny Lind for whom Verdi wrote *I masnadieri*.

---

[1] Benjamin Lumley, *Reminiscences of the Opera*, pp. 142–3.

Lablache had to content himself with the comparatively minor role of Count Moor.

Three years later, after he had composed *Luisa Miller*, Verdi suggested various ideas for subjects to Salvatore Cammarano, who had collaborated with him on the libretti for *Alzira*, *La battaglia di Legnano* and *Luisa Miller*. One of his suggestions was *King Lear*: he sent Cammarano a complete scenario that he had drafted, and was keen to discuss the subject in detail. "At first glance," wrote Verdi, "*King Lear* seems so huge and complex a drama that it would appear impossible to adapt it into an opera. But, having examined it closely, I consider that the difficulties, though great, are by no means insuperable. After all, we must not make *King Lear* into the usual kind of opera. We can treat it in a completely new manner, on a large scale, without regard to conventions of any kind. . . . It seems to me that the principal parts could be reduced to five: Lear, Cordelia, the Fool, Edmund, Edgar. Two secondary parts: Regan and Goneril (perhaps the latter would have to be made a second lead). Two secondary bass parts (as in *Luisa Miller*): Kent, Gloucester. All the rest minor parts."[1]

Verdi's detailed synopsis of the libretto makes it clear that his understanding of the play was no mere superficial excitement over its theatrical possibilities. His feeling for Shakespeare was real and intense. The synopsis reveals that Verdi intended the opera to be in four acts, with eleven scenes. It is far too long a document to be quoted here in full; but one scene, Verdi's Act II, Scene 4, based on Shakespeare's Act III, Scene 6, will give some idea of his sensitivity, his theatrical expertise, and his fidelity to Shakespeare:

> The Fool asks Lear "whether a madman be a gentleman or a yeoman?" Lear answers "A king, a king"—Song—The delirious Lear, still obsessed with the ingratitude of his daughters, wishes to arrange a court of judgment. He calls Edgar "most learned justicer", the Fool "sapient sir" and so on. Extremely bizarre and moving scene. Finally Lear tires and gradually falls asleep. All weep for the unhappy king. End of second act.[2]

Had Cammarano responded to the composer's suggestions about *Lear*, this might well have become the first great middle-period Verdi opera. At about the same time, Verdi's friend Giulio Carcano, poet and Italian translator of Shakespeare, offered to write him a *Hamlet* libretto. This Verdi declined. "Unfortunately," he wrote, "these huge subjects take up too much time. I have had to put *King Lear* aside at the moment, and commission Cammarano to work on the play whenever convenient. but if *King Lear* is difficult, *Hamlet* is far more so. I am caught between two promises, and if I am to fulfil my obligations I must choose easier and shorter subjects."[3] These were indeed his galley years: the opera he proceeded to write was *Stiffelio*.

[1] *Copialettere*, p. 478.   [2] Op. cit., p. 480.   [3] Op. cit., pp. 482–3.

Three years passed, years in which, after *Stiffelio*, Verdi had composed three masterpieces: *Rigoletto*, *Il trovatore* and *La traviata*. Again his thoughts returned to *King Lear*. Throughout the spring and summer of 1853 he brooded on the idea. A well-known playwright, Antonio Somma, had written to him, hoping to collaborate on an opera, and had suggested various subjects. Verdi informed Somma that he preferred Shakespeare to all other dramatists, including the Greeks. In the same breath he refers to *Rigoletto* as the best subject he has set so far. This is interesting, for Hugo's *Le Roi s'amuse*, on which *Rigoletto* was based, is a romantic melodrama as strongly influenced by Shakespeare as was Hugo's contemporary Byron, whose poem, *The Corsair*, Verdi had made into the opera, *Il corsaro*.

Verdi drew Somma's attention to *Lear*. He himself re-read the play, and in his ensuing correspondence with Somma the possibility of composing *Lear* was discussed in some detail. Verdi's ideas were still based on the synopsis he had prepared for Cammarano, who meanwhile had died. Somma eventually began to write a libretto in close consultation with Verdi, who advised him every step of the way. "There are two things about this project that worry me," wrote Verdi:

Firstly, it seems to me that the opera is turning out to be too long, especially in the first two acts. So, if you can find anything to cut out or to shorten, do so: the effect can only benefit. If this is not possible, do your best to be as brief as possible in the lesser scenes. Secondly, it seems to me there are too many changes of scene. The one thing that has always prevented us from writing more Shakespeare operas has been precisely this necessity to change the scene all the time. It used to annoy me greatly when I went to the theatre: I felt as if I were watching a magic lantern. In this, the French have the right idea. They plan their dramas with only one scene for each Act, and so the action flows freely without hindrance and with nothing to distract the public's attention. I completely understand that in *Lear* it would be impossible to have only one scene for each Act, but if you could manage to dispense with some of them, that would be fine. Think it over and, when you have written the verses for a few scenes, send them to me.[1]

Verdi's detailed criticism, after he has received Somma's Act One, is quite fascinating:

The stanzas of the Fool are very good, but from the moment Goneril enters I'm at a loss to know what to do. Perhaps you intended the six-line stanzas as an ensemble. But they are written as dialogue, the characters must answer one another and so they can't be used as ensemble. So there would need to be a further ensemble with eight-line stanzas when Regan

[1] Werfel and Stefan, pp. 148–9.

enters. At the end you have Goneril and Regan exit, leaving Lear to finish the Act alone. This is fine in tragedy, in spoken drama, but in music the effect would be cold, to put it mildly.[1]

For over two years the long and richly absorbing correspondence continued, with Verdi making close criticisms scene by scene, and continually checking Somma's tendency to expand. Verdi's genius was for contraction: he never went on too long. "In the theatre," he told Somma, " 'long' is synonymous with 'boring', and the boring is the worst of all styles."[2]

Eventually Somma's libretto was finished, and Verdi paid him for it. But by this time the composer was at work on *Les Vêpres siciliennes* for the Paris Opéra, so *Lear* was again put aside. "Perhaps it's just as well, for I shall be able to devote myself later to this opera with all the necessary leisure, and shall make, I don't say something new, but something a little different from the others."[3]

In October of the following year, a few days after rehearsals of *Les Vêpres siciliennes* had begun in Paris, Sophie Cruvelli, the prima donna, disappeared without explanation and rehearsals had to be suspended. Verdi decided to take this opportunity of pressing forward with *Lear*. The new Teatro Carlo Felice in Genoa had asked him to write an opera, and Verdi's publisher Tito Ricordi, who of course knew of the composer's desire to write *Lear*, suggested that opera. But the force of destiny intervened. Madame Cruvelli suddenly returned from her unexplained leave of several weeks. She had merely gone to the country with her lover, and was now ready for work again. Rehearsals for *Les Vêpres siciliennes* were resumed, and *Lear* faded into the distance of Verdi's intentions.

Two years passed and again negotiations for the production of *King Lear* were opened, this time with the management of the Teatro San Carlo in Naples. Somma's libretto was again closely scrutinised:

> I am not sure the fourth Act of *King Lear* is good in the form in which you sent it to me, but I do know that you cannot impose so many recitatives on the audience, one after another, especially in the fourth Act. These are not merely a composer's caprices. I would be willing to set even a newspaper or a letter to music, but in the theatre the public will put up with anything except boredom. . . . I'm not quite sure what it is, but something doesn't satisfy me. It certainly lacks brevity, perhaps clarity and perhaps truth.[4]

Preliminary casting was discussed. Verdi thought the Fool should be sung by a contralto, he wanted a baritone for Lear, and had a particular soprano, Maria Piccolomini, in mind for Cordelia. But the San Carlo could not procure the services of Maria Piccolomini, and Verdi refused

[1] Werfel and Stefan, p. 150.   [2] Op. cit., p. 155   [3] Op. cit., p. 153.
[4] Op. cit., pp. 160–1.

to accept the soprano they offered. He would not have singers foisted upon him, he said, "not even if Malibran were to return from the grave".[1] I have the feeling that here, as elsewhere, Verdi was grasping at excuses to postpone tackling *Lear*. He was apparently determined not to go ahead with the opera without Piccolomini, yet he sent a message to assure her that "if she thinks there is the slightest disadvantage to her in the proposition, she should have no scruples, for I shall not be at all offended if she refuses".[2]

So the project foundered, and Verdi set to work on *Simon Boccanegra* for Venice. I sometimes wonder if any of Verdi's Lear–Cordelia sketches made their way into the music for Boccanegra and his daughter—into the recognition duet, "Figlia, a tal nome io palpito", for instance.

In Paris in 1863 it was suggested that Verdi should set a libretto based on Flaubert's *Salammbô*. The composer was interested but said he would prefer to do *Lear*. He still had Somma's libretto, which he was determined sooner or later to set to music. Nothing came of *Lear* in 1863, but five years later, after Somma's death when a collected edition of the poet's works was about to be published, Verdi would not allow the *Lear* libretto to be included. He still intended to write the opera, though the chances of his actually doing so became increasingly remote.

We hear of *Lear* again many years later, when Verdi agreed to meet Boito with a view to collaborating on a Shakespeare opera. But the opera which emerged was, of course, *Otello*. Towards the end of Verdi's life, after *Falstaff*, there were rumours that he and Boito were to work together on *Il re Lear*. It is true that Boito began to adapt the play as a libretto and that Verdi tried to resume work on his sketches for the music. But by then it was too late. In 1896, the 83-year-old composer offered his synopsis and Somna's libretto to the young Mascagni. Mascagni says he asked Verdi why he had never written the opera. "Verdi closed his eyes for a moment, perhaps to remember, perhaps to forget. Then softly and slowly he replied: 'The scene in which King Lear finds himself on the heath terrified me.' "[3]

As he had wished, all of Verdi's sketches for unfinished compositions were destroyed at his death. But it is quite likely that he had frugally made use, in other operas, of some of the material he had sketched out for *Lear*. I have already suggested the possibility of some *Lear* music having found its way into *Simon Boccanegra*, an opera he wrote at the period of his most intense interest in *Lear*. Perhaps other operas in the period immediately following the years of Verdi's closest concern with

---

[1] *Copialettere*, p. 197. Verdi persisted in this attitude throughout his life. In 1891 when Marchesi wrote suggesting that his wife's pupil and protegée Nellie Melba should visit Verdi to study Desdemona with him in the hope of singing the rôle in Paris, Verdi icily rejected the proposal. After Verdi's death, Melba spread the story that she had met the composer and studied Desdemona and Traviata with him!

[2] *Copialettere*, p. 195. [3] *Carteggi Verdiani*, Vol. II, p. 64.

the *Lear* project contain some music originally intended for that work. Might he not in 1861 have incorporated some *Lear* sketches into *La forza del destino*? A few lines of Somma's *Lear* libretto suggest that he did. Cordelia's cavatina contains the lines:

Me pellegrina ed orfana	(A pilgrim and orphan
Lunge dal ciel natio	far from my native skies)

and, further on,

Non ho per te che lagrime,	(I have only tears for you.
Dolce Inghilterra, addio	Sweet England, farewell)

These lines, very slightly altered, occur in *La forza del destino* whose libretto is by Piave:

Me pellegrina ed orfana	(A pilgrim and orphan
Lunge dal patrio nido	far from my country's heath)

and

Ti lasciò, ahimè, con lagrime	(I leave you, alas, with tears.
Dolce mia terra! Addio	My sweet country, farewell)

They are part of Leonora's cavatina in the opening scene, which must surely be based on Cordelia's music.

The practical explanations why Verdi never wrote his *Lear* are all feasible. The psychical reason for his failure to attempt something he so clearly wanted to do is obscure. Perhaps, as he told Mascagni, he was terrified by Lear's madness. He himself was gloomy of temperament, neurotic and given to psychosomatic upsets. But, more likely, he was terrified by Lear's feeling for Cordelia. The father-daughter relationship had a special meaning and emphasis for him. Might not *Lear* have proved too overwhelming an exposition of it, or have led Verdi to too deep an exploration? My surmise is that, throughout his life, Verdi's sub-conscious protected him from *Lear*.

II

After that lengthy digression, let us return to 1843 and the Teatro la Fenice, Venice. Having finally rejected several other subjects as well as *Lear*, Verdi and the Fenice director Count Mocenigo settled on Victor Hugo's play *Hernani*, which had been first produced in Paris in 1830 with great success.[1]

[1] A few months after the Paris production of *Hernani*, Bellini and his librettist Felice Romani undertook to prepare an *Ernani*, of which sketches for five numbers survive in the Museo Belliniano at Catania. Some of this music made its way into other operas, particularly *Norma*.

Verdi himself drafted the outline of a libretto, and it was agreed that a Venetian poet Francesco Maria Piave, a friend of one of the Fenice officials, should write the actual verses. Since Piave was completely inexperienced as a librettist, Verdi made it perfectly clear that he intended to have his own way should any differences of opinion arise. The amiable Piave appears not to have objected.

After the obligatory wrangles with the censorship, settled after some slight changes had been made to a few lines in the libretto, Verdi encountered a more serious difficulty when he proposed to bring a hunting horn onstage in the last act. The Fenice authorities were of the opinion that this would lower the tone of their distinguished theatre. However, Verdi had his way. He even won a battle against his prima donna, Sophie Loewe, who did not think much of the idea of ending an opera with a trio, as Verdi intended *Ernani* should end. An excited solo cabaletta for herself would, in her opinion, bring the curtain down more effectively. She actually ordered Piave to write the verses for it, and Piave, by then accustomed to taking orders, wrote them only to be told by Verdi to throw them away. Loewe gave in with an ill grace.

Immediately after the first performance, Verdi wrote to a friend in Milan to say that the opera had been a success, and that if his singers had been at all competent it would have been even more successful. "[Carlo] Guasco had no voice at all and was so hoarse that it was frightening. And it is impossible to sing flatter than Loewe did last night. Every number, big or little, was applauded, with the exception of Guasco's cavatina."[1]

Ernani grew in popularity after the first performances. When it was revived two months later at another Venetian theatre, the Teatro San Benedetto, with even greater success than at La Fenice, people left the theatre after the performance cheerfully humming its tunes.

III

Piave's compression of Hugo's play is expertly done. Even if we give Verdi the credit for selecting the scenes and reshaping the plot, Piave deserves a certain amount of praise for his verses, which are simple, direct and immensely singable. Not infrequently they are a direct translation of Hugo, but there is much that is completely original. What has been lost in the process of adaptation is the incidental humour of Hugo's text. The romantic poet and playwright displays in *Hernani* a quality rare in romantic drama, an ability to laugh at himself. In saying this, I have in mind not so much the somewhat bitter irony of certain of Hernani's utterances as the outright comedy which occasionally bursts through the romantic gloom. For instance, Elvira's lady-in-waiting or duenna, who in Piave–Verdi is Giovanna, the usual colourless

[1] *Copialettere*, p. 425.

comprimario mezzo, useful solely as a feed in recitative. In Hugo's play she is the outspoken, rather coarse Donna Josefa. In the opera's second scene she merely and demurely accepts Carlo's order to send Elvira to him, with an obedient "Sia". This is a reduction of a quite funny scene in the play, the opening scene in fact, in which Donna Josefa is awaiting, on her mistress's behalf, the arrival of Ernani. When she hears a knock on the secret door, she opens it with a gaily expectant "Bonjour, beau cavalier", and then is appalled to find it is not Ernani. Whispering, "Deux mots de plus, duègne, vous êtes morte," Carlo proceeds to question her jealously about Elvira's lover ("un cavalier sans barbe et sans moustache encore"), to which Donna Josefa replies, "Vous m'avez défendu de dire deux mots, maître." She continues to bandy words with him, and, when bribed, insists he hide in a cupboard while she finds Elvira. Carlo, as he enters the cupboard, mutters, "Serait-ce l'écurie où tu mets d'aventure/Le manche du balai qui te sert de montre?" ("Is this where you put your witch's broomstick?") Earlier, when Donna Josefa exclaims, scandalised, "Un homme ici!", Carlo asks sarcastically, "C'est une femme, est-ce pas, qu'attendait ta maîtresse?"

These crackling exchanges are missing from Piave's *Ernani*. Mercifully, most of Hernani's longer rhetorical outbursts are missing as well: Piave's ability to compress meaningfully was a decided asset to him as a librettist. Hugo's Hernani declares to Charles V that he is no bandit but a nobleman in a long speech beginning

> Je prétends qu'on me compte!
> Puisqu'il s'agit de hache ici, que Hernani,
> Pâtre obscur, sous tes pieds passerait impuni,
> Puisque son front n'est plus au niveau de ton glaive,
> Puisqu'il faut être grand pour mourir, je me lève.
> Dieu qui donne le sceptre et qui te le donna
> M'a fait duc de Sergorbe et duc de Cardona,
> De Gor, seigneur des lieux dont j'ignore le comte . . .

and continuing for several more lines. Piave's Ernani at this moment makes his point more succinctly. The lines quoted above are compressed into

> Decreta dunque, o Re, morte a me pure.
> Io son conte, duca sono
> Di Segorbia, di Cardona.

For the most part, Piave has followed the play closely. His short opening scene, set in the bandits' hideout in the mountains of Aragon, does not appear in Hugo, and in the final Act where Ernani is offered alternative methods of suicide, poison or dagger, in Hugo he chooses poison, in Piave the dagger. Interestingly, in Hugo's play Silva kills himself as well. In Piave, when the curtain falls he is exulting in his vengeance. In general, Piave's libretto conveys the essence of Hugo's play, and his verses have a theatrical effectiveness and point, almost a terseness, which were precisely the qualities Verdi sought in his librettists.

The opera is in four acts. Act I, Scene 1 is set in the mountains of Aragon in the camp of Ernani, the bandit, and his followers. It is nearly sunset, and the bandits are eating, drinking, playing cards or cleaning their rifles. Ernani tells them of his love for Elvira. Her uncle and guardian, the aged Don Ruy Gomez de Silva, whose castle can be glimpsed in the distance, intends to marry her himself on the morrow, and Ernani asks his comrades to help him abduct Elvira. She has sworn that she loves him and will follow him gladly. The bandits agree to kidnap her from Silva's castle.

The scene changes to Elvira's apartment in the castle, that same evening. Elvira sings of her distaste for Silva and her hope that Ernani will rescue her. With him by her side, even a desert would seem an Eden of delight. Her ladies-in-waiting arrive to adorn her with Silva's gifts of jewels, but she spurns them and leaves the room. Don Carlo (Charles V of Spain) enters, asking that Elvira be sent to him. When she returns, he declares his love for her, but sensibly she distrusts him and asks him to leave. He knows of her love for the bandit Ernani, and his jealousy drives him to attempt to take her by force. Ernani enters through a secret door in time to prevent this abduction. Although the King recognises the outlaw, he chivalrously offers to allow him to depart. Accusing Carlo of having caused the death of his, Ernani's, father, the bandit declares his hatred for the King. Elvira, furious with both King and lover for conducting their quarrel in her rooms, threatens to plunge a dagger in her breast unless they desist. At this moment the door is flung open and Silva and his attendants enter. Silva is appalled to find two young men in his fiancée's apartments, and considers that his family has been dishonoured. He sings of his disillusionment with Elvira, and his desire for immediate vengeance upon the two men, but his steward Jago then enters with the King's aide-de-camp who, of course, immediately recognises and identifies Carlo. The astonished Silva falls to his knees. He is pardoned by Carlo, who says he had made his visit incognito because he wished to consult Silva on a secret matter. The King claims hospitality for the night and, unwilling to take advantage of his rival Ernani in this situation, pretends that the bandit is a member of his retinue, and secures his escape simply by ordering him to depart immediately. Ernani reluctantly takes the opportunity to escape, but swears to himself he will pursue Carlo until his father's death has been avenged.

Act II takes place in a magnificent hall in Silva's castle. The walls, says the libretto, are adorned with portraits of Silva's ancestors, and beneath each portrait there stands a complete suit of equestrian armour of the appropriate period. It is the wedding-day of Silva and Elvira, and Silva is receiving the congratulations of his dependants. A pilgrim, Ernani in disguise, comes to ask for shelter, and Silva makes him welcome. Elvira enters, and when the pilgrim learns from his host that he is to marry her within the hour, he cries, "I wish to offer you a wedding gift—my head!" and flings off his disguise. He is being pursued by the King's soldiers, he says, and suggests that Silva take him prisoner and claim the reward. This offends the old man, for within his walls a guest is as sacred as a brother. He rushes off to the battlements with his retainers. During his absence Elvira persuades the embittered Ernani that she still loves only him and had intended to stab herself at the altar. Silva returns to find the lovers clasped in each other's arms. Absolutely certain now that he has been dishonoured, he is about to challenge Ernani when the arrival of the King and his troops is announced. Silva's laws of hospitality will not allow him to denounce Ernani to the King, so he hides the bandit in a secret compartment behind one of the portraits. Elvira retires to her own apartments, and the King and his retinue enter. Carlo is certain that Ernani is within the castle, and orders Silva to produce him. Silva replies that he cannot betray a guest. Carlo calls him a traitor, has him disarmed, and orders his men to search the castle. They fail to find Ernani, and Carlo offers Silva a choice: "Il tuo capo, o il traditore" ("Your head or the traitor"), but the old man cannot betray his own code of honour. When Elvira rushes in to plead with Carlo, the King suddenly alters his conditions. He will leave the castle either with Ernani or with Elvira as hostage. As Silva is still bound by his sense of honour, Carlo and his followers depart, taking Elvira with them. First taking two swords from an armoury near the portraits, Silva then opens Ernani's hiding-place. Tersely he calls to Ernani to follow him outside and fight. Ernani refuses on the grounds of Silva's age, but the old man repeats his challenge. "You saved my life," says Ernani. "Now kill me. But first let me see Elvira." When Silva tells him that the King has taken her as hostage, Ernani exclaims, "Old man, what have you done? He is our rival." That the King is in love with Elvira had not occurred to Silva. Now he summons his vassals to arms. He will first kill Ernani, and then pursue Carlo. Ernani begs to be allowed to share his vengeance: he is willing to die, but only after he has rescued Elvira. Silva asks him to pledge his word, and Ernani gives him his hunting horn. "When I hear you call on this horn," he tells Silva, "I shall take my own life." He swears it on the soul of his dead father, and brandishing their swords he, Silva and his men rush off to pursue Carlo.

Act III is set in the catacombs in Aquisgrana, in the vault containing the tomb of Charlemagne, over whose bronze door can be seen the inscription "Karolo Magno". There are also several less imposing tombs, and doors to other vaults. Carlo and his equerry Riccardo enter. It is here that the League is about to assemble to conspire against Carlo, and he intends to conceal himself in Charlemagne's tomb and spy on them. Elsewhere, the Electors of the Holy Roman Empire are at that moment deliberating the choice of Emperor. Carlo hopes that he will succeed to the throne of the Holy Roman Empire, and asks Riccardo to signal with three cannon shots if the Electors should choose him, and then return to the vault with Elvira. Left alone, Carlo broods on the greatness and moral stature of his illustrious namesake, Charlemagne, and resolves to emulate him. He unlocks the door of the tomb and enters it.

The members of the League now enter severally and cautiously from various directions. Finally, Silva and Ernani appear. Lots are drawn to decide who is to assassinate Carlo, and the name drawn is that of Ernani. Silva offers to release Ernani from his suicide oath if he will allow Silva the honour and pleasure of killing Carlo. Ernani refuses. The conspirators sing a stirring chorus, "Si ridesti il Leon di Castiglia" ("Let the Castilian lion arise"). The Castillian Lion which once fought against the Moor has reawakened; freedom is dearer even than life. Suddenly the loud boom of a cannon is heard. And a second, third. The door of Charlemagne's tomb opens, Carlo steps forth, and the fearful conspirators exclaim, "Carlo Magno Imperator". In a thunderous voice, he corrects them: "Charles V, you traitors!"

A ceremonial procession of six Electors dressed in gold brocade now appears. Pages carry on cushions the crown and sceptre of the Holy Roman Empire. An assemblage of German and Spanish nobility surrounds the new Emperor. Elvira and her lady-in-waiting are led in by Riccardo, Carlo is proclaimed Emperor and calls for the arrest of the traitors. The commoners shall be conveyed to prison; the noblemen are to be executed. Ernani proudly proclaims his nobility, and Carlo agrees he should die with the others. But when Elvira pleads with him, Carlo remembers the great Emperor whose virtues he would assume, pardons the entire League and offers Elvira to Ernani in marriage. "Glory and honour to Carlo Magno," he cries. The assembled company joyfully echoes his cry, changing the words "Carlo Magno" to "Carlo Quinto", Charles V.

The short Act IV is set on a terrace of the palace of Don Giovanni of Aragon in Saragossa, where the wedding festivities of Elvira and Ernani are in progress. Dancers and revellers sing the praises of the happy pair, while a sombre figure in a black mask makes his way slowly through the crowd, as though searching for someone. Ernani and Elvira come out on to the terrace from the ballroom and sing of their love and their happiness. Suddenly the distant sound of a horn is heard. Ernani recognises it. Elvira notices his distress, and he pretends he is not well and asks her to search for a doctor. When she has gone, the masked figure appears, reveals himself as Silva, reminds Ernani of his pledge and offers him poison or a dagger. Momentarily, Ernani's courage fails him. "Now that heaven has just begun to smile on me, after years of misery, let me sip awhile the cup of love," he pleads. "Where is Spanish honour?" Silva sneers. Ernani takes the dagger as Elvira returns. At first she threatens Silva but then, checking herself, she pleads with him. He is adamant. Elvira tells him she loves Ernani. "All the more reason for him to die" is the reply. Again he quotes Ernani's oath. Ernani stabs himself, Elvira tries to snatch the dagger to use against herself, but the dying Ernani bids her live to remember and love him. He dies, she faints, and Silva stands gloating.

IV

Ernani's short, tuneful *adagio* prelude begins with the horn motif which will summon Ernani to his death at the end of the opera, then relaxes into a warm and compassionate cantilena before returning to the horn theme. After a few bars of filling-in music, we are plunged straight into the drinking chorus of the bandits, acceptable enough as an opening number but hardly memorable. Toye ingeniously discerns a rhythmical similarity to Iago's drinking song in *Otello*, but does not mention Ernani's aria "Come rugiarda al cespite", a graceful *andante* separated from its lively and by no means brutal cabaletta by one of those funny conspiratorial choruses (there was one in the first act of *I Lombardi*) alternating *sotto voce* whispers with *forte* explosions. Ernani's cavatina, incidentally, calls for several trills from the tenor: I have rarely heard them in performance.

Elvira's cavatina and cabaletta in the next scene are deservedly popular. The cavatina, "Ernani, involami", is both melodic and expressive; even its ornamentation is meaningful as well as decorative [Ex. 17].

Ex. 17

un E - den, un E - den di de - li - zia sa - ran   que - gli antri a   me,

The *allegro* cabaletta, "Tutto sprezzo che d'Ernani", has both individual character and force, and the rhythm of the female chorus which precedes the cabaletta reminds us that we are in Spain. The duet in which the King attempts to seduce Elvira begins with a glorious tune written high in the baritone's range [Ex. 18]. Elvira's reply has a fierce Castilian rhythm, and there is something Spanish, too, in the frequent use of the soprano's chest register here and throughout the opera. Ernani's entrance and recognition by Carlo turn the duet into a trio, "Tu se' Ernani", which ends in a stirring *allegro vivacissimo*. The first Act finale begins on Silva's entry. His cavatina, "Infelice!" is a most impressive piece of writing for the bass voice, and its cabaletta is irresistibly martial. When Carlo is recognised as king, a slow ensemble

Ex. 18

Andantino cantabile

Da quel di che t'ho ve - du - ta bel - la co - me un pri - mo a -
mo - - re, la mia pa - ce fu per - du - ta, tuo fu il
pal - pi - to, tuo fu il pal - pi - to del co - re.

builds up and, after further recitative, Ernani bursts out with his threat against Carlo, to a tune echoed by Elvira. The phrase to which he sings the words "L'odio inulto che m'arde nel core" will turn up again at a famous moment in *Attila* [Ex. 35]. A bustlingly quick ensemble brings the curtain down.

The opening chorus of Act II is great fun, as long as it is accepted in the right spirit. It would be, admittedly, a more suitable accompaniment to Saturday night dancing in Busseto than to the wedding festivities of a Spanish grandee. Verdi redeems himself with the extended trio for Silva, Ernani and Elvira which incorporates a great deal of dramatic action, and whose middle section is a duet for the lovers. Carlo's aria, "Lo vedremo, veglio audace", addressed to Silva, is a fine example of Verdi's habit of writing for the upper reaches of the baritone voice. The agitated accompaniment and Silva's chromatic interjections add to its effectiveness. After the chorus has admitted its failure to discover Ernani, and Elvira has made her unsuccessful plea to Carlo, Silva confesses his love for her in a touchingly dignified *moderato*. To no avail, however, for in a deceptively suave cabaletta Carlo reaffirms his intention to take Elvira as a hostage. When he and his retinue have departed with Elvira, Silva and Ernani launch into an energetic duet which, when they are joined by the chorus, ends the act.

Act III opens with a slow, atmospheric prelude which leads into Carlo's recitative and aria, "Oh de' verd' anni miei". The aria is first-rate, its accompaniment consisting solely of a repeated figure on solo cello until, at the climactic phrase which no one but Verdi could have

written, "E vincitor de' secoli il nome mio farò" [Ex. 19], the full
orchestra comes in to support the voice. The postlude, a mere eight bars,
is on the way to being one of those rare but beautiful moments in Verdi
where the composer allows his orchestra a compassionate comment on
the characters' situation. The postlude to Fiesco's "Il lacerato spirito"

Ex. 19

e vin - ci - tor   de'   se - co-li   il   no - me   il no-me mi - o fa - rò;

in *Simon Boccanegra*, and the tune which accompanies the penitents in
the *auto da fè* scene of *Don Carlo* are two more such moments of particularly memorable beauty.

The scene of the conspirators possesses a seriousness of purpose
lacking from many another conspiratorial scene in Verdi. It culminates
in "Si ridesti il Leon di Castiglia", the first of Verdi's stirringly active
patriotic choruses, as opposed to the masochistically nostalgic choral
numbers exemplified by "Va, pensiero" in *Nabucco*. Out of context,
the Lion of Castile chorus sounds banal, but in the opera it not only
serves its immediate purpose admirably but also is capable of awakening feelings of group solidarity and togetherness, as is proved by the
meaning the Venetians imposed upon it, and the use they made of it in
substituting "Venezia" for "Castiglia".

The third act finale includes a fine trio begun by Ernani with the
terse information, "Io son conte, duca sono", a précis of several lines of
Hugo. Elvira contributes an eloquent plea for clemency which, throughout its length, descends the scale from F down to A below middle C.
After Carlo has displayed his generosity, an impressive ensemble
ensues which includes the famous cry "A Carlo Quinto sia gloria ed
onor", sung to an emotionally affecting phrase [Ex. 20] which was

Ex. 20

A   Car - lo Quinto sia gloria ed o - nor   glo - - ria   e o -

nor! .... glo - ria e o nor!

picked out by Roman audiences three years after its Venice première
and turned into a paean of praise for the newly elected Pope Pius IX,
of whom the liberals had great hopes. "A Pio Nono sia gloria ed onor",
they sang.

The very short fourth act opens with Verdi's gay but somewhat rustic idea of festive music. Elvira and Ernani have a few brief and, in retrospect, tragic moments of happiness before Silva's horn is heard and the final, inexorable trio begins. All else pared away, the protagonists confront one another and the last questions are answered. Ernani and Elvira sing one phrase in which their love becomes real and felt; then the horn is heard and Ernani realises he must die. The trio is one of Verdi's finest; expressive, and of great melodic and harmonic beauty. Forty years later, the Viennese critic Hanslick, writing of *Tristan und Isolde*, used Verdi's *Ernani* as a stick to beat Wagner with. Why should Tristan take a whole hour to die, he asks, when Ernani manages it "in a few modest bars"?[1]

The weak pages in *Ernani* are comparatively few. What is most impressive is the opera's wealth of beautiful and gloriously singable tunes, "profuse strains of unpremeditated art". And perhaps it is worth pointing out the obvious: that Silva's horn theme is Verdi's earliest use of a primitive form of the *Leitmotif*, which he has often been accused of appropriating from Wagner. He had heard no Wagner in 1844. *Der fliegende Holländer* was new, had not yet been published, and had not been performed in Italy. *Tannhäuser* was composed and awaiting production, which it achieved in Dresden in 1845. There is really no Wagner influence anywhere in Verdi, and no such influence would even have been possible at this stage of the Italian composer's career. It is much more likely that *Der fliegende Holländer* contains music written under the influence of Verdi and Donizetti.

Although the characters in *Ernani* may not strike us today as particularly interesting or subtle in their behaviour, they did provoke Verdi to paint them in strong musical colours. The opera marks an advance on *Nabucco* and *I Lombardi* in that Verdi's musical characterisation is becoming more assured. *Nabucco* is finer because it is a finished work of its kind. Its kind, however, is that of the Rossinian *opera seria. Ernani* looks to the future. Its theatrical effectiveness is due more to Verdi's endeavours than to Piave's. Until the time of his collaboration with his final librettist Boito, Verdi was almost invariably to supervise the writing of his libretti. His habit was to tell the poet what he wanted, and how much of it. Perhaps this is why he never managed to persuade the finest librettist of the early nineteenth century, Felice Romani, to write for him. In *Un giorno di regno* he had set an old libretto by Romani, and for his next opera *I due Foscari* he was to attempt, unsuccessfully, to secure Romani's services. Would Romani, I wonder, have responded politely to being used as a kind of literary secretary by Verdi?

The elegant irony of Hugo's *Hernani* has vanished in its transition to Verdi's *Ernani*, and only the full-blooded romanticism remains. It is enough.

[1] Eduard Hanslick, *Music Criticisms, 1846–99* (London, 1963), p. 227.

V I

I due Foscari

Dramatis personae

Francesco Foscari, Doge of Venice	(baritone)
Jacopo Foscari, his son	(tenor)
Lucrezia Contarini, Jacopo's wife	(soprano)
Jacopo Loredano, member of the Council of Ten	(bass)
Barbarigo, Senator, member of the Giunta	(tenor)
Pisana, friend and confidante of Lucrezia	(soprano)
Officer of the Council of Ten	(tenor)
Servant of the Doge	(bass)

LIBRETTO by Francesco Maria Piave, based on the play *The Two Foscari* by Lord Byron

TIME: 1457
PLACE: Venice

FIRST PERFORMED at the Teatro Argentina, Rome, November 3, 1844, with Marianna Barbieri-Nini (Lucrezia); Edvige Ricci (Pisana); Giacomo Roppa (Jacopo); Achille De Bassini (Doge); Gaspare Pozzolini (Barbarigo); Mirri (Loredano)

I due Foscari

RETURNING TO MILAN immediately after the Venice production of
Ernani, Verdi found himself offered contracts to write for several Italian
theatres. He was now, at the age of thirty, the coming composer and the
obvious heir to Donizetti. Milan society did its best to cultivate him,
but Verdi was not temperamentally suited to the world of the salon:
at this stage of his life he had few interests outside his work. He entered
into negotiations with the Teatro San Carlo in Naples to write *Alzira*,
became interested in a play about Attila and drafted from it a libretto
which he sent to Piave to versify, and accepted an invitation from the
new management of the Teatro Argentina in Rome to write the *opera
d'obbligo* or customary new opera for the coming autumn season.
This Rome commission gave him about four months in which to choose
a subject, have a libretto written, compose, cast and rehearse the opera.
He put aside his other projects, including the Attila idea which he
probably considered could not be brought to fruition in so short a time,
and suggested to Rome an opera on Lorenzino de' Medici. This was
rejected by the papal censors, so Verdi turned to Byron's play *The Two
Foscari*, one of the subjects he and Piave had considered in Venice before
deciding on *Ernani*. *The Two Foscari* as outlined by Verdi proved acceptable to Rome, so he and Piave immediately set to work. As usual,
Verdi closely supervised the writing of the libretto, continually making
suggestions regarding dialogue and characterisation. During the
composition of the opera he became afflicted with the psychosomatic
illnesses which for the remainder of his life were to attend his creative
processes. He complained first of headaches and pains in the stomach,
and then of a continually sore throat. Even a few weeks spent at Busseto
failed to effect a cure. Finally, however, work on *I due Foscari* was
complete except for the orchestration, and at the end of September
1844, Verdi travelled to Rome, where he spent the month of October
orchestrating the opera and rehearsing it. He conducted the first
performance on November 3rd and, as was customary, the second and
third performances as well. On the first night, although the opera was
enthusiastically received, a certain amount of irritation was expressed at
the increase in admission prices made by the management. The later
performances, at regular prices, played to cheering audiences: on the

second night Verdi himself took more than thirty curtain-calls. The critic of the *Rivista di Roma* wrote in glowing terms of the opera: "It seems to me that Verdi, even more than in *Ernani,* has endeavoured to shake off his former manner, to return to the springs of affection and passion. . . . Every personage speaks his own language; every character expresses his own passions in a manner eminently dramatic."[1]

II

Verdi's supervision of the writing of the libretto was close. In one of his letters to Piave, he wrote:

So far everything is going beautifully, except for one small thing. I notice that up to here nothing has been said about the crime for which Foscari is sentenced. It seems to me that that should be emphasised.

In the tenor's cavatina, two things are bad. First, Jacopo remains on the stage after he has sung his cavatina, which always weakens the effect. Secondly, there is no contrasting idea to set against the *adagio*. So just write a piece of dialogue between the soldier and Jacopo, and then have an officer say "Bring in the prisoner!" Follow this with a cabaletta, but make it a good, rich one for we are writing for Rome. And then, as I say, the character of Foscari must be made more forceful. The woman's cavatina is excellent. At this point I think you should insert a short recitative, followed by a solo for the Doge and a big duet. This duet, coming at the end, should be quite short. Get yourself into a really inspired mood and write some beautiful verses. In the second Act, write a romanza for Jacopo, and don't forget the duet with Maria,[2] then the great trio, followed by the chorus and finale. In the third Act do just as we agreed, and try to make the gondoliers' song blend with a chorus of citizens. Could it not be arranged for this to happen towards evening, and so have a sunset too, which is always so beautiful?[3]

Although the provenance of the libretto is definitely Byron's play, Piave does not mention Byron in his Introduction to the published libretto, which I reproduce in its entirety:

On 15 April 1423 Francesco Foscari was raised to the Ducal throne of Venice, his rival being Pietro Loredano. Pietro did not cease opposing him in council, to such an extent that the irritated Foscari once said openly in the Senate that he could not believe himself truly Doge as long as Pietro Loredano lived. By a fatal coincidence, some months afterwards Pietro and his brother Marco suddenly died, and—as it was rumoured—by poison. Jacopo Loredano, Pietro's son, supposed this, believed it, carved

---

[1] *Toye*, p. 40.

[2] This was the name of Jacopo's wife in Byron's play. Eventually, in the libretto, her name was altered to Lucrezia.

[3] *Copialettere*, p. 426.

it on their tombstones, and, noting in his account books that the Foscari were his debtors for two lives, coldly waited to make them pay.

The Doge had four sons, of whom three were dead. The fourth, Jacopo, married to Lucrezia Contarini, having been accused of receiving gifts from foreign princes, according to Venetian law was banished first to Napoli di Romania, then to Treviso. Meanwhile it happened that Ermalao Donato, head of the Council of Ten which had condemned Jacopo, was assassinated on the night of November 5, 1450, while returning to his palace from a session of the Council. Since Oliviero, Jacopo's servant, had been seen the day before at Venice, and on the morning following the crime had spoken of it publicly in the boat going to Mestre, suspicion fell on the Foscari. Master and servant were immediately brought to Venice and, after torture which failed to extract a confession, were exiled for life to Candia. Five years later, Jacopo, having vainly sought pardon, unable any longer to live without seeing his beloved homeland again, wrote to the Duke of Milan, Francesco Sforza, begging him to intercede with the Signoria. This letter fell into the hands of the Ten; Jacopo, brought back to Venice and tortured once more, confessed to having written the letter but with the sole desire of seeing his homeland again—even at the cost of returning as a prisoner. He was condemned to return for life to Candia, to endure there first, however, a year of rigorous imprisonment, and he was threatened with penalty of death if he again wrote comparable letters. The unfortunate octogenarian Doge, who with Roman fortitude had attended the interrogation and torture of his son, was able to see him privately before he left, and to counsel obedience and resignation to the Republic's will. Subsequently, it happened that a Venetian nobleman, Nicolò Erizzo, being about to die, revealed himself as the murderer of Donato and wished to publish such information to exculpate the innocent Jacopo Foscari. Some leading senators were already disposed to seek his pardon, but meanwhile the unhappy man had died of anguish in his prison at Candia.

The wretched father, afflicted by so many bitter blows, lived in isolation and seldom attended council meetings. Meanwhile Jacopo Loredano, who had been raised to the dignity of one of the Ten in 1457, believed that the hour of his revenge had come, and he secretly plotted to force the Doge to abdicate. At two other times during his tenure as Doge, Foscari had wanted to resign, but not only were his wishes then not heeded, he was also further required to swear that he would die in full exercise of his power.

Despite the oath, he was compelled to leave the Ducal palace and to return as a simple private citizen to his own household, having refused a munificent pension offered him by the public Treasury.

On October 31, 1457, hearing the bells ring to announce the election of his successor, Pasquale Malipiero, Foscari experienced such strong emotion that by the following day he was dead. As if he had died still reigning, he was given a splendid funeral, which Malipiero attended in the plain costume of a senator. It is said that Jacopo Loredano then wrote in his accounts, opposite the item cited above, these words: "*The Foscari have paid me.*"

This is the fragment of history upon which my tragedy is based. For
its effect and the inevitable requirements of this kind of composition, I
have had to take some easily detectable liberties, and for those I crave the
cultivated reader's indulgence.

Byron's *The Two Foscari*, though written in dramatic form, was
according to the poet "not composed with the most remote view to the
stage". It was based on the historical story which he found in P. Daru's
L'Histoire de la République de Venise. Written in blank verse, the play
nevertheless contains very little poetry. It does, however, have about
it an atmosphere of gloom, restraint and embittered despair, something
of which, though suppressed in Piave, curiously reappears in Verdi.
Piave followed the structure of the play very closely, making only those
excisions necessary to reduce the text to operatic proportions. Given
the neurotic intensity of Jacopo's love for his native city, the sequence of
events (or, rather, of feelings, since there are few events in the play)
is believable.

> My beautiful, my own,
> My only Venice—*this is breath*! Thy breeze,
> Thine Adrian sea-breeze, how it fans my face!
> Thy very winds feel native to my veins,
> And cool them into calmness! How unlike
> The hot gales of the horrid Cyclades,
> Which howl'd about my Candiote dungeon, and
> Made my heart sick.

Verdi has captured the feeling in these lines of Byron, and given it
far more effective expression, in Jacopo's cavatina, "Dal piu remoto
esilio". Indeed, throughout the opera, whenever Verdi touches upon
the same vein as Byron, he enriches it. It is true that, in compressing
play into libretto, Piave has inadvertently lessened an emphasis here,
given undue prominence to an incident there, but the emotional balance
is redressed in Verdi's sombrely magnificent score.

Act I, Scene 1 is a hall in the Doge's Palace. On the right are two
doors, one of which leads to the Doge's private apartments and the other
to the street outside. There are two more doors on the left, leading to
the Chamber of the Council of Ten and to the state prison. The members of the Council and of the Giunta are assembling. When Barbarigo
and Loredano arrive, their numbers are complete, and they enter the
Council Chamber to resume the trial of Jacopo Foscari. Jacopo is
brought in, under guard, from the prison. He sings of his love for
Venice, and is led into the Council Chamber.

The next scene is a hall in the Palazzo Foscari. Lucrezia, Jacopo's wife, is determined to go the Doge to beg for Jacopo's life. Her servants and staff attempt to dissuade her from thus giving joy to her enemies, and assure her that heaven will take pity on the prisoner. Persuaded by their arguments, Lucrezia prays. Pisana enters to announce that the Council in its clemency has condemned Jacopo to renewed exile, but this news incites Lucrezia to fulminate against the cruelty of the Council, in a cabaletta, "O patrizi, tremate".

The scene changes back to the large hall in the Doge's Palace. The members of the Council and Giunta return from the Council Chamber, discussing the trial and its outcome, and congratulating themselves on their impartiality.

In the fourth scene of Act I, set in the Doge's private apartments, the octogenarian Doge soliloquizes unhappily. He feels his every move, every gesture, is observed by the Ten, and is powerless to help his son Jacopo. In any case, he feels bound to observe the laws of Venice. He gives way to his despair in an aria, "O vecchio cor, che batti". Lucrezia enters, accusing him of having unjustly condemned his own son, and the Doge attempts to make her understand his position, crippled by his stern sense of duty to the State and by the power of the Ten. "Di Venezia il principe in ciò poter non ha," he tells her. (The prince of Venice is powerless in this matter.)

The first scene of Act II is set in Jacopo's dungeon in the state prison. Weakened by torture and illness to the point of delirium, Jacopo is beset by visions of horror. Lucrezia visits him, and at first he does not recognise her. She tells him he has again been sentenced to exile and that neither she nor their two sons are allowed to accompany him. The Doge enters to say farewell to his son, and Jacopo takes some comfort in knowing that, despite his stern judicial attitude, his father still loves him. Loredano now appears to summon Jacopo back to the Council Chamber to hear his sentence. In the quartet finale, Jacopo and Lucrezia, the Doge, and Loredano give voice to their various feelings.

Act II, Scene 2 is the Council Chamber. The Ten and the Giunta are ready to announce their sentence to the prisoner. The Doge, preceded by Loredano and attended by his officers and pages, makes a ceremonial entrance. When he is seated upon his throne, the entire assembly sits and the prisoner is brought in. His sentence is handed to him to read. "In its clemency," says Loredano, "the Council spares your life." But handing back the parchment Jacopo says simply, "Nell' esilio morirò." (I shall die in exile.) He appeals to his father, but the Doge can say only

> Il Consiglio ha giudicato;
> Parti, o figlio, rassegnato.

(The Council has passed sentence. Depart, o son, in resignation.)

When Jacopo asks his father if they will ever meet again, the terse reply is "Perhaps in heaven; on earth no." And Loredano demands that Jacopo's departure for exile should be immediate. At this moment Lucrezia rushes into the Council Chamber with her two children, followed by several other women, among them Pisana. Jacopo embraces his children, and Lucrezia alternately harangues and pleads with the Councillors, who are shocked by her audacity. Barbarigo is moved to pity, and asks Loredano if he is not similarly affected. He is not. The Council informs Lucrezia that her tears are in vain, and that the sentence must stand. Lucrezia swoons as Jacopo is led away.

Act III begins in St. Mark's Square. It is carnival time, and "tutto è gioia". Masked revellers throng the square. The galley ship arrives to bear Jacopo off to exile, he and Lucrezia sing a last farewell to each other, and he is taken on board the galley.

The scene changes to the Doge's apartments, where the old Doge laments the loss of all his sons, three by death and now Jacopo by exile. Barbarigo enters to announce that a dying man has just confessed to the murder for which Jacopo was originally exiled. The Doge is overcome with joy, but in the next instant Lucrezia rushes in crying that at the moment of departure, Jacopo had dropped dead. Piling Pelion upon Ossa, the Council of Ten now visits the Doge. At the instigation of Loredano, they have come to invite him, in consideration of his great age, to abdicate. The Doge reminds them that twice previously when he had wished to abdicate he was not allowed to do so. Now he refuses. He is made to realize, however, that he has no choice, a decision having already been reached by the Ten. He relinquishes his ring of office, but when Loredano attempts to help him remove his crown and mantle, he indignantly disdains aid. "Non mi toccare, o misero; n'è la tua destra indegna" (Do not touch me, wretched man. Your right hand is not worthy to do so), he cries, as he hands crown and mantle to another senator. As the bells of St Mark's are heard tolling to announce his successor, the Doge collapses and, with a last despairing cry of "Mio figlio", falls dead. "Pagato ora sono", "Now I have been paid" remarks Loredano as he writes the words in his notebook. The opera ends here, as does Byron's play:

> BARBARIGO: What art thou writing,
>   With such an earnest brow, upon thy tablets?
> LOREDANO (*pointing to the Doge's body*): That he has paid me.
> CHIEF OF THE TEN: What debt did he owe you?
> LOREDANO: A long and just one: Nature's debt and mine.
>   (*The curtain falls*)

III

I due Foscari is one of the operas to which I feel earlier Verdi commentators have done less than justice. Carlo Gatti complains that though it contains some lovely passages, it reflects Verdi's weariness and boredom and the depression of the age in which he lived; Dynley Hussey concludes that it is "dead past revival"; even Toye sums it up as "not a good opera" but one with "a certain amount of music that compels admiration as well as interest". To me it seems an often beautiful expression of the melancholy which predominated in Verdi's temperament. It is true that his first attempts to identify his characters by their own individual themes are neither particularly subtle nor very effective. But even they are of some use in serving to refute the suggestion that, by giving individual themes to characters in his later operas, Verdi was influenced by Wagner's use of the *Leitmotif*. What is most remarkable about *I due Foscari*, however, is its atmosphere and the way in which this is created in the orchestra. Verdi gives more prominence here to woodwind instruments than in earlier operas, from the solo clarinet and flute writing in the Overture to the clarinet and bassoon colours which contribute to the shadowy gloom which predominates throughout the opera. In these, his galley years, Verdi's orchestral technique does not stand still: it develops steadily from opera to opera. Although he often expressed the opinion that, unlike German music, Italian music was not by nature instrumental, Verdi was from his earliest days aware of the importance of the orchestra in opera. In this he differed strongly from Bellini and Donizetti. True, the orchestration in *Oberto* and *Un giorno di regno* is largely done in blocks, but as early as *Nabucco* Verdi began to experiment with more individual instrumentation. The orchestra is still subjugated to the voice, but it becomes an increasingly active junior partner, not only in the use of an instrument to double the voice for emphasis at a climax but also in the exposed solo passages in the introductions to arias. In every way, *I due Foscari* is an important step forward for Verdi.

The Prelude, an agitated *allegro* with a slow middle section which in the opera is associated with Jacopo's despair, leads into the opening chorus of senators, an attractively lilting piece. Jacopo's recitative and cavatina, "Dal piu remoto esilio", are preceded by an orchestral introduction consisting of the *andante* tune heard in the Prelude. The accompanying figure to the recitative is marvellously evocative of water-lapped Venice [Ex. 21] and the aria itself is both expressive and graceful. Its cabaletta has a splendid Verdian energy, but seems out of place in this context. Verdi was sparing with his cabalettas in *I due Foscari*, and rightly so. The opera's atmosphere is one of gloom and resignation rather than resolution.

The theme allotted to Lucrezia, a few bars of hurry-music in triplets, is the least happy of Verdi's character motifs. It is heard now to herald her appearance, and to serve as introduction to her cavatina, "Tu al cui sguardo onnipossente", a beautiful Bellinian aria whose decorated

Ex. 21

vocal line is somewhat reminiscent of "Casta diva" [Ex. 22] as, too, is
the way in which her solo voice floats above the chorus. The attractive
cabaletta, this time an appropriate one, has a forcefulness forged from
Lucrezia's desperation. She is the one character in the opera who

attempts to defy the status quo. The senators' chorus which comprises
Act I, Scene 3 is comparatively featureless.

The Doge's recitative, preceded by his theme, and his slow aria,
"O vecchio cor che batti", are really first-rate. From his opening bars
the Doge, Francesco Foscari, is given stature and authority. He is more
than just a sketch for that not dissimilar baritone Doge, Simon Boccanegra. Foscari's aria is dignified and moving, and Verdi wisely did
not burden it with a cabaletta. His sound dramatic sense is beginning to
dominate his musical conservatism. The duet between the Doge and
Lucrezia, "Tu pur lo sai che giudice", one of the finest numbers in the
score, melodically generous and dramatically apposite, is also one of
that series of long, unfolding duets between father or father-figure—
in this case father-in-law—and daughter.

The second Act opens, like *Fidelio*'s Act II, in the prisoner's dungeon.
After a distinctly Beethovenian orchestral introduction, Jacopo's first
words in recitative, "Notte, perpetua notte qui regni", are virtually a
translation of Florestan's "Gott! Welch' Dunkel hier!" Jacopo's aria,
"Non maledirmi, o prode", is a restless and agitated *andantino*. The

prison scene as a whole is particularly satisfying in construction. Its form is simple, Jacopo's aria being followed by a duet with Lucrezia, which is in turn followed by a trio at the entry of the Doge, and a quartet when Loredano appears. The parallels with *Fidelio* need not further be stressed: the manner in which the scene builds firmly to its climaxes is quite masterly, and Verdi's prodigality of melodic invention is in full flow. The duet "No, non morrai", which follows the joyful moment of reunion of Lucrezia and Jacopo, is particularly moving. The happiness of husband and wife at seeing each other again even in such appalling circumstances is nicely conveyed in the vocal line. At one moment, the light-hearted song of the gondoliers is heard in the distance, and for a few bars Lucrezia sings in unison with them, ironically remembering a world of happiness and freedom.

The entry of the Doge launches a magnificent trio. Its first section is quick and joyful, but it is the hectic and fleeting joy of unexpected reunion which gives way to sadness as father, son and daughter-in-law face the reality of the situation. The D flat *andante* section, "Nel tuo paterno amplesso", is most affecting [Ex. 23], and Lucrezia's passage of

Ex. 23

plaintive minor seconds at "Di questo affanno orrendo farai vendetta, o ciel" is not only particularly moving but also unusually striking. [Ex. 24.]

Ex. 24

The quartet which ensues after Loredano enters is hardly on the same level. A quick waltz, it is inappropriately whoopsy enough to put one in mind of a chorus from Johann Strauss's *Eine Nacht in Venedig*.[1] [Ex. 25.]

[1] Since writing this, I have discovered that the Viennese in 1845 thought it sounded like Johann Strauss the Elder. The day after the first Viennese performance of *I due Foscari* on April 3rd, Donizetti who was in Vienna wrote to his publisher: "Last evening the first performance by the Italians: *I due Foscari*. By a hateful chance, the Waltz in the trio made them laugh. They called it a Strauss waltz." (Herbert Weinstock: *Donizetti* (London, 1964), p. 230).

Ex. 25

Ah! si, il tem-po che mai non s'ar-re-sta re-chi pure a te un' o-ra fa-ta-le, e l'af-fan-no che man-ge mor-ta-le più tre-men-do ri-ca-da su te

Act II, Scene 2, opens with a chorus of councillors whose prelude is the by now familiar motif associated with the Ten. The finale, introduced by Jacopo's melodically eloquent plea, turns into a sextet with chorus, a heart-warming ensemble of great power and that peculiarly Verdian creative energy which glows at even the steadiest of tempi. With what mysterious significance Verdi invests even the apparently simple rhythmic accompaniment. It is absurd that his occasional use of the "big guitar" orchestration should once have been so roundly sniffed at. It was, after all, a device handed on to Verdi by Italian opera of the eighteenth century, and for that matter by Mozart's Italian operas. In the process of slowly developing beyond it, Verdi humanised the marking rhythm accompaniment.

Act III, Scene 1, opens with a joyful chorus of Venetians and a barcarolle. The former is silly, the latter pleasant, but both are naïvely transparent attempts to lighten the atmosphere of gloom for a few moments. Jacopo's melancholy *andante* theme introduces his final aria, "All' infelice veglio", whose pathos is achieved by a plain but expressive vocal line, a most effective accompaniment, and appropriate ensemble support.

The final scene in the Doge's apartments opens interestingly with the Doge's arioso-like *andante* to which Lucrezia's anguished outburst when she rushes in to tell of Jacopo's death, acts as a kind of stretta or cabaletta. The finale, which consists of the Doge's aria, "Questa dunque è l'iniqua mercede", followed by a superb ensemble scene which he dominates, is perhaps the finest part of the opera. The darkly pessimistic orchestral colour never seems merely applied to the vocal line, but is used as an intrinsic element in the sound texture. As Verdi once wrote to a correspondent: "The idea comes to me all of a piece, and I hear immediately whether a certain note ought to be played by flute or violin. The difficulty lies in getting it down on paper quickly enough and in attempting to express the musical idea exactly as it enters my mind."[1] Of *I due Foscari* it would, I feel, be true to say that Verdi almost completely succeeded in setting down as an integrated whole the vision of gloom and *accidia* which Byron's play suggested to him.

[1] Verdi to Quintino Sella. *Copialettere*, p. 599.

VII

Giovanna d'Arco

Dramatis personae:

Carlo VII, King of France	(tenor)
Giacomo, a shepherd	(baritone)
Giovanna, his daughter	(soprano)
Delil, one of the King's officers	(tenor)
Talbot, in command of the English army	(bass)

LIBRETTO by Temistocle Solera, based on the play *Die Jungfrau von Orleans* by Friedrich Schiller

TIME: *c.* 1429
PLACE: France

FIRST PERFORMED at La Scala, Milan, February 15, 1845 with Erminia Frezzolini (Giovanna); Antonio Poggi (Carlo); Filippo Colini (Giacomo); Napoleone Marconi (Delil); Lodetti (Talbot)

Giovanna d'Arco

RETURNING FROM ROME to Milan at the end of November 1844, Verdi immediately found himself involved in producing a revival of *I Lombardi* to open the season at La Scala on December 26. He had also promised Merelli to write a new opera for production in the same season, and he began to compose it during the rehearsal period of *I Lombardi*. The subject chosen was Joan of Arc, and Solera concocted a libretto based on Schiller's play, *Die Jungfrau von Orleans*. The *Lombardi* rehearsals were stormy; standards and discipline had apparently deteriorated badly, and Verdi had cause to complain vociferously of the inadequate strength of the orchestra and its unsatisfactory distribution in the pit, the indolence and arrogance of the principal singers, the incompetence of the chorus, and the lack of care in preparation of décor and costumes. It was hardly a propitious moment to begin writing a new opera for La Scala.

Verdi's young pupil and amanuensis, Emmanuele Muzio, corresponded regularly with their common benefactor Antonio Barezzi in Busseto, and several of his letters in December 1844 mention music already composed for *Giovanna d'Arco*. It is clear from his descriptions of musical numbers that Verdi must have begun composing the opera immediately he arrived back in Milan from Rome. Muzio was completely uncritical of Verdi, whose every page seemed to him the greatest ever written. According to him, the "terrifying introduction" was inspired by the rocky precipices of the Apennine passes through which the composer travelled on his way up from Rome. This is in a letter dated December 9th which continues: "The magnificent piece ("Maledetti cui spinse rea voglia") will amaze every poor mortal. The demons' choruses are original, popular, truly Italian. The first ("Tu sei bella"), is a most graceful waltz, full of seductive motifs that, after two hearings, can be sung straight away. The second ("Vittoria, vittoria, s'applauda a Satana"), is music of diabolical exaltation, music that makes one shudder and tremble."[1] On December 22nd Muzio writes: "This morning the Signor Maestro wrote the march for *Giovanna*. How beautiful it is."[2] And on the 29th: "Yesterday I heard the great duet between Giovanna and Carlo, when they fall in love. This is

[1] Garibaldi: *Verdi nelle lettere di Muzio e Barezzi*, p. 175.   [2] Op. cit., p. 178.

the grandest and most magnificent piece in the opera. I have heard the third act finale which has one of the most beautiful melodies that has ever been heard."[1]

A great part of *Giovanna d'Arco*, therefore, had been written before the end of 1844. Nevertheless, there is no doubt that the opera was a rushed job. The 31-year-old galley slave must have composed it in no more than eight weeks, during half of which time he was conducting rehearsals of *I Lombardi*, at which, according to Muzio, he "shouted like a madman and stamped his feet so much he looked as though he were playing the organ. He sweated so profusely that the perspiration dripped on to the score."[2]

Verdi refused to attend the opening night of his own production on December 26th. Nevertheless, the revival was successful. *Giovanna d'Arco* then went into rehearsal, and opened on February 15th. It was extremely popular with audiences, less so with the critics, and was played four nights each week until the end of the season. Productions in other towns followed. In Palermo, two years later, police objections to the subject necessitated the music being fitted to a new libretto, with the title of *Orietta di Lesbos*.

After the Scala première of *Giovanna*, Merelli asked Verdi to supervise the revival of *Ernani* later in the season. Bitterly disappointed with the way Merelli was running the opera house, Verdi refused, stating that he would have nothing further to do with La Scala. The fact that, some months later, Merelli put on *I due Foscari* with the second and third Acts in reverse order did nothing to help matters. Verdi was determined never to allow La Scala another première. A quarter of a century passed before he relented. During that quarter-century Verdi's operas, including several of his most important works, received their initial performances in Naples, Venice, Florence, London, Paris, Trieste, Rome and St. Petersburg. The leading Italian opera house was boycotted by the leading Italian composer.

II

Solera's libretto for *Giovanna d'Arco* is generally thought of as the epitome of the really silly opera libretto, and the fact that it is adapted from a play by Schiller is often used to imply that a certain degree of desecration or travesty has been indulged in as well. It is certainly true that Solera's *Giovanna d'Arco* has virtually no point of contact with the historical Jeanne d'Arc, but then neither has Schiller's *Jungfrau von Orleans*. Before, however, we condemn Schiller for having written a piece of high-flown romantic nonsense, we ought to consider what his aims were, and how far he went towards realizing them in *Die Jungfrau*.

[1] Garibaldi: op. cit., p. 179.   [2] Garibaldi: op. cit., pp. 177–8.

I suppose the St. Joan play which comes closest to portraying the actual fifteenth-century events, as well as being the least partisan, is Shaw's *St. Joan*. His Joan is the simple peasant girl who thought she heard voices from heaven telling her to drive the English out of France, the maid whose faith was so strong that she allowed herself to be burned at the stake for it. Schiller's Joan is given to indulging in flights of theatrical rhetoric: she is a figure of the stage rather than of life, and she dies a theatrically effective death after being wounded in battle. But Schiller's play, written in 1801 while Voltaire's satirical poem on Joan, *La Pucelle*, was still being widely read, made no pretence to historical accuracy. In his correspondence with Goethe, Schiller had expressed the belief that art could flourish best by avoiding the mere imitation of nature. This he imagined could most appropriately be achieved by introducing symbolic aids to take the place of the object represented. Such symbolism as Schiller believed would purify theatrical art, raising it to the level of poetry, was employed in *Die Jungfrau von Orleans*. Schiller's interest was not in historical reality but in poetic truth, and to him the inner symbolic truth of Joan of Arc rendered her death at the stake unnecessary. In an essay on Schiller, Thomas Mann referred to *Die Jungfrau* as a "word-opera". Verdi had already intuitively realised this: his mistake lay in imagining that the play's poetic identity could survive the inevitable compression required by adaptation to the lyric stage. Solera not only cut several scenes, but also made significant alterations, the most damaging of which is his making Joan fall in love with the French Dauphin instead of, as in Schiller, with the handsome young Englishman, Lionel. Joan's dilemma, in Schiller's play, is brought about by the opposing pulls of her mission and her love. Solera's plot reduces the action to a completely personal level, the protagonists being Joan, her father and the Dauphin. It was understandable that the romantic Schiller, like Byron and Hugo, should appeal both to Verdi's temperament and his political liberalism, but it was a pity that Solera had not sufficient intellect to understand the plot's intentions.

In Schiller's play, Joan, who is one of three sisters, renounces Raimond, the suitor her father has chosen for her. She is convinced she has been chosen by heaven to save her country. In the royal palace at Chinon, despair is uppermost. The Duke of Burgundy is in alliance with the English, and the Dauphin cannot grasp the situation. When his soldiers begin to leave him because he has no money to pay them, his mistress Agnes Sorel offers her jewels. News comes of a battle against the English in which an unknown girl has led the French to victory. It is Joan who, when she arrives at Chinon, recognises the Dauphin among his courtiers (this incident is also used in Shaw's *St. Joan*) and persuades him to let her command the army. After further victories, Joan wins the Duke of Burgundy over to the French cause. Two of her generals,

Dunois and La Hire, are in love with her, but she claims to have no interest in earthly love. The English general Talbot is killed in battle, and Joan learns from the apparition of a Black Knight that her own downfall is imminent. She defeats the young Englishman Lionel in combat, but when she sees his face clearly she experiences love for the first time and spares his life. From this moment she feels guilty of having betrayed her voice and her country. When, at the Dauphin's coronation, Joan's father accuses her of witchcraft, she is incapable of uttering a word in her own defence, and is sentenced to exile. Wandering in the forest during a storm, followed only by the faithful, rejected suitor Raimond, she is captured by the English. Lionel, the young English knight whose life she had spared, tries to win her love; but, strengthened by her shame, Joan recovers her sense of divine purpose and resists him. The French, apprised of her capture, attack in order to rescue her. An English soldier watching the battle from a window of the tower in which Joan is imprisoned, narrates the fighting to her. When she hears that the French King has been captured, she prays for strength and, bursting her bonds, rushes out to fight. She rescues the King, but is killed in battle.

Solera's libretto cuts this plot away to a bare minimum. He dispenses with all the minor characters, and several of the major ones as well. Agnes Sorel, Queen Isabel the Dauphin's mother, the Duke of Burgundy, Dunois, La Hire—none of these exists in Solera's *Giovanna d'Arco*, which is firmly centred on Giovanna, Carlo VII, and Joan's father Giacomo. Little more than the barest outline has been retained of Schiller's play. The coronation scene interrupted by Giacomo, and the narration of the battle from Joan's prison follow the play reasonably closely, though in the opera it is Joan's father who narrates the battle. In the play, Joan has a long speech, a famous set piece in German, in which she says farewell to the forests and mountains of her childhood as she prepares to leave her native countryside and take up the life of a warrior. It begins:

> Lebt wohl, ihr Berge, ihr geliebten Triften,
> Ihr traulich stillen Täler lebet wohl!
> Johanna wird nun nicht mehr auf euch wandeln,
> Johanna sagt euch ewig Lebewohl.

(Farewell, you mountains and beloved pastures,
You friendly, quiet valleys, now farewell.
Johanna will no more upon you wander,
Johanna says forevermore farewell.)[1]

Something of this sentiment remains in Giovanna's aria, "O fatidica foresta". In general, however, very little of Solera's dialogue is a direct

[1] Tchaikovsky's setting of the same lines in his opera *The Maid of Orleans* is well-known.

translation of Schiller, nor is there much more connection between the motivation of his characters, when it can be discerned, and that of Schiller's. Judged purely on its own terms, without reference either to Schiller or to history, the libretto of *Giovanna d'Arco* is average stock.

Giovanna d'Arco consists of a prologue and three Acts. The first scene of the prologue takes place in Domrémy, in the courtyard of the King's apartment. (Although not yet crowned, he is referred to throughout the opera as the King.) People are questioning officials about the war and the disastrous defeats France has suffered at the hands of the English. The King, Carlo VII, enters, announces his intention of abdicating, and tells the assembled crowd of a vision he has had in which a statue of the Virgin, near an old oak tree, commanded him to lay his sword and helmet at her feet. He describes the spot, and the chorus, recognising it as a haunted part of the forest where devils and witches congregate, warns him against going there. The King chides them for their superstition and sets out to find the place.

The scene changes to a clearing in the forest with a shrine to the Virgin near the entrance to a cave. Giovanna's father Giacomo enters in order to keep watch on his daughter, who is so attracted to this notorious spot that he suspects her of witchcraft. He hides in the cave as Giovanna appears. After singing of her desire to fight for France, she falls asleep. Carlo enters, kneels by the statue of the Virgin, and prays, placing his sword and helmet on the ground. In her sleep Giovanna is tempted by a chorus of demons, and exhorted by a chorus of angels to do as heaven commands. When she awakes, she finds Carlo's helmet and sword and, considering them a sign from heaven, takes them up and persuades Carlo, whom she recognises, to accompany her to battle, promising him victory. Seeing them depart together, Giacomo is convinced they are lovers.

Act I opens in the English encampment not far from Rheims. Thanks to Giovanna's leadership of the French forces, the war is now going badly for the English. Giacomo visits the English commander Talbot and offers to join them. Believing as he does that France is now ruled by the powers of hell, he promises to deliver Giovanna into the hands of the English.

The second scene of Act I is set in a garden at Rheims where Carlo has his Court. Now that her task is accomplished, Giovanna longs to return to her simple life, and to the countryside she loves. Carlo begs her to remain, declaring his love for her. In a moment of weakness she confesses that she loves him and immediately hears angelic voices warning her against worldly love. Carlo, not hearing the voices, cannot understand her distress, and when one of his officers, Delil, enters to announce that preparations are now complete for the coronation,

Carlo persuades Giovanna to accompany him to the cathedral. Demon voices proclaim their victory over Giovanna, and the wretched girl realises she has betrayed her sacred purpose.

Act II takes place in the square outside the cathedral at Rheims. After the procession, followed by the cheering populace, has entered the church, Giacomo appears, still determined to bring about Giovanna's downfall. When Giovanna comes rushing out of the cathedral in great agitation, followed by Carlo, who announces that she is the patron saint of France, Giacomo steps forward and, before the entire crowd which has now emerged from the cathedral, accuses the King of blasphemy and Giovanna of witchcraft. Giovanna, as a penance, refuses to say a word in her own defence, but when the crowd asks for a sign that Giacomo is speaking the truth they are rewarded by immediate thunder and lightning. The people denounce Giovanna as a witch and demand that she be banished. Giacomo himself leads her away to be handed over to the English and burned at the stake.

Act III takes place in an English fortress near the battlefield. Giovanna, in chains, prays to God to free her. Overhearing her, Giacomo eventually realises that her allegiance is to heaven and that he has accused her unjustly. He frees her from her chains, and she rushes off to join the battle. Under her leadership the French are victorious, but she is mortally wounded. Her funeral procession is interrupted as she momentarily revives to see the heavens opening and the Virgin herself calling her. Ecstatically, Giovanna bids farewell to earth and dies.

III

The Overture to *Giovanna d'Arco* is an excellent piece, a sinfonia in three sections, *allegro, andante* and *allegro*. The pastoral *andante*, presumably intended to suggest Giovanna's life before she received her sense of vocation, is particularly beautiful, scored for solo flute, clarinet and oboe. Toye, after mentioning a German critic's claim "that the Overture was subsequently used for *I vespri siciliani*", continues, "but between the two published versions at any rate I can find no connection." This is very curious, as is the fact that no other book on Verdi that I have consulted mentions any connection between the two Overtures. There is, nevertheless, a connection, to put it mildly, and it is astonishing that, if Toye was actually searching for a similarity between them, he should have failed to find it; for the final *allegro* theme of the Overture to *Giovanna d'Arco* [Ex. 26] is, in fact, virtually identical with the big central tune in the Overture to *I vespri siciliani*. [Ex. 27.] They are basically the same tune, and the only important difference is in tempo: in *Giovanna d'Arco* it is quick, while in *I vespri siciliani* it is moderate. This is, incidentally, the only instance I can discover in Verdi of conscious self-borrowing, a practice in which his older contemporaries frequently indulged.

The opening ensemble is noteworthy more for the firmness and individuality of its orchestral writing than for its vocal line, though the "Maledetti" section which young Muzio admired has a typically and

Ex. 26

lovably Verdian *slancio*. Carlo's cavatina, "Sotto una quercia", is charming, the chorus in which the citizens tell of their horror of the haunted spot is, surprisingly, a by no means unworthy forerunner of the storm music in *Otello*, and Carlo's cabaletta is attractively individual.

The scene in the haunted forest opens with a marvellously eerie orchestral introduction which would not seem out of place in *Der Freischütz*. Giacomo's arioso-like recitative is eloquently urgent: the Verdi of *Oberto* would have followed it with a cavatina, but the experienced opera composer of *Giovanna d'Arco* does no such thing. He has nothing against the accepted forms, in fact as late as *Aida* he will ask his librettist to allow for cabalettas, but he is ready now to sacrifice form to the requirements of the drama. Giovanna's cavatina, "Sempre all' alba", is exquisitely beautiful, one of those early manifestations of Verdi's genius which somewhere illumine every score he wrote in those "galley" days. The accompaniment is translucent, the vocal figuration

Ex. 27

delicate yet strong. When it is over, Giovanna does not launch into a cabaletta: she sings a few bars of arioso and goes to sleep.

The chorus of demons is not at all frightening. Verdi was doubtless aiming at something like the seductively dangerous sweetness of the Erlking's utterances in Schubert's song, but his demons in 3/8 time remain disarmingly jolly. [Ex. 28.] The chorus of angels, curiously, is somewhat more Schubertian, and rather beautiful in the manner of "Ave Maria". The angels are given a harp-and-accordeon accompani-

Ex. 28

ment, while the demons have harmonium and percussion. (The demons' chorus, "Tu sei bella", was immediately taken up by the barrel organs of Italy.) Giovanna awakens and now sings her cabaletta, a really delicious one, in duet with Carlo, its two verses interrupted by an unaccompanied trio as Giocomo spies on them.

The similarity of the chorus of English soldiers in Act I to "Hearts of Oak" has been mentioned by other writers. Giacomo's unusual cavatina exists at two tempi: an *andante* in the vocal line, below which a more quickly pulsating accompaniment provides energy and direction. Giacomo's cabaletta is deliberate in pace, as though weighed down by sadness.

In the following scene, the introduction to Giovanna's *andantino*, "O fatidica foresta", quotes the demons' chorus. The little aria itself is first-rate, like a water-colour sketch for the oil painting of Aida's "O patria mia", with the most delicate woodwind writing. The naïve and charming love duet is interrupted by angels, after which it loses its innocence, as we can hear from the orchestral figure that punctuates Carlo's "T'arretri e palpiti" and the knowingly seductive cantabile vocal line of his "È puro l'aere, limpido il cielo" [Ex. 29], as well as

Ex. 29

È pu - ro l'a - e - re, lim-pi-do il cie -lo, sic-co - me il ve - lo di no-stradi no - stra fè.

from the change that comes over Giovanna. For the remainder of the duet she tends to sound like the *Trovatore* Leonora. When Delil and the chorus remind Carlo that he is about to be crowned, with the insinuating voice of the serpent he persuades Giovanna to accompany him: "Vieni al tempio". She hears the demons mocking her while he continues to woo her. The effect is tremendous, out of all proportion to the absurd yet touching means.

In the triumphal march which opens Act II, Verdi makes splendid use of his favourite device of the stage band. The broad tune of the march, sheer Verdi, is quite indefensible against the charge of banality, but it can reduce to tears anyone who deeply responds to the composer. Others will recognise it only as the ancestor of a certain chorus in *The Pirates of Penzance*. [Ex. 30.] Giacomo's aria in which, remorse-ridden,

Ex. 30

he is yet driven on by shame and horror, foreshadows the accents of the similarly convention-bound Germont in Act II of *La traviata*. A Te Deum is sung off-stage, in the cathedral, and, after a few bars of recitative from Giacomo, Giovanna and Carlo return. Giacomo denounces her, and the great second-act finale gathers momentum. Giacomo's *moderato* has an uneasy, almost turbulent accompaniment. From the ensemble, Giovanna's lovely "L'amaro calice" emerges magnificently. The final *allegro* is unremarkable.

Act III begins with one of Verdi's father-daughter, baritone-soprano scenes. After Giovanna's opening *allegro* and her charming prayer, Giacomo joins her in a duet, "Ella innocente e pura", which again looks forward to *La traviata*, but is also tenderly beautiful in its own right. The duet cabaletta is equally heart-warming. Although the battle music is no better than workaday, from here to the end the opera is simply superb. Carlo's romanza, with its delicately textured accompaniment, has a quiet, grave quality of its own, and the ensemble of this finale is rendered memorable by the sheer flourish of Giovanna's gloriously drawn phrase, "Addio terra, addio gloria mortale". [Ex. 31.] In this

Ex. 31

form, it occurs once only. Verdi was so prolific a melodist that it never occurred to him to "plug" his best tunes as, for instance, Bellini did. (I yield to no one in my enjoyment of "Qui la voce", but we do hear rather much of it in *I Puritani*.) The angels welcome Giovanna to heaven, while the demons sulkily admit defeat. The end is serene.

I cannot agree with Toye's summing-up of this opera: "It was not lack of care but lack of the necessary technique, coupled perhaps with a certain paralysis of imagination, characteristic of Verdi's work at this time, which made *Giovanna d'Arco* a comparative failure." It seems to me a comparative success containing, as did *I due Foscari*, a great deal of evidence that Verdi's imagination was anything but paralysed at the time. *Giovanna d'Arco* is a work that would repay revival. Solera's characters may be two-dimensional on the page, but Verdi's are fully rounded in the opera house. Interpreted by stylish and imaginative Verdi singers such as Leontyne Price, Nicolai Gedda and Tito Gobbi, *Giovanna* would surely win its way back into the repertoire. Yet Gatti says of it, "The music has no particular value except for the bellicose strain." Can these Verdi commentators not have heard some of the operas they dismiss so easily and unimaginatively? How can anyone who loves and understands Verdi fail to respond to the melodic generosity and youthful resilience of these early works? One can love

Tristan or *Die Walküre* while remaining impervious to *Die Feen, Das Liebes verbot* or *Rienzi,* for Wagner's early efforts are heavily charmless; but I distrust the man who says he adores *Falstaff* yet has no soft spot for *Il corsaro* or *I masnadieri. Giovanna d'Arco* has a curiously primitive but pervasive charm of its own that sets it apart from bigger works like *Nabucco* and *Ernani.* It is also a perfectly viable and hugely enjoyable work of art in a style which modern audiences are learning to appreciate.

VIII

Alzira

Dramatis personae:

Alvaro, Governor of Peru	(bass)
Gusmano, his son	(baritone)
Ovando, Spanish Duke	(tenor)
Zamoro, Chief of a Peruvian tribe	(tenor)
Ataliba, Chief of another Peruvian tribe	(bass)
Alzira, Ataliba's daughter	(soprano)
Zuma, her sister	(mezzo-soprano)
Otumbo, Peruvian warrior	(tenor)

LIBRETTO by Salvatore Cammarano, based on the play *Alzire* by Voltaire

TIME: Mid-sixteenth century
PLACE: Peru

FIRST PERFORMED at the Teatro San Carlo, Naples August 12, 1845 with Eugenia Tadolini (Alzira); Salvetti (Zuma); Gaetano Fraschini (Zamoro); Filippo Coletti (Gusmano); Marco Arati (Ataliba); Domenico Ceci (Ovando); Giuseppe Benedetti (Otumbo); Gaetano Rossi (Alvaro)

Alzira

I

VERDI'S NEXT CONTRACT was with the Teatro San Carlo in Naples, to write an opera for performance in June 1845, only four months after the première of *Giovanna d'Arco*. The subject already chosen was Voltaire's *Alzire*. Verdi was not in good health and, when his usual nervous headaches, sore throats and stomach pains came on during composition of the new work, he was obliged to ask for a postponement of two months. This was granted only with the greatest reluctance by the Neapolitan impresario Vincenzo Flauto who, not disposed to take Verdi's illnesses seriously, wrote telling him his health would be sure to improve in sunny Naples. This, of course, intensely infuriated Verdi. "We artists are never allowed to be ill,"[1] he wrote to his librettist Cammarano. He arrived in Naples in June, having almost completed the score. He must have composed it very quickly, for a letter to Cammarano on May 23rd reveals that he had not yet started work on it. "I have received the synopsis of *Alzira*," he wrote, "and I am completely satisfied with it. I have read Voltaire's tragedy: in your hands it will make an excellent libretto. I am accused of liking a great deal of noise and neglecting the singing. But if you put enough passion into it, you will see that I write reasonably well."[2]

Salvatore Cammarano was a Neapolitan librettist who had already achieved a certain fame for his work with Donizetti, Mercadante and Pacini. For Donizetti he had provided seven libretti, among them *Lucia di Lammermoor*, *Roberto d'Evereux* and *Maria di Rohan*, for Mercadante two, including *La vestale*, and for Pacini the immensely popular *Saffo*. He was to collaborate with Verdi on four operas altogether. His virtues as a librettist were not dissimilar to those of Piave, though he was the more experienced of the two at this time, a sound literary craftsman with a real feeling for theatrical effect. Some years later, Verdi entrusted him with the Neapolitan production of *Macbeth*.

The leading Neapolitan composers of the day, Mercadante and Pacini, were hostile to Verdi: both were considerably older than he, and jealous of his success. Saverio Mercadante (1795–1870) composed in the style we think of today as Donizettian, though with considerably more care over orchestration than Donizetti was wont to display. A twentieth-

[1] *Copialettere*, p. 13.   [2] *Copialettere*, p. 429.

century Mercadante enthusiast named Biagio Notarnicola has claimed that the majority of Verdi's ideas were, in fact, stolen from the older composer! This is demonstrably nonsensical: there are probably traces of Mercadante in the early operas of Verdi, but one may as well accuse him of stealing from Beethoven and Bellini. Giovanni Pacini (1796–1867) who wrote seventy-three operas was rather more Rossinian than Donizettian, with less interest in orchestration than Mercadante, but greater melodic variety. His *Saffo*, much admired when it was first performed at Naples in 1840, sounds today rather stiffly contrived.

After the first performance of *Alzira* on August 12th, Verdi wrote to his friend Giuseppina Appiani: "Thank heaven this is over now. *Alzira* has been put on. These Neapolitans are ferocious, but they applauded. . . . The opera will stay in the repertoire and what is more important, will go on tour like its sister operas."[1] He was mistaken. *Alzira* was a mixed and moderate success in Naples, and was received stonily some months later in Rome. One of the Neapolitan critics, Vincenzo Torelli, accused Verdi of writing too hastily: "No human talent is capable of producing two or three grand operas a year."[2] A Milanese critic, however, writing of the Naples première, accused the Neapolitans of being prejudiced against a composer from Lombardy. And in Naples the following piece of deathless verse achieved a wide circulation in the coffee houses:

> Tu in prima scrivesti il *Nabucco*
> E gli astanti rimaser di stucco,
> *I Lombardi* scrivesti in appresso
> Si restò press'a poco lo stesso;
> Tu per terzo scrivesti gli *Ernani*
> E cessò quello batter di mani,
> *I due Foscari* in Roma scrivesti,
> Ti ricordi che fiasco facesti?
> A Milano *Giovanna* fu data,
> E ben due volte fu spenta e bruciata;
> A San Carlo scrivesti l'*Alzira*
> E il Sebeto, sbuffando dall'ira,
> Così disse: Chi è mai lo sfrontato
> Che a San Carlo l'*Alzira* ha portato?
> Forse è ignota all'ardito mortale
> Che a San Carlo si fa *La Vestale*,
> Che a San Carlo vi scrive Pacini,
> Che rapì coi suoi canti Bellini?
> Che credea con barba e mustacci
> Ritirarsi così dagli impacci?
> A San Carlo si vuol melodia,

---

[1] A. M. Cornelio, *Per la storia* (Pistoia, 1904), p. 29.
[2] In the Neapolitan paper, *L'Omnibus*. Quoted by Walker, p. 138.

Regolata con grande armonia.
Ci vuol canto che sia declamato,
Non cantaccio da perdervi il fiato
E costringer fin anche a stonare,
Ma Fraschini che mai potè fare?
Qui si tacque il Sebato, ed accenna
Che si rechi all'istante una penna.
A punir l'enorme delitto
Ipso facto emanò quest'editto:
"Quel colore cotanto gradito
Da' nostr'occhi sia tosto bandito,
Trovi il verde se alcuno lo brama
Sotto il gel del *Vascello di Gama.*"[1]

This important Neapolitan folk-poem now appears for the first time in English:

To begin with you gave us *Nabucco*,
Which simply turned spectators to stucco.
So *I Lombardi* was your next try,
Leaving the audience almost as dry.
Your third shot, *Ernani*, was heard
In a silence no clapping disturbed.
For *I due Foscari* Rome was the site.
You've not forgotten the flop of that night?
Next at Milan *Giovanna* was played.
And proved just another pyre for the Maid.
When at the San Carlo *Alzira* was staged
Sebeto swelled visibly, deeply enraged,
Demanding: "Whoever is the insolent fellow
Daring to bring *Alzira* to the San Carlo?
Isn't it known to the foolhardy creature
That at San Carlo *La Vestale*'s the feature,
That San Carlo is also the home of Pacini
Whose music used once to enrapture Bellini?
Does he think, hiding behind moustaches and beard,
He'll escape from all the trouble he's stirred?
At the San Carlo we expected to hear melody,
Composed—what is more—with considerable harmony.
It's music that's truly for voices we like—
Not horrible notes that the singer can't strike,
While forcing himself to grow tuneless and flatter.
Now, granted the foolery, how to deal with the matter?"
Here Sebeto fell silent, having commanded a pen
Which was instantly brought to him—whereupon then,
For the awful crime to have punishment so strict,
Ipso facto, he sternly issued this edict:

[1] F. Schlitzer, *Mondo teatrale dell' ottocento* (Naples, 1954), pp. 137–8.

"That colour so long thought pleasant and bright
Shall be sentenced to banishment, out of our sight;
If you're asked to find 'verde' in the panorama,
Look under the ice of *Vascello di Gama*."[1]

Although Verdi had at first leaped to the defence of *Alzira*, within a few months he had come to see that it was not likely to achieve the success of most of his earlier operas. After the Rome performances in the autumn, he wrote to a friend: "I am very thankful to you for your news about poor, unfortunate *Alzira*, and even more for the suggestions you are kind enough to make. In Naples, I too saw those weaknesses before the opera was produced, and you can't imagine how long I thought about them. The flaw is too deeply rooted, and retouching would only make it worse."[2] Years later, Verdi is reported to have said of *Alzira*: "Quella è proprio brutta"[3] (That one is really awful). But, having attempted to rescue one or two of the earlier operas from what I consider to be the unjust dismissal of other critics, I shall endeavour later in this chapter to defend *Alzira* from this unwarranted denigration by its own composer.

II

Voltaire's *Alzire* is subtitled "Les Américains", the Americans in question being the Incas of Peru. Cammarano has reduced the five-act tragedy to a libretto consisting of a prologue and two acts. The prologue brings on to the stage an incident merely referred to in the play, while the two acts are a compression of Voltaire's five. Cammarano has given titles to the separate Acts: the Prologue is "Il prigioniero" (The Prisoner), Act I is "Vita per vita" (A Life for a Life) and Act II "La vendetta d'un selvaggio" (The Revenge of a Savage). As in the play, the action takes place in and around Lima, in the middle of the sixteenth century.

The Prologue is set on a vast plain at sunrise near the banks of the river Rimac. Alvaro, the Spanish Governor of Peru, has been captured by a group of what both Verdi and Voltaire refer to as Americans, and what we had better agree to call Incas, led by Otumbo. They tie Alvaro to a tree and, dancing fiercely around him, threaten to kill him. His life is saved by the intervention of Zamoro, the chief of the tribe, who arrives in a canoe. Freeing Alvaro, Zamoro tells him to return to his own people and inform them that his life has been spared by a savage. Alvaro leaves, escorted back to civilisation by some members of the tribe. When Otumbo tells him that Alzira, his betrothed, and her

---

[1] *La Vestale* and *Vascello di Gama* are operas by Mercadante.
[2] *Copialettere*, p. 432.   [3] *Copialettere*, p. 432.

father Ataliba are prisoners of the Spaniards, Zamoro calls on the tribe to follow him in battle and rescue them.

The first scene of Act I takes place in a public square in Lima where Alvaro is ceremonially resigning as Governor of Peru. He presents his son Gusmano to the crowd as his successor, and Gusmano's first act is to declare peace with the Incas. His second is to announce that, although he has conquered in many battles, he cannot conquer the feelings of his heart: he loves Alzira, a Peruvian girl, and asks her father Ataliba, as a sign of friendship between the two races, to give her to him in marriage. The second scene, in Ataliba's apartments in the Governor's palace, introduces Alzira and her younger sister Zuma. Alzira awakens from having dreamed of Zamoro, whom she believes to have been killed in battle. Her father enters to tell her that she must marry the Spaniard Gusmano. She refuses, but her father warns her he is adamant, and leaves. Alzira has just sworn she would rather die than be unfaithful to the memory of Zamoro, when suddenly Zamoro appears. Their joyous reunion is interrupted by the entrance of Gusmano. Zamoro and Gusmano recognise each other: Gusmano is Zamoro's most hated foe against whom he has sworn vengeance. Summoning his guards, Gusmano takes Zamoro prisoner, despite the fact that, in so doing, he is violating the peace agreed between Spaniard and Inca. Alvaro enters and recognises Zamoro as the young chieftain who had behaved mercifully to him when he was captured. He kneels before his son Gusmano to beg for Zamoro's life. But it is only when Gusmano hears that the Incas have crossed the river Rimac and are marching on Lima that he orders Zamoro to be set free, vowing that they shall meet in battle.

The second act consists of three scenes, the first of which takes place inside the fortifications of Lima, where the Spanish forces are celebrating their victory over the Incas. Prisoners are brought in, among them Zamoro, who is sentenced to be burned at the stake at dawn. Alzira pleads with Gusmano, who tells her that Zamoro's fate is in her hands. If she will marry him, he will give Zamoro his freedom. Overcoming her horror at the proposal, Alzira consents.

In the next scene, Zamoro and his followers are sheltering in a cave in the countryside near Lima. Zamoro is told of Alzira's imminent marriage to Gusmano and, cursing her for being unfaithful to him, he swears vengeance and returns immediately to Lima.

The final scene is a huge hall in the Governor's palace, where the wedding ceremony is being held. As Gusmano is about to take Alzira's hand in marriage, he is stabbed by the disguised Zamoro, who then allows himself to be taken prisoner. The dying Gusmano unexpectedly matches Zamoro's magnanimity as displayed in the Prologue, pardoning him and returning Alzira to him. Gusmano says a final farewell to his father, and dies.

Cammarano's libretto follows the events of Voltaire's play reasonably closely, though there are minor divergences; but it completely fails to capture either the play's mood or its meaning. Critics have doubted whether Voltaire can really have meant to display the superior virtues of Christianity as opposed to those of the noble savage. It is true that *Alzire* is dramatically so inept that it can be made to mean almost anything, but I think the words and the tone of Voltaire's introduction to the play must be accepted at their face value:

> On a taché dans cette tragédie toute d'invention et d'une espèce assez neuve, de faire voir combien le véritable esprit de religion l'emporte sur les vertus de la nature.
>
> La religion d'un barbare consiste à offrir à ces dieux le sang de ces ennemis. Un chrétien mal instruit n'est souvent guère plus juste. Etre fidèle à quelques pratiques inutiles, et infidèle aux vrais devoirs de l'homme, faire certaines prières, et garder ses vices; jeûner, mais haïr; cabaler, persécuter, voilà sa religion. Celle de chrétien véritable est de regarder tous les hommes comme ses frères, de leur faire du bien et de leur pardonner le mal. Tel est Gusman au moment de sa mort; tel Alvarez dans le cours de sa vie; tel j'ai peint Henry IV, même au milieu de ses faiblesses.
>
> On trouvera dans presque tous mes écrits cette humanité qui doit être le premier caractère d'un être pensant; on y verra (si j'ose m'exprimer ainsi) le désir du bonheur des hommes, l'horreur de l'injustice et de l'oppression; et c'est cela seul qui a jusqu'ici tiré mes ouvrages de l'obscurité où leur défauts devaient les ensevelir.[1]

Cammarano's departures from Voltaire are a violation of these expressed intentions. In a way, they humanise the characterisation and even, in places, improve the plot. But Voltaire's approval of Christian morals becomes lost in Cammarano's rather brutal adventure story. I wonder what initially attracted Verdi to the play. He favoured Christian virtue, but had no feeling for Christian mysticism. His liberal agnostic-

---

[1] This tragedy, a work of complete fiction and almost of a new species, was written with the intention of showing how far superior the spirit of true religion is to the virtues of nature.

The religion of a barbarian consists in offering up to his gods the blood of his enemies. A badly instructed Christian is seldom more just. To be a faithful observer of certain unnecessary practices yet to neglect the true duties of mankind, to repeat certain prayers yet to retain his vices, to fast but to hate, to plot and to persecute, that is the religion of such a person. That of a real Christian is to regard all men as his brothers, to do good to them and to forgive the evil they do. Such is Gusman at the moment of his death, such Alvarez throughout his life. As such a character have I painted Henry IV, despite his weaknesses.

In almost all my writings will be found that humanity which ought to be the first characteristic of a thinking being. In them will be found, if I may say so, the desire that men should be happy, a horror of injustice and oppression. It is that alone which has so far rescued my works from the obscurity to which their faults ought really to consign them.

ism was allied with the kind of nineteenth-century Italian political anti-clericalism that made him detest all talk of religion. He would not have been interested in proving the Christian God morally superior to the Inca gods. Indeed, he probably encouraged Cammarano to minimise the religious element in the play. Perhaps it was the exotic locale which appealed to him, though he made no attempt to write Indian music for it, in the way that he was to invent Egyptian music for *Aida* a quarter of a century later. Cammarano's principal contribution to the enterprise, was to replace the plodding verse in which Voltaire's characters sneer at one another's religion—

> Dieu? ta religion? Quoi! ces tyrans cruels,
> Monstres desaltérés dans le sang des mortels,
> Qui dépeuplent la terre, et dont la barbarie
> En vaste solitude a changé ma patrie

—with a brutally terse poetry for Verdi to translate into rhythmic vigour and unsubtle melodic charm.

III

There is a thematic connection, but not much affinity of spirit, between the Overture to *Alzira* and the remainder of the opera. The Overture, which opens exotically on woodwind and drums alone, is a delightful piece, exquisitely scored, full of pleasant and catchy tunes, though something a little more sombre seems to be called for. Verdi wrote it in Naples after the opera had been rehearsed and had been found rather too short, and he received an additional fee for it. The opening chorus of Incas inviting Alvaro to "die covered with insults" (muoia coverto d'insulti), a remarkably sprightly number for the occasion, is followed by the arrival of Alvaro's rescuer Zamoro, whose cavatina, "Un Inca, eccesso orribile", and stretta, "Dio della guerra", comprise the remainder of the Prologue. Both look ordinary on the printed page and spring to life in performance. They are separated by a curious *allegro* section marked to be sung *sotto voce*.

In the Prologue and throughout the opera, although Verdi achieves some interesting effects within the arias, cabalettas, choruses, duets and ensembles, he retains in the shape of his scenes the old formula of introductory chorus, recitative, cavatina, recitative, cabaletta. In earlier operas he had occasionally forsaken these closed forms, and in the future he was more and more frequently to break free of them. But, perhaps because the opera was written in haste, Verdi appears in *Alzira* to have accepted the conventional formal structure without question. The structure itself was, after all, not completely inflexible. The introduction might be orchestral or choral, extended or brief. In recitative,

the character could either lead quickly into his aria, or advance the
action in arioso. The second recitative, between aria and cabaletta,
could likewise consist either of a few phrases of plot delivered by a
messenger, or could be expanded into a full-scale chorus.

The first-act opening chorus is largely declamatory, above a lilting
tune in the orchestra which has already been heard in the Overture.
Gusmano's aria and cabaletta, formally conventional, again are of the
kind that is immediately effective in performance. I am hardly the first
person to have noticed that, in early Verdi, what looks dull on paper and
sounds pointless when played on the piano, more frequently than not
completely justifies itself in stage performance. The point to be stressed
about the early Verdi is that, even when he is not a great composer, he
is almost invariably a great opera composer. He wrote for the stage, and
with such assurance and skill that it is usually difficult to fault him in
performance. He should no more be studied away from the stage than
Shakespeare or Chekov.

Alzira's cavatina, "Da Gusman, su fragil barca", and cabaletta,
"Nell' astro che più fulgido", are both excellent. The cavatina has
both dramatic strength and grace, and the strikingly individual cabaletta calls for a sound coloratura technique. Even better is the lively and
unusual duet for Alzira and Zamoro, a potential show-stopper. The
finale to Act I is rich: beginning with Zamoro's outburst, "Teco sperai
combattere", it moves through the beautiful baritone-bass duet in
which Alvaro pleads with Gusmano ("Nella polve, genuflesso"), and
builds up, first with Alzira's moving *andante*, and then with the entries
of the other principals, into a large, exciting, vintage early-Verdi first-
rate ensemble [Ex. 32]. A vigorous *allegro* section begun by Gusmano

Ex.32 Andante

Ah!.... il con-ten - to fu per no - i bre - ve so - gno men - ti - to - re!

brings the Act to an end.

An unintentionally funny chorus, this time of exultant Spaniards,
opens the second Act. The duet for Alzira and Gusmano after he
has told her his price for allowing Zamoro to live, "Il pianto, l'angos-
cia", is a touching and attractive number, with a typically Verdian
energy animating its moderate pace. Its *allegro* cabaletta fits naturally
into the dramatic situation: Gusmano's elation at having won Alzira
and her desperation at having had to resort to marriage with Gusmano
to save Zamoro are both admirably conveyed in their separate stanzas,
which then combine in duet. The orchestral introduction to the following scene, though brief, is almost symphonic in stature, and Zamoro's
elegantly melancholy aria, "Irne lungi ancor dovrei," is followed by
a really exhilarating and applause-making cabaletta, "Non di codarde
lagrime" [Ex. 33].

The last scene of the opera consists simply of a joyous wedding chorus, which is livelier in the orchestra than in the voices, and Gusmano's recitative and aria, "É dolce la tromba", which leads, after his stabbing by Zamoro, straight into the finale. The aria is sweet and assured: it is Gusmano's moment of real triumph and happiness and, as such, rather touching. It is also not unlike the love song of that other character driven by sexual passion to villainy, Di Luna in *Il trovatore*.

Zamoro knifes him and flamboyantly offers himself for punishment, but the dying Gusmano enunciates his suddenly acquired doctrine of Christian forgiveness in a beautiful *andante* punctuated by the en- ensemble. He receives his heartbroken father's blessing, and dies.

I cannot agree with the conventional view that in *Alzira* and *Il corsaro* Verdi had struck rock-bottom. They may be his least successful operas, but I cannot see that they lag so very far behind *Oberto*, *I Masnadieri*, *Attila* and *Aroldo*, in all of which I find much to admire and enjoy. *Alzira*'s years of neglect, incidentally, were interrupted by a production at the Rome Opera in 1967 which, though not particularly well sung, and somewhat limply conducted, was adequate enough to reveal that the score still has plenty of life in it.

IX

Attila

Dramatis personae:

Attila, King of the Huns   (bass)
Ezio, Roman general   (baritone)
Odabella, daughter of the Lord of Aquileia   (soprano)
Foresto, Aquileian knight   (tenor)
Uldino, a young Breton, Attila's slave   (tenor)
Leone, an old Roman   (bass)

LIBRETTO by Temistocle Solera, based on the play *Attila, König der Hunnen* by Zacharias Werner

TIME: A.D. 454
PLACE: Italy

FIRST PERFORMED at the Teatro La Fenice, Venice, March 17, 1846 with Sophie Loewe (Odabella); Carlo Guasco (Foresto); N. Constantini (Ezio); Ignazio Marini (Attila); Profili (Uldino); Romanelli (Leone)

Attila

BACK IN MILAN in August 1845, Verdi dismissed *Alzira* from his mind, and addressed himself to his immediate commitments. He had offers from Paris and London which in due course were to mature into firm contracts. Meanwhile, he agreed to write an opera for Francesco Lucca, a rival of Verdi's regular publisher Ricordi. The opera was to be delivered to Lucca who undertook to arrange for its production at one of the leading Italian theatres. It is about this time that Verdi's business arrangements become rather complicated. Writing one opera hard on the heels of another is hectic enough, but Verdi found himself committed simultaneously to several projects, and having to offend one impresario or publisher in order to satisfy another. He wrote a group of six songs (see pp. 456–7) which he gave to Lucca, perhaps in order to keep him quiet, and then began work not on Lucca's opera but on one he had already agreed to write for the Teatro La Fenice, Venice. The subject chosen was Attila the Hun, a subject which Verdi and his Venetian librettist Piave had already seriously considered earlier. As mentioned in the chapter on *I due Foscari*, Verdi had in fact sketched out a draft synopsis for a libretto, based on a German play about Attila, and had asked Piave to provide the verses:

> I shall send you the original Werner play in a few days, and you must have it translated, for there are passages of tremendous power in it. Read also Madame de Staël's *De l'Allemagne* which will throw great light on it for you. I advise you to study the subject thoroughly and to keep everything well in mind; period, characters and so on. Then block it out, but in detail, scene by scene, with all the characters, so that all you will have to do will be to write the verses. This way you will encounter less difficulty. Read Werner, especially the choruses which are magnificent.[1]

The Attila idea had been dropped at that time in favour of *I due Foscari* which Piave and Verdi wrote for Rome. Now, three operas later, Verdi returned to the subject. Deciding that the gentle Piave was really not the right man for Attila, Verdi took it away from him and engaged the more colourful Solera to write the libretto. Lazy and unreliable, Solera

---

[1] *Copialettere*, p. 438.

took his time over the job. On August 13, 1845, young Muzio wrote to
Barezzi:

> The Signor Maestro has written to Solera that he is coming to Milan
> especially to collect the libretto of *Attila* from which he will make his
> most beautiful opera, but that lazy dog of a poet hasn't done a thing. . . .
> This morning at eleven o'clock he was still in bed, so it seems that he is
> not working.[1]

But Solera was capable of putting a spurt on when pressure was
applied: five days later he had almost finished the libretto. Now it was
Verdi's turn to sink into a condition of neurotic sloth. He went to
Busseto for a few weeks, but found it difficult to work. Earlier in the
year he had told his friend Giuseppe Demaldè: "I look forward to the
passing of these next three years. I have six operas to write, and then farewell to everything."[2] And on November 5th, his mood was sufficiently
unstable to be reflected quite dissimilarly in letters to two correspond-
ents. To one he wrote: "*Attila* keeps me busy. What a wonderful, wonderful subject. The critics can say whatever they like, but I say 'What
a wonderful libretto for music'."[3] To the other: "Thanks for the news of
Alzira, but more for remembering your poor friend, condemned continually to scribble musical notes. God save the ears of every good
Christian from having to listen to them! Accursed notes! How am I,
physically and spiritually? Physically I am well, but my mind is black,
always black, and will be so until I have finished with this career that I
abhor. And afterwards? It's useless to delude oneself. It will always be
black. Happiness does not exist for me."[4]

He took to his bed with rheumatism, and had to be massaged continually by the faithful Muzio. When he arrived in Venice in December to
produce the opera on New Year's Eve, he had written hardly any of it.
Some alterations to the fourth act of the libretto were necessary, and,
as Solera had taken himself off to Spain, Piave was called upon. The
opening night had to be postponed. Early in January, Verdi succumbed
to a severe form of gastric fever and was confined to bed for three weeks.
He continued to work on *Attila*, but suffered a relapse, took to his bed
again, had to be bled, and eventually finished composing the opera in
bed in what he himself referred to as "an almost dying condition".
Finally, eleven weeks late, *Attila*'s première took place at the Fenice, on
March 17, 1846. It was a huge success. Naturally the Venetian audience
responded happily to the scene in which the refugees from Aquileia
arrive at the lagoon to found the city of Venice, and less happily to the
political implications of battle between Italians and Huns. When, in
a duet with Attila, the Roman general Ezio sang the line, "Avrai tu

---

[1] Garibaldi, op. cit., pp. 177–8.   [2] Walker, op. cit., p. 180.
[3] *Copialettere*, p. 432.   [4] Walker, op. cit., pp. 180–1.

l'universo, resti l'Italia a me" (You take the universe, but leave me Italy), there were shouts from the crowded theatre of "A noi! L'Italia a noi!" It is incredible that the Austrian censorship authorities had passed the scene for performance. Verdi found himself fêted as a hero by the Venetians and escorted to his hotel "with flowers, bands and torchlights". To his friend the Countess Maffei, he wrote: "*Attila* had, on the whole, a very cheerful reception. The applause and calls were too much for a poor invalid. . . . My friends maintain that this is the best of my operas. The public questions that. I think it is not inferior to the others. Time will tell."[1]

II

Zacharias Werner (1768–1823), the author of the play *Attila, König der Hunnen* on which the libretto of *Attila* is based, was a minor German playwright who had first become known in 1808 through the sponsorship of Goethe. He wrote a new species of drama which he called *Schicksalsdrama*, or fate-play, one example of which, *Der vierundzwanzigste Februar* (The twenty-fourth of February), Goethe produced in Weimar. Werner himself was a curious character: Goethe considered him a "very gifted man", but eventually lost interest in him when Werner became converted to Catholicism as a result, he claimed, of reading Goethe's *Wahlverwandtschaften*. Werner gave up the theatre and ended his life in Vienna as a popular evangelist. His *Attila* is a very long tragedy in five acts, highly romantic but, one would have imagined, much more suitable operatic fodder for Wagner than for Verdi, with its celebration of the old German gods and its superior Teutonic attitude to the childish southerners. Verdi, however, was particularly impressed by the character of Attila and by Werner's almost operatic use of the stage chorus. He, Piave and Solera among them simplified the play considerably and made such radical alterations to the plot that it is pointless to seek in the play parallels to the opera's scenes. Most of the characters have been renamed, one is entirely invented, and several who are important to the play, including the entire Roman court, do not appear in the opera. The play's twenty-four speaking parts are reduced to six solo roles in the opera. The scene in the opera in which the survivors from Aquileia arrive at the lagoon to found the city of Venice has no counterpart in the play: it is simply a piece of clever public relations work on Verdi's part. (It is also, musically, very beautiful.) One of Werner's finest scenes, in which, while news is brought of the approach of Attila, the boy-emperor Valentine sits playing dice with Heraclius, the Greek envoy, is omitted from the opera.

---

[1] *Copialettere*, p. 441.

Werner's fierce Attila, known as "Gottes Geissel" (God's scourge), makes frequent references to Wotan and Valhalla. Informed that he has lost seven thousand soldiers in battle, he exclaims:

> Sie trinken in Walhalla bei den Vätern,
> Und laben sich an Wodan's Freudenmahl.
> (They drink in Valhalla with their fathers, and refresh themselves
> at Wotan's joyful feast.)

The play's "hunnisches Mädchen", Hildegunde, daughter of the Lord of Aquileia, becomes the opera's Odabella. A Roman consul Aetius does at one point voice patriotic sentiments not dissimilar to those of Ezio in the opera, and behaves as traitorously. But Ezio is a cipher by comparison with Aetius, who is given to philosophising in this vein:

> Wo ist denn Rom? In diesen Steinkolossen?
> Rom ist wo Römer sind. Wo giebts noch Römer?
> Der Römer lebte, starb für's Vaterland,
> Wir leben, sterben—keiner weiss wofür.
> (Where then is Rome? In this colossus of stone? Rome is where
> Romans are: where are they today? The Romans lived and died
> for their fatherland. We live and die, but no one knows what for.)

Werner's play, despite the turgidity of its sentiment and, to a lesser extent, its language, is a more complex work of art than Verdi's opera, though not necessarily a more valid one. Werner was concerned to make a statement about the concept of fate, while Verdi merely set out to write an opera about patriotism. Indeed, he and Solera were so convinced of the rectitude of the Italian cause that they appear not to have noticed how, in their libretto, it is the Italians who behave treacherously, the Hun who is magnanimous. If Solera's *Attila* is not a patch on Werner's, it is not the fault of his verse, which, like Piave's, is serviceable and to the point:

> Ella in poter del barbaro, fra le sue schiave avvinta!
> Ahi, che men crudo all'anima fora il saperte estinta!
> Io ti vedrei fra gl'angeli, almen né sogni allora,
> E invocherei l'amora dell'immortal mio di.

It is Solera's haphazard construction and lack of interest in providing adequate motivation for his characters that cause his downfall. Fortunately, Verdi's music is forceful enough to overcome this defect to a large extent.

The opera is written in a prologue and three acts. Scene 1 of the Prologue, corresponding roughly to Act I of Werner's play, takes place in the main square of Aquileia. The town has been razed by Attila's hordes of Huns and Ostrogoths. Attila, King of the Huns, enters and congratulates his jubilant troops. Most of the vanquished Aquileians have been slain, but Attila's slave Uldino has contrived to save the lives of a band of women who fought under the leadership of Odabella, whose father, the Lord of Aquileia, had been killed by Attila himself. Impressed by Odabella's courage, Attila offers her whatever she most desires. When she asks for her sword to be returned to her, he gives her his own, which she swears to herself she will use on him, to avenge her father.

Attila asks for the envoy from Rome to be brought in and, when Ezio enters, greets him as a valiant soldier and worthy adversary. Ezio announces that he must speak privately with Attila. They are left alone, whereupon Ezio proposes a secret pact by which he and Attila will divide Italy between them. The Eastern ruler, he points out, is heavy with age ("Tardo per gli anni, e tremulo" is his taut phrase), while the Roman Emperor is still a child. Why should they not agree to share the spoils? Verdi's audiences, who cheered Ezio's rousing phrase, "Avrai tu l'universo, resti l'Italia a me", seem not to have realised either that, in the context of A.D. 454 "l'universo" meant Italy and "l'Italia" meant Rome, or that Ezio was not, in effect, saying "Leave us in peace", but "I'll help you to the rest if you allow me to take over Rome." This is stated explicitly in Werner's play:

AETIUS:
    So hör auch mich! Ich hab' geträumt wie Du,
    Von Menschenrecht, Gefühl und Pflicht und Tugend;
    Doch beim Erwachen schwand der Morgentraum,
    Nur eines blieb: die Kraft, die selbst sich Gott ist!
    Das ist die Freiheit, jenes Sklaverei;
    Willst Du die Welt befrei'n—entfessle Dich!
ATTILA (*erstaunt*): Aetius!
AETIUS: Ich bin Dictator Rom's;
    Ein Stoss in's Herz das Kaiserlichen Knaben,
    Und ich bin Kaiser!—Dass—ich muss es sein—
    Und ging die Menschheit, ging ich selbst zu Grunde!
ATTILA: Und was soll ich—
AETIUS: Dem Kindertraum entsagen!
    Ich, Du! Wir sind die Welt. Was sonst dafür
    Sich ausgiebt—'s ist nur unsre Bühne—Menschen
    Sind Puppen—Tugend, Pflicht—es ist Verzierung!
    Die Erd' ist gross, sie reicht wohl für uns Beide!
    Behalte was Du hast; (Du hast schon viel)
    Mir lass den Rest—doch, bei dem Gott in mir,
    Den muss ich haben.

(AETIUS: Listen to me. I, like you, used to dream of the rights of man, of feelings, duty and virtue, but when I awoke only one thing remained real: might itself is God. That is freedom, all else slavery. If you want to set the world free, loose your own chains.

ATTILA (*astonished*): Aetius!

AETIUS: I am Rome's Dictator. One blow to the heart of the young Emperor, and I should be Emperor of Rome. That I must be, even if I destroy mankind and myself in achieving it.

ATTILA: And what should I do—?

AETIUS: Renounce your youthful dream. You and I are the world; it is our stage. What else matters? Men are puppets, virtue and duty mere ornaments. The earth is large enough for us both. Keep what you have (you already have enough), and leave the rest to me, because, by the spirit in me, I swear I must have it.)

Attila rejects Ezio's offer, calls him a traitor to his country, and prepares to march on Rome.

The second scene of the Prologue takes place by the Adriatic lagoon which was to become the site of Venice. The landscape is bare but for a few wooden huts and an improvised altar. It is just before dawn: a storm is raging, but subsides during the scene as the sun rises. A hymn praising God is sung by a number of holy men, described by Solera as "a chorus of Christian hermits"! Boats appear, bearing Foresto and other survivors and refugees from Aquileia. The survivors hail Foresto for having led them to safety, but Foresto laments the fact that his beloved Odabella is a prisoner of Attila ("Ella in poter del barbaro"). Rousing himself, he exhorts his followers to build a new and wonderful city on this desolate spot.

Act I, Scene 1, takes place by moonlight in a forest near Attila's camp. Odabella weeps for her father and for Foresto who she believes died with him ("Oh, nel fuggente nuvolo"). Foresto arrives, disguised. He reveals his identity to Odabella, but her joy at finding him alive is cut short by his accusations of treachery and infidelity. Reminding him of the story of Judith and Holofernes, Odabella finally convinces Foresto that she is no traitress, and explains her plan to murder Attila.

The second scene of Act I is set in Attila's tent. Attila is asleep in bed, and stretched asleep on the floor covered only by a tiger skin is his slave Uldino. Attila calls out in his sleep, and Uldino awakens him. The King tells the boy he has had a dream in which he was stopped at the gates of Rome by an old man who prophesies disaster for Attila unless he turns back. Now properly awake, Attila is ashamed of his fear, and calls his soldiers and Druids together for an immediate assault on Rome. They sing a hymn of praise to Wotan, but from the distance the sound of quieter singing is heard. A procession of maidens dressed in white and waving palms approaches, singing a Christian hymn. Leading the procession is Leo, a Roman bishop, later to become Pope Leo I. (In Werner's play, Leo is an important character who has already been introduced in the Roman scenes, and who has announced his intention of going out to meet Attila.) Attila recognises him as the old man of his dream and, struck with fear when Leo repeats the old man's words, falls to the ground in terror.

Act II opens in Ezio's camp outside Rome. Ezio reads a despatch from the Emperor Valentine ordering him to return to Rome, as a treaty has been concluded between the Huns and the Romans. Ezio objects to being so tersely recalled by the "coronato fanciul", and reflects on the bitter contrast between Rome's present decadence and its former days of glory. A group of slaves arrives, bearing an invitation from Attila to a banquet. One of them remains behind: it is the still disguised Foresto, who, making himself known to Ezio, suggests they combine to bring about Attila's downfall. Ezio readily consents.

The second scene of Act II is the banquet in Attila's camp. The action is presented somewhat confusedly in the libretto, but what happens is that the slave Uldino, bribed by Foresto, attempts to poison Attila. (Uldino has some reason for his disaffection: his country, Brittany, had been subjugated by Attila.) Odabella, determined that Attila shall die by her hand and no other, prevents him from drinking the wine proffered by Uldino. Foresto throws off his disguise, announcing that it was he who had attempted to poison Attila. Odabella pleads for Foresto's life, and Attila, grateful to her for having saved him, announces that he will marry her, places Foresto under her supervision, and prepares to resume the attack on Rome.

Act III takes place in the forest. It is morning. Uldino informs Foresto that plans are proceeding for the wedding of Attila and Odabella. Ezio enters, and he and Foresto plot to ambush the Huns, while in the distance the sound of wedding festivities can be heard. Odabella appears, Foresto again accuses her of treachery, and she pleads with him to believe her ("Te sol quest' anima"). Attila suddenly arrives to find Odabella with his enemies, and reproaches all three of them in turn. As Roman soldiers are heard approaching, Attila realises he has been betrayed. Odabella stabs him with the sword he had given her. "You too, Odabella?" he murmurs, echoing the phrase of an earlier and greater conqueror in a similar situation, and falls dead. "God, people and king are avenged," the three conspirators cry.

III

The Prelude to *Attila* is a short, dark, yearning *largo* whose intense string writing startlingly anticipates the style Verdi was to develop in *La traviata*. The opening chorus of Huns, Eruli and Ostrogoths, lively and undistinguished, is interrupted by Attila's recitative as he enters and greets his warriors. Obadella's "Allor che i forti corono", with its melody frequently doubled by first violins and cellos in octaves, is a superb piece of musical invective. Although its tempo is moderate, the aria itself, because of the ferocity of the sentiments expressed, has something of the character of a cabaletta. The preceding recitative contains a scale passage from top C to B below middle C, and the aria's tuneful vigour is irresistible in the theatre [Ex. 34]. Its brilliant cabal-

etta generates an even higher voltage of fury. The famous line, "Avrai tu l'universo, resti l'Italia a me" is verbally and musically the most effective moment in the duet between Attila and Ezio [Ex. 35].

The second scene of the prologue is the finest in the opera. As the diminished sevenths of the tempest die away, the dramatic tension is eased, the storm abates and the sun rises, and the chorus "of hermits" gives thanks to God in an affirmative C major. The orchestral figure accompanying the arrival of the refugees from Aquileia is cleverly effective, and Foresto's aria ("Ella in poter del barbaro") and cabaletta are both excellent.

Preceded by a warmly beautiful orchestral introduction, Obadella's cavatina, "Oh, nel fuggente nuvolo", is exquisitely scored for flute, English horn, harp and cellos, which give the voice most delicate yet expressive support. In place of a cabaletta, there is a vigorous duet for Odabella and Foresto, "Si, quello io son, ravvisami!" which more than compensates in energy for what it lacks in thematic distinction. The next scene in which Attila first dreams of and then is in reality confronted by the old man is first-rate almost throughout. Attila's dramatic aria, "Mentre gonfiarsi l'anima", is let down by a particularly empty cabaletta, though even this can be used to dramatic advantage to underline the hollowness of the King's apparent recovery of his courage. His forces assemble, but their battle-cry of "Glory to Wotan" is interrupted by the distant hymn. The dramatic conflict is expressed with superb directness in purely musical terms. After Leo's pronouncement, Attila's broken, declamatory phrases give way to a sadly sweet legato melody at "Spiriti, fermate", out of which the beautiful ensemble finale to the act grows. A few bars earlier, the orchestral phrases that precede Attila's "No, non è sogno" look forward across the years to the "Mors stupebit" of the Requiem.

The second act is patchier. Ezio's aria, "Dagl' immortali vertici", is an excellent example of Verdi's early middle-period writing for the baritone, both elegant and suave. His obvious, yet lovable and indeed effective device of doubling the voice part in the strings for emphasis is brought into play at "Roma nel vil cadavere". After the aria, a brief and urgent passage in duet with Foresto leads into the cabaletta, not a very good one. The banqueting scene is distinguished by an interesting orchestral figure here, a telling vocal phrase there, rather than by overall excellence, though the great ensemble which develops when a sudden gale extinguishes the lights and the Huns fall to the ground in superstitious terror is Verdi at his most splendid. A quirky little staccato figure [Ex. 36] alternates with a beautiful legato phrase swell-

Ex.36

L'or - ren - da, l'or - ren — da pro - cel - la spa - rì,

ing from piano to forte in two bars [Ex. 37]. The attempted poisoning is rushed and confused, and the final *allegro* a wild scramble, though undeniably exciting in the threatre.

There are incidental felicities in the very brief final act, but only the elegiacally lovely trio, "Te sol quest' anima", can be called really

Ex.37

di cal - ma no - vel - la il ciel si ve - stì!

vintage Verdi. Foresto's aria, "Che non avrebbe il misero", has a certain pale charm, but the quartet finale, "Tu, rea donna", is disappointingly perfunctory.

Despite Verdi's enthusiasm for the libretto, and the presence in the score of a few really first-rate numbers and some telling phrases, I cannot bring myself to regard *Attila* as among the most successful early Verdi operas. Toye says "it can by no means be considered, like *Alzira*, an utter failure", and his own opinion of *Alzira* is that it "is undoubtedly the worst of Verdi's operas". To my ears, however, despite the conventionality of *Alzira*'s musical language, its standard of achievement is more consistently high than that of *Attila*. Both operas, in fact, work very well on the stage: it must be remembered that Toye had no opportunity to see or hear the vast majority of the early Verdi operas performed. *Alzira* may well be one of the least successful operas, but it is at least as enjoyable a work as *Attila*, and no more intrinsically absurd as a theatrical experience. *Attila* perhaps improves on the earlier work in that Verdi's imaginative use of the orchestra continues to take, if not strides, at least firm steps forward. His musical characterisation, however, is temporarily at a standstill. Foresto is a complete cipher, Ezio and Odabella are flat, one-sided characters, and Attila himself is as much a confusing as confused character. It seems obvious to me that Verdi was on the edge of a nervous breakdown when he wrote this opera.

X

Macbeth

Dramatis personae:

Macbeth, a General in King Duncan's army   (baritone)
Banquo, another General   (bass)
Lady Macbeth   (soprano)
Macduff, a Scottish nobleman   (tenor)
Malcolm, the King's son   (tenor)
Gentlewoman, attendant on Lady Macbeth   (mezzo-soprano)
Doctor   (bass)
Servant of Macbeth   (bass)
Murderer   (bass)
Herald   (bass)

LIBRETTO by Francesca Maria Piave, based on the play *Macbeth* by Shakespeare

TIME: 1040
PLACE: Scotland

FIRST PERFORMED at the Teatro della Pergola, Florence, March 14, 1847 with Marianna Barbieri-Nini (Lady Macbeth); Felice Varesi (Macbeth); Michele Benedetti (Banquo); Brunacci (Macduff). Revised version first performed at the Théâtre Lyrique, Paris, April 21, 1865, with Rey-Balla (Lady Macbeth); Ismaël (Macbeth); Bilis Petit (Banquo); Monjauze (Macduff)

Macbeth

IMMEDIATELY AFTER THE production of *Attila* in Venice in 1846, Verdi was expected to go to London to write an opera for the impresario Benjamin Lumley, to be produced at Her Majesty's Theatre. But he was in no condition to travel, and, in fact, his doctors forbade it. He appears, at this time, finally to have succumbed to that nervous exhaustion to which his temperament rendered him peculiarly vulnerable. His doctors insisted that he give up all engagements and take six months' complete rest. Verdi was in no condition to resist: for six months he did absolutely nothing, living the life of a complete invalid, faithfully looked after by Muzio. His mood varied between lethargy and irritability. Unable to work and unwilling to think about working, he endured this, for him, unusual condition of neurotic sloth, taking the medicines prescribed, exercising himself with long walks, and in the summer taking the waters at Recoaro as ordered by his Venetian doctor.

Those commentators who have expressed themselves sceptically on the subject of Verdi's illness in the middle of his "galley years" exhibit a distinct lack not only of sympathy but also of imagination. In the case of a busy professional like Verdi, a sudden and prolonged unwillingness or inability to work is symptomatic of a more serious condition than mere malingering. To argue that Verdi simply wanted to get out of unwelcome commitments is to fail completely to understand his temperament. The "mens sana in corpore sano" Verdi we still read about is an absurd simplification of the whole man. He had his fair share of the artist's schizophrenia: he was both healthy, shrewd, common-sensible farmer, and melancholic, listless and pessimistic musician. The psychosomatic sore throats, headaches and stomach upsets were suffered by the musician: the musician's tantrums were tolerated by the peasant-farmer.

At last, in the autumn of 1846, Verdi felt confident enough to direct attention once more to the world of contracts, impresarios, singers and agents. As usual, he had several libretti in mind, in various stages of negotiation, as well as a few nebulous plans for the future. His friend Count Maffei, who had accompanied him to Recoaro, intended to adapt Schiller's play *Die Räuber*, and this would in time become the opera *I masnadieri*. Verdi also planned to set Grillparzer's *Die Ahnfrau*, to be called *Avola*, and Shakespeare's *Macbeth*. He was still not willing to undertake the journey to London, which he postponed, agreeing first to write an opera for Alessandro Lanari, the impresario of the Teatro della Pergola in Florence. He had also to write a new opera for the publisher Francesco Lucca, had thought of doing *Il corsaro* and then decided against it. For the time being, Lucca, and his wife Giovanna who was the real business head of the firm, had to wait as patiently as they could. Verdi's thoughts began to crystalise around *I masnadieri* and *Macbeth* simultaneously. He began work upon both. Maffei produced his libretto for *I masnadieri* and Verdi started to compose the music, at the same time writing the *Macbeth* libretto himself in prose, and sending it to Piave to be turned into verse. He began to discuss singers with the Florentine impresario. For *I masnadieri* he needed a strong tenor, and was keen to have Gaetano Fraschini, who had sung Zamoro in *Alzira*. But Fraschini was not free, and Napoleone Moriani[1] was suggested. Verdi went to Bergamo to hear Moriani sing, but found that the tenor's voice had badly deteriorated. No other acceptable tenor being available, Verdi and Lanari decided on *Macbeth* as the Florence opera, as Verdi intended the character of Macbeth to be a baritone role, and so would require no leading tenor. He abandoned the nearly half-completed *Masnadieri* which he decided he would finish in London the following year, and began to compose *Macbeth*. He worked slowly, refusing to take on other commissions or to discuss future engagements. He felt, it seems, more deeply committed to *Macbeth* than to its immediate predecessors. Indeed, some months later, in dedicating the vocal score to his old benefactor Barezzi, he wrote: "Here now is this *Macbeth*, which is dearer to me than all my other operas, and which I therefore deem more worthy of being presented to you."[2]

Verdi concerned himself with every aspect of the production of *Macbeth*, which he was determined would be something more than just another new opera in a busy season. To the scene designer, who had imagined the period of the play to be contemporaneous with Ossian and the Roman Empire, he read a lesson in Scottish history. While he was still composing the opera, he wrote several letters to Lanari, containing detailed instructions:

When you receive the music you will see there are two choruses of the utmost importance, so don't be economical about the number of singers and you'll be happy with it. Do make sure that the witches are always divided into three groups, the best way being in groups of six, making eighteen in all. Take particular care in choosing the tenor for Macduff.

[1] The tenor whose illness in 1839 had caused the postponement of the *Oberto* première.
[2] *Copialettere*, p. 451.

See that the small-part singers are good too, because the ensembles will need good voices. I'm much concerned about these ensembles.

I can't tell you exactly when I shall be in Florence, because I want to finish the opera here [Milan] in peace. Don't worry, I shall arrive in time. Hand out the solo and chorus parts to everyone so that when I arrive we can begin to work with the orchestra after only two or three rehearsals . . . I am annoyed that the singer who is to do Banquo doesn't want to come on as his ghost. Why is this? Singers must be engaged to sing and to act. It is high time we stopped being lenient in this way. It would be monstrous for someone else to play the ghost, for Banquo's ghost must be immediately recognisable as Banquo.[1]

Piave's libretto underwent a certain revision, and Maffei was prevailed upon to re-write the Witches' Chorus and the Sleepwalking scene in particular. Verdi continued nervously to supervise everything. He wrote to London to discover how the appearance of Banquo's ghost was usually staged, and told Lanari he had "consulted prominent scholars as to period and costumes". He showed himself to be well swotted up on the British Isles: "Macbeth assassinated Duncan in 1040", he wrote, "and was himself killed in 1057. In England in 1039 the King was Harold, called Harefoot. He was Danish, and was succeeded in the same year by Hardicanute, half-brother of Edward the Confessor, etc."[2]

A letter of Verdi's, written the following year to Salvatore Cammarano, who was producing *Macbeth* in Naples and at the same time writing the libretto of *La battaglia di Legnano* for Verdi, contains the composer's much quoted description of the kind of voice he wanted Lady Macbeth to have:

I understand you are rehearsing *Macbeth*; and, as this opera interests me more than my others, please allow me to say a few words about it. Madame Tadolini, I believe, is to sing Lady Macbeth,[3] and I am astonished that she should have undertaken the part. You know how highly I regard Madame Tadolini, and so does she, but for the sake of us all I feel I must say that her qualities are too fine for this role. This may sound absurd, but Madame Tadolini is a handsome woman with a beautiful face, and I want Lady Macbeth to be ugly and evil. Madame Tadolini sings to perfection,

---

[1] *Copialettere*, pp. 447–8.

[2] *Copialettere*, p. 448. This letter was quoted in George Martin's *Verdi*. Harold was called "King of the Hares", and the author commented that "Verdi by his unfortunate mis-translation had libelled an entire nation." And indeed there is a quaint footnote in the Copialettere to "Re di lepre" in the text: "Non *Re di lepre* ma piede di lepre (Hare-foot) fu detto Aroldo". (Harold's nickname was not King of the hares but hare-foot.) The point is miniscule, but may as well be cleared up. It is hardly likely that Verdi or anyone else could have mistaken "foot" for "king". It is, on the other hand, very likely that Verdi's spidery handwriting was misunderstood when the letter was transcribed for publication in Italy, and that, although what was printed was "re", (king) what Verdi in fact wrote was "pie" (foot).

[3] Three years earlier, she had been Verdi's first Alzira.

and I don't want Lady Macbeth to sing at all. Madame Tadolini has a wonderful voice, clear, flexible and strong, while Lady Macbeth's voice should be hard, stifled and dark. Madame Tadolini has the voice of an angel, and Lady Macbeth's should be that of a devil. Please bring these comments to the notice of the directors, of Maestro Mercadante who will understand my ideas better than anyone, and of Madame Tadolini herself. Do what you think best. Tell them that the most important numbers in the opera are the duet between Macbeth and Lady Macbeth and the Sleep-walking scene. If these two numbers fail, then the entire opera will fail. And these two numbers definitely must not be sung. They must be acted and declaimed, with hollow, masked voices. Otherwise it will make no effect. The orchestra *con sordini*. The stage extremely dark. In the third Act, the apparitions of the kings (I have seen this in London) must take place behind a special opening at the back, with a thin, ash coloured veil in front of it. The kings must not be puppets, but eight men of flesh and blood. The spot they pass over must be a kind of mound, and you should be able to see them ascend and descend. The stage must be completely dark, especially when the cauldron disappears, with light only where the kings appear. The music from underneath the stage will have to be reinforced for the large San Carlo theatre. But take care there are no trumpets or trombones. The sound must seem far away, muffled, so it must be composed of bass clarinets, bassoons, contra-bassoons and nothing else.[1]

Verdi arrived in Florence in February 1847, accompanied by Muzio who was to play for the piano rehearsals, and soon the company found themselves working much harder than was usual for them. Verdi told Felice Varesi, the Macbeth, to study the dramatic situation and the words, and to attempt to "serve the poet before the composer". The Lady Macbeth, Marianna Barbieri-Nini, has left an account of the rehearsal period, and of how thoroughly she and Varesi were made to rehearse their first act duet.

And imagine this. The evening of the final rehearsal, with the theatre full of guests, Verdi made the artists put on their costumes, and when he insisted on something woe betide those who contradicted him. When we were dressed and ready, with the orchestra in the pit and the chorus already on stage, Verdi beckoned to me and Varesi to follow him into the wings. We did so, and he explained that he wanted us to come out into the foyer for another piano rehearsal of that wretched duet.

"Maestro", I protested, "we are already in our Scottish costumes. How can we?"

"Put cloaks over them."

Varesi, annoyed at this strange request, dared to raise his voice: "But, for God's sake, we've already rehearsed it a hundred and fifty times."

"I wouldn't say that if I were you, for within half an hour it will be a hundred and fifty-one."

[1] *Copialettere*, pp. 61–2.

He was a tyrant whom one had to obey. I can still remember the black look Varesi threw at Verdi as he followed the Maestro into the foyer. With his hand clutching the hilt of his sword, he looked as though he would murder Verdi just as later he would murder Duncan. But even Varesi gave in, and the one hundred and fifty-first rehearsal took place, while inside the theatre the audience clamoured impatiently.[1]

Allowing for prima donna hyperbole, it remains clear that the young Verdi was taking advantage of his popularity and fame to effect a raising of the standards of operatic production and performance and, in due course, a profound change for the better in the art-form of Italian opera itself. He was not content continually to churn out, à la Donizetti, the kind of thing he could do easily and successfully: though he professed no self-conscious theories, he was an artist and he inevitably developed in stature and artistic integrity.

The première of *Macbeth* on March 14th was an enormous success. Verdi took thirty-eight curtain calls, and even Barbieri-Nini realised that the intensive rehearsals had been worthwhile. She received an ovation after her Sleepwalking scene:

The storm of applause had not yet died down, and I was standing in my dressing-room, trembling and exhausted, when the door flew open—I was already half undressed—and Verdi stood before me. He gesticulated and his lips moved as if he wanted to speak but could not utter a word. Between tears and laughter, I too could say nothing. But I saw that his eyes were red. He squeezed my hand very tightly and rushed out. That moment of real feeling repaid me many times over for the months of hard work and continuous agitation.[2]

Eighteen years later, a year or two after the première of *La forza del destino* in St Petersburg, Verdi's French publisher Léon Escudier suggested a French translation of *Macbeth* for the Paris Opéra, and asked the composer if he would consent to revise the opera, adding the obligatory ballet sequence. Verdi agreed. It is generally this 1865 revision of the opera which is performed today; the differences between it and the 1847 original, less significant than has frequently been supposed, will be discussed later in this chapter. The Paris production was only moderately successful. When a critic suggested Verdi did not know his Shakespeare, the composer wrote with a splendid and indignant pride to Escudier:

Oh, there they are greatly mistaken. It may be that I did not do *Macbeth* justice, but to say I do not know, I do not understand and do not feel Shakespeare, no, by God, no! He is my favourite poet. I have known him from my childhood and read and reread him continually.[3]

---

[1] Monaldi, *Verdi, 1839–1898*. Second edition, p. 75.   [2] Op. cit., pp. 76–7.
rteggi Verdiani, Vol. IV, p. 159.

II

Verdi himself, as we have seen, was largely responsible for the libretto of *Macbeth*. He not only planned its shape and decided which scenes from the play should be included, but also wrote the entire libretto in Italian prose, leaving Piave to turn it into regular verse patterns. His reduction of the play to a reasonable libretto-length has been carefully and sensitively achieved. The libretto is less than half the length of the play, and it necessarily lacks the play's poetry; a poetry, however, which the music re-provides most successfully.

The opera begins with the third scene of the play. Congregating on the heath in thunder and lightning are not three witches but three covens of at least six witches each. And why not? They make a more effective noise than three. Their dialogue closely follows Shakespeare's. In fact, throughout the entire opera, the words are more often than not a literal translation of Shakespeare. Macbeth and Banquo enter, and Macbeth's opening line, "So foul and fair a day I have not seen", is retained: "Giorno non vidi mai sì fiero e bello". The witches hail Macbeth as Thane of Cawdor and as King of Scotland, and further prophesy that Banquo shall beget kings though he himself will not reign. The witches vanish, and immediately messengers from King Duncan (in the play there are only two of them, Ross and Angus) arrive to announce that the King has made Macbeth Thane of Cawdor. Macbeth ponders on the witches' utterance, and Banquo warns that "often times, to win us to our harm, the instruments of darkness tell us truths". Verdi omits the scene in the royal palace at Forres when Duncan greets Macbeth and Banquo; the opera's Scene 2 is the play's Act I, Scene v, a room in Macbeth's castle at Inverness. Lady Macbeth reads a letter from her husband in which he tells her of the strange circumstances of his advancement. Her aria and cabaletta, separated by the messenger's announcement that "the king comes here tonight", follow the shape of Shakespeare's scene. The aria, "Vieni t'affretta", parallels

> Hie thee hither,
> That I may pour my spirits in thine ear,
> And chastise with the valour of my tongue
> All that impedes thee from the golden round,
> Which fate and metaphysical aid doth seem
> To have thee crown'd withal.

And, after the messenger's lines, the spirit and substance of

> Come to my women's breasts
> And take my milk for gall, you murdering ministers

are perfectly caught in the cabaletta "Or tutti sorgete, ministri infernali". Macbeth enters, and they implicitly agree that the King must die.
The King and his courtiers arrive. Shakespeare gives him a polite
exchange with his hostess: Verdi, who has restricted Duncan's role to
this one scene, merely shows his ceremonial entry in procession across
the stage and off to the apartments set aside for him. The "If it were
done when 'tis done" scene is omitted. Macbeth, left alone on stage,
imagines a blood-stained dagger hovering in front of him ("Mi si
affacia un pugnal?"). This scene follows Shakespeare's lines closely. The
bell rings, and Macbeth enters the King's apartments with the words

> Quel bronzo, ecco, m'invita!
> Non udirlo, Duncano! È squillo eterno
> Che nel cielo ti chiama o nell' inferno.
>
> (The bell invites me.
> Hear it not, Duncan, for it is a knell
> That summons thee to heaven, or to hell.)

Lady Macbeth enters, and Macbeth returns with the dagger still in
his hand. Already he is at the mercy of his conscience. The duet follows
Shakespeare's words. He refuses to go back and leave the dagger to
incriminate the grooms sleeping in the room next to Duncan, so Lady
Macbeth seizes the dagger and goes to Duncan's chamber. When she
returns, her hands are as bloodstained as Macbeth's. As a loud knocking
at the gate is heard, they both retire.

Verdi dispenses with Shakespeare's comical porter. Macduff and
Banquo enter. Macduff has been bidden to awaken the King early. He
goes off to do so, and returns shocked and horrified, calling that
Duncan has been murdered. Everyone assembles, including the Macbeths. Banquo, who has gone to the King's apartments, returns to
confirm the dreadful news. The act ends with a huge ensemble in which
all express their stupefied horror.

Several scenes of the play are now omitted. Verdi's Act II is set in
Macbeth's castle. (In the play, though most Shakespeare productions
fail to make this clear, Macbeth and his wife, having been crowned,
take up residence in the royal Palace at Forres.) Macbeth is brooding
on the witches' prophecy that Banquo would father kings, and determines, encouraged by Lady Macbeth, to have Banquo and his son
Fleance assassinated. This is Shakespeare's Act III Scene ii. Lady
Macbeth's aria, "La luce langue", at the end of the scene, in which
she sings of the necessity of their crimes, and of her exaltation at having
attained the throne, has no exact parallel in the play. In the next scene,
the castle park, the murderers (three in Shakespeare, a double chorus
in Verdi) lie in wait for Banquo and his son, who have been invited to a
banquet by Macbeth. In the play Banquo has no soliloquy, but in the

opera he is given an aria, "Come dal ciel precipita", expressing his troubled thoughts. He is ambushed by the assassins and killed, but Fleance escapes.

The third scene of the act is the Banquet at the castle. Macbeth is informed secretly by one of the murderers that Banquo has been killed but that his son has fled. Lady Macbeth leads the guests in a rousing drinking song, interrupted by a distraught Macbeth who, about to sit down, has found his chair occupied by the ghost of Banquo. The apparition is not visible to the rest of the company, who are amazed at his behaviour. Lady Macbeth exhorts him to pull himself together, but the ghost reappears to him and again he cries out in terror. He recovers, and Lady Macbeth repeats her drinking song more determinedly. Suddenly Macbeth cries out in fear a third time. The act ends in an ensemble in which Macbeth determines to learn more from the witches, while his guests speculate on his erratic outbursts.

Two of Shakespeare's scenes are omitted, and the opera's Act III resumes at the play's Act IV, Scene i, the witches' cave. Sounds of thunder and lightning are heard. In the centre of the cave a cauldron is boiling, and around it the witches are dancing. Macbeth enters and asks what they are doing. Shakespeare's Macbeth addresses them as "secret, black and midnight hags"; Verdi's, more polite, calls them "misteriose donne". However they are addressed, their reply is the same: "Un' opra senza nome", a deed without a name. Macbeth demands that they reveal the future to him, and they obligingly ask if he will hear it from them or from their masters. "Call 'em; let me see 'em", replies Macbeth, and the powers of darkness are called up. First, a helmeted head arises from the cauldron, warning Macbeth to beware Macduff. A child covered in blood next appears, assuring him that "none of women born shall harm Macbeth". Another child, crowned, and holding a branch in his hand, prophesies that

> Macbeth shall never vanquished be until
> Great Birnham wood to high Dunsinane hill
> Shall come against him.

Considerably relieved to hear this, Macbeth still wants to know "shall Banquo's issue ever/Reign in this kingdom?" "Seek to know no more", the witches cry as their cauldron vanishes into the earth. But they conjure up a silent parade of eight kings, the last of them Banquo carrying a mirror and pointing at the others as though to indicate that they are his offspring. Macbeth faints, and the witches vanish. At this point the play brings on Lenox to announce that Macduff has fled to England, and Macbeth decides to seize his castle and murder his family. In the opera Lady Macbeth enters, and Macbeth tells her what he has seen and heard. The act ends with their duet voicing similar sentiments to those which, in the play, Macbeth utters as an aside: a determination to plunge even deeper into villainy.

Act IV, Scene 1, of the opera is set in the countryside, not far from Birnham Wood, just over the English border. Refugees from Scotland sing of their oppressed country. The content of their lament, though not the actual wording, has its provenance in Ross's speech in Shakespeare's Act IV, Scene iii, beginning "Alas, poor country!/Almost afraid to know itself". Macduff's aria, "Ah, la paterna mano", mirrors his lines in the play:

> Sinful Macduff!
> They were all struck for thee. Naught that I am,
> Not for their own demerits, but for mine,
> Fell slaughter on their souls . . .
>   . . . . front to front
> Bring thou this fiend of Scotland and myself;
> Within my swords's length set him; if he 'scape,
> Heaven forgive him too!

Malcolm enters at the head of a troop of English soldiers. He offers Macduff the joys of revenge, to which Macduff makes the desperate and heart-breaking Shakespearian reply, "Di figlio è privo" (He has no children). Macduff and Malcolm lead their forces against Macbeth, Malcolm first ordering every soldier to cut a branch from Birnham Wood and bear it before him as camouflage.

The second scene is set in a hall of Macbeth's castle at night. Lady Macbeth has for several nights been walking and talking in her sleep, and a gentlewoman is waiting with a doctor to observe her. Lady Macbeth enters, walking in her sleep. From her repeated gesture of hand washing, and the confused speech ("Una macchia è qui tuttora": Out damned spot) in which she rehearses the story of Duncan's murder, they realise they are overhearing an appalling confession.

In Scene 3, a room in the castle, Macbeth reflects on the bloody course of events, and realises that, for all he has gained, he has lost the compassion, respect and love of his fellows. ("Pieta, rispetto, amore"):

> My way of life
> Is fall'n into the sere the yellow leaf;
> And that which should accompany old age,
> As honour, love, obedience, troops of friends,
> I must not look to have.

The gentlewoman (in the play, Seyton, an officer) enters to say "The queen, my lord, is dead". Unfortunately, so soon after his last aria Verdi was obviously reluctant to give Macbeth another one. So there is no aria-equivalent of the great speech that begins "She should have died hereafter". Instead, Verdi merely sets the words "Life—what does it matter. It is a tale told by an idiot, full of sound and fury, signifying nothing."

Soldiers enter to announce that Birnham Wood is on the move, and Macbeth rushes off to battle. In the next scene, the play's Act V, Scenes vi and vii, a nearby plain where the battle is being fought, he encounters Macduff, and warns him to flee: "I bear a charmed life, which must not yield to one of woman born." Macduff's reply is unnerving:

> Despair thy charm,
> And let the angel whom thou still hast serv'd
> Tell thee, Macduff was from his mother's womb
> Untimely ripp'd.

They fight, and Macbeth is killed. Malcolm is hailed king, amidst general rejoicing.

III

The Prelude to *Macbeth* is a short piece in the composer's terse, Beethovenian manner. Verdi's reverence for and close study of Beethoven is revealed just as clearly by certain moments in his music as by the fact that many Beethoven scores are still to be seen in the cabinet beside his bed at Sant' Agata. The influence can be discerned in various parts of Macbeth, and not least in the *adagio* of the Prelude. Martial and pathetic strains alternate, the tune which in the opera serves to introduce Lady Macbeth's Sleepwalking scene being used to fine effect. It is, in fact, Lady Macbeth who dominates the Prelude, as she does the opera. She has two motifs here, a nervously jabbing figure and a tragically elegiac theme. It is the latter which, on its last appearance in the Prelude, seems to resound with the composer's sympathy for his unsympathetic character. For a moment, one imagines oneself in the boudoir of the dying Violetta. The opening chorus of witches is not particularly outstanding, though the orchestral evocation of night and storm is successful. Verdi's *Macbeth* score is full of detailed instructions to the singers. Above the opening bars of the chorus he has written "Nè dimenticarsi che sono streghe che parlano." (Don't forget it's witches who are talking) "Cupo" has replaced "con slancio" as a guide to style. The old forms are treated with increasing fluidity. The scene of Banquo and Macbeth with the witches does not consist of recitative, *andante* aria, chorus interruption, cabaletta. Macbeth and Banquo have only a few bars of recitative after the witches vanish, and Macbeth's reaction to the male chorus's information that Duncan has made him Thane of Cawdor is expressed in a poignantly uneasy *andante*. Lady

Macbeth's scena is formally more conventional. Yet her aria, "Vieni, t'affretta", and cabaletta, "or tutti sorgete, ministri infernali", are strikingly successful: dramatically meaningful and exciting not only in terms of nineteenth-century Italian opera, but also as parallels of Shakespeare's scene at this point in the play. It is when Verdi, as here, takes a bold imaginative leap, trusting in his own genius, that he lands closest to Shakespeare. The confident, curiously sinuous line of her aria paints Lady Macbeth's character and intentions with unwavering strokes: the majestically fierce determination of the cabaletta can be spine-tingling in performance.

The music for the procession of Duncan and his court into Macbeth's castle is frequently cut almost to nothing by nervous conductors who have been persuaded by critics of its banality. I have been guilty of gibes about the Busseto town band on occasion, but never with reference to this stage band music for Duncan's entrance. It is true that Verdi's first impressions of ceremonial music must have involved the Busseto band, true that the speech and the song he heard around him in the tavern at Le Roncole were those of rough farmers' baritone voices rather than the cultivated tenors of the Milan salons. But how splendid that he was led thus to define the baritone voice for the stage, how superb the series of great baritone roles he created. How right his stage band music for so many of the occasions on which he utilised it: wandering through the Palazzo ducale in Mantua today, one can more easily imagine Verdi's Duke frolicking to the rustic rhythms of his *Rigoletto* music than to more elegant Parisian dances. Verdi's use of apparent banality in the *Macbeth* processional music creates an admirable distancing effect. It is perhaps the earliest instance of what we think of now as Brechtian *Verfremdungseffekt*. Duncan's two earlier scenes have been deliberately excluded from the libretto, and even for this one appearance Verdi robs the character of speech. He is merely the king in the procession: he is not to figure importantly in our feelings. This is not a story of the murder of a kindly old king—it is an exploration of the psyches of Macbeth and Lady Macbeth. Duncan, soon to be despatched to another world, already exists in another sound-world as far as we are concerned. Verdi's tune is eerie, significant in the same way that Mahler's sudden intrusion of a simple hurdy-gurdy tune into a complex symphonic argument is significant, bringing its own immediately chilling and curious resonance from another world. No, the real Verdi conductor does not duck the challenge of the band music. That Duncan's march was misunderstood and dismissed as vulgar and trivial by the critics of 1847 is perhaps hardly surprising. It is, however, perplexing to find contemporary post-Freudian critics still sneering at it.

The duet which follows is the one that Verdi's singers complained of rehearsing a hundred and fifty times. It is preceded by the urgent recitative-arioso of Macbeth's dagger scene. As Macbeth tries to screw his courage to the sticking-place, his voice rises semitone by semitone only to fall again, and again to rise [Ex. 38].

He goes off to murder Duncan, and Lady Macbeth enters. The duet proper begins on his return, at "Fatal mia donna!" If one can put one's finger on a particular place in the score and say "Here is where Verdi lifted Italian opera out of its stagnant conventions," this is it. Conventions, of course, to which he himself was to return whenever he felt

Ex.38   **Andante**
misterioso

Sul - la me-tà   del   mon-do or mor-taè la   na - tu - ra:

or   l'as - sas - si - no   co - me fan - ta - sma per l'om-bre si   striscia:

Allegro

or con-su-man le   streghe   i   lor   mi - ste - ri.

like it, for Verdi is difficult to fit into any allotted groove, even that of the *avant garde* liberator. He needed no theories, he had genius instead. To infuse dramatically meaningful material, not into free recitative which any fool can do, but into the formal operatic duet is an ability possessed by Mozart and, fitfully, by Donizetti. After *Macbeth*, it became an obligation for composers of Italian opera.

The characters of Macbeth and Lady Macbeth share the same basic flaw, but their characteristics are very different, representing dissimilar temperaments. Her music in the duet abounds in nagging staccato ("Quell' animo trema, combatte, delira") [Ex. 39] while he is inclined

Ex.39   **Allegro**
sotto voce

Quell'a - ni-mo trema,   com-bat - te,   de - li - ra... Chi

mai   lo   di - reb - be l'in - vit - to   che   fu!

to resort to a desperately swelling legato ("Com' angeli d'ira vendetta tuo narmi") [Ex. 40]. Throughout this scena and duet, the manner in

Ex.40   **Allegro**   *a voce spiegata*

Co - m'an - ge - li   d'i - ra, ven - det - ta tuo - nar - mi   u -

-drò   di Dun - ca - no   le   san - te   vir - tù.

which the meaning of the words is conveyed within the formal shape of the music is masterly. In one of his letters to Escudier during the preparations for the Paris production of 1865, Verdi wrote:

> In the first act duet between Macbeth and Lady Macbeth, the first part always makes a big effect, and includes the words "Follie, follie, che sperdono i primi rai del di". The French translator should use the actual words "follie, follie", for it may be that that very word, indicating Lady Macbeth's secret scorn, contains the whole secret of the effectiveness of this number.[1]

Banquo's brief soliloquy is supported by a poetic and imaginative use of solo wind instruments, oboe and clarinet, creating an effect of chilly and inhuman lament. The ensemble which builds up after the discovery of Duncan's murder, and which concludes the first act, is magnificent: the swinging *grandioso* section, "L'ira tua formidabile e pronta" is both typically Verdian and strangely moving in context. Almost the whole of this act dates from the original 1847 version. In revising it for the Paris production of 1865, Verdi merely added a chorus for the witches after the exit of Banquo and Macbeth ("S'allontanarano") and altered twenty-four bars of the concluding *presto* of the duet between Lady Macbeth and Macbeth, beginning at "Oh potessi il mio delitto dalla mente cancellar". Significantly, the fifty-two-year-old composer did not make any alteration to the "commonplace" *banda* music for Duncan and his retinue. He saw that it was good.

The introductory bars of Act II quote the *Angst*-ridden duet from Act I. After Macbeth and Lady Macbeth have discussed killing Banquo, he goes off to commission the murderers while she, in a superb aria, "La luce langue", broods on the necessity for yet another crime. This was written for the 1865 version to replace a completely different aria, "Trionfai! secure alfine", in the 1847 score. The earlier aria was a fast, exciting and excited cabaletta, whereas "La luce langue" is a marvellous piece of musical characterisation, expressive in its instrumentation and harmony of the guilt and doubt which already begin to torture Lady Macbeth. She is both stronger and weaker than her husband: stronger in determination and ambition, but stronger, too, in imagination. His lack of imagination is the strength which sustains him until the end, while she, the more sensitive of the two, succumbs to her fears. "La luce langue" is not only musically superior to the 1847 aria—it is also a rich gain to the psychology of the drama to have such a piece immediately follow Macbeth's decisive exit.

The murderers' staccato chorus is innocuous, in fact rather charming. Banquo's "Come dal ciel precipita", darkly apprehensive, is one of Verdi's finest bass arias, scored in masterly fashion. At "e il mio pensiero

[1] *Copialettere*, p. 454.

ingombrano" he indulges his endearing habit of suddenly bringing
in his strings to double the voice, with fine effect. The banquet scene
works remarkably well on the stage. Lady Macbeth's drinking song,
"Si colmi il calice", a jovial enough tune in itself, is used by Verdi
to superb dramatic effect. After its first stanza, Macbeth has his *sotto
voce* conversation with the murderer, who has come to report only
partial success. Returning to his seat at the table, he finds it occupied
by Banquo's ghost and cries out in terror. Failing to bring him to his
senses, Lady Macbeth desperately launches into a second stanza of "Si
colmi il calice", in an attempt to save the situation. She has no sooner
landed on her final B flat than Macbeth sees the spectre again and cries
"Va! Spirto d'abisso". If one has merely read the score, one might
perhaps sneer at the *brindisi* as "the shoddy stuff favoured by the
composer in the matter of social festivities" (Toye), but no one at all
sympathetic to Verdi could continue to hold this opinion after seeing
and hearing the banquet scene adequately performed. The effect of
dramatic irony achieved by Verdi with this aria is as magnificent as the
similar stroke he was to bring off a few years later in *Rigoletto* with an
even more banal tune, "La donna è mobile".

When he finally succeeds in banishing Banquo's ghost from his vision,
Macbeth has a brief exchange with Lady Macbeth which I find
disturbingly reminiscent of that wonderful moment of reconciliation
between the Count and the Countess at the end of *Le nozze di Figaro*
[Ex. 41]. The Macbeths' reconciliation is not verbal, but the music

clearly reveals it to us. Macbeth, in one of those magical phrases that
Verdi was able to draw from simple ascending or descending scale
passages, sighs with relief "La vita riprendo" (Life returns to me).
Lady Macbeth's whispered words to him are "Shame on you, sir"
(Vergogna, signor), but her musical phrase is imbued with a curiously
tender, if momentary, sympathy. She forgives his kind of waywardness,
just as Mozart's Countess forgives her husband his kind [Ex. 42].

A short solo *adagio* for Macbeth ("Sangue a me") leads into the final ensemble, a splendid sextet with chorus.

Apart from the inclusion of "La luce langue", Act II is virtually the same as it was in 1847 except for differences in the setting of Macbeth's words during both appearances of the ghost.

The first scene of Act III, in which Macbeth returns to the witches, who conjure up apparitions for him, is considerably altered from the 1847 version. The ballet music at the beginning of the scene was, of course, written for the Paris production of 1865. It is generally, and rightly, omitted from stage performances today, as it disrupts the dramatic tension Verdi has so magnificently built up throughout the opera. But the music itself, lasting about ten minutes, is excellent. Verdi's ballet scenario will be found in the letter to Escudier, quoted below. The opening *allegro vivacissimo*, for the arrival of the spirits who dance

Ex.43

contando, con espansione

O Mac-duf-fo, tua vi - ta per - do - no, tua vi - ta per - do - no!

about the cauldron, is skilfully and originally orchestrated: in particular, there is a daring use of the brass. Hecate, for her mime, is given an almost noble *andante* theme, and the catchy *allegro* finale is a kind of *valse un peu macabre*.

The orchestral theme used for the appearance of the eight kings is scored for an unusual woodwind combination of two oboes, six clarinets, two bassoons and contra-bassoon. Macbeth has a moment of compassion for Macduff when he is told that "none of women born" could harm him and, to a phrase of anguished tenderness, cries "O Macduffo, tua vita perdono" [Ex. 43] but immediately repents of his weakness and decides that Macduff must die.

The scene ends with a duet for the Macbeths, "Ora di morte e di vendetta", which did not exist in the 1847 version. It is not, to my mind, the equal of the dramatically and psychologically gripping duet in the first act. The original version of this scene ended with a vigorous aria for Macbeth which rings true in a way in which the duet does not. It would be interesting to hear it tried in performance.

To Escudier, Verdi gave his reason for writing a duet to end this scene, and also his advice on the staging of the ballet:

I close the Act with a duet between Macbeth and Lady Macbeth. It seems to me quite logical that Lady Macbeth, who watches constantly over her husband, should have found out where he is. The end of the Act is better this way. The machinist and the regisseur will enjoy this Act! You will see that there is a little plot in the ballet which fits very well with the rest of the drama. The appearance of Hecate, Goddess of Night, works well:

she interrupts the devilish dances with a sober, severe *adagio*. I don't need to tell you that Hecate should not dance, but mime. Nor need I point out that this *adagio* must be played by the basset horn or bass clarinet, as is specified, so that in unison with cello and bassoon it produces a hollow, forbidding tone which suits the situation. Please ask the conductor to keep an eye on the dance music so that the dancers keep to the tempi I have laid down. You know ballet dancers always change the tempo. (At the Opéra, for example, they say the Tarantella can't be danced the way I want it. But any street urchin in Sorrento or Capua could dance it very well at my tempo.) If the tempi are changed, the witches' ballet will lose all its character, and won't produce the effect of which I think it capable. Now I have something to call to the attention of M. Deloffre: during the apparition of the eight kings, he must be sure to have the players of the small orchestra grouped under the stage. This little ensemble, two oboes, six clarinets in A, two bassoons and a contra-bassoon, produces a strange, mysterious, very still kind of sound which no other instruments could duplicate. It must be arranged under the stage, but under an open trap-door wide enough to enable the sound to spread through the entire theatre—but it must sound mysterious as though from a distance.[1]

The chorus of exiles which begins Act IV was re-written for Paris. It is a not unimpressive piece, much subtler in style than that prototype exiles' chorus, "Va, pensiero", though no less expressive. Falling semi-tones in the accompaniment are marked by Verdi to be played "come un lamento": the effect is almost Moussorgskian in its realism. Mac-duff's graceful yet melancholy aria, "Ah, la paterna mano", is followed, by way of cabaletta, by a rousing call to arms sung in duet by Macduff and Malcolm, and responded to by their troops.

Lady Macbeth's Sleepwalking scene is superb. Its alternation and combination of strings and woodwind curiously delineates the tender scorn for her consort which she half expresses in dream. As she goes off to bed again, Verdi asks for a *fil di voce* on a phrase rising to D flat. The scene is one of the highlights of the score, and one of the most dramatic-ally effective pieces of music Verdi ever composed, eloquent, insinuat-ing and absolutely right in every bar. Its dramatic truth is fully the equal of Shakespeare's. Verdi, many years later in a letter to the Coun-tess Maffei, wrote "To copy real life may be a good thing, but to invent real life is better, much better."[2] Here he has finely invented real life.

Macbeth's "Pieta, rispetto, amore" which, like the sleepwalking scene, dates from the original 1847 score, is beautiful in the serenity of its despair. Macbeth's reaction to the news of Lady Macbeth's death, which in Shakespeare is the famous, bleak "Tomorrow and tomorrow and tomorrow" soliloquy, is brief and stunned. In a few bars of arioso he muses on the futility of life: "La vita, ch'importa? È il racconto d'un

---

[1] *Copialettere*, pp. 452–3.
[2] *Copialettere*, p. 624. Verdi uses "il vero": "truth" or "natural life".

povero idioto! Vento e suono che nulla dinota!" (What does life matter? It is a tale told by a poor fool! Sound and fury signifying nothing!) From here until the end of the opera, there are differences between the two versions, but the original score is by no means notice-ably inferior to Verdi's second thoughts of eighteen years later. Neither version, consisting of battle music, recitative, and final chorus of vic-tory, is completely satisfactory. Nor, for that matter, is Shakespeare's ending. Again, Verdi's remarks to Escudier are valuable:

> The whole chorus at the beginning of the fourth act is new. The tenor's aria is touched up and re-orchestrated. And all the scenes from the baritone's romanza to the end are new, that is the description of the battle and the final hymn of victory. You will laugh when you see I have written a fugue for the battle !!! I, who detest everything that smacks of theory. But I assure you that in this case, the fugue form is permissible. The mad chase of subjects and counter-subjects, and the clash of disson-ances, the general uproar, can suggest a battle quite well. Oh, if you only had our trumpets which sound so bright and full-toned!! Your *trompettes à pistons* are neither one thing nor the other.[1] Nevertheless, the orchestra will enjoy themselves.[2]

A soliloquy for Macbeth, who dies on-stage in the 1847 version, is deleted from the revision. This is no real loss. Attempts by producers today to incorporate the 1847 death scene into the 1865 finale are aesthetically misguided. The 1865 victory chorus, which effectively combines and contrasts enthusiasm and reflectiveness, makes a really stirring finale.

The opera as we know it today is still basically the work of the thirty-four-year-old composer. The alterations and additions of middle-age are not particularly significant: it is good, of course, to have "La luce langue", but one should remember that all the other great moments in the opera were there from the beginning. Verdi's *Macbeth* is worthy to stand beside Shakespeare's. To claim that it is the earliest of Verdi's great works is not to denigrate the splendidly impressive achievement of *Nabucco*. And there are plenty of other early works, *I Lombardi*, *Ernani*, *Giovanna d'Arco* and *I due Foscari* among them, not to mention the sport, *Un giorno di regno*, which reveal their creator's genius. But with *Macbeth* Verdi takes an immense leap forward: a leap away from the conven-tional demands of the time, and towards dramatic truth and a musical style which combines psychological depth with a continuing abundance of that prolific and individual melodic gift which was never to desert him. His intuitive feeling for Shakespeare was obviously to a large extent responsible for this. English music critics are prone to be wary of Verdi's *Macbeth*. While acclaiming *Otello* and *Falstaff*, we tend to speak

---

[1] "né carne né pesce", literally "neither flesh nor fish".   [2] *Copialettere*, p. 456.

of *Macbeth* with a nervous, jocular and, in effect, patronising affection. But we have only to listen and to experience it in the theatre to know, directly and instinctively, that *Macbeth*, warts and all, is a great opera.

The path to *Otello* and *Falstaff* remains a tortuous one: With the three operas that immediately followed *Macbeth*, Verdi was back in the galleys, writing against time again, pouring gold and dross into the same vessel, behaving as though he were merely a first-class professional supplier of operatic ware.

XI

I masnadieri

Dramatis personae:

Massimiliano, Count Moor	(bass)
Carlo, ⎫ his sons	(tenor)
Francesco, ⎭	(bass)
Amalia, orphan, and niece of the Count	(soprano)
Arminio, a servant of the Moor family	(tenor)
Moser, a clergyman	(bass)
Rolla, companion to Carlo	(tenor)

LIBRETTO by Count Andrea Maffei, based on the play *Die Räuber* by Friedrich Schiller

TIME: Beginning of the eighteenth century
PLACE: Germany

FIRST PERFORMED at Her Majesty's Theatre, London, July 22, 1847, with Jenny Lind (Amalia); Italo Gardoni (Carlo); Filippo Coletti (Francesco); Luigi Lablache (Count Moor); Leone Corelli (Arminio); Lucien Bouché (Moser)

I masnadieri

I

BEFORE HE HAD begun to compose *Macbeth*, Verdi had written a prose
libretto based on Schiller's play, *Die Räuber* (The Brigands), and had
commissioned his friend Andrea Maffei to turn it into verse. At his
time, the Count and Countess Maffei had been among Verdi's closest
friends for about five years. Her salon was the most important in Milan,
while he was a poet of some elegance, and a respected translator from
English and German. The Maffeis separated in 1846, but Verdi
remained friendly with them both. At the time of his collaboration with
Verdi on *I masnadieri*, Maffei was in his late fifties, and had translated
all of Schiller's plays for Italian publication.

It had been agreed between the London impresario Benjamin
Lumley and Verdi that *I masnadieri* (*Die Räuber*) would be the work
Verdi was to write for Her Majesty's Theatre, and that he would
travel to London to produce it in the spring or early summer of 1847.
Verdi had actually begun to write the opera in the autumn of 1846 at a
time when he still expected to give it to Florence. When he decided to
do *Macbeth* for Florence, he had shelved *I masnadieri* for some months.
Now, the arrangements with Lumley having been finalised, he returned
to Milan immediately after the première of *Macbeth*, and almost
finished the opera except for the orchestration which, as usual, he left
until his arrival in London to rehearse with the company. With Muzio
to accompany him, Verdi set out from Milan at the end of May to
travel to London via Paris. Muzio's letters are full of stories of their
travelling experiences. From Milan to Paris by rail, coach and Rhine
steamer was a complicated journey of more than ninety hours. Verdi
stayed in Paris for a few days, sending Muzio on ahead to London. He
probably visited his friend the singer Giuseppina Strepponi, who was at
this time living and teaching in Paris: his love affair with her most
likely dates from this visit rather than from their earlier professional
encounters. Finally, Verdi arrived in London, where Muzio had already
found an apartment for them both. "For three rooms I wanted to
take," Muzio wrote to Barezzi, "they asked £5 a week, and ten shillings
for the maid. So I have taken only two rooms, and have had a bed put
in the parlour for myself, which during the day turns into a most

splendid divan.''[1] In another letter, a few days later, Muzio describes Verdi's working methods in London:

> We get up at five in the morning and we work until six in the evening, which is supper time. Then we go to the theatre for a while, and come back at eleven to go to bed, so as to be up early the next morning. The opera is progressing, two acts are already at the copyists', and the rest may be finished by next Monday.[2]

Lumley had placed at Verdi's disposal a box at Her Majesty's Theatre, and whenever he used it he was the centre of attention. The ladies, one newspaper reported, "devoured poor Verdi with their opera-glasses." Although it was June, the weather was, apparently, foul, and Verdi complained bitterly of the rain, mist and smoke. The following month, after he had left London, he wrote to a friend, Emilia Morosini:

> Although the London climate was horrid, I took an extraordinary liking to the place. It isn't a city, it's a world. Its size, the richness and beauty of the streets, the cleanliness of the houses, all this is incomparable. One stands amazed and feels insignificant when, in the midst of all this splendour, one surveys the Bank of England and the Docks. Who can resist the people? The surroundings and the country outside London are marvellous. But I do not like many of the English customs, or rather they do not suit us Italians. How ridiculous it looks when people in Italy imitate the English![3]

The climate, according to Muzio, made Verdi even "more eccentric and melancholy" than usual. But work progressed, rehearsals proceeded fairly amicably, and Verdi seems to have liked Jenny Lind, the "Swedish nightingale", who was to sing in his opera, and who had made her London début earlier in the season in Meyerbeer's *Robert le Diable*. Refusing the countless social invitations he received, refusing even to meet Queen Victoria who had expressed a desire to know him, Verdi concentrated on his work. His sore throat and stomach pains returned to plague him, and the weather continued to encourage his hypochondria. To Maffei and his wife he wrote separately to exclaim at the beauty of London and to complain of its climate.

By command of the Queen, *I masnadieri* was to have its first performance on July 22nd, and Parliament, which ended its session that day, was to attend in full dress. As the date approached, London society became increasingly excited. Verdi was the first of the great nineteenth-century composers to write an opera specifically for London, and the social occasion promised to be a memorable one. At first reluctant to conduct the première himself, Verdi agreed to do so upon being petitioned by the Russian Ambassador and a deputation of English

[1] Garibaldi, op. cit., p. 327.   [2] Garibaldi, op. cit., p. 328.   [3] *Copialettere*, pp. 460–1.

noblemen. The first night was a decided success. The Queen and Prince Albert, Prince Louis Bonaparte, the Duke of Wellington and several other notabilities attended. Muzio described the scene:

> The opera created a furore. From the Overture to the Finale there was nothing but applause, *evvivas*, recalls and encores. The Maestro himself conducted sitting on a chair higher than the others, with bâton in hand. As soon as he appeared in the orchestra pit, applause broke out and continued for a quarter of an hour. Before it had finished, the Queen and Prince Albert her consort, the Queen Mother and the Duke of Cambridge, uncle of the Queen, the Prince of Wales, son of the Queen, and all the royal family and a countless number of lords and dukes had arrived. It suffices to say that the boxes were full of elegantly dressed ladies, and the pit so crowded that no one could remember having seen so many people there before. The doors had been opened at half past four, and the crowd had burst in with an enthusiasm never previously seen . . . The Maestro was cheered, called on to the stage, both alone and with the singers, and pelted with flowers. All you could hear was "Evviva Verdi! Bietifol" [beautiful].[1]

The press was for the most part favourable. *The Times*, incredibly, praised Maffei's rather poor libretto, and remarked that Verdi's writing emphasised the ensemble more than the solo singers. *The Morning Post* was enthusiastic, and *The Illustrated London News* claimed that "the music is dramatic in the extreme and somewhat excels the masterpieces of Meyerbeer and other composers of the German romantic school". One critic, Chorley, stood out. In the *Athenæum*, he wrote: "We take this to be the worst opera which has been given in our time at Her Majesty's Theatre. Verdi is finally rejected. The field is left open for an Italian composer."

In his memoirs, published seventeen years later, the impresario Lumley wrote of *I masnadieri*:

> On Thursday, July 2nd, "I masnadieri" (after wearying rehearsals, conducted by the composer himself), was brought out, with a cast that included Lablache, Gardoni, Coletti, Bouché, and, above all, Jenny Lind, who was to appear for the second time only in her career, in a thoroughly original part composed expressly for her.
>
> The house was filled to overflowing on the night of the first representation. The opera was given with every appearance of a triumphant success: the composer and all the singers receiving the highest honours. Indeed, all the artists distinguished themselves in their several parts. Jenny Lind acted admirably, and sang the airs allotted to her exquisitely. But yet the "Masnadieri" could not be considered a success. That by its production I had adopted the right course, was unquestionable. I had induced an Italian composer, whose reputation stood on the highest pinnacle of

[1] *Copialettere*, p. 459.

continental fame, to compose an opera expressly for my theatre, as well as to superintend its production. More I could not have done to gratify the patrons of Italian music, who desired to hear new works.

It may be stated, in confirmation of the judgment of the London audience, that "I masnadieri" was never successful on any Italian stage. The *libretto* was even worse constructed than is usually the case with adaptations of foreign dramas to the purpose of Italian opera. To Her Majesty's Theatre the work was singularly ill-suited. The interest which ought to have been centred in Mademoiselle Lind was centred in Gardoni; whilst Lablache, as the imprisoned father, had to do about the only thing he could not do to perfection—having to represent a man nearly starved to death.[1]

Verdi conducted the opera once again, and then handed the remaining performances over to Balfe (the composer of *The Bohemian Girl*) and went to Paris, where he spent the next few weeks turning *I Lombardi* into *Jérusalem*. He took with him an offer from Lumley to return to London as Musical Director of Her Majesty's Theatre at a very large salary, and to compose for that theatre one new opera each year for ten years. Various perquisites were to include a country house and a carriage. Insufficiently enthusiastic, Verdi wrote to Lumley from Paris naming his terms. Nothing came of the offer.

II

I masnadieri is in four acts. As in the play, *Die Räuber*, the action takes place in the early eighteenth century in Franconia, Saxony and Bohemia. The events, according to Schiller, extend over a period of two years; according to Maffei, three years. The opera's first act has three scenes. In the first, a tavern on the Saxon border, Carlo, the elder of Count Moor's two sons, is discovered reading Plutarch. His opening remark, as he puts the volume aside, is "Quando io leggo in Plutarco, ho noia, ho schifo di quest' età d'imbelli." (When I read Plutarch, I feel bored and disgusted with this decadent age.) A restless, dissatisfied youth, he had left home and joined a band of wild companions whom Maffei, literally translating Schiller, describes among the dramatis personae as "coro di giovani traviati, poi masnadieri", though in the opera they are well and truly "masnadieri" from the beginning. Carlo can hear them carousing outside the inn. He regrets the turning his life has taken and has written to his father Count Massimiliano Moor, to ask whether he will be forgiven if he returns to the fold. He longs for his parental home, and sings too of his love for his cousin Amalia. Rolla and some of the other brigands enter hurriedly with a letter for Carlo. He takes it eagerly, sure that it contains his father's pardon, but, having read it, he rushes out in despair crying that the

[1] Benjamin Lumley, *Reminiscences of the Opera*, pp. 192–3.

letter was from his brother, and flinging it away. Rolla picks it up and reads it. It advises Carlo not to return, as his father, far from having forgiven him, will have him placed in solitary confinement on a diet of bread and water. Not realising that the letter to his father had been intercepted by his unscrupulous brother, Carlo renounces the bourgeois law-abiding life for ever, and agrees to become the captain of the band of brigands.

The scene changes to a room in Count Moor's castle in Franconia. Francesco congratulates himself on his villainy. Determined to inherit his father's title and estate, and having got his elder brother out of the way, he now plans to hasten the death of his aged father. Calling one of the servants, Arminio, whom he believes he can trust, he orders him to disguise himself as a soldier and announce to Count Moor the death of Carlo on the field of battle outside Prague.

The third scene takes place in a bedroom of the castle. The aged and ailing Count is asleep on a settee, watched over by his niece Amalia, who sings of her love for Carlo and her bewilderment at his desertion of her. The old man awakens from a dream of his favourite son, Carlo, and longs to see him again before he dies. Francesco enters, introducing the disguised Arminio who has, he says, sad news for the Count. Arminio dutifully announces that he and Carlo were among the troops who fought for King Frederick outside Prague, that Carlo had been mortally wounded but, before dying, had handed Arminio his sword, saying, "Take this bloodstained sword to my father, and tell him that his unwanted son died a desperate death in the slaughter of war." Francesco points out that Carlo has written on the sword, in blood, "My death, Amalia, releases you from your vow. Francesco, you must marry Amalia." Amalia cries that Carlo can never have loved her, the old Count vents his wrath on Francesco and falls, apparently dead. Francesco joyously shouts that he is now lord and master.

Act II has two scenes, the first of which is set in the graveyard of the church attached to the castle. There are several gothic monuments, on one of which the name of Count Massimiliano Moor can be seen. Amalia enters to pray at her uncle's tomb, having fled from a banquet being given by Francesco at the castle. A repentant Arminio appears to confess the deception he had practised. He tells Amalia not only that Carlo is not dead, but that her uncle is alive as well, and rushes off before she can question him. In a cabaletta, Amalia sings of her joy at this extraordinary news. Francesco enters, wondering why she has left the banquet. He declares his love for her, and asks her to marry him. When Amalia vehemently refuses him, Francesco threatens to take her by force, but she manages to snatch his sword from him and make her escape.

Scene 2 takes place in a Bohemian forest just outside Prague. Some of the brigands enter, talking of how Carlo is at that moment rescuing

Rolla from a prison in Prague, and setting fire to the town. The flames are glimpsed through the trees, and terrified women can be heard crying that it must be the end of the world. Rolla enters with more of the brigands, who describe the rescue operation, and finally Carlo appears. After the brigands have wandered off, Carlo apostrophises the sunset, and contrasts the beauty of nature with his own moral deformity. Aroused from this gloomy introspection by Rolla and the brigands, who announce that an army of a thousand soldiers is pursuing them, Carlo exhorts his followers to fight for their lives.

Act III opens in a part of the forest not far from Count Moor's castle, where Amalia has fled to escape Francesco. She hears the sound of the approaching bandits and fears for her safety. When Carlo enters, she does not immediately recognise him, and begs for mercy. He reveals himself to her, though without telling her he is the leader of the bandits. They are overjoyed at finding each other, but when Carlo asks her why she is wandering in the woods, Amalia begins her unhappy account of Francesco's attack on her virtue, a story interrupted by the return of the brigands.

The scene changes to another part of the forest, near the ruins of a tower. It is night, and as Carlo keeps watch he soliloquises on his fate. Drawing a pistol, he considers putting an end to his unhappy life, but decides that he must live and suffer. Arminio enters stealthily, bringing food for Count Moor, whom he has hidden in the ruined tower. When Carlo surprises him, he runs off crying that he had not the heart to do as he was ordered. Hearing a voice within the tower, Carlo discovers the wasted frame of his father. The old man does not recognise his son, but tells him that Francesco, when he realised his father was not dead but merely in a swoon, still determined to bury him, and that he was rescued by Arminio. The old man faints. Carlo, rousing his brigands, sends them to capture Francesco.

Act IV, Scene 1, is a room in the castle. Having had a terrifying nightmare, Francesco calls the servants and sends for the local pastor. Meanwhile, he relates his dream to Arminio. It was a version of the last day of judgment and of his eternal damnation. Pastor Moser enters and, when Francesco asks him which sin is the least forgivable, replies that parricide and fratricide are the foulest. Hearing the brigands storming the castle, Francesco asks Moser to give him absolution, but Moser says he cannot. In desperation, Francesco rushes out, shouting that he will outwit the fires of hell.

The final scene takes place next morning, near the ruined tower. Carlo receives the blessing of the old Count, who, still unaware of his real identity, bewails the loss of his favourite son. The brigands return, announcing that they were unable to capture Francesco. "Non è qua, n'uscì di mano," they proclaim. (He wasn't there; he escaped.) Carlo reacts joyously to this. Henceforth mercy, he swears, will be the watchword of the robbers. In Schiller's play, Karl von Moor's reaction is similar, but there what he has been told is that Franz was "tot gefunden": found dead, having strangled himself with the golden cord from his hat.[1]

Amalia is now dragged in by the brigands. Realising that he can no longer hide, from her or from his father, the shame of his being the leader of the brigands, Carlo reveals his identity to his dying father. Amalia swears she will marry Carlo, whatever life he has chosen to lead, but, rather than have her involved in the shame and disgrace which cover him, Carlo quickly stabs her. "Ora al patibollo!" (And now to the gallows) he cries as he rushes off.

Die Räuber, Schiller's earliest play, is a long, sprawling work, written in an extraordinary prose that gathers up such diverse influences as those of Goethe, the Bible, and demotic German speech into a new and heady style of its own. It was first published in 1781; a second edition followed a few months later, omitting what Schiller called "those equivocal sentences which were offensive to the more fastidious section of the public", and including musical settings of the songs scattered throughout the play, by Johann Zumsteeg, the ballad composer who was a close friend of Schiller, and whose songs influenced the young Schubert. A third, acting edition also appeared, which considerably reduced the play's length and made important alterations to the plot.

Schiller's brigands, or at any rate eight of them, are an interesting collection of villains, individually characterised. In the opera, they are reduced to the status of a chorus. Schiller's Karl von Moor is the victim of his own extravagant sensibility as much as of his brother's machinations. A romantically restless youth, he progresses in the play from the attitude of an adolescent disaffected with society to that of a conscienceless monster. From Jimmy Porter to Iago. At all stages of his career, he is given to moralising. Similarly, his brother Franz indulges in long philosophical justifications for his own misdeeds. Nevertheless, the play, for all its blemishes, is fascinating to read. Maffei's reduction of it has necessarily to omit several scenes, the greater part of the dialogue and almost all of the soliloquies, retaining only certain key sentences which, however, are meaningless out of their original context. For instance, Maffei translates, in précis, Karl's opening lines about Plutarch. In Schiller, the remark[2] sparks a long discussion with Spiegelberg, in

---

[1] According to Schiller's first edition. In the acting edition, Franz attempts to throw himself into the flames of the burning castle, but is captured alive and brought back to Karl who, Pontius Pilate-like, embraces and forgives his brother then hands him over to the brigands who thrust him into the dungeon in which he had immured his father.

[2] "Mir ekelt vor diesem tintenklecksenden Säkulum, wenn ich in meinem Plutarch lese von grossen Menschen." (I am disgusted with these puny scribblers when I read about great men in my Plutarch.)

which he tempts Karl towards the lawless life. In Maffei's libretto, Plutarch leads to nothing. And throughout the libretto there are frequent occasions where only by consulting Schiller can one discover the librettist's meaning. If, for instance, one wonders why, in the opera's Act II, Scene 2, the entire city of Prague appears to be on fire, the answer is to be found in some lines given in the play to Schwarz, who says Karl has sworn ". . . that he would light a funeral pyre for him [Rolla], such as had never graced the bier of royalty, one that would burn them all to cinders. I fear for the city. He has long borne a grudge against it for its intolerable bigotry, and you know that when he says 'I'll do it', a thing is as good as done."

(. . . Er wolle ihm [Roller] eine Todesfackel anzünden, wie sie noch keinem König geleuchtet hat, die ihnen den Buckel braun und blau brennen soll. Mir ist bang für die Stadt. Er hat schon lang eine Pike auf sie, weil sie so schändlich bigott ist, und du weisst, wenn er sagt: Ich wills tun!' so ists so viel, als wenns unsereiner getan hat.)

Rolla is the only one of the opera's gang of brigands who has a solo role. He also takes over some of Spiegelberg's lines. There is more telescoping of characters: the opera's Arminio is a concoction from Schiller's Daniel, an old servant of Count von Moor, and Hermann ("the natural son of a nobleman"), who had been Karl's rival for the hand of Amalia.

Something of Schiller's manic-depressive Karl remains in Maffei's and Verdi's Carlo, but not much. In one of his most splendid long speeches in Schiller's play, he fulminates against Christian intolerance, covetousness and hypocrisy. It is an effective tirade whose opportunities the Verdi of *La forza del destino* would have seized gratefully. The Verdi of *I masnadieri* was not ready for it. At all events, he seems not to have objected to Maffei's omitting it. The curious episode in which Karl returns to Amalia, courts her under another name, and is distressed when she succumbs to him, is mercifully also omitted. A real loss to the opera, however, by omission, is Schiller's famous and touching scene by the Danube at sunset, when, overcome by the glory of the setting sun, Karl bursts into an ecstasy of nostalgia for his childhood innocence, and longs to return to his mother's womb (though a little of this finds expression in Carlo's aria in the Bohemian forest scene of the opera). It is in this scene of the play that Karl tries to express his gratitude to the entire gang of thieves for having saved him from capture. "So wahr meine Seele lebt," he swears, "Ich will euch niemals verlassen." (As truly as my soul lives, I shall never forsake you.) Schweitzer urges him not to swear such an oath, as he may repent it; but Karl repeats, "Ich will euch niemals verlassen." The strength of this scene makes somewhat more dramatically feasible the finale in which Karl, unable to condemn Amalia to a life of shame, kills her. In the opera, his action seems unmotivated and completely senseless.

III

The Prelude to *I masnadieri* is an attractive, romantically melancholy *andante* for solo cello and orchestra. When the curtain rises it is not upon a lusty chorus of brigands, but on Carlo reading Plutarch in the village inn. His aria, "O mio castel paterno", though pleasant, is somewhat conventional, but its cabaletta has a fierce excitement. Francesco's opening recitative can be animated by a really good dramatic baritone into a meaningful soliloquy, while his aria "La sua lampada vitale", is melodically generous. Its cabaletta, too, is first-rate, with a splendid desperation and attack. In fact, the individuality and distinction of *I masnadieri* lie to a great extent in the tension between its darkly romantic arias and the jagged energy of its cabalettas. Like *Ernani*, it succeeds by virtue of its combination of tunefulness and vigour. Its orchestration is not uninteresting, particularly in the more significant use Verdi makes of his woodwind instruments, but its sombre violence is what really distinguishes this opera. Structurally, Verdi is marking time.

Amalia's first, and somewhat jaunty aria, "Lo sguardo avea degli angeli", abounding in tricky fioriture, is interesting as an example of the kind of music in which Jenny Lind excelled. It was presumably tailored for her: some of the decoration looks and sounds as though Verdi added it to a vocal line conceived more plainly. But the duet for Amalia and the Count, "Carlo, io muoio", is superb, with Verdi's father-daughter feeling pervading the music as the old man sings of his son to his quasi-daughter. Throughout the duet the vocal writing, sincere and direct, basks in its own beauty [Ex. 44].

Ex.44 Andante

Car-lo!io muo-io... ed,ahi! lon-ta-no tu mi sei, tu mi sei nel-l'ul-ti - m'o - re.

Arminio gives his false message in an urgent arioso. His is more than just another tenor comprimario rôle, for his voice is important to the ensuing quartet, a brilliant piece of dramatically characterised ensemble writing with all the assurance and melodic beauty of the *Rigoletto* quartet.

The churchyard scene begins with a superb scena for Amalia, who prays at the old Count's tomb while sounds of revelry are heard coming from the castle. The flexible, lengthy recitative is worthy of *Aida*, while Amalia's passionate bel canto aria, "Tu del mio Carlo al seno", is arguably the finest number in the score, a great set-piece for a soprano with elegaic style and well-founded technique. The brilliant cabaletta after Amalia learns from Arminio that Carlo is still alive, is full of assured, tuneful and rhythmically exciting vocal writing, and perfectly judged accompaniment. The duet for Amalia and Francesco, "Io t'amo, Amalia", is hardly less effective. The villainous Francesco is unfairly allowed some ravishingly lovely tunes.

The robbers' chorus in the Bohemian forest, in which they observe the flames of Prague and note with satisfaction that their Captain has kept his word, is disappointingly tame stuff, but Verdi recovers his form later in the scene when Rolla enters and his rescuers narrate their adventure. After they have wandered off, Carlo contemplates the setting sun, and sings his romanza, "Di ladroni attorniato". Both the romanza [Ex. 45] and its preceding recitative are beautifully set, to a

Ex.45 Andante ♩=50 con espressione   morendo   ppp
Di la-dro-ni at-tor-ni-a - to, al de-lit - to in-ca-te - na - to

line at once expressive and graceful. This is one of the most exquisite numbers not only in *I masnadieri* but in the whole of pre-*Rigoletto* Verdi. The chorus finale, as the brigands reassemble to fight the soldiers who are pursuing them, is rushed and perfunctory. I note with amused surprise that Rolla claims they are being chased "da mille soldati", by only a thousand soldiers. Schiller's figure was "Viele Tausend Husaren, Dragoner und Jäger" (Thousands of hussars, dragoons and huntsmen), and one would have expected this to escalate in Italian operatic translation.

The orchestral introduction to Act III and to Amalia's recitative looks forward to *La forza del destino*. The recitative is, as always in Verdi, both expressive and dramatically apt, and Amalia's duet with Carlo, "T'abbraccio, o Carlo", is fine, once it progresses beyond its hectic unison beginning, the andantino section being particularly appealing and the final allegro roughly exciting. The robbers' chorus is worthless but in the next scene Carlo's recitative, in which he contemplates suicide, is absolutely gripping, helped enormously by the sensitivity of the orchestral writing. What an absurdly uneven work this is, but at its best how splendidly it catches the glow of Schiller's romantic and cynical age.

Carlo's suicide recitative leads into the third act finale, in which old Count Moor is found wasting away in his ruined tower. The anxious accompaniment figure to the old man's narration remains hauntingly in the ear. Carlo's call to vengeance limps somewhat until the oath ensemble beginning at "Giuri ognun", which is highly effective, and makes a superb theatrical curtain to Act III.

Act IV opens with Francesco's terrified account of his vision of the

Dies Irae. Rushing string arpeggios set the scene brilliantly, and low brass and woodwind chords emphasise his terror. His scene with Moser is scored with equal brilliance and dramatic power. As the tension mounts, the clergyman Moser assumes almost the stature of Don Giovanni's stone guest. The pirates storming the castle sound like tormenting demons from hell, and the baritone villain rushes off in despair accompanied by an orchestral sound and fury that are not unlike, and by no means unworthy to be compared with, Mozart's in *Don Giovanni*. The opera's final scene contains two beautiful numbers, a duet for Carlo and his father, "Come un bacio d'un padre amoroso", and a trio in which they are joined by Amalia and the chorus of robbers. The trio, "Caduto è il reprobo", ends the opera magnificently, revealing Verdi's unique gift of being able to infuse pace and energy into a movement whose tempo is no livelier than that of a steady *andante*. And it possesses the typically Verdian melodic richness and, almost, bitterness [Ex. 46]. Part of the secret of the tempo is the composer's trick of

rarely allowing bars of purely orchestral sound in his vocal ensembles. The vocal phrases cunningly overlap. If some of the solo singers are taking a breath, others are singing a linking phrase that keeps the vocal melody going. The energy thus generated is remarkable. The emotional effect is calculated to a nicety.

Despite its admitted unevenness, *I masnadieri* is one of the most interesting and one of the most inspired of the works which emerged from those much maligned years in which Verdi obsessively chain-composed. He responded to Schiller's extremely Byronic hero even more strongly than to the authentic Byronic protagonist of his next opera *Il corsaro*, and dressed Carlo and the other three principals in the most glorious melodies. Bernard Shaw, a great Verdian, kept a vocal score of *I masnadieri* on a shelf by his piano. He is said to have played and sung it, quaveringly, in his ninety-fourth year. It *is* an opera that stays in one's affections.

XII

Il corsaro

Dramatis personae:

Corrado, pirate chieftain	(tenor)
Giovanni, a pirate	(bass)
Medora, Corrado's mistress	(soprano)
Seid, Pasha of Corone	(baritone)
Gulnara, favourite member of Seid's harem	(soprano)
Selimo, one of Seid's warriors	(tenor)
Eunuch	(tenor)
Slave	(tenor)

LIBRETTO by Francesco Maria Piave, based on the poem *The Corsair* by Lord Byron

TIME: Beginning of the nineteenth century
PLACE: An Aegean island, and the Turkish city of Corone

FIRST PERFORMED at the Teatro Grande, Trieste, October 25, 1848 with Marianna Barbieri-Nini (Gulnara); Carolina Rapazzini (Medora); Gaetano Fraschini (Corrado); Achille De Bassini (Seid); Giovanni Volpini (Giovanni); Giovanni Petrovich (Selimo)

Il corsaro

Il corsaro, which Verdi wrote in Paris in the winter of 1847–8, had been brewing for some time. It is usually suggested that Verdi simply did not want to write the opera, that he composed it in a hurry only in order to fulfil a contract. This is, as far as it goes, perfectly true; but there was a time when Verdi most certainly did want to compose *Il corsaro*: when it was his intention to write the opera for Francesco Lucca to publish and for Benjamin Lumley to stage in London. The subject was chosen by Verdi himself, and it seems a not unlikely choice when one considers how popular Byron's poem was with the patriotic Italians at the time. The romantic Greek pirate fighting the wicked Turks could all too easily be seen as a gallant Italian opposing his Austrian overlords. Corrado, "il corsaro", might have been their own Garibaldi. And a poem by Byron must have seemed a most appropriate subject for a London opera.

It was when Verdi considered the subject in close detail that he began to have doubts about its suitability as an opera. By this time, however, Lucca, who had warmed to the idea, tried to hold the composer to it. This was no way to deal with the obstinate Verdi, who had in any case begun work on *Macbeth* for Florence. Nevertheless, when, after London and *I masnadieri*, Verdi found himself supervising the production of *Jérusalem* at the Paris Opéra in November 1847, he decided to stay on in Paris and dash off the opera for which Lucca was now clamouring even more insistently. He had written to Lucca from Paris in August, offering to get down to work on the opera, to be performed at one of the leading Italian theatres during the Carnival season of the following year. He was then still toying with other possible subjects, including *Medea*, but finally agreed to do *Il corsaro*, and he began writing it after the première of *Jérusalem* on November 26, 1847. At this time he was regularly seeing Giuseppina Strepponi. At first she, then the political events of 1848, and finally a bad cold kept Verdi from attending the première of *Il corsaro* in Trieste, though it has to be admitted that he went about the creation of the opera in a peculiarly cold-blooded manner, determined not to write an important work for "that tiresome and ungrateful man", as he called Lucca.[1] Had Verdi gone to Trieste,

[1] *Copialettere*, pp. 461–2.

he would undoubtedly have done some revision of the opera on the spot. As it was, he sent off to Lucca a hastily written first draft. Piave had produced a libretto whose events closely follow those of Byron's poem, and for once Verdi seems not to have hectored his librettist, but simply to have accepted what was provided. It was in February 1848, the month in which revolution broke out in Paris, sparking off political uprisings all over Europe, that Verdi finished *Il corsaro*, and sent it off to Muzio in Milan with instructions to deliver it to Lucca. A feverish cold had prevented him from taking the opera to Italy himself. To his friend the sculptor Vincenzo Luccardi, he wrote:

> I have written an opera for the publisher Lucca in Milan, and I had intended taking it to Italy myself, but I decided to send it because I didn't feel up to the long and tiring journey at this time of year. Now I shall rest for a few days or a few weeks, and then begin work on the opera for Naples.[1]

He recommended Muzio to Lucca as producer and conductor of *Il corsaro*, which was performed in Trieste in October. The first performance was not a success: two of the numbers were well applauded, but at the end of the evening only the scene-designer took a curtain-call. There were productions at the Teatro Carcano in Milan, in 1852, and in Novara, Venice, and Malta in 1853, after which *Il corsaro* disappeared from the stage for over a century, to re-emerge in Venice in 1963, where it was badly done, and at St Pancras, London, in 1966, where a modestly staged but robustly sung performance was enthusiastically received.

II

No one appears ever to have thought very highly of Piave, except perhaps Verdi. When Piave's libretti were attacked, as frequently happened, Verdi was usually quick to defend him, on one occasion pointing out that the two scenes in Piave's *Macbeth* which attracted the most abuse had, in fact, been written by Maffei. It is undeniable that Piave was anything but a brilliant librettist: his theatrical sense was deficient, and his verses were frequently poor. Yet in many ways he suited Verdi's purposes. In the composer-librettist relationship with Verdi, Piave's rôle, as we have seen in considering *Ernani*, *I due Foscari* and *Macbeth*, was a comparatively subservient one. In the case of *Il corsaro*, however, he was left to his own devices, and what he presented to Verdi turned out to be a sometimes absurd, sometimes inscrutable, always haphazard collection of scenes. Paradoxically, it also turned out to be one of Piave's best libretti. It is, for one thing, faithful to Byron.

[1] *Le cronache musicali*, 1.2.1901: "Una lettera inedita di Giuseppe Verdi," E. Faustina-Fasini.

Of course, it is easier to transfer to the operatic stage the plot of an eighty-page narrative poem with few characters than that of a lengthy five-act melodrama with a huge cast. On the other hand, it is more likely that something of a prose playwright's essence will remain in adaptation than that the flavour and character of a poet's verse can be preserved. Byron's poem is really not very good, but it does contain an occasional splendid line, sometimes an excellent entire stanza. That which is most easily extractable from the poem for operatic purposes, its plot, is unfortunately its least impressive feature. But Piave has constructed his separate scenes skilfully and sensibly. The result is a workman-like job, uncluttered, surprisingly and mysteriously coherent, and a worthy peg for Verdi's music.

There had been two earlier stage versions of Byron's poem, a ballet performed at La Scala in 1826 and an opera, also staged at La Scala in the Carnival season of 1831–2, with music by Giovanni Pacini and a libretto by Jacopo Ferretti, the author of *La cenerentola* for Rossini and four libretti for Donizetti. Piave knew Ferretti's libretto, for he appears to have borrowed one or two scenic ideas from it, but he remained closer to Byron than the earlier librettist had.

The plot of *The Corsair* is slight. Conrad, a pirate, leaves his mistress Medora, and his island, and sails off to attack a Muslem city. He is captured, but escapes with the aid of the Pasha's favourite harem girl, Gulnare, who returns with him to his island, where they find Medora dead. The pirate mysteriously disappears, never to be seen or heard of again. Byron's poem, written in heroic couplets and published in 1814, is one of his minor works, eminently readable but rarely gripping as narrative or thrilling as poetry. The pirate chief Conrad (whose name Piave, or perhaps Verdi in order to make it easier to sing, altered to Corrado) is a typically Byronic creation. Man of action, yet introvert, he has opted out of the social contract and taken to a life of adventure and excitement. He commands his crew easily:

> That man of loneliness and mystery,
> Scarce seen to smile, and seldom heard to sigh;
> Whose name appals the fiercest of his crew,
> And tints each swarthy cheek with sallower hue;
> Still sways their souls with that commanding art
> That dazzles, leads, yet chills the vulgar heart.

A spiritual kinsman to Schiller's Karl von Moor, hero of *Die Räuber* and *I masnadieri*, Conrad "knew himself a villain—but he deem'd/The rest no better than the thing he seemed". The opera ends with Corrado killing himself by leaping from a cliff into the sea as Medora breathes her last. In the poem, Medora is already dead when Conrad returns. Heart-broken, he gazes on her corpse, and then

> The sun goes forth—but Conrad's day is dim;
> And the night cometh—n'er to pass from him.
> There is no darkness like the cloud of mind,
> On Grief's vain eye—the blindest of the blind!
> Which may not—dare not see—but turns aside
> To blackest shade—nor will endure a guide!

Not only does Conrad's mind cloud over, he also physically disappears, presumably into the sea, and is seen no more. The poem ends

> And fair the monument they gave his bride:
> For him they raise not the recording stone—
> His death yet dubious, deeds too widely known;
> He left a Corsair's name to other times,
> Link'd with one virtue, and a thousand crimes.

The poem's finest passages are those in which Byron writes with a buoyant and lyrical enthusiasm of the Aegean sea and sky. His description of the pirate's return from their Turkish exploit, for instance, though it contains some poor lines, is vivid in texture:

> They gain by twilight's hour their lonely isle.
> To them the very rocks appear to smile;
> The haven hums with many a cheering sound,
> The beacons blaze their wonted stations round,
> The boats are darting o'er the curly bay,
> And sportive dolphins bend them through the spray;
> Even the hoarse sea-bird's shrill, discordant shriek,
> Greets like the welcome of his tuneless beak!
> Beneath each lamp that through its lattice gleams,
> Their fancy paints the friends that trim the beams.
> Oh! what can sanctify the joys of home,
> Like Hope's gay glance from Ocean's troubled foam?

Unfortunately, nothing of these descriptive passages remains in Piave's libretto. There is, after all, no character into whose mouth the words could appropriately be put.

The opera is in three acts, the first of which is set on the pirates' island in the Aegean. Corrado is alternately railing at the world and regretting his lost innocence, when Giovanni, his lieutenant, hands him a message warning him against the Pasha Seid. Corrado rallies the pirates to attack Seid's city of Corone. The second scene occurs in Medora's apartment in an old tower facing the sea. She is singing of her love for Corrado when he enters to tell her he must leave her for a time. She attempts to dissuade him, but he assures her he will return safely. The sound of a cannon signals the imminent departure of his ship. Corrado rushes out, and Medora swoons.

The second act is set in the Turkish harbour town of Corone. In Pasha Seid's harem, slave-girls are attending the Pasha's favourite, Gulnara. (In a note to the poem, Byron explains that Gulnare means "the flower of the pomegranate".) Gulnara sings of her hatred of Seid and of her longing for freedom and love. A eunuch announces that she is invited to the Pasha's banquet to celebrate, prematurely, Seid's certain victory over the pirates. Gulnara unwillingly agrees to attend. The scene changes to the Turkish kiosk in which the banquet is being held. Seid enters, followed by Selimo and other warriors, and orders a hymn of praise to Allah to be sung. A slave enters to announce that a Dervish who has escaped from the pirates begs to be admitted. He is brought in, and Seid questions him. Suddenly, flames are seen lighting up the night sky: the Pasha's fleet has been set on fire. The Dervish reveals himself as Corrado, his men swarm into the banquet hall, and a fierce battle ensues. At first the pirates are successful, but, in rescuing Gulnara and the other occupants from the burning harem, Corrado inadvertently gives Seid and his followers time to recover. Finally, the pirates are routed; Corrado is taken prisoner and, despite the pleas of Gulnara and the ladies of the harem, is condemned to be tortured to death.

In the first scene of Act III, Seid is in his private apartments rejoicing over his victory, but fearful that Gulnara may have fallen in love with the pirate who rescued her from the flames. He sends for her, and talks of Corrado's fate in order to test her reactions. When she pleads for Corrado's life, he is unable to contain his jealous rage, and threatens her. He rushes out, and Gulnara determines to be avenged. The next scene is set in Corrado's prison. By bribing a guard, Gulnara gains entrance and explains that, far from loving Seid, she detests and fears him. She has fallen in love with Corrado, and offers to help him escape if he will kill the Pasha. This his conscience or, more likely, his honour will not allow him to do, so Gulnara herself murders Seid, and returns to free Corrado. The two of them escape.

The final scene takes place on the pirates' island, on a promontory near Medora's tower. She is dying, surrounded by the pirates and their women, and longs to see Corrado once more. A ship is sighted, and within seconds Corrado and Gulnara appear. Medora confesses that, unable to live without Corrado whom she had believed dead, she has poisoned herself. Gulnara in turn confesses to Medora that she too loves Corrado, but in vain. Medora dies in Corrado's arms, and he, in despair, throws himself into the sea.

III

"Since, with the exception of *Alzira*, this is the worst opera ever written by the composer, little more need be said about it. *Il corsaro*

contains an excellent scene, that depicting the hero in prison; otherwise, the only point of interest about the opera is that it provides almost
the only instance of a lapse of Verdi's part from the standards of
conscientious craftsmanship. He took the execrable libretto exactly as it
came from Piave; he displayed no interest in the production. We may
dispose of it as summarily as he did."

That was Toye's verdict. With the exception of those commentators
who thought *Il corsaro* actually worse than *Alzira*, critical opinion
tended to agree with him, at any rate until critics were able to see
the opera on the stage for the first time in the 1960s, and hear it with their
own ears. Prior to that, most books on Verdi dismissed *Il corsaro*
unheard, and possibly even unlooked at, in a couple of lines. "Another
piece of hackwork", is the comment of *Grove's Dictionary*.

While I cannot pretend to consider the opera another *Trovatore*, I do
think it dangerous completely to dismiss unheard anything written by
Verdi, however unpromising the circumstances of composition (and,
in this instance, I agree that they were indeed unpromising). A sympathetic reading of the vocal score ought to have led critics to suspect
what the 1966 St. Pancras performances clearly revealed: that *Il corsaro*
does not deserve the contempt cast upon it by generations of writers on
Verdi who, not having seen it staged, were content to echo one another's
opinions.

Musically and dramatically, *Il corsaro* leaves much to be desired. The
characters are almost completely wooden, and Verdi was not able,
perhaps because not sufficiently involved in the proceedings, to bring
them to life in musical terms. But, number by number, much of the
music is immensely enjoyable, and if the whole mysteriously adds up to
less than a sum of its parts, the parts themselves are well worth
listening to.

The Prelude is short and tempestuous with a gentler middle section.
The opening pirates' chorus, with interrupting recitative by Corrado, is
undistinguished stuff, but Corrado's *andante* aria, "Tutto parea sorri-
dere", is not only beautiful but, when Verdi gives the tune to the strings
while the voice punctuates the melody with short phrases of recitative,
interesting and unusual as well. Throughout the opera, even when the
voice parts are conventional, the orchestral writing is original and
exciting. After Corrado's aria, Giovanni's message is delivered in
fifty-five ploddingly consecutive crotchets, but the rousing cabaletta
it sparks off is wonderfully gutsy, a splendid *polacca* in the best kind of
brutal bad taste.

The next scene opens with a recitative and aria for Medora which, in
atmosphere, is highly suggestive of Leonora's first scene in *Il trovatore*
of five years later. (Corrado and Medora require, in fact, Manrico and
Leonora voices.) The opening phrase of the orchestral introduction

eventually became "Amami, Alfredo" in *La traviata* (Ex. 72). The aria proper, which Medora accompanies on her harp, begins as though it is going to rival "D'amor sull' ali rosee", but disappointingly fails to develop. An exciting, not altogether convincing tune, it calls for a rock-like technique, and possesses some intervals that are not easy for the voice to negotiate. Corrado enters, and he and Medora sing a ravishingly tuneful duet with an urgent accompanying figure. A bridge passage leads to the necessary cabaletta, and by this point in the opera Verdi has really found his form, for the music is curiously sweet yet unusual in melodic shape, and immensely effective.

The chorus sung by the Pasha's harem at the beginning of Act II has a pleasantly light, springy rhythm. Gulnara's cavatina, "Vola talor dal carcere", is an appealing, delicately scored and exquisitely decorated Bellinian *andante*, and is followed by an absolutely glorious cabaletta which really justifies the convention, and contains some fiercely exciting coloratura. The cabaletta is introduced in a typically Verdian manner: the orchestra announces the theme, then suddenly breaks off. A pause then the voice repeats the theme and the cabaletta is on its way. Gulnara, the most fully characterised figure in the opera, is made of sterner stuff altogether than Medora, a fact which is reflected in her music.

The Pasha's banquet begins with a brief but lively chorus, after which Seid himself, a Di Luna-like figure, leads the chorus in a hymn to Allah which is admittedly somewhat more pompous than anything Di Luna ever sang, both tune and accompaniment for once being utterly conventional, though the choral interjections carry Verdi's inimitable signature and, more specifically, echoes of "Va, pensiero". The brief exchanges between Seid and the disguised Corrado are telling, and the finale to the act is first-rate, with superb writing for the ensemble and, from Gulnara, a soaring line in true Verdian style. Though the battle music is undistinguished, the scene as a whole has life and movement, and the stretta of the finale, despite the ordinariness of its melody, is fascinating because of the way Verdi varies the formula with each return of the tune.

The third act opens with Seid's jealous aria, "Cento leggiadre vergini", a splendid piece which would not seem out of place in *Il trovatore*. The orchestra adds swell and emphasis, and a magnificent introduction to the swinging cabaletta. The duet for Seid and Gulnara is one of the most dramatically effective numbers in the score. The following scene in Corrado's prison is musically the finest in the opera, expressive and delicately scored. The orchestral introduction, consisting of a plangent melody over a curiously nervous, repeated triplet figure in the accompaniment, put Toye in mind of "Madre, pietosa vergine" or of Beethoven. I think, however, of the third variation in the last movement of Mozart's Clarinet Quintet. The figure survives under Corrado's recitative [Ex. 47].

Gulnara enters, and Verdi adapts the form of their long duet to suit the demands of the dramatic action. She begs Corrado to escape with her, in a phrase [Ex. 48] that adumbrates "Di quell' amor" in *La traviata* (see Ex. 70). When Gulnara goes off to kill Seid, the orchestra

romantically conjures up thunder and lightning which subside when she returns shattered by the enormity of her crime.

The final scene opens with the dying Medora and a sorrowful chorus. The sudden excitement of Corrado's return, and the brief but blissful ensemble as he and Gulnara enter, are heart-warmingly beautiful in performance. The final magnificent trio builds up into a finely paced ensemble of real feeling. This is Verdi at his simplest and most effective, not unlike the trio in the last Act of *Il trovatore*. Medora dies, there is a final yell from Corrado as he flings himself into the sea. Abrupt end.

Il corsaro is, it must be admitted, the type of work from which Verdi was eventually to rescue Italian opera. But I strongly doubt whether anyone who really loves middle-period Verdi will be able to resist a more than sneaking affection for this opera which the composer, though he succeeded in not making it "important", failed to make unenjoyable.

XIII

La battaglia di Legnano

Dramatis personae:

Federico Barbarossa	(bass)
First Milanese Consul	(bass)
Second Milanese Consul	(bass)
Mayor of Como	(bass)
Rolando, a leading Milanese warrior	(baritone)
Lida, his wife	(soprano)
Arrigo, Veronese warrior	(tenor)
Marcovaldo, German prisoner	(baritone)
Imelda, servant to Lida	(mezzo-soprano)
A herald	(tenor)

LIBRETTO by Salvatore Cammarano

TIME: 1176
PLACE: Milan and Como

FIRST PERFORMED at the Teatro Argentina, Rome, January 27, 1849 with Teresa De Giuli-Borsi (Lida); Marchesi (Imelda); Gaetano Fraschini (Arrigo); Filippo Colini (Rolando); P. Sottovia (Barbarossa); Gaetano Ferri (Marcovaldo)

La battaglia di Legnano

I

IN 1847, VERDI was in contact with several of the leaders of the liberal and nationalist political movement, and their literary supporters, one of whom was the poet Giuseppe Giusti who was keen to enlist him as the movement's composer. Disturbed when Verdi, after setting several subjects with acceptable patriotic overtones, then turned to Shakespeare's *Macbeth*, Giusti wrote to the composer in an attempt to set his feet on the right path again:

> You know that it is the chord of sorrow which finds the readiest echo in our breasts. Sorrow, however, assumes different aspects depending on the time and nature and condition of this or that nation. The kind of sorrow that now fills the minds of us Italians is the sorrow of a race that feels the need of a better destiny, the sorrow of one who has fallen and wishes to rise, the sorrow of one who repents and waits, longing for regeneration. Accompany, my Verdi, this high and solemn sorrow with your noble harmonies. Do what you can to nourish it, to strengthen it and direct it to its goal.[1]

Verdi's reply, written less than a fortnight after the première of *Macbeth*, is interesting:

> Yes, you put it very well. "It is the chord of sorrow which finds the readiest echo in our breasts." You speak about art like the great man you are, and I shall certainly take your advice, for I understand what you are saying. Oh, if only we had a poet who knew how to produce a drama of the kind you mean! But unfortunately, you yourself will admit it, if we want anything at all effective we are forced, shamefully, to accept foreign things. How many subjects there are in our own history![2]

Verdi was quite sincere about this. He had already half finished *I masnadieri* for London, and after that had to get Lucca's *Il corsaro* off his hands. Then, as soon as he was free of these commissions, he began to look for a patriotic Italian subject for his next opera. As he had said to Giusti, the difficulty was to find young poets capable of writing libretti. In his view, there were no original young talents on the scene. The youngsters, Verdi complained, thought they had attained

[1] *Copialettere*, pp. 449–50. [2] *Abbiati*, I, pp. 691–2.

perfection if they could claim to write like Romani or Cammarano. What he sought was a poet who would not write like his predecessors, but who would produce an operatic text with scope, power, freedom from convention, variety and novelty.

Verdi's implication is that he himself is the composer to do justice to such a libretto. Hardly modest, but then modesty is only the fig-leaf worn by mediocrity, and Verdi was anything but mediocre. Operatic subjects were continually being suggested to him; most were useless, but even the possible ones were just not to his taste. "The artist," wrote Verdi to Giuseppina Appiani, "must give himself up to his own inspiration and, if he has true talent, he feels and knows better than anyone else what his needs are. I should feel perfectly confident to compose any subject that moved me, even if every other composer condemned it as unsuitable for music."[1]

In March 1848, the Milanese rebelled against their Austrian over-lords, in the famous "cinque giornati". During these five days, there was desperate fighting in the streets, barricades were put up, the entire city rallied and, after skirmishes in all parts of the town including the roof of the Duomo where Alpine troops had taken up their position, the Austrians were driven out. When Verdi, in Paris, heard of the "cinque giornati", he hastened to return to Milan. In a letter to Piave, he wrote: "Honour to these brave men! Honour to all Italy, which at this moment is really great! Be assured, her hour of liberation has come. It is the people who demand it, and there is no absolute power that can resist the will of the people. . . . A few more years, perhaps only a few more months, and Italy will be a free, united republic. What else should she be?"[2]

But the fact that the Austrians, rather than destroy the entire city, had allowed themselves to be driven out of Milan did not, of course, mean the withdrawal of Austria from northern Italy. The Milanese appealed to Piedmont to come to their aid, and the Piedmontese reluctantly declared war on Austria. The Italian states, however, far from being united, began to quarrel among themselves over allegiances and pledges. When Carlo Alberto, King of Sardinia and Piedmont, drove the Austrians out of Venice, that city joyfully declared itself a republic. Nor had Milan any wish to annex itself to Piedmont. From the south, a move was afoot to unite all the Italian states with the Pope as their temporal as well as spiritual head. Meanwhile, the war between Austria and northern Italy continued: there was to be no easy victory. Since Milan was no longer the centre of events, Verdi decided to return

[1] *Copialettere*, p. 538. Although Verdi would like to have found Italian subjects, the libretti of twenty-one of his twenty-six operas have their provenance in foreign literary or dramatic works.

[2] *Una lettera di Giuseppe Verdi finora non pubblicata*, ed. A. Bonaventura (Florence, 1948).

to Paris, his unfinished business affairs and Giuseppina Strepponi. On the way, he wrote to Cammarano in Naples about an idea for an opera which the librettist had suggested, an idea which linked up with Giusti's patriotic exhortations to the composer. Cammarano had proposed a propaganda piece urging Italy to unite to expel the invader. Verdi was enthusiastic.

Cammarano's libretto took as its subject the defeat of Barbarossa, the German King and Holy Roman Emperor in 1176, by the Italian cities which had combined to form the Lombard League, at the battle of Legnano. He knew his audiences would understand that his libretto was really about the situation in 1848, though for censorship reasons he had to write about a war in 1176. During the summer, he and Verdi corresponded about it, and Verdi wrote the opera in Paris surrounded by civil strife, the revolt of the Parisian workers and its savage defeat.

In Italy the war went badly. The Piedmontese Carlo Alberto signed an armistice with the Austrians, by the terms of which he was to return to Piedmont. As his troops retreated through Milan, their fellow-countrymen denounced them as traitors and tried to take the King prisoner. Refusing to allow his troops to fire on fellow-Italians, Carlo Alberto managed to escape, and Milan was reoccupied by the Austrians. From Paris, Verdi sent the revolutionary leader Mazzini a patriotic song he had written, "Suona la tromba" (see pp. 457–8).

Verdi's opera was to be called *La battaglia di Legnano*. In addition to having been the scene of a decisive battle in 1176, Legnano was in 1848 one of the many Lombard towns still occupied by Austria. Having made his usual number of alterations and additions to Cammarano's libretto, by the end of the year Verdi had completed the score. The work was offered by Ricordi to Rome and was, of course, accepted. But the composer was displeased by the tone of the letters he received from the management of the Teatro Argentina, who appeared to think, according to him, that they were doing him a favour in accepting his score. He wrote to the baritone Filippo Colini who was to sing Rolando in the opera:

You know I have never put myself under an obligation to anyone, nor have I ever begged to have my scores accepted, or received favours of charity from anyone, not even when I badly needed them. You can therefore imagine that I am not going to put up now with even the slightest humiliation. As you know, I am under contract to write the opera for Ricordi. Apart from that, I have no obligations. So, if I have intervened in this matter, it has been to help to get things settled. If I have agreed to come to Rome, it is not out of self-interest, quite the reverse. I am making a sacrifice, for, as you know, a thousand francs is not enough to defray the expenses of the journey from Paris to Rome and back.[1]

[1] *Copialettere*, p. 63.

Political life in Rome was as violent as in the north. The Pope, Pio Nono (Pius IX), had escaped from Rome, following the murder of his chief administrator Count Pellegrino Rossi by local republicans, as a consequence of the refusal of Pio Nono and Rossi to join with Lombardy against Austria, or to send any help to the north. For two days the Pope had been besieged in the Quirinal Palace by an armed crowd of several thousands, but on November 24th, with the aid of the French and Bavarian ambassadors, he escaped disguised as an ordinary priest. In his absence from Rome, the government was controlled by the Republicans, who called an election at which all citizens were entitled to vote. From his exile in Gaeta, a seaside town south of the Papal State, the Pope condemned the election and forbade Catholics to vote. Consequently the Republicans won by an overwhelming majority. The newly elected Assembly was to meet for the first time in February when it was expected to declare the Papal State a republic. This was the situation when Verdi came to Rome in January to conduct the première of *La battaglia di Legnano*, so it is no wonder that the opera was a riotous success. The republican leaders Mazzini and Garibaldi had arrived in Rome, the atmosphere on January 27th was electric with excitement, and the Teatro Argentina was packed to the rafters. Verdi's music roused the entire house to a frenzy of enthusiasm. Newspaper accounts tell us that, when the first words of the opera's opening chorus were heard, "Viva Italia! Sacro un patto/Tutti stringe i figli suoi" (Long live Italy. A sacred pact binds all her sons), there were hysterical and delirious cries of "Viva Verdi" and "Viva Italia". At the end of Act III, when the hero, with a cry of "Viva Italia", leaps off a balcony into the moat in order to rejoin his regiment, a soldier in the fourth tier was so overcome that he flung his sword, his coat and his epaulettes on to the stage, followed by all the chairs in his box. In some accounts, he is said then to have flung himself as well.

The entire fourth act of the opera was encored, not only on the first night but at every subsequent performance of the season. The première was hardly a musical occasion. Even the critic of the *Pallade* who managed to hear, amid the shouting, that Verdi's music was breaking the shackles of the old forms, felt constrained to phrase his comment in political terms: "Far from following the old conventions, Verdi has felt that his spirit needs freedom just as Italy needs independence."[1]

La battaglia di Legnano received a few performances in other Italian towns and then succumbed to the Austrian censorship. Twelve years later, it was revived in Milan as *L'assedio di Haarlem* (The Siege of Haarlem), with the Germans and Italians turned into Spaniards and Dutchmen in a story of the Dutch revolt against Spanish occupation in the sixteenth century. When it was performed at the Teatro Regio,

[1] Quoted by Toye.

Parma, just after the Italian victories of 1869, the opera was cheekily subtitled *La disfatta degli Austriaci* (The Defeat of the Austrians).

II

Verdi's letters to Cammarano while they were working on *La battaglia di Legnano* reveal that what he wanted from his librettist was "a short drama, interesting, swift-moving and full of passion".[1] For the beginning of the last act, he had specific requirements:

At the beginning, outside the church of Saint Ambrose, I should like to combine two or three different melodies. For example, I should like both the priests inside and the people outside to have words in the same poetic metre, and Lida to have a song in a different metre. Leave the task of combining them to me. You might even, if you think it a good idea, give the priests some Latin verses. Do whatever you think best, but be sure that the situation is dramatically effective.[2]

The obliging Cammarano did exactly as he was asked. Sometimes Verdi's requests were couched in more general terms, allowing the poet a certain latitude:

Since the woman's role seems to me not to have the importance of the other two, I should like you to add, after the funeral chorus, a great agitated recitative in which she expresses her love, her despair at Arrigo's imminent death, her fear of being discovered and so on. After a beautiful recitative, let the husband arrive and give them a moving little duet. Have the father bless his son, or something of the kind. And so on.[3]

The wonder is that, intending to write a piece of propaganda pure and simple, Verdi and Cammarano should have produced the valid work of art that *La battaglia di Legnano* undoubtedly is. Cammarano's libretto effectively combines patriotism with the obligatory love interest, while Verdi's intention was to preach the desirability of a united Italy. Both composer and poet fervently believed in what they were doing, which probably explains why they did it so well.

The opera's four acts have separate sub-titles. Act I, "Egli vive!" (He is Alive) is set in Milan, close by the gates of the city. Soldiers of the Lombard League are arriving in Milan. The League has been formed by several Lombard cities to fight Federico Barbarossa, the German King who is invading their country, and the citizens of Milan have assembled to greet the various contingents. At the head of the troops from Verona is Arrigo, who is recognised by his old friend Rolando, a

[1] *Copialettere*, pp. 55–6.   [2] *Copialettere*, p. 56.   [3] *Copialettere*, p. 60.

Milanese leader, who had thought him killed in battle. The two friends embrace, and Arrigo explains that he had been wounded, captured and imprisoned by the enemy. The Milanese consuls greet the warriors of the League, who all swear to give their lives for the defence of their country.

The second scene of Act I takes place in the shade of a cluster of trees presumably somewhere on Rolando's estate. His wife Lida, surrounded by her ladies-in-waiting, sings of her horror of a war which has already robbed her of her brothers and her parents. She has often prayed to God to relieve her of life, but she is a mother and must care for her child. Marcovaldo, a German prisoner of war to whom Rolando has given his freedom, approaches. He is in love with Lida, who has always rejected his advances. Imelda, Lida's companion, appears and announces to Lida that her husband is returning, bringing Arrigo with him. Lida and Arrigo had been betrothed many years earlier, and she too had believed him dead. Her joy at hearing he is alive is noticed by Marcovaldo, who correctly supposes that she still loves Arrigo. Rolando and Arrigo enter, and Arrigo finds it difficult to conceal his emotion at finding that his friend's wife is his own ex-sweetheart. He manages to dissemble until Rolando is called away by a Herald on business of the Senate. When he and Lida are finally left alone together, Arrigo upbraids her for what he considers her faithlessness. The fact that he had been considered dead does not lessen his anger and bitterness. He rushes off, leaving Lida desolate.

The second act, "Barbarossa", takes place in the town of Como, in a ceremonial hall of the municipal building. The leaders and magistrates are assembling to receive a deputation from the League. The Mayor asks that the messengers from the League be brought in. They are Arrigo and Rolando, who attempt to persuade the representatives of Como to end their old feud with Milan and join the League. The Mayor points out that Como has signed a pact with Barbarossa, a pact which Rolando denounces as shameful:

> Dell italico linguaggio,
> Ma nell' opre, nei pensieri
> Siete barbari stranieri!

(Your language may be Italian, but in deeds and thoughts you are foreign barbarians.)

Arrigo adds his voice, calling the assembled leading citizens of Como traitors and parricides. Impatiently he asks what answer they are to convey to Milan. Suddenly, Barbarossa himself appears and gives Arrigo his answer. He orders the windows to be flung open to reveal, on the hills outside the town, his assembled army. Rolando asserts that his mercenaries are no match against a people fighting for their own freedom, and Arrigo tells Barbarossa that he cannot hope to change Italy's great destiny, to which the King replies: "Il destino d'Italia, son io!" (I am Italy's destiny.) In an ensemble which ends the act, they all voice their differing opinions and threaten one another with pitiless warfare.

Act III, "L'infamia" (The Disgrace), opens in the crypt of the church of St Ambrose in Milan, where a meeting of the Campioni della Morte, or Death-Champions, a select group of Lombard League warriors, is taking place. Arrigo is elected a member of the band who all swear to drive the invaders out of Italy or die in the attempt. The second scene of the act is set in Rolando's castle. Lida, fearful that Arrigo will be killed in the fighting, sends Imelda to him with a letter. Rolando enters to say farewell to his wife and child. After Lida and the child have left the room, Arrigo enters and is told by Rolando that he, Rolando, has been chosen to lead the Campioni della Morte. If he should not return, he asks Arrigo to take care of his wife and child. Arrigo swears to do so, and the two friends embrace and say their farewell. Arrigo leaves, and Marcovaldo enters. He has intercepted Lida's note to Arrigo, and shows it to Rolando as proof that his wife has been unfaithful to him. Rolando reads the note, in which Lida has asked Arrigo to visit her before he departs, in the name of their former love. Wild with rage, Rolando determines to be avenged on them both.

The last scene of Act III takes place in Arrigo's room, which has a balcony overlooking the castle's moat. Arrigo is writing to his mother when Lida enters. Having had no reply to her note, she has called to say goodbye. She admits to Arrigo that she still loves him, but says they must part, he to live for the sake of his mother, she for her child. Rolando's voice is heard at the door, and Lida just has time to hide on the balcony before he enters. Pretending to look for the approaching dawn, he steps out on to the balcony and discovers her. In a cold fury, Rolando disowns his wife, disregarding Arrigo's assurances that she is innocent. He is about to kill Arrigo, who offers no resistance, when he suddenly decides instead that disgrace will be a worse punishment. He rushes out, locking the door behind him. The sound of the departing battalions can be heard, and Arrigo goes to the balcony to see Rolando's contingent already setting off. Determined to join his troops, Arrigo leaps over the balcony with a cry of "Viva Italia!"

Act IV, "Morire per la patria" (To Die for one's Country), takes place in a Milan square, in front of the church. The citizens, Lida and Imelda among them, are awaiting the return of the soldiers. After they have prayed for victory and the safe return of their heroes, a Consul appears and announces that the Lombards have won. Arrigo has himself killed Barbarossa. There is a general rejoicing, and then the sound of a funeral march is heard. The mortally wounded Arrigo is being carried back, followed in procession by Rolando and other warriors. Arrigo swears to Rolando that he and Lida have not betrayed him, the friends are reconciled, and Rolando embraces his wife. As the choir inside the church intones a Te Deum, Arrigo dies, kissing his country's flag. The populace calls on God to open the gates of Paradise for the brave patriot.

III

The Overture to *La battaglia di Legnano*, planned on a large scale, is one of Verdi's finest, utilising various themes from the opera, in particular the march of the Lombards. The structure of the Overture is basically a–b–a, the middle section being a very beautiful *andante* of a somewhat Bellinian kind. It is heard again in the opera when Arrigo writes to his mother. The opening march and chorus effectively set the mood of patriotic fervour and martial determination of the entire work. Arrigo's cavatina, "La pia materna mano", expressive and tuneful, is an excellent example of Verdi's natural and skilful vocal writing at this time. After a brief reprise of the choral march, the joyful reunion of the two friends Arrigo and Rolando is effected in a lively arioso. Rolando's aria, "Ah! m'abbraccia", serves as cabaletta to Arrigo's, and Rolando leads the ensemble in "Giuramento", the swearing of the patriotic oath, after which the orchestral postlude's use of the march gives a unity to the entire scene which, though it consists of the usual separate units, combines them into an organic whole. The scene itself becomes a valid musical form rather than merely a succession of numbers. In later operas, of course, Verdi's methods were to become consistently more sophisticated, but the solution he chose in *La battaglia di Legnano* to the formal problems posed is entirely appropriate to this type of opera and its intent.

The chorus of women at the beginning of the second scene is noteworthy more for its inventive accompaniment than for its voice parts. Lida's cavatina, "Quante volte come in dono", is charming, and makes meaningful use of ornamentation. This is a role for a soprano spinto of flexibility and range, for trills and top Cs are frequent. Lida's cabaletta after she has heard that Arrigo is alive and has returned is a brilliant piece of vocal writing, really irresistible in performance. The next piece of plot is negotiated in workaday recitative, and is followed by the duet for Arrigo and Lida, "È ver? Sei d'altri", a number which is of no great musical interest out of context, but whose dramatic thrust is entirely appropriate to the demands of the plot at this point. Here, as elsewhere, Verdi's sense of drama is unerring.

The second act is very short, consisting merely of an opening chorus of Como officials, a duet-scene in which Arrigo and Rolando attempt to sway Como to the common Italian cause, and a concerted finale when Barbarossa himself makes an unexpected appearance. The varying attitudes, Barbarossa's proud scorn, the Lombards' defiance, and the vacillation of the citizens of Como are all magnificently portrayed. The duet, in which the two representatives of the Lombard League harangue the assembly, abounds in rousing phrases, but the entire scene is musically and dramatically so effective that it is impossible to single out individual moments for praise. The remarkable, and remarkably exciting, thing about this opera is the manner in which each succeeding scene makes even more of an effect than the preceding one, generating an infectious and mounting enthusiasm.

The conspiratorial atmosphere of Act III, Scene 1, is admirably conveyed in the orchestral prelude. Indeed, the orchestral writing throughout this scene is worthy of Beethoven. The great oath chorus, "Giuriam d'Italia por fine ai danni", is as stirring as one would expect, but what is particularly noteworthy is the way in which Verdi, though he is writing a popular essay in propaganda. refuses to subordinate the dramatic situation to cheap effect. The musical integrity of the scene is never violated: the dark, questioning mood, in which the orchestra began the scene, returns in the postlude after the "*fff tutta forza*" ending of the chorus. The orchestra has the last thirteen bars, and they are sprinkled with reminders to play *ppp*.

In the following scene, Lida's dramatic recitative leading to her duet with Rolando contains the phrase [Ex. 49] which, four years later, was

Ex.49   Andante

Ma   Dio mi vol - le

to become Violetta's great cry, "Amami, Alfredo", in the second Act of *La traviata* [Ex. 72]. The broad melodic sweep of the duet, "Digli ch'è sangue italico", is brilliantly effective, and Rolando's aria, "Se al nuovo dì pugnando", with phrases contributed by Arrigo, has a forthright sincerity which is immensely moving. The orchestral comment in the following recitative is always apt, and Rolando's cabaletta, when he learns of Arrigo's apparent seduction of Lida, has an invigorating energy if a little less than usual of Verdi's melodic genius.

The final scene of Act III develops from Arrigo's *parlante* as he writes to his mother, through his affecting scene with Lida, into a superb trio, "Ah! d'un consorte, o perfidi", at Rolando's entrance. Arrigo's figure [Ex. 50] turns up again in *Il trovatore* as Manrico's "Ah, che la morte

Ex.50   Andante mosso

no   ah! no:tra fit - to,e - san - gue

ognora". The trio ends, and Rolando leaves, locking Arrigo in his room. The finale of the act, with the sound of the departing warriors off-stage and Arrigo's cry as he leaps from the balcony to join them, is tremendously exciting in the theatre.

The extremely short Act IV, a mere fifteen minutes in performance, opens dramatically with the dialogue of Lida and Imelda against a background of liturgical chanting, followed by Lida's prayer, effective in the manner of Leonora's music in the last act of *Il trovatore*. The hymn of victory, with bells pealing, is brilliantly effective, and the beautiful trio when the dying Arrigo is carried in, can be criticised only for its brevity. Arrigo dies, and the ensemble's cry to heaven to receive his soul ends the opera.

If, in drawing attention to phrases which occur in later and more popular operas, I have given the impression that *La battaglia di Legnano* is valuable primarily for the light it casts on those later works, let me immediately correct that impression. Commentators are always searching through the early Verdi operas to find traces of his later greatness. Indeed, when London first heard *Un giorno di regno* a few years ago, one critic poked about in the score for such passages as though it were a Christmas pudding from which he wanted to extract only the sixpences. Those of us who ate the pudding as well found the taste most enjoyable. *La battaglia di Legnano*, too, is enjoyable in itself. In a work where his sympathies were so closely engaged, Verdi could hardly have failed to write stirring, exciting and apt music. His score is by no means rhythmically complex, but the sweep of the melodies is such that its sound always falls most gratefully on the ear. Throughout the opera, too, the orchestral tone-colouring is always dramatically expressive, particularly in the accompaniments to recitatives and in the introductions to scenes. The concision of the musical ideas is striking: a baritone cabaletta is shorn of its usually obligatory second stanza; a delicate soprano cavatina has hardly begun before it is interrupted and abandoned in the interests of dramatic truth. There are no wasted notes.

La battaglia di Legnano is an opera with a purpose. Parts of Verdi's earlier operas had frequently been taken up by the fighters of the Risorgimento, but this time the composer had given the movement its own opera. It was his contribution to Italy's future as a united nation: it was also a valid work of art. Thoroughly effective, it did not aim purely at effect. This dramatically self-contained piece is, on its own terms, as viable a piece of *Musiktheater* as *Don Giovanni*, *Otello* or *Tristan und Isolde*, though it is by no means the exalted masterpiece that each of those works is.

XIV

Luisa Miller

Dramatis personae:

Luisa Miller	(soprano)
Miller, her father, a retired soldier	(baritone)
Count Walter	(bass)
Rodolfo, his son	(tenor)
Federica, Duchess of Ostheim, the Count's niece	(mezzo-soprano)
Wurm, in the employ of the Count	(bass)
Laura, a village girl	(mezzo-soprano)
A peasant	(tenor)

LIBRETTO by Salvatore Cammarano, based on the play *Kabale und Liebe* by Friedrich Schiller

TIME: The early seventeenth century
PLACE: A village in the Tyrol

FIRST PERFORMED at the Teatro San Carlo, Naples, December 8, 1849, with Marietta Gazzaniga (Luisa); Salvetti-Manzi (Laura); Salandri (Federica); Settimio Malvezzi (Rodolfo); Achille De Bassini (Miller); Antonio Selva (Walter); Marco Arati (Wurm)

Luisa Miller

I

AFTER LAUNCHING *La battaglia di Legnano* in Rome at the beginning of 1849, Verdi returned to Paris and to Strepponi. During the following months, things went badly for the liberal cause in Italy: a recurrence of the fighting in the north led to the abdication of the King of Sardinia and Piedmont, and the victory of Austria. The Roman Republic collapsed, and the Pope called on France, Austria, Spain and Naples to intervene. "Force still rules the world," wrote Verdi. "And justice? What use is it against bayonets? We can only weep over our wrongs and curse the instigators of so many misfortunes."[1] He and Giuseppina returned to Italy. In order to help Cammarano out of a difficulty with the management of the Teatro San Carlo, who were threatening to sue him because he had failed to deliver a libretto, Verdi had agreed to collaborate with him on an opera for Naples. Their first intention was to use an historical novel, *L'assedio di Firenze* (*the Siege of Florence*), by Francesco Domenico Guerrazzi as the starting-off point of their opera, but the Neapolitan censors refused to allow this, as Guerrazzi's novel, which had been published in 1836, was political propaganda disguised as historical fiction. Cammarano then reminded Verdi of Schiller's play, *Kabale und Liebe* (Intrigue and Love), which the composer had considered earlier, and Verdi agreed to write an opera based on the play. Cammarano immediately began work on his libretto, and Verdi was even able to begin composing the opera before he left Paris. He continued working on it in Busseto, where he arrived at the end of August 1849. He had brought Giuseppina to live with him, thus outraging the locals and estranging himself from several of his old friends. And he had bought the Villa Sant' Agata, two or three miles outside Busseto, which was to be his and Giuseppina's home for the remainder of their lives.

By the end of October Verdi had completed *Luisa Miller*, based on Schiller's play but renamed after its heroine. He set out for Naples, accompanied by old Barazzi, but because of the cholera outbreak was held up by quarantine regulations in Rome for over a fortnight. In Naples, Verdi took his ex-father-in-law sight-seeing. They visited Herculaneum, Pompeii, Pozzuoli, the island of Ischia and several other

[1] *Copialettere*, p. 475.

places of tourist interest. Verdi had never really come to terms with Naples, and this time he had trouble with the management of the San Carlo, who first demanded that he hand over the score, then refused to pay for it and threatened to have the composer arrested if he attempted to leave Naples without official permission. Verdi refused to be intimidated, announced that he would take himself and his opera on board one of the French warships in the bay, and demand protection from the French against the Kingdom of the Two Sicilies. The authorities backed down, but Verdi's Neapolitan troubles were not ended. A local composer called Vincenzo Capecelatro, said to have the evil eye, kept trying to waylay Verdi whose friends therefore felt constrained to keep constant guard over him. In their opinion Capecelatro had been responsible for the failure of *Alzira* in Naples four years earlier. On the first night of *Luisa Miller*, however, the "mal occhio" managed to make his way back-stage, and part of the scenery collapsed, narrowly missing Verdi. Nevertheless, *Luisa Miller* was a success, which almost made bearable the habitual Neapolitan intrigues, gossip and invasion of privacy. Almost, but not quite. Verdi had never really got used to the absurd idol worship and scandal-mongering of the Neapolitans, and this time the San Carlo's attempt to invoke its royal status against him really infuriated him. A week after the opening of *Luisa Miller* he left Naples, vowing he would never produce another opera there. He kept his vow.

II

Cammarano's libretto reduces Schiller's five acts to three, subtitled "L'amore" (Love), "L'intrigo" (Intrigue) and "Il veleno" (Poison). Act I, set in the village square, shows the exterior of Miller's house as well as the village church. In the distance, through the trees, can be glimpsed the towers of Count Walter's castle. It is the birthday of Luisa, Miller's daughter, so her friend Laura and the other villagers have assembled to sing her praises. Luisa and her father enter, and she looks anxiously around for Carlo, with whom she is in love. Her father attempts to warn her against Carlo, who is a stranger in the village, but she is sure of her love for him and his for her. The villagers approach to present Luisa with flowers and, from among them, dressed as a hunter, Carlo suddenly steps forward. The young lovers sing of their happiness, but Miller is still disturbed. When the church bell rings, the assembled company, including Luisa and Carlo, dutifully enter the church. Miller is stopped by Wurm, an employee of Count Walter. Wurm is in love with Luisa, and has had Miller's promise to recommend him to his daughter. Miller reminds Wurm that he has no intention of coercing Luisa into marriage against her will, and the jealous Wurm reveals that Carlo is, in fact, the Count's son Rodolfo. Miller is now convinced that Carlo's intentions towards Luisa are far from honourable.

The second scene of Act I takes place in a room in Count Walter's castle. Wurm informs the Count of his son's love for a simple village girl, but the Count is determined that Rodolfo shall marry his niece, Rodolfo's cousin, the widowed Federica, Duchess of Ostheim. He sends for Rodolfo, and tells him he has already spoken to Federica, who had grown up with Rodolfo and who is not only willing to accept him as a husband but has also confessed her love for him. The Duchess is announced, and the Count, leaving Rodolfo alone with her, goes off to the hunt. Rodolfo decides to tell Federica the truth and place himself at her mercy. He explains, therefore, that he loves someone else, and would rather kill himself than be unfaithful to her. Federica's unsatisfactory reply is that, while she would forgive him with her dying breath if he were to kill her, she will be pitiless where any rival is concerned.

The third and last scene of Act I takes place in Miller's house. A hunting chorus is heard in the distance as Luisa awaits Carlo, who has promised to visit her after the hunt. Her father enters to tell her she has been deceived, and that her beloved, who is really the Count's son, is at this moment preparing to marry the Duchess. Rodolfo-Carlo arrives and swears he is sincere in his love for Luisa. Kneeling with her before her father, he vows to marry her. Miller is forced to recognise his sincerity, but fears the consequences of his defying his father. Rodolfo mysteriously announces that he has secret information which, were he to reveal it, would bring his father to his senses. The Count arrives unexpectedly, claiming that he has come to save his son from ruin. He insults Luisa, and her father angrily challenges him. The Count calls on his archers to arrest Miller and his daughter. Rodolfo attempts to bluff his father by threatening first to kill him and then, rather than allow her to be taken prisoner, to kill Luisa. His father, however, is not taken in by any of this bravado, and finally Rodolfo is forced to mutter privately to him that, unless Miller and Luisa are released, he will reveal to the world how his father became Count Walter. This has an immediate effect: Luisa and her father are released, Rodolfo rushes out and the Count anxiously follows him.

There are two scenes in Act II, the first of which is Miller's house again. A group of villagers enters to tell Luisa that just outside the village they have seen her father being dragged in chains to the Count's castle. She is about to rush off to the castle when Wurm enters and, dismissing the villagers, tells her that her father was arrested for having threatened the Count. He will be sentenced to death unless Luisa follows the instructions of Wurm, who has been sent by the Count. She is to write Wurm a letter swearing that she loves only him, that her only interest in Rodolfo had been to secure an advantageous match, and that she wishes to elope with Wurm at midnight. Luisa can hardly bring herself to write such a letter, but Wurm points out that the alternative is the execution of her father. Hurriedly, she writes as directed. Wurm tells her she must also go with him to the castle and repeat before the Count and the Duchess that she loves only Wurm. In desperation, Luisa agrees.

In the next scene, a room at the castle, the Count is brooding over his son's disobedience when Wurm enters to report that Luisa has written the necessary letter. Walter and Wurm recall how, many years earlier, they had ambushed and killed Walter's cousin so that Walter would inherit the title. Walter tells Wurm that Rodolfo knows of this, having being told by the dying man, and that Rodolfo has threatened to reveal it. The Count cannot understand this ingratitude: it was, he claims, only for Rodolfo that he desired advancement. Wurm, terrified that the truth may become known, retires to fetch Luisa as the Duchess enters. Count Walter tells the Duchess that Rodolfo's infatuation for Luisa is over, that Luisa had in any case never cared for him, and that she will hear Luisa herself confess this. Luisa is brought in by Wurm, and forces herself to lie to Federica, saying that she cares nothing for Rodolfo and that she is enamoured of the unprepossessing Wurm.

The third scene of Act II is set in the garden outside Rodolfo's apartment in the castle. A peasant, bribed by Wurm, brings Rodolfo Luisa's letter to Wurm, with a story that Luisa had given instructions that Rodolfo was not to see it. Rodolfo dismisses the peasant with a tip, reads the letter, and is foolish enough to believe it. He is more sad than bitter at the discovery, as he thinks, of Luisa's betrayal of him, and he sings of the happy hours they used to spend together. Wurm enters and Rodolfo, showing him the letter, challenges him to an immediate duel and thrusts a pistol upon him. Refusing to fight, Wurm fires his pistol in the air, which brings the Count and his retainers on to the scene. The broken-hearted Rodolfo kneels at the feet of his father, who pretends to have relented and to be willing to allow him to marry Luisa. Rodolfo cries that Luisa has betrayed him, and the Count advises him to take another bride, the Duchess Federica, in order to be avenged on Luisa. Beyond caring now, Rodolfo agrees to marry Federica.

The third act is set in Miller's house, where the miserable Luisa sits writing, watched by Laura and some of the villagers, who try in vain to cheer her up. She asks why the church across the square is so gaily lit, and Laura tells her that it is for the wedding of the Duchess Federica, but does not say to whom, fearing the truth might kill Luisa. Miller, released from the castle, enters, and the villagers depart. Miller knows of the sacrifice his daughter has made, and is disturbed by her calm remoteness. Luisa hands him the letter she has written, asking that it be given to Rodolfo. Miller reads the letter, in which she explains how she was tricked into giving Rodolfo up, asks his forgiveness, and requests that he come to her "when the church bells toll at midnight". Luisa admits to her father that she intends to kill herself, but when the old man begs her to have pity on him, she relents and swears she will stay with him for the rest of his life. They plan to leave the village early next morning, Miller goes to his own room, and Luisa kneels in prayer. Rodolfo enters, ordering his servant to go to the castle and tell the Count where he is to be found. While Luisa continues to pray, Rodolfo pours poison from a phial into the jug of water on the table. He then interrupts her to show her the letter she wrote to Wurm, and asks her to confirm that it is her writing. When Luisa simply says yes, he asks for a glass of water. Luisa pours a glass from the jug, and he drinks. Complaining of the bitterness of the water, he requests Luisa to taste it, which she does. He reproaches her for her disloyalty, and when the church bell begins to ring, he tells her they have both been poisoned. Crying that death releases her from her promise, Luisa tells Rodolfo the truth, and he is overcome with remorse and despair. Miller enters to find the lovers dying. The Count and Wurm arrive as Luisa dies, and Rodolfo finds strength enough to run his sword through Wurm before falling lifeless to the ground.

Though Cammarano's well-constructed libretto in three acts appears to pay lip service to the five acts of Schiller's *Kabale und Liebe*, it is really even further removed from its original than is usually the case with operatic libretti. Schiller's title, *Intrigue and Love*, was carefully and deliberately chosen. His play contrasts idealism and expediency, self-less romanticism and self-interested practicality, and his concern, beneath the trappings of romanticism, is not in itself romantic: his proposition is that love does not always triumph over all obstacles, that worldliness can too easily pervert love, and that the machinery of political intrigue is more than a match for the spirituality of romantic feeling. In reducing the play to a reasonable libretto length, Cammarano had naturally to make most of his excisions in the scenes of "Kabale" rather than in those of "Liebe". Love, after all, is simple; intrigue is complex. The love scenes, being all of a piece, lose little of their individual flavour in reduction. The complex strands of intrigue are more vulnerable: remove some of them, and the face of intrigue is changed. Cammarano dispenses with two of Schiller's most important characters, Lady Milford and the Court Chamberlain, Baron von Kolb. In the play, it is Lady Milford with whom Ferdinand's father would force him into marriage. Federica is merely mentioned as a possible alternative. Lady Milford is a high-born Englishwoman who had fled to Germany at the age of fourteen as a political refugee, and had eventually become the mistress of a German prince in whose court much of the action of the play takes place. When Ferdinand (Rodolfo in the opera) is told by his father that he must marry Lady Milford, whose name is presumably known to him, the young man scornfully replies: "Welcher Schandsäule im Herzogtum ist sie das nicht!" (To what brothel throughout the Dukedom is she not known!) He defies his father, the Prime Minister, saying that, although he will call on Lady Milford, it will not be to ask her hand in marriage. In the scene between Ferdinand and Lady Milford, one of the most effective in the play, he leaves her in no doubt of his feelings:

Und wenn du auch noch dann meine Hand verlangst—im Angesicht des versammelten Adels, des Militärs und des Volks—umgürte dich mit dem ganzen Stolz deines Englands—ich verwerfe dich—ein deutscher Jüngling.

(Then, if you should still demand my hand, in the presence of the assembled nobles, the soldiers and the populace, you may gird yourself with all your English pride, but I, a German youth, will spurn you.)

By placing the action of the opera in a Tyrolean village instead of a princely court, and substituting a local lord of the manor for Schiller's Prime Minister, Cammarano made it impossible for so high-powered a character as Lady Milford to fit into the plot. So Federica, Duchess of Ostheim, a childhood friend of Rodolfo, is pressed into service. Schiller's amusingly Pandarus-like Baron von Kolb is found similarly expendable. In the play, it is he who is named as Luisa's lover and who is challenged to a duel by Ferdinand, while in the opera the Count's retainer Wurm (called, in the play, the Prime Minister's Private Secretary) is used to fulfil this function. Cammarano's Miller is no longer the local music teacher, but a retired soldier.

Generally speaking, the "intrigue" element in the opera is less weighty, certainly less convoluted. The opera could hardly have been called *Intrigo ed amore*, for there is less political intrigue than parental opposition. The enclosed world of Schiller's eighteenth-century German court is replaced by the pseudo-pastoral atmosphere of Cammarano's operatic seventeenth-century Tyrolean village. His opening scene, set in the village square with a chorus of locals serenading Luisa, who anxiously awaits her beloved, acknowledges a certain debt to the first act of Romani's libretto for *La sonnambula*. Verdi took the reference, and composed a quasi-Bellinian scene to fit the text.

Though it is inadequate as an adaptation of Schiller's excellent play, Cammarano's *Luisa Miller* is, in its own right, a very fine libretto. Luisa's mother who, in the play existed only to be the butt of her husband's invective, is dispensed with, and the weight of the action is shared firmly and equally by Rodolfo, Luisa, their fathers and Wurm. Federica, though necessary to the mechanics of the plot, is really no more than a pawn in the Count's game. What is particularly interesting about the libretto, especially when one considers it in context with and in contrast to Cammarano's preceding libretto, *La battaglia di Legnano*, is the domesticity of the story as opposed to the larger, public nature of the earlier opera. Verdi's *Luisa Miller*, his first attempt at portraying something of bourgeois "respectability" on the stage, is a direct predecessor of *La traviata*, which deals, among other things, with bourgeois hypocrisy. The nature of the story calls for a more intimate style of vocal writing than was required by the larger-scale tragedies which had comprised the majority of Verdi's earlier operas, and in *Luisa Miller* we see the composer come some distance towards providing it, at least in the latter part of the opera.

III

The splendid Overture is gracious in manner and pleasantly pastoral in tone, due mainly to the predominance of the solo clarinet. Admirably planned as a sonata-form symphonic first movement, it is based on a elegant figure [Ex. 51] which will be heard again in the introduction

Ex.51   Allegro ♩ = 126

to the third Act. The decidedly Bellinian opening scene echoes the beginning of *La sonnambula*, though Verdi's orchestra is considerably more interesting than Bellini's. An idyllic chorus of villagers is followed by Luisa's aria, "Lo vidi, e il primo palpito il cor senti d'amore", which uses coloratura not simply as embellishment but as significant expression. After Rodolfo's arrival, the expected cabaletta is provided, but it is in the form of a joyful duet for Rodolfo and Luisa, and builds up into a superb ensemble. Here the style of Bellini is overlaid with the originality and the theatrical excitement of Verdi. Miller's aria and cabaletta bring Act I to a close. The aria, "Sacra la scelta è d'un consorte", is rather beautiful: the cabaletta, on the other hand, is ordinary.

Count Walter's aria, "Il mio sangue", at the beginning of Scene 2, can be made to sound effective by a good dramatic bass, but is by no means foolproof. Rodolfo's exchanges with his father and then with Federica, though they usefully and speedily advance the action, contain nothing especially worth noting. The act recovers itself in the last scene in Miller's house where, after a somewhat frenetic hunting chorus, the situation between the Walters, father and son, and the Millers is worked into a dramatic finale in which Luisa's top line, less decorated now than in Scene 1, dominates the magnificent ensemble.

The first scene of Act II, in which Wurm explains to Luisa the terms of her father's freedom, built on the simple plan of recitative-aria recitative-cabaletta, is none the less immensely effective. The recitative, both before Luisa's aria and after, is really extended arioso, and beautifully expressive. The clarinet is used eloquently to express Luisa's anguish. Her aria, "Tu puniscimi, o Signore", and, despite its unusual minor opening, the cabaletta as well, look back to *I masnadieri* rather than forward to *La traviata*. It can hardly be denied, however, that the aria is affecting and the cabaletta exciting.

Act II, Scene 2, opens with a splendid duet for the two basses, Wurm and Walter, "L'alto retaggio non ho bramato", which manages to be both dramatically and psychologically apt, as well as memorably melodic [Ex. 52]. This is music which puts one in mind of the scene for

Philip and the Inquisitor in *Don Carlo*. The quartet for Walter, Wurm, Luisa and Federica, part of it unaccompanied, just misses the chance to provide one of the great moments of the opera, though it usefully and more than capably advances the action. The aria, "Quando le sere al placido", in the last scene of the act, is justly the most famous single number of the score, a lyrical *bel canto* melody of great beauty in which Rodolfo nostalgically recalls past happiness and broods on his present situation [Ex. 53]. This is the aria of which, years later, Boito wrote:

"Ah, if you knew the kind of echo and ecstasy that this divine cantilena awakens in the soul of an Italian."[1]

The last act looks forward in structure and accent to Act II, Scene 1, of *La traviata*: the level of inspiration may not be so consistently high, but the scene flows steadily and inexorably to its conclusion, without

[1] To Bellaigue. Quoted by Toye, p. 65.

an ounce of musical fat. All is to the purpose. The formal plan is simple: the introduction makes use of the Overture's principal theme, now in 3/4 time, and after an opening chorus there follows a splendid long duet for Luisa and her father, in which Verdi's vocal writing is both fluent and natural, and at times sounds positively Schubertian. The climactic scene for Luisa and Rodolfo, in which Luisa's music takes on the accents we are later to associate with the dying Violetta in *La traviata*, culminates, with the re-entrance of Luisa's father, in one of those wonderfully expressive trio finales into which Verdi poured so many of his finest melodic inventions. The real world of feeling so finely and fully explored, the composer as usual wastes no time over the brute facts: in a few mechanically hasty bars the Count and Wurm enter, Wurm is despatched by Rodolfo's sword, and Rodolfo himself falls dead by Luisa's side.

Luisa Miller is, in addition to being an affecting and enjoyable opera, an important transitional work, marking both the end of Verdi's first period and the beginning of his second. The change can almost be said to occur between Acts II and III, the first two acts inhabiting the world of Bellini and Donizetti, a world which Verdi leaves with the tender regret of "Quando le sere al placido", while Act III is both a real anticipation of the musical style and dramatic atmosphere of *La traviata*, and a confident assertion of the composer's by then complete independence from the past. The intimate, domestic tone is new and exciting; equally exciting are the increasing mastery of orchestration and, especially in the last act, the freedom and flexibility of form, the easy confidence of the vocal writing, the quality of the melodic recitative, and the general widening of Verdi's expressive range of feeling.

XV

Stiffelio and *Aroldo*

Dramatis personae:

Stiffelio, evangelical
   minister (tenor)
Lina, his wife (soprano)
Stankar, an elderly colonel
   and Imperial Count, Lina's
   father (baritone)
Raffaele, a nobleman (tenor)
Jorg, an elderly minister (bass)
Federico di Frengel (tenor)
Dorothea, Lina's
   cousin (mezzo-soprano)

Aroldo, Saxon knight (tenor)
Mina, his wife (soprano)
Egberto, elderly knight,
   Mina's father (baritone)

Godvino, a knight (tenor)
Briano, a holy man (bass)
Enrico (tenor) and
Elena, cousins of Mina (mezzo-
   soprano)

LIBRETTO by Francesco Maria Piave, based on the play *Le Pasteur* by Emile Souvestre and Eugène Bourgeois

TIME: Beginning of the nineteenth century
PLACE: Germany

FIRST PERFORMED at the Teatro Grande, Trieste, November 16, 1850, with Marietta Gazzaniga (Lina); Gaetano Fraschini (Stiffelio); Filippo Colini (Stankar); Raineri Dei (Raffaele); Francesco Reduzzi (Jorg)

LIBRETTO by Francesco Maria Piave, based on his *Stiffelio* libretto

TIME: *c.* 1200

PLACE: England and Scotland

FIRST PERFORMED at the Teatro Nuovo, Rimini, August 16, 1857, with Marcellina Lotti (Mina); Giovanni Pancani (Aroldo); Carlo Poggiali (Egberto); Cornago (Godvino); Gaetano Ferri (Briano)

Stiffelio and *Aroldo*

I

VERDI RETURNED FROM Naples to Busseto in December 1849 after the first three performances of *Luisa Miller*, and began to fling ideas for operas at Salvatore Cammarano. He had already suggested the librettist should look at Victor Hugo's play, *Le Roi s'amuse*, "a beautiful play with tremendous dramatic situations",[1] and now he also recommended "*El Trovador*, a Spanish play by García Gutiérrez. It seems to me very fine, rich in ideas and strong situations. I should like to have two female roles. First the gypsy, a woman of strange character, after whom I want to name the opera. The other role would be for a supporting singer."[2]

These were in due course to become *Rigoletto* and *Il trovatore*, though it was Verdi's other tame librettist, Francesco Maria Piave, who was to write the *Rigoletto* libretto. To Cammarano at this time Verdi also sent his synopsis of *King Lear* (see p. 78). But the opera which followed *Luisa Miller* was none of these. Verdi had agreed to provide Ricordi with a new opera for production in the autumn of 1850 in any one of the leading Italian theatres "except La Scala, Milan".[3] Leaving Cammarano to study Hugo, García Gutiérrez and Shakespeare for future purposes, Verdi asked Piave to suggest an immediate subject, and Piave recommended a French play, *Le Pasteur*, by Emile Souvestre and Eugène Bourgeois, which he had seen on the stage in an Italian translation, as *Stiffelius*. The subject of *Stiffelius*, which was first produced in Paris in February 1848, is the floundering marriage of a German Protestant clergyman whose wife has committed adultery. Verdi accepted the idea, and Giovanni Ricordi arranged to have the opera, *Stiffelio*, produced at the Teatro Grande, Trieste, in November 1850, under the composer's supervision.

The plot of *Stiffelio* was not an easy one for Italian audiences to understand or to believe: a priest with a wife, a husband who thinks it Christian to forgive marital infidelity—these were stumbling-blocks in the way of their enjoyment of Verdi's excellent score. There were censorship difficulties as well. A scene in the church in which the clergyman quotes the New Testament was regarded as blasphemous, and was severely mutilated; and, in the penultimate scene, Lina's addressing

---

[1] Abbiati, Vol II, p. 61.   [2] Monaldi: Second edition, p. 119.
[3] Abbiati, Vol. II, p. 49.

her husband as "ministro", and confessing to him as a priest was not allowed. The opera was quite well received in Trieste, the theatre was sold out for several performances, three of which omitted the offending third act, and most of the numbers were enthusiastically applauded. A critic wrote: "This is a work at once religious and philosophical, in which sweet and tender melodies follow one another in the most attractive manner, and which achieves . . . the most moving dramatic effects without having recourse to bands on the stage, choruses or superhuman demands on vocal cords or lungs."[1] It was, in fact, to a certain degree an extension of Verdi's *Luisa Miller* manner. That, although it was produced in Rome and Florence within months of its première, it did not catch on is surely due to the unsuitability of its libretto. In Rome and Florence, and within the following four years in Catania, Palermo and Naples, the opera was staged as *Guglielmo Wellingrode*, to comply with censorship requirements. The character of Wellingrode was not a parson, but the prime minister of a German principality, and the action was moved back to the beginning of the fifteenth century.

In the course of time, Verdi obviously came to feel that *Stiffelio/ Wellingrode* was being hampered by its libretto. At first, he had merely been concerned to see that *Stiffelio* was produced elsewhere without alterations. When, several weeks after the Trieste première, he heard that La Scala wanted to produce the opera, he wrote to Giovanni Ricordi:

> If it absolutely must be given, the censors must convince themselves that the libretto contains nothing offensive to politics or religion. They should leave the libretto as it is, with all the text and its requisite staging intact. Nothing should be changed, nothing emasculated, and everyone should endeavour to do his best for it. It should be especially observed that the effect of the final scene depends on how the chorus is arranged on the stage. There must be, not just the usual single stage rehearsal, but ten or, if necessary, twenty. Unless these conditions are met, I cannot permit *Stiffelio* to be given at La Scala. And remember that if it should fail of its effect through poor performance, I shall hold you, Signor Giovanni Ricordi, responsible for any damage which may result. Farewell. Farewell. P.S. I cannot possibly come to Milan to stage *Stiffelio*.[2]

In 1854, Verdi wrote to Cesare de Sanctis: "Among my operas which are not in circulation, there are some I must forget about, because their subjects were at fault. But there are two I should not like to be forgotten: they are *Stiffelio* and *La battaglia di Legnano*."[3] He went on to say that he had already written to Piave about *Stiffelio*. And two years later, in March 1856, after he had returned from the première of *Les Vêpres siciliennes* in Paris, and while engaged in negotiations with the

---

[1] *Gazzetta Musicale*, 4.12.1850.   [2] *Copialettere*, p. 112.
[3] *Carteggi Verdiani*, Vol. I, p. 25.

San Carlo Theatre over the possibility of writing *Il re Lear* for them, Verdi called Piave to Sant' Agata to confer about fitting a new libretto to the music of *Stiffelio*. Piave's suggestion was to alter the setting to a medieval period and make Stiffelio a Crusader. But "I've already told you I don't want to make Stiffelio a Crusader. Something newer and more exciting. Think about it,"[1] commanded the composer. Piave held out for his Crusaders, and the eventual result was *Aroldo*, whose leading character is an English Crusader.

Aroldo was the inaugural production of the new opera house a Rimini, on August 16, 1857. Verdi and Piave themselves supervised the production, and Angelo Mariani, who was beginning to make a name for himself as an interpreter of Verdi, was the conductor. Piave accepted the lavish hospitality offered by the citizens of Rimini, but Verdi, who was accompanied by Giuseppina, preferred to stay at a hotel.

> Accompanied by Piave, he visited the tailor to examine the costumes, which he ordered to be made and re-made, being always hard to please. The sociable librettist chatted with the women in the establishment and told them risqué stories, at one of which the usually gloomy and sulky Verdi smiled broadly. . . . At rehearsals, which he attended regularly, nothing escaped his hawk-like attention. The village bell that was to sound the Ave Maria in Act IV of *Aroldo* was out of tune, and Verdi worked on it with a file until he obtained the right note.[2]

At one rehearsal, when Mariani was haranguing the orchestra for being unable to play the storm music as he wanted it, Verdi listened silently for some time, then finally approached the conductor and told him not to persist, but to proceed with the next number. After the rehearsal, when Mariani protested that he would eventually have got the orchestra to play it properly, Verdi smiled and pointed out that it was not the fault of the players—the orchestration was quite wrong, and he intended to re-do it overnight.

Aroldo was less of a success than *Stiffelio*, though this fact was at first obscured by the excitement in the town over the opening of the new theatre, and the presence of Italy's most famous composer.

> Rimini was crowded with visitors. Expectation ran high. Portraits of Verdi appeared in shop windows, on walls, in the windows of houses everywhere. Epigraphs were written in praise of Italy's genius. The brilliant Overture was the most popular number in the score, but the rest of the opera failed to excite the audience. Discreet applause greeted the last notes of this "warmed-up *Stiffelio*" as it was called, and everyone preferred the old version in which there was at least more sincerity, a more coherent style, and more expression and inspiration.[3]

[1] *Copialettere*, p. 185.
[2] Girolamo Bottoni, *Giuseppe Verdi a Rimini* (Rimini, 1913), p. 69.
[3] Op. cit., p. 74.

Until recently, it was as *Aroldo*, rather than as *Stiffelio*, that the opera survived, and even then, only just. After years of neglect, *Aroldo* was broadcast in Italy in 1951, the fiftieth anniversary of Verdi's death, and since then it has been performed in Florence, Trieste, Wupperthal, Hamburg, Karlsruhe, Wexford, London and New York. But a production of *Stiffelio* by the Teatro Regio, Parma, in December 1968 proved the opera to be perfectly viable in its original form. There seems now no reason why it should not be performed in addition to *Aroldo*.

II

The authors of *Le Pasteur*, Souvestre and Bourgeois, were minor French romantics. Bourgeois is completely forgotten today, and Souvestre (1806–54) is known, if at all, chiefly for his writings about his native Brittany and its customs. The *Biographie Nationale Française* accuses his work of a tendency towards "une sorte de prédication morale" and says that his plays, "languissants et ternes", have fallen into oblivion.

Le Pasteur appears to have had more success in its Italian translation, *Stiffelius*, than in France. It was hardly noticed when it opened in Paris. The *Journal des Débats*[1] was kind ("C'était une de ces compositions heureuses qui s'adresse de préférence aux gens honnêtes, aux imaginations innocentes, aux cœurs fidèles"), but *Le Pasteur* was unable to compete with the rival attractions of Edouard Mazères and Eugène Scribe.

The characters, if not the events, of *Le Pasteur* were to some extent based on real life. In the play, Pastor Müller assumes the name of Stiffelius. In fact, a Protestant preacher named Stiffelius flourished around 1816 in Hemsdorf, near Dresden, and was one of the circle of a famous divine, Professor Müller. Piave did not set the earlier acts of the play. When the curtain rises on *Stiffelio*, much has already taken place: Müller, the leader of a German Protestant sect called Assassverians,[2] has had to flee from his home to avoid being persecuted for his religious ideas. He has found refuge at the castle (on the bank of the "Salzbach" river) of Count Stankar, an elderly colonel and member of his sect, and has assumed the pseudonym of Stiffelio. He has also fallen in love with, and married, the Colonel's daughter Lina. For a time he had to leave the castle on business of the faith, and during his absence Lina succumbed to the advances of a young nobleman, Raffaele di Leuthold. The opera begins at the moment of Stiffelio's return to the castle.

Until their final scenes (*Stiffelio*'s Act III, Scene 2, and *Aroldo*'s Act IV), the operas' plots are identical. Here, briefly, is the story of

---

[1] On February 19, 1849.

[2] The "Ashaverien" sect is an invention of the authors of *Le Pasteur*. Presumably the name derives from Ahasuerus, the wandering Jew, a figure frequently met with in nineteenth-century literature. Wagner's Kundry is his female equivalent.

Stiffelio. In Act I, Scene 1, set in a room in the castle, the elderly minister Jorg has been reading a copy of Klopstock's *Messias* while he awaits the return of Stiffelio, who arrives with Lina and some of the guests including Lina's lover Raffaele. Stiffelio tells how a sailor handed him a wallet which had been dropped by a young man the sailor had espied at dawn with a lady at a window of the castle overlooking the river. The guilty lovers tremble, but Stiffelio magnanimously flings the wallet into the fire without having examined it. Old Stankar, however, is aroused to suspicion by the narrative. Other guests, members of Stiffelio's sect, arrive. When Lina and Stiffelio are finally alone, Lina is overcome with remorse at having been unfaithful to him and comes near to revealing her guilt. Stiffelio leaves the room, and she begins a letter of confession. She is interrupted by her father, Stankar, who forbids her to stain the family honour by telling her husband the truth. Lina reluctantly agrees. After she and Stankar have left the room, Raffaele enters and, observed by Jorg, hides a letter to Lina within the pages of the Klopstock volume. A moment later, Lina's cousin Federico enters and borrows the volume.

The scene changes to a large hall of the castle where a reception is being held to welcome Stiffelio's return. When Jorg reveals what he has seen, Stiffelio seizes the book from Federico, whom he suspects of being his wife's lover, and breaks the clasp. The letter falls out, but Stankar retrieves it and refuses to give it to Stiffelio. In the ensuing ensemble, Stankar invites Raffaele to meet him in the churchyard and fight a duel.

Act II is set in the cemetery adjoining the church. Lina enters and prays at the tomb of her mother. When Raffaele arrives and speaks of his love for her, she tells him she regrets their liaison and asks him to return to her a ring she had given him, as well as her letters. Raffaele refuses. Stankar enters, carrying two swords, and challenges Raffaele to fight. The noise of fighting brings Stiffelio to the scene, and he interrupts the duel. But when he greets Raffaele warmly, Stankar in a rage reveals that Raffaele has been his betrayer. At this, Stiffelio himself attacks Raffaele, but is stopped by the sound of voices from the nearby church. Jorg enters, calling on Stiffelio to pardon his wife. Torn between the demands of his blood and of his conscience, Stiffelio swoons on the steps of the church.

The first scene of Act III takes place in a room in the castle. Fearing that Lina may have fled with Raffaele, Stankar contemplates suicide. However, when Jorg informs him that Raffaele has returned to the castle, he is overcome with joy at the thought that he will again be able to challenge him. He leaves the room, and Stiffelio enters with Raffaele, whom he asks to wait in an adjoining room while he speaks to his wife. Lina enters, and Stiffelio gives her documents of divorce to sign. He will dedicate himself henceforth to God, she to the man her heart has chosen. Lina is reluctant to sign, but Stiffelio insists. Stankar re-enters, his sword stained with blood. He has killed Raffaele and avenged the honour of his family.

The final scene takes place in church. The congregation, including Lina and Stankar, has assembled, and Stiffelio enters the pulpit. Opening the Bible, he reads from the New Testament story of Christ and the woman taken in adultery. When he reaches the passage in which Christ pardons the woman, he is moved to forgive Lina.

Stiffelio was in three Acts. Act III of *Aroldo* breaks off before the final scene of forgiveness in Stiffelio's church and substitutes an improbable Act IV, set, some time later, on the banks of Loch Lomond or, as Piave will have it, "Lago Loomond". His earlier acts have taken place in the county of Kenth [*sic*] or, to quote the libretto again, "la dimora d'Egberto presso Kenth", Egberto's castle *near* Kent!

At the beginning of Act I of *Aroldo*, a banquet is being held to celebrate the return of Egberto's son-in-law, Aroldo, from Palestine, where he has taken part in the Crusade. Mina, Egberto's daughter and Aroldo's wife, enters the empty drawing-room, in a state of guilty agitation. During her husband's absence, she has been unfaithful to him with Godvino, but she now regrets this, and prays for forgiveness. Aroldo enters with Briano, a holy man who had saved his life in Palestine and who now travels with him as a kind of spiritual adviser. Briano leaves the husband and wife together, and Aroldo tells Mina that he thought of her constantly while he was away, which merely increases her feelings of guilt and shame. Aroldo notices that she is no longer wearing the ring his mother had given her. She can hardly explain why, for she has given it to Godvino. Briano returns and takes Aroldo off to join the celebrations, while Mina, left alone, decides to write a letter of confession to her husband. She is engaged in doing this when her father Egberto enters. He reads the letter and dissuades her from showing it to Aroldo, asserting that the shock of learning that his wife had committed adultery would kill him.

The second scene of Act I takes place in a big hall in the castle. Knights and their ladies are sauntering about, but the hall is momentarily empty when Godvino enters with a letter he has written to Mina, who has, of late, been avoiding him. He leaves the letter in a huge locked book which lies on a table, and of which he has a key. He is observed by Briano, who thinks he recognises Godvino as a friend of Aroldo, but does not know his name. Other guests begin to appear, and when Aroldo, Mina and Egberto enter, Briano tells Aroldo what he has seen, but wrongly identifies the man who put the letter in the book as Enrico, Mina's cousin, who happens to be dressed like Godvino. Asked by the guests to relate the story of King Richard's exploits in

Palestine, Aroldo instead tells of the book and the letter. Seizing the book, he asks Mina to produce the key and, when she fails to do so, he breaks the lock. The letter falls out, but Egberto picks it up and, refusing to give it to Aroldo, tears it into pieces. During the ensemble which brings the act to an end, Egberto orders Godvino to meet him later in the graveyard.

Act II is set in the castle's ancient graveyard. On the right is a church, and to the left the castle can be seen in the distance. The moon is shining. As Mina is praying at her mother's tomb, Godvino enters and professes his love for her, but she denounces him, calling down the curses of her mother, whose tomb, she says, he desecrates. Egberto arrives carrying two swords, and challenges Godvino to defend himself. At first Godvino refuses, pleading Egberto's age as an excuse, but finally he is taunted into fighting. At this moment, Aroldo enters and orders them to cease their duel. When Aroldo greets Godvino in a friendly manner, Egberto in a fury reveals the truth about him and Mina. Aroldo invites Mina to deny the charge, but she cannot. He grabs Egberto's sword and is about to attack Godvino when Briano suddenly appears and reminds him that a Christian is bound to forgive his enemies.

Act III takes place in an ante-room in the castle. Godvino has fled, and Egberto, unable now to wipe out the stain on his family's honour, contemplates suicide. He is about to swallow the contents of his poisoned ring, when Briano enters to announce that Godvino has been captured and is being brought back to the castle. Egberto is overjoyed to think that he will again have a chance to fight Godvino. Swearing that one of them will not leave the castle alive, he rushes out. Aroldo and Godvino enter. Aroldo, after asking Godvino to decide whether he values more his own freedom or the future of the woman he has betrayed, orders him to wait in an adjoining room. He then sends for Mina and, when she enters, tells her he has arranged for a divorce. He hands her the separation agreement, which he has already signed, and insists that she too sign it. Heartbroken, Mina does so, and then declares her love for her husband. Suddenly Egberto enters with a blood-stained sword in his hand, having killed Godvino. Briano immediately appears and takes Aroldo off to the church to pray, while Mina begs heaven for forgiveness.

Act IV, which takes place some time later, is set in Scotland by the banks of Loch Lomond, near a modest hut in which Aroldo and Briano live in seclusion from the world. A chorus of shepherds and hunters is heard in the distance as the sun sets. As a village church bell sounds the Angelus, Aroldo and Briano kneel to pray, and then enter their hut. A fierce storm breaks out, during which a boat on the lake is driven ashore. Villagers rush to rescue the sailors, who are Egberto and Mina. Seeking shelter, they knock at the door of the hut, which is opened by

Aroldo. He attempts to drive Mina away, while Egberto exhorts him to be merciful and she begs for forgiveness. Again, Briano appears to remind Aroldo that only he who is without sin should cast the first stone. As though inspired by heaven, Aroldo forgives Mina. They embrace, and all exclaim that the divine law of love has triumphed.

III

The Overture to *Stiffelio* is pleasant and, in its latter stages, lively. The opening arioso for Jorg is simple and dignified, putting one in mind of Fiesco's utterance in the Prologue of *Simon Boccanegra* seven years later. In the ensemble which follows, with the entrance of Stiffelio and friends, Stiffelio's narrative is concise but unmemorable. The septet sounds better on stage than it looks on paper, but the stretta of the introduction, a chorus of welcome, is quite conventional. It is when Stiffelio and Lina are left alone on stage that Verdi begins to steep himself in the situation. The arioso passage in which Lina recalls fondly the name—Rodolfo Müller—by which she first knew Stiffelio is gently touching, and Stiffelio's aria, "Vidi dovunque gemere", with interjections from Lina, is free in form and generously melodic, though some of its 6/8 section, from "Ah no, il perdono è facile", is rather square and predictable. The grand tune of "Allor dunque sorridimi" is authentically Verdian, and the stretta which Stiffelio begins in a voice stifled with rage leads into a splendid trio-coda as Stankar enters to announce that they are awaited by their friends.

Lina's prayer, "A te ascenda", preceded by dramatic recitative, just misses being a really first-rate piece, though it is by no means ineffective in performance. The duet, "Dite che il fallo a tergere", is not one of Verdi's most perceptive baritone father-soprano daughter scenes, despite some fine phrases in the final *allegro assai moderato*, "Or meco venite". A brief scena in which Raffaele places his letter in the volume of Klopstock, which is then borrowed by Federico, brings the first scene to an end.[1]

Act I, Scene 2, of *Stiffelio* is, in fact, the finale of the act, consisting of an ensemble scene made up of four sections. The opening chorus is appropriately festive. The dramatic action is advanced in the next section, which leads into the third part, a *largo* ensemble with a typically Verdian swinging movement, and the fourth, a violent stretta, both of which are among the opera's most successful numbers. *Stiffelio*'s music in this scene is almost *Otello*-like in its force and intensity.

The two scenes of *Aroldo*'s Act I contain some music newly composed for the later version. The Overture remains basically the same with minor alterations and excisions; however the curtain goes up not on a

---

[1] The 1968 Parma production placed this episode before Lina's prayer, thus ending Act I, Scene 1, with the duet. This seemed to me an improvement.

solo bass scena, but on an off-stage festive chorus which makes an effective prelude to Mina's agitated recitative. Her expressive yet restrained prayer, "Salvami tu, gran Dio", replaces the prayer in *Stiffelio*. The vocal writing in "Salvami tu" is assured: the means are simple, the result suggests a richness of resources. In the next number, which is theoretically a cavatina and cabaletta for Aroldo, Verdi advances the dramatic action not in the recitative but within the melodic framework. Aroldo sings a tender *andante*, "Sotto il sole di Sina", about his longing for Mina while he was away. Then, for recitative and cabaletta Verdi substitutes a slightly faster, still lyrical section, which is "Allor dunque sorridimi" taken from the *Stiffelio* score. The duet in which Egberto forbids Mina to confess to Aroldo is "Dite che il fallo a tergere", which existed in the same form in *Stiffelio*.

The second scene of *Aroldo*'s Act I is virtually the same as *Stiffelio*'s, the differences being inconsequential. As in *Stiffelio*, a 3/4 version of a tune which occurs in common time in the overture is heard in the opening chorus.

Act II of *Stiffelio* opens with a darkly brooding, beautifully written orchestral introduction to Lina's scena and aria, "Ah! dagli scanni eterei". Her recitative is in Verdi's finest middle-period style, with the orchestra playing an important part in building up the atmosphere of the scene, and her superb aria is worthy of those other guilt-ridden Verdian heroines, Amelia, and the Leonora of *La forza del destino*. After her exchange with Raffaele, she sings an *allegro* cabaletta which is honestly constructed but not at all noteworthy. The duet between Stankar and Raffaele is not particularly interesting, but onward from Stiffelio's impassioned outburst, "Ah, era vero; ah, no! e impossibile" [Ex. 54], the vocal and orchestral writing is first-rate, and the quartet

Ex.54 *con disperazione* **Largo** ♩ = 56

Ah! e - ra   ve-ro?   Ah no   è im-pos-si-bi-le!   Che ho men-ti - to almen mi di-te

that follows is one of the highlights of the score. Jorg, the voice of Stiffelio's protestant conscience, intervenes, supported by a pious chorus, and the act ends quietly. Apart from an occasional alteration in recitative or cadenza, Act II of *Aroldo* utilises the *Stiffelio* music, with one important exception. The cabaletta to the aria, "Ah! dagli scanni eterei", now sung by Mina, is new. It begins with a gloomy minor section which is followed by a vigorous major conclusion.

Act III, Scene 1, of *Stiffelio* begins with Stankar's aria, preceded by a long and eloquent passage of recitative. The aria, "Lina, pensai che un angelo", is excellent, and its cabaletta, "Oh gioia inesprimibile", is one of the most imaginative Verdi ever wrote. Stankar is delighted that Raffaele has returned to the castle. He can hardly wait to avenge the

family honour. Verdi requires the baritone not to belt out the entire
cabaletta fortissimo, but to sing it, up to the concluding phrases,
"estremamente piano". The effect is tremendously exciting as Stankar,
"con voce soffocata e convulsa" (with a convulsed, suffocating voice),
whispers his way through the *allegro agitato*, with finally a diminuendo
and a vocal effect of being breathlessly overcome with joy [Ex. 55]

before suddenly launching into the final bars *tutta forza*. After a passage
in recitative the scene ends with a duet for Lina and Stiffelio, "Opposto
è il calle, che in avvenire", in which he insists on their divorce. Melodically prodigal and dramatically expressive, in feeling its first section is not
unlike the Violetta–Germont scene in Act II of *La traviata*. Its stretta is
crude but effective. The entire scene exists almost unchanged in *Aroldo*
as that opera's Act III, though not always in the same key.

It is in their respective final scenes (*Stiffelio*'s Act III, Scene 2,
Aroldo's Act IV) that the operas diverge. The final scene of *Stiffelio*, set
in the church, contains two numbers. The first, preceded by an organ
voluntary, is an *andante* prayer sung by the congregation, with separate
vocal lines for Lina and Stankar [Ex. 56]. It is followed by the brief

scena in which Stiffelio preaches the gospel story of the woman taken in
adultery, which he narrates in recitative. When he is suddenly moved
to forgive Lina, his voice rises from the narrative chant to his top A on
"perdonata". The congregation echoes him, Lina ecstatically thanks
God with her top C, and the curtain falls.

The fourth Act of *Aroldo*, the Loch Lomond Act, was newly composed. The opening chorus of huntsmen and shepherds is unexceptionable, nor is there much to be said for the "Angiol di Dio" chorus led by Aroldo and Briano, though this contains a clear reminiscence of the "Confido in te" ensemble from *Stiffelio* [Ex. 56]. But the storm music is marvellous. Chromatic passages in doubled thirds represent the wailing of the wind, and stark woodwind figures conjure up lightning. The chorus, not humming as in *Rigoletto*, but singing the vowel sound "ah" in addition to verbal interjections, contributes to a magnificent effect. The final trio, leading into a quartet when Briano appears and quotes the New Testament, just misses being one of Verdi's most successful and beautiful finales. It is too short, and does not avoid sounding perfunctory. But what there is of it can hardly be faulted.

Aroldo and *Stiffelio* are unjustly neglected works. The earlier opera makes the better dramatic sense, but one would not willingly consign the new Act IV of *Aroldo* to oblivion: there is a good case for refraining from making a choice between them. Both are anything but dull in performance, and *Stiffelio* marks another step, though perhaps a faltering one, on the domestic path that leads from *Luisa Miller* to *La traviata*.

XVI

Rigoletto

Dramatis personae:

The Duke of Mantua	(tenor)
Rigoletto, his jester, a hunchback	(baritone)
Sparafucile, a professional assassin	(bass)
Count Monterone	(baritone)
Marullo	(baritone)
Borsa	(tenor)
Count Ceprano	(bass)
An usher	(bass)
Gilda, Rigoletto's daughter	(soprano)
Giovanna, her nurse	(mezzo-soprano)
Maddalena, Sparafucile's sister	(contralto)
Countess Ceprano	(mezzo-soprano)
A page	(mezzo-soprano)

LIBRETTO by Francesco Maria Piave, based on the play *Le Roi s'amuse* by Victor Hugo

TIME: Sixteenth century
PLACE: Mantua

FIRST PERFORMED at the Teatro La Fenice, Venice, March 11, 1851, with Teresa Brambilla (Gilda); Annetta Casaloni (Maddalena); Raffaele Mirate (Duke); Felice Varesi (Rigoletto); Paolo Damini (Sparafucile); Feliciano Ponz (Monterone)

Rigoletto

I

SOME MONTHS BEFORE the première of *Stiffelio* in 1850, Verdi had been asked by the directors of the Fenice Theatre in Venice to write a new opera for the following carnival season. Having enjoyed his two earlier engagements in Venice with *Ernani* and *Attila*, he agreed to provide an opera for performance in February 1851, and began immediately to discuss possible subjects with Piave. It was in these circumstances that, as related in the previous chapter, Verdi urged Piave to look at *El Trovador* and Hugo's *Le Roi s'amuse*. He also drew the librettist's attention to *Kean* by the elder Dumas, a play about the amorous exploits of the great English actor, Edmund Kean. Eventually, *Le Roi s'amuse* was decided upon: Verdi called it "one of the greatest subjects and perhaps the greatest drama of modern times." "Tribolet", he said, "is a creation worthy of Shakespeare."[1] Tribolet is the hunchback jester in Hugo's play who was to become Verdi's Rigoletto.

Piave blithely assured Verdi that the Austrian censors would not object to the subject, and set to work on his libretto. It must therefore have been something of a shock to them both when, a mere three months before the proposed date of the opening night, the management of the Fenice Theatre received the following communication from the Austrian authorities:

His Excellency the Military Governor Chevalier Gorzkowski in his respected despatch of the 26th instant N.731, directs me to communicate to you his profound regret that the poet Piave and the celebrated maestro Verdi should not have chosen a more worthy vehicle to display their talents than the revolting immorality and obscene triviality of the libretto of *La maledizione* submitted to us for intended performance at the Teatro Fenice.

His above mentioned Excellency has decided that the performance shall be absolutely forbidden, and wishes me at the same time to request you not to make further enquiries in this matter. I am returning the manuscript sent to me with your accompanying letter of the 20th instant. N.18.

> The Imperial and Royal Central Director,
> Martello[2]

---

[1] Letter to Piave. Abbiati, Vol. II, p. 62.   [2] *Copialettere*, p. 487.

However, further enquiries were made. In fact the discussion continued for several weeks during which Verdi stayed put in Busseto, awaiting the outcome. It is hardly surprising that the censorship authorities objected to a story which showed a reigning monarch as debauched and conscienceless, which offended religious proprieties by displaying the working out of a curse, and which was, by the standards of the time, immoral and obscene. It is almost as though, today, Henze had decided to put Apollinaire's *The Debauched Hospodar* on to the lyric stage. Hugo's play had created a scandal on its opening night in Paris in 1832, and had been banned after its first performance for, according to Hugo, political reasons. But Verdi was determined to fight for the subject on which, by this time, he had done so much work. From Busseto, he wrote defending his choice. Piave had compliantly re-cast the libretto along the lines now required by the censors, but Verdi rejected this revised version:

I have had very little time to examine the new libretto. But I have seen enough to know that in this form it lacks character and meaning, and the dramatic points have all been nullified. If the names of the characters had to be changed, then the scene of action should also have been changed, with a prince or duke of some other locality, for instance a Pier Luigi Farnese, or else place the action further back before Louis XI, when France was not yet a united kingdom, and have a Duke of Burgundy or Normandy. In any case an absolute ruler. In the fifth scene of Act I, the courtiers' fury at Triboletto doesn't make sense. The old man's curse, so terrifying and sublime in the original, is made ridiculous here, for the motive that drives him to utter the curse no longer has the same force, and he no longer addresses his king so daringly. Without this curse, what point or sense is left to the drama? The Duke becomes a cipher, but it is essential that he should be a libertine. Otherwise there is no reason for Triboletto's fear that his daughter will emerge from her hiding-place, and the entire drama is impossible. Why should the Duke go, in the last Act, to a remote tavern, alone, unless he has had an invitation to a rendezvous? I don't understand why the sack has been eliminated. What difference does a sack make to the police? Are they afraid it won't be effective? But let me ask this: why do they think they know more about it than I do? Who can be sure? Who can say this will work and that will not? We had the same difficulty with the horn in *Ernani*. Well, did anyone laugh at the horn? If there is no sack, it is improbable that Triboletto would talk to the body for half an hour without a flash of lightning revealing it to be his daughter's. Finally, I note that Triboletto is not to be ugly or a hunchback. Why? A singing hunchback? Why not? Will it be effective? I don't know. But if I don't know, neither does the person who proposed these changes. In my view, the idea of this character, outwardly ridiculous and deformed, inwardly filled with passion and love, is superb. It was precisely because of these original and characteristic traits that I chose the subject, and if they are cut out I shall not be able to write the music. If I am told that my music will do just as well for this drama as for the other, I must answer that I don't understand such reasoning. I tell you frankly that my music, whether good or bad, is never fortuitous, and that I always try to give it a distinct character. In short, an original and powerful drama has been turned into something completely ordinary and uninteresting. I much regret that the Board did not answer my last letter. I can only repeat what I said in it, that my artistic conscience will not allow me to set this libretto to music.[1]

Eventually, a compromise was arrived at which satisfied Verdi, by which the situations in Hugo's play were, for the most part, left intact, only the locale and the names of the characters being changed. Verdi, Piave and Guglielmo Brenna, the Secretary of the Fenice Theatre, drew up a document in Busseto, "at the residence of Maestro Giuseppe Verdi", on December 30, 1850, setting out the agreed changes:

In accordance with the contract received on 27th December from the President of the Board of Management of the Teatro La Fenice, the undersigned Secretary of the President invites Maestro Verdi to specify the changes which he consents to make in the libretto submitted under the title of *La maledizione*, in order that this libretto may be composed for the current season, Carnival and Lent, 1850–51, according to the contract of April 23rd. The changes are made in order to remove the objections which the State authorities place in the way of its performance.

In consultation therefore, with the poet Francesco Maria Piave, the following is agreed:

1. The scene shall be changed from the French court to that of an independent Duke of Burgundy or Normandy, or to the court of a minor absolutist Italian state, preferably that of Pier Luigi Farnese, and in the period most suitable for scenic and dramatic effect.

2. The original characters of the drama *Le Roi s'amuse* by Victor Hugo shall be retained, but other names shall be found for them, dependent on the period chosen.

3. The scene in which Francesco appears determined to use the key in his possession to enter the room of the abducted Bianca shll be omitted. It shall be replaced by another, which preserves the decencies, but does not detract from the interest of the play.

4. The King or Duke shall come to the rendezvous in Magellona's tavern as the result of a pretended invitation brought to him by the Triboletto character.

5. In the scene in which the sack containing the corpse of Triboletto's daughter appears, Maestro Verdi reserves to himself the right to make such changes as he considers necessary.

6. The above mentioned changes require more time than was originally supposed. Therefore Maestro Verdi declares the new opera cannot be performed before February 28th or March 1st.

Accordingly, this document has been signed and agreed upon by those present: G. Verdi. F. M. Piave. G. Brenna, Secretary.[2]

[1] *Copialettere*, pp. 109–11.   [2] *Copialettere*, pp. 489–90.

The jester's name was changed from Triboletto to Rigoletto, from the French "rigoler", to guffaw, and this also became the title of the opera. Verdi is said to have completed his score in forty days, but it had been in his head for most of the preceding year, and parts of the music had already been written down.

Rigoletto was an enormous success at its first performance on March 11, 1851, and it has continued to be an enormous success ever since, triumphing over haphazard production, inelegant singing, and cliché-ridden conducting. Soon after its Venice première, the opera was being played all over Italy, though in order to get past the various local censors it was produced under a variety of names, among them *Viscardello*, *Clara di Perth* and *Lionello*. In its first Paris season, *Rigoletto* was performed over one hundred times. Victor Hugo resented its popularity, but when he finally heard the opera he was forced to admit its greatness. Of the famous quartet, he exclaimed: "If I could only make four characters in my plays speak at the same time, and have the audience grasp the words and sentiments, I would obtain the very same effect."[1]

II

Rigoletto is in three acts, of which the first has two scenes. Act I, Scene 1, is set in a magnificent hall of the Ducal Palace in Mantua. Doors at the back open into other rooms, all of which are splendidly lit. An elegant assembly of courtiers and ladies moves through the rooms, pages come and go, there is a general air of festivity. From off-stage come the sounds of dance music and occasional laughter. The Duke of Mantua enters with one of his courtiers, Borsa, and strolls through the crowd talking of the beautiful girl he has been pursuing, incognito, for the past three months. He first saw her in church, and has followed her to her home, a small house in a dark, narrow lane. A mysterious man, the Duke has noticed, visits her there every evening. At this point in his narrative, a group of women crosses his field of vision, and the Duke's attention is diverted from his story of the beautiful commoner. He praises the beauty of the Countess Ceprano, and when Borsa warns him not to let Count Ceprano overhear him, the Duke expounds his philosophy that one pretty woman is the same as any other. Today this one pleases him, tomorrow that. He dances with the Countess Ceprano, to the annoyance of her husband. Rigoletto, the hunchbacked court jester enters and taunts Ceprano, implying that the Duke is enjoying the favours of the Countess. The Duke and the Countess wander off to an adjoining room, and Rigoletto follows them. Another courtier, Marullo, enters to tell the others he has discovered that old Rigoletto has a mistress whom he visits every night. This occasions great merriment. The Duke and Rigoletto return, and the Duke

[1] Abbiati, Vol. II, p. 111.

mutters to him that though the Countess Ceprano is adorable, her husband is in the way. The malevolent Rigoletto banteringly suggests prison, exile or execution for the Count, a remark which that gentleman overhears. All the courtiers have at one time or another suffered from Rigoletto's tongue; so, when Ceprano asks them to meet him later that evening to plan revenge on the hunchback, they readily agree. Suddenly a voice outside is heard demanding admittance. It is that of Count Monterone, who bursts in to confront the Duke who has seduced his daughter. Rigoletto makes fun of the old man, and, when Monterone continues to denounce him, the Duke has him arrested. As Monterone is being led off to prison, he curses both Duke and jester. Rigoletto is terrified.

The second scene of Act I is so arranged that one sees both the courtyard of Rigoletto's house and the lane on the other side of its wall. In the courtyard are a large tree and a marble seat. A door in the wall leads into the lane, and above the wall is the balcony of the house, connected with the courtyard by a staircase. On the other side of the lane can be seen the wall of Ceprano's palace. It is night. Rigoletto, a cloak wrapped around him, comes along the lane, followed by a man who now introduces himself as Sparafucile, a professional assassin, and offers his services at reasonable charges. He tells Rigoletto that outside the town he keeps an inn, to which his victims are lured by his young sister. Rigoletto says he has no present need for his services, but makes a point of asking how he can be found. When Sparafucile has departed, Rigoletto soliloquises on the similarity between himself and the assassin. Both are paid to wound, one with his tongue, the other with his sword. He curses the fate that brought him into the world deformed, and expresses his loathing for the courtiers. He keeps remembering the old man's curse, but, shaking off his disturbed mood, he enters the courtyard of his house and greets his daughter, Gilda. He enjoins upon her that she must never leave the house on her own, for he is fearful that she will fall a victim to one of the courtiers. Gilda asks her father why he never mentions their family name, or her mother, and Rigoletto can only reply: "Ah, don't speak to a miserable man of his lost happiness." He calls Gilda's nurse, Giovanna, and reminds her to watch carefully over his beloved child. Thinking he hears a noise outside, he rushes into the street. As he does so, the Duke slips into the courtyard, noticed only by Giovanna, to whom he throws a purse, and hides behind the tree. Rigoletto, having assured himself that no one is loitering outside, returns to say goodnight to Gilda. He addresses her as daughter, which surprises the Duke. When her father has gone, Gilda confesses to Giovanna her remorse at not having confided to him that she has frequently been followed by the handsome young man she saw in church. She murmurs to herself that she loves him and, as she utters the phrase, the Duke steps out from his hiding-place and repeats it.

They sing a love duet, and he tells her he is Gualtier Maldè, a poor student. Footsteps are heard in the street outside and, fearful that it may be her father returning, Gilda insists that the young man leave. After he has gone, she repeats his name tenderly to herself, sings of her love for him and goes into the house. The voices she had heard outside were those of the courtiers who, all of them masked, have assembled to take their revenge on Rigoletto. The jester returns, and they persuade him that their intention is to abduct Ceprano's wife from the palace opposite and take her to the Duke. Rigoletto agrees to join them and allows them to bandage his eyes. He holds the ladder for them as they climb over his own wall, enter his house and carry off Gilda. Finding himself alone, he becomes suspicious and, tearing off the bandage, rushes into his house to find his daughter gone. The old man's curse is working out.

The second act takes place in a drawing-room in the Ducal Palace. On the walls are full-length paintings of the Duke and the Duchess, and the furniture includes a large chair near a velvet-covered table. The Duke enters in a state of agitation: he has returned to Rigoletto's house to find it deserted. Certain that Gilda has been abducted, he is torn between rage that anyone should dare so to cross him and pity for the girl who, he says, has awakened for the first time feelings of constancy and affection in his heart. Marullo, Ceprano, Borsa and the other courtiers enter and gleefully narrate their adventures of the previous night when, with his unwitting collaboration, they had stolen the girl they believed to be Rigoletto's mistress. Realising that they are referring to Gilda, the Duke is delighted when they inform him they have brought her to the palace. He rushes off, intending to console her and tell her that he loves her. A moment later, the grief-stricken Rigoletto enters, attempting to conceal his distress beneath his usual banteringly cynical manner. He looks about uncertainly for clues, even snatching up a handkerchief from the table in the hope that it may be Gilda's. He asks for the Duke, and is told he is still asleep. But when a page enters to say that the Duchess wishes to speak to her husband, the courtiers pretend that he has gone hunting. Rigoletto suddenly realizes the Duke must be with Gilda. The courtiers tell him to look for his mistress somewhere else, but, with a cry of "Io vo' mia figlia" (I want my daughter), he turns on the astonished but not noticeably abashed assembly, alternately threatening and pleading with them. Suddenly, Gilda runs in and throws herself into her father's arms. Overjoyed that she is safe, Rigoletto is willing to believe the escapade was nothing but a harmless joke, until Gilda's tears and obvious shame convince him the matter is more serious. "Let me blush before you alone," Gilda says, and her father orders the courtiers to leave them. When they are alone, Gilda confesses that she had been attracted by a young man whom she had seen at church and who followed her home. When she was kidnapped she was brought to the Palace, where, she implies, she has just been raped by him. As Rigoletto attempts to comfort her, Monterone crosses the room, under guard, on his way to prison. He pauses before the Duke's portrait to exclaim

Poichè fosti invano da me maledetto,
Nè un fulmine o un ferro colpiva il tuo petto,
Felice pur anco, o Duca, vivrai.

(Since I have cursed you in vain, and no thunderbolt or sword has struck you down, you live happily still, o Duke.)

As Monterone is led out, Rigoletto calls after him that he is mistaken, and that he will be avenged. He then swears a terrible vengeance on the Duke, while Gilda in vain tries to counsel forgiveness so that they too may be forgiven by heaven.

Act III takes place outside the town, on the right bank of the Mincio, near a dilapidated two-storeyed house, Sparafucile's inn. One can see, on the ground floor, a room used for drinking and public entertaining, with a narrow staircase leading to an attic with a bed and an unshut-tered balcony. A door in the ground-floor room leads outside to the river bank. It is night. Sparafucile sits at a table polishing his belt. Outside, watching through a chink in the wall, are Rigoletto and Gilda. Gilda has told her father that she is still in love with the Duke, and that she believes he really returns her love. Rigoletto has brought her here to prove that her lover is worthless and inconstant. He tells her to wait and watch, and soon she sees the Duke enter the inn from another door, and hears him order some wine and a room for the night. He sings a cynical song about the fickleness of women and the inadvisability of believing or loving them. Sparafucile brings a bottle and two glasses, and knocks on the ceiling with his sword, which is the signal for his sister Maddalena to appear. At this, a young girl in gypsy attire runs down the stairs. The Duke rushes to embrace her, but she laughs and skips away from him. While they are engaged in this preliminary sex-play, Sparafucile goes outside to Rigoletto, whom he has been expecting, and, taking him aside so that Gilda shall not hear, asks if he has decided whether the man is to live or to die. Rigoletto promises to return later and let him know. Sparafucile exits behind the house, and Gilda and Rigoletto remains outside while the Duke flirts with Madda-lena in the tavern. Gilda, disillusioned and heart-broken, is persuaded by her father to return home, dress in male attire, and set out on horse-back for Verona, whither her father will follow the next day. When she pleads with him to come now, he says that he cannot: there is some-thing he still must do. Gilda goes, and Rigoletto disappears behind the house, returning with Sparafucile and counting out money, which he hands over, promising to pay the remainder when the job is done. It is arranged that he is to return at midnight to collect the body. Sparafucile casually asks the victim's name, to which Rigoletto's splendidly extravagant reply is

> Vuoi saper anche il mio?
> Egli è *Delitto, Punizion* son io.

(Do you want to know my name as well? His is crime, and mine is punishment.)

This is not Piave's invention, but an exact translation of Hugo's

> Veux-tu savoir le mien également?
> Il s'appelle le crime, et moi le châtiment.

Rigoletto departs, a storm begins to brew, the Duke arranges to spend the night with Maddalena and is shown up to his room. Attracted by the handsome young stranger, Maddalena attempts to dissuade her brother from murdering him. But Sparafucile does not understand this sentiment: after all, the sum of twenty crowns is at stake. "Why not kill the old hunchback instead, and still take the money?" Maddalena suggests, thus offending her brother's professional honour. One does not murder one's own clients, Sparafucile points out. At this moment Gilda reappears outside, dressed in male riding clothes. She approaches the inn and overhears the brother and sister arguing over which of the two shall die, her lover or her father. Sparafucile offers his sister a compromise: if, before Rigoletto's return at midnight, another stranger should chance to call at the inn, he will be murdered. Otherwise, Maddalena's handsome young man must die. Maddalena fears that so late on such a stormy night, no one is likely to arrive. She weeps, and Gilda, touched by her sympathy for the Duke, resolves to give her own life for him. Summoning up her courage, she knocks at the door calling, "Have pity on a beggar who wants shelter for the night." Sparafucile takes his dagger and stands behind the door, which Maddalena opens after having extinguished the light. In the darkness Gilda screams "God forgive them", and then all is silent.

A few moments later, Rigoletto returns. The violence of the storm lessens, midnight strikes, and Sparafucile comes out of the inn dragging a sack which, he says, contains the dead body Rigoletto has asked for. He offers to throw it into the river, but the hunchback prefers to give himself that satisfaction. Sparafucile disappears, but, as Rigoletto is about to push the sack into the river, he hears in the distance the Duke's voice singing his song about the fickleness of women. He opens the sack, and a flash of lightning clearly reveals Gilda's face. She is still alive, but dies in his arms, asking for his blessing. Rigoletto remembers Monterone. "Ah, la maledizione," he cries.

Apart from altering the locale from Paris in the 1520s to Mantua in an unspecified period in the same century, and turning François I, Triboulet, Blanche, M. de Saint-Vallier, Saltabadil and the other characters respectively into the Duke of Mantua, Rigoletto, Gilda, Count Monterone, Sparafucile and so on, Piave and Verdi closely followed Hugo. In the play several characters, including the King, bear historical names. François I was, apparently, as black as Hugo painted him, but Diane de Poitiers, the seduced daughter of M. de Saint-Vallier, was not exactly snow-white in her purity. Verdi and Piave were not allowed by the military censors to set the scene in the play in which Blanche is brought before the King whom she is astonished to find is her young admirer. The King laughs at her plight, offers to make her his official mistress and, when she runs off into another room to escape from him, takes out a key, follows her in and locks the door, the poor girl having chosen to seek sanctuary in, of all places, the King's own bedroom. With the exception of this scene, however, composer and librettist were extremely faithful to the original. Piave's Italian is, for the most part, a direct, though necessarily abridged, translation of Hugo. Rigoletto's magnificent soliloquy in Act I, Scene ii, for instance,

> Pari siamo! Io la lingua, egli ha il pugnale;
> L'uomo son io che ride, ei quel che spegne!

to which Verdi's music gives a truly Shakespearian stature, exists in the same form in *Le Roi s'amuse*:

> Nous sommes tous les deux à la même hauteur.
> Une langue acérée, une lame pointue.
> Je suis l'homme qui rit, il est l'homme qui tue.

(We are alike, I with my tongue, he with his dagger. I am the man who laughs, he the one who kills.)

The only noticeable difference between play and opera occurs in the very last scene, where Piave and Verdi are a distinct improvement upon Hugo. In the play, a crowd gathers around Rigoletto and Gilda's corpse, and the half-crazed father enacts a scene of distracted grief with the onlookers. A doctor pushes his way through the crowd, examines Gilda, and announces in clinical, almost Büchner-like language:

Elle est morte.
Elle a dans le flanc gauche une plaie assez forte.
Le sang a dû causer la mort en l'étouffant.

(She's dead. She has a very deep wound in her left side. The flowing of the blood caused death by suffocation.)

Triboulet falls senseless, after a cry of "J'ai tué mon enfant" (I have killed my child). But the opera's scene for father and daughter alone, with its last line recalling Monterone's curse both verbally and musically, is formally more satisfying, and certainly more in accord with the mood of both play and opera.

III

Rigoletto is undoubtedly one of Verdi's masterpieces: even those critics who would consign the pre-*Rigoletto* works to oblivion are agreed on this. It also marks the beginning of his second or middle period. As I have stressed earlier, Verdi was in no sense a conscious innovator. Or, if he was conscious of the significance for Italian opera and for opera in general of what he was doing, he chose not to draw attention to the fact. Unlike certain avant garde artists of our own age whose creative work seems merely an unnecessary adjunct to their theorising, Verdi was content to leave the theoretical justification to others. He was a creator, not a theorist. In *Rigoletto* he continued the process he can be seen to have begun in the last act of *Luisa Miller*: a move towards opening the closed forms of nineteenth-century Italian opera. He continued basically to write his operas in separate numbers, but with so flexible an approach that, as with Wagner, it is not always easy to tell where one number ends or the next begins. Now completely confident of his gifts, he moves with arrogant ease from number to number, linking them not by the jerky recitative and contrived situations of the past, but in whatever way he chooses. Sometimes his most beautiful inventions will occur in what used to be the no-man's-land between the end of an aria and the beginning of an ensemble. Sometimes, as in *Rigoletto*, he will almost by-pass the aria altogether and conceive the work as a series of duets.

The first three operas of Verdi's middle period—*Rigoletto*, *La traviata* and *Il trovatore*—are, as the popular guides to opera point out, "treasure houses of glorious melody", but they are something more than that: they are a practical demonstration of Verdi's utter lack of subservience to the formal patterns frequently accepted by Rossini, Donizetti and Bellini (though the evidence of Bellini's last opera, *I Puritani*, suggests that he intended to move in the direction Verdi was to take). Where he continued to find these forms of use, Verdi employed them: *Il trovatore*, for instance, is more the apotheosis of *Oberto* than the adumbration of *Otello*. But Verdi had won through to an ability to use, to create, form rather than be used by it. From then on, he was completely master of the situation.

To emphasise the technical innovation in *Rigoletto*, however, is to do the opera an injustice. What is remarkable about the work is its sustained level of inspiration. As in its companion operas, *La traviata* and *Il trovatore*, an uncanny psychological acumen is allied with a wonderfully spontaneous outpouring of melody, a gift shared only by Mozart and Schubert.

In *Rigoletto*, Verdi's working unit is no longer the aria, but the scene. In replying to the husband of Teresa De Giuli-Borsi, the soprano who was to sing Gilda in the Rome production, and who wanted him to insert a new aria for her, Verdi wrote:

> If *Rigoletto* can stand on its feet as it is, any new number would be superfluous. And where would it be put? Words and music can be written, but would make no effect without the right time and place . . . As to "Caro nome", I do not understand what you mean by its "agility". Perhaps you have not understood the tempo, which should be *allegretto molto lento*. At a moderate pace, and sung throughout in a quiet *sotto voce*, it should not be difficult. But to return to the first question, let me add that my intention was that *Rigoletto* should be one long series of duets, without arias and finales, because that is how I felt it. If anyone replies, "But you could have done this or that or the other," I can only say, "That may be, but I did not know how to do any better."[1]

It is true that *Rigoletto* does not contain anything like the typically Verdian ensembles in *Macbeth* in the past, or *Traviata*, *Un ballo in maschera* or *Otello* in the future (and the four titles I have chosen as examples demonstrate that Verdi felt free to return to the huge ensemble, if he felt it necessary, at every stage of his career). And it is also true that the backbone of *Rigoletto* is the series of duets between Rigoletto and Gilda, Rigoletto and Sparafucile, Gilda and the Duke. But the formal unit is the scene. It may contain arias, duets, recitative dialogue and choruses, but the length and position of these will depend on the structure of the entire scene. In the past, the scene had merely been the total of the independent units of aria, recitative, cabaletta and ensemble contained within it.

The short, ominous Prelude to *Rigoletto*, a mere thirty-five bars, is based on the phrase associated with Monterone's curse, first heard on trumpets and trombones [Ex. 57]. It leads straight into the festive

[1] *Copialettere*, p. 497.

Ex. 57   Andante sostenuto ♩=66

music of the opening scene, music whose rustic "Busseto town band"
atmosphere seems to me ideally suited to the quality of life in the court
of Mantua in the sixteenth century, or at any rate in the mythical
Mantua in which the events of *Rigoletto* are set. The Duke's ballata,
"Questa o quella", emerges naturally and informally from the surrounding dialogue and merges as easily into the formal dance which
follows it. Verdi is concerned with characterisation, not with applause-
catching top notes: most of the high notes one hears in the music of the
Duke, Gilda and Rigoletto are singers' interpolations not to be found
in the score. The rakish rhythm of "Questa o quella" is enchanting, a
forerunner of 1920's swing. To the more proper rhythm of the minuet,
an imitation, though probably an unconscious one, of the *Don Giovanni*
minuet, the Duke flirts elegantly with the Countess Ceprano. Some of
the guests dance a *perigordino*, or *périgourdine*, a lively French country
dance in 6/8 time, whose name comes from Périgord where, presumably,
it originated. An appropriate dance, Verdi must have felt, for the
court of François I; and it remained when the locale was changed to
Mantua.

The gay chorus in which Marullo arouses the interest of the other
courtiers in plotting against Rigoletto, and the dialogue of the Duke
and Rigoletto, fit easily into the festive dance rhythms which still
predominate. The joyous atmosphere is dissipated by Monterone's
entrance, Rigoletto's arioso mocking the outraged father, accompanied
by orchestral figures which vividly illustrate the evil, destructive side
of the hunchback's nature, and by Monterone's curse, which in context
is as chilling as the music of the Commendatore's statue in *Giovanni*. In
this short opening scene, lasting about fifteen minutes, the plot of the
drama is considerably advanced. The old Italian opera would in this
time have got no further than overture, opening chorus, and aria
revealing the hero or heroine's state of mind. No wonder that, as early
as *Rigoletto*, Verdi was accused of succumbing to German influences.
But the German influence to which he succumbed, that of Haydn and
Beethoven, was apparent in his first opera, twelve years before *Rigoletto*.

The duet between Rigoletto and the assassin Sparafucile which opens
the second scene of Act I is beautifully atmospheric, the scene itself
being set as vividly by clarinet, bassoon and lower strings as by the
scenic designer. Verdi's use of the orchestra is masterly, as is his decision

to give the gloomily sinister melody of the duet to the instruments, leaving the two voices to converse freely over it [Ex. 58]. The voices, baritone and bass, are dark of timbre, as are the instruments playing the melody: solo cello and double-bass, both muted, supported by clarinets, bassoons, violas, cellos and double-basses. Sparafucile tells Rigoletto that he comes from Burgundy, thus betraying the French provenance of

the plot. Piave ought to have noticed this and altered "Borgognone" to, say, "Bolognese". The assassin makes his exist on a sustained low F.

Rigoletto's soliloquy, "Pari siamo", part recitative, part arioso, is another example of Verdi's extraordinary ability to harness his psychological insight to his melodic genius. "Pari siamo" is not an aria, and it contains no tunes, but phrase after phrase is searingly memorable. It is, as I suggested earlier, equal in stature to one of Hamlet's soliloquies, and is given the variety of pace of a spoken monologue by the six changes of tempo which Verdi calls for. The G at the end, on "è follia", regularly heard in the opera house, is an E in Verdi's score. The tempo quickens to a happy *allegro vivo* as Rigoletto greets his daughter. Their extended duet is one of the finest of that long series in which Verdi explored the father-daughter relationship. It is surely not entirely by accident that he found himself so frequently writing for baritone fathers

and soprano daughters. He had lost his own children soon after they
were born; his relationship with his parents was the uneasy and
embarrassed one of a child who has moved out of his parents' social
and intellectual class into a world they cannot share; and his sister died
of meningitis in her teens. Perhaps the lack of close relationships of
this kind led Verdi to create them on the stage. The long,. free-ranging
duet in this scene encompasses a variety of moods, all of them sketched
economically yet clearly in themes of melodic beauty. Rigoletto's
andante section, "Deh non parlare al misero", in which he tenderly
remembers his dead wife, is both expressive and consoling, as are the
moving phrases in his reply to Gilda's question about family, friends
and country [Ex. 59]. The demands of the drama are all-important. A

reprise of the lovely "Veglia, o donna" is broken off in mid-phrase so
that the suspicious Rigoletto may investigate a noise in the street.

The arioso leading to "È il sol dell' anima" is as melodically charged
as is the entire opera. Has anyone noticed that the phrase to which
Gilda sings "No, che troppo è bello" [Ex. 60] is yet another rehearsal for

Violetta's great "Amami, Alfredo" in *La traviata* [Ex. 72]? It had already
made appearances in *Il corsaro* and *La battaglia di Legnano* [Ex. 49].[1] The
duet itself, particularly the Duke's elegantly insincere solo beginning,
is exquisite, though the excitement of its concluding *allegro* is fairly
conventional. Again, it is enhanced by Verdi's strikingly original, and
in this instance also strikingly simple, instrumentation: high violins
and violas playing as lightly and softly as possible.

Some English critics have found difficulty in accepting passages of
coloratura from the supposedly artless Gilda. This seems to me to be
carrying Anglo-Saxon distrust of the baroque too far. Gilda's fioriture
are always dramatically or emotionally meaningful, and are never used
for purposes of aimlessly dazzlingly display. Gilda's E major aria in this
scene, "Caro nome", in which she muses on the name of her beloved,
is not only a most beautiful piece of music but is also completely in

[1] The "Amami, Alfredo" phrase first occurs not in Verdi but in Donizetti's *Pia de'
Tolomei*, to the words "Pia mendace". Donizetti's opera was produced in Venice
in 1837. Giuseppina Strepponi sang Pia in Rome in 1838, and in Milan in the spring
of 1839 when Verdi is almost certain to have heard the opera.

character, though its beauty and its psychological suitability are sometimes obscured in performances by *prime donne* who insist on inter-
polating top notes, and altering the ending. I do not wish to sound
puritanical about the thrill of the high note. Certain Bellini and
Donizetti arias, and some of Verdi's, are positively enhanced by the
singer's inserting a note unthought of by the composer. And it is, I
think, a legitimate pleasure to hear the second stanza of a cabaletta
decorated. But "Caro nome" is not this kind of music. Like several of
Verdi's most memorable tunes, it grows from a simple scale, in this
case descending from E to F sharp [Ex. 61]. This delicate aria must be

Ex. 61 **Allegro moderato**

Ca - ro no - me che il mio cor fe - sti pri - mo pal - pi - tar,

sung as written, to achieve its proper effect, with the ending, a long
diminuendo trill on E, sung off-stage as Verdi intended, while the
courtiers are gathering in the street outside. The entire piece has a
unique quality of virginal young love, trustfulness and innocence,
underlined by the delicacy and imagination of the accompaniment.

The abduction scene is fine, though the chorus, "Zitti, zitti", has by
now come to sound like the hackneyed prototype of all conspiratorial
choruses. At first hearing, it must have been deliciously effective.

The second act opens with the Duke's recitative "Ella mi fu rapita"
and aria "Parmi veder le lagrime". Both recitative and aria are, in
themselves, pleasant, but for once Verdi's grasp of character falters.
Perhaps because Piave's words do not give any indication of whether
the Duke is at this moment sincere, or at any rate deluded into thinking
himself sincere, Verdi's music could as easily be sung by one of his
earlier tenor characters. Incidentally it is, of course, untrue to say that,
by making his tenor an anti-hero, Verdi was breaking new ground in
Rigoletto. Surely Corrado in *Il corsaro* and Carlo in *I masnadieri* are anything but conventional tenor-heroes.

The courtiers recount their adventure of the previous night in a lively
and tuneful chorus with amusing and effective juxtaposition of fortissimo and pianissimo, and the Duke reacts in a cabaletta, "Possente
amor", on which the commentators pour scorn and which is therefore
invariably omitted from stage performance. It is a by no means despicable piece and, like Alfredo's cabaletta in Act II, Scene 1, of *La
traviata*, which is also usually suppressed, it deserves to be heard
[Ex. 62].

Ex. 62 **Allegro**
deciso

Pos - sen - te a-mor mi chia - - ma, vo-lar io deg - gio a le - i;

Rigoletto's scene with the courtiers is one of the most affecting in the opera. The studied indifference of "La ra, la ra", behind which he desperately searches for a clue to Gilda's whereabouts, the tremendous outburst of fury in "Cortigiani, vil razza dannata", and the pathetic attempt to gain Marullo's sympathy in the second section of the aria with its cello obbligato, are all, in context, extremely moving. The sudden entry of Gilda, and Rigoletto's realisation that she has been raped by the Duke, are most effective if the producer remembers that this is also the first time Gilda has seen her father dressed as a jester. She discovers his shame at the same moment as he discovers hers. Gilda's "Tutte le feste" is equally touching. Its solo oboe opening sets a tone of elegiac melancholy which becomes more impassioned as the aria proceeds. Rigoletto's reply, "Solo per me l'infamia", possesses a pathetic dignity: each of these numbers merges into the next with the minimum of formal gesture. The entire scene flows smoothly from Rigoletto's entrance to the end of the act. The duet for Rigoletto and Gilda, "Piangi, fanciulla", is most affecting, her disjointed, tearful phrase contrasting with his legato, while the violins play a beautiful accompanying figure. As so often, Verdi's genius produces music of heart-rending beauty by the simplest and most economic means. Monterone's appearance on his way to prison sparks off the final section of the duet, "Si vendetta, tremenda vendetta", which provides a legitimately exciting conclusion to the act.

The final act is superb from its first note to its last. Though it contains a song for the Duke, a quartet, a trio and a final duet, none of these numbers can easily be extracted from its context, not even the famous or infamous "La donna è mobile". The entire act is an arioso of genius, simmering at climactic moments into various melodic units, aria, duet, quartet, but never losing its essential unity, its sense of forward movement, or the sheer perfection of its musical structure. Verdi was right not to give the tenor the music of "La donna è mobile" until the last possible moment. It is a vulgar, catchy tune, and he did not want its effect vitiated in advance. It is also precisely the right kind of tune for that character to sing in that context, and to complain of it in terms of pure music is to misunderstand the art of opera. It is in character, and it is immediately identifiable, as it needs to be, when it is used again at the end of the opera, at the moment when Rigoletto thinks he has the Duke's body in a sack. The words,

> La Donna è mobile
> Qual piume al vento,
> Muta d'accento
> E di pensiero

are a reasonably faithful translation of the words sung by the King in Hugo's play:

Souvent femme varie,
Bien fol est qui s'y fie!
Une femme souvent
N'est qu'une plume au vent!

(Women are frequently fickle: he who trusts them is mad. A woman is often like a feather in the wind.)

"Souvent femme varie" was a famous dictum of the historical François I. Hugo merely expanded the sentiment into a song.

Verdi ends "La donna è mobile", not on the high B so beloved by many exponents of the role, but an octave lower. In its context, the Duke's song is a stroke of genius. So, of course, is the quartet, "Bella figlia dell' amore", in which the Duke, Maddalena, Gilda and Rigoletto voice their widely differing feelings in themes which, each individually suitable, blend into a harmonious and very beautiful whole. This is one of the highlights not only of *Rigoletto* but of all Italian opera. The four parts, individual not only in melody but also in the type of emotion expressed, add up to a quartet which is astonishing in its pyschological complexity and sheer musical persuasiveness. This is the kind of thing that opera is uniquely equipped to do, and no one has done it more magnificently than Verdi. Sopranos are apt to alter the composer's vocal line and end their part in the quartet an octave higher than written. Verdi's more sensitive, less sensational ending is to be preferred.

In the storm music into which the ensuing trio is incorporated, brilliantly atmospheric music whose economy of means is again masterly, Verdi by a stroke of real genius uses the humming of an off-stage chorus to represent the sound of the wind, thus anticipating Debussy by half a century. Graphic phrases for flute and piccolo represent lightning. The repetition of the tenor's "La donna è mobile" when Rigoletto is about to throw the sack into the river is another masterstroke, the cynical indifference of the tune underlining the tragedy. This is operatic writing at its finest, real music theatre as opposed to the concert-in-costume of a great many pre-Verdian Italian operas. The final duet of Rigoletto and the dying Gilda is also first-rate. Verdi's dying music was almost invariably effective, mainly because of the combination of its simple sincerity with the composer's ability to draw beautiful tunes out of the air. The perverse and pathetic joy of Rigoletto's "Quest' è un buffone, ed un potente è questo", deflated by the offstage sound of the Duke's cynical song, is turned to an equally pathetic despair by his discovery that the sack contains the dying Gilda, and finds release in the simple beauty of "Lassù in cielo" with its ethereal instrumentation. As Gilda dies, both Rigoletto and the orchestra recall Monterone's curse.

A use of the orchestra as appropriate and frequently as skilful as that of Berlioz, brilliant delineation of the minor characters, in particular Sparafucile, Maddalena and Monterone, a prodigality of melodic invention, an advance towards integral structure, and brilliant psychological insight into character motivation: these are a few of the attributes which combine to make *Rigoletto* one of the most popular of operas, as well as one of the finest musically and dramatically. A resilient work, it triumphantly survives non-production, determinedly wrongheaded production, and the vain foibles of musically illiterate singers. Conversely, what superb opportunities it offers to the intelligent singer of the role of Rigoletto, so memorably "burnt into music by Verdi", as Bernard Shaw wrote. The role, indeed the entire opera, is infused with a humanity which puts one in mind of Mozart. In a very real sense, beneath the obvious surface differences, *Rigoletto* is Mozartian, as are all of Verdi's great middle-period operas. His concern, like Mozart's, is with characterization and with the dialogue of one human being with another. Verdi's ensembles look back to Mozart, not forward to Wagner. He has Mozart's sense of dramatic movement and interplay of character. "Bella figlia dell' amore" moves, in the way that the first-act finale to *Don Giovanni* moves, and Wagner's static set-pieces do not. In *Rigoletto*, Verdi appears to be approaching a quasi-Wagnerian endless melody, but its roots are in the organically developing ensembles of *Don Giovanni* and *Le nozze di Figaro*, though the opera itself spurns the usual ensemble finales. Act I ends with Rigoletto alone on stage; Acts II and III end with duets for Rigoletto and Gilda.

From *Rigoletto* onwards, each Verdi opera acquires a strong individual flavour. Arias and duets from *Oberto*, *I Lombardi* and *La battaglia di Legnano* could perhaps be interchanged, just as they could in several operas of Rossini, Donizetti and Bellini. But there is no mistaking pages of *Rigoletto*, *La traviata* or *Il trovatore* for one another. Each has its distinctive range of orchestral colour, its melodic shape and its overall dramatic form. During rehearsals, Verdi had said to his Rigoletto, Felice Varesi (who had also been his first Macbeth), that he never expected to do better than the quartet, "Bella figlia dell' amore". In a sense, he was right. No one could do better: Verdi continued to do differently.

It was *Rigoletto* which impelled Rossini to remark that at last he could recognise Verdi's genius. And so he ought to have done: it was, in 1851, one of the greatest operas written since Mozart's *Don Giovanni* of sixty years earlier.

XVII

Il trovatore

Dramatis personae:

Count di Luna, a young nobleman of Aragon	(baritone)
Ferrando, Captain in di Luna's army	(bass)
Manrico, an officer in the Prince of Vizcaya's forces, and the supposed son of Azucena	(tenor)
Leonora, lady-in-waiting to the Princess of Aragon	(soprano)
Ines, her confidante	(soprano)
Azucena, a Vizcayan gypsy woman	(mezzo-soprano)
Ruiz, a soldier under Manrico's command	(tenor)
An old gypsy	(bass)

LIBRETTO by Salvatore Cammarano, completed by Leone Emanuele Bardare, based on the play *El Trovador* by Antonio García Gutiérrez

TIME: Fifteenth century
PLACE: The provinces of Vizcaya and Aragon in northern Spain

FIRST PERFORMED at the Teatro Apollo, Rome, January 19, 1853, with Rosina Penco (Leonora); Emilia Goggi (Azucena); Carlo Baucardé (Manrico); Giovanni Guicciardi (Di Luna); Balderi (Ferrando)

Il trovatore

AFTER THE PRODUCTION of *Rigoletto* in Venice, Verdi returned to Busseto and to various problems, both personal and professional. He was openly living with Giuseppina Strepponi, which scandalised Busseto; and his, to piously conventional minds, extremely *louche* choice of operatic subjects, such as adultery in *Stiffelio* and rape in *Rigoletto*, gave a certain amount of offence as well. A year or so later, he was to outrage his audiences still further by apparently combining the personal and the professional in *La traviata*, a kind of emotional memoir of his relationship with Giuseppina. Because his parents quarrelled with her, Verdi had bought them a small property outside Busseto, and sent them to live there. In June 1851, his mother died. Some months later, his old benefactor and ex-father-in-law Barezzi took him to task for not legalising his union with Giuseppina. In reply, Verdi wrote:

> There lives in my house a lady, free and independent, who, like myself, prefers a solitary life, and in possession of a fortune that caters for all her needs. Neither I nor she is obliged to account to anyone for our actions. But who knows what our relations are? What affairs? What ties? What rights I have over her or she over me? Who knows whether she is my wife or not? And if she is, who knows what the reasons may be for not publically announcing the fact? Who knows whether that is a good or a bad thing? Might it not be a good thing? And even if it is a bad thing, who has the right to ostracize us? I will say this, however: in my house she is entitled to as much respect as myself, more even. And no one is allowed to forget that for any reason. And finally she has every right, both because of her conduct and her character, to that consideration she habitually shows to others.[1]

Verdi's biographers have speculated about the composer's apparent reluctance to marry Strepponi until they had lived together in Busseto and Sant' Agata for twelve years. The life they lived was that of a respectable married couple; perhaps Verdi found the religious aspect of the actual marriage ceremony distasteful to him. His lack of interest in religion both perplexed and infuriated Giuseppina. Many years

[1] *Copialettere*, p. 130.

later she described to Cesare Vigna, the alienist, the habitual result of her occasional attempts to persuade Verdi of the existence of God:

> It's wasted breath. He laughs in my face, and my oratory, my divine enthusiasm, are ignored. "You are mad," he says. And unfortunately he says it in good faith.[1]

By his example, Verdi even created doubts in Giuseppina's mind. "For some virtuous natures," she wrote,

> belief in God is a necessity. Others, equally perfect, while observing strictly every precept of the highest moral code, are happier believing nothing. Manzoni and Verdi! These two men give me food for thought. My imperfections and my ignorance, alas, leave me incapable of solving so complicated a problem.[2]

Verdi was never belligerent in his agnosticism. He had, after all, submitted easily to marrying his first wife in a church. The theory has been advanced that he had promised his dying wife not to marry again. It is even said that Strepponi herself told a friend that this was the reason, though nothing exists on paper to support such an assertion. Whatever the truth of the matter, Verdi and Giuseppina Strepponi withstood the outraged attitude of the Busseto townsfolk in 1851, and made no move towards marriage for another eight years. They spent the winter of 1851–2 in Paris, by which time Verdi had already begun work on *Il trovatore*.

Cammarano had acquired a copy of *El Trovador*, as instructed by Verdi in January, and had sent the composer a draft synopsis for a libretto. On April 9, 1851, just a month after the *Rigoletto* première, Verdi wrote to Cammarano: "I have read your sketch. As a gifted and most exceptional man, you will not be offended if I humbly take the liberty of saying it would be better to give up this subject if we cannot manage to retain all the boldness and novelty of the Spanish play." After setting out his own suggested outline for the libretto, the composer concluded:

> Please excuse my presumption. I'm probably wrong, but at least I had to tell you how I feel about it. Incidentally, my first suspicion that you didn't like the play now seems confirmed. If this is so, we still have time to think of a substitute. Rather that, than have you do something that doesn't appeal to you. I have prepared another subject, simple and passionate, which can be said to be almost complete as it is. If you wish, I'll send it to you and we'll forget *Il trovatore*. Write me a word about it. And, if you have a subject, tell me what it is.[3]

[1] *Carteggi Verdiani*, IV, p. 285.   [2] Strepponi's Letterbooks in MS. at Sant' Agata.
[3] *Copialettere*, p. 118, and pp. 120–1.

The other subject to which Verdi refers was *La Dame aux camélias*: in the stage adaptation which Dumas fils had made from his own novel, it was indeed almost perfect for musical setting. Cammarano, however, chose to persevere with *Il trovatore*, so Verdi postponed any further work on the Dumas play. While he and Giuseppina were in Paris, he also signed a contract to write a new work on a libretto to be provided by Scribe, for production at the Paris Opéra two years later. The announcement of this led to a request from Vienna for this opera, coupled with a hint that Verdi might be appointed to the post of Hofkapellmeister, which Donizetti had once held. Returning to Busseto in March 1852, Verdi continued working on *Il trovatore*, though held up somewhat by the librettist's illness and by worry over his own father, who was also ill. He began to correspond with Piave concerning another opera for Venice, eventually deciding that this should be *La Dame aux camélias* or, as it came to be called, *La traviata*.

In July, Cammarano died in Naples, leaving the *Trovatore* libretto unfinished. To his Neapolitan friend, Cesare de Sanctis, Verdi wrote: "I was thunderstruck by the sad news of Cammarano. I can't describe the depth of my sorrow. I read of his death not in a letter from a friend but in a stupid theatrical journal. You loved him as much as I did, and will understand the feelings I cannot find words for. Poor Cammarano. What a loss."[1]

Part of the third and all of the fourth act of the libretto remained unwritten, but Verdi paid Cammarano's widow six hundred ducats instead of the agreed five hundred and, through De Sanctis, engaged a young Neapolitan poet, Leone Emanuele Bardare, to sort out Cammarano's notes for the last act, and complete the libretto.

Il trovatore had not been commissioned: Verdi had suggested it to Cammarano because he had been struck by the play. After all, he no longer had to worry about getting an opera accepted for performance. At first, he intended offering it to the San Carlo in Naples because of Cammarano's connections with that theatre. But his principal concern was that the opera should be staged by whichever theatre had the most suitable singers for it, and finally he decided to allow the first production to be staged by the Apollo Theatre in Rome. The date chosen for the première was January 19, 1853.

Verdi had, by this time, agreed to have *La traviata* ready for performance at the Fenice in Venice on March 6th, so while he was rehearsing *Il trovatore* in Rome he was also composing *La traviata*. He is said to have composed the whole of *Il trovatore* during the month of November 1852. This may be literally true, in that the actual writing down of the notes was done in that month, but Verdi had, of course, been thinking about *Il trovatore* for almost a year. He arrived in Rome

[1] *Carteggi Verdiani*, I, p. 9.

in December to rehearse the opera, whose première in January was an overwhelming success. The *Gazzeta Musicale*[1] described the music as "heavenly", and continued:

> The composer deserved this splendid triumph, for he has here written music in a new style, imbued with Castilian characteristics. The public listened to each number in religious silence, breaking out into applause at every interval, the end of the third Act and the whole of the fourth arousing such enthusiasm that their repetition was demanded.

In short, the opera was immediately recognized as the masterpiece it is, and, in the years immediately following its Rome première, was performed all over the civilised world. Several critics, however, complained that Verdi was killing off the art of *bel canto* by the impossible demands he made on his singers, and many people objected to the violence and gloom of *Il trovatore*'s plot. "People say the opera is too sad, and that there are too many deaths in it," wrote Verdi to the Countess Maffei. "But, after all, death is all there is in life. What else is there?"[2]

II

'Death is all there is in life. What else is there?" The observation is by no means unexpected from someone of Verdi's pessimistic temperament. And it should be remembered by those who scoff at the plot of *Il trovatore* with its baby flung into the fire, that even so gruesome a detail as this probably did not seem particularly melodramatic or far-fetched to Verdi. As a baby, had he not narrowly escaped from the sabres of a Russian regiment which had slaughtered many of the women and children in his village? What reason had he to baulk at the idea of a baby tossed into the flames?

Gutiérrez's *El Trovador* reads to us now like one of the worst excesses of romantic melodrama. But when it was first performed in Madrid in 1836, its audiences were impressed by its power and originality, and the twenty-three-year-old playwright immediately became famous. Gutiérrez was, as might be expected, a disciple of Victor Hugo. He was also strongly influenced by a fellow Spaniard, the Duke of Rivas, and in particular by his play *Don Alvaro*, which, in due course, Verdi was to turn into *La forza del destino*. The romantic characters of Byron, Hugo and their followers always exercised a strong appeal to Verdi. Gutiérrez's play is a sprawling romantic-historic melodrama set against the background of a fifteenth-century Spanish civil war. Cammarano had to eliminate most of the politics, and indeed compressed the plot to such an extent that, in the opera, it is difficult to follow. Difficult, but

---

[1] On January 20th, 1853.   [2] *Copialettere*, p. 532.

not impossible: Cammarano's *Il trovatore* is continually referred to by English-speaking critics as the epitome of the confused and silly operatic libretto, but this betrays a certain mental laziness. Admittedly, much of the exposition is buried in ensembles or recitatives, but an intelligent reading of the libretto makes everything perfectly clear, though not necessarily perfectly believable. The plot is complicated, but it makes sense. If one is willing to look back, beyond the Gilbert and Sullivan parody on the switch of babies in *The Gondoliers*, to the original effect of the melancholy yet violent drama, it becomes quite easy to follow and less absurd: a perfectly viable romantic melodrama created by Cammarano from the huge and apparently unwieldy canvas of the original play, a play which, incidentally, is still considered a classic of Spanish drama.

Gutiérrez's *drama caballeresco*, as he called it, is a play of unbridled romantic passions. The three leading characters, Leonor, Manrique and Don Nuño (who, in the opera, becomes the Conte di Luna) take nothing into account but their sexual feelings. The play is partly in prose and partly in verse, in the manner of Elizabethan drama. The most important difference between play and libretto is that the libretto eliminates an important character, Leonora's brother, whose attitude to her and to their family's honour is very similar to that of that other Leonora's brother in *Don Alvaro* (*La forza del destino*). The libretto also emphasises the importance of Azucena, the gypsy woman torn between love for her *fils adoptif* and the desire to avenge her mother's death. Verdi, perhaps more than usually sensitive to the subject of filial and maternal love because of his mother's death, continually urged upon Cammarano the importance of Azucena to the drama. "It seems to me that this woman's two great passions, filial love and maternal love, are no longer present with all their original force,"[1] he said in criticism of Cammarano's first draft. And, concerned to preserve Azucena's significance and importance to the drama right to the very end, he specifically advises his librettist on the last act. "Don't make Azucena go mad. Exhausted with fatigue, suffering, terror and sleeplessness, she speaks confusedly. Her faculties are weakened, but she is not mad. This woman's two great passions, her love for Manrico and her wild desire to avenge her mother, must be sustained to the end. When Manrico is dead, her feeling of revenge overwhelms her, and in the utmost agitation she cries: 'Yes, he was your brother . . . Fool! . . . Mother, you are avenged!'"[2] To Verdi, Azucena was the leading female character in the opera, and he lavished all his compassion upon her.

The four acts of Cammarano's libretto are each sub-titled, and each act has two scenes. Act I is "Il duello" (The Duel). Its first scene is set

---

[1] *Copialettere*, p. 118.   [2] *Copialettere*, p. 120.

in a hall in the Palace of Aliaferia. The Princess of Aragon is in residence, and Ferrando and a number of the Count di Luna's retainers are
resting by a door that leads to the Count's apartments. The soldiers are
tired, and, in order to keep them awake so that they may serve the
Count, who sometimes spends entire nights beneath the balcony of his
beloved Leonora, Ferrando recounts to them the story of how, many
years earlier when the Count was a child, his baby brother was be-
witched by a gypsy who claimed she merely wanted to tell the baby's
fortune. The baby became ill, and the gypsy was burnt as a witch. But
the gypsy's daughter exacted a terrible revenge. She kidnapped the
baby, and later, on the spot where her mother had been put to death,
the half-burned skeleton of a child was found. The old Count could
never bring himself to believe his son dead, and when he himself lay
dying he charged his other son, the present Count di Luna, to continue
to search for his brother. Ever since that day, the Count has looked for
the gypsy's daughter who stole, and probably killed, his brother.

The superstitious soldiers react with terror to Ferrando's narrative.
They recall that the gypsy who had been burned at the stake had
reappeared in the form of an owl to one of the old Count's men who
had tortured her, and had frightened him to death. A bell in the
Palace strikes midnight, and all combine to curse the witch.

Scene 2 takes place at night in the Palace gardens, where Leonora, a
Lady-in-waiting of the Princess, and her confidante Ines are strolling.
Leonora is upset that so long a time has passed since she has seen the
troubadour with whom she has fallen in love. Ines asks where she first
saw him, and Leonora explains that it was at a tournament when she
presented the prize to him, an unknown warrior. Then civil war broke
out, and she did not see him again until one night she heard her name
repeated in a troubadour's song. Rushing to her balcony, she found that
the singer was her unknown warrior. Ines advises her to forget this man,
but Leonora swears her love is so great she could die for him. The two
ladies leave the gardens by way of a marble staircase that leads up to
their apartments, and the Count di Luna enters. Seeing a light burning
in Leonora's window, he goes towards it but is halted by the sound of his
rival the troubadour serenading Leonora from a distance. Leonora
comes down into the garden and, mistaking the Count for the troubadour in the darkness, confesses her love for him. A voice from beyond the
trees calls "Faithless woman," and Leonora realises her mistake. She
convinces the troubadour that she was confused by the darkness and
swears that she loves him, to the intense fury of the Count, who challenges his rival, whose face is hidden by his visor, to reveal himself.
The troubadour lifts his visor and announces his name, Manrico. A
follower of the rebel Prince Urgel, pretender to the throne, he has been
sentenced to death, and dares Di Luna to hand him over to the executioner, The jealous Count, however, is determined on a quicker ven-

geance, and challenges Manrico to an immediate duel. Despite Leonora's entreaties, the two men rush off to fight.

The first scene of Act II, "La gitana" (The Gipsy), is set in a ruined dwelling on a mountain-side in Vizcaya, where a tribe of gypsies have made their camp. Azucena sits by a fire, and Manrico lies near her, wrapped in his cloak and staring moodily at his sword, which he holds in his hands. It is almost daybreak, and the gypsies sing a chorus in praise of the dawn, work, wine and gypsy girls. Azucena sings about a woman being burned to death by a mob, and then, turning to Manrico, murmurs "Mi vendica" (Avenge me). The gypsies go off to forage for food in a nearby village, and Manrico questions Azucena, whom he has always believed to be his mother, about the event alluded to in her song. She tells him of his grandmother's death, accused of witchcraft by the old Count di Luna, and of how she, Azucena, with her own baby in her arms, watched her mother die. As she was driven to the stake by the swords of the Count's soldiers, she had cried to Azucena, "Avenge me!" Azucena had managed to steal the Count's baby and take him to the spot where the fire was still burning. For a moment the child's tears had softened her crazy resolve, but as she gazed into the fire she seemed to see again the face of her tortured mother and to hear her cry, "Avenge me". Still staring into the fire, she had involuntarily grabbed the baby and flung him into the flames. When she came to, and looked about her, there was the Count's son by her side. She had burned her own son.

Horrified, Manrico interrupts her. If she killed her own son, who then is he? Azucena rouses herself from rapt contemplation of the past and assures him that he is her son. He must realise that, whenever she remembers that dreadful event, she is not responsible for her words. Has she not always been a loving mother to him? Manrico admits this. When he was left for dead on the battlefield, she came to bury him, found him still alive, and nursed him back to recovery. Manrico's wound had been inflicted by Di Luna. Curious thanks, says Azucena, for Manrico's action in sparing Di Luna's life when he had defeated him in the duel they fought. What, she asks, can have come over Manrico to make him behave with such absurd magnanimity? Manrico himself cannot explain it. His sword was about to descend when suddenly he heard a cry from heaven: "Non ferir!" (Do not strike!) Azucena drily observes that Di Luna heard no such voice when the situation was reversed, and makes Manrico swear not to hesitate if ever he has Di Luna at his mercy again. At this moment, a messenger arrives from Manrico's lieutenant, Ruiz. The fortress of Castellor is now in the hands of the rebel forces, and Manrico, who has been chosen to supervise its defence against the royalists, is ordered to proceed there immediately. Ruiz adds that Leonora, believing Manrico killed in battle, is about to enter a convent. Manrico rushes off to stop Leonora from taking so desperate a step, paying no heed to Azucena's cries that his wounds are not properly healed.

The second scene of Act II takes place in the courtyard of a convent in the neighbourhood of Castellor. Di Luna, Ferrando, and some of their retainers enter cautiously. Driven almost to madness by the force of his love for Leonora, Di Luna is determined to abduct her. He and his followers conceal themselves and await the procession of nuns which is to accompany Leonora into the convent. Leonora and Ines enter, and as Leonora is saying farewell to her friend, Di Luna steps forward, crying, "Per te non havvi che l'ara d'imeneo" (The only altar you will embrace is the nuptial one). Suddenly, to everyone's astonishment, Manrico and his followers appear. The rival factions fight, Di Luna and his men are driven back, the nuns flee into the convent, and Manrico drags Leonora off with him.

Act III is "Il figlio della zingara" (The Gypsy's Son), and its first scene is Di Luna's camp, from which the towers of Castellor can be seen in the distance. Soldiers are playing at dice. A new reinforcement of archers arrives in preparation for the attack on Castellor, which is planned for the next morning. The soldiers sing a martial chorus and then disperse. The Count emerges from his tent and looks across towards Castellor: he cannot bear to think that Leonora is now in the arms of his rival, and is determined to separate them. The guards bring before him a gypsy woman they have caught prowling near the camp. It is Azucena. When she admits she comes from the mountains of Vizcaya, Ferrando thinks he recognises her as the daughter of the gypsy they burned. He questions her, and in desperation she calls on Manrico to come and save her. Realising that he has Manrico's mother in his clutches, Di Luna is overjoyed, and Azucena is dragged off to be tortured.

Scene 2 takes place in a hall in the castle of Castellor, adjoining the chapel where Leonora and Manrico are about to be married. Manrico sings of his love and of their future happiness. The chapel organ is heard, but as they are about to enter for the ceremony, Ruiz rushes in to announce that Azucena has been captured and that even now the stake is being prepared for her. Summoning his soldiers, Manrico rushes off to save his mother.

Act IV, "Il supplizio" (The Punishment), opens in a courtyard of the palace of Aliaferia. At one corner is a tower with barred windows. It is night. The Count's army has recaptured Castellor; Manrico has failed to rescue his mother and has been taken prisoner. Ruiz leads Leonora in, and leaves her, after pointing out the tower in which the State's prisoners are held. A chorus of monks can be heard singing a Miserere for Manrico, who is to be executed at dawn. As Leonora sings of her anguish, Manrico's voice from the tower joins her in a song of farewell. Leonora is determined to save Manrico's life; when Di Luna appears, she offers herself to him if he will allow Manrico his freedom. Di Luna agrees, but Leonora's real intention is to kill herself rather than be unfaithful to Manrico. Surreptitiously swallowing poison from a ring, she exclaims, "M'avrai, ma fredda, esanime spoglia" (You will have only my cold, lifeless corpse).

The final scene is set in the prison cell shared by Manrico and Azucena. The gypsy woman lies on a blanket, exhausted and half-crazed with terror. Manrico tries to comfort her, but her mind keeps returning to the day, so many years before, when her mother was burned. Manrico lulls her into an uneasy sleep, and Leonora is let into the prison. She tells him he is free to go, but, suspecting the price she has paid for his freedom, he denounces her. In vain Leonora tries to persuade him to flee before it is too late. It is only when she falls, dying, that Manrico realises the nature of the sacrifice she has made for him. She dies in his arms as the Count enters the prison cell. Angrily, he orders his guards to take Manrico out to the execution block. Azucena awakens and asks for her son. "He has gone to his death," Di Luna replies. The gypsy begs him to stop the execution, but he draws her to the window to show her that Manrico is already dead. "He was your brother!" cries Azucena. "You are avenged, mother!" Horrified, Di Luna exclaims, "E vivo ancor!" (And I still live!)

III

Il trovatore's effects are broad and immediate. The wealth of melody, the passionate melancholy of Leonora's music, the dark beauty of the orchestral colouring, the almost brutal vigour and speed of the entire opera, whose characters, as Hanslick said, arrive on the stage as if shot from a pistol; these are some of the ingredients that have ensured the opera's popularity since the day of its first performance. Too popular for its own good, perhaps, as it was for many years a non-favourite with critics who, unimpressed by Verdi's honest directness of purpose, could hear in his score only the death of *bel canto*.[1] To enlightened ears, however, *Il trovatore* is the veritable apotheosis of the *bel canto* opera, with its demands for vocal beauty, agility and range. It is as though Verdi had decided to do something which he had been perfecting over the years, and to do it so beautifully that he need never do it again. Formally, *Il trovatore* is a step backwards after *Rigoletto*; but Verdi had an extraordinary ability to move simultaneously in a number of different directions. In his next opera, *La traviata*, he was to travel into completely new territory. His humanity never degenerated into bourgeois sentimentality, but his range of sympathy could embrace the cosily

---

[1] "It seemed rubbish on the whole to me", wrote Charles Dickens to Georgina Hogarth after a Naples performance in 1853. (*The Letters of Charles Dickens*, Vol. I [London, 1880], p. 328.)

domestic as well as the fabled world of high romance. My feeling is that in *Il trovatore* he was consciously saying goodbye to that fairy-tale world. There are several connecting links between *Il trovatore* and Verdi's first produced opera, *Oberto*. The later opera is an essay in pessimistic nostalgia for the innocent virtues of the earlier one. *Il trovatore*'s muscular energy is compelling, its lyrical romanticism irresistible. Its covert temperamental reference to the turmoil and sadness of the composer's own life at the time of its composition is veiled but unmistakable. Above all, it is for its tuneful spontaneity and its sincerity of purpose that it continues to be one of Verdi's best-loved operas, and to symbolise the quintessential soul of Italy. The conductor Gianandrea Gavazzini has called *Il trovatore*, "the Italian St Matthew Passion."

The opera's brief twenty-seven bars of orchestral introduction range from soft drum-rolls, through clarion-like figures as though rousing for battle, to softly romantic calls on the horn. The mood thus set, the opera begins without further preamble with Ferrando's recitative and narration of the burning of the gypsy many years before. From the very beginning, we hear the opera's considerable narrative elements being squeezed into melodic form. Here, as throughout *Il trovatore*, the melodies are so glorious that one hardly attends to the words. Hence the legend that the story is incomprehensible. Most of Ferrando's scena is in a minor key, which fact emphasises the vigorous determination of the chorus's final yell on a chord of A major, as they disperse.

Leonora is Verdi's most Mozartian heroine: her arias possess something of the stature and elegance of the music of the Countess Almaviva, and call for a style in performance reaching back beyond that of early-nineteenth-century *bel canto* to eighteenth-century formality. Her 'Tacea la notte placida" is one of Verdi's most beautiful soprano arias. Again, its tunes are found simply, are eminently vocal, and are at their most irresistible when, on the page, they appear merely to be ascending or descending a scale [Ex. 63]. This phrase, incidentally, was to grow

Ex. 63   Andantino
animando un poco con espansione
dol - ci   s'u - di - ro e   fle - - bi - li

into Violetta's repeated cry, "Ah, perchè venni, incauta! Pietà, gran Dio, pietà di me!", in Act II, Scene 2 of *La traviata* [Ex. 73]. Verdi had already used the phrase fifteen years earlier in the song "In solitaria stanza" [Ex. 133].

Of the cabaletta, "Di tale amor", Toye incredibly writes: "the less said about [it] the better; it is, exceptionally, a mere excuse for virtuosity". He can surely never have heard it meaningfully sung, for it is one of Verdi's most attractive and tuneful cabalettas, splendidly expressive of Leonora's joyful anticipation [Ex. 64].

Ex. 64 Allegro giusto

Di ta - le amor che dir - - si mal può dal-la pa-ro - - la,

Manrico's off-stage song to harp accompaniment, "Deserto sulla terra", is typical of the troubadour's elegant yet forceful utterance. The *allegro* trio for Leonora, Manrico and Di Luna which ends the act is the apotheosis of early Verdi as, in a sense, is the entire opera. Its excitement is almost elemental; its energy and panache are irresistible.

In the second scene, the Gypsy Chorus, utilising triangle and anvil to great effect, needs no description. It has become part of Italian musical consciousness and acquired a stature as the Ur-operatic chorus. But then *Il trovatore* is the repository of most operatic folk-lore. Its plot is *the* opera plot, Manrico's "Di quella pira" is *the* tenor aria, and "Ai nostri monti" the epitome of all those "gems from opera" to be found in the old song-books. To fight against *Il trovatore* is futile; it is as indisputably there as the Colosseum, the Mona Lisa and the book of Genesis.

Azucena's "Stride la vampa" is a simple and effective introduction to the character, and to Verdi's first important mezzo-soprano role. Even here, where it is ostensibly merely providing a rum-ti-tum accompaniment, Verdi's orchestra repays examination. His skilful use of the violins, his taste and his tact, all are remarkable. Azucena's monotone, "Mi vendica", is followed by the departure of the gypsies, still singing their chorus. Manrico and Azucena are left alone, and the expressive accompaniment to Azucena's "Condotta ell' era in ceppi" again makes one pause and admire. It is typical of Verdi's use of the orchestra throughout the opera. The old *canard* about big guitar-strumming accompaniments cannot hold good anywhere if it cannot hold good in *Il trovatore*. And it cannot. The allusive orchestral comment under Azucena's recital is superbly placed. When Verdi, elsewhere, wishes to resort to a purely rhythmical, marking accompaniment, he does so. But it is always used for a purpose, and by no means frequently.

In their duet, Azucena's unaccompanied "strana pieta", just before Manrico launches into the beautifully lyrical narration, "Mal reggendo", achieves an effect out of all proportion to the simplicity of its means, just as the *Oberto* Leonora's "Generosa" had done, in Verdi's first produced opera. And the gypsy's "Ma nell' alma dell' ingrata" has a nagging maternal affection that permeates the entire Manrico-Azucena duet [Ex. 65]. Verdi's writing for the voice, always grateful, achieves an even richer melodic eloquence in this scene.

The second scene of Act II perfectly catches the growing intensity of

Ex. 65
Meno mosso ♩=92

Ma nell' al - ma dell' in - gra - to non par - lò del ciel un
det - to, non par - lò del cie - lo un det - to!

Di Luna's jealous fury. His aria, "Il balen del suo sorriso", a beautiful cantabile melody, is a glowingly romantic love song whose passion borders on madness. In this song, Verdi uses the baritone range as he would a tenor's, and Di Luna's high Gs have the climactic effect of a tenor's B flat. Again, the effectiveness of the orchestration calls for comment. In the first part of the aria, the violins are silent. They enter, to wonderfully heart-lifting effect, doubling the vocal line where it broadens at "Ah! l'amor, l'amore ond'ardo" [Ex. 66].

Ex. 66 Largo
con espansione

Ah! l'a - mor l'a - mo - re on-d'ar - do

The Count's passion is given really crazed utterance in the following chorus, where, from the ensemble of his followers, his "Per me ora fatale" bursts forth, unable to contain itself, the voice part doubled by solo trumpet. Di Luna is a man whom desire has driven virtually to madness, and this is reflected in his music. He is not an evil, Iago-like figure, but an *homme plus sensuel* pushed completely off balance: Verdi's music conveys this with a Mozartian precision.

The finale to the act is a brilliantly successful fusion of lyrical melody and dramatic intent. Leonora's joyous reaction to the unexpected appearance of Manrico is a perfect example of this. Her breathless excitement is indicated by the shortness of the phrases, the proliferation of the rests, yet the passage is one of memorable tunefulness [Ex. 67]. In no other opera is Verdi's melodic generosity to be found in such

Ex. 67 Andante mosso ♩=76
con tutta la gioia

E deg - gio e pos - so cre - derlo? Ti veg - go a me d'ac-can - to!

abundance. Where other composers would work a passage like this to death [Ex. 68], Verdi is content to offer it once, at the very end of the Finale.

Ex.68 Andante mosso

Sei tu dal ciel di - sce - so o in ciel son io con te?

In the first scene of Act III, the opening chorus, staccato in character, is soon followed by a second chorus, sung by Ferrando and the soldiers, which needs, as they say, no introduction. As well known out of context as Mendelssohn's Wedding March or Handel's Hallelujah Chorus, it is probably often confused with the Soldiers' Chorus from *Faust*.

For the French version of the opera, *Le Trouvère*, presented at the Paris Opèra four years after the Rome première, Verdi wrote ballet music which was inserted after the soldiers' chorus, the ballet being danced for the delectation of the soldiers by gypsies. It is a pity that this music is almost completely unknown, for, although the ballet holds up the drama for a good quarter of an hour, Verdi's music is really fine. He could have been the Tchaikovsky of Italian ballet; in fact, he could have helped to create Italian ballet. His dances are lushly and romantically scored, rhythmically rather than melodically alive, in short perfect ballet music. Themes from the Gypsy Chorus of Act II are woven into the dances, which is unusual, for Verdi's ballet music in other operas is completely unrelated to the rest of the score. The four ballet numbers are Pas de bohémien, Gitanilla and Ensemble; Sevillana; Bohémienne; Galop. It is the opening number which utilises the Anvil Chorus, as well as having a lively bolero section. The interior movements are engaging, and the Galop finale is infectiously lively.

Azucena's "Giorni poveri vivea" cannot fail to touch the heart in adequate performance, and her fierce stretta, "Deh, rallentate, o barbari", makes an exciting conclusion to the scene. At the beginning of Act III, Scene 2, Leonora and Manrico experience their one moment of happiness. They are expecting Castellor to be attacked the following day, but for the immediate present their thoughts are able to rest on their love and their imminent marriage. Manrico's graceful "Ah si, ben mio" is reminiscent, in mood and style, of Mozart. It does not fit easily into the Italian tradition: its ancestors are not "Quando le sere al placido" and "Ah, la paterna mano", but "Dalla sua pace" and "Un' aura amorosa". The sweet little bridge passage about the joys of pure love, a sequence of imitation, and the nearest that Manrico and Leonora get to a love duet, is followed by Manrico's warlike "Di quella pira", the cabaletta to end all cabalettas. It is heard to best effect if both verses are sung: neither contains the top C invariably inserted, but the C has become such a fixture that the tenor who cannot manage it will transpose the cabaletta down and interpolate a note he hopes will pass for C, rather than perform the music as written.

The entire fourth act could hardly be bettered. A brief orchestral introduction uses the lower tones of clarinet and bassoon to paint a picture of night and gloom. Leonora's recitative, "Timor di me", with the dark woodwind instruments still featured, and her aria, "D'amor sull' ali rosee", are poignantly beautiful, and the string writing is, as usual, masterly. The aria is not unworthy of Mozart's Countess or Pamina: I can think of no higher praise. The Miserere, victim of its own popularity, has become hackneyed over the years. But what a superb piece of invention it is, in its melodic richness and brave humanity. Over the grave, obscurantist beauty of the monks' "Miserere", with the entire orchestra's throbbing ostinato accompaniment, the lost, passionate, and completely human cry of the lovers rises with tremendous effect, particularly Manrico's "Ah, che la morte ognora", accompanied only by harp. If one did not know of Verdi's anti-clericalism and impatience with organised religion, one could deduce it from this number.

Most performances of *Il trovatore* suffer a particularly disfiguring cut after the Miserere. They omit Leonora's magnificently effective cabaletta, "Tu vedrai che amore in terra", which is linked to the end of the Miserere by a splendid bridge passage. This cabaletta should never be omitted from the performance of what is, after all, a short and almost brutally swift-moving opera.

No less heart-warming than the preceding scene are the humanity and compassion of Leonora's scene with Di Luna, consisting of two exciting duets in which the soprano's coloratura is used to fine dramatic effect. "Mira d'acerbe lagrime" contrives to be both elegant and eloquent, while the *allegro*, "Vivrà! Contende il giubilo", adds a vigorous excitement. The unadorned pathos of the scene for Manrico and Azucena in prison, culminating in the nostalgic duet, "Si, la stanchezza", is deeply moving. The scene has begun with a series of slow *ppp* chords from the entire orchestra, and the duet grows out of the exhausted calm which follows Azucena's ravings. To a delicate pizzicato accompaniment, the old gypsy tries to rest while Manrico sings to her his gently consoling lullaby, "Riposa, o madre". At the risk of being considered repetitive, I must again draw attention to the simplicity of means to which the extraordinarily moving quality of this duet is allied.

The final trio, "Parlar, non vuoi", contains, in Leonora's dying music, one of those incredibly simple "scale passage" tunes which no other composer has found so easily [Ex. 69]. On the page, those notes

Ex. 69   Andante ♩=50

Pri - ma che d'al-tri   vi - ve - re .... i - o   vol-li tua   mo - rir!....

are simply ascending a scale. In performance, they soar.

Manrico is led out to execution. Awakening from her restless slumber just a second too late to save him, Azucena tells the Count that he has killed his brother. In a final phrase, rising to her top B flat, she cries "Sei vendicata, o madre" (You are avenged, mother). For the Paris production of 1857, Verdi expanded and, to my mind, improved the Finale, giving more dramatic emphasis to the role of Azucena. But the version invariably performed, at any rate outside France, is the original one of 1853.

I have so frequently found myself in disagreement with Francis Toye that it is a particular pleasure to admit I can find no more suitable words to describe my feelings about *Il trovatore* than his:

> Some of the effects, since repeatedly copied by many other composers, may strike us as commonplace. Nevertheless, there is quality in *Il trovatore*, democratic, if you will, rather than aristocratic, but none the less impressive. It is this, in conjunction, of course, with its extraordinary wealth of melody, which has assured the triumph of the opera. Periodically, after a succession of conventional or trivial pages, something emerges and hits you, as it were, between the eyes, something elemental, furious, wholly true. *Il trovatore* has been reproached with vulgarity and the reproach is not unfounded. But this vulgarity is the vulgarity of greatness, a by-product of the vitality and passion without which there can be no great art. Is Shakespeare never vulgar? Or Beethoven?[1]

[1] Toye, *Verdi*, p. 320.

XVIII

La traviata

Dramatis personae:

Violetta Valéry	(soprano)
Flora Bervoix	(mezzo-soprano)
Annina, Violetta's maid	(soprano)
Alfredo Germont	(tenor)
Giorgio Germont, his father	(baritone)
Gastone, Viscount de Letorières	(tenor)
Baron Douphol, Violetta's protector	(baritone)
Marquis d'Obigny, Flora's protector	(bass)
Doctor Grenvil	(bass)
Giuseppe, a servant	(tenor)

LIBRETTO by Francesco Maria Piave, based on the play *La Dame aux camélias* by Alexandre Dumas *fils*

TIME: Around 1850
PLACE: Paris and surroundings

FIRST PERFORMED at the Teatro La Fenice, Venice, March 6, 1853, with Fanny Salvini-Donatelli (Violetta); Lodovico Graziani (Alfredo); Felice Varesi (Germont)

La traviata

ONLY A FEW weeks separate the premières of *Il trovatore* in Rome and *La traviata* in Venice. After the first three performances of *Il trovatore*, Verdi returned to Busseto and to his villa at Sant' Agata, which was now finally habitable, and completed *La traviata*. Piave, who had been entrusted with the libretto, had been busily re-writing, in the light of the composer's criticism that some sections of it would send the audience to sleep. A large amount of the music had been written simultaneously with that of *Il trovatore*, which demonstrates how completely Verdi was able to immerse himself in the characters and atmosphere of his subjects. The worlds of *Il trovatore* and *La traviata* could hardly be more different. Having found his way into them both, Verdi was able apparently to turn from one to the other with ease. He was the most objective of composers, which goes some way towards explaining why he is one of the greatest composers of opera. But, within the context of this objectivity, he managed to lay bare his own feelings. It is rare for Verdi to identify himself with any one character in his operas, but when he does lavish his compassion upon a particular character, the occasion is sure to be a very revealing one.

Most of the music of *La traviata* was written while Verdi was *en route* to Rome to produce *Il trovatore*, in Rome during the rehearsal period, or at Sant' Agata immediately after the première. The final act was written at Sant' Agata in an atmosphere of pessimistic gloom highly suitable to its content. Both Verdi and Giuseppina were unwell, and Verdi was convinced that the cast engaged by the Fenice Theatre would not be able to do justice to the opera. Piave stayed at Sant' Agata to complete the libretto. "When it rains," he wrote to the Fenice Secretary, Guglielmo Brenna, "I assure you it's a case of looking at oneself in the mirror to see if one is still in human form, or whether one hasn't been turned into a toad or a frog."[1] He was instructed to convey to the Fenice Verdi's conviction that, unless different singers were engaged, the opera would fail. When an anonymous letter warned the composer that, unless the soprano and baritone at least were replaced, the performance would be a disaster, Verdi gloomily passed it on to Piave, adding, "I know, I know". But he arrived in Venice on February

---

[1] Giovanni Cenzato, *Itinerari Verdiani* (Parma, 1949), p. 98.

21st, orchestrated the opera, and supervised the rehearsals. He had good reason to fear the worst: the soprano was unsatisfactory, the tenor not in good voice, and even the baritone Felice Varesi, who was used to working with Verdi, felt unhappy in so unusual a work: a purely domestic background, no intrigues, no duels, none of the trappings of high romance. The singers were probably convinced that this absurd *avant garde* work would fail. And so it did. The first performance was on March 6th, and in letters to various friends the following day Verdi reports disaster. The most quoted letter is the terse note he wrote to Muzio: "Dear Emanuele: *Traviata* last night—a fiasco. Was it my fault or the singers? Time will tell."[1] He wrote also to Tito Ricordi: "Unfortunately I have to send you sad news, but I can't conceal the truth from you. *Traviata* was a fiasco. Don't try to work out the reason, that's just the way it is."[2] And to Angelo Mariani, who had conducted *Aroldo*: "*La traviata* was a great fiasco and, what is worse they laughed. Still, what can I say? I'm not upset by it. Am I wrong or are they? I myself believe that the last word on *La traviata* was not heard last night. They will hear it again—and we shall see! Meanwhile, dear Mariani, note the fiasco."[3]

The tone of these brief reports is calm, the calm of resignation and of conviction. The first-night audience had laughed at the thought of Fanny Salvini-Donatelli, an extremely stout lady, dying of consumption. Some Verdi commentators have suggested that the Venetian audiences were also not used to seeing modern dress on the operatic stage. But at the first performances this is not what they saw. True, one of Verdi's reasons for setting Dumas' play was his fascination with the idea of using a contemporary subject. No one had ever done it in a serious opera, though he himself had come close to it in *Stiffelio*, set at the beginning of the nineteenth century. While he was composing *La traviata*, he wrote to Cesare de Sanctis: "A subject from our own time. Another person would perhaps not have composed it because of the costumes, because of the period, because of a thousand other foolish objections, but I am delighted with the idea. Everybody complained when I proposed to put a hunchback on the stage. Well, I enjoyed composing *Rigoletto*."[4] But someone at the Teatro Fenice had got cold feet, and, when *La traviata* was produced, the period and costumes were those of Louis XIV, early eighteenth century.

Verdi's letters about the "fiasco" were, of course, written before the newspaper reviews were published. The reviews, though mixed, were by no means entirely unfavourable. One critic, after praising various parts of the score, refused to judge the opera *in toto* until he had heard a better performance. Ten performances were given during the season, but for over a year the opera was not produced anywhere

[1] *Copialettere*, p. 533.   [2] *Copialettere*, p. 533.   [3] Abbiati, Vol. II, p. 227.
[4] *Carteggi Verdiani*, I, pp. 16–17.

else, Verdi having instructed Ricordi not to allow a production unless he, Verdi, could be in charge of it. He toyed with the idea of producing it in Rome, but was forestalled by a request from Venice, not from the Fenice, but from a smaller theatre, the Teatro San Benedetto, to stage the work again in that city. The impresario offered to collect a first-rate cast, engage Piave to direct the production, and allow unlimited rehearsal time. The Louis XIV period, however, was to be adhered to. Apparently it would have been tempting providence to show the audience themselves on the stage. After an initial hesitation, Verdi agreed, and the Venetians heard *La traviata* again on May 6, 1854. This time the opera was an overwhelming success, a success which spread immediately. It was produced throughout Italy, and elsewhere in Europe, though always in the 1700 costumes, and soon became the most talked-of opera of its day. Verdi was pleased, but remarked on *La traviata*'s vindication in Venice that it was the same audience listening to the same opera.

II

La Dame aux camélias was first produced in Paris on February 2, 1852, and Verdi saw a performance there during that winter. Dumas' novel of the same name, from which he adapted the play, had been published in 1848, only a few months after the death of Marie Duplessis, the original of Dumas' Marguerite Gautier.

Marie Duplessis was a famous Parisian courtesan of great beauty and wit, who at various times had liaisons with such eminent men as Musset, Liszt and Dumas himself. She was only twenty-three when she died of consumption. There are very strong autobiographical elements in both novel and play, and it is quite reasonable to assume that Armand Duval, who shares his author's initials, was intended as a self-portrait. Dumas' first meeting with Marie Duplessis took place in conditions not unlike those described in the novel, and he lived with her in the country near Paris during the summer months of 1845. It was not Dumas père, however, who was responsible for the breaking up of the relationship, but financial problems and Marie's infidelity. The elder Germont's intervention in novel and play appears to have no basis in the reality of Dumas' life. But that the story is largely true is attested to by the novel's opening paragraphs:

> Mon avis est qu'on ne peut créer des personnages, que lorsque l'on a beaucoup étudié les hommes, comme on ne peut parler une langue que lorsqu'on l'a sérieusement apprise.
>
> N'ayant pas encore l'âge où l'on invente, je me contente de raconter.
>
> (In my opinion, one can create characters only when one has closely studied people, just as one can speak a language only when one has learned it conscientiously. Not having yet reached the age when I can invent, I have contented myself with recounting.)

Dumas was in his early twenties when he wrote his novel, which, though widely admired at the time, has today fallen into obscurity. The play, however, remains obstinately alive, not only because of its suitability as a vehicle for great romantic actresses such as Sarah Bernhardt, Greta Garbo and Edwige Feuillère, but also because of its emotional honesty and formal simplicity, qualities which triumph over the fact that it has now completely lost its initial power to *épater les bourgeois*.

Much, perhaps too much, has been written about Marie Duplessis by *La traviata*'s commentators. After all, Verdi was not one of that lady's lovers. If one wishes to search for some extra-aesthetic reason for the composer's interest in *La Dame aux camélias*, it is to Giuseppina Strepponi that one's attention should be directed. At the time when he made the acquaintance of the play, Verdi's relationship with Giuseppina was scandalising the citizens of Busseto to such an extent that his father-figure, Antonio Barezzi, felt obliged to write rebuking him for his thoughtless behaviour. It is quite possible that Verdi saw in the play something of the emotional truth of his own situation, with Giuseppina, mother of two illegitimate children[1] from an earlier relationship, as Marguerite, and Barezzi as the elder Germont. Certainly it is true that *La traviata* occupied a special place in his affections and that, in style, it is a much more intimate and personal work than anything else he had written up to that time.

Piave's libretto follows the Dumas play fairly closely. The play is in five acts. Piave omits the second act in which Marguerite decides to live with Armand in the country and dismisses Count de Giray. In doing so, he improves the form of the drama at the expense of its content, for, at the end of Act I, Marguerite, or Violetta as she becomes in the opera, has apparently determined to continue her life as a high-class courtesan, yet is next seen at the beginning of the opera's Act II (the play's Act III) living in domestic bliss with Armand. But the four scenes of the opera add up to a satisfying musical and dramatic shape, and Dumas' Act II is not really necessary either to the plot or to the boldly sketched characterisation.

As well as omitting this act, Piave reduced the number of subsidiary characters, thus placing an even greater emphasis on Marguerite, Armand and his father Georges Duval. I cannot understand why he introduced Duval père (now called Giorgio Germont) into Act II, Scene 2, Flora's party, where his presence is both unnecessary and highly unlikely. Basically, however, Piave was faithful to Dumas. Whatever the play meant to him and, more importantly, to Verdi, it has resonances which linger today. The situations are basic, the characters both romantic and, paradoxically, prosaic, and the emotional truth of the drama, as opposed to its creaky plot, is indisputable.

---

[1] One, a boy, is known to have been still alive in 1849, aged eight. The other probably died in infancy.

Marguerite undergoes hardly any change at all in her transformation into Violetta. She retains her warmth, impulsiveness and doomed fascination. Piave was careful to retain as many of her speeches as possible, at least in outline. Revealing her intrinsically good breeding to M. Duval, Marguerite reacts to his brusqueness with: "Pardonnez-moi, monsieur, mais je suis femme et je suis chez moi, deux raisons qui devraient plaider en ma faveur auprès de votre courtoisie. Le ton dont vous me parler n'est pas celui que je devais attendre d'un homme du monde que j'ai l'honneur de voir pour la première fois, et—[Duval: et?] je vous prie de permettre que je me retire, encore plus pour vous que pour moi-même."[1] In the opera the sense of this speech is retained, and the words compressed to: "Donna son io, signore, ed in mia casa. Chi'io vi lasci assentite, più per voi che per me."[2]

When Germont speaks to Violetta of his two children, Violetta is surprised. "Di due figli?" she asks. (Your *two* children?) She has not known that Alfredo has a sister. In the play, Marguerite makes the same remark, "De ces *deux* enfants?", which is curious because, in the preceding act, she has mentioned Armand's family. "Si vous saviez," she says to her friend Prudence, "quel bon coeur il a, comme il parle de sa mère et sa soeur." (If only you knew how kind-hearted he is, how he speaks of his mother and his sister.)

Marguerite-Violetta begins her great scene of renunciation similarly in play and opera:

Marguerite: Ordonnez, je suis prête.	*Violetta:* Imponete.
Duval: Il faut lui dire que vous ne l'aimez plus.	*Germont:* Non armarlo ditegli.
Marguerite: Il ne me croira pas.	*Violetta:* Nol crederà.
Duval: Il faut partir.	*Germont:* Partite.
Marguerite: Il me suivra.	*Violetta:* Seguirammi.
Duval: Alors . . .[3]	*Germont:* Allor . . .[3]

La traviata is one of Piave's finest libretti, and in some respects it even improves upon the play from which it is taken.

---

[1] "Pardon me, sir, but I am a woman and in my own house, two reasons which should appeal in my favour to your courtesy. The tone in which you speak to me is not that which I should expect from a man of the world whom I have the honour of seeing for the first time, and [Duval: And?] so please permit me to retire, more for your sake than for my own."

[2] "I am a woman, sir, and in my own house. Allow me to leave you, more for your sake than for my own."

[3] Command me, I am ready.
Tell him you no longer love him.
He won't believe me.
Leave.
He will follow me.
Well, then . . .

Act I takes place in Violetta's house in Paris, where a party is in progress. Guests are still arriving, among them Gastone, who has brought his friend Alfredo Germont, a young man who has, he says, for a long time been in love with Violetta from afar. According to Gastone, Alfredo came to enquire after her every day during a recent illness. Violetta is touched to hear this, and gently chides her protector Baron Douphol for not having done as much. "I've known you only a year," replies the Baron. Alfredo is called upon to propose a toast, and does so. Hearing music in the next room, the guests decide to dance, but Violetta, who suffers from consumption, suddenly feels ill and has to sit down. She insists that her guests go and dance, and they all go off to the next room—except Alfredo, who stays to look after her. He confesses his love for her, which both amuses and moves Violetta. There is no place in her life for romantic love: she can neither love nor accept so great a love, and she asks Alfredo to forget her, as she can offer him only friendship. As he is about to go, she hands him a camellia and asks him to bring it back to her. "When?" asks Alfredo, and her reply is, "When it has faded." "Tomorrow!" Alfredo exclaims in a transport of happiness. He leaves, and so, too, do the other guests. Left alone, Violetta ponders on Alfredo's declaration, and wonders whether she dare allow herself to fall in love. Though strongly attracted to Alfredo, she persuades herself it would be madness to abandon the life she now leads as a fashionable courtesan. Love would be painful, and she prefers to live for pleasure. Trying to ignore Alfredo, whom she can hear singing below her balcony, Violetta repeats her determination to live for the moment.

Act II, Scene 1 (Dumas' Act III), is set in the ground-floor drawing-room of a country house outside Paris where Violetta has been living with Alfredo for the past three months. Alfredo comes in from hunting, and sings of their happiness together. Violetta's maid Annina returns from Paris, whither she had gone at her mistress's request to arrange the sale of her horses, carriages and most of her possessions in order to meet living expenses. Alfredo is covered in shame when he realises that Violetta has been paying all their bills. When Annina tells him that yet more money is required, he leaves for Paris in order to raise it. Violetta enters, and a servant hands her a letter from her friend Flora inviting her that evening to a party in Paris. She disinterestedly throws the invitation aside. A gentleman is announced, and Violetta imagines it is a business caller she has been expecting in connection with the sale of her Paris house. The visitor, however, is Alfredo's father, who at first addresses her impolitely but then finds himself impressed by her style and dignity. When Violetta proves to him that, far from living on Alfredo, she is supporting them both, Germont realises he has completely misjudged her. Nevertheless, he appeals to her to leave Alfredo, whose young sister's forthcoming marriage is being jeopardised by the scandal of Alfredo's affair. Violetta pleads with Germont not to ask so great a sacrifice of her. She feels she has not long to live, and would not want to spend her remaining days without Alfredo. But Germont cruelly points out that their liaison is not blessed by heaven. The day will come when Alfredo's carnal desire for her will lessen. What will happen to her then? Would she not rather now be the consoling angel of his family and ensure the happiness of Alfredo's sister? Violetta is defeated and, in tears, agrees to leave Alfredo immediately. Knowing that he will be bitterly hurt, she asks his father to wait in the garden and be ready to comfort him. Germont gratefully bids her farewell and goes into the garden. Violetta writes to her former protector Baron Douphol, and then begins a letter to Alfredo, who enters just as she finishes it. He is worried by a stern note he has received from his father, whom he is expecting. Violetta, greatly agitated, makes Alfredo tell her again how much he loves her. Crying, "Amami, Alfredo, amami quant' io t' amo" (Love me, Alfredo. Love me as much as I love you), she embraces him and rushes out. Alfredo basks contentedly in the light of her love for a few moments, and is not perturbed even when the servant informs him that Violetta has left by coach for Paris. A messenger enters and hands him the letter that Violetta had written. He begins to read, "Alfredo, by the time you receive this letter . . ." and breaks off with a cry of alarm, collapsing into the arms of his father, who has just come in. Germont senior attempts to console his son by reminding him of the joys of his parental home in Provence, but Alfredo, consumed with jealousy and despair, can pay no attention. He notices Flora's invitation on the writing-desk and, convinced he will find Violetta and Douphol at Flora's party, rushes out, followed by his father.

The second scene of Act II (the play's Act IV) takes place in Flora's salon, where she is receiving her guests. There are gambling tables as well as tables loaded with food and flowers. A crowd of masked revellers appears, the women dressed as gypsies and the men as matadors and picadors, and dance for Flora's guests. Alfredo enters and, when Flora enquires after Violetta, says he knows nothing about her, and proceeds to the gambling table. Violetta arrives with Baron Douphol, who forbids her to speak to Alfredo. The Baron plays cards with Alfredo, who wins every hand. When supper is announced, all the guests go off to the dining room, but Violetta immediately returns, having sent a message to Alfredo to follow her. He enters, and she begs him to leave before Douphol challenges him to a duel, at which he remarks bitterly that a single shot would deprive her of both lover and keeper. Violetta tries to convince him that it is his life she fears for, but he forces her to say she loves Douphol and then calls all the guests back to witness that he has repaid Violetta all he owes. He flings at her the money he has won, and she faints in Flora's arms. At this moment Alfredo's father, who has followed him to the party, enters and expresses his contempt for his son's behaviour. Distraught with jealousy, shame and love, Alfredo gives voice to his remorse, and an ensemble builds up, under cover of which Douphol quietly challenges Alfredo, who is led away by his father.

The fourth Act (Act V of the play) takes place several weeks later. Violetta is in bed, seriously ill. The shutters are drawn, and Annina sits dozing by the fire. Violetta awakens and asks for water and, a moment later, when the Doctor arrives, she insists on rising and going to sit on a sofa. The Doctor utters encouraging words, but as he is leaving he admits to Annina that Violetta can have only a few hours to live. Violetta asks Annina to distribute to the poor half the money left in her purse. When Annina has gone, she takes from her bosom a letter from Giorgio Germont, which she re-reads. It tells her that, having wounded the Baron in their duel, Alfredo has gone abroad. Germont has relented and revealed Violetta's sacrifice to Alfredo, who will return and beg her to forgive him. But Violetta knows she is dying, and sings a farewell to all her happy dreams of the past. Annina returns to announce Alfredo, who hastens to Violetta and embraces her. He promises her they will leave Paris and spend their lives together in happiness, but after the first ecstasy of reunion he realises how ill she is. Violetta, on the other hand, is determined to live, now that Alfredo has come back to her, and tries to stave off the approach of death. Annina has run out for the Doctor, and returns with him and Germont senior. Violetta gives Alfredo a miniature portrait of herself, and asks him to marry some pure young girl, and to give her the portrait, the gift of one who will pray for them both in heaven. Suddenly, Violetta begins to feel life and strength returning to her, rises to her feet joyfully, and falls dead.

III

La traviata is remarkable for the way in which its separate numbers arise from and merge into the general melodic background. Even less than in *Rigoletto* are there set arias and cabalettas or convenient applause-breaks in the music. Each act has a structural unity which makes itself felt in performance to such an extent that the opera could almost be thought of as a four movement symphony for voices. The Prelude to Act I is a beautiful *adagio* movement in which the strings predominate. The opening bars for violins divided into four parts bring the *Lohengrin* Prelude to mind. The two operas are roughly contemporary, though, at the time he was composing *Traviata*, Verdi had not heard a bar of Wagner's music. The second theme of the Prelude is the affecting "Amami, Alfredo" tune of Violetta's great outburst in Act II Scene I [Ex. 72]; when it is repeated by the cellos, the first violins play a staccato counter-melody. The curtain rises to brilliant party music over

which Violetta and her guests project phrases of arioso and *parlante*.
After the Brindisi, "Libiamo", a gay and tuneful *allegretto* led by
Violetta and Alfredo, when the guests go into the next room to dance,
the *parlante* conversation of Violetta and Alfredo continues over the off-
stage waltz. The orchestra re-enters as Alfredo begins his confession
of love, "Un dì felice". His beautiful legato melody, "Di quell' amor",
the very spirit of romantic love, later becomes for Violetta a motto of
their love. She sings it in her aria, "Ah fors' è lui", a few minutes later
[Ex. 70].

When Alfredo has concluded his lyrical stanza of the duet, Violetta
replies in a contrastingly florid manner, with nervously agitated figuration. Verdi uses decoration here not for its own sake but to characterise
the brittle and superficial life Violetta has led, a life and past which she
now attempts to use as a shield against Alfredo's affection and her own
finer feeling. When the duet ends, the orchestra falls silent and the
conversation continues again over the music of the off-stage *banda*.
Only when Alfredo exclaims "Io son felice", do the strings steal in,
marking the rhythm in pizzicato notes. To a reprise of the music which
began the act, the guests return from the ballroom and sing a gay
chorus as they fly off to another party. Violetta is left on-stage alone to
end the act with her long *scena*. Its form is simply that of the old recitative and *andante* aria, followed by further recitative and quick cabaletta.
But Verdi makes quite brilliant dramatic use of the conventional form.
In the first recitative, "È strano", Violetta considers the possibility of a
changed life with Alfredo. The aria, "Ah fors' è lui", is a lyrical yearning for such a life. Then, fearful that she has been deceiving herself, she
attempts to appraise the situation more realistically and, in the hectic
and fevered gaiety of "Sempre libera", determines to continue her
search for immediate though transitory pleasure. Outside her window,
Alfredo's song of love can be heard. Violetta momentarily weakens,
but in the meaningful coloratura of the second stanza she pushes all
thoughts of romantic love from her and, with a brittle self-pity which is
reflected in the music's sharp edge and hysterical agility, reaffirms her
intention of going to hell her own way. Verdi's dramatic use of coloratura in this cabaletta is masterly.

At the beginning of Act II, Alfredo's recitative and aria, "De' miei
bollenti spiriti", is hardly one of the score's most inspired passages,
but its graceful lyrical ardour can sound appealing when elegantly
sung. Its cabaletta, "Oh mio rimorso", is frequently omitted in performance. This is a pity for, though it looks unexceptional on the page,

this impetuous piece can be exciting in the theatre and it also reveals Alfredo in unusually lively mood. Its omission leaves an awkward hole. Violetta's great scene with Giorgio Germont displays Verdi's dramatic writing at its finest. Violetta's indignation, pride, anxiety, distress and resignation are conveyed as surely as Germont's initial harshness, his growing sympathy and his constant parental concern for Alfredo, and all in tunes of firm character and melodic richness. Germont's "Pura siccome un angelo" would seem over-sweet out of context, but how perfectly it pleads his cause with Violetta. And how apt the frantic vivacissimo of her "Non sapete quale affetto" in reply [Ex. 71]. The

inexorable logic of Germont's demands continues through "Un dì, quando le venere". Violetta succumbs in "Dite alla giovine", an affecting *cantabile* to which Germont contributes the consoling melody of "Piangi, piangi", and Verdi's cellos come in to give unison support. The concluding section of the duet has a determined and pathetic animation. After Germont has left, it is to the accompaniment of solo clarinet, an instrument that has already contributed its tone colour as an obbligato in "Ah, fors' è lui", that Violetta writes her letter of farewell to Alfredo. Alfredo enters, and Violetta's frenzied outburst of love culminates in the great arching span of "Amami, Alfredo" [Ex. 72]. This is led

up to by ominously agitated trills in the orchestra, betraying Violetta's real state of mind as she tries to behave cheerfully for Alfredo. The emotional outpouring itself, the most tremendously affecting bars in the entire opera, is superbly scored. Unfortunately, few sopranos give anything like their proper value to the notes in the last half-dozen bars, thus spoiling the proportions and the effect of Verdi's great melodic arch.

The remainder of the act, consisting of the elder Germont's aria and cabaletta, is less noteworthy. The aria, "Di Provenza il mar, il suol", is uninterestingly square, but in context is a most effective piece of musical characterisation; its stodgy sentimentality is just right for

Germont père. The aria is popular with baritones because it displays their top to advantage. The naggingly insistent character of the caba-letta, "No, non udrai rimproveri", is dramatically appropriate. This number is usually omitted in performance; but the practice of cutting those parts of a score thought to be the least successful is a dangerous one, and should be resorted to only with extreme caution. The musical and dramatic shape of a scene can be ruined by a thoughtless cut. It is usually far more satisfactory to play a score complete, as most attempts at improvement are little better than mutilation. None of Shakespeare's sonnets is improved by the omission of the less good lines.

The party music and the gaily rhythmic choruses of gypsies and matadors at the beginning of Act II, Scene 2, might appear to be mere padding, but in fact they serve a valid dramatic purpose. After the unvarying mood of the previous scene, a degree of relaxation is neces-say to prepare for the next emotional onslaught. The choruses of masked guests fulfil their relaxing function admirably. As always, Verdi's timing is impeccable: the whole of this party music is not a bar too long. The tension begins to mount again after Violetta's arrival with Baron Douphol. From the *parlante* above the tense orchestral figuration, Violetta's angui-shed span of melody arises three times, with the accompaniment slightly altered and intensified at each repetition [Ex. 73].

Ex.73 Allegro agitato

(Ah per - chè   ven-ni, in-cau - ta! Pie-tà, gran Dio, pietà, gran Dio, di   me!)

Dramatically and musically the rest of the scene is superb, the music relentlessly pushing the action forward until Alfredo, in his hurt and bewilderment, insults Violetta and then instantly is covered in shame and remorse. The final ensemble would melt the coldest heart: per-fectly controlled, never lingering self-pityingly, it is of a most affecting beauty. Violetta's top line is one of those long melodies that only Verdi knew how to find, combining Bellinian grace with a completely Verdian expressiveness.

The Prelude to Act III, an exquisite and poignant *andante* for strings, not only sets the atmosphere of the scene perfectly, but is also in itself one of the loveliest orchestral pieces in Verdi's entire oeuvre. Its first eight bars are identical with those of the Act I Prelude, but a semi-tone higher. The delicately sensitive writing for voices and strings at the beginning of the act leads into Violetta's reading of Germont's letter, while two violins play the love theme. Verdi's use of the speaking voice here is poignantly effective. Violetta's *andante* aria, "Addio del passato bei sogni ridenti", bids an elegaic farewell to the happy dreams of the past. It is, incidentally, in this aria that the word "traviata" occurs. Violetta asks God to "smile on the desires of the fallen woman" (della traviata sorridi al desio). The last notes have hardly died away when, in ironic juxtaposition, the sound of a banal carnival chorus is heard from the street outside.

The eight bars of unison writing for Violetta and Alfredo at their moment of reunion are followed by the gracefulness and gentle charm of their duet, "Parigi, o cara". In the arioso after the duet, Violetta asks Annina to tell the Doctor that she has regained the will to live and is given an immediate answer by a stern chord on the brass, an unmistakable intimation of mortality. Violetta bursts into her desperate "Gran Dio, morir sì giovine", and Alfredo joins in her protest at the blind cruelty of fate. The end is brutally swift. After Violetta's moving "Se una pudica vergine", she imagines, as the strings remember the love theme, that she is recovering. The music uncannily depicts the cruel delusion of the consumptive. She cries "Oh gioia" on a high B flat, and falls lifeless to the floor.

La traviata is not only one of Verdi's finest and best-loved operas but is also one of the world's great music dramas. That it was not immediately recognised as such can only have been because of its melodic wealth. It seems hardly fair that a superb music dramatist should also be able to invent such a prodigality of tunes, but it is an indisputable fact. And in *La traviata*, more completely than in *Luisa Miller*, whose plot still retains elements of romantic melodrama, Verdi has brought a new domestic milieu into opera and, despite the Louis XIV costumes of the first production, has written about the bourgeois world of his own day.

Much of the opera's atmosphere of pathos derives from Verdi's beautifully expressive writing for the strings. Each of his great middle-period operas has its own distinctive sound. The dark, melancholy hues of *Il trovatore* give way in *La traviata* to a warmer, more pathetic string sound. The role of Violetta is splendidly conceived, the glittering coloratura of her artificial Paris life of Act I giving way to the more direct and unembellished simplicity of her utterance in the later acts. This raises a certain problem in casting. Agile coloratura Violettas who can toss off the *fioriture* of "Sempre libera" with accuracy and ease are frequently unable to rise above the orchestra at "Amami, Alfredo". The ideal voice for the part is a reasonably flexible *spinto*: it is, after all, less important to negotiate the end of Act I than it is to cope with the dramatic requirements of the remaining two acts.

La traviata is so well known to us today, its melodies are so much a part of every musician's experience, that it is difficult to stand sufficiently far away from the work to appraise it afresh. It is an opera in which all of Verdi's finest qualities are to be perceived: his technical mastery, his clarity, his humanity, his psychological penetration, his unerring taste. It was that great transmogrifier, Proust, who said that in *La traviata* Verdi had lifted *La Dame aux camélias* into the realm of art.

XIX

I vespri siciliani
(Les Vêpres siciliennes)

Dramatis personae:

Guido di Monforte, Governor of Sicily	(baritone)
Bethune, French official	(bass)
Count Vaudimont, French official	(bass)
Arrigo, a young Sicilian	(tenor)
Giovanni da Procida, Sicilian physician	(bass)
The Duchess Elena, sister of Duke Federigo of Austria	(soprano)
Ninetta, her Lady-in-waiting	(contralto)
Daniele, Sicilian	(tenor)
Tebaldo, French soldier	(tenor)
Roberto, French soldier	(bass)
Manfredo, Sicilian	(tenor)

LIBRETTO by Eugène Scribe and Charles Duveyrier

TIME: 1282
PLACE: Palermo

FIRST PERFORMED at the Paris Opéra, June 13, 1855 with Sophie Cruvelli (Hélène); Sannier (Ninette); Louis Gueymard (Arrigo); M. Bonnehée (Montfort); Louis-Henri Obin (Procida)

I vespri siciliani
(Les Vêpres siciliennes)

I

VERDI SPENT MUCH of the spring and summer of 1853 at Sant' Agata, working on the land and corresponding with Antonio Somma about the projected *King Lear* which was very much in his thoughts at this time. (The *Lear* correspondence is discussed in Chapter V.) His next contract was to write a new work for the Paris Opéra, to be performed during the Great Exhibition of 1855. This would be his first opera to have its première in Paris, the earlier *Jérusalem* having been merely an adaptation of an existing work. In October, a few days after his fortieth birthday, Verdi left for Paris with Giuseppina. The subject of the opera was to be the Sicilian Vespers, the famous massacre in Palermo in 1282; and the Opéra's ubiquitous Eugène Scribe, together with one of his numerous collaborators, Charles Duveyrier, was to provide the libretto. The libretto was delivered at the end of December, and Verdi spent most of 1854 in Paris slowly composing the opera. There were difficulties from the very beginning, perhaps the most nearly insuperable of them being the formal requirements of French opera at the time. The tradition decreed that a "grand opera" had to be a spectacular affair in five acts, with huge choruses, splendid effects, magnificent scenery and a great deal of ballet: in other words, the kind of opera that composers such as Meyerbeer and librettists like Scribe had been turning out for years. This type of old-fashioned show was diametrically opposed to the swift, clear and truthful drama towards which Verdi had been moving; but, realising it was hopeless to attempt to alter Parisian taste, he did his best to adapt himself to the task of providing the opera that Paris wanted and that Scribe's libretto presupposed. "A work for the opera is enough to stun a bull!" he wrote to a friend. "Five hours of music. Phew!"[1] But, although he knew what kind of libretto he could expect from Scribe, he was dismayed when he read the imbecilic hotch-potch that was presented to him. It was, he felt, an inane travesty of the historical events of 1282. Nevertheless, he set to work composing it, spending the winter months in Paris, and the summer in the country, at Mandres. By October he had completed

[1] *Carteggi Verdiani*, I, p. 26.

four of the five acts, and rehearsals began. After a few days, however, the leading soprano Sophie Cruvelli disappeared. Verdi was all for giving up the entire project and returning to Italy to work on *King Lear*: a new opera house was being built in Genoa, and the authorities had approached Verdi requesting a new opera as well as his permission to name the theatre after him. He refused the latter request, and the theatre became the Paganini, but he seriously considered writing the opening opera. Tito Ricordi suggested *King Lear*, knowing how deeply Verdi had been thinking about that subject, and the opera would probably have been written except that Madame Cruvelli returned from what had been simply an impromptu holiday with her lover, and rehearsals were resumed.

Verdi's troubles with Scribe, with the management of the Opéra, and with the Parisian concept of opera, snowballed rapidly, and on January 3, 1855 he wrote to Louis Crosnier, Director of the Opéra:

> I feel it my duty to let no more time pass without making a few observations concerning *Les Vêpres siciliennes*.
>
> It is both upsetting and mortifying for me that M. Scribe will not take the trouble to improve the fifth Act, which everyone agrees is uninteresting. I fully realise that M. Scribe has a thousand other things to concern him which are perhaps more important to him than my opera! But if I had been able to foresee his complete indifference I should have stayed in my own country where, really, I was not doing so badly.
>
> I had hoped that M. Scribe would find it possible to end the drama with one of those moving scenes which bring tears to the eyes, and whose effect is almost certain, since in my opinion the situation lends itself to that. Please note that this would have improved the entire work, which has nothing at all touching in it except the romanza in the fourth Act.
>
> I had hoped that M. Scribe would have been kind enough to appear at rehearsals from time to time, to be on the look out for any unfortunate lines which are hard to sing, to see whether anything needed touching up in the numbers or the Acts and so on For example, the second, third and fourth Acts all have the same form: aria, duet, finale.
>
> Finally, I expected M. Scribe, as he promised me at the beginning, to change everything that attacks the honour of the Italians.
>
> The more I consider this, the more I am persuaded it is dangerous. M. Scribe offends the French, because Frenchmen are massacred; he offends the Italians by altering the historic character of Procida into the conventional conspirator beloved by the Scribe system, and thrusts the inevitable dagger into his hand. Good Lord, there are virtues and vices in the history of every race, and we are no worse than the rest. In any case, I am first of all an Italian, and whatever happens I will not become an accomplice in offending my country.
>
> It remains for me to say a word about the rehearsals in the foyer. Here and there I hear words and remarks which, if not actually wounding, are at least inappropriate. I am not used to this, and I shall not tolerate it. It is

possible there are people who do not think my music worthy of the Opéra. It is possible there are others who think their rôles unworthy of their talents. It is possible that I, for my part, find the performance and style of singing other than I would have wished! In short it seems to me, unless I am strangely mistaken, that we are not at one in our way of feeling and interpreting the music, and without perfect accord there can be no possible success.

You see that everything I have just said is serious enough for us to stop and consider how to avoid the catastrophe which menaces us. For my part, I see but one means and I do not hesitate to propose it: the dissolution of the contract. I quite realize you will answer that the Opéra has already lost some time and money, but that is little in comparison with the year I have lost here, during which I could have earned a hundred thousand francs in Italy. You will go on to say it is all very well to annul a contract when there is a deficit, to which I reply that I should by now have paid it if my losses and expenses here were not already too great.

I know you are too just and reasonable not to choose the lesser of two evils. Trust my musical experience: under the conditions in which we are working, a success is really improbable. A half-success profits no-one. Let each of us try to make up for lost time, try to arrange everything calmly, and we may both gain by it.

Accept, sir, the assurance of my great esteem.

P.S. Excuse my bad French. The important thing is that you understand.[1]

The Opéra refused to release Verdi, and Scribe appears to have made none of the required changes. The situation dragged on, as did the rehearsals, for another five months. *Les Vêpres siciliennes* was finally produced at the Opéra on June 13th. Ironically, it was an enormous success with the Parisian public and critics. Verdi's style, the clarity of his vocal and orchestral writing, his restraint and economy were all praised. The critic of *La Presse* wrote: "Verdi's music has conformed to the procedure invented by French genius without losing anything of its Italian ardour."[2] The French composer Adolphe Adam, writing in the *Assemblée Nationale*, was particularly impressed by the quality of Verdi's melody. The *Débats* drew attention to the manner in which the composer improved upon his predecessors, Bellini and Donizetti: "He has carried further the respect for dramatic proprieties and dramatic truth. His writing for the orchestra shows colours and accents previously unknown in Italian music."[3]

Les Vêpres siciliennes notched up fifty performances at the Opéra in its first season. It was immediately translated into Italian, and produced in Italy. For censorship reasons it was known variously as *Giovanna di Braganza*, *Giovanna di Guzman*, *Giovanna di Sicilia*, and even *Batilde di Turenna*, before it acquired its proper title, *I vespri siciliani*, six years later, when Italy had finally achieved independence. The opera's

[1] *Copialettere*, pp. 157–9.   [2] Quoted by Toye, p. 93.   [3] Quoted by Toye, p. 93.

popularity was short-lived although, in its Italian version, it has survived. After the initial enthusiastic reception of Verdi's melodic inspiration had died down, it was found that the work really pleased no-one. The Italians were offended at being portrayed as villainous and cowardly, the French at seeing themselves massacred by foreigners, and the Austrians in Italy at the idea of Italians driving out an occupying power.[1]

II

Historically, the event known as the Sicilian Vespers is the massacre of the French by Sicilians at Palermo on March 30, 1282; an event of immense significance in European history, leading as it did to the destruction of the huge empire of Charles, Count of Anjou and Provence, King of Sicily, Albania and Jerusalem, and to the collapse of the Papacy's already tottering moral authority. The story leads, to quote from Sir Steven Runciman's admirable study, *The Sicilian Vespers*, "through schism and disillusion to the troubles of the Reformation."

Charles seldom visited his island kingdom, which was run for him by French administrators reputed to be both oppressive and corrupt, most of whom made no attempt to learn the islanders' language. The downtrodden and discontented Sicilians harboured their resentment of the French officials, knowing that the day of rebellion was sure to come. A conspiracy was organised with money and support from Constantinople, and arms were smuggled on to the island. The first moment of action may, however, have been spontaneous. Here is Runciman's description:

> There was gossiping and singing in the square as everyone waited for the service to begin. Suddenly a group of French officials appeared to join in the festivities of Easter Monday. They were greeted with cold, unfriendly looks, but they insisted on mingling with the crowd. They had drunk well and were carefree; and soon they treated the younger women with a familiarity that outraged the Sicilians. Among them was a sergeant called Drouet, who dragged a young married woman from the crowd and pestered her with his attentions. It was more than her husband could bear. He drew his knife and fell on Drouet, and stabbed him to death. The Frenchmen rushed up to avenge their comrade and suddenly found themselves surrounded by a host of furious Sicilians, all armed with daggers and swords. Not one of the Frenchmen survived. At that moment the bell of the

[1] Italian audiences still react politically to Verdi, it seems. The reviewer of a performance of *I vespri siciliani* in Trieste on November 4, 1968, wrote: "Given the particularly patriotic atmosphere that reigned in our city during the celebrations for the 50th anniversary of the liberation from the Austro-Hungarian Empire, this piece was an excellent choice, and the audience rose enthusiastically to the occasion." (*Opera*, February, 1969, p. 118.)

Church of the Holy Spirit and of all the churches of the city began to ring for Vespers.

To the sound of the bells messengers ran through the city calling on the men of Palermo to rise against the oppressor. At once the streets were full of angry armed men, crying "Death to the French"—"moranu li Franchiski" in their Sicilian dialect. Every Frenchman that they met was struck down. They poured into the inns frequented by the French and the houses where they dwelt, sparing neither man, woman, nor child. Sicilian girls who had married Frenchmen perished with their husbands. The rioters broke into the Dominican and Franciscan convents; and all the foreign friars were dragged out and told to pronounce the word "ciciri", whose sound the French tongue could never accurately reproduce. Anyone who failed in the test was slain.[1]

By the following morning, over two thousand of the French were dead, and the rebels had taken over Palermo. Uprisings took place in other parts of the island in the next few days.

In Scribe's absurd libretto, one of the leaders of the rebellion is Giovanni da Procida (Jean de Procida). The historical John of Procida was an eminent physician who was born in Salerno in 1210. He had been the personal physician of the Hohenstaufen Emperor, Frederick II, who rewarded him with several gifts of land, including the island of Procida. He became a political intriguer devoted to the Hohenstaufen cause, and his intrigues took him to Germany, to Spain and to Constantinople. The stories about this international conspirator and his legendary exploits are innumerable: he is thought by many historians to have played an important part in the Vespers, and Gibbon states in *The Decline and Fall of the Roman Empire* that the revolt was "inspired by the presence or the soul of John of Procida". Scribe's Procida is too cardboard a character to bear a resemblance either to the historical character or to any person who ever lived.

Scribe, the incredibly prolific dramatist and librettist whose complete works comprise seventy-six volumes each containing several titles, was born in Paris in 1791, and thus was twenty-two years older than Verdi. At the time of their collaboration, he had been turning out scripts for nearly half a cen ury and had accumulated a vast fortune. It is hardly surprising, therefore, that he was disinclined to go out of his way to satisfy Verdi. He had written for Meyerbeer, Adam, Auber (for whom he provided thirty-eight libretti!), Boieldieu, Donizetti, Halévy, Rossini and many others, and was also the author of hundreds of comedies for the stage. The incredibly high output-rate of the Scribe factory was maintained until his death in 1861. In addition to reading three of his libretti in the course of writing this book, I dipped into a few of the plays and vaudevilles in the collected edition, and hastily formed the opinion that they could have been written in his sleep.

[1] Runciman, *The Sicilian Vespers*, pp. 214–15 (Cambridge, 1958).

Les Vêpres siciliennes may not have been written in M. Scribe's sleep, but it was certainly not an original work created for Verdi, and it is difficult to understand why Scribe took so long over it. All he did was use an old libretto he had written for Donizetti, called *Le Duc d'Albe*, altering the names of the characters and some details of the plot. Basically, the story is the same, and so is much of the actual dialogue.[1] Scribe's *Le Duc d'Albe* was written in 1839 for the Paris Opéra, and by the following year Donizetti had composed most of the music. For various reasons the opera was not produced in Donizetti's lifetime. Scribe took court action to obtain his fee, which he eventually received, so the libretto was presumably the legal property of Donizetti: at any rate it was not Scribe's. Donizetti died in 1848, but *Le Duc d'Albe* did not reach the stage until 1882. Meanwhile, the dishonest and avaricious Scribe patched up the libretto and re-sold it to Verdi in 1853 as *Les Vêpres siciliennes*. In 1882, at the time of the posthumous première of Donizetti's opera, Verdi wrote to his friend Senator Giuseppe Piroli:

> I have seen D'Arçais's article on *Il Duca d'Alba*. I never knew that Scribe had made use of *Il Duca d'Alba* in writing *I vespri siciliani*. It is true, however, that Vasselli, Donizetti's relative, mentioned it to me *en passant* when I was in Rome for *Un ballo in maschera* in 1859, but I paid no attention and thought it was only a suspicion, an idea of Vasselli's. Now I understand and truly believe that *I vespri* was taken from *Il Duca d'Alba*.[2]

Le Duc d'Albe deals with the Spanish occupation of Flanders in the sixteenth century. Its story and the relationships of its characters are virtually the same as those of *I vespri siciliani*, except that in Act V of *Le Duc d'Albe* there is, of course, no massacre, only an attempted assassination. The Duke of Alba, Marcello and Amelia become, in *I vespri siciliani*, Monforte, Arrigo and Elena, and John of Procida is pasted on to the existing plot. In a bold attempt to camouflage the lack of any connection between his plot and the historical events in 1282, Scribe appended to his libretto[3] a lengthy footnote which begins thus:

> A ceux qui nous reprocheront, comme de coutume, d'ignorer l'histoire, nous nous empresserons d'apprendre que le massacre général connu sous le nom de Vêpres Siciliennes n'a jamais existé. Ce point historique une fois reconnu, il doit être à peu près permis à chacun de traiter ce sujet comme il l'entend. C'est ce qu'ont fait tous les auteurs dramatiques qui nous ont précédé. Du reste, notre ouvrage n'a, malheureusement pour nous, aucun rapport avec celui de Casimir Delavigne.[4]

[1] Verdi's Piave also wrote a libretto on this subject, *Il Duca d'Alba*, for Pacini in 1842.

[2] *Carteggi Verdiani*, Vol. III, p. 152.

[3] Scribe: *Œuvres Complètes*, 3rd series, Vol. VI (Paris, 1888), pp. 73–4.

[4] Delavigne was the author of a verse tragedy, *Les Vêpres siciliennes*, from which Scribe borrowed what few ideas he had about John of Procida.

(To those who make the usual accusation that we have ignored history, we hasten to point out that the general massacre known as the Sicilian Vespers never existed. This historical point once acknowledged, it must be left to each to treat the subject as he thinks proper. This is what those authors who have preceded us have done. For the rest, our work has, unfortunately for us, no connection with that of Casimir Delavigne.)

It is a great pity that the Sicilian Vespers, a subject which Verdi must have realised could provide splendid encouragement to the cause of the Risorgimento, should have been so mishandled by Scribe, to whose demented imagination one massacre was no doubt very like another, and who certainly failed to distinguish the Sicilian Vespers of 1282 from the slaughter of the Huguenots in 1572. In 1842, a decade before Verdi's concern with the subject, Michele Amari, a distinguished Sicilian historian, published *La guerra del Vespro Siciliano* in which he gave a scholarly account of the events and into which he also infused a great deal of anti-Bourbon propaganda in an attempt to rouse his fellow Sicilians to the cause of the Risorgimento. What formidable collaborators he and Verdi would have been.

The first of *I vespri siciliani*'s five Acts takes place in the main square of Palermo. French soldiers are drinking and carousing, watched by a mob of sullen and discontented Sicilians. The Duchess Elena appears, in mourning for her brother, Federigo of Austria, who has been executed by the French for treason. (As a matter of historical fact, the executon of the teen-age Frederick took place fourteen years earlier, in 1268.) Roberto, a French soldier, orders Elena to sing for the entertainment of his colleagues. She does so, but her song is an exhortation to the Sicilians to rise against their oppressors. Under cover of singing about the perils of the sea, she reminds her countrymen: "Il vostro fato è in vostra mano" (Your fate is in your own hands), and launches into a rebel-rousing incitement to violence. Naturally a fight breaks out in the square between Sicilians and French, stopped only by the arrival on the scene of Monforte (Guy de Montfort), the French Governor of Sicily. The crowd disperses, and Arrigo, a young Sicilian, enters. He has just been acquitted of a charge of treason, but his inflammatory remarks to Elena are overheard by Monforte, who, ordering Elena to leave, questions the young man about his name and family. Arrigo's replies are defiant, but Monforte offers him service with the French, an offer which Arrigo, of course, indignantly refuses. Ignoring Monforte's order not to associate with the suspect Elena, he immediately strides off towards Elena's palace.

The second act is set in a valley outside Palermo, by the sea. Giovanni da Procida, returned from exile to lead the revolutionaries, sings of his love for his native land and his determination to set it free from foreign dominion. He has arranged to meet Elena and Arrigo, and when they arrive several chapters of history are covered in two lines of dialogue:

Procida: Bisanzio e Spagna scorsi chiedendo ovunque aita!
Elena: Di Pietro d'Aragona è nostro il voto?

Procida: I have sought help from Byzantium and Spain.
Elena: Is Peter of Aragon for us?

Peter of Aragon will help if the whole of Sicily joins the uprising. Procida depends on Arrigo's aid to bring this about. When Procida has left, Arrigo declares his love for Elena, who promises to be his if he will avenge her brother's death. This he swears to do. Bethune, a French officer, arrives with a message from Monforte inviting Arrigo to a ball and, when he scornfully refuses the invitation, he is arrested and led away. Procida returns, and discovers a way of arousing the Sicilians from their apathy. Young men and girls arrive to dance at a festival of betrothal, and Procida suggests to the drunkenly amorous French soldier Roberto that he and his companions should abduct some of the girls, hoping thus to arouse the fury of the Sicilian males. The plan succeeds, and the Sicilians are made even more furious when a vessel sails past carrying elegantly attired French officers and Sicilian women, all singing a barcarolle as they sail to the Governor's ball at Palermo.

The first scene of Act III is set in Monforte's study in his palace. The Governor is seated at his desk brooding over a letter he has received from a woman he seduced years earlier, in which she boasts of having brought up his son, Arrigo, to hate Monforte. Bethune enters to announce that Arrigo, having refused the invitation, has been arrested, and Monforte asks that he be brought in. He sings of the emptiness in his heart, and of his desire to be loved by his son. When Arrigo enters, Monforte tells him they are father and son, to which news Arrigo reacts in great consternation. Not only are the demands on his feelings too confusing for him, he also realises that as Monforte's son he has no hope of gaining Elena's hand. Monforte appeals in vain to Arrigo to recognise their relationship and to accord him the filial love that is his due. Arrigo rushes out, calling on his mother to pray for him.

The second scene of Act III is set in a great ballroom at the palace. After they have been entertained by the ballet of "The Four Seasons", the guests dance. Among them are Elena and Procida, both masked. Procida tells Arrigo, who has turned up after all, that there are several conspirators among the guests and that Monforte is to be assassinated. The conspirators wear silk ribbons, and Procida pins one on Arrigo's costume. Arrigo attempts in vain to warn Monforte of the danger surrounding him and, when the conspirators advance upon the Governor, Arrigo steps forward to defend him. Monforte has the conspirators arrested, and thanks Arrigo for saving his life, while Elena, Procida and the Sicilians denounce Arrigo as a traitor.

In Act IV, set in the courtyard of the fortress where Elena and Procida are imprisoned, Arrigo comes to visit Elena. At first she treats him with contempt. But, when he explains that Monforte is his father and that he feels he has now paid his debt of filial respect and is free to rejoin the conspirators, Elena relents, and she and Arrigo reaffirm their love for each other. Procida is brought in, and whispers to Elena that a ship laden with arms for the cause is lying in the harbour. Monforte arrives, demands the immediate execution of the prisoners, and refuses to listen to Arrigo's pleas on their behalf unless Arrigo acknowledges him publicly as his father. At the sight of Elena being led to the scaffold, Arrigo accepts his father's terms, and Monforte releases the prisoners and announces the wedding of Elena and Arrigo to celebrate the amnesty. When Elena hesitates, Procida whispers that she must accept for the sake of her country and her brother. The act ends in general rejoicing, under cover of which Procida makes his plans for rebellion.

The last act is set in the gardens of Monforte's palace, where a crowd has assembled for the wedding celebrations. Elena sings a gay song of thanks to the guests for the flowers they have given her, and she and Arrigo sing of their blissful future. The fanatical Procida enters, and informs Elena that, when the bells ring out to announce the wedding, the armed Sicilians will fall upon the French and slaughter them all. Elena is aghast. She cannot bring herself to denounce Procida, so can only refuse to proceed with the ceremony without giving a reason, to the mystified despair of Arrigo. Monforte enters and overrules Elena's decision, which he is sure she cannot really intend. He orders the bells to be rung, and immediately the Sicilian mob, armed with swords and daggers, rushes into the garden and advances menacingly as the curtain falls.

III

The Overture to *I vespri siciliani* is a splendid piece, of great character and excellent construction, built around a big tune which, as I mentioned earlier, made its first appearance in *Giovanna d'Arco* (see pp. 113–14). The tune [Ex. 27] is heard again in the opera, in the Act III duet between Arrigo and Monforte. Other themes from the opera heard first in the Overture are the massacre music and the gentle pianissimo subject with tremolando strings which occurs in the prison scene of Act IV. The opening chorus of French soldiers and Sicilian citizens is, like most of the opera's choral writing, so conscientiously well-made that it could almost be by Meyerbeer, and the same is true of most of the recitative-cum-arioso in which the action is advanced. The Parisian influence on Verdi, though fleeting, is undeniably baleful. Elena's aria, "Deh! tu calma, o Dio possente", with its fierce *allegro* section, "Corragio", inciting the Sicilians to rebel, is quite a lively number, though the ensuing ensemble, when the French and Sicilians fight, lapses into emptiness. Verdi seems frequently in this opera to have lost his touch. The quartet, "D'ira fremo all' aspetto tremendo", technically excellent, is curiously dead, lacking the authority and the imagination which he had displayed sixteen years earlier in the *Oberto* quartet. Nor is the duet between Arrigo and Monforte, which ends the act, much more successful, although Arrigo's cantabile, "Di giovine audace" contributes a certain distinction [Ex. 74].

Ex.74

Di gio - vi - ne au-da - ce   ca - sti - ga   l'ar - dir:

Act II begins promisingly with Procida's "O tu, Palermo", deservedly one of Verdi's most popular bass arias, a lyrical cantabile of great beauty. Its exciting cabaletta, "Nell' ombra e nel silenzio", accompanied by the chorus basses, is less well known [Ex. 75]. The duet for

Ex.75   Allegro

San-to a - mor,..... che in me fa - vel - li,   par-la al cor.............de' miei fra - tel - li;

Elena and Arrigo, "Quale, o prode, al tuo corragio", just misses being first-rate, but contains much that is effective in performance. Scribe has written a second act finale of an impressive mindlessness, but Verdi salvages the situation to some extent by the quality of the dances he has written, a gay and lively tarantella and a very pretty barcarolle, the latter effectively punctuated by the discontented muttering of the Sicilians.

Act III has two scenes, the first of which consists simply of an aria for Monforte followed by a duet with Arrigo. The aria, "In braccio alle dovizie", is one of the score's most attractive numbers, and the superb duet, one of Verdi's many attractive tenor-baritone pieces, makes good use of the tune from the Overture. At first Monforte sings it, and later it is taken up by Arrigo [Ex. 76].

Ex.76

Om - bra   di - let - ta,........... che in   ciel   ri - po - si,

la.......... for - za   ren - di - mi che il   cor   per - dè.

The second scene of Act III, in the ballroom of Monforte's palace, opens with the ballet of the Seasons, performed for the delectation of the Governor's guests. The first season is Winter, whose dances are appropriately glittery, with glissandi, much staccato, and a section of pizzicato. The final *allegro* is invigorating. Spring is more shimmering, warm and Tchaikovskian in its first dance [Ex. 77], sprightlier in the

others. There is much use of solo woodwind instruments throughout the ballet. Summer has a pleasant and rhythmically lively *vivace*, while Autumn follows an exciting opening *allegro* with a sadly beautiful *andante* punctuated by more agitated passages. The whole of the ballet music is deliciously scored, the woodwind writing in Spring being particularly notable. The brighter orchestral colour of the ballet music does something to lighten the otherwise unrelieved appropriately dark gloom of the scoring. At the conclusion of the ballet, the guests sing a festive chorus. The music for the attempt on Monforte's life is no more than passable, but the finale ensemble, while it is by no means Verdi at his best, generates something of the old energy and spirit.

The orchestral introduction to Act IV, Arrigo's lengthy recitative and his aria, "Giorno di pianto" [Ex. 79] are all excellent, though the

aria is strongly reminiscent of the Duke of Mantua's "É il sol dell anima" in *Rigoletto* [Ex. 78]. The duet for Elena and Arrigo, "Volgi il

guardo a me sereno", is first rate, particularly the reconciliation after he has explained that Monforte is his father. Elena, a dramatic soprano d'agilità, sings a cadenza which takes her from top C to the F sharp below middle C. The final section of the duet, "É dolce raggio", has a charmingly graceful melody. The quartet, "Addio, mia patria amata", is extremely moving, as is Procida's solo farewell which precedes it, but the finale, the kind of ensemble on various levels which Verdi brought off superbly on other occasions, fails to cohere.

After the opening chorus of Act V, Elena sings "Mercè, dilette amiche", an exciting coloratura display piece which, in addition to exploiting the soprano's range above the stave, twice asks of her an audible A below middle C. This is the number often referred to as the Bolero, although the score labels it Siciliana. A Siciliana is, as its name implies, a Sicilian dance rhythm, in 6–8 or 12–8 time, while a Bolero is a lively Spanish dance in 3–4 time. Verdi's Bolero-like Siciliana is in 3–4 time. The brief duet, "La brezza aleggia intorno", for Arrigo and Elena, begins with a sweetly appealing melody for Arrigo, and ends on his heroic flourish reaching up to the tenor's D natural [Ex. 80].

Part of the trio for the lovers and Procida in the finale is interesting and effective, but the massacre at the end of the opera is botched and brutally swift. Incidentally, a comparison of the French and Italian versions reveals no significant difference in detail. Verdi himself translated the libretto into Italian, and made the necessary slight changes to the vocal line. If anything, the Italian text declaims more naturally than the French.

Verdi's dislike of the sprawled lifelessness of Scribe's libretto and of its inane offensiveness was hardly likely to lead to the composition of a masterpiece. But the more one looks at and listens to *I vespri siciliani*, the more frustrated one feels at the thought of so much splendid music married not only to so impossible a text but also to so unviable a form as that of the five-act French grand opera. These lines, as it happens, are being written a day or two after a London revival, or resuscitation, in concert form, of Meyerbeer's *Les Huguenots*, probably the most successful work ever written in that *genre*. But how cumbersome the dead beast is. Had the performance been given without cuts, it would have lasted nearly six hours, yet musically, apart from a few ensembles which might prove immediately effective in the theatre, with adequate visual aid, all that one can admire is a phrase in the fourth act duet. The rest is a *tableau morte* of gargantuan proportions. The inflated form is conducive to inflated music.

It says something for Verdi's taste and sensitivity that he was unable to produce a monster of this kind, and something more for the quality of his musical imagination that he poured so much excellent music into the work. It is occasionally performed today, and rightly so, for it is by no means a despicable piece. Toye makes the point that "Scribe's artificiality seems to have paralysed Verdi in whom complete unabashed sincerity was a primary virtue." True, and the finest pages of the opera are those in which this sincerity burns through the deadwood of the libretto: the Overture, the duet between Arrigo and Monforte in Act III, the ballet music (which I was delighted to find an operatic reference book dismissing with the words: "The bastard French ballet music is frightful trash"[1]), and much of the fourth act. It is perfectly clear that Verdi's art, always one of concision and directness, was ill-suited to the prolix form and empty professionalism of Meyerbeerian opera.

Tastes differ. In 1864, in his own short-lived magazine *Figaro*, Boito, who was later to become the librettist of Verdi's last two, and perhaps greatest, operas, but who at the time was no out-and-out Verdian, wrote of *I vespri siciliani*: "It would take a long time to enumerate all the graces and the strength of this solemn opera, for one would have to stop and admire every piece."[2]

[1] Brockway and Weinstock, *The World of Opera* (London, 1963), p. 308.
[2] Walker, p. 452.

X X

Simon Boccanegra

Dramatis personae:

Simon Boccanegra, a buccaneer in the service of the Genoese republic, later Doge	(baritone)
Jacopo Fiesco (also known as Andrea)	(bass)
Paolo Albiani, goldsmith, later favourite courtier of the Doge	(baritone)
Pietro, citizen, later courtier	(baritone)
Maria, Boccanegra's daughter, also known as Amelia Grimaldi	(soprano)
Gabriele Adorno, Genoese nobleman	(tenor)

LIBRETTO by Francesco Maria Piave, revised by Arrigo Boito, based on the play *Simón Boccanegra* by Antonio García Gutiérrez

TIME: 1339 and 1363
PLACE: Genoa

FIRST PERFORMED at the Teatro Fenice, Venice, March 12, 1857. With Luigia Bendazzi (Maria); Carlo Negrini (Gabriele); Leone Giraldoni (Boccanegra); Giacomo Vercellini (Paolo); Giuseppe Echeverria (Fiesco). Revised version first performed at La Scala, Milan, March 24, 1881, with Anna d'Angeri (Maria); Francesco Tamagno (Gabriele); Victor Maurel (Boccanegra); Federico Salvati (Paolo); Édouard de Reszke (Fiesco)

Simon Boccanegra

AFTER THE PREMIÈRE of *Les Vêpres siciliennes* Verdi stayed on in Paris for several months in order to cope with a number of business and legal problems connected with the copyright, publication and performance of his operas. These involved a visit to London to prevent a pirated production of *Il trovatore* from taking place. Finally, in December 1855, he returned to Sant' Agata, his immediate chore being to adapt *Stiffelio*. The pliable Piave was summoned and ordered to find a new subject; one which would be acceptable to the censorship, and to which the *Stiffelio* music could easily be adapted. This, as we know, became *Aroldo*, which was eventually produced in Rimini in August 1857. In March 1856, Verdi went to Venice, where he conducted a successful revival of *La traviata* at the Fenice. While there, he agreed to write a new opera for the Fenice, to be produced during the 1856–7 season. The subject he chose was another play by the Spanish playwright Antonio García Gutiérrez. Called *Simon Boccanegra*, it was written around the historical character of that name who became Doge of Genoa in 1339. Piave was asked to prepare the libretto under the composer's guidance. During 1856, Verdi not only worked on this new opera, having first planned the libretto for Piave to turn into verse, but also went on his travels again to Paris and London in order to protect his interests. While in Paris, he supervised the French production of *Il trovatore*, for which he wrote ballet music and made alterations to the finale, and also found time to correspond with Piave about *Simon Boccanegra*. The usual trouble over censorship arose, for the Doge Boccanegra had been a man with a vision of a united Italy, but Verdi this time made it clear that he would not consider any alterations. In the end, he was not asked to make any. He worked on the opera throughout the year, but when he left Paris at the beginning of 1857 to return to Sant' Agata, he had by no means completed it. Dissatisfied with parts of Piave's libretto, he had asked Giuseppe Montanelli, a politician and former professor of law living in exile in Paris, to re-write certain scenes. Montanelli complied quickly and competently, but when Verdi arrived in Venice in mid-February to rehearse, he still had one act to compose and the entire score to orchestrate. The opera was produced at the Fenice on March 12th, but was not a success.

To the Countess Maffei, Verdi wrote: "*Boccanegra* was almost a greater fiasco in Venice than *Traviata*. I thought I had done something fairly good, but now it seems I was mistaken."[1]

If it failed with the public in Venice, however, the opera interested the critics. The music was praised for its fidelity to the text, the orchestration for its elegance, the melody for its inspiration. "There is something for every taste," wrote the *Gazzetta Musicale*, "but the various tints, as is always the case in Verdi's operas, are invariably subordinated to the general atmosphere and to the logic of the whole."[2]

Twenty-three years later, in 1880, the sixty-seven-year-old Verdi, with *Aida* behind him and *Otello* in the process of gestation, was persuaded by Ricordi to take another look at *Boccanegra*. Verdi was easy to persuade, having always had a fondness for the opera, and was full of ideas for the revision of the libretto. He wrote to Giulio Ricordi:

> The score as it stands is impossible. It is too sad, too desolate. There is no need to touch anything in the first or last acts, and nothing but a few odd notes in the third. But the whole of the second act must be revised and given more relief, variety and animation. From a musical point of view, we could retain the soprano's cavatina, the duet with the tenor, and the other duet between father and daughter, despite the cabalettas! (Open, earth, and swallow us up!) Anyway, I am not afraid of cabalettas, and if a young man were to appear tomorrow who could write any as good as, for example, "Meco tu vieni" or "Ah, perchè non posso odiarti", I would listen to him with all my heart, and let the harmonic imagination and refinements of our learned orchestration go. Ah, progress, science, realism. Oh dear, be as realistic as you like, nevertheless. Shakespeare was a realist, but he did not know it. He was a realist by inspiration; we are realists by design, by calculation. So there, all things considered, the cabalettas are still better. The joke of it is that in the whirl of progress, art is turning about and going backwards. Art without spontaneity, naturalness and simplicity is not art.
>
> To get back to Act II, who could revise it? I have said that in general it needs something to give life and variety to the drama's excessive gloom. But what? A hunting scene? Not suitable for the stage. A festival? Too ordinary. A battle with African pirates? Not very entertaining. Preparations for war against Pisa or Venice? In that connection, I remember two magnificent letters of Petrarch's, one to Boccanegra, the other to the Doge of Venice, warning them against starting a fratricidal war, and reminding them that both were sons of the same mother, Italy, and so on. This idea of an Italian fatherland at that time was quite sublime! All this is political and undramatic, but a clever man could surely turn it into drama. For instance, Boccanegra, struck by this thought, intends to take the poet's advice. He calls a meeting of the senate or privy council, and expounds the idea of Petrarch's letter. Great indignation, quarrels, even accusations of treachery against the Doge, and so on. The argument is interrupted by the business of Amelia's abduction.[3]

[1] *Copialettere*, p. 553.   [2] Quoted by Toye, p. 98.   [3] *Copialettre*, pp. 559–60.

The task of improving the libretto was entrusted to Boito, who was later to provide Verdi with the libretto for *Otello* and who was, in fact, already at work on it. For some months the two men collaborated on the *Boccanegra* project. Boito wanted to provide a completely new act, but this eventually became the Council Chamber scene. Verdi wrote:

> Having, unfortunately, to renounce this Act, we must agree on the Council Chamber scene which, as written by you, I have no doubt will be effective. Your criticisms are justified but, immersed in more important work and thinking of *Otello*, you are aiming here at an unattainable perfection. I do not aim so high and so am more optimistic than you, and by no means in despair. I admit the table is shaky, but if we adjust the legs a little I think it will stand up. I also admit that none of the characters will make anyone exclaim, "How well delineated"; but this is always very rare. Nevertheless, it seems to me there is something worth salvaging in the characters of Fiesco and Simone.[1]

Boito wrote the new scene, and Verdi commented on it:

> This scene in the Council Chamber is most beautiful, full of movement, of local colour, with your usual very elegant and forceful verses. I agree about the verses to be altered at the beginning of the third act, and the poisoning of the Doge in that way will do very well. But to my misfortune the piece is vast in the extreme, difficult to set to music, and I don't know whether, now that I am no longer *dans le mouvement*, I shall be able to get back into practice in time to do this, and patch up all the rest.
>
> Allow me now a few remarks, simply to clarify things to myself:
>
> 1 Do you think it necessary to let it be known in the beginning that Amelia is safe, and is *calling for justice*?
>
> 2 Do you think that the affair of Tartary is alone sufficient to call the Council together? Could one not add some other affairs of state, a Corsair raid, for example, or even the war with Venice, cursed by the poet? All that, of course, in passing, in a few lines?
>
> 3 If Adorno says: "I killed Lorenzino because he carried off my betrothed" and Amelia: "Save my betrothed!" we spoil the scene in the third act between the Doge and Amelia—a scene not very important in itself but which prepares very well for the Doge's sleep and the terzetto. It seems to me that the action would lose nothing if when the Doge says: "Why did you take up arms?" Gabriele replied: "You had Amelia Grimaldi carried off. Vile crowned Corsair, die!"
> Doge: "Strike, then!"
> Gabriele: "Amelia!"
> All: "Amelia!"
> Doge: "Adorno, you protected this maiden; I admire you and absolve you. . . . Amelia, tell us how you were carried off," etc., etc.
> The rest will do very well. Stupendous from "Plebeians! Patricians! People!" to the end, which we will close with "Be accursed!"[2]

Ten days later, Verdi wrote again to his librettist:

[1] *Copialettere*, p. 316.   [2] Walker, p. 481.

Don't blame yourself for having wasted my time. So far I have done nothing about the music. Now however I am thinking about it, indeed I have been thinking all day about this *Boccanegra*, and this is what it seems to me could be done:

I pass over the Prologue, of which I'll perhaps alter the first recitative and a few bars here and there in the orchestra.

In the first act I should take out the cabaletta of the first piece, not because it's a cabaletta but because it's very ugly. I should alter the prelude, to which I should link Amelia's *cantabile*, changing the scoring, and making them *one single piece*. At the end I should take up again an orchestral movement from the prelude, over which Amelia would say "Day has dawned . . . he's not coming!" or something similar. So patch me up a couple of short lines in broken phrases. I should not want that expression of jealousy on Amelia's part!

The tenor's offstage romanza would stay as it is.

In the following duet I should alter the line: "You agree to our marriage." If the audience doesn't catch the word "humble" it would not understand anything further. If he said, for example, "Listen . . . a deep secret!" etc., etc—these are words that always make an audience prick up its ears. And therefore, if you think fit, add a couple of lines—or don't, just as you wish. What really matters to me is to alter the duet between Fiesco and Gabriele: "Tremble, O Doge!" It's too ferocious, and says nothing at all. Instead I should like Fiesco, who is almost Amelia's father, to bless bride and bridegroom to be. A pathetic moment could result which would be a ray of light amid so much gloom. To maintain the atmosphere introduce too a bit of local patriotic feeling. Fiesco can say: "Love this angel . . . but after God . . . our country," etc. All good words to make the ears prick up. . . .

Eight lines then for Fiesco and as many for Gabriele, simple, touching, affectionate, on which to write a bit of melody, or something that at least resembles it. Ah, if one could bring Amelia back into the scene, and write an unaccompanied terzettino! How delightful to write for three voices! Amelia and Gabriele kneeling, Fiesco, above, blessing them! But I can understand that, apart from the difficulty of bringing Amelia back, we should have an almost identical final scene in the last act.

Have I made myself clear? I'm not quite sure. Try to guess at what I haven't been able to say and send me meanwhile those few verses as soon as possible, and tomorrow or the next day I'll tell you about the rest. Meanwhile I shall set to work on the first piece of this first act, to get myself in practice before I come to the finale.

I would like to do everything in order, as if a new opera were concerned.[1]

The correspondence continued throughout the winter, as the two men became immersed in their joint task. At last the revision was complete, and *Simon Boccanegra* was produced at the Scala on March 24, 1881. The ten performances were triumphantly successful. Boccanegra was sung by the famous French baritone Victor Maurel, and Verdi admired him sufficiently to promise, during one of the rehearsals, to write the role of Iago for him.

[1] Walker, p. 482.

II

The opera is based, loosely, both on historical fact and on the play *Simón Boccanegra* written fourteen years earlier by the prolific Spanish dramatist Antonio García Gutiérrez whose *El Trovador* had already provided Verdi with operatic material. In the 1857 libretto there are considerable divergences from the play, and after Boito's re-writing of 1881 there is, of course, an even wider gulf between play and opera. The character of Boccanegra in both play and opera is an amalgam of the historical Simon and his brother Egidio, the fictional Simon being saddled with Egidio's sea-faring occupation. García Gutiérrez had, for a time, been the Spanish Consul at Genoa, which is where, presumably, he acquired his interest in mediaeval Genoese history.

The historical Simon was elected first Doge of Genoa in 1339 and, as in the opera, it appears that he accepted the office with a certain reluctance. Once elected, he attempted to keep peace between patricians and plebeians and, among the patricians, between the Guelph and Ghibelline families; he nevertheless found himself compelled to fight the patricians on several occasions. After five years of battle and intrigue, Simon resigned and took his family off to voluntary exile in Pisa. Ten years later, hearing that the patricians planned to take over the city of Genoa with the aid of the Milanese Visconti family, Simon decided to return and lead the people against the nobles. This he succeeded in doing, and was again appointed Doge in 1356. Refusing to indulge in revenge against the conquered patricians, he merely banished them from Genoa, and established a period of prosperity and peace in the city state. Finally, his enemies triumphed. He was given poisoned wine at a banquet in March 1363, and died in great agony watched by the gloating patricians.

Piave's Boccanegra is basically the character that García Gutiérrez created: a naval hero, a pirate, perhaps not unlike an Elizabethan sea adventurer, he at first accepts political office in order to facilitate his marriage to the daughter of a patrician family, but then brings his own personal qualities of weak amiability to affairs of state in an attempt to create peace and stability. Boito's additions a quarter of a century later have the effect of strengthening Boccanegra's personality and of giving him, in the Council Chamber scene, a greater stature. One still, however, has to accept on trust his sea-faring and buccaneering qualities. In the opera he is far from being a man of action. It would be absurd to pretend that the final libretto is anything more than a second-hand, patched up job, but it is certainly a distinct improvement upon the first draft.

The opera consists of a Prologue and three Acts. The Prologue, which takes place in 1339, is set in a square in Genoa. In the background the church of San Lorenzo can be seen, and on the right is the town palace of the Fiesco family, a house with a large balcony and, on its outside wall, a figure of the Madonna illuminated by a lantern. It is dark, just before dawn. Paolo Albiani, political leader of the plebeian faction, is plotting with his colleague Pietro. A Doge is to be chosen, and they are determined to undermine the power and influence of the patricians by having a plebeian candidate elected. Paolo persuades Pietro to urge upon the people the name of Simon Boccanegra, a buccaneer who has won the gratitude of the Genoans by ridding their coast of African pirates. Pietro pledges the people's vote in return for a promise of "gold, power and honour" from Paolo, whose motives for wishing to overthrow the patricians are also not entirely selfless. Pietro leaves to organise the plebeians, and Simon enters, having been summoned from Savona by Paolo, who now asks him if he would like to be Doge. Simon is at first not interested, and agrees only when Paolo points out to him that as Doge he will be able to overcome the opposition of the wealthy and powerful Jacopo Fiesco to his marriage with Fiesco's daughter. She has already had a child by him. Simon leaves, and Paolo withdraws into the shadows as groups of sailors and workmen begin to enter the square. Pietro returns and moves among them conspiratorially, urging the cause of a popular plebeian candidate for Doge. When the crowd asks who this candidate is, Paolo steps forward and announces the name of Boccanegra. The people ask how the Fiesco family is likely to react, and Paolo assures them that the Fieschi will do nothing. Pointing to their palace, he tells of the beautiful Maria, who for three months now has not been allowed out of the house. Suddenly, a flame appears in one of the windows of the Fiesco palace, an indication that someone has just died. Crossing themselves superstitiously, the crowd disperses, expressing their allegiance to Simon Boccanegra.

When the square is deserted, Jacopo Fiesco comes out, bidding his palace a last farewell. His daughter Maria has just died, and he calls down a curse on Simon, who had seduced her. As he sings a lament for his daughter, a chorus of women inside the palace can be heard chanting a Miserere, and a procession of mourners led by a priest leaves the palace and slowly crosses the square. After they have gone, Simon returns and is immediately confronted by Fiesco. Simon begs the old man to forgive him, but Fiesco is implacable in his hatred of the man he considers responsible for his daughter's death, and swears there can be no peace between them until one of them dies. Simon invites him to strike now, but Fiesco scorns to act as an assassin. He offers, instead, to forgive Simon if he will hand over Maria's child, a daughter. The unhappy Simon is forced to confess that he cannot do this. He had entrusted the child to the care of an old woman, but one day, when he went to visit them, he found the old woman dead. The frightened child had wandered off, and although he had searched everywhere for her, she was not to be found. Repeating coldly that if Simon cannot produce the child there can be no reconciliation, Fiesco leaves. Deciding to gain entry to the palace to see Maria, Simon is surprised to find the front door open. He goes inside, and Fiesco immediately steps forward from the shadows where he had been watching. This is the beginning of his revenge. "T'inoltra e stringi gelida salma," he cries. "Go in and embrace a cold corpse." From within the house there is a cry as Simon discovers the dead Maria. Heart-broken, he staggers out into the square while a crowd in the distance is heard acclaiming him Doge. The crowd enters, led by Paolo and Pietro who announce to Simon that he has been elected, but the stricken Simon is in no condition to pay attention to the people swarming about him or the pealing of the bells.

Between the Prologue and the rest of the opera there is, according to the libretto, a leap of twenty-five years. This would bring us to 1364, but as the historical Boccanegra died in 1363, Piave's arithmetic is out by one year. Act I, Scene 1, takes place in the garden of the Grimaldi palace on the coast not far from Genoa. The Mediterranean can be seen in the background. It is dawn, and Amelia Grimaldi awaits the arrival of Gabriele Adorno, with whom she is in love. Adorno is a young nobleman who, together with her guardian Andrea, is engaged in plotting against Boccanegra, the Doge. Gabriele arrives, and Amelia, fearful of the danger to which his activities expose him, attempts to dissuade him from his political conspiracies. Pietro enters to announce that the Doge, on his way back to Genoa from the hunt at Savona, wishes to visit Amelia. She is convinced the Doge wishes to force her into marriage with his favourite, Paolo, and to forestall this she begs Gabriele to make immediate plans for their wedding. She hurries into the palace. As Gabriele is about to leave he meets her guardian Andrea, who is in fact Fiesco living under an assumed name. Knowing of Gabriele's love for Amelia, Fiesco considers it his duty to inform the young man that she is not really a member of the high-born Grimaldi family. The Grimaldi child had died years ago, and a foundling was brought up in her place as Amelia Grimaldi, in order to stop the Doge from confiscating Count Grimaldi's estate. Gabriele reaffirms his love for Amelia, whoever she may be, and Fiesco gives him his blessing. The distant sound of trumpets heralds the approach of the Doge, so the two men depart. The Doge enters, attended by Paolo and a party of huntsmen, and Amelia returns to meet him. Boccanegra dismisses his followers and disarms Amelia by presenting her with a document pardoning her exiled Grimaldi brothers. He asks her if she is in love; Amelia replies that she is and that she detests the attentions of Paolo, whom she accuses of merely coveting the Grimaldi fortune. She confides in the Doge that she is not really a Grimaldi, and speaks of her childhood with an old woman in a cottage on the seashore near Pisa. Before the woman died, she had given Amelia a locket containing a portrait of her real mother.

Boccanegra, beginning to suspect Amelia's identity, questions her, and she tells him she also remembers being visited by a sea-faring man. Was the old woman's name Giovanna, Boccanegra asks? Learning that it was, he produces a locket which Amelia compares with her own. They contain similar portraits. "Maria!" cries the Doge, and tells her that she is his daughter. A scene of tearful reunion follows, after which Amelia goes indoors. When Paolo enters, Boccanegra curtly orders him to renounce all hope of marrying her. The Doge leaves, and Paolo immediately enlists the aid of Pietro in planning to abduct Amelia. They intend to kidnap her at dusk and take her to Lorenzino's mansion. (Lorenzino is a completely unnecessary character who, though he never actually appears in the opera, is mentioned several times.)

The second scene of Act I is set in the Council Chamber. The Doge is seated on his throne, with twelve patrician councillors on one side of him, twelve plebeians, among them Paolo and Pietro, on the other. At the beginning of the scene, the Doge is accepting pledges of peace and lavish gifts from the Emperor of Tartary. As the Tartar emissaries bow and depart, Boccanegra addresses his councillors on another matter. He has received a letter from the poet Petrarch, urging that Venice be left in peace. Paolo immediately shouts that the poet should stick to his verses in praise of his "bionda Avignonese", Laura, his blonde mistress from Avignon. The councillors agree and call for war on Venice. Boccanegra tries to convince them that both the Adriatic and Ligurian coasts are part of one fatherland, Italy, but the councillors reply that Genoa is their fatherland. The debate is interrupted by the noise of a rioting mob outside. Looking out of a window, the Doge sees Gabriele Adorno fighting an angry crowd. Pietro quietly suggests to Paolo that he should flee, but Boccanegra, who has been watching Paolo, orders the doors to be guarded. "Anyone who attempts to leave is a traitor," he cries. The crowd outside is now shouting "Death to the patricians" and even "Death to the Doge". Boccanegra sends a herald to announce to the crowd, nobles and plebeians alike, that he does not fear their threats, but waits to hear their complaint. After the herald has addressed the crowd, there is a moment of silence followed by a cry of "Long live the Doge". "So much for the people," is Boccanegra's understandably sarcastic comment. The mob now bursts into the Council Chamber with Gabriele and Andrea (Fiesco). Gabriele announces that he has killed Lorenzino, who was attempting to kidnap Amelia. Before he died, Lorenzino had admitted that he was in the employ of a "man of great power". When the Doge asks for this man's name, Gabriele admits that Lorenzino had died before he could reveal it, but implies that in his opinion it was the Doge himself. He raises his sword against Boccanegra, but Amelia, entering suddenly, steps between the two men. Begging Boccanegra to forgive Gabriele, she tells how she was seized by three ruffians and carried off to Lorenzino's house. She says she knows who was behind the plot, and she is about to denounce Paolo when the patricians swear it must have been a plebeian, and the plebeians accuse the patricians. A fight seems imminent when Boccanegra intervenes with a call to reason. He makes an impassioned appeal for peace and amity between the factions, and his words have an immediate effect. Gabriele gives himself up as the Doge's prisoner, and he and Fiesco are led away, the Doge allowing him, however, to retain his sword. Turning to Paolo, the Doge pretends he is unaware of the identity of the culprit, and commands him to join in uttering a curse on whoever it may be. The terrified Paolo has no choice but to obey. He repeats the curse after the Doge, and rushes from the Council Chamber in panic.

Act II takes place that evening in a private apartment in the Doge's palace. Determined to be revenged on Boccanegra, Paolo empties a phial of poison into his jug of drinking water. In order to make doubly sure of Boccanegra's death, he has Fiesco and Gabriele brought in and attempts first to bribe Fiesco to assassinate the Doge while he is asleep. Fiesco naturally refuses to perform so dishonourable a deed, and is taken back to his cell. With Gabriele, Paolo uses different tactics, telling him that Amelia is the Doge's mistress. Left alone, Gabriele broods on this information, and, when Amelia enters, he accuses her. Unable to divulge the truth, she merely says she loves Boccanegra but is true to Gabriele. The Doge is heard approaching, and Gabriele hides, vowing to kill him. Amelia confesses to her father that she loves Gabriele, which appals him as he has just discovered Gabriele's name on a list of those who have been plotting against him. When Amelia convinces him of the depth of her love, Boccanegra agrees to try to find a way to pardon Gabriele. He asks her now to leave him as he has work to do. Fearing that, if she departs, Gabriele will return and kill her father, Amelia tries to refuse, but the Doge insists. Left alone, he drinks some of the poisoned water and comments that even spring water tastes bitter to him. He sits at his desk, but is overcome by sleep. Gabriele enters and is about to stab him when Amelia reappears. The Doge awakens and accuses Gabriele of robbing him of his one treasure, his daughter. Astonished, Gabriele begs Amelia to forgive him, and the Doge decides to pardon him as well. A commotion is heard outside, signalling the beginning of the patrician uprising. Boccanegra tells Gabriele he is free to join his friends, But Gabriele now refuses to fight against the Doge. Instead, he offers his services as a messenger of peace. Boccanegra, in return, gives his consent to Gabriele's marriage to Amelia.

Act III takes place in another part of the palace. Through the balcony windows Genoa and the sea can be seen. The plebeians have defeated the patricians, and cries of "Long live the Doge" are to be heard. Fiesco is released from prison and given back his sword by the Captain of the Archers. Paolo enters under guard, on his way to execution, having fought on the side of the rebels. He tells Fiesco that although Simon has condemned him to die, he has already condemned Simon to death by poisoning. He is tortured by the sounds of the wedding hymn celebrating the marriage of Gabriele and Amelia, and confesses to Fiesco that it was he who had planned her abduction. He is led out, and Fiesco hides as he hears the Doge approaching. A herald announces from the balcony that, as a sign of respect for those who have died in the fighting, the city's lights are to be extinguished. Then Simon enters, walking unsteadily because the poison is taking effect. Looking out to sea, he nostalgically remembers his early sea-faring days. When Fiesco suddenly confronts him, Simon at first fails to recognise him but, realising who he is, is overjoyed. At last he can give Fiesco his granddaughter. He tells Fiesco who Amelia really is and claims his pardon. The contrite Fiesco warns the Doge that he is dying. Amelia and Gabriele enter with their attendants, and Simon tells Amelia that the man she knew as Andrea, her guardian, is her mother's father. He blesses the newly married couple, names Gabriele as his successor, and dies as the last lights in the city are extinguished.

III

It is astonishing that, given the history of its composition, *Simon Boccanegra* should be the masterly work it is. The revision it underwent was much more thorough than appears at first glance. Certainly Verdi dug more deeply than Boito, fusing his styles of 1857 and 1881 into a homogeneous whole. The opera's orchestral colour is almost unrelievedly gloomy, but Verdi was invariably at his best when he allowed his own pessimistic temperament to infiltrate into every corner of a libretto. It was not until his final opera *Falstaff* that the obverse side of his temperament emerged in his music. In *Simon Boccanegra*, his orchestration combines the subtlety of a Debussy with the kind of spontaneity that Berlioz occasionally achieved. And he continues his move away from the division into self-contained numbers, in the direction of a continuing and dramatically truthful melody. That this amalgam-opera of 1857 and 1881 does not strike the listener of today as a patchwork of styles is in some part due to the fact that, although Verdi developed continuously and enormously over the years, he never swerved from his ideal of dramatic truth expressed in melodic terms. His most brilliant effects all stem from a concern to present his melody in the best possible light.

Although the score of *Boccanegra* is not set out on the page in separate numbers, its various arias, duets and ensembles, for all their fluidity of form, are in fact identifiable, just as they continued to be in *Otello* and *Falstaff*. Or, for that matter, in *Tristan und Isolde, Capriccio* or *Peter*

Grimes, all of whose climactic moments emerge from their surroundings as distinctly as in Donizetti, though very differently. The difference really lies in the added interest given to the surroundings. What was once arid recitative is now musically significant material, and for this Verdi is to be thanked equally with Wagner.

After a few solemn bars of orchestral prelude, the prologue to *Simon Boccanegra* begins with a scene of dialogue for Paolo and Pietro, later for Paolo and Boccanegra, in Verdi's dramatic arioso style. Then the chorus of sailors and workmen trickles onstage to an accompaniment of orchestral stealth. When Paolo tells them whom they are to vote for, the initial reaction of the chorus is one of surprise. An example of the thoroughness with which Verdi revised his score in 1881 can be found here. In the 1857 version, the choral exclamation, "Simone? Il corsaro?" (Simon? The buccaneer?) is marked *ff*. In the later version, in a different key and with slight rhythmic and melodic changes (for instance, there is no longer a rise in pitch on the second syllable of "corsaro"), the initial cry of "Simone?" is still *ff*, but "il corsaro" drops to a sudden and highly effective shocked pianissimo. Paolo's "L'altra magion vedete", though not the musically self-sufficient kind of aria that survives out of context, fulfils its function perfectly in the opera. Its similarity to Ferrando's scene at the beginning of *Il trovatore*, where he narrates part of the plot to his captive audience, is emphasised by the chorus's sudden irrational terror. In *Il trovatore* it is the cry of an owl that frightens them. Here it is a light in the Fiesco palace. They disperse, crossing themselves, while the orchestra steals away with them into silence only to assert itself again with solemn chords as Fiesco emerges from his palace. Fiesco's recitative and aria, dramatically and musically superb, are almost as effective divorced from context. The aria, "Il lacerato spirito", perfectly mirrors Fiesco's grief, dignity and determination. His noble phrases are interspersed with plangent cries of "É morta" and "Miserere" from the offstage chorus of mourners. The tremolando strings that accompany the aria add considerably to its beauty, and the orchestral postlude is one of those rare and moving passages in which Verdi allows his compassion for a character to intrude into the drama. A tune of great consolation from the strings, it baths Fiesco in its glow. I know of no other composer who does precisely this, though Mozart and Britten come close to it in different ways. It is a gesture that Verdi makes sparingly, but always to overwhelming effect.

The scene for Fiesco and Boccanegra is a marvellous example of Verdi's mature style, ranging freely among arioso, recitative, *parlante* exchanges and formal melody, though in fact it dates from the original version of the opera. Verdi's duet scenes for baritone and bass are always interesting. He inclines to use the high fifth of the baritone range for contrast, but does not write particularly low bass parts, relying more on the bass's distinctive tone colour. Fiesco opens the scene angrily but has a, for him, unexpectedly tender passage when he asks Boccanegra for his daughter's child. Simon's off-stage discovery of Maria's death is portrayed in masterly fashion. The pianissimo phrase played by the violins as he enters the house is particularly beautiful. Most impressive are the restraint and taste with which Verdi ends the Prologue: the populace acclaims Boccanegra as Doge, to a cheerily banal tune used to superbly ironic effect, while he, lost in his private grief, remains silent.

Act I opens with a delightful orchestral prelude, all shimmering strings and delicate pianissimi, evoking sunrise over the sea. It leads into Amelia's aria, "Come in quest' ora bruna", whose stunning use of the orchestra completes the sound picture of dawn and the rippling of waves in the sunlight. The dancing wave-like figure persists under Amelia's vocal line [Ex. 81]. In the delicacy and translucence of its

Ex. 81

texture as well as the freshness of its colouring, the orchestra calls to mind the accompaniment to Mina's aria in Act II of *Stiffelio*.

Gabriele is heard off-stage singing a brief, Manricoish serenade with harp accompaniment. The *andantino* section of the duet for Amelia and Gabriele is both charming and elegant, its *allegro brillante* stretta less so. Fiesco's solemn benediction of Gabriele, "Vieni a me, ti benedico", is the most impressive element in their scene together. The great recognition scene in which the Doge rediscovers his lost daughter is planned with careful strategy. The first *parlante* exchanges of Simon and Maria, over a violin figure, lead to Amelia's still somewhat prosaic "Orfanella il tetto umile", with its oboe introduction, a tune whose emotional temperature is deliberately kept fairly low, though rising passion gives it a melodic lift at "Mi bacio, mi benedisse". The Doge's hopeful yet incredulous interjection, "Ah! se la speme", is almost heart-rending in its pathos, but even here Verdi is holding back. Tension increases during the ensuing arioso question and answer, until the moment of certainly is reached. Then, after a loud orchestral climax, pizzicato strings introduce the Doge's moving "Figlia! a tal nome io palpito", [Ex. 82]. At the end of the duet, the orchestra swells into the same tune,

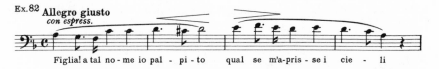

Ex.82 Allegro giusto *con espress.*

Figlia! a tal no - me io pal - pi - to   qual se m'a-pris - se i   cie - li

harp arpeggios accompany Amelia's exit, the Doge repeats, dolcissimo, "Figlia!" and the harp arpeggios fade into silence. Would Verdi's Lear and Cordelia have shared a duet similar to this, I wonder?

Opinions differ sharply about the brief recitative exchanges between the Doge and Paolo, and then between Paolo and Pietro, with which the scene ends. Some critics consider the end an anti-climax, and indeed Tito Gobbi's Covent Garden production of 1965 brought the curtain down on Boccanegra's "Figlia!" (though when the production was revived in the producer-baritone's absence, the omitted scene was restored). It seems to me that, as usual, Verdi knew best, and that the conspiratorial exchanges end the scene most effectively, if unconventionally.

The second scene of Act I, set in the Doge's Council Chamber, dates from the 1881 revision of the opera, and speaks the language of *Otello*, a work Verdi was already planning. This brilliantly constructed ensemble scene, whose largely declamatory style broadens into melody for the important solo utterances of Amelia and the Doge, is the pivotal point of the opera, the scene towards which the work has been moving both musically and dramatically, and from which the later two very short acts tend to trail into anti-climax. It is also the only scene in the opera, with the possible exception of the brief exchange between the Doge and Amelia in Act I, Scene 1, when he pardons the Grimaldi brothers, where the Doge's clemency and statesmanship are displayed in action.

There is much of interest in the scoring of this scene. The first distant noise of the rioting crowd is achieved with agreeably insolent economy by the humming of the off-stage chorus. As the crowd gets nearer, the sound becomes a sustained note sung to the vowel "ah". The silence after the herald's trumpet is dramatic, composed silence, provided by soft drum beats. When the mob bursts into the Council

Chamber, it is to a violent *allegro agito* that foreshadows the storm in Act I of *Otello*. Amelia's narrative of her abduction is the one passage in this scene which was not composed for the 1881 revision but was lifted from the first version.

The scene reaches its climax with the Doge's stirring call for peace and unity. Interrupting the accusations and counter-accusations with "Plebe! Patrizi! Popolo dalla feroce storia" (Plebeians, patricians, you people with a fierce history), an apparently declamatory passage which also serves as the beginning of an *andante* aria that moves through the majestic appeal of "Piango su voi" to the great Verdian phrase with which Boccanegra appeals for peace and love [Ex. 83]. Throughout the

Ex. 83   Andante mosso

e vo gridan-do: pa - ce!   e vo gridan-do: a-mor   e vo gridan-do: a-mor!

scene, the Doge's music characterises him perfectly. This kind of writing is a far cry from the tuneful but relatively anonymous baritone arias of the earliest Verdi operas. Here, the call for peace is taken up and developed by the other characters, who voice their differing sentiments in an ensemble of beauty and dramatic effectiveness. Amelia contributes a new and gentle theme, Fiesco plunges the music into a minor contrasting section, and, at the end, the volume of sound diminishes to *ppp* and Amelia is left to end unaccompanied on an F sharp trill and an octave drop. The Doge's curse on the malefactor is introduced violently by the orchestra's brass. In Boccanegra's address to Paolo, the orchestral tension mounts, emphasised by Verdi's imaginative use of the bass clarinet, until he utters the curse and insists on Paolo repeating it. "Sia maledetto!" The bass clarinet continues its insinuations as a terrified Paolo utters the words. The ensemble then repeats the oath before dispersing to a further *pp* repetition in unison. The lowest instruments of the orchestra add their dark comment, and with the brass loudly insisting on Paolo's guilt the curtain falls.

Act II opens strongly with Paolo's almost Iago-like soliloquy, in which he broods on the curse he was forced to put on himself, a short scene whose dramatic intensity heightens Paolo's stature as a fully conceived character. It is an addition by Boito to Piave's libretto. Gabriele's aria of jealousy and despair, though it fails to find quite the right shape for itself, is by no means ineffective in context. Its fierce opening gives way to a lyrical section in which a solo oboe echoes the weeping figure of the tenor's "Io piango". The duet for Amelia and Gabriele is more interesting orchestrally than vocally. A trumpet announces the approach of the Doge, and the short, rushed passage in which Amelia attempts to persuade Gabriele to flee, while he reiterates his determination to kill Simon, is, to say the least undistinguished.

From Boccanegra's entrance to the end of the act, however, the music is more assured, and the orchestration full of felicitous touches: the orchestra's warning as Boccanegra drinks the poisoned water, the very quiet phrases on violins and violas as he falls into uneasy sleep, the reminiscence of "Figlia! a tal nome io palpito" on flute, clarinet and oboe as he dreams of Amelia. The finely expressive trio, "Perdon, perdon, Amelia", is vintage in its sense of movement and its melodic warmth. Gabriele begins it solo by expressing his remorse and shame, and his phrase, "Dammi la morte", has a splendidly heroic ring. The trio existed in the 1857 version of the opera, but was extensively re-written for 1881.

Warlike noises are heard in the distance. The off-stage chorus sings a rousing call to arms, and the scene ends in a state of orchestral and vocal flurry reminiscent of *Nabucco*.

The very short Act III achieves continuity with the second by means of its brief orchestral introduction, which makes use of material from the end of Act II. The scene between Fiesco, who has just been given his freedom, and Paolo, who is on his way to the scaffold, is magnificent of its kind. Paolo's confession is peculiarly touching for so unsympathetic a character, except that in Verdi there are very few completely unsympathetic characters, or very few for whom he cannot find a certain sympathy. "Everything human we comprehend." The unaccompanied wedding chorus of Gabriele and Amelia continues in the background throughout this grim confrontation.

To a dignified unison phrase for horns, a trumpeter enters with the Captain of the Archers, and calls the populace below to attention. The Captain makes his announcement, and he and the trumpeter depart to the same horn phrase. The dying Boccanegra enters, his condition revealed by the confused fever of the orchestra. His soliloquy, in which his feeling for the sea finds apt expression, is exquisitely scored for strings. The climactic duet for the two old enemies Boccanegra and Fiesco is impressive and, finally, very moving as Boccanegra's joy at the reunion melts Fiesco's wrath. Fiesco's tears are portrayed by Verdi's familiar semitone figure, this time a rising semitone. At the end of the duet, the orchestra repeats its warning of Boccanegra's imminent death as Fiesco tells the Doge he has been poisoned. The simple but affecting passage in which the Doge blesses Amelia and Gabriele leads into a final ensemble begun by Amelia's "No, non morrai". But he does die, and the crowd calls for peace on his soul as the curtain falls.

It is easy to understand the initial lack of success of *Simon Boccanegra* in 1857. Verdi's audience must have felt somehow cheated: instead of the profuse melody of *Rigoletto, Il trovatore* and *La traviata*, they were offered a score in which the melodic plums, though as ripe as those of the past, were considerably less numerous, and in which the emphasis was upon dramatic characterisation. By the time *Otello* was composed, his audience was ready for it. But Verdi had been ahead of them for several years before they caught up. By any standard, the musical characterisation in *Simon Boccanegra* is first-rate. The villain of the piece, Paolo, is more than just a rather striking study for Iago. Boito has given him a roundness and a stature which he lacked both in García Gutiérrez's play and in Piave's libretto. It is Paolo's pure hatred of Boccanegra, rather than his desire for wealth and power, which controls his behaviour, and Verdi, who had written, "I will see to it that Paolo is no ordinary villain," succeeded in conveying this in the music he wrote for this introverted version of Iago. His instinctive comprehension of the incomprehensible rarely failed him. Curiously, Paolo is viewed by his creators almost more sympathetically than the stoical old Fiesco who, nevertheless, emerges from the score with something of the dignity and strength of Verdi himself. I think Verdi must momentarily have identified himself with Fiesco in the scene where the old man laments the death of his daughter—it obviously had a real significance for the composer, whose deeply felt postlude to Fiesco's "Il lacerato spirito" keeps returning to my mind's ear as I write.

Amelia's music has a lightness and innocence which, to some extent, alleviate the sombre melancholy of most of the score, but it is Boccanegra who really bestrides the opera like a colossus. The beauty and eloquence of his music and the forcefulness and consistency of his characterisation make him one of Verdi's most successfully realised rôles. He is both statesman and dreamer, and the two aspects of him are given full weight in his musical and dramatic utterance. It is by Boccanegra alone that, finally, the opera must stand or fall. And, to pursue Verdi's metaphor of the table, it does not fall, it is no longer even shaky. It stands.

XXI

Un ballo in maschera

Dramatis personae:

Riccardo, Count of Warwick, Governor of Boston	(tenor)
Renato, a creole, Riccardo's secretary	(baritone)
Amelia, Renato's wife	(soprano)
Ulrica, a negro fortune-teller	(contralto)
Oscar, a page	(soprano)
Silvano, a sailor	(bass)
Samuel, enemy of the Count	(bass)
Tom, enemy of the Count	(bass)
A judge	(tenor)
Amelia's servant	(tenor)

LIBRETTO by Antonio Somma, based on Eugène Scribe's libretto *Gustave III*

TIME: The end of the seventeenth century
PLACE: In and around Boston

FIRST PERFORMED at the Teatro Apollo, Rome, February 17, 1859, with Eugenia Julienne-Dejean (Amelia); Pamela Scotti (Oscar); Zelinda Sbriscia (Ulrica); Gaetano Fraschini (Riccardo); Leone Giraldoni (Renato); C. Bossi (Samuel); G. Bernadoni (Tom); S. Santucci (Silvano)

Un ballo in maschera

I

A FEW MONTHS after the première of *Simon Boccanegra* in March, 1857, Verdi found himself involved in the production at Rimini of *Aroldo*, the revised *Stiffelio*, which we have discussed in Chapter XV. But for some time he had also been negotiating with the San Carlo Theatre, Naples, about *King Lear*, for which he proposed to use the libretto provided for him by Antonio Somma, the well-known Venetian playwright with whom he had been corresponding for some years on the project. A contract was signed with the theatre, but in Verdi's mind much depended on the availability of Maria Piccolomini to sing Cordelia; when it became clear that she would not be available during the 1858 season, he decided to shelve *Lear* for the time being, and search quickly for another subject for the opera which the contract stipulated should be produced in January 1858. His choice fell upon an existing libretto by his ex-collaborator Scribe, *Gustave III ou Le bal masqué*, written for Auber's opera, which had been produced in Paris a quarter of a century earlier, in 1833. The libretto had also, in 1843, been translated and adapted as *Il reggente* by Cammarano for Saverio Mercadante, whose opera was produced in Turin. Its subject, taken from history, was the assassination of Gustavus III of Sweden at a masked ball in 1792. Verdi asked his *Lear* librettist, Antonio Somma, to re-translate Scribe's French five-act libretto, and to re-cast it in three acts. This decision was not made until October 1857, three months before the proposed production date, but Somma worked quickly and by the end of the month had sent Verdi the first act. On November 6th, the composer wrote from Busseto:

> I have received your pleasant letter of November 1st with the rest of Act I. These verses are quite good: there are only a few very small points, which you can quickly correct. The scene between Amelia and the Witch is good. The stanzas, "Della citta all' occaso", are very beautiful. Also the following recitatives. I find the three stanzas for Amelia, the Witch and Gustav somewhat weak, though I may be wrong. Perhaps they need to have a little more of your inspiration breathed into them.
>
> The whole scene of the chorus entrance and Gustav's song are very good, and particularly beautiful is the following recitative up to "scritto e lassu". In the following quartet, make certain we have a chorus of conspirators. They'll need something to say, so write a stanza for them. In this

quartet with chorus, you can also use that breath of inspiration already mentioned. The only place that needs improving is from "Strega mia" to "ti tradi". All this is not sufficiently dramatic. I admit you say all there is to say, but the words are not vivid. Consequently, neither Gustav's indifference nor the Witch's surprise nor the conspirators' fear is sufficiently emphasised. As the scene at this point is lively and important, I want the words to be right. Is it the metre or the rhyme that bothers you? You could, if you like, turn this passage into recitative. I much prefer a good recitative to a poor piece of verse.[1]

Two weeks later, Verdi wrote again to Somma:

I have received Act II. The duet between Riccardo and Amelia is beautiful, wonderful. It has all the warmth and agitation of real passion. That is what I should have liked the preceding aria for Amelia to be like. Perhaps it is the form that ruins it. The two stanzas weaken the situation.[2]

Verdi had submitted a prose synopsis of the libretto to the censor, anticipating that there might be some difficulty in showing on the stage the assassination of a ruling monarch. He probably expected to be asked to make the characters fictitious, and even to alter the locale. In fact, he and Somma had dicussed this. Somma proposed moving it all back to the twelfth century, but in a letter of November 26th, after he had received Act III, Verdi rejected this suggestion.

Dear Somma, I really think the twelfth century is a little too remote for our Gustav. It is such a raw and brutal period, especially in those countries, that it seems a serious contradiction to use it as a setting for characters conceived in the French style as Gustav and Oscar are, and for such a splendid drama based on customs nearer our own time. We shall have to find some great prince or duke, a rogue whether of the North or not, who has seen something of the world and caught something of the atmosphere of the court of Louis XIV. When you have finished the drama, you can think about this at your convenience.

I've written to you about Act II, now here's what I think of Act III. The opening dialogue between Ankarstroem and Amelia is cold, despite the liveliness of the situation. In the French there is the phrase, "Il faut mourir", which keeps occurring, and which is very dramatic. I know that "Apparecchiati alla morte" and "Raccomandati al Signore" mean the same thing, but on the stage they don't have the effect of that simple "Bisogna morire". And almost all those lines are too difficult for music. What's more, the words essential to be heard don't stand out strongly enough. The four stanzas of Amelia's cantabile are good, except for the first two lines which seem ordinary: "Ah mi concedi in grazia/Ancor una volta almeno". The whole of Ankarstroem's aria is good. But the scene between him and the conspirators needs more pace. Condense it somehow, and change "Vi diletta giocar di noi?" The stanza, "Tutti stretti", is good.

[1] Abbiati, Vol. II, p. 454.   [2] Op. cit., p. 457.

In the French, the scene where Amelia enters and draws the name of her husband is beautiful and terrifying. In the verses you have sent me, it does not affect me in the same way. The characters aren't well dramatized, the language is weak, and the great moment passes almost unnoticed. Think about it carefully, because this is an important point. From the words, "Signora, ho un invito", up to the following stanzas, it is all too long.[1]

Eventually, Verdi and Somma agreed to move the action from eighteenth-century Sweden to seventeenth-century Stettin, in Pomerania, and to alter the title from *Gustave III* to *La vendetta in domino*. It was not until Verdi had arrived in Naples in January that he discovered the censor had refused to allow the opera to proceed, with or without the changes in time and place. On January 14th, a bomb had been thrown under the carriage of Napoleon III on his way to the Paris Opéra, an incident which naturally increased the nervousness of the Neapolitan monarchy. Naples was, in any case, sufficiently aware of the danger of regicide. In the previous year, the reigning king had been attacked with a bayonet by one of his own soldiers. From Naples, on February 7th, Verdi broke the news to his librettist:

I'm drowning in a sea of troubles. It's almost certain the censors will forbid our libretto. I don't know why. I was quite right to warn you to avoid every sentence, every word which could offend. They began by objecting to certain phrases and words, and then entire scenes and finally the whole subject. They made the following suggestions, but only as a special favour:
1. Change the hero into an ordinary gentleman, with no suggestion of sovereignty.
2. Change the wife into a sister.
3. Alter the scene with the fortune-teller, and put it back to a time when people believed in such things.
4. No ball.
5. The murder to be off-stage.
6. Omit the scene of the drawing of the name.
And, and, and!!...

As you can imagine, these changes are out of the question, so no more opera. So the subscribers won't pay the last two instalments, so the government will withdraw the subsidy, so the directors will sue everyone, and already threaten me with damages of 50,000 ducats. What hell! Write and tell me your opinion of all this.[2]

The San Carlo management prepared an altered libretto which met the censor's requirements, called *Adelia degli Adimari* and set in Florence in the fourteenth century. Verdi refused to accept it, and the theatre threatened legal action. Verdi and his lawyer issued a counter-claim. The case was settled out of court, and an agreement reached in which

[1] Abbiati, Vol. II, pp. 458–9.   [2] Op. cit., pp. 469–70.

the contract was dissolved, and the composer allowed to offer *La ven-detta in domino* elsewhere, on condition that he return to Naples in the autumn to produce *Simon Boccanegra*, which had not yet been staged there.

While the lawyers were still fighting, Verdi had already offered the opera to the Teatro Apollo in Rome, which had accepted it, subject, of course, to the approval of the Papal censor. Returning to Sant' Agata for the summer, the composer continued to correspond both with the Rome impresario Vincenzo Jacovacci and with Somma about the opera. The Papal censor gave his qualified approval to the libretto, but insisted that it should be set in some non-European country. Verdi and Somma considered several places, including the Caucasus, before settling on Boston at a time before the American War of Independence. On August 6th, Verdi wrote to Somma:

> Arm yourself with courage and patience. Particularly with patience. As you will see from the enclosed letter from [Antonio] Vasselli,[1] the censor has sent a list of all the lines he disapproves of. If on reading this, you feel a rush of blood to the head, lay it down and try it again after you have eaten and slept well. Remember that under present conditions our best plan is to present the opera in Rome. The lines and expressions deleted by the censor are numerous, but it could have been worse. In any case, it is better like this, since now we know how to proceed, what we can leave in and what must go. Also a great many lines would have had to be changed, since the king is now only a Governor. Don't worry about the gallows in Act II, I'll try to obtain permission for it. Cheer up, amend the lines marked and try to arrange that you have fifteen or twenty days free during the Carnival season, so that you can come to Rome where I hope we shall have a good time together.[2]

Scribe's original sub-title, *Le bal masqué* now became, in Italian, the new title of the opera, *Un ballo in maschera*. That the libretto as we know it represents the final, though doubtless harrassed, intentions of Verdi and Somma is attested to by the amount of work they continued to do on it before the Rome première. Once having decided on colonial Boston, Verdi closely re-examined the entire libretto. His letters to Somma reveal the amount of editing and re-arrangement that he felt necessary. The Papal censorship made final alterations, to Somma's disgust. In December, a harassed Verdi wrote to his friend Cesare Vigna, the alienist:

> From Rome I have received the variants for *Ballo in Maschera*. Somma writes that he is "nauseated" by them (the word is not polite), and I am, more than he. But what could I have done? Did he want me to protest and

---

[1] Donizetti's brother-in-law, who lived in Rome.   [2] Abbiati, Vol. II, p. 506.

start a law suit like last year? A second litigation would have been scandalous and ridiculous. In the theatre, of course, one has to make sacrifices, and it's useless for anyone who hasn't the courage to do this to expose himself to this severe trial.[1]

In Rome, however, everything went smoothly, despite the feverish political situation. The première was fixed for February 17, 1859, Verdi and Giuseppina arrived in Rome in January and were moderately pleased with the cast assembled. The first night was a brilliant success: this was the occasion when the cunning acrostic "Viva Verdi" was first shouted. The cry was taken up all over Italy, painted on walls, displayed on banners and, in northern Italy, shouted in defiance of the Austrians. For V-e-r-d-i meant not only Verdi but also Vittorio Emanuele, Re D'Italia. It was a cry from deep down in the Italian psyche. Nothing in *Un ballo in maschera* seems capable of having aroused such feelings; nothing, that is, but the emotive power and resonance of Verdi's genius. He spoke most strongly to his audience when he was least conscious of attempting to influence its actions. He was not so much its spokesman as its soul.

In addition to its popularity as a focal point of patriotic feeling, the opera was a success in its own right. Audiences responded enthusiastically to it from the beginning, and the Rome critics wrote of it as a step forward in a new direction for Verdi, drawing attention to the warmth and brilliance of its orchestration and to its unique marriage of dramatic truth and melodic appeal.

II

The historical King Gustavus III of Sweden was a reasonably colourful character. A nephew of Frederick the Great, he was, like his uncle, homosexual. Though he acquitted himself bravely in battle, he was considerably more interested in the arts than in war. He patronised artists, wrote plays, and drew about himself a court of culture, elegance and learning. He possessed the agnostic's intelligent interest in theology, as well as an eccentric curiosity regarding the occult. He is said to have more than once consulted the famous Stockholm fortune-teller Madame Arvidson, who appears to have been as much notorious intriguer as foreteller of the future. Gustavus was twenty-six when he succeeded to the throne in 1772 on the sudden death of his father from a surfeit of muffins. He immediately antagonised the nobility by reducing their privileges in the process of enlarging his own, though he remained popular with the mass of the people. It was after he had reigned for twenty years that Gustavus was assassinated. The leaders of the conspiracy against him were two young noblemen in their mid-twenties,

[1] *Bulletin* of the Institute of Verdi Studies, No. 2, p. 647.

Count Ribbing and Count Horn; the man chosen to murder the king was Captain Ankarstroem, an ex-officer of unbalanced personality who had resigned his commission several years earlier, and who professed some kind of personal animosity towards Gustavus. Whatever its basis was, it was certainly not that the king was having an affair with Ankarstroem's wife. The assassination was carried out at a masked ball in the Royal Opera House. Ankarstroem shot Gustavus in the back at close range, using a pistol which had been loaded with rusty nails to ensure that, if the wound was not immediately fatal, gangrene would set in.

A Polish officer present at the ball wrote an extremely interesting account of the assassination.[1] He mentions that, just before going to the ball, Gustavus received an anonymous note (which he claims was from a Guards officer called De Lilienhorn) containing the pencilled words: "Je suis encore de vos amis, quoique j'aie des raisons pour ne le plus être. N'allez pas au bal ce soir. Il y va de votre vie." (I am still one of your friends, though I have reasons not to be. Do not go to the ball this evening. You will lose your life there.) At the ball, the Polish officer was close enough to Gustavus when he was shot to hear him cry, "Je viens d'être blessé par un grand masque noir."

The King took thirteen days to die in great agony; he asked that all the conspirators be pardoned, but in fact the unrepentant religious fanatic Ankarstroem was beheaded, though not before the hand which fired the shot had been severed. His body was quartered and displayed in public. Counts Horn and Ribbing were exiled.[2]

Those, briefly, are the historical facts. What did Scribe make of them when, forty years after the event, he wrote his five-act libretto for Auber? The answer, predictably, is that he made them over into the standard Scribe libretto. He introduced, as the basis of the plot and the reason why Ankarstroem turned against the king, a love affair between Gustavus and Amélie, Ankarstroem's wife. Curiously, he also invented a page-boy, Oscar, with whom Gustavus would have been much more likely to have had an affair. Scribe used simply the names, not the characteristics, of the real people involved in the events, and produced a neat, well-constructed melodrama which bore absolutely no relation to the life and times of Gustavus III. His Gustave is just another stage lover. The historical Gustavus, who, by the time of his assassination, was

[1] *Histoire de l'Assassinat de Gustav III, Roi di Suède, par un officier Polonais, témoin oculaire* (Paris, 1797).

[2] During the course of my background reading for this chapter, I dipped into two or three volumes of the *Collection des Ecrits politiques, littéraires et dramatiques de Gustav III*, published in Stockholm eleven years after his death. Gustav's literary style seemed to me stiff and impossibly elevated, as might have been expected. I was amused to find that the list of subscribers to the volumes included the names of "Arfvedson (Madame)", "Horn (le Comte), Lieutenant général" and "Ribbing (le Baron) Capitane".

showing signs of becoming a serious ruler and a statesman of erratic genius, was a strange amalgam of clemency and cruelty far removed from Scribe's cardboard cut-out. Somma's translation and adaptation of Scribe added a further distancing effect, even before the character became Riccardo, Governor of Boston.

Although for the most part Scribe used the characters' real names, his libretto turned Count Ribbing into Count Warting, presumably because Ribbing was still alive and living in Paris in 1833. After the success of Auber's opera, several Italian composers became interested in the possibility of writing a Gustavus III opera. Bellini, shortly before his death in 1835, thought of doing so for the Teatro San Carlo, Naples, and at least two operas based on Scribe's libretto actually reached the stage before *Un ballo in maschera*. One, *Clemenza di Valois*, by the Bolognese composer Vincenzo Gabussi (1800–46), whose librettist was Gaetano Rossi, was performed at the Fenice in 1841, with the action transferred to the thirteenth century. Another, Saverio Mercadante's *Il reggente*, with libretto by Verdi's erstwhile collaborator Salvatore Cammarano, was produced in Turin in 1843, the scene this time being sixteenth-century Scotland.

Verdi and Somma, apart from a few matters of detail, stayed fairly close to Scribe's *Gustave III*, although they removed from their portrait of Riccardo Scribe's references in Act I to the intellectual and artistic aspects of Gustavus. Ulrica's invocation, "Re dell' abisso", simply translates Madame Arvedson's, "Prince des nuits", and the laughter of the Swedish conspirators when Amélie is unmasked—

> Admirable conquête!
> Quoi! ces époux heureux,
> Tous deux, en tête-à-tête,
> Se trouvaient en ces lieux

—has the same mocking quality that the Americans Samuel and Tom reveal in Somma's version. And so on. But there is no counterpart in Scribe to "Eri tu", Renato's bitter outburst of jealousy and rage against Riccardo. In the French libretto, Ankarstroem admits the conspirators immediately Amélie has left the room.

One or two recent productions of *Un ballo in maschera* have reverted to the historical Swedish setting and characters. And conservative opera lovers who had become used to Renato, Riccardo and Ulrica, found themselves having to cope with Ankarstroem, Gustave and Madame Arvedson. I cannot see that any great harm is done to the opera by using the historical names, though there is not the slightest need to use them. Verdi's music is no more Swedish in character than it is American. It does, however, as he himself claimed, have something of the eighteenth century in its elegance, wit and lightness of touch. But whether Amelia's lover is called Riccardo, Gustavus, Gustavo or Gustave, seems hardly to matter. The character has little in common with King Gustavus III of Sweden, and there is no more justification for giving Verdi's Riccardo the name of Scribe's Gustave than there would be in changing the Duke of Mantua in *Rigoletto* back into Victor Hugo's François I. To call Riccardo Gustavus is harmless enough, but to attempt to superimpose the historical Gustavus III on to the character that Verdi has delineated is, of course, immensely harmful to the opera. I have seen a Swedish production in which Gustavus was made to mince about like a revue-sketch homosexual and flirt heavily with Oscar the page. What this has to do with the Riccardo whose great love duet in Act II is, after all, sung not with Oscar but with Amelia, was never made clear.

The scene, then, is Boston around the year 1700. Act I, Scene 1, is set in a reception room in the Governor's residence. It is morning, and a number of deputies, citizens and officials await an audience with Riccardo, Earl of Warwick, Governor of Boston. Most of the crowd sing a hymn of praise to the noble Riccardo, but a group of conspirators headed by Samuel and Tom utter quite different sentiments. Preceded by his page, Oscar, Riccardo enters, greets the assembly, accepts their petitions and promises justice for all. Oscar shows Riccardo the invitation list for a masked ball that is being planned; when he sees on it the name of Amelia, whom he loves, Riccardo momentarily loses himself in thoughts of her. He dismisses the crowd, and Renato enters. He is the Governor's friend and secretary, and also the husband of Amelia. When he tries to warn the Governor of a plot against his life, Riccardo, serene in his certainty that God and his people will protect him, refuses to listen. Oscar announces the Chief Justice, who asks Riccardo to sign a paper banishing a Negress fortune-teller, Ulrica, whom the people regard as a divine oracle. Oscar defends Ulrica, while the judge pleads with Riccardo to sign the banishment order. Riccardo summons the crowd back, and light-heartedly invites them to join him, all suitably disguised, in a visit to the fortune-teller. Renato tries in vain to dissuade Riccardo from what he considers a dangerous enterprise. The scene ends with a gay ensemble in which all agree to meet later at Ulrica's hut.

Scene 2 takes place in Ulrica's hut. There are front and back doors to the hut, with a view of the harbour through a window. The fortune-teller is seated before a steaming cauldron, and a group of townsfolk is listening as she invokes the king of darkness. Riccardo, disguised as a fisherman, arrives and joins the onlookers. A sailor named Silvano pushes his way through the crowd, asking Ulrica to tell his fortune. Taking his hand, she studies it and tells him that wealth and rank will soon be his. In order to fulfil her prophecy immediately, Riccardo quickly scribbles a note and slips it, with some money, into the sailor's pocket. A moment later the astonished Silvano discovers the money and reads the note offering him a commission. The crowd acclaims Ulrica as a great oracle.

Suddenly a knocking is heard at the smaller of the two doors. Ulrica opens it and admits a man whom Riccardo recognises as one of Amelia's servants. The servant informs Ulrica that his mistress wishes to consult her privately. Riccardo hides, Ulrica gets rid of Silvano and the on-lookers, and Amelia enters. She asks Ulrica to help her overcome her love for Riccardo. Ulrica tells her that a certain magic herb will cure her of her love, but that she must gather it herself at midnight from beneath the gallows outside the city. Amelia, though terrified, promises to go there that night, and Riccardo mutters to himself that he too will be there. Voices are heard outside calling Ulrica. Amelia departs by the back door, while Ulrica opens the other door to admit Oscar and the gentlemen and officers from the first scene, including—in various disguises—Samuel and Tom and their faction. Riccardo joins them and, approaching Ulrica, asks her to tell his fortune. Examining his hand, Ulrica says it is that of a great man, but rather abruptly refuses to say more. Riccardo insists, and reluctantly she informs him that he is soon to die at the hand of an assassin. Riccardo laughs at her prophecy and asks who the assassin will be. "The next man who shakes your hand," replies Ulrica, whereupon Riccardo cheerfully offers his hand to all, none of whom will touch it. At that moment Renato arrives and, going up to Ricardo, shakes his hand. Everyone breathes freely again: the oracle was obviously mistaken. Riccardo tells Ulrica that the hand he has just clasped is that of his dearest friend. He reveals his identity to her, and hands her a purse of money. Accepting it quite unabashed, Ulrica again warns him of a traitor "or perhaps more than one", at which Samuel and Tom start guiltily. All present, with the exception of the conspirators, join in a song of praise for their Governor.

In Act II, it is midnight as Amelia approaches the deserted field outside the city which is used as a place of execution. She is attempting to pluck up sufficient courage to gather the herb when suddenly Riccardo appears and, declaring his love for her, begs her to admit that she loves him. The unhappy, conscience-stricken Amelia confesses that she returns his love. Their duet is interrupted by Renato, who has followed Riccardo to warn him that an ambush is being prepared for him. He does not recognise his wife, who has lowered her veil. Riccardo is persuaded to escape before the assassins arrive. He extracts from Renato a promise that he will escort the veiled lady back to the city gate, without attempting to discover her identity. Riccardo leaves, and almost immediately Samuel, Tom and their friends appear. Dis-concerted when they discover that their quarry is Renato, they ask to see who his companion is. Renato draws his sword, but in the ensuing scuffle Amelia's veil falls. The conspirators are delighted at the situation, but the humiliated Renato asks Samuel and Tom to call at his house in the morning. The conspirators saunter off, still laughing, and Renato reminds Amelia that he has sworn to escort her back to the town.

The first scene of Act III takes place later the same night in the library of Renato's house. On one wall is a full-length portrait of Riccardo. Renato enters with Amelia, who has been attempting to persuade him that her only guilt lay in being found in the admittedly compromising situation of the earlier part of the evening. Renato, however, is convinced of her adultery, and tells her he intends to kill her. He takes up his sword, but Amelia begs to be allowed first to see their only son. Renato sends her upstairs to say farewell to the child and then, addressing the portrait of Riccardo, accuses his former friend of having completely destroyed his life and his love for his wife. Samuel and Tom arrive, and Renato offers to join them in their plot to kill Riccardo. They find it difficult to believe in his change of heart, but when he offers his own son as a hostage, the conspirators are convinced. Each wants for himself the honour of killing Riccardo, but they agree to draw lots. Renato writes their names on three pieces of paper which he places in a vase. When Amelia enters to say that Oscar has arrived with an invitation from the Governor, Renato orders her to choose a name from the vase. Fearfully and unwillingly, she does so. The name she draw is Renato's, and from his joyful shout of vengeance, she realises he plans to kill Riccardo. Oscar is called in, and announces that the Governor has invited Renato and Amelia that evening to a masked ball. Samuel and Tom murmur that they too will attend. The scene ends with a quintet in which the conspirators conspire, Amelia considers how to warn Riccardo, and even wonders if she should consult Ulrica again, and Oscar prattles on about how splendid a ball it will be.

In Scene 2, next evening, Riccardo is revealed seated at a desk in an ante-room of his palace. At the back is a huge curtain beyond which is the ballroom. Riccardo has honourably decided to renounce Amelia, and signs a document sending her and Renato back to England. He is oppressed by forebodings, but when Oscar enters with an anonymous letter delivered by an unknown woman warning Riccardo that his life is in danger, he refuses to be intimidated by it, and prepares to enter the ballroom.

The final scene takes place in the ballroom where a huge crowd of guests, most of them masked, are dancing or promenading. The masked Renato asks Oscar to describe how Riccardo is dressed. At first, Oscar facetiously refuses to disclose so important a secret, but when Renato claims that his business with Riccardo is urgent, the page reveals that the Govenor is wearing a black cape with a pink ribbon. During the dancing, Amelia and Riccardo meet and recognise each other. Amelia begs him to fly from the immediate danger, but he refuses. Telling her that he has arranged for her and Renato to leave America, he bids her a last farewell. Renato steps between them with a cry of "Accept my farewell too", and stabs Riccardo. Members of the crowd rush forward and seize Renato, tearing off his mask. But the dying Riccardo orders them to release him and, swearing to Renato that his wife is innocent, produces the documents ordering their return to England. He pardons all the conspirators, says farewell to his friends and his country, and dies.

III

Out of all the censorship difficulties, the alterations, reworkings and compromises, one of Verdi's finest operas was born. *Un ballo in maschera* shows, musically and dramatically, none of the scars one might, in the circumstances, have expected to find. It is one of the middle-period masterpieces, a work whose characters are rich in humanity, whose melodies combine the warmth and vigour of the old Verdi with the lightness and elegance that had entered his work with *La traviata*. An opera whose instrumentation reveals the composer continuing to move towards a greater variety and flexibility of orchestral colour, with more detail in the inner voices and a masterly use of woodwind. An opera whose musico-dramatic form is aesthetically satisfying, in the way that *La traviata* is satisfying, or *Otello* or *Falstaff*. *Un ballo in maschera* is a complete work of art. Somma's libretto, if one forgets history and Gustavus, is tautly constructed and ripe for music, though flowery in style and less direct in manner than the work of Verdi's more professional collaborators such as Piave and Cammarano. The music which clothes it is not only sumptuously scored but also perfectly attuned to the style of its subject, and impeccably in character. In addition to the drama of the events, there is a great deal of laughter in the score, ranging from Oscar's quick gaiety through Riccardo's amused irony to the mocking taunts of the conspirators, all depicted with brilliant accuracy.

The short Prelude to Act I is based on three themes, all of which are heard early in the opening scene. The first becomes the rather solemn hymn of praise which the chorus sings to Riccardo, the second is a staccato tune associated with the conspirators, and the third is Riccardo's "La rivedrà nell' estasi", his song of love for Amelia, a tune as simply beautiful as its words are inflatedly banal [Ex. 84]. The curtain rises, and the first scene repeats and expands upon the Prelude's material. The hushed and reverent opening chorus is interrupted by the staccato mutterings of Samuel, Tom and the other conspirators, and is followed, after recitative for Riccardo and Oscar, by Riccardo's

Ex.84   Poco meno mosso

La ri-vedrà nel-l'e - sta-si rag-gian - te di pal - lo - - re...e
qui so-nar d'a-mo - re la sua pa - ro - - laudrà, sonar d'a-mo - re.

romantic reverie [Ex. 84], in the second part of which he is joined by
Oscar and both the loyal and disloyal elements in the chorus who voice
their differing sentiments. The days of the cabaletta, it would seem,
have vanished forever. Ten years earlier, "La rivedrà" would have been
followed by a rousing allegro in which, on one or another flimsy pretext,
Riccardo's feelings would have taken a more violent turn. Now, his
ardent love song is supported by a complex ensemble and followed by
the entrance of Renato and his tuneful *andante*, "Alla vita che t'arride".
Actually, Renato's aria is formally not dissimilar to those Verdi was
writing for the baritone voice ten years earlier, but it fits naturally
into its present context, and it too is now able to dispense with what
used to be the statutory cabaletta. The aria's old-fashioned aspect is
emphasised by its accompaniment and, in particular, its cadenza.
Oscar's *ballata*, "Volta la terrea", pleading Ulrica's cause, is a lively
and sparkling piece in two identical stanzas, calling for a light and
flexible soprano. But Oscar, the page, ought not to be too soubrettish
of voice: he sometimes has to lead a huge ensemble. The scene ends
with a very jaunty stretta ensemble led by Riccardo. Verdi has caught
the jocular mood of Riccardo's invitation to visit the fortune-teller to
perfection, and has provided a delicious *allegro brillante* of positively
Offenbachian frivolity. Gaiety did not come easily to him: the beginning of *La traviata*, for all its apparent light-heartedness, has a hectic,
feverish quality psychologically suited to the situation. But this ensemble is one of Verdi's few genuinely gay pieces of music. There is
laughter of a kind to be heard elsewhere in *Un ballo in maschera*, but
nothing as spontaneous as this: Riccardo's "É scherzo od é follia" in
Scene 2 has an ironic edge, and the conspirators' laughter in Act II is
distinctly sardonic.

The second scene begins with Ulrica's "Re dell' abisso, affrettati",
whose orchestral introduction, after three *ff* chords to focus the attention, conjures up eerie atmosphere by means of the low notes of the
clarinet as well as by suitably deployed strings. The female chorus,
themselves sounding not unlike Verdi's witches in *Macbeth*, admonish
one another to attend carefully to the witch, Ulrica, who proceeds to
call upon the King of the Abyss in an *andante* whose mysterious orchestral
colouring beautifully supports a vocal line both dignified and intense.
The arrival of Riccardo leads to the second part of Ulrica's invocation,

a cabaletta-like section in slightly faster tempo than the opening of her aria, ending with Ulrica growling at her onlookers to be silent, on an unaccompanied low G. Silvano's brief scene is followed by a trio for Riccardo, Amelia and Ulrica, "Della citta all' occaso", begun by Ulrica as she describes her cure for love in a perhaps unsuitably agreeable cantabile. The trio contains Amelia's prayer, "Consentimi, o Signore", one of Verdi's simple but immensely telling melodic arches [Ex. 85] which he makes orchestral use of, later in the opera. Riccardo's

song, in his disguise as a sailor, "Di' tu se fedele il flutto m'aspetta", is a gaily pleasant piece, if a trifle sophisticated for a humble sailor. The ensemble, "È scherzo od è follia", led by Riccardo now in his own character, splendidly assembles the moods of various characters: Riccardo amused and sceptical, Ulrica somewhat affronted, the conspirators disturbed, the usually flippant Oscar genuinely concerned for Riccardo, and the crowd credulously astounded. Verdi's musical characterisation is so assured that he is able to distinguish with ease between the styles of Riccardo as sailor and Riccardo as aristocrat. In *propria persona*, in the ensemble, Riccardo reverts to his usual style of expression. Verdi uses the frequent rests, often between syllables, to emphasise a certain tenseness behind the levity at this point. At the beginning of this century, the tenor, Alessandro Bonci, introduced an effect of his own here by inserting rhythmical "ha-ha's" into the rests, since when tenors have tended to copy him. The effect is harmless but unnecessary. The Act I finale, "O figlio d'Inghilterra", moves from the march in which Riccardo's praises are sung to the enthusiastic reply by Riccardo and Oscar, and finally combines the two tunes fortissimo.

Act II opens with Amelia's recitative and aria, "Ma dall' arido stelo divulsa". The orchestral introduction begins stormily but soon gives way to the melody of Amelia's "Consentimi, o Signore" from the preceding scene [Ex. 85], heard first on solo flute accompanied by tremolando strings, then repeated by violins and cellos. The music becomes agitated again, and Amelia launches into her terrified recitative. In the aria itself, a fine example of Verdi's middle-period style of writing for his soprano heroines, musical characterisation, dramatic situation and pure melodic inspiration are made to cohere excitingly. The love duet is well on the way towards the perfection of the Act I duet in *Otello*. A little of the pre-*Rigoletto* crude vigour returns to date it as obviously earlier than *Otello*, but the central outburst [Ex. 86]

is as breath-takingly lovely as anything in the *Tristan und Isolde* love music, and indeed not dissimilar to it. Riccardo's opening mezza voce utterance in the duet ("Non sai tu che se l'anima mia") sets the mood of tenderness from which the duet's later passion erupts. When Amelia confesses her love for him, Riccardo expresses his joy in a rapturous dolcissimo passage in which Amelia then joins him. But the throbbing heart of the duet is contained in the passage I have quoted. The urgent and exciting trio in which Renato and Amelia persuade Riccardo to flee is dramatically and musically first-rate. In fact, there are remarkably few blemishes on the entire score of this opera. As music drama, it stands up confidently under the closest scrutiny. The Act II finale, with the sardonic laughter of the conspirators taunting Renato, is an inspired piece of operatic writing. An ensemble develops in which Amelia's poignant lament soars in legato phrases above the staccato amusement of Samuel and Tom, and Renato's fury: a dramatic adumbration of a method to be put to comic use years later in *Falstaff*. The act ends as Renato prepares to escort Amelia to the city while the mocking laughter of the conspirators dies away in the distance.

Amelia's aria, "Morrò, ma prima in grazia", at the beginning of Act III is preceded by stormy exchanges between her and Renato. The aria, moving and richly yet subtly tuneful, is enhanced by its solo cello obbligato. Renato's "Eri tu che macchiavi quell' anima", though less complex, is no less affecting. It consists simply of two contrasted sections. The first is an angry and bitter denunciation of Riccardo, its accompaniment marked by a martial string figure and fortified by brass; and the second, in which Renato recalls past happiness, is an expressive cantabile of great beauty and simplicity in which the brass is replaced by the gentler sound of harp and flute [Ex. 87].

The scene and trio in which Renato, Samuel and Tom swear to assassinate Riccardo is brilliantly written. The conspirators enter to their by now familiar figure and, when Renato agrees to join their plot, they combine in a somewhat early-Verdian martial episode. As

Renato writes the names to be drawn from a vase, the orchestra comments in a suspense-laden passage which calls to mind the oath music in *Götterdämmerung*, which was still several years in the future. It is Verdi's superb writing for solo trumpet which provides most of the tension here. The sudden *ppp* that he demands from the orchestra at the moment when Amelia draws the name is tremendously effective in a really good performance. Renato's name is announced, and he, Samuel and Tom return in unison to their oath theme, while Amelia adds her agitation. The quintet finale works well, Oscar's sprightly coloratura contrasting strongly with the style of Amelia and the three low male voices.

The short solo scene for Riccardo is permeated with references to his love theme [Ex. 84]. The first violins use it to introduce the scene, and it continues to be referred to underneath Riccardo's recitative. His aria, "Ma se m'è forza pederti", is pleasant, touching in its dignity, and imaginatively scored. During Riccardo's conversation with Oscar, the music of the ball can be heard intermittently in the background, but as Riccardo anticipates his final meeting with Amelia, the orchestra swells up to cover the off-stage band music, and Riccardo sings his love theme again.

The action of the ballroom scene is kept moving forward to the rhythm of the dance music, right up to the moment when Renato stabs Riccardo. Oscar's teasing song, "Saper vorreste", in two stanzas like his earlier one, is very pretty and high-spirited, its orchestral colour lightened by the prominence of the piccolo part. To a change in the dance music, Riccardo and Amelia meet and sing their sad farewell. When Renato suddenly appears from the surrounding dancers and stabs Riccardo, there is a horrified cry from the crowd which is stilled by the dying Riccardo. The dance music trickles to an end, and, to the accompaniment of four violins playing in two parts, and the clarinet in its low register, Riccardo swears to Renato that Amelia is innocent. The voices of Amelia, Oscar and Renato are added, Riccardo gathers his strength for a final farewell, and dies in mid-phrase. After a loud, swift cry of horror from the ensemble, the curtain falls. So ends one of Verdi's masterpieces, a music drama worthy of its place in the great Italian operatic tradition that began with *Orfeo* and stretched across three centuries to end with *Falstaff*.

XXII

La forza del destino

Dramatis personae:

Il Marchese di Calatrava	(bass)
Donna Leonora di Vargas, his daughter	(soprano)
Don Carlo di Vargas, his son	(baritone)
Don Alvaro	(tenor)
Preziosilla, a gypsy girl	(mezzo-soprano)
Padre Guardiano ⎱ Franciscan monks	(bass)
Fra Melitone ⎰	(baritone)
Curra, Leonora's maid	(mezzo-soprano)
Trabuco, muleteer and vendor	(tenor)

LIBRETTO by Francesco Maria Piave, based on the play *Don Alvaro o la fuerza del sino* by Angel Saavedra, Duke of Rivas, and on a scene from the play *Wallensteins Lager* by Friedrich Schiller

TIME: About the middle of the eighteenth century
PLACE: Spain and Italy

FIRST PERFORMED at the Imperial Theatre, St Petersburg, November 10, 1862, with Caroline Barbot (Leonora); Constance Nantier-Didiée (Preziosilla); Enrico Tamberlick (Alvaro); Francesco Graziani (Carlo); Achille De Bassini (Melitone); Gian Francesco Angelini (Padre Guardiano). Revised version first performed at La Scala, Milan, February, 20, 1869, with Teresa Stolz (Leonora); Ida Benza Nagy (Preziosilla); Mario Tiberini (Alvaro); Luigi Colonnese (Carlo); Giacomo Rota (Melitone); Marcel Junca (Padre Guardiano)

La forza del destino

THE TEMPO OF life for Verdi and Giuseppina was now more leisurely than it had once been. They stayed on in Rome for several weeks after the February 1859 première of *Un ballo in maschera*, before returning to Sant' Agata for the summer. In the autumn Verdi was elected to an Assembly in Parma, and was one of the small group deputed to carry the Assembly's deliberations to Vittorio Emanuele in Turin. While there, with the help of the British ambassador he managed to meet the statesman, Count Camillo Cavour. He also, under conditions of the greatest secrecy, married Giuseppina on August 29, 1859, in the small town of Collonges-sous-Salève in Savoy. The legalising of their union made no apparent difference to the lives of the couple, and it is useless now to speculate on why, after having lived as man and wife for twelve years, they descended upon a church in Collonges, bringing with them a priest from Geneva to perform the ceremony, and told the local priest to "go for a walk".

The winter was spent in Genoa, most of 1860 at Sant' Agata. When the unification of Italy was achieved in 1861, Verdi at first resisted all attempts to persuade him to stand for election as the Busseto representative in the first Italian parliament. He was an artist, he insisted. He had neither the aptitude nor the desire to be a politician. But when Cavour himself urged him to stand, Verdi could resist no longer. He was elected, and in February he and Giuseppina travelled to Turin for the opening of the first Parliament by Vittorio Emanuele. Verdi was assiduous in his attendance at the sessions, but made a point always of voting as Cavour did. When Cavour died in June, Verdi organised a memorial service in Busseto at which, as he wrote to his friend Arrivabene, "The priest officiated without charge, which is quite something."[1]

The death of Cavour was a disaster for the newly-formed country. For Verdi, it meant the loss of a man he had always revered, and the end of his brief political career. Having gone into politics only because Cavour wished it, he now gradually extricated himself. He returned to Turin for a session of Parliament, but while he was there he signed a contract with the Imperial Theatre in St Petersburg to write an opera for production in the winter of 1861–2. His first choice of subject was

[1] *Verdi Intimo* (ed. Alberti), p. 9.

Victor Hugo's *Ruy Blas*, but this play about a valet who becomes the Empress's lover and his country's Prime Minister invested the common man with too great a dignity and nobility to commend itself unreservedly to the Tsarist régime. By the time the authorities had reluctantly decided to allow it, Verdi had lost interest in the play. He finally decided on a Spanish play he had considered once before, *Don Alvaro o La Fuerza del Sino* (Don Alvaro, or The Force of Destiny) by Don Angel de Saavedra, Duke of Rivas. Entrusting the libretto to Francesco Maria Piave, he worked on the opera throughout the summer. "The play is powerful," he wrote to Léon Escudier, "unusual and extremely vast. I like it immensely."[1]

The correspondence between Verdi and Piave reveals that the composer-librettist relationship was much as it had always been between them. Verdi harrassed Piave, complaining frequently of the ugliness and the incomprehensibility of his verses:

> All the verses of the terzetto are quite bad. "Ed io ti dovrei spezzare?/Nol debbe la mia mano". One can't say that. From "La mia presenza" to the end, everything must be done again. Finally, "Maledetta"—what does that mean?—must be changed to "Ti maledico!"
>
> For God's sake, my dear Piave, let's think about this carefully. We can't go on like this: it's absolutely impossible with this drama. The style must be tightened up. The poetry can and must say all that the prose says, and in half the words. So far you're not doing that . . .[2]

Giuseppina made elaborate preparations for the journey to Russia, and ordered large quantities of wine, pasta, cheese and salami to be sent in advance to St Petersburg. The leading tenor of the St Petersburg opera was an Italian, Enrico Tamberlick, who was also popular in London: it was he who had unofficially acted as Verdi's agent in negotiations with the management, and the role of Don Alvaro was written for him. As soon as Verdi and Giuseppina arrived, rehearsals began of the opera which Verdi had decided to call *La forza del destino*. Unfortunately, the soprano became ill. As Giuseppina wrote to Count Opprandino Arrivabene,

> The voices of singers are as fragile as . . . (I leave you to finish this phrase) and the voice of [Emma] La Grua is, to her and Verdi's misfortune, an upsetting example of this fragility. So, lacking the prima donna for whom he had written, and there being no other singer here suitable for the role, Verdi asked to be released from the contract.[3]

A few more lines of Giuseppina's letter are worth quoting for the picture they give of the Russian winter and the contrast between the luxury of the rich and the miserable condition of the poor.

[1] *Rivista Musicale Italiana*, Vol. XXXV, 1928, p. 22.
[2] Abbiati, Vol. II, p. 647.   [3] *Verdi intimo*, p. 14.

Nevertheless, this terrible cold has not bothered us in the least, thanks to our apartments. One sees the cold but doesn't feel it. But, be quite clear, this curious contradiction is a benefit only of the rich who are able to shout, "Hurray for the cold, the ice, the sleighs and other joys of this world." But the poor people in general, and the coachmen in particular, are the most miserable creatures on earth. Just think, dear Count, many of the coachmen stay sometimes all day and some of the night sitting still on their boxes, exposed to freezing cold, waiting for their masters who are guzzling in beautifully warm apartments while some of these unhappy beings are freezing to death. Such horrible things happen all the time. I shall never get used to the sight of such suffering.[1]

The production of *La forza del destino* was postponed until the following autumn, and in February 1862 the Verdis left Russia. Verdi wrote to Tamberlick:

Here I am in Berlin after a trip with no sinister events except the appalling cold from Dunaberg to Kovno. We travelled three or four miles in an open train in thirty-three degrees of cold to join the train of a Grand Duke who had stopped at the fort. It is a terrible thing to be at the disposition of others, even a Grand Duke! Now I understand the meaning of cold, and there was one moment when I seemed to feel all the swords of the Russian army in my head. If I could believe in another world, an inferno of ice as Papa Dante calls it, I should begin tomorrow to recite the Rosary and Miserere, and ask for pardon for all my sins of commission and omission. The railway carriages that took us from Dunaberg to Kovno were unheated, and even the wine—a good one at five roubles a bottle—turned to ice![2]

As Verdi had reluctantly accepted a commission to represent Italy at the London Exhibition of 1862, he and Giuseppina did not return to Italy but travelled on to London via Paris (see pp. 458–60). Eventually, they arrived back at Sant' Agata, and shortly afterwards tragedy struck: their dog Loulou died. "Our Loulou, our poor little Loulou is dead! Poor little animal! My sadness is great, but Peppina is absolutely desolate!"[3] Verdi buried Loulou underneath a willow tree in the garden, and erected a headstone with the inscription: "To the memory of one of my most faithful friends". He set to work perfecting the orchestration of *La forza del destino*, and in the autumn he and Giuseppina returned to St Petersburg. This time all went smoothly, and the opera was produced with great success on November 10, 1862, or October 29th according to the Russian calendar. The critic of the *Journal de St.-Pétersbourg* wrote, immediately after the first performance:

[1] Op. cit., p. 14.　　[2] *Bulletin of Institute of Verdi Studies*, Vol. V, p. 1096.
[3] Verdi to Arrivabene, August 1, 1862 (*Verdi intimo*, p. 21). Loulou, or Lulu as Giuseppina always spelled the name, was a male dog.

It is midnight. We have just left the first performance of the new opera which Maestro Verdi has written expressly for the Italian Theatre of St Petersburg. We should not want this issue of the paper to go to press without mentioning the brilliant success of this beautiful work.

We shall speak again at leisure about this magnificent score and about this evening's performance; but for the moment we wish to report the composer's victorious success and the ovations for the artists who, in order to comply with the insistent demands of the entire audience, had on several occasions to drag the celebrated composer on to the stage, to the sound of wild cheering and prolonged applause.

It is our opinion that *La forza del destino*, of all Verdi's works, is the most complete, both in terms of its inspiration and the rich abundance of its melodic invention, and in those of its musical development and orchestration.[1]

At one of the later performances, a group of supporters of the Russian nationalist school of composition staged a demonstration against the opera, but this merely had the effect of inciting the vast majority of the audience to a counter-demonstration of enthusiastic applause.

The version of *La forza del destino* performed at St Petersburg differs in several respects from the opera as we know it today. Despite its successful première, Verdi was not entirely satisfied with the work. Within a few months of its Russian performances, the opera was produced in Rome (as *Don Alvaro*), and in Madrid, where Verdi himself supervised the staging, and the elderly Duke of Rivas, author of the play, was in the audience. The following years saw performances in New York, Vienna, Buenos Aires and London. But for its production at La Scala in 1869 Verdi revised the opera, omitting some numbers, changing the order of scenes, generally re-editing, completely altering the finale, and adding the present overture. The necessary alterations to the libretto were made by Antonio Ghislanzoni, the poet, playwright, novelist, and editor of the Milan *Gazzetta Musicale*, who some months later was to turn the French synopsis of *Aida* into an Italian libretto. The revised *Forza* was triumphantly successful, though Verdi himself considered it a somewhat old-fashioned work in comparison with his *Don Carlo* of 1867: "It is a strange thing, and at the same time discouraging. While everyone cries, 'Reform, Progress', in general the public applauds and the singers prefer arias, romances and songs."[2] When Filippo Filippi, the music critic of *La Perseveranza*, called Leonora's aria, "Pace, pace mio dio", an imitation of Schubert's "Ave Maria", and then wrote to Verdi in explanation and apology, the composer replied at some length:

I know nothing about what happened between you and Ricordi, but it may be that Giulio, who, unless I am mistaken, prefers Leonora's *cantabile* to many other compositions, lost his temper somewhat when he read that you thought it an imitation of Schubert. If it is, then I am as surprised as

[1] No. 245, Nov. 11th (Oct. 30th Russian style).   [2] *Copialettere*, p. 619.

Giulio, for musically illiterate as I am I couldn't say how many years it has been since I heard Schubert's "Ava Maria". It would have been difficult for me, therefore, to copy it. Please don't think when I speak of my great musical ignorance that I'm simply exaggerating. It's the pure and simple truth. In my house there is very little music. I have never gone to a music library or to a publisher to refer to a piece of music. I keep up with a few of our best modern operas not by studying them but by hearing them occasionally in the theatre. You will understand my purpose in all this. So I repeat that, of all composers of past or present, I am the least erudite. Let us understand each other: I repeat, this is no modesty. I am referring to erudition, not to musical knowledge. It is true that, in my youth, I studied long and hard. That is why now I have the confidence generally to succeed in shaping the sounds so as to achieve the effects I want. And if I write something that breaks the rules, I do so because in that case I can't get what I want within the rules, and because I don't really believe that all the rules are perfect. The counterpoint textbooks must be revised.[1]

II

Don Angel Saavedra, Duke of Rivas, the author of *Don Alvaro o la fuerza del sino*, was one of the leading Spanish playwrights of his day. Born in Córdoba in 1791, he was poet and man of action, soldier and diplomat. Because of his liberal opinions, much of his early life was spent in exile from Spain; in Malta, France and England. After the death of Ferdinand VII, an amnesty was granted by Queen Maria Cristina, and Rivas returned to Spain where, after a further short period of exile in Lisbon, this time because the new liberal tide of opinion considered him reactionary, he eventually achieved stability as a diplomat and became ambassador first to Naples and then to France. He died in Madrid in 1865.

As a playwright, the Duke of Rivas was part of the romantic movement. His own work was influenced by such writers as Sir Walter Scott, and, in particular, Victor Hugo, and Rivas in turn exercised a strong influence on other Spanish poets and playwrights, among them García Gutiérrez whose *El Trovador*, produced in 1836, owes much to Rivas's *Don Alvaro* of 1835. Verdi had twice gone to the plays of García Gutiérrez for operatic subjects (*Il trovatore* and *Simon Boccanegra*), before, in 1861, turning his attention to *Don Alvaro* which was, by then, a quarter of a century old.

Don Alvaro is typical of the sprawling, loose-limbed romantic expressionism which evolved from the comparatively ordered *Sturm und Drang* of Schiller and the German romantic movement. The formal structure of Rivas's play is virtually schizoid: the dramatic unities are flung to the winds, the action ranging over five years and see-sawing between Spain and Italy. Behind its ferociously absurd yet somehow

[1] *Copialettere*, pp. 616–17.

tenuous plot, the play is about the contrast between the contemplative life and the life of action, if it is about anything at all. Verdi, I think, understood this intuitively, and emphasised the element of contrast; this is particularly true of his 1869 revision of the opera. The crowd scenes in Rivas, the scenes of local colour in which the dramatic action is forgotten as in a rambling aside of Dickens, Manzoni or Dostoevsky, are an integral part of his overall stage picture. They are, one might have thought, the very stuff to be considered expendable in transition to the operatic stage. That Verdi chose not only to retain this element but also to add to it indicates that he was well aware of the nature of Rivas's achievement, even if he may have overestimated its extent.

The play's eponymous hero remains firmly in the foregound, but in the opera Don Alvaro is only one of at least three equally important characters. In the opening scene of the play, not included in the opera libretto, Don Alvaro is discussed by the populace. He has newly arrived in Spain from the Americas, and his origins are as obscure as the provenance of his immense wealth. Said to be half Inca, he is elegant, generous, and the finest toreador in Spain. Leonora's two brothers are telescoped into one in the libretto, but otherwise the principal characters and the general narrative outline remain reasonably faithful to the play. Piave's verses lean heavily on F. Sanseverino's Italian translation of Rivas's play, published in Milan in 1850. Some of the opera's recitative relates directly to Rivas's soliloquies. For instance, when Don Alvaro, in the opera, recalls the night in Seville when he inadvertently killed Leonora's father, his phrase, "O notte ch'ogni ben mi rapisti!" (Oh night that robbed me of all that is good), is a reasonable translation of the play's, "¡Noche en que ví de repente mis breves dichas huir!"

Rivas's play ends, after the duel and the death of Leonora, with Alvaro's suicide. He rushes to the cliff edge as the Father Superior and the monks appear on the scene. When the Father Superior calls him by his monastic name, Rafaele, he cries: "You can search for Father Raphael, you fool. I am a messenger from hell. I am the spirit of destruction. . . . Hell, open your mouth and swallow me. Let the heavens collapse! Let mankind perish!" And, with a final shout of "Extermination, Annihilation", he flings himself over the cliff. The opera also ended thus in its original St Petersburg version. The gentler ending as we know it today stems from the Milan revision of 1869.

The latter part of Act III, Scene 3, one of the scenes of life in the military camp, derives not from *Don Alvaro* but from Schiller's play *Wallensteins Lager* (*Wallenstein's Camp*). Verdi had known the Wallenstein plays for several years, and as early as 1849 had drawn Cammarano's attention to the very scene which, in 1861, he was to remember and encourage Piave to plunder for *La forza del destino*. It is not only, as is sometimes stated, Melitone's comical sermon which derives from

Schiller: the very shape and movement of the scene, and even part of the stage directions, are lifted straight out of *Wallensteins Lager*. The utterances of Trabuco, the begging peasants, the reluctant recruits and the vivandières are all adaptations of Schiller, while Melitone's sermon is a direct translation of the opening lines of a harangue delivered by a Capuchin friar to Wallenstein's troops. The friar's

> Kümmert sich mehr um den Krug als den Krieg,
> Wetzt lieber den Schnabel als den Sabel. . . . .
> Die Christenheit trauert in Sack und Asche,
> Der Soldat füllt sich nur die Tasche[1]

emerges from Melitone's mouth as

> Ben più facenda
> Le bottiglie vi dan che le battaglie!
> E invece di vestir cenere e sacco
> Qui si tresca con Venere e con Bacco.[2]

La forza del destino is in four acts, the first of which takes place in the castle of the Marquis of Calatrava, near Seville. The Marquis's daughter Leonora is saying goodnight to her father, who believes she has recovered from her infatuation for a foreigner unworthy of her. When the Marquis has gone, the conversation of Leonora and her maid Curra reveals that, far from having given up her foreign lover, Leonora is planning to elope with him that evening. She is, however, very much in two minds about the entire enterprise, wavering between joyful anticipation and guilt-stricken fear. Oppressed by the rival claims of her love and respect for her father, and her passion for Don Alvaro, Leonora finds it impossible even to know her own true feelings. When her maid accuses her of not loving Alvaro, she protests that, on the contrary, she is planning to forsake family and country for him. Nevertheless, when midnight strikes and Alvaro has not yet arrived, she is almost pleased that the elopement may have to be postponed. Suddenly the sound of an approaching rider is heard, and soon Alvaro enters from the balcony to claim his bride. When Leonora hesitates, he at first attempts to persuade her to hurry, but is finally struck by her indecision. Incoherently, she tries simultaneously to reassure him of her love and to postpone their flight. Coldly, Alvaro offers to release her from her vow if she is uncertain of her love for him. At this, Leonora realises the strength of her love, and swears to follow him to the ends of the earth.

[1] [The army] cares more about bottles than battles, and moistens its beaks more readily than its swords. . . . Christendom mourns in sackcloth and ashes, while the soldier fills his own pockets.

[2] Bottles give you more trouble than battles; and, instead of wearing sackcloth and ashes, here you intrigue with Venus and Bacchus.

As they are about to depart, the Marquis returns brandishing his sword and exclaiming, "Vile seducer! Infamous daughter!" Alvaro chivalrously announces that he alone is guilty, and invites the Marquis to kill him. But the haughty Calatrava considers Alvaro of too lowly an origin to be struck by a nobleman, and orders his servants to arrest him so that he can die at the hands of the public executioner. Outraged, Alvaro again protests Leonora's innocence and, offering himself as the Marquis's prisoner, flings his pistol to the ground. It goes off, mortally wounding the Marquis who, as he dies, curses his daughter. Alvaro leaves, dragging Leonora after him.

The first scene of Act II is set in an inn in the village of Hornachuelos. The host and hostess are about to serve supper to the assembled company of peasants and muleteers. Among them is Leonora's brother, Don Carlo di Vargas, disguised as a student. As they sit down to their meal, Leonora, who is staying at the inn disguised as a man, appears at a door leading to the upper storey but withdraws when she catches sight of her brother. We are to understand, and in fact are explicitly though abruptly informed in the next scene, that in their flight Leonora became separated from Alvaro.

The company at supper, which includes an itinerant vendor named Trabuco, is enlivened by the appearance of a young gypsy girl, Preziosilla, with whom everyone immediately begins to flirt. She is asked to tell fortunes, and advises the men to go and fight in Italy, where war has broken out against the Germans. Everyone shouts "Death to the Germans", and offers to go off and enlist, at which Preziosilla bursts into a militant song in praise of war in general. Don Carlo offers his hand for his future to be read, and Preziosilla shrewdly murmurs that, though she will keep his secret, she realises he is no student. A band of pilgrims celebrating Holy Week passes by, and all in the inn suddenly drop their warlike aspect and fall to their knees in prayer. Leonora reappears at the top of the stairs, calling on heaven to protect her from her brother. Don Carlo has, without actually recognising his sister, noticed the "personcina" who arrived at the inn in Trabuco's company, and teases the vendor about the sex of his travelling companion. "È gallo, oppur gallina?" he asks. "Is it a cock or a little hen?" The discomfited Trabuco goes off to bed, and Don Carlo is invited to tell the company about himself. He informs them that he is Pereda, a Bachelor of Arts from Salamanca, and that he is a friend of Di Vargas, whose sister's foreign lover had killed their father. He and Di Vargas pursued the villain to Cádiz, where they learned that Leonora had died and that the seducer had escaped back to America. Di Vargas had followed Leonora's lover to America, and he, Pereda, had returned to his studies. Preziosilla comments sarcastically on Carlo's story, and gives him to understand she doesn't believe a word of it. The company disperses for the night.

Act II, Scene 2, takes place in the courtyard of a monastery on a mountainside not far from Hornachuelos. To the right is a rocky precipice, centre-stage is the façade of the church of the Madonna of the Angels, and to the left is the entrance to the monastery. In the courtyard is a rough stone cross at the top of four steps. It is night. Leonora enters, still in her male disguise, having overheard her brother's narrative and fled from the inn. Believing Alvaro to have gone to America, she is in a state of acute distress, and falls to her knees calling on the Virgin to forgive her and to help her forget the lover who has, as she thinks, deserted her. She hears the monks chanting in the distance, and rings the bell of the monastery door. Brother Melitone answers, and she asks to see the Father Superior. Irritably, Melitone goes off and returns with the Father Superior, to whom Leonora reveals that she is the infamous Leonora di Vargas, and that she longs to be allowed to live near the monastery as a hermit, as another unhappy woman had apparently done before her. The Father Superior tries to persuade her to enter a convent, but Leonora is adamant that she must devote her life to God in strict solitude. Finally he agrees and calls the monks to appear before the high altar. The door of the church opens, the monks file in, and Leonora, now clad in a monk's habit, kneels before the Father Superior, who informs the monks that an unhappy soul has come to expiate his sins in the sacred cave nearby, and that no one must approach this place of asylum. When the ceremony of dedication is over, Leonora sets out alone for her nearby retreat.

For all three scenes of Act III, the action moves to Italy and to the battle of Velletri. The first scene takes place in a wood near Velletri on a dark night. Offstage the voices of soldiers playing cards can be heard. Don Alvaro, now a captain in the army, appears. In a soliloquy he reveals something of his past life. His parents, failing to regain the crown of the Incas, had been executed: he was born in prison and raised in the desert. He thinks Leonora dead and calls on her soul to look down in pity on him. The sound of a fierce quarrel is heard, and Alvaro rushes off to defend a man calling for help. He returns with Carlo, having saved his life, and the two men exchange vows of eternal brotherhood, though each gives the other a false name. At the sound of a call to arms, they run off in the direction of the fighting.

The scene changes to the Spanish officers' quarters near the battlefield. It is morning, and sounds of battle can be heard. An army surgeon and some orderlies are watching the progress of the fighting from a window. The Spanish grenadiers, led by Alvaro, put the Germans to flight, but Alvaro is wounded. He is carried in on a stretcher, followed by Carlo, who attempts to comfort him. When Carlo assures him that for his bravery he will be awarded the Order of Calatrava, Alvaro exclaims "Never!" Thinking himself close to death, he gives Carlo the key of a casket he always carries with him, and makes him swear to extract from it a package which he must burn without opening. Carlo gives his word, and the surgeon has Alvaro carried into the next room to be operated upon. Left alone, Carlo broods on his new friend's violent reaction to the name of Calatrava, and wonders if he can be Leonora's seducer. The key will reveal all, but Carlo's sense of honour will not allow him to betray his friend's trust. Curiosity drives him to compromise: he opens the box and, in addition to the package which he scrupulously does not disturb, discovers a portrait of Leonora. "The wounded man is Don Alvaro," he cries. "Now let him be saved to die at my hand!" The doctor calls from the adjoining room that Alvaro will live, and Carlo rejoices at now being able to avenge the family honour.

The third scene of Act III takes place in another part of the military encampment near Velletri, at night. A patrol passes by, and Alvaro, recovered from his injury, enters, deep in thought. He is followed by Carlo who, when he has satisfied himself that Alvaro is now strong enough to fight a duel, reveals his own identity and challenges him. Alvaro is reluctant to fight a man who, he says, had first offered him friendship. He tries to persuade Carlo that the killing of his father was an accident. He himself lost Leonora that night, and searched for her for a year before being convinced of her death. Carlo informs him that Leonora is still alive, but will die when he finds her. His threats against Leonora arouse Alvaro's anger, and the two men draw their swords and begin to fight. The patrol comes running up and manages to separate them. Carlo is dragged away, and the wretched Alvaro decides to enter a monastery. Throwing his sword away, he rushes out.

The sun rises. Reveillé is sounded. Spanish and Italian soldiers, boys, male and female camp-followers enter. (From here to the end of the scene, the material derives not from Rivas, but from Schiller.) Preziosilla, who has followed the army to Italy, begins to tell fortunes. Trabuco appears, peddling his wares. Some peasants enter, begging food, and are followed by a group of conscripted recruits bewailing their fate. Preziosilla cheers them up and leads the company in a lively dance. This is interrupted by Brother Melitone, who has also followed the troops to war. He attempts to preach a sermon chastising the soldiers for their vices, but this leads to a quarrel between the Italians, who fling abuse at him, and the Spaniards, who rush to his defence. Preziosilla restores amity by leading everyone in a chorus, "Rataplan".

Act IV takes place back in Spain, after the war is over. In Scene 1, the poor are being fed by Melitone in the courtyard of the monastery near Hornachuelos, while the Father Superior paces up and down reading his breviary. Melitone is bad-tempered with the beggars, who complain that Father Raphael used to be more charitable. Father Raphael, Melitone tartly informs them, has had enough of them for the time being, and has deputed to him the irksome task of feeding such rabble. Kicking the cauldron of soup over, he chases the beggars away. The

Father Superior gently chides him for his lack of charity, and Melitone begins to gossip about the saintly Father Raphael, of whom plainly he is jealous. He recalls that when, the previous day, he had said jokingly "You're working as hard as a mulatto," Father Raphael had clenched his fists and looked grim. We realise, if we have not done so already, that Father Raphael is Alvaro. The Father Superior enters the monastery as Melitone goes to answer a ring at the front gate. Melitone returns with Don Carlo, who asks for Father Raphael. "We've two", says Melitone, "One, from Porcuna, is fat and deaf, and the other dark with eyes like—" "The one from hell," answers Carlo, and the description suffices. Melitone goes off to find Father Raphael, whom he sends out to the visitor. Carlo reveals that he has been searching for Alvaro for five years. He offers him a sword, but Alvaro answers that he is doing penance for his sins and will not resort to violence. Carlo taunts him with cowardice, and twice Alvaro almost rises to the challenge only to remember his vows and beg for forgiveness. Carlo renews his insults, and slaps Alvaro's face, whereupon Alvaro flings aside his Christian humility, and the two men rush outside to fight.

The final scene follows immediately, outside Leonora's nearby cave. Leonora enters and prays for an end to her sufferings. She is still tormented by her love for Alvaro, and expects to find peace only in death. Disturbed by the sound of fighting nearby, she retreats to her cave. Carlo's off-stage voice is heard calling for a priest, and Alvaro enters, sword in hand. He runs to the door of the cave, calling for someone to come and comfort a dying man. Leonora refuses, but Alvaro is insistent. Finally, Leonora rings the bell to summon help from the monastery and then comes to the door of the cave. She and Alvaro recognise each other, and the broken-hearted Alvaro tells her to keep away from him, for his hands are again stained with her family's blood. Leonora runs off to her brother, and then is heard to utter a sudden cry. The Father Superior enters, supporting Leonora, whom her brother had stabbed before he died. Alvaro begins to curse, but the Father Superior calls on him to repent, and Leonora, too, promises him God's pardon. Throwing himself at her feet, Alvaro cries, "Leonora, io son redento" (I am redeemed). Leonora dies serenely, believing they will meet again in heaven.

This substitution, in the 1869 revision of the opera, of Christian resignation for the wild romantic gesture of the original version, was arrived at only after an inordinate amount of discussion between Verdi and various people whose advice he sought. As early as October 1863, Verdi had written to Piave: "We've got to think about the ending and find some way to avoid all those dead bodies."[1] He consulted his publisher, Tito Ricordi, whose only suggestion for improving the opera was to delete the character of Melitone. Verdi did not think much of

[1] Abbiati, Vol. II, p. 722.

this. "I'm not yet sure exactly what I'll do," he replied to Ricordi, "but I can tell you right away that I don't intend to cut out Melitone."[1] Another friend came up with a happy ending, Ricordi suggested calling in García Gutiérrez or Antonio Ghislanzoni, and Verdi himself wrote to Count Opprandino Arrivabene. The problem was debated sporadically for four or five years. When Piave became seriously ill, Ghislanzoni was finally called in to help, and his idea of ending the opera with Alvaro's redemption was accepted. At least there was one dead body fewer.

III

La forza del destino, often referred to as a flawed masterpiece, is as tuneful a work as *Il trovatore*. Despite this, and despite the fact that the Spanish plays on which the two operas are based have much in common, *La forza del destino* is not really very like the earlier opera. In fact, it is not very like anything else in Verdi's *œuvre*. Much of it betrays the circumstance that it was composed for Russia: the choral writing, the almost Dostoevskian monks with their dark bass voices, the sprawling formlessness of the action, the military scenes. And much of it, surely— particularly Melitone and the chorus scenes—influenced Moussorgsky when he came to write *Boris Godunov* six years later.

The full-scale Overture, a compendium of some of the opera's best tunes, held together by the destiny motif associated with Leonora [Ex. 88] was composed for the 1869 revision to replace the original

Ex.88 Allegro agitato e presto ♩ = 96

orchestral prelude. Three Es in unison on the brass are used, like the prompter's knocks in French theatre, to direct the attention. A pause, the sequence is repeated, and then the overture begins with a full statement of the destiny theme which continues to be heard threateningly beneath the potpourri of tunes that follows, which includes a sadly graceful *andantino* for flute, oboe and clarinet, later to be sung by Alvaro in Act IV, Scene 1; the great arching phrase of Leonora's "Deh, non m'abbandonar" [Ex. 89], heard here on the violins in octaves, playing very softly; and a passage from the duet for Leonora and the Father Superior, played first by solo clarinet with harp accompaniment. By way of a rather grandiose brass sequence, the overture moves to an exciting conclusion. The opening conversation between

[1] Abbiati, Vol. II, p. 782.

Leonora and her father is in Verdi's most flexible recitative. Leonora's brief aria, "Me pellegrina ed orfana", moving in its tender self-regard, may well be, as I have suggested elsewhere in this book, part of the lost *King Lear* music. Leonora's vacillation is beautifully conveyed in the recitative preceding Alvaro's arrival. Though she loves him, it is with joy and relief that she persuades herself it is now too late for him to arrive. When he does, their duet begins urgently. It is only during the course of it that Leonora's hesitancy, which Alvaro counters by gentle expression of his love, finally betrays her. Her secret fear, and now his, is that her love for him is not deep enough, and in an extraordinary passage Leonora protests her love while the vocal line and the orchestra both refute her actual words and express her subconscious doubts and fears. When Alvaro's dignified reaction brings her to a sudden realisation that he is all-important to her, the duet takes on a more conventional aspect. At its conclusion they are about to depart when, to the accompaniment of the destiny theme, the Marquis enters. The scene moves quickly to its conclusion: sensibly, Verdi wastes no time here on reflection or ensemble. After the fatal accident, the lovers utter a cry of horror and flee.

The second scene begins with the same call to attention that preceded the Overture, but this time the music that follows is in a light-hearted 2/4 rhythm to which the crowd sings and dances. Preziosilla's gay song in praise of war, taken up by the assembled company, is followed by a typically Verdian ensemble in which everyone, inspired by a passing band of pilgrims, kneels in prayer. Carlo's teasing of Trabuco is carried on in the effortlessly free conversational manner which Verdi had developed during his middle period. Carlo's lying narrative, "Son Pereda", is sung to a lilting and persuasive melody. When the company disperses for the night, recapitulating several of the themes it has enjoyed during the evening, Carlo's "Buona notte" is answered, first graciously by the entire chorus, and then, meaningfully and flirtatiously by Preziosilla.

The second scene of Act II begins with Leonora's great prayer, "Madre, pietosa Vergine". Its orchestral introduction is, of course, the destiny motif, its recitative is free-ranging and tremendous in its effect, and the aria itself is beautiful, its climax the superb, broadly sweeping phrase we have already heard in the Overture [Ex. 89]. Formally, the

Ex. 89   Andante mosso
            con passione

deh! non m'ab-ban - do-nar. pie - tà,   pie-tà   di   me,   Si-gno - re.

aria is particularly interesting. Its agitated minor beginning, the voice anguished, the strings disturbed and disturbing, gives way to the consoling major key of the phrase quoted. Behind it, we hear the monks chanting in the church, a sound which brings comfort to Leonora. "Ah, que' sublimi cantici," she sings, and repeats her heartfelt prayer. A second repetition of "Deh, non m'abbandonar" [Ex. 89] is given added emphasis by the full weight of the orchestra. After Leonora's brief exchanges in recitative with Melitone, the orchestra insists on the destiny motif again, and Leonora prays to the Virgin while a solo clarinet above tremolando strings softly but expressively offers the big tune. The long and absolutely magnificent duet for Leonora and the Father Superior recalls the Oberto-Leonora duet in Verdi's first produced opera, *Oberto*. The duet moves through several sections, each melodically more captivating than its predecessor. A declamatory beginning gives way to the relaxed *andante* of Leonora's "Più tranquilla l'alma sento" and a cantabile section in which the Father Superior joins her. Leonora's vocal line abounds in features which have come to be thought of as typically Verdian, not because Verdi uses them to excess, but because they are unique to him. The rising and falling arch is one; another is the masterly ability to draw expressive melody from what looks on the page to be little more than a scale passage [Ex. 90].

Ex.90 Andante

nè ter - ri - bi - le l'a - scolto la sua fi - glia ma - le dir,—

Ex.91 Andante

È que - sto il por - to; chi tal con-for - to mi to-glie-

- rà, chi tal con-for - to mi to - glie - rà?

eases into confidence. Although the duet undergoes several gradations of tempo, these are all variations on a basic natural *andante* pace. When the Father Superior calls Melitone, the latter's entrance phrase is accompanied by an orchestral statement of his grumbling remark from earlier in the scene.

The finale begins with an organ voluntary, whose harmonic implications suggest Leonora's aria and the monks' chant which accompanied it. Then two violins steal in with "Deh, non m'abbandonar" over tremolo strings. "Il santo nome", in which the Father Superior instructs the monks, is the beginning of an exciting ensemble of wide dynamic and vocal range: the chorus of monks sounds more fervent when called on to curse than when required to bless. The *adagio* "La Vergine degli angeli", sung first by the monks, then solo by Leonora, and finally by Leonora and the monks, is a touchingly simple tune which gives the soprano a chance to show off the purity of her legato and provides an impressively quiet close to the act.

Act III opens with a noisy orchestral tutti and off-stage chorus phrases from a group of men playing cards. The melancholy, intro-spective yet graceful introduction to Alvaro's aria, "Oh, tu che in seno agli angeli", features an important solo clarinet part. Alvaro narrates his recent history in an alternation of unaccompanied recitative and accompanied arioso. The aria itself, both tuneful, though subtly so, and expressive of Don Alvaro's accidie, is a splendidly effective piece of dramatic characterisation in beautifully lyrical terms. The upward leap from C to A flat in its opening phrase is indicative of the mood of desperate yearning which imbues the entire aria [Ex. 92].

The friendship duet which follows the episode of the off-stage quarrel is deliberately kept brief: a mere two phrases in A flat. Verdi obviously knew he had more important tenor-baritone business looming up a page or two later. Off-stage trumpets play a call to arms, and a scene change is effected during the ensuing battle music.

The duet for Alvaro and Carlo, "Solenne in quest' ora", is beautiful and, in context, most affecting. There is a simple but quite breath-takingly moving key-change from C minor to C major at Alvaro's "Or muoio tranquillo". Don Carlo's aria, "Urna fatale", is broodingly impressive and eminently singable. Its recitative is almost as varied in mood and tempo as Rigoletto's "Pari siamo", and its cabaletta has an exhilarating vengeful energy. This, incidentally, is the only cabaletta in the opera.

The next scene opens with a superbly written chorus, an 1869 addi-tion to the score, conjuring up an atmosphere of night and stillness. As dawn breaks, Don Alvaro appears, and with him the solo clarinet motif from his aria in Act III's Scene 1. After his dramatic duet with Carlo, the remainder of the scene consists of a number of sound-pictures of life in the military camp. A gay chorus of vivandières and soldiers praises the military life; Preziosilla has a lightly scored strophic song ending with a flourish up to top C; Trabuco's arietta as he peddles his wares to the soldiers combines a Donizettian frivolity with an earthi-ness which it is not too fanciful to imagine may have had its effect on Moussorgsky (it could almost be part of *Sorochintsy Fair*); a mournful chorus of starving peasants is followed by an equally sad chorus of young recruits, who are first taunted by the vivandières to a tuneful figure which the orchestra has already played during Trabuco's song, and then teased in somewhat better-humoured fashion by Preziosilla; a lively tarantella is danced and sung by all; Melitone's declamatory sermon is followed by a Rataplan chorus which Preziosilla leads and which can hardly fail to remind one of either Donizetti in *La Fille du régiment* or Meyerbeer in *Les Huguenots*.

At the beginning of Act IV, Melitone's scene with the hungry beggars rounds out the characterisation of this curiously un-Verdian character. Un-Verdian, that is to say, in the light of the earlier operas, but in some ways an adumbration of Falstaff and his companions. In the little duet with the Father Superior, Melitone retains his buffo characteristics in contrast to his superior's more solemn legato. Moussorgsky surely bore Melitone in mind when he came to write Varlaam's music in *Boris Godunov*. The scene ends with a magnificent duet for Alvaro and Carlo. To a tune which has already been heard in the Overture, Alvaro asks for mercy [Ex. 93]. The tune returns between Carlo's renewed taunts,

utilising the tenor's lower register down to B flat. Finally, goaded into action, Alvaro agrees to fight, and the duet concludes with a brief, noisy coda. The last scene opens with Leonora's familiar fate motif, which fades before her *andante* plea for peace, "Pace, pace, mio dio". This is the aria that the music critic Filippo Filippi contended was a copy of Schubert's "Ave Maria". The two have a phrase in common, as well as an arpeggio accompaniment, but the very slight likeness is obviously coincidental. The aria is one of the loveliest Verdi ever wrote, from its gentle opening to its brief, violent coda. It is Mozartian, not only in its simplicity of means but also in its testing of the soprano's technique. The sudden leap to a pianissimo B flat at "Invan la pace" is a *locus classicus*: the effect, if brought off, is stunning, and Verdi made use of it again in the final movement of his Requiem [Ex. 115]. Isolated passages in the finale to Act II have looked forward to the Requiem as well.

The last, desperate events of the drama are quickly and dramatically told. The brief passage in which the dying Leonora tells how Carlo stabbed her has a dramatic effect out of all proportion to the economy of its means: the woodwind instruments, pitted against brass and strings, are both poignant and eloquent. All is resolved in the great final trio launched by the Father Superior, an 1869 alteration to the score, which provides a moving, quiet end to Verdi's rich, sprawling, immensely lovable essay on the respective values of the contemplative life and the life of action.

To call this opera, as some critics do, "flawed", simply because it does not observe the Aristotelian unities seems to me absurd. It covers a vast canvas, from the personal to the social, in the manner of Elizabethan theatre or the nineteenth-century novel: it is the opera of a man who has read Manzoni's *I promessi sposi*. The Preziosilla scenes, frequently cut in performance, are as integral to the work as the scenes of plot involving Leonora, Alvaro and Carlo, and it is the task of the producer to reveal them as such, not to avoid the question by omitting them.[1]

I am not sure that the opera deserves that other epithet, "uneven", which has also been hurled at it. The emotions expressed in the military camp scenes are simple and banal and so, frequently, is the music which portrays them. These glimpses of popular life, it seems to me, perfectly complement, and indeed make their own implicit comment on, the drama of the Calatrava family and the Indian outcast, Alvaro. *La forza del destino* is not a flawed but a complex masterpiece. To us now, the opera appears to consist of a string of glorious arias, but in fact Verdi was, in it, continuing his move away from strict aria form towards a greater fluidity and an apportioning of more orchestral and melodic interest to the recitative, or arioso as it was fast becoming. Verdi himself knew the kind of work he had composed. In a letter to his friend Vincenzo Luccardi, after the Rome production of 1863, he wrote: "It is certain that in *La forza del destino* the singers do not necessarily have to know how to manage *solfeggi*, but they must have soul, and understand the words and express their meaning."[2] On paper, *La forza* looks both messy in shape and old-fashioned in content. But an adequate performance can reveal it as the valid work of music drama it really is.

---

[1] Franz Werfel's adaptation and translation of the opera into German as *Die Macht des Schicksals* in 1926 was one of the early successes of the Verdi revival in Germany and Austria. The translation, though not always faithful to Piave, is excellent, and the only rearrangement of scenes occurs when the Act III duet for Alvaro and Carlo is placed after the Rataplan scene, instead of before it, in order to end the Act with a return to the plot line. Werfel calls Act I a prologue. Thus his version is "in einem Vorspiel und drei Akten".

[2] *Copialettere*, p. 612.

XXIII

Don Carlo

Dramatis personae:

Don Carlo, Infante of Spain	(tenor)
Elizabeth de Valois	(soprano)
Philip II, King of Spain	(bass)
Rodrigo, Marquis of Posa	(baritone)
Princess Eboli	(mezzo-soprano)
Grand Inquisitor	(bass)
Tebaldo, page to Elizabeth	(soprano)
Count Lerma	(tenor)
A Friar	(bass)
A Royal Herald	(tenor)
A Voice from Heaven	(soprano)

LIBRETTO, based on Friedrich Schiller's play *Don Carlos*, by Joseph Méry and Camille du Locle, translated into Italian by Achille de Lauzières and Angelo Zanardini

TIME: 1568
PLACE: France and Spain

FIRST PERFORMED, in French as *Don Carlos*, at the Paris Opéra, March 11, 1867, with Marie-Constance Sass (Elizabeth); Pauline Gueymard (Eboli); A. Morère (Carlo); Jean-Baptiste Faure (Rodrigo); Louis-Henri Obin (Philip); M. David (Inquisitor). Revised four-act version, in Italian, first performed at La Scala, Milan, January 10, 1884, with Abigaille Bruschi-Chiatti (Elizabeth); Giuseppina Pasqua (Eboli); Francesco Tamagno (Carlo); Paul Lhérie (Rodrigo); Alessandro Silvestri (Philip); Francesco Navarrini (Inquisitor).

Don Carlo

THE YEARS IMMEDIATELY following the Russian première of *La forza del destino* in 1862 were occupied by Verdi in travel, business negotiation, and revivals of earlier operas. After the Madrid production of *Forza*, Verdi and Giuseppina took the opportunity to spend some weeks sight-seeing in Spain. In Paris, the composer agreed to direct a new production of *Les Vêpres siciliennes*, but quarrelled with the orchestra, which he considered had been insolent to him, and returned to Sant' Agata. A great deal of his time was spent now living the life of a farmer; he did not even bother to attend the rehearsals in Paris of his revised *Macbeth*. In the autumn of 1865, he went to Paris to discuss a proposed French production of a revised *Forza*. The plan came to nothing, for Verdi and the Opéra could not reach agreement on several points, but he agreed to write a new opera for performance during the Paris Exposition of 1867. The subjects considered included *King Lear*, but Verdi had been flirting with *Lear* for too long. Although he thought seriously of attempting it at last, and wrote to Léon Escudier about it, he finally decided against *Lear* with the comment that, magnificent though it was, it would hardly be spectacular enough for Parisian taste. The subject eventually chosen was Schiller's play *Don Carlos*. An elderly librettist, Joseph Méry, who had worked with Auber, was entrusted with the task of adapting Schiller, but died before he had completed the work. Camille du Locle was called in to finish the libretto, which Verdi took back to Sant' Agata with him in March 1866. After he had worked for two months on the opera, the Austro-Prussian War broke out, in which Italy was involved on the side of Prussia. This, and a return of the psychosomatic sore throat, slowed down Verdi's progress, but at the end of August he and Giuseppina returned to Paris with a virtually complete opera. Rehearsals began, with the usual Parisian delays, postponements and irritations, in the middle of which Verdi received the news that his father had died. *Don Carlos* finally had its première on March 11, 1867, and the following day Verdi left for the farm at Sant' Agata to deal with his family problems. The opera had been only a moderate success.

To Count Opprandino Arrivabene, Verdi wrote: "Last night *Don Carlos*. It was not a success. I don't know what the future may hold, but

I shouldn't be surprised if things were to change".[1] The work was performed at the Opéra forty-three times during the season, so it was certainly no failure. But the Empress Eugénie found it offensive, which gave many people their cue, and there was, too, a certain amount of resentment that a foreign composer had been honoured by so important a commission. The press notices were, on the whole, favourable, though some critics spoke of the influence of Meyerbeer and even of Wagner. This Verdi deeply resented. He wrote to Escudier: "I have read in Ricordi's *Gazetta* the account of what the leading French papers say of *Don Carlos*. In short, I am an almost perfect Wagnerian. But if the critics had only paid a little more attention they would have seen that there are the same aims in the trio in *Ernani*, in the sleep-walking scene in *Macbeth*, and in other pieces. But the question is not whether the music of *Don Carlos* belongs to a system, but whether it is good or bad. That question is clear and simple and, above all, legitimate."[2]

Verdi's indignation was genuine. At this time he had yet to hear a Wagner opera, nor was he to do so until after he had scored *Aida*. The Verdi progression is a natural one, requiring no reference to Wagner. The taunts of Meyerbeerism are equally wide of the mark. Of course, the formal structure of *Don Carlos* was that of a Meyerbeer opera: this was virtually a condition of composing for the Paris Opéra. But Verdi's music has little in common with Meyerbeer's. His operatic style is, in *Don Carlos* as elsewhere, that of a genuine musical dramatist, whereas Meyerbeer possessed more sense of display than of drama.

In Italian, as *Don Carlo*, the opera was produced in Italy, first in Bologna and then at La Scala. Seventeen years later, at a time when he and Boito were already preparing to begin work on *Otello*, Verdi was persuaded to revise *Don Carlo* for a production in Vienna. When the production was cancelled, the revision was first seen at La Scala. Verdi made several changes, wrote some new music, and deleted the whole of the first act from which he salvaged only Carlo's aria, which he inserted into the former second act. On the whole, this new four-act adaptation was neither more nor less popular with the public than the original version, and structurally it is less satisfactory than the original. For some years the opera continued to be performed in four acts. But the most satisfactory solution of the *Don Carlo* problem, and the one increasingly adopted today, is to restore the first act to the revised four-act version of 1884 (which was, in fact, done as early as 1887). This, of course, necessitates the removal of Carlo's aria from its new position. It also makes a long opera even longer, though the ballet music is usually, and in this instance I think excusably, omitted.

A further point: it is *Don Carlo*, the Italian translation, which is universally known today, not the French *Don Carlos*. Curiously, the advocates of opera in the original language appeared not to be unduly

---

[1] *Verdi intimo*, p. 75.   [2] Abbiati, Vol. III, pp. 131–2.

worried when Covent Garden produced its Italian *Don Carlo* in 1958, though I imagine their sensibilities would have been affronted and their disgust vociferously expressed had the opera been performed in English. I, who take no sides or rather both sides, on the question of vernacular or original, find myself perfectly happy with *Don Carlo* in Italian. It was, after all, Verdi's own language, and the only one he spoke fluently. His knowledge of French, though extensive, was imperfect, and I do not think that he set it particularly well. I certainly cannot agree with the view that the French of *Don Carlos* lies more easily and naturally on the vocal line than the Italian of *Don Carlo*. As with the adaptation of *Les Vêpres siciliennes* to *I vespri siciliani*, Verdi made what alterations were necessary to fit the music to the Italian text. (And it should be remembered that, when he came to compose *Aida*, Verdi refused to set a French libretto by Camille du Locle, and himself worked closely on an Italian libretto with Antonio Ghislanzoni who translated du Locle's French). All things considered, Verdi's *Don Carlo* is to be preferred to his *Don Carlos*.

II

Schiller's play, *Don Carlos*, his first to be written in verse, is no more historically accurate than are Shakespeare's histories. Like Shakespeare, Schiller was concerned with poetic truth; to achieve it, he was willing to sacrifice mundane fact whenever necessary (*vide Die Jungfrau von Orleans*, which Verdi had set as *Giovanna d'Arco*). *Don Carlos*, though it takes place in late sixteenth-century Spain, and though it purports to deal with the Marquis of Posa's attempts to save Flanders from the despotic misrule of his sovereign, Philip II, is really a play of abstract ideas, a play about determinism and free will, and the dialogue, still current in Schiller's age and by no means irrelevant today, between the liberal attitude and the obscurantist religious mind. A sub-theme running through the play, the sacrificing of romantic love to larger concerns, fits awkwardly into the action. *Don Carlos* could exist without Carlos and Elisabetta, but not without Philip and Posa. In its compression into an operatic libretto, Schiller's lengthy play has undoubtedly suffered. What his librettists were forced to omit, Verdi was able to restore in music; but, where they actually altered or invented, it was usually for the worse.

The principal differences between play and libretto are these: the libretto adds a new first act showing the meeting of Elisabeth and Carlos at Fontainebleau, which is only referred to in Schiller; the *auto-da-fé* scene, again only mentioned in the play, is new; Schiller's emphasis on Posa has been shifted, and in the libretto Posa is sketchily drawn in comparison with Carlos; two important characters in Schiller, Domingo and the Duke of Alba, are omitted from the libretto. The most unfortunate difference lies in the ending. The librettists, taking their cue from the play's mention of the spirit of Charles V being seen in the robes of a monk, actually produce this ghost or monk, and allow him to help Carlos escape. In Schiller, the ghost rumour is there merely to be taken advantage of by Carlos when he visits the Queen at midnight: he dresses as a monk, and the terrified sentries disperse as he approaches. The play ends chillingly with the King handing his son Carlos over to the Grand Inquisitor, with the words "Kardinal, ich habe das Meinige getan. Tun Sie das Ihre." (Cardinal, I have done my duty. Do yours.)

Schiller's liberties with history are considerable: his play is set in 1558, the year in which the historical Don Carlos died, yet it contains a reference to the Armada of 1588. The real Carlos was not only an epileptic cripple but also a viciously sadistic madman, while Schiller's romantic young prince is merely a trifle over-excitable. But Schiller's characters are superbly realised, and Philip II's Spain is fully sketched as their background. The libretto of Méry and Du Locle, despite the serious shortcomings already noted, stays for the most part sufficiently close to the play to be able to offer Verdi what he most relished: interesting, believable characters, and strong dramatic situations. Enough of his old revolutionary ardour remained for him to warm to the Marquis of Posa and his political idealism. Indeed, *Don Carlo* is the one Verdi opera in which political activities are discussed in adult terms. The conflicts between the public and private life, between church and state, between despotism and liberalism, Catholic and Protestant, tensions which influence the actions of the main characters, all these were gratefully seized upon by Verdi.

Act I of the five-act libretto is set in the forest of Fontainebleau outside Paris, at dusk. Foresters and their wives can be seen at work. Elizabeth de Valois, daughter of the French King Henry II, enters with her page Tebaldo and a party of huntsmen. After distributing alms to the foresters, she and her suite move on. When the scene is deserted, Don Carlo, son of Philip II of Spain and heir to his throne, emerges from the shadows. He has been, for reasons of state, betrothed to Elizabeth, and has come to France secretly in order to see his future wife, whom he has never met. The brief glimpse he has now had of her suffices to make him fall ardently in love with her. Noticing that night has fallen, he is wondering how he will find his way back to the palace of Fontainebleau, when Elizabeth and her page return. Carlo steps forward and introduces himself as a Spanish gentleman, and member of the retinue of the Count of Lerma, the Spanish Ambassador. Tebaldo the page hastens off to procure a suitable escort back to the palace for Elizabeth, and Carlo discusses with Elizabeth her imminent marriage to the Infante of Spain, which is to procure peace between France and Spain. He hands her a miniature portrait of the Infante, and she is astonished and delighted to find that it is, in fact, a likeness of the young man who now kneels before her. They declare their love for each other. Tebaldo returns with the Spanish Ambassador, pages, ladies-in-waiting and a crowd of commoners, and salutes Elizabeth as Queen of Spain. Her father has offered her in marriage, not to Carlo, but to his father, Philip II, who hopes she will accept him. Elizabeth and Carlo are in despair, but when she is pressed for an immediate answer, Elizabeth knows that for the sake of her country she must acquiesce. The crowd rejoices, the unhappy Elizabeth is borne away in a litter, and Carlo is left alone to lament the cruelty of fate.

The rest of the opera takes place in Spain. The two scenes of Act II are set at the monastery of San Giusto. In the first scene, a cloister within the monastery, a Friar is discovered in prayer before the monument to Charles V (the Carlo Quinto of *Ernani*, and the grandfather of Don Carlos). Carlo enters, and is startled by the Friar's voice, which he thinks he recognises as that of his dead grandfather. The Friar withdraws, and Carlo has hardly recovered from his shock when Rodrigo, Marquis of Posa, enters. The two friends greet each other warmly, and Carlo confides to Rodrigo that he is in love with Elizabeth, now the Queen and his step-mother. Rodrigo advises him to attempt to forget his passion by engaging in the worthy task of helping the oppressed people of Flanders, who are suffering under the repressive Catholic rule imposed on them by Philip, Carlo's father. Carlo just has time to agree, before Philip and Elizabeth arrive to pay homage at the tomb of Charles V. Carlo is disturbed at encountering Elizabeth again, but joins Rodrigo in a duet in which they swear undying friendship and their determination to aid the cause of freedom in Flanders.

The second scene of Act II takes place immediately afterwards, outside the monastery, where Elizabeth's ladies-in-waiting are passing the time while awaiting her return. One of them, the Princess Eboli, entertains the others with the Song of the Veil, about the Moorish King who, thinking he was courting an unknown veiled beauty, found he was making love to his own wife. Elizabeth returns, and Tebaldo announces the Marquis of Posa. Rodrigo, under cover of delivering a letter to the Queen from her mother, hands her a note from Carlo, and asks her to see him once more. Eboli, who is attracted by Carlo, wonders to herself if Carlo could be in love with her and, if so, why he does not declare himself. The Queen agrees to give Carlo an audience, and the others all discreetly withdraw. Carlo enters, and asks the Queen to persuade his father to send him as Governor to Flanders. She agrees to do so and, herself upset by their meeting, attempts formally to dismiss him. But Carlo cannot contain himself and, confessing that he still loves her, reproaches Elizabeth for her coldness. He swoons at her feet in a fit of over-excitement and, when he comes to, continues to speak of his passion for her. Elizabeth brings him to his senses by reminding him that he can have her, only by killing his father and then leading his mother to the altar. Carlo rushes out, and Philip and his suite arrive from the monastery. The King is furious at finding the Queen unattended and, establishing that the Countess of Aremberg should have been in attendance, banishes the Countess to her native France. The ladies-in-waiting have now returned, and Elizabeth takes a tender farewell of the Countess. All leave, but Philip calls Rodrigo back to ask him why he has never sought advancement at Court. He wishes to reward Rodrigo for his achievements and his loyalty. Rodrigo replies that he requires nothing, but that others are in need of Philip's help. He speaks of Flanders and of the rule of violence established there by Philip, and begs the King to adopt a more liberal attitude. Philip is impressed by Rodrigo's idealism, but is insistent that his own harsh rule is the only way to establish peace. He warns Rodrigo to beware of the Grand Inquisitor, confides to him his suspicions regarding the Queen and his son, and asks Rodrigo to keep an eye on both Elizabeth and Carlo, granting him free entry to the Queen's presence at all times. Encouraged by the King's confidence to imagine that he may in time be able to persuade him to a more humane attitude in Flanders, Rodrigo accepts the commission. As they part, Philip once more warns him of the Inquisition.

Act III, Scene I, takes place at midnight in the Queen's Gardens in Madrid. Carlo has received an anonymous letter, which he believes to be from the Queen, making an assignation with him. When a veiled woman appears, he embraces her and they declare their love for each other. The lady removes her veil, and Carlo is mortified to discover that it is not the Queen but the Princess Eboli. At first he attempts to dissemble, and Eboli warns him of the danger that threatens him, mentioning that she has heard Philip and Rodrigo discussing him. Finally, she realises it was not she whom he expected to meet, and, guessing that it is the Queen he loves, threatens to reveal this to Philip. Rodrigo arrives and attempts first to cajole and then to frighten her out of this resolve, but she departs determined upon vengeance. Rodrigo asks Carlo to let him have any incriminating documents he may be carrying. After an initial momentary suspicion of his friend, who is, after all, an intimate of the King, Carlo hands over the documents.

In the second scene of Act III, a crowd has assembled in the huge square outside the Cathedral of Our Lady of Atocha, to watch the *auto-da-fé* or burning of the heretics. Monks lead in those who are condemned to die, and Elizabeth arrives in procession with the Court, nobles and various dignitaries. The Royal Herald calls for the door of the Cathedral to be opened, revealing the King wearing his crown and surrounded by monks. As the King descends the cathedral steps to join the procession, a deputation from Flanders, led by Carlo, appears. The envoys kneel before Philip, begging him to show clemency and mercy to their country. Philip orders them to be removed from his sight, but Carlo intervenes, asking Philip to give him the Governorship of Flanders and Brabant. Philip rejects him scornfully and, when Carlo is foolish enough to draw his sword, calls on his guards to disarm him. No one moves, and Philip himself furiously seizes a sword, but Rodrigo quickly steps between the King and his son and, in order to save Carlo, asks him to surrender his sword. The astonished Carlo does so, Rodrigo presents the sword to Philip, who immedately dubs him Duke, and the procession continues as Carlo is led off under guard. Flames fly up from the stake, and a celestial voice is heard welcoming the souls of the heretics to heaven.

Act IV, Scene 1, takes place in the King's study at dawn. Philip is sitting at his desk, bitterly soliloquising about his loveless marriage, the cares of state and the impossibility of ruling wisely. The Grand Inquisitor is announced, and enters, a blind old man of ninety supported by two monks. Philip has summoned the Inquisitor to advise him how best to deal with Carlo's rebellion. The choice appears to him to be between exile and death, and the Inquisitor assures him of the Church's approval if he should decide to condemn his son to death. Philip asks how he a Christian, can be expected to sacrifice his own son, and is reminded that God, after all, sacrificed his. Unwillingly, Philip agrees to the death of Carlo. When the Inquisitor asks if there is not also some other matter on which the King wishes his advice, Philip answers in the negative, and the Inquisitor himself refers to Rodrigo, Marquis of Posa, denouncing him as a dangerous heretic. Philip protests that in Rodrigo he has at last found a loyal friend, and the Inquisitor retorts that a real King would have no need of another man. Philip angrily orders him to be silent. ("Tais-toi, prêtre", appears to have been the line in the original French production that the Empress Eugénie most strongly objected to; it has become, in Italian, "Non più, frate".) At this, the Inquisitor accuses Philip of having been influenced by dangerously liberal ideas which seek to overthrow the Catholic church. He demands that the King deliver up Rodrigo, and when Philip replies "Never!" the Inquisitor warns him that, if he had not been summoned to the royal presence today, he would tomorrow have had the King arraigned before the Inquisition. He leaves, and Philip comments bitterly that apparently the throne must always give way to the altar.

Suddenly, Elizabeth enters in a state of agitation. Her casket of jewels has been stolen, and she demands that Philip discover and punish the thief. In answer, he hands Elizabeth the casket, which has been lying on his desk, and asks her to open it. When she refuses, he breaks it open and discovers a miniature portrait of Carlo. Elizabeth reminds him that she was once betrothed to Carlo, and asserts her innocence. When Philip calls her an adultress, she swoons and the King calls for aid. Eboli and Rodrigo enter and, in the quartet which ensues, each of them voices his own feelings. Rodrigo reproaches Philip, and later broods on the fact that he may have to sacrifice himself for Spain. Philip is ashamed of his suspicions, and Elizabeth, when she regains consciousness, feels herself alone and forsaken in a foreign land. Philip and Rodrigo retire. Left alone with the Queen, Eboli confesses not only that it was she who had stolen the casket but also that she has been the King's mistress. Deeply shocked, Elizabeth dismisses Eboli, ordering her to choose between exile and a nunnery. Elizabeth leaves her, and Eboli, bitterly repentant, curses her own beauty which has led her into this situation. She vows to enter a nunnery, but not before she has made an attempt to save Carlo from his imminent death. Act IV, Scene 2, takes place in the dungeon in which Carlo is confined. He is visited by Rodrigo, who has come to sacrifice his life for his friend and for the sake of the liberal cause in Flanders. Rodrigo has allowed the incriminating papers he had taken from Carlo to be found on his own person, thus ensuring that he, and not Carlo, will now be identified as the leader of the Flanders revolt and that Carlo will be released and thus be able to escape to Flanders and organise a rebellion. While the friends are talking, two men, one of them in the uniform of the Inquisition and the other carrying an arquebus, enter the dungeon stealthily. The armed man, having had Rodrigo pointed out to him, fires. Rodrigo falls, but before he dies manages to tell Carlo that the Queen will be waiting for him at the monastery of San Giusto the next day, to bid him farewell. He begs Carlo to rescue Flanders from oppression, and dies. As the distraught Carlo falls weeping upon the body of his friend, King Philip enters with members of his Court, Eboli in disguise, and the Grand Inquisitor. Philip attempts to embrace his son but Carlo repulses him, crying that his hands are stained with blood. Philip is moved to remorse at the sight of Rodrigo's body and, falling to his knees cries, "Who will give this man back to me?"

Sounds of commotion are heard, and a crowd of citizens, enraged at the Infante's imprisonment, shouts for him to be released. At the King's command, the crowd is admitted to the prison, and Philip presents Carlo to the populace. During the confusion, Eboli urges Carlo to leave, which he does. The Grand Inquisitor suddenly reveals himself and quells the citizens who fall to their knees praying to heaven for mercy, while the noblemen cry, "Long live the King!"

The final act takes place in the cloisters of the San Giusto monastery. Elizabeth enters and prays before the tomb of Charles V. She has come to say farewell to Carlo, and recalls the happiness of their brief meeting at Fontainebleau. Carlo arrives, and Elizabeth reminds him of his promise to Rodrigo that he would lead Flanders to peace and happiness. He assures her that he has now sublimated his love for her in his determination to liberate Flanders, and he and Elizabeth say their farewells, hoping to meet again in Heaven. They have both cried, "Per sempre addio" (Farewell forever), when Philip who has entered quietly with the Grand Inquisitor and Officers of the Inquisition, echoes them: "Si, per sempre" (Yes, forever). Seizing the Queen by the arm, he calls on the Inquisition to arrest her and Carlo. To the Grand Inquisitor he says, "Il dover mio farò. Ma voi?" (I shall do my duty. But you?), which is virtually a translation of the closing lines of Schiller's play. But the opera moves on quickly to an improbably happy ending. Drawing his sword, Carlo retreats towards the tomb of his grand-father, Charles V. The Friar whom he had earlier heard at prayer suddenly appears, dressed in the royal robes and crown of Charles V, and drags Carlo into the cloister, while Philip, the Inquisitor and the guards exclaim that it really is Charles V. The curtain falls, leaving the audience completely bewildered. *Is* it Charles V, and was he then not dead? (In historical fact, he died ten years earlier, in 1558). Is it his spirit? The ending to this otherwise magnificent work is completely unsatisfactory, and one is tempted to suggest that producers revert to Schiller's ending. This could be managed without any great violence being done to the music, merely by stage production and by suppressing a few bars of the score, or possibly only of the vocal parts.

III

The edition of *Don Carlo* discussed here is the complete five-act Italian version of 1887. The opera begins with a short orchestral introduction in which horns alternate with the full orchestra, while a few exclamatory phrases are contributed by an off-stage hunting chorus. As the hunting horns fade into silence, a melancholy solo clarinet introduces and punctuates the arioso-like recitative leading to Carlo's aria, "Io la vidi", a graceful romanza. In the brief following scena, in which the approach of night is economically conveyed by distant horn calls and pianissimo timpani, Carlo and Elizabeth meet. Their scena and duetto move through arioso dialogue exchanges to the lyrical melodic outbursts of "Di qual amor", an exquisite tune accompanied by clarinet and pizzicato strings. As the duet reaches its climax, after the cannon shots announcing peace, Elizabeth expresses her excitement with a repeated exclamation descending from a for-tissimo B natural. The effect is brilliant. The duet's opening theme returns, and is sung in unison, after which the action is advanced by Tebaldo in recitative. The duet ends with an agitated section elo-quently accompanied by woodwind. The act-finale is built up from an unaccompanied chorus in praise of Elizabeth, followed by recitative in which the Count of Lerma asks for her reply. After her unwilling "Si", the choral rejoicing continues against the anguished outbursts of the lovers. As the royal party leaves, Carlo is left to utter broken phrases of despair. The entire scene, written with remarkable freedom and flexibility, is impressive, too, in that, in a short period of time, a great deal is shown to happen without seeming brutally rushed.

The first scene of Act II opens with a prelude played by four horns, which creates the appropriately sombre and elegaic atmosphere for the chorus of monks with its solo lines for the monk whose voice Carlo finds so like that of Charles V. The whole of this opening chorus is kept dark in mood by the predominance of lower strings and wind in the accompaniment. The little scena for Don Carlo and the mysterious monk leads into the duet-scene for Carlo and Rodrigo. (In the four-act version of the opera, Carlo's aria from the Fontainebleau scene, "Io la vidi", is inserted here.) The beginning of the duet is a splendid example of Verdi's late conversational style, in which dialogue is fitted in masterly fashion into the orchestral format with no sacrifice of flexibility. The duet ends in one of Verdi's tenor-baritone friendship tunes: this one is noted more for its openhearted sincerity than its subtlety, but its theme [Ex. 94] is put to good orchestral use at key

Ex.94

moments later in the opera. As the curtain falls on this scene, it is played fortissimo by the orchestra.

The second scene of Act II begins with a chorus for the Queen's ladies-in-waiting. In the lively orchestral introduction, Verdi introduces brighter colours into his orchestra. This is the one place in the entire opera where the tension is momentarily lifted. The orchestra gives way to the quiet, placid three-part chorus in which the Queen's ladies sing of their delight in their surroundings. Eboli's Song of the Veil, accompanied visually by Tebaldo on his mandolin, but audibly by the entire orchestra, is more than simply a showpiece for the mezzo: Verdi takes its Saracen origins seriously, and inserts in both stanzas a series of flamenco-like flourishes in the chest register. The rhythm of the song is that of the seguidilla, and its orchestral colour deliberately exotic. Each verse has a refrain in which first Tebaldo and then the chorus of ladies joins Eboli.

Although the score of *Don Carlo* is still laid out in numbers, the flexibility of Verdi's style is now such that, in performance, one number moves as smoothly into the next as in any Wagner opera. This opening-out of the form is reflected in the titles given to the numbers in the score. The next few minutes of Act II, Scene 2, until the entrance of Carlo, are called, somewhat awkwardly, "Scena, terzettino dialogotato; Romanza di Rodrigo"; what one hears is a freely composed scena in which, although the vocal writing ostensibly plays second fiddle to the musical structure, which in turn is determined by the dramatic demands of the libretto, the melodic interest is as strong and as varied as in the old "aria-recitative-cabaletta" scheme of the earlier years. The social gossip of Eboli and Rodrigo is carried on in flirtatious dialogue to an elegant tune, into which Elizabeth inserts her anguished *sotto voce* phrases. This pleasant little trio is characteristic of Verdi's genius for advancing the dramatic action under cover of apparently inconsequential melodic dalliance. Rodrigo's solo romanza in two stanzas is suavely beautiful. The stanzas are separated by phrases in which both Eboli and the Queen remember Carlo, and Eboli first considers the hopeful possibility that it is she whom Carlo loves.

The "Gran Scena e Duetto" for Elizabeth and Carlo begins almost conversationally, but Carlo becomes increasingly agitated as he talks to Elizabeth, while she tries to keep her replies on a purely formal level. Carlo's music follows him through moments of despair, pleading, exaltation, bitterness, and an ecstatically self-pitying remembrance of their meeting at Fontainebleau. Verdi's orchestration is here at its most eloquent and imaginative. A plangent figure for flute and oboe underlines Carlo's pleading; a very gentle, delicate woodwind accompaniment weaves its way through the exquisite lyrical passage beginning, "Perduto ben, mio sol tesor". Carlo's delirious "Qual voce a me dal ciel", has a sensuous *Tristan*-like beauty [Ex. 95]. Elizabeth's

Ex.95 Meno mosso

Qual voce a me dal ciel scende a par - lar d'amor? E - li - sa - bet - ta! tu, bell' ado - ra - ta,

angry and sarcastic *piu animato* sends Carlo rushing off on a sustained B flat, while she brings the scene to an end with one of those big arching phrases around which Verdi often constructed his soprano arias.

Philip's stern recitative, and a murmured phrase of comment by the chorus lead to Elizabeth's romanza, "Non pianger, mia compagna", sung to the Countess Aremberg whom the King has just banished. This affecting and compassionate aria in two stanzas, each of which moves from minor to major, has a meltingly beautiful cor anglais introduction. The instrument continues to play an important accompanying role throughout the gentle, affectionate farewell, and emerges again, after a coda in which Elizabeth is joined by the other characters in ensemble, in the postlude, where it echoes one of Verdi's magical, scale-climbing tunes which Elizabeth has sung to the words, "Ritorna al suol natio, ti seguirà il mio cor" [Ex. 96].

Ex.96 Andante assai sostenuto

ri - tor - na al suol na - ti - o, ti se - gui-rà il mio cor...........

The scene ends with an extended duet between Philip and Rodrigo, one of the most impressive parts of the entire score, and one of the two scenes (the other being the confrontation of King and Inquisitor in Act IV) which give *Don Carlo* its unique flavour. These pages, in which Verdi has written the Italian equivalent of Wagnerian dialogue, look forward clearly to *Otello*. The orchestra reflects every thought, every change of mood, whether or not expressed in dialogue; the form is flexible, yet beautifully fitted to the requirements of the drama as expressed by the text. This is not so much a duet as a dramatic dialogue, for it is not until towards the end that the two characters sing at the same time. Until then, they converse. Although Verdi has written their conversation in the free style which is so prominent a feature of his late operas, he does not abandon melody. On the contrary, he dispenses it with an even greater prodigality than usual. Many of the lyrical tunes are heard only once to express the sense of a particular phrase, and are never used again. Verdi's use of the orchestra is equally flexible and imaginative. As dramatic and lyrical vocal phrases follow each other quickly, the orchestra keeps pace by harmonic means as well as rapidly changing colours. There is a dramatic climax halfway through the scene, when Rodrigo angrily shouts that the King's peace is that of the grave. Loud, ominous growlings from the lowest register of trombones and tuba give way to quietly sinister clarinets, as Rodrigo warns the King that history may consider him another Nero. The debate continues: the next point of emphasis occurs when Philip warns Rodrigo to beware of the Inquisition. When Philip goes on to speak of his personal sorrows, his suspicions of his wife and his son, and authorizes Rodrigo to watch them, Rodrigo gives way to his excitement in an arioso which consists principally of the repetition of this eloquent phrase [Ex. 97].

Ex.97 Allegro moderato

In - a-spet-ta - - - - ta au - ro - ra in ciel ap - par!

The scene has now become a duet proper, with the King and Rodrigo simultaneously giving voice to their separate thoughts. Finally, the King again warns Rodrigo of the Grand Inquisitor. His words, quiet but meaningful, are punctuated by pianissimo chords from the full orchestra, with one final fortissimo chord after the last vocal phrase, "Ti guarda", sung forte. A grand orchestral flourish brings the curtain down.

The third act has a gravely beautiful orchestral prelude based on Carlo's Act I romanza, "Io la vidi". By no means merely an orchestral restatement of the aria, it develops the theme into a romantic mood-picture of a moonlit night, but adds in the lower voices just a hint of the rôle the Grand Inquisitor is going to play in Carlo's personal drama. This brief but magical tone poem replaces the ballet music of the original Paris production of the opera. (Act III of the Paris version opened with a short scene in which Eboli despatched a page with her note of assignation to Carlos. This was followed by a ballet in which the Queen of the Waters and all the pearls of the ocean paid homage to the most beautiful pearl of all, the Queen of Spain. The five numbers, Introduction, Andante and Waltz, Variations, Pantomime and Galop Finale, are among Verdi's most successful ballet music, though in places still as curiously Tchaikovskian as his earlier ballet music for the French productions of *Il trovatore* and *Les Vêpres siciliennes*.) The scene in the Queen's Gardens is written as one number, which Verdi has called "Scena, duetta e terzetto". After Carlo's opening recitative, his duet with Eboli begins, *allegro agitato*, at her entrance. When she removes her mask, a passage of recitative leads into the duet's lyrical *andante mosso*. At Rodrigo's entrance, the trio, "Al mio furor", begins, the two men developing a lyrical theme against Eboli's excited and more florid line. After the final *allegro agitato* section, "Trema per te", Eboli leaves, and the troubled dialogue for Carlo and Rodrigo, in which the former momentarily suspects his friend, is resolved in a brief cadenza and is followed by an orchestral restatement of the friendship duet.

The *auto-da-fé* constitutes the *gran finale* of Act III. A brassily martial orchestral introduction, a pompous festive chorus, and a darker-coloured orchestral *marcia funebre* usher in the procession of heretics condemned to the stake, while a unison bass chorus of monks chants of the day of reckoning. Their sickly, depressing monotone is immediately followed by a most beautiful tune played by the cellos: a *cantabile espressivo* melody of consoling compassion, of the kind which Verdi used sparingly but always most movingly. (The postlude to Fiesco's "Il lacerato spirito", in *Simon Boccanegra*, comes immediately to mind.) It is as though Verdi himself has intervened to offer his blessing to the suffering victims of the church militant [Ex. 98].

Ex.98

Verdi never "plugs" his tunes *à la* Puccini. This one vanishes to reappear only once, appropriately, when sung by a celestial voice at the end of the scene. The populace continues its rejoicing, and a brass fanfare introduces the official procession. The march is heard first in A major, then is repeated immediately in C. The effect is of a sudden heightening of the excitement, though the *poco piu animato* section which follows smacks more of bucolic Busseto than of Spain. The chorus bursts in again, and the march comes to an animated conclusion. The Herald's eight bars of unaccompanied arioso are repeated by the chorus in harmony, but also unaccompanied, and after more orchestral pomp the King's recitative is greeted jubilantly by the crowd. Carlo and his six Flemish deputies now interrupt the procession: the six bass voices of the deputies sing—in unison to mark their unanimous solidarity—their expressive *cantabile* whose dark colouring is matched by the accompaniment, in which the lower strings double the voice parts. The King reacts in an angry arioso which sparks off a superb ensemble, from which the melody of the Flanders deputies emerges and with which it blends. Carlo's *allegro* outburst and the King's reply, conducted in free melodic-recitative exchange, lead to the tense recitative of the incident in which Carlo draws his sword on his father. The friendship theme is played quietly by clarinets to enormous effect, as Rodrigo demands that Carlo give up his sword. The festivities resume in chorus and orchestra, and the funeral march of the heretics is heard again. The compassion tune [Ex. 98] is sung by a solo soprano, accompanied by harp and harmonium: "Una voce dal cielo (molto lontana)" (A voice from heaven—very far away), as the vocal score states with presumably unconscious sarcasm. The chanting of the monks continues underneath the trills of the heavenly voice, which rises to a top B and finally rests into silence on E sharp at the top of the stave. The crowd echoes the King's cry of "Glory to Heaven", and the curtain falls.

The first scene of Act IV opens with Philip's great scena. A poignant orchestral introduction, containing a prominent part for solo cello, sets the mood of world-weariness and despair. Philip's recitative, "Ella giammai m'amò", is, in fact, an inspired arioso, much of it sung pianissimo. The aria proper, "Dormirò sol nel manto mio regal", is an *andante cantabile* of expressive beauty and sadness, with a slightly more agitated contrasted section. Its form is ABAB, but the repeat of B is confined to the lower instruments of the orchestra, above which Philip utters three phrases of recitative. As coda to the aria, a truncated version of the arioso, "Ella giammai m'amò", swells from *piano* to *forte* with, at the words, "amor per me non ha", a heart-raising lift to the bass's top E on the second syllable of "amor". The entire scena is not only musically one of Verdi's finest, but also an illuminating piece of three-dimensional dramatic characterization. It is followed by an almost equally superb scena for the King and the Grand Inquisitor.

After three *fortissimo* chords, the Inquisitor is announced, and enters to a sinister theme on the lower strings and woodwind which suggests the strength and intransigence of the Inquisition. The entire scene is remarkable for the way in which its perfect formal structure serves the requirements of the drama, and for Verdi's genius in creating so richly varied a sound from two bass voices and a sombre orchestra. The two basses converse in to-and-fro dialogue, never singing together in duet proper. As their quarrel reaches its height, the Inquisitor's threats are punctuated by strident brass, the King's protests supported by *fortissimo* chords from trombones, tuba and bassoons. The Inquisitor departs to the sound of the Inquisitional theme and, in a remarkable phrase spanning two octaves from F to F, Philip bitterly refers to the uneven battle between church and state.

Elizabeth's distraught entry, the King's accusation of adultery, her collapse and his call for Rodrigo and Eboli to come to her aid, lead to a quartet which is easily the equal of the quartet in the last act of *Rigoletto* in its masterly characterisation, and possibly its superior in purely musical terms. The tune, unusually, is given to the lowest voice, the King's, though it is first heard played by cellos and bassoon behind his *parlante* phrase [Ex. 99].

Ex.99   Largo

The King and Rodrigo leave and, in an exquisitely scored dialogue scene, Eboli makes her confession to the Queen. Eboli's aria, "O don fatale", an exciting *allegro giusto* with a contrastingly tender middle section, never fails to bring the house down with its climactic B flats, if the mezzo can encompass them. Earlier in the aria, she has been expected to produce a C flat.

The music of Act IV, Scene 2, is given the title of "Morte di Rodrigo e Sommossa" (Death of Rodrigo and Rebellion), which describes it precisely. The *andante* orchestral introduction, based on a sombre string figure, also contains a brief reference by solo oboe to the love duet of Act I. After recitative dialogue for Rodrigo and Carlo, Rodrigo's *andante*, "Per me giunto è il dì supremo", reverts to Verdi's earlier middle-period type of baritone aria. It is a sweetly affecting tune, and calls for a trill which it does not always get in performance. In the following *parlante*, at the phrase, "Carlo mio, a me porgi la man", Verdi offers an alternative on "la"; the upper note, the baritone's E flat, gives an effect of tender sweetness. The second part of the aria retains the same tempo, as the now dying Rodrigo bids farewell to his friend. The accompaniment is light and ethereal: at one moment it recalls a phrase from the friendship duet. Some modern productions end the scene with the death of Rodrigo: authority for this goes back to the cuts Verdi made after the première. But by 1884 Verdi not only had restored the rest of the scene, but was insisting rigorously on it being performed without cuts.[1] Musically, the remaining two or three minutes are hardly outstanding, but dramatically they are necessary. The entry of the King and his court, the Inquisitor and, later, the easily quelled rebels, leads to an abrupt and noisy conclusion.

The last act consists of two numbers: Elizabeth's aria, and the farewell duet and finale. The aria, "Tu che le vanità conocesti del mondo", is preceded by an orchestral introduction, the first twelve bars of which consists of the monks' chant from Act II, played pianissimo by wind instruments. As the curtain rises and Elizabeth enters, the chant continues, punctuated now by urgent string interjections which soon engulf it and spread out into a tune of passionate intensity. The broad, sweeping lines of the aria break up into smaller lyrical units, and twice the woodwind instruments recall moments from the love music of the Fontainebleau scene. In the following duet, the past is recalled again with the moving theme from the encounter of Elizabeth and Carlo in Act II. The *marziale* section of the duet, with one of Verdi's curiously military harp accompaniments, is usually cut in performance, which is a pity; for, although it is itself undistinguished, it is part of the setting for the pearl that follows, the closing *cantabile* passage which begins "Ma lassù ci vedremo". Here, all passion spent, the lovers sing with tender resignation of their parting, and their hope to meet in a better world. This is one of Verdi's most imaginative moments, of a fragile, distilled beauty. (The mediocre *marziale* is, incidentally, not, as Toye claims, "a product of [Verdi's] revision, the only instance, perhaps, of a definitely bad afterthought". It was part of the original Paris score.)

From the sudden appearance of Philip, the Inquisitor and their guards, to the end of the opera, the action is rushed and the music no more than dramatically serviceable. The curtain falls to the sound of a brass restatement of the monks' chant, as Carlo is dragged off by a monk, by Charles V, or by his ghost.

---

[1] Since I wrote this, Spike Hughes's *Famous Verdi Operas* (London, 1968) has appeared, in which Mr Hughes states (p. 364): "In all public performances and all recordings except the exemplary 1966 Decca version, the act comes to an end with the death of Rodrigo." This is not so. The 1955 HMV recording certainly includes the rest of the scene, and so did the production at the Vienna State Opera which I last saw in 1960. I have a vivid recollection of Hans Hotter's appearance in the prison as the Inquisitor. The scene was also restored to the Covent Garden production when it was revived in the spring of 1968.

It would, as I have suggested elsewhere in this chapter, be an easy task to substitute Schiller's ending for the present nonsensical one. The stage picture could reveal Carlo being handed over to the Inquisition. Carlo's lines, "Dio mi vendicherà! Il tribunal di sangue sua mano spezzerà!" (God will avenge me! His hand will demolish the tribunal of blood), could either be omitted or be sung as he struggled in vain with the guards. The Friar's voice could still be heard, without any suggestion of his being Charles V, so long as he was dressed as a Friar, and not as the dead King! The Inquisitor's "È la voce di Carlo", the King's "Mio padre", and the guards' "È Carlo Quinto" could be verbally altered to other, harmless ejaculations, or omitted. The orchestral parts need not be tampered with.

I gather that the Sadler's Wells 1951 production, which I did not see, reverted to Schiller's ending. But Norman Tucker, who was responsible for the version performed, apparently succumbed to a *folie de grandeur* and rearranged virtually the entire opera for no valid reason. If an article in *Opera* (January 1951) is accurate, the two scenes of Act II were merged into one, the order of scenes was changed and music lifted from one was dumped into another, the great encounter between the King and the Grand Inquisitor was transferred to the prison scene, Carlo and his deputies appeared in a scene devised by Mr Tucker which included Elizabeth's "Giustizia, giustizia, Sire", now meant as a plea for Carlo and not for the return of her jewel box. Various numbers were omitted, among them Eboli's Song of the Veil and Rodrigo's "Per me giunto il dì supremo". The final sentence of the *Opera* article deserves to be quoted: "Most of all, perhaps, criticism will be levelled at Mr Tucker for omitting the famous *auto-da-fé* scene, but it should be borne in mind that a scene obviously written as a vehicle for the pageantry and splendour of nineteenth century Paris is not very suitable for twentieth-century Islington, and it is specifically for Sadler's Wells that this new version has been made."

The question of the ending apart, the less *Don Carlo* is messed about with, the better it will play. For all its shortcomings, the libretto, with Schiller's great play looming behind it, is extraordinarily interesting, and Verdi's setting both illuminates and rarifies it. The dark orchestral colouring, the rich, complex musical characterisation, and the quality of the melody combine to make *Don Carlo* one of the most rewarding of operas to encounter in the theatre. The charges of Wagnerism and Meyerbeerism need hardly be answered. Verdi was his own Wagner; and though he had no choice but to cast *Don Carlo* in the Parisian mould, there is, as I have already indicated, a world of difference and of quality between his music and that of Meyerbeer. This is the one opera in which Verdi can be said to have forsaken his customary sharp conciseness; nevertheless, the work can hardly be called prolix, and even the *auto-da-fé* scene, comparatively weak when one examines it in detail, adds up to triumphantly more than the sum of its parts. Above all, the opera glows with Verdi's humanity, which he has been able to breathe into characters who, on the printed page, must have seemed to him at first acquaintance to be frigidly formal.

I suggested, in the chapter on *La forza del destino*, that that opera may have influenced Moussorgsky. *Don Carlos* reached St Petersburg at the beginning of 1869 while Moussorgsky was composing *Boris Godunov* there. I submit that either Verdi, in the confrontation of the King and the Inquisitor, looks forward to Moussorgsky, or Moussorgsky, in much of Pimen and Boris, glances keenly back at one of Verdi's greatest operas.

XXIV

Aida

Dramatis personae:

The King of Egypt	(bass)
Amneris, his daughter	(mezzo-soprano)
Aida, her slave	(soprano)
Radames, Captain of the Guards	(tenor)
Amonasro, King of Ethiopia	(baritone)
Ramfis, High Priest	(bass)
A Messenger	(tenor)

LIBRETTO, based on a synopsis by Auguste Mariette (Bey), by Camille du Locle; translated into Italian by Antonio Ghislanzoni

TIME: The age of the Pharaohs
PLACE: Memphis and Thebes

FIRST PERFORMED at the Cairo Opera House, December 24, 1871, with Antonietta Pozzoni (Aida); Eleonora Grossi (Amneris); Pietro Mongini (Radames); Francesco Steller (Amonasro); Paolo Medini (Ramfis); Tommaso Costa (King)

Aida

AFTER THE PARIS première of *Don Carlos* in 1867, Verdi returned
for a time to farming. In the summer, when his old friend and benefactor Antonio Barezzi died at the age of seventy-nine, the fifty-four-
year-old composer was at his bedside. Understandably much affected
by the death of the man who had been all to him that his father was
never able to be, Verdi became even more melancholy when he heard
that his old collaborator Piave had suffered a paralytic stroke. Piave
lived on, unable to move or speak, for eight years, during which time
Verdi gave generous financial support to his wife and daughter. In the
winter of 1867–8, he and Giuseppina moved into the winter apartment
they had permanently rented in Genoa. The following spring Verdi
went to Milan for the first time in twenty years, to meet his idol Manzoni.
In the summer, a new opera house in Busseto was opened. Verdi had
had several fights with the Busseto Council about this theatre, having
objected not only to the proposal to call it the "Teatro Verdi" but also
to the Council's assumption that he would contribute a large part of
the building costs. The Teatro Verdi still exists, a tiny, pretty, but
badly neglected house which looks as if it could not seat more than a
couple of hundred. At the opening performance on August 15, 1860,
the audience heard *Rigoletto*, preceded by an overture, "La Capric-
ciosa", said to have been written by Verdi at the age of twelve. The
composer's box was conspicuously empty: he and Giuseppina stayed
away from Busseto until the day after the opera season ended. Two
months later, Rossini died in Paris, and Verdi attempted to organise
the leading Italian composers to combine in writing a Requiem to be
performed on the first anniversary of his death. His idea was that
several composers should each write one movement, that there should
be only one performance, after which the score would be deposited in
the Liceo Musico in Bologna, where Rossini spent his student years, and
that neither composers nor performers should receive a fee for their work.
An organisation committee was set up in Milan, and the composers,
chosen by lot from a selected list, were: Antonio Bazzini, Raimondo
Boucheron, Antonio Buzzolla, Antonio Cagnoni, Carlo Coccia, Gaetano
Gaspari, Teodulo Mabellini, Alessandro Nini, Carlo Pedrotti, Enrico
Petrella, Pietro Platania, Federico Ricci, and (fortunately) Verdi. Most,

if not all, of these composers submitted their finished movements in good time. Verdi certainly completed the "Libera me" which it had fallen to him to contribute. But, incredibly, difficulties in organising a chorus proved insuperable. The committee suggested postponing the performance, Verdi refused to consider this, and finally the composers received their manuscripts back. By this time Verdi had supervised the successful revival of *La forza del destino* at La Scala, and had been carrying on a correspondence with Camille du Locle, the librettist of *Don Carlos*, who was continually suggesting ideas for new operas. Verdi, distinctly reluctant to write again for the Paris Opéra, tried to explain his attitude to Du Locle. A letter in which he complains of Parisian taste and conditions, and remarks that even the genius of Rossini was defeated, in *Guillaume Tell*, by the "fatal atmosphere" of the Opéra, continues: "The conclusion to be drawn from this is that I'm no composer for Paris. I don't know whether or not I lack the talent, but certainly my ideas about art are very different from those of your country. I believe in inspiration; you believe in construction."[1]

Du Locle nevertheless kept trying, and various possible operatic subjects were raised and dropped in their correspondence: *Froufrou* by Meilhac and Halévy, Molière's *Tartuffe*, and a play by the contemporary Spanish playwright López de Ayala. Du Locle sent Verdi a copy of the Spanish play, but included with it a four-page synopsis of an opera to be set in ancient Egypt. Verdi dismissed the Spanish play from his mind, but expressed interest in the Egyptian synopsis, praising it and asking who had written it.

The answer was that Du Locle had written it, from a story by a French Egyptologist, Auguste Mariette. Mariette, who had been given the title of Bey by the Khedive of Egypt, had printed a limited edition of his story and suggested to the Khedive that it could be made into a splendid opera to celebrate the opening of the Suez Canal. Mariette entrusted Du Locle with the task of interesting an internationally known composer in the project. Verdi was the first choice, but the Khedive was willing that Gounod and then Wagner should be approached if he refused. By the time the synopsis came into Verdi's hands in the spring of 1870, the Suez Canal had been open for several months, so the persistent story that *Aida* was first performed at the opening of the Canal must be disregarded. The opera was not even, as one also still reads, commissioned for the inauguration of the Cairo Opera House, for the Opera House opened (with *Rigoletto*), on November 1, 1869, two weeks before the Canal.

Verdi agreed to write the opera, which became *Aida*. He would have only six months to work on it, since the contract stipulated that it was to have its première at the Cairo Opera House in January 1871. Du Locle drafted a complete libretto in French, but Verdi insisted that the opera

[1] *Copialettere*, pp. 220–1.

be Italian, and hired Antonio Ghislanzoni to translate the text. Ghislanzoni, who a few months earlier had provided some verses for the revised *Forza*, was a musical journalist ten years Verdi's junior. He had originally intended to have a medical career, then became an operatic baritone, after which he turned to literature.[1] He was the kind of librettist Verdi liked: the kind he could bully. His correspondence with Ghislanzoni reveals how great a part Verdi played in the writing of the libretto, reveals in fact that the completed libretto was much more the product of his imagination than of Du Locle's or Ghislanzoni's. Verdi's letters show this clearly, and are of absorbing interest for the picture they give of the way in which he approached the composition of an opera. Here are some extracts:

> This is not the moment to write to Mariette, but I've thought of something for the consecration scene. If it doesn't seem appropriate to you, we can try something else. Meanwhile, it seems to me that we might make rather an effective musical scene of this. It would consist of a litany chanted by the priestesses, to which the priests respond. Then a sacred dance with slow, sad music, a short recitative powerful and solemn, like a biblical psalm, then a prayer of two stanzas for the Chief Priest, and repeated by everyone. It should have an air of serenity about it, as different as possible from the other choruses at the end of the first scene and in the second Act finale which have a touch of the Marseillaise about them.
>
> I think the litanies should be composed—and once again forgive my boldness—of short stanzas, each with one long line and one five-syllable line or, perhaps even better so as to be able to say everything, two eight-syllable lines. The five-syllable line would be the *Ora pro nobis*. So there would be short stanzas of three verses each, six in all, and that would be more than sufficient.
>
> Rest assured, I have no aversion to cabalettas, but I insist always on a situation which justifies them. In the duet in *Un ballo in maschera* there was a magnificent justication. After that entire scene, if I say so myself, an outburst of love was inevitable.[2]

Let me say once and for all that I am never criticising your verses which are always good, but merely expressing my opinion of their theatrical effect. The duet between Radames and Aida in my opinion is much less good than that for father and daughter. That may be due to the situation or to the form which is more ordinary than the earlier duet. I am sure that the succession of lyrical verses of eight lines each, sung by one character and then repeated by the other, will not keep the dialogue alive.[3]

The eight verses for Aida, "Let's flee", and the first four for Radames are good. But in the later four I don't much like the idea of the bride. Would

[1] The American critic, translator and Verdi expert, William Weaver, says that Ghislanzoni's melodramatic novel *Gli artisti da teatro* is a mine of information about backstage life in Italian opera houses in the first part of the nineteenth century (*High Fidelity*, October 1963).

[2] *Copialettere*, p. 642.   [3] *Copialettere*, p. 651.

it not be better to say, as in the scenario, "Here, where I was born, where I grew up, where I became my country's saviour"? You have omitted Aida's outburst "And my gods shall be your gods. Home is where one loves". This must be said, either in the verses you have done, or, if you prefer, as recitative. Then the following transition must be made more significant:

Aida: Go, you do not love me.

Radames: Not love you? No man on earth or god in heaven has ever loved more passionately.

(Whether these or different words hardly matters, but the phrase must be a theatrical one that grips you.[1]

At the end, I should like to avoid the conventional death scene, and not have words like "My senses fail me. I go before you. Wait for me. She is dead, but I still live", and so on. I want something sweet, ethereal, quite a short duet, a farewell to life. Then Aida should sink quietly into the arms of Radames, while Amneris, kneeling on the vault above should sing a *Requiescat in pace*, and so on. I shall write out the last scene, to make my meaning clearer.[2]

And he does so, actually giving Ghislanzoni the words of the final duet and asking him to improve them. Later, he writes, "Dear Ghislanzoni, I received your verses. They are beautiful, but they aren't quite right for my purpose. And since you sent them so late, in order to save time I had already composed the music to the monstrous verses that I sent you."[3]

So, in addition to composing the music of the beautiful final duet, "O terra, addio", Verdi also wrote the "versi mostruosi", which are, in fact, by no means monstrous but simple, sincere and, in their context, extremely moving.

It took Verdi no more than four months to write the opera, which he completed well ahead of schedule. However, the Franco-Prussian war, which had begun in July, was at its height. Paris was under siege, and the scenery which had been constructed there could not be shipped to Egypt. Consequently, the Cairo première was delayed by eleven months. It finally took place on December 24, 1871, and the first Italian performance followed six weeks later at La Scala.

Before the *Aida* première, Wagner's *Lohengrin* was staged in Italy for the first time, in November, and Verdi went to Bologna to hear the opera conducted by Angelo Mariani. He sat at the back of a box with a vocal score on which he scribbled over a hundred notes during the performance, which apparently was a poor one. (Mariani agreed that it was.) He thought parts of the opera beautiful, but "The action moves as slowly as the words and therefore is boring," was his summing-up, scribbled on the score which is preserved at Sant' Agata.

[1] *Copialettere*, p. 652.   [2] *Copialettere*, p. 669.   [3] *Copialettere*, p. 671.

The first night of *Aida* was a glittering affair. The Khedive had invited the leading French and Italian critics to Cairo, and one of them, Filippo Filippi, contacted Verdi in advance, offering to do his best for the new opera. Verdi was so outraged that he wrote to his publisher threatening to destroy the score, and insisting that there be no organised réclame, which he regarded as the most mortifying humiliation. To Filippi he replied strongly, and at some length. "You in Cairo? That would be the finest advertisement imaginable for *Aida*," he declares sarcastically. The letter ends:

> Journalists, musicians, singers, directors and so on must all contribute their stone to the temple of publicity, to build a cornice out of nonsensical gossip that adds nothing to the worth of an opera, but merely obscures its true merits. This is deplorable, absolutely deplorable. Many thanks for your kind offers for Cairo, but I wrote in full detail yesterday to Bottesini[1] on the subject of *Aida*. All I want for that opera is good and, above all, intelligent singing, playing and stage production. For the rest, *à la grace de Dieu*. That's how I began my career, and that's how I wish to end it.[2]

Verdi did not go to Cairo. He stayed in Italy and rehearsed the singers for the Scala production, which was conducted by Franco Faccio.[3] For this production, he wrote an Overture to replace the Prelude, but decided against using it. It is still in manuscript at Sant' Agata, unplayed since the Milan rehearsals. He also composed a new recitative and aria, "O patria mia . . . O cieli azzurri", for Aida.

Both the Cairo and Milan premières were enthusiastically received. The French composer and disciple of Wagner, Sigurd Reyer, writing after the Cairo performance, was impressed by Verdi's harmonic sense, his unexpected modulations, the originality of his melodic line and the richness of his scoring. Over the Milan production, Verdi had taken great pains, concerning himself not only with the choice of conductor and cast but also with every detail of the orchestra, and even making use of one of Wagner's ideas, as this letter to Giulio Ricordi reveals:

> You know the libretto of *Aida*, and you know that Amneris requires an artist of dramatic stature who can dominate the stage. How can anyone expect to find this quality in a near-beginner? The voice alone, however beautiful (which, incidentally, is hard to judge in a room or empty theatre), is not sufficient for this role. So-called vocal perfection means little to me: I like to have roles sung the way I want them, but I am

---

[1] Giovanni Bottesini, who conducted the première, was also a double-bass virtuoso and composer.

[2] *Copialettere*, pp. 272–3.

[3] Faccio (1840–91) was also to conduct the first performances of *Otello* fifteen years later. A composer as well as conductor, he had achieved some success in 1865 with his own Shakespeare opera, a setting of *Hamlet*. The libretto of this *Amleto* was written by his close friend, and Verdi's eventual Shakespeare collaborator, Arrigo Boito.

unable to provide the voice, the soul, that indefinible spark understood by the phrase "to have the Devil on your back".

I wrote to you yesterday what I thought of Waldmann, and I repeat it now. Although finding an Amneris will not be easy, we are discussing it in Genoa. But that isn't enough, and you have not yet told me whether the terms I have set out in several letters are acceptable.

Remember this, my dear Giulio, that if I come to Milan it will not be for the empty pleasure of performing my own opera, but in order to ensure a really artistic performance. To achieve that, we must have the means. So please give me definite answers as to whether, besides the company of singers,

1. The conductor is decided upon.
2. The chorus conductors are engaged as I directed.
3. The orchestra has been drawn up according to my directions.
4. The drums are being exchanged for much bigger instruments than you had two years ago.
4a. The standard pitch is being retained.
5. The orchestra has accepted this standard pitch, in order to avoid the flattening that I have heard on other occasions.
6. The orchestra will be seated this time as I indicated in the sketch I made last winter in Genoa.

This seating of the orchestra is much more important than is usually assumed, for the blending of the instrumental colour, for the sonority, for the effect. Such minor improvements ought to prepare the way for other innovations that will come one day. Among these in particular I mean the disappearance of spectators' boxes from the stage. The curtain must come right up to the footlights. And then the invisible orchestra. This idea is not mine, but Wagner's, and it is an excellent one. It is absurd today to have to tolerate horrid white ties and tails against Egyptian, Assyrian and Druid costumes, to set the orchestra, which should be part of an imaginary world, in the middle of the floor in the middle of the crowd as it applauds or hisses. And think too how annoying it is to have harps, double basses, to say nothing of the conductor's windmill arms, all jutting up into the view.

Answer me categorically and decisively: because if you cannot promise me what I ask, it will be useless to continue negotiations.[1]

Verdi's comments on the casting of Amneris are those of a true musical dramatist. And, some may be tempted to add, a Wagnerian dramatist at that. But the evidence of his requirements for *Macbeth* a quarter of a century earlier is an immediate corrective. It is worth repeating: from the very beginning, Verdi was a man of the theatre. Though his methods altered, and his style matured, his goal remained constant. It was nothing less than the creation of an Italian musical theatre, and in a life-time of endeavour he achieved it. But, arrogant though Verdi could be in inessentials, he was intrinsically too modest to allow such a claim to be made for him. He found occasion to write to Giulio Ricordi:

[1] *Copialettere*, pp. 263-5.

I cannot take your statement that "the complete salvation of the theatre and of art is in your hands" as anything but a joke. No, no. Have no doubt of it, there will always be composers, and I too would repeat the toast proposed by Boito to Faccio after the performance of his first work: "Perhaps the man is already born who will smash the altar". Amen![1]

The day after the Milan première of *Aida*, Verdi wrote briefly to Count Opprandino Arrivabene:

Last night *Aida*. Very good. Performance of ensemble and soloists excellent, production also. Stolz [Aida] and Pandolfini [Amonasro] very good. Waldmann [Amneris] good. Fancelli [Radames] beautiful voice but nothing else. The others good, and the orchestra and chorus fine. As for the music, Piroli will speak to you about it. The audience liked it. I don't want to play modest with you: this is by no means the worst thing I've written, and time will give it the place it deserves. In short, it's a success and will pack the theatre. If I'm wrong, I'll write to you. Meanwhile, farewell in haste.[2]

The audience certainly did like it, and Verdi was forced to take several curtain calls. But the accusation of Wagnerism made by several critics distressed and annoyed him. "A fine thing," he complained to Ricordi, "after thirty-five years to end up as an imitator."[3]

Not every member of the public loved *Aida*. One dissatisfied customer wrote to the composer from Reggio, stating that he had travelled twice to Parma to hear the opera which, in his opinion, if it were not for the magnificent scenery, no audience would endure to the end. Claiming that the expense of these operatic excursions prayed on his mind like a terrible spectre, he enclosed an account for L. 31.80, the amount he had expended on two railway journeys, two opera seats, and two disgustingly bad dinners at the station. Verdi instructed his publisher to send the gentleman L. 27.80, having deducted the costs of the dinners which "he could perfectly well have eaten at home". He added: "Naturally he must send you a receipt, as well as a written undertaking not to attend another new opera of mine, so that he won't expose himself again to the danger of being pursued by spectres or involve me in further travel expenses."[4] The sum was paid, and the receipt and undertaking duly given.

II

It has generally been assumed that Mariette's story, expanded by Du Locle into a libretto which was translated by Ghislanzoni for Verdi, who also had a hand in the Italian text, was an original work. It now appears that the plot of *Aida* did not originate with Mariette.

[1] Gaetano Cesari, "L'arte superstite del Maestro" (*Corriere della Sera*, Jan. 27, 1926).
[2] *Verdi Intimo*, pp. 138–42. [3] Cesari, op. cit. [4] Abbiati, Vol. III, pp. 571–2.

I do not suggest that Auguste Mariette, the eminent archaeologist responsible for some of the most important Egyptian finds of the nineteenth century, including temples and tombs of the Pharaohs at Giza, Abydos, Sakkara and Thebes, was a conscious plagiarist; though it is interesting and amusing to discover that his own brother had no qualms against making such an assertion. In his biography Edouard Mariette claims that when, in the summer of 1866, he accompanied Auguste on a journey through Upper Egypt, he amused himself by sketching out a novel which he intended to call *La fiancée du Nil*, based on old Egyptian legends. His manuscript lay for weeks on a table in the tent he and his brother shared. Three years later, Auguste sent him a précis of his scenario which was to be set by Verdi, and Edouard was astonished to find a great similarity to his novel.

Speculation about whether Edouard was telling the truth would be fruitless. His biography of Auguste was published only after the latter's death. But Auguste Mariette's knowledge of Egyptian legends must surely be presumed to have been at least the equal of his non-archaeologist brother's. His synopsis was set in a period of history he knew well, and he may of course have drawn upon, or used as his starting point, an old legend, or even an historical incident. The conflict between Egypt and Ethiopia extended over several hundred years. Around 1000 B.C., the time of the *Aida* story, there were a number of wars in which, for a generation or two, Ethiopia gained the upper hand, only to be defeated again, for a period, by the Egyptians. Both countries at the time worshipped Amon, the Sun God, and many of the names of royal personages began with the sacred prefix "Am". Thus, in Mariette's synopsis, the Egyptian princess Amneris and the Ethiopian king Amonasro.

In his book *Opera as Drama*, published as long ago as 1957, Joseph Kerman drew attention to a claim[1] that the plot of *Aida* had been taken from a libretto by Metastasio[2] called *Nitteti*. Curiously, none of the books on Verdi that have appeared in English since then discusses or even mentions this claim, and Abbiati does so only cursorily. I felt I should at least examine Metastasio's *Nitteti*; and I am glad I did so, for it proved clearly to be one of the sources of the plot of *Aida*.

In the "Argomento" which precedes the printed text, Metastasio states that *Nitteti* is based on historical facts which are to be found in Herodotus and in Diodorus of Sicily. There is, in Herodotus, an account of Apries, a Pharaoh of the twenty-sixth Dynasty, and of his General, Amasis: this is the provenance of the plot of *Nitteti*. At the beginning of

[1] Made by F. Pérez de la Vega in *La Prosapia de Aida* (Mexico City, 1950).

[2] Metastasio (1698–1782) was one of the most admired librettists of the eighteenth century. Born in Rome, he worked for the greater part of his life in Vienna where he died. His libretti include *La Clemenza di Tito*, set by Caldara, Gluck and Mozart among others, *Il rè pastore*, *Siroe* and *L'Olympiade*.

Metastasio's Italian libretto, the dying king Aprio has declared Amasi to be his successor, and has confided to him that his daughter the Princess Nitteti is lost, and that the woman known as Nitteti is really the daughter of a shepherd. He asks Amasi to find the real Nitteti and give her to his, Amasi's, son Sammete in marriage, so that one day the families of Aprio and Amasi will unite to reign over Egypt.

Here is my synopsis of the three acts of Metastasio's *Nitteti*:

Act I. In the gardens of the palace at Canópo, Amenofi, King of Cirene, is awaiting the return of his friend Sammete, son of Amasi, the Egyptian king. Sammete, who had gone to visit Beroe, a shepherdess whom he has been wooing disguised as a shepherd, returns in despair, having failed to find Beroe who, he is told, has been captured by Egyptian soldiers. He leaves, and Beroe and Nitteti are led in between guards. Amenofi, who loves Nitteti, assures her she will soon be at liberty. He goes, and Beroe confesses to the princess Nitteti that she loves a shepherd called Dalmiro, while Nitteti in return admits she loves Prince Sammete. The Captain of the Royal Guards takes Nitteti to King Amasi, whose arrival is imminent. Sammete enters, now in his princely attire, and Beroe recognises him as her beloved Dalmiro. She is confused and distressed when she discovers he is the son of the new king, but he assures her that he loves her and will marry her. When he has gone, Beroe remembers that Nitteti has confessed she loves Sammete.

The scene changes to a public place by the walls of Canópo, festively adorned for Amasi's triumphal entrance. "On the right is a high, richly decorated throne, around which stand some of the sacred priests holding the royal insignia in golden vessels. In the background is a huge and majestic triumphal arch. Musicians and spectators are seated in rows. The triumphant Egyptian army can be seen approaching from the distance. The new and victorious king advances slowly, majestically seated upon a splendidly decorated white elephant, and passes under the arch, preceded by representatives of the defeated provinces carrying their respective tributes." Amasi is acclaimed as king by the populace. He gives back to Amenofi the conquered kingdom of Cirene. If his daughter Amestri were still alive, he would offer her in marriage to Amenofi. He wishes his son Sammete to marry Nitteti, daughter of the late king Aprio, whom he had promised that this marriage would take place. Amenofi tells Beroe that her shepherd-prince has no choice but to marry Nitteti. Beroe and Sammete meet to bewail their fate and affirm their love for each other.

Act II. Beroe soliloquises unhappily. Nitteti enters in a state of agitation. She has been offered to Sammete in marriage, but he has refused her. She longs to know with whom he is secretly in love. Beroe reveals that it is she, and that he and Dalmiro are the same person.

Beroe acquaints the king with her miserable situation. He absolves her from blame, but reminds her that it is now her duty to renounce Sammete. Beroe tells the king she will become a priestess in the temple of Isis. Sammete abducts her from the temple, but, in a scene by the shore with ships in the background, they are captured by the guards. They are brought before the king, who accuses his son of filial ingratitude. He orders him to prison.

Act III. Nitteti pleads with Amasi for Sammete's life. Amasi decides to offer Sammete the choice of death by entombment in the vaults of an ancient tower, or marriage to Nitteti. Sammete chooses to die. Beroe visits Sammete in his dungeon, and begs him to live and marry Nitteti. It is only when she threatens to kill herself that he consents to save his own life. Beroe departs and, when Nitteti arrives to urge him to flee, Sammete refuses.

The scene changes to a hall in the palace. The High Priest has discovered a document proving that the shepherdess Beroe is, in fact, Nitteti, and that she whom all have believed to be Nitteti is the long-lost Amestri, daughter of Amasi. Amasi, to the joy of all, proposes the marriage of Sammete to the real Nitteti, and of Amenofi to Amestri.

Though the plot of *Nitteti* is not that of *Aida*, they are close enough to each other in several places for one reasonably to suspect that *Nitteti* was known to one of the authors of *Aida*. The triumphal scene in which the victorious Amasi is crowned; the rivalry of (ostensibly) princess and lowly shepherdess for the love of Sammete; the fact that Beroe is really of as royal blood as Nitteti; the scene in which Sammete spurns Nitteti's offer to save his life; the threatened entombment; all these have their parallels in *Aida*.

Mariette may or may not have known his Metastasio, but it is very likely that a professional opera librettist like Du Locle would know other libretti, particularly so successful a libretto as *Nitteti*. Metastasio wrote it in Vienna for Niccolò Conforti (1727–65), whose opera was produced in 1756, the year of Mozart's birth.[1] The libretto was subsequently used by several other composers, among them Ignaz Holzbauer (Turin, 1757), Niccolò Piccinni (Naples, 1757), Tommaso Traetta (Reggio, 1757), Johann Adolph Hasse (Venice, 1758), Niccolò Jommelli (Stuttgart, 1759), Luigi Gatti (Mantua, 1773), Ferdinando

[1] This is according to the title page of the copy of *Nitteti* I consulted, which states "Dramma scritto dall' autore in Vienna, per la Real Corte Cattolica; ed ivi alla presenza de' Regnanti con superbo apparato rappresentato la prima volta con Musica del Conforti, sotto la magistrate direzione del celebre Cavalier Carlo Broschi, l'anno 1756." Grove calls the composer Conforto, and says he settled in Spain in 1756 and that *Nitteti* was first produced at Buen Retiro on September 23rd of that year. Carlo Broschi, who produced the opera, was the famous castrato known as Farinelli. He lived in Spain from 1737 onwards, and in 1750 established the Italian opera at Buen Retiro. He left Spain in 1759 to spend his remaining years in Italy.

Bertoni (Venice, 1786) and Johann Nepomuk von Poissl (in German translation, Darmstadt, 1817).

It is possible, I would say probable, that Du Locle knew the *Nitteti* libretto and inserted some of its detail into Mariette's story. But Metastasio may not have been the only author Du Locle plundered. Struck by a curious sentence in Toye's chapter on *Aida*,[1] I decided to renew my acquaintance with Racine. In *Bajazet*, a tragedy set in seventeenth-century Constantinople, an Amneris-Radames-Aida situation among Roxane, the favourite of Sultan Amurat, Bajazet, the Sultan's brother, and Atalide, a maiden of royal blood, is embedded in a plot which bears no other similarity to *Aida*. In two scenes (Act II, Scene 1, and, in particular, Act V, Scene 5) between Roxane and Bajazet, the Amneris-Radames confrontation of *Aida*'s Act IV, Scene 1, is quite clearly adumbrated; and Racine's Act IV, Scene 3, is surely the provenance of Act II, Scene 1, of *Aida*, in which Amneris tricks Aida into declaring her love for Radames. Here are a few lines of Racine (Roxane has just shown Atalide a letter she has received from the Sultan, commanding her to have Bajazet put to death):

> *Roxane*: Hé bien?
> *Atalide* (à part): Cache tes pleurs, malheureuse Atalide.
> *Roxane*: Que vous semble?
>
> . . . . .
>
> *Atalide*: Quoi donc: qu'avez-vous résolu?
> *Roxane*: D'obéir.
> *Atalide*: D'obéir!
> *Roxane*: Il le faut; et déjà mes ordres sont donnés.
> *Atalide*: Je me meurs.
>
> . . . .
>
> *Roxane*: Ma rivale à mes yeux s'est enfin déclarée. . . .[2]

(The remainder of this long speech by Roxane is very much in Amneris's style.)

---

[1] "Prime-Stevenson is right, I think, in tracing here a certain affinity with Racine: the scene [Act IV, Scene i] definitely suggests one of the great monologues of French classical tragedy." (Toye, *Verdi*.) *Long-Haired Iopas* by Edward Prime-Stevenson (Florence 1928) is on Toye's list of books he consulted. It is unknown to me. (I have still not read Prime-Stevenson but, since writing this, my attention has been drawn to the fact that he continues [p. 169]: "The libretto makes the situation of Radames much like that of Bajazet.")

[2] *Roxane*: Well?
Atalide (aside): Hide your tears, unhappy Atalide.
Roxane: What do you think?
Atalide: What have you resolved?
Roxane: To obey.
Atalide: To obey!
Roxane: I must, and already my orders are given.
Atalide: I shall die.
Roxane: My rival has at last declared herself to my face.

My conjecture is that Du Locle, concerned to give artistic verisimilitude to Mariette's bald and unconvincing narrative, filled out the Egyptologist's sketch with detail and characterisation from Metastasio, Racine and, I dare say, several other dramatists. No doubt some of his borrowings were less conscious than others. Here, then, with acknowledgements to whom it may concern, is the plot of *Aida*:

The opera, set in the time of the Pharaohs, is in four acts, of which all but the third are in two scenes. Act I, Scene 1, takes place in a hall of the King's Palace at Memphis. Through a door at the back, temples, palaces and the pyramids can be glimpsed. Radames, a captain in the Egyptian army, is conversing with Ramfis, High Priest of Egypt. Ramfis tells Radames that it is rumoured the Ethiopians are again planning to attack. He has consulted the goddess Isis, who has named the supreme commander of the Egyptian troops. With a meaningful glance at Radames, Ramfis says that the man chosen is young and brave, and that he is about to take his name to the King. He goes, and Radames expresses the hope that it is he who has been chosen, and that he can return, crowned with the laurels of victory, to his beloved Aida, the Ethiopian slave of the Princess Amneris. Amneris, herself in love with Radames, enters followed by Aida, and tries to discover, by oblique questions, whether Radames is in love, and, if so, with whom. She suspects it may be her slave. Aida, who returns Radames's love, attempts to conceal her feelings from Amneris. The King enters, accompanied by his court, guards and priests, and announces that a messenger has just arrived from the Ethiopian border. The messenger reports that the Ethiopians have already invaded Egypt, destroying fields and crops as they advance towards Thebes, led by their King, Amonasro. In an aside, Aida reveals that Amonasro is her father. The Egyptian King declares that Isis has appointed Radames General-in-Command of the army, and orders him to hasten to the Temple of Vulcan for the ceremony of the consecration of his armour. When all have departed, Aida soliloquises on her divided feelings. Unable to wish for the defeat of either her father or the man she loves, she calls on the gods to have pity on her suffering.

Scene 2 is the interior of the Temple of Vulcan, where priests and priestesses, led by Ramfis, evoke the God Fthà. A silver veil is placed over the head of Radames while the priestesses perform a sacred dance. At the end of the ceremony, the holy sword is given to Radames.

The first scene of Act II is a room of Amneris's apartment in the palace. The Princess is surrounded by her slave-girls, who are helping her to dress for the victory celebrations. The male slaves dance for her as she dreams of the imminent return of Radames. Aida enters and, in order to discover the truth, Amneris tells her that Radames is dead. Aida's tears almost betray her. Her joy, when Amneris reveals that she was lying and that Radames is alive, finally convinces Amneris that she and her slave are rivals. Aida admits her love for Radames, and begs Amneris, who has so much else of happiness and power, to relinquish him. Amneris refuses and leaves Aida, who again calls on the gods to pity her.

Act II, Scene 2, the great triumphal scene, takes place in a public square near one of the gates to Thebes. A huge crowd has gathered to witness the return of the victorious army. The King and his court, Amneris with Aida and other slaves, priests, standard-bearers and officials all enter ceremonially. The citizens sing a song of victory as the troops march in, followed by chariots of war, sacred statues carried in procession, as well as various spoils. Finally, Radames himself is borne in on a canopy. The victor's crown of laurels is placed on his brow by Amneris, and the King swears to give him whatever he should ask. Radames orders the Ethiopian prisoners to be brought in, and Aida discovers her father among them, disguised as an ordinary soldier. Muttering to Aida not to reveal he is the Ethiopian King, Amonasro publically admits he is her father. Radames asks that the King grant life and liberty to the prisoners. The Egyptian people support him, but the priests demand death for all the Ethiopians. A compromise is reached: all are freed except Aida's father, who is to remain in Egypt as a hostage. The King then rewards Radames by offering the hand of his daughter Amneris in marriage. In a huge ensemble, all give voice to their own reactions to this announcement.

Act III takes place on the banks of the Nile, near a Temple of Isis, on a clear, moonlit night. From within the temple, a chant to Isis is heard. A boat draws up to the bank, and from it steps Amneris, with Ramfis and their attendants and guards. Ramfis invites Amneris, on this the eve of her marriage to Radames, to pray in the Temple. They go in. Aida arrives for an assignation with Radames who, she imagines, wants merely to say farewell to her. Heartbroken, she contemplates drowning herself in the Nile. Suddenly her father appears. Having realised that she and Radames love each other, he asks his daughter to help him discover the route the Egyptian army will take the following day. His own people are in arms again, and waiting to attack. As Radames is to lead the Egyptians, she should be able to prise the information from him. Aida is horrified at the suggestion, but when Amonasro angrily tells her she is no longer his daughter, and is fit only to be a slave of the Pharaohs, she tearfully agrees to obtain the knowledge he requires. Amonasro hides as Radames approaches. Aida repulses Radames, reminding him that he is about to marry Amneris. He swears to her that, once he has put down the latest Ethiopian uprising, he will beg the King to allow him to marry Aida. Aida points out the futility of this, crying that the vengeance of Amneris would descend on her and her father. Their only chance of happiness, she says, is to flee from Egypt to Ethiopia. Radames can hardly bear to think of abandoning his country, but when Aida accuses him of not loving her, and tells him to join Amneris at the altar, he agrees to flee with her immediately. She asks what road they had best take to avoid the army, and Radames reveals that the gorge of Nápata is where the army will be found. "The gorge of Nápata! My warriors will be waiting!" cries Amonasro as he steps forward, announcing himself to Radames as King of Ethiopia. Radames exclaims bitterly that he is dishonoured, that he has betrayed his country. Amonasro and Aida try to persuade him to flee with them, but at that moment Amneris, Ramfis and their guards come out of the Temple. Amneris cries "Traitor!" Amonasro rushes towards her with a dagger but is restrained by Radames who, ordering him and Aida to escape, steps forward and gives himself up to Ramfis.

The first scene of Act IV is a hall in the King's Palace. On the left, is a door to the underground chamber of judgment. On the right, a passage leads to Radames's prison. Amneris broods on her love for him, and is furious that Aida has succeeded in escaping. She has Radames brought to her, and offers to plead with the King for his life. She reveals that, although Amonasro has fallen in battle, Aida is miss-ing. If Radames will swear to forget Aida, his life can be spared. He refuses, and the jealous Amneris, torn between hate and love for him, collapses in tears as he is led away to the chamber of judgment. She overhears Ramfis and the priests calling Radames "Traitor", and wait-ing for him to defend himself. He remains silent, and is sentenced to be entombed alive beneath the altar of the god he has offended. As the priests come out of the chamber, Amneris alternately pleads with them and curses them.

The final scene reveals two levels of the Temple of Vulcan. Above is the interior of the Temple, while below is a crypt in which Radames stands while two priests close the stone above him. As Radames tells himself he will never see Aida again, she suddenly appears, having hidden herself in the tomb so as to die with him. The priestesses are heard chanting in the distance as the lovers utter their farewell to earth and calmly anticipate the bliss of heaven. Amneris, in mourning robes, appears in the Temple above, and prostrates herself on the stone over the tomb, calling on Isis to grant peace to Radames and receive him into heaven.

III

The orchestral prelude is based on two themes which recur in the opera. The first, which is later associated with Aida's love for Radames, is heard at the beginning played *andante* and pianissimo by muted violins later joined by violas [Ex. 100]. The second, contrasting theme, is

Ex.100 Andante mosso

a descending scale figure expressive of the priests' intransigence [Ex. 101]. First played very quietly by muted cellos, it builds up to fortis-

Ex.101 Andante mosso

simo, and is heard in conflict with Aida's theme. The dramatic idea is simple, its musical expression most satisfying. The conflict subsides, and the first violins ascend and fade.

Ramfis's conversation with Radames, carried on in an easy and eloquent arioso, is followed by Radames's recitative, "Se quel guerrier io fossi", and aria, "Celeste Aida". The recitative is punctuated by martial fanfares on trumpets and trombones; the aria is a simple and direct romantic declaration, with a strikingly delicate accompaniment. Verdi's score asks the tenor to end on a top B flat pianissimo and morendo. Few tenors are willing to do this, and Verdi himself suggested to an early performer of the rôle who found it difficult, that he should sing the B flat forte, and then repeat the words, "vicino al sol", *pp*, an octave lower.[1] The printed ending is preferable: if the tenor really cannot produce his B flat pianissimo, he should be able to compromise on a reasonable mezzoforte.

Amneris enters to a coiling violin figure whose suavity characterises one aspect of her. Her duet with Radames moves from graceful insinuation to a more agitated state as she attempts to pry into his feelings. An accompanying figure, which recurs throughout the opera to denote Amneris's jealousy, is heard here for the first time [Ex. 102]. When

---

[1] Verdi's sketch of the suggested addition is reproduced in *Carteggi Verdiani*, Vol. II, p. 42.

Ex.102
Andante mosso

p dolciss.

Aida appears, to a statement of her theme [Ex. 100] on solo clarinet, a trio develops which, though brief, admirably exposes the situation and feelings of the three characters. As it ends, a sumptuous fanfare heralds the entrance of the King and his court. The action is advanced by dramatic recitative for Ramfis and the Messenger, with choral interjections. How easily, economically and concisely the dramatist Verdi sets the situation before us. The Messenger ends his report with the name of the warrior leading the Ethiopians: "Amonasro". "Il Re" (The King), cries the assembly. "Mio padre" (My father), mutters Aida. What would be comically brutal in modern spoken drama is turned into a master-stroke of lyrical theatre which is the modern equivalent of Greek classical theatre, one of whose conventions it here revives.

When he is announced as General, Radames indulges in a cadenza-like vocal flourish, decorated by the asides of Amneris and Aida, and the *ppp* repetitions of his name by the crowd. The King launches into a rousing martial tune, "Su! del Nilo", which forms the basis of a splendid ensemble. When, for eight bars, Radames has the tune, Aida sings a more agitated melody in shorter notes above it. This brief passage is quite remarkable, not only musically, for its shifting of the harmonic emphasis, but also dramatically, for the way it contrasts the situations of Aida and Radames: she hesitant and anxious, he exhilarated and determined.

The others depart, and Aida ends the scene with her recitative, "Ritorna vincitor", and aria, "L'insana parola". "Ritorna vincitor" is no mere formal recitative, of course, but a brilliant piece of dramatic writing. The aria begins with an urgent intensity, makes a reference to Aida's love theme, and finally moves beyond passion into the unearthly serenity of "Numi, pietà" [Ex. 103]. The rare beauty of this tune has

Ex.103

Nu - mi, pie - tà　del　mio sof - frir!　Spe-me　non　v'ha　pel　mio do-lor...

not been achieved easily; its simplicity is magical. On the printed page it appears banal. Transposed into sound, it is clearly one of Verdi's most sensitive inspirations.

The second scene of Act I is written as one long number described in the score as "Grand Scene of the Consecration and First Finale". It begins with the solo soprano voice of the Grand Priestess, supported by a chorus of priestesses and accompanied by harps, invoking the God, Fthà. The tune, which will be heard again at the end of the opera, sounds decidedly exotic [Ex. 104]. It is not, however, in the slightest

Ex.104 **Andante con moto**

Pos - - - sen - te, pos-sen - te Fthà,............

degree Egyptian, and, if it sounds so to us today, this is because Verdi has persuaded us that it does. Ramfis and the priests respond in unaccompanied chant, and the process is repeated twice. The Sacred Dance of the Priestesses, which follows, is a rather quaint allegretto with a middle section scored for three unison flutes and pizzicato strings. It, too, is heard again at the end of the opera. Ramfis and the priests address Radames in a declamatory arioso, after which Ramfis invokes Fthà in an impressive legato melody, "Nume, custode e vindice di questa sacra terra" (God, custodian and guardian of this sacred land), which is taken up by Radames and the priests. During its rests, the off-stage priestesses are heard. On- and off-stage forces combine, and the invocation comes to an end with a fortissimo cry of "Immenso Fthà".

The first scene of Act II is laid out as two numbers in the score, though in performance there is no perceptible break. The curtain rises to the sound of Verdi's harps in march rhythm. This is presumably to let us know, as Amneris's slaves also let us know in their chorus, that Radames has been victorious. To Verdi, the harp appears to have had connections more martial than celestial. The triumphant sound is succeeded by music in a more tender vein. Giving way to violins, the harps confine themselves to an arpeggio accompaniment as the slave girls sing. In completion of the musical sentence they have begun, Amneris sings the sensuous phrase [Ex. 105]. The opening vocal section

Ex.105 **Allegro giusto**

(Ah! vie - - ni. vie-ni a-mor mio, m'i-neb - bria, fammi be-a-to il

morendo

cor, fammi be - a-to il cor.)

is repeated to different words, when it leads straight into the dance of the young moorish slaves, an agreeably light and lively tune, after which a truncated version of the opening vocal section is heard without the martial beginning. Sung for the third time, Amneris's voluptuous phrase of love and yearning is now accompanied by the pianissimo sustained notes of her female slaves, and by tremolando strings.

Aida's love theme, suitably downcast on lower strings and bassoon, announces her entrance, and is heard again briefly as an agitated *sotto voce* in the ensuing duet. In the duet, notable both for the quality of its melody and for the manner in which the dramatic argument is pursued, Amneris tricks Aida into revealing her love for Radames. Aida's plea, "Pietà ti prenda dal mio dolor" (Have pity on my sorrow), is an appealing tune accompanied sparsely by two flutes, clarinet and bassoon. Towards the end of the duet, the King's "Su! del Nilo" march from Act I is heard off-stage, fortissimo, while Amneris continues to taunt Aida. When Amneris scornfully sweeps out on her top A flat, Aida repeats her moving prayer from the end of Act I, Scene 1, "Numi, pietà", again accompanied by quiet tremolando strings.

The triumphal scene, Act II, Scene 2, is really the epitome of so-called grand opera. Its renown, out of context, is such that it effectively obscures the fact that *Aida*, for all the pomp and ceremony of its trappings, is really an intimate opera. Much, indeed most, of the music for its three principal characters, Aida, Radames and Amneris, is scored with the clarity of texture of chamber music. But the public spectacle of Act II, Scene 2, is a legitimate and highly enjoyable aspect of *Aida*. It opens with twenty-four bars of *allegro maestoso* orchestral introduction to the chorus, "Gloria all' Egitto", a splendid tune which so impressed the Khedive at the dress rehearsal that he wanted to use it henceforth as the Egyptian National Anthem. A contrasting cantabile section is sung by the female voices. The priests enter with a statement of their theme [Ex. 101] for which the orchestra momentarily provides its darker colours, but the populace joins in the chorus again to restore a more convivial atmosphere. The moment the singing has ceased, three trumpeters on-stage begin the famous march known far and wide as the "Grand March from *Aida*". Verdi ordered the six trumpets required for this scene, three in A flat and three in B, to be made to his specifications in Milan and sent out to Egypt. These long, straight instruments are his version of the ancient Egyptian trumpet. While writing the opera, he had given some thought to using Egyptian instruments for authentic colouring. He went to Florence to examine an ancient Egyptian flute in the museum there, but scornfully dismissed it as "a reed with four holes in it like the ones our shepherds have." Hence, his invention of six ancient Egyptian trumpets. The three in A flat play the march tune in unison [Ex. 106]. Immediately, the remain-

Ex.106   Allegro maestoso

ing three trumpets repeat the march in their key of B. The sudden modulation is one of the most effective and exciting moments in Verdi or, for that matter, in opera. The A flat trumpets return to finish the tune, which is immediately followed by a lively ballet movement in which the full orchestra is engaged, with emphasis on piccolo and triangle. After the ballet, the "Gloria all' Egitto" chorus returns to different words, new material is added to it, and the priests' theme continues underneath as the ensemble builds up to the triumphal entry of Radames, who is greeted with cries of "Gloria!"

The King's recitative, a *ppp* reference to Amneris's theme in the orchestra as she places the crown of laurels on Radames's head, and a restatement of the priests' theme, darkly accompanied, as the Ethiopian prisoners are brought in, lead to Amonasro's recognition by Aida, and his brief but dramatic aria, "Anch'io pugnai", with its beautiful legato section at "Ma tu, Re" on which an ensemble, the scene's semi-climax, is built. A solo cadenza for Aida introduces a pianissimo restatement by the ensemble of "Ma tu, Re". Aida's top line at moments takes on an almost Mahlerian shape [Ex. 107]. The closing bars take Aida to a

top C. Radames, in recitative, asks for the release of the prisoners, and is supported pianissimo by the people but opposed forte by Ramfis and the priests. Over tremolando strings, the King offers Amneris to Radames in marriage, in a passage which is sung almost completely on the note of B flat. After a phrase from Amneris, the crowd bursts into "Gloria all' Egitto" again, the priests contribute their theme, the principals their comments in quintet, and the scene moves to a splendid finale in which chorus, orchestra and stage band are joined by the three A flat trumpets. The final orchestral bars consist of the beginning of the "Grand March" which, after five bars, disintegrates into a brilliant flurry of chords.

Act III of *Aida* contains some of the most glorious music in Verdi's entire œuvre. The sixteen bars of orchestral introduction are magical in their evocation of a hot, shimmering moonlit night by the river. The atmosphere is produced by rustling strings, the muted violins playing staccato spread octaves very softly, and a solo flute used with the simplicity of genius. A chorus of priests is heard praying in the temple as Ramfis and Amneris appear. In a passage of tuneful conversation, Amneris's phrase, "Si, io pregherò" must be singled out [Ex. 108]. It is too transparently simple to be analysed, but one would

have to be completely insensitive to sound not to be struck by its expressive beauty. In these five notes, Verdi has secured our sympathy for Amneris. Aida's theme, played by flutes in unison, heralds her entrance Her recitative, "Qui Radames verrà", and aria, "O cieli azzurri", were added to the score by Verdi for the Milan production. After the recitative in which, when Aida talks of drowning herself, we hear the rushing and swirling waters of the Nile for four bars in the orchestra, a sinuous solo oboe introduces the yearning arioso passage, "O patria mia". This leads into the aria proper, whose vocal line and evanescent accompaniment are both exquisite and original. The exposed instrumentation underlines the elegant yet affecting melancholy of the aria, whose climax takes the singer to a top C to be sung dolce. The quiet orchestra postlude is suddenly interrupted by the arrival of Amonasro. His duet with Aida begins in dramatic *parlante*, moves through the persuasive cantabile of "Rivedrai le foreste imbalsamate" (You shall see again our perfumed forests), which Aida joyfully repeats after her father, to the lyrical and moving plea of "Deh! fate, o numi" (Grant, o Gods). When Aida at first refuses to trick Radames into betraying his country Amonasro turns on her in a savage *allegro*. Her cry for pity is set most movingly, and his unexpectedly tender reply is given in one of Verdi's broad, heart-rending ascending phrases [Ex. 109] which bears a strong

Ex.109   Andante assai sostenuto

Pen - sa   che un po - - - po-lo vin - to, stra-zia - to

resemblance to "Deh, non m'abbandonar" in *La forza del destino* [Ex 89]. This is the one moment in the opera when Amonasro behaves like a Verdian father to his daughter. Elsewhere, he is always the single-minded warrior King. "O patria, o patria, quanto mi costi" (Oh, my country, how much you cost me), cries Aida, and, just as one feels the sadness of the situation to be almost unbearable, it is interrupted by sounds of action and excitement in the orchestra, signalling the approach of Radames. His attempts to begin an enthusiastic love duet are thwarted by Aida. To an orchestral background of the theme denoting Amneris' jealousy, she reminds him that he is betrothed to the Princess. In a more lyrical passage, after she has suggested they flee from Egypt, Aida sings nostalgically of the flowers and forests of her native land. In another of Verdi's most expressive and beautiful phrases [Ex. 110] Radames

Ex. 110

Andantino

ab - ban - do - nar   la   pat - ria,   l'a - re de' no - stri Dei !

wonders how he could possibly leave the country he loves. This ravishingly lovely section of the duet gives both tenor and soprano more than
one chance to float soft, sweet B flats. Even those tenors who fail the
test of "Celeste Aida" are usually inspired to produce the right kind of
note on the final syllable of "il ciel de' nostri amori". Finally, Radames
is persuaded. He and, after him, Aida sing of their flight, to a new and
resolute tune, and then combine in unison in the love duet which
Radames had earlier found difficult to begin without Aida. This is the
apotheosis of the old cabaletta.

The plot is advanced in dramatic recitative. After Radames realises
that he has inadvertently betrayed his country, Aida attempts to
console him in a beautiful repeated phrase, but he replies with insistent
cries of "Io son disonorato" (I am dishonoured). After Amneris's
appearance and cry of "Traitor", the scene moves swiftly to its end.
Radames's exciting final phrase, "Sacerdote, io resto a te" (Priest, I am
your prisoner), with its repeated top As, is followed by a series of
emphatic chords as the curtain falls.

The first scene of Act IV opens with an orchestral passage in which
Amneris's jealousy theme [Ex. 102] is heard *allegro agitato* and pianissimo on first violins. In her recitative, Amneris ranges from bitter
despair to tenderness. When she sings of her love for Radames, she
does so with a reference to the suave theme associated with her tenderer
feelings. The great duet for Amneris and Radames, "Già i sacerdoti
adunansi" (Already the priests are sitting in judgment), is expounded
in a series of splendid tunes, each with its appropriate dramatic
character. The duet begins with a broad, noble melody sung by each in
turn. A few bridging bars usher in the next lyrical section sung first by
Amneris and then, altered, by Radames. Another *parlando* passage in
which, when Radames sings of Aida, a few bars from "Celeste Aida"
are echoed, leads to an angry outburst from Amneris and to the next
great tune, in which Radames almost ecstatically anticipates death.
His "È la morte un ben supremo" (Death is a supreme reward) is sung
to a tune of serene assurance. Amneris joins him only at the climax of
the musical sentence, which has a deliberate melodic ambiguity. For her
it expresses desperation, for him determination [Ex. 111]. The duet

Ex. 111

moves quickly to a climax. Radames is led away and, as the priests'

theme is heard on muted basses, Amneris soliloquises on her despair in
simple but eloquent phrases set low in the voice. The priests' theme
continues as Radames is led to trial. While the trial proceeds in an
underground chamber, Amneris listens above, the desperate warmth
of her cries to the gods for pity contrasting with the cold brutality of
the proceedings below. Three times Radames is accused and told to
defend himself. Three times there is no reply but the characterised
silence of a *pianissimo* roll on the bass drum. The sequence is pitched a
semitone higher at each repetition. Verdi's falling-tear cadences are
heard in Amneris's unavailing cries. When sentence is pronounced,
her pleading turns to fury, and she denounces the heartless priests in a
deeply felt outburst which reminds one of the unwavering strength of
Verdi's anti-clericalism, and of his probable equation of Ramfis and
his priests with the nineteenth-century Italian clergy, for whom he had
little but contempt. He may easily himself have written the words
Amneris sings: "O, gl' infami! Ne di sangue son paghi giammai. E si
chiaman ministri del ciel!" (Oh, the infamous creatures. They can never
have enough bloodshed. And they call themselves ministers of heaven!)

The priests file out of the judgment chamber, impervious to Amneris's
despairing fury. Calling down the vengeance of heaven on them, she
rushes off, as the orchestra brings violently to an end a scene which has
something of the grandeur of classical tragedy.

The final scene begins with Radames's monotone phrases, which
broaden into melodic recitative as he discovers Aida. Her moving
declaration that she has come to die with him is very gently accomplished, and his "Morire! Si pura e bella" is sung to an arioso melody of
great tenderness, against a delicate accompaniment of pizzicato strings
occasionally reinforced by two clarinets. Aida's "Vedi? di morte
l'angelo", a staccato, semi-delirious passage, is brilliantly scored in
Verdi's most ethereal style. The chanting of the priests is heard above,
and after a last few bars of agitation while Radames tries to lift the
stone and free Aida, the music moves into the heavenly serenity of the
final duet, "O terra, addio" [Ex. 112].

Ex.112

This sublimely ravishing Italian *Liebestod* in which the lovers sink
themselves, singing its melody first separately and then together in
unison, is almost Mozartean in its pure spirituality, as truly an
apotheosis of the horror of the realistic dramatic situation as the last
pages of *Tristan und Isolde*. I have always felt an appoggiatura should be
sung on "pianti". I don't know that Verdi was consistent or, for that
matter, insistent about appoggiature, but in the last scene of *Otello* his

direction "a tempo prestissimo, senza appoggiature" implies that he normally expected them.

The chanting of the priests and the heart-broken phrases of Amneris are added to the lovers' hymn. The voices of Aida and Radames fade into silence, and, as the first violins quietly play the final bars of "O terra addio" in their highest register, Amneris whispers her last "pace t'imploro, pace, pace", the priests add their "Immenso Fthà" in the background, and Verdi's most original opera comes to an end *pppp*.

Aida is a remarkable work which has almost become the victim of its own popularity. In a sense, it falls between two Verdian stools, possessing neither the rough vigour of the early works nor the psychological penetration of *Otello* and *Falstaff*. In purely musical terms, however, it is nothing less than a miracle of melodic beauty and imaginative orchestration. For all its public scenes, it is the most intimate of "grand" operas, and at its heart one senses Verdi's profound melancholy. The sounds he has created are not picturesquely Egyptian: Verdi has created his own Egypt just as surely as his beloved Shakespeare did in *Antony and Cleopatra*. His dramatic use of recurring musical motives is nicely judged, and his balancing of objective description and subjective feeling is perfect. He has written four superb roles for singers; and in Amneris, who almost steals the opera from Aida, he has created perhaps the greatest of his mezzo-soprano characters. Both in its spectacular and its intimate aspects, *Aida* is a triumph of the creative imagination.

XXV

Messa da Requiem

For soprano, mezzo-soprano, tenor, bass, mixed chorus and orchestra

FIRST PERFORMED, to commemorate the first anniversary of the death of Alessandro Manzoni, on May 22, 1874 in the church of San Marco, Milan. The soloists were Teresa Stolz (soprano); Maria Waldmann (mezzo); Giuseppe Capponi (tenor); Armando Maini (bass); the composer conducted.

Messa da Requiem

I

FOR SOME MONTHS after the Milan production of *Aida* in February 1872, the fifty-eight-year-old Verdi divided his attention between his farm and productions of his operas in Parma, Padua and elsewhere. Towards the end of the year he travelled to Naples, where he had agreed to produce *Don Carlo* and *Aida*. Teresa Stolz, the Aida of the Milan production, was to sing in both operas, but, when she became ill after *Don Carlo* had opened, the *Aida* rehearsals were postponed. With time on his hands, Verdi occupied himself by writing a String Quartet (see pp. 461–2).

In May 1873, Alessandro Manzoni, one of Verdi's heroes, died in Milan at the age of eighty-nine. "Now all is over," said Verdi, "and with him ends the most pure, the most holy, the greatest of our glories."[1] This was not how the Catholic church saw Manzoni: the obituaries in the clerical papers were mostly disguised attacks on him. But he was mourned by the workers, and by Verdi, who, too upset to attend the funeral, went to Milan a week later to visit his grave. Through Giulio Ricordi, he suggested to the Mayor of Milan that he might compose a Requiem Mass to be performed on the first anniversary of Manzoni's death. He himself would bear the expenses of having the music printed if the city would pay the costs of the first performance. The Mayor agreed, and during his summer holiday in Paris with Giuseppina, Verdi began work on the Mass.

Manzoni, the author of *I promessi sposi* (*The Betrothed*), the one internationally known Italian novel before *Il gattopardo*, was one of the great figures of the Risorgimento. Far from being a hot-headed revolutionary, however, he was a poet who, though violently anti-clerical in his extreme youth, became converted to Catholicism at the age of twenty-five, wrote one or two volumes of Catholic apologetics, two verse tragedies on patriotic themes, an ode on the death of Napoleon, and then devoted his life to writing *I promessi sposi*. Its effect, on its first publication in 1827, was extraordinary, and its success immediate. Manzoni continually revised it as it went through edition after edition, until he produced his definitive version in 1840. It is still by far the most popular novel in the Italian language. From the beginning, it

[1] *Copialettere*, p. 283.

appealed not only to the educated classes, but also to almost everyone who could read or be read to. Though it was not an overt propaganda novel, it spoke directly to emergent Italian patriotism. The huge response to *I promessi sposi* was undoubtedly extra-aesthetic, many people being inspired by it to attach themselves emotionally to the new liberal cause. The novel deals with events in Lombardy in the first half of the seventeenth century, at a time when the people were being oppressed by their Spanish overlords. But Manzoni's nineteenth-century readers were perfectly capable of making the transposition to the Italy of their own day, suffering under the Austrians. The local patriotism of the novel's submerged meaning worked on its public in the same way that Verdi's first operas did.

Verdi revered Manzoni, but for years was too shy to meet him. When his old friend the Contessa Maffei took Giuseppina to meet Manzoni, a visit Verdi did not hear about till afterwards, he was both delighted and envious. The two men finally met in 1868 in Milan, and Verdi wrote to the Contessa: "What can I say of Manzoni? How to describe the extraordinary, indefinable sensation the presence of that saint, as you call him, produced in me."[1]

By April 1874, Verdi had finished the Requiem. He had chosen the church of San Marco in Milan for the performance, as having the best acoustics, and he rehearsed assiduously his chorus of a hundred and twenty and orchestra of a hundred. The performance was an enormous success, and the work was acclaimed a masterpiece; three days later Verdi had to conduct a second performance at La Scala, and Franco Faccio conducted a further two. Never before had a Requiem Mass been greeted like this. But then, never before had there been a Requiem Mass like this: agnostic, dramatic, popular.

The German conductor and Wagnerian, Hans von Bülow, happened to be in Milan on the day of the first performance. In the following day's newspaper he inserted an announcement stating that "Hans von Bülow was not present at the spectacle presented yesterday at the Church of San Marco. Hans von Bülow must not be counted among the foreigners gathered in Milan to hear Verdi's sacred music."[2] Elsewhere, Bülow described the Requiem as "Verdi's latest opera, in ecclesiastical dress",[3] an ignorant gibe which is, nevertheless, sometimes quoted with approbation by admirers of the work. Brahms, when he heard of Bülow's remark, examined a score of the Requiem, and declared: "Bülow has made a fool of himself. This is a work of genius."[4]

The Requiem was taken on a triumphal tour of Europe. Verdi conducted seven performances in Paris at the Opéra-Comique, and a further eight the following year, 1875, when the French Government made him a Commander of the Legion of Honour; four performances at

[1] Abbiati, Vol. III, p. 215.   [2] Gatti, Vol. II, p. 274.   [3] Op. cit., p. 273.
[4] Op. cit., p. 273. Gatti's translation of Brahms is: "Bülow ha preso una cantonata."

the Hofoper in Vienna, where he received the Order of Franz Josef and attended a performance of *Tannhäuser*; three performances at the Royal Albert Hall in London, where press criticism was amusingly divided. The *Pall Mall Gazette* thought the work the most beautiful sacred music since Mozart's Requiem, while the *Morning Post* objected to the "shouting of the chorus in the 'Dies Irae'," and the "canine vociferation" of the "Libera me". It continued: "There is no melody that the mind can receive consonant with the words, and the breaking of those words into short, sharp ejaculations, like a series of barks or yells, is certainly not indicative of reverence."[1] The *Daily Telegraph* was enthusiastic, and referred to "Puritans who think all sacred music should conform to English standards".[2] Giuseppina's comment on the critics is pertinent:

They talk a lot about the more or less religious spirit of Mozart, Cherubini and others. I say that a man like Verdi must write like Verdi, that is according to his own way of feeling and interpreting the text. And if the various religions have a beginning, a development, changes and modifications according to the time and the country, then the religious spirit and the way in which it finds expression must bear the imprint of its time and, surely, the personality of its author. I would have repudiated a Mass by Verdi that had been modelled on those of A, B or C.[3]

II

Is Verdi's *Messa da Requiem* sacred music? Since it is a setting of a liturgical text, the answer must be, by definition, yes. The term "sacred music" can have no other meaning, except perhaps loosely to separate the good from the bad. In the latter sense, Bach's deeply emotional St Matthew Passion, Mozart's joyous Masses and his incomplete and only partly impressive Requiem, Beethoven's probing Missa Solemnis, Verdi's dramatic Requiem and Fauré's sweetly serene one, are *not* sacred music, and Stainer's *The Crucifixion*, for instance, is. But, to Verdi, music was good or bad: he preferred not to consider such classifications as sacred and secular, artistic and popular. In the *Messa da Requiem*, his intention was to express the emotional meaning and implications of the liturgical text, just as in his operas he was concerned to express the meaning of the words and situations with which he was presented by his librettists. The only significant difference was that this time he was unable to bully the librettist into altering the words.

A Requiem Mass takes its text from the Roman Catholic liturgy (though Brahms composed his *Deutsches Requiem* on passages from the Lutheran Bible). The Requiems of some composers are so written that they can be used, movement by movement, as part of the religious

[1] Toye, p. 169.   [2] Toye, p. 169.   [3] Giuseppina's Letterbooks.

service. Needless to say, Verdi's is not. He intended it as a work for concert performance. The primitive imagery of the medieval Latin text, filtered through Verdi's humanist imagination, emerged transformed into music which, ostensibly celebrating the dead, is more desperately concerned with the situation of the living. The seven movements are Requiem and Kyrie; Dies Irae; Offertorio; Sanctus; Agnus Dei; Lux aeterna; Libera me.

1. *Requiem and Kyrie*

The Requiem begins very quietly, with muted cellos playing a slow, descending phrase which is taken up by the rest of the strings as the chorus enters with its monotone chant. After sixteen bars, in the change from A minor to A major, a simple yet, in context, miraculously beautiful violin phrase ushers in the possibility of "lux perpetua" and the chant broadens out into quasi-archaic, imitative unaccompanied melody at the words, "Te decet hymnus". The hushed opening section is repeated, and at "Kyrie eleison" the soloists enter one by one, on a generously expansive lyrical theme over a chromatically descending accompaniment. They combine in a quartet accompanied by the chorus. The ensemble is one of great beauty and fervour. As it dies away after its climax, the chromatic accompaniment leads to a final pianissimo chant of "Christe eleison".

2. *Dies Irae*

This is the longest movement, consisting of several sections linked together by key relationships as well as by references to the movement's opening theme. The orchestra begins its tumultuously Michelangelesque picture of the day of wrath with four shattering G minor chords and a wildly swirling theme which ushers in the chorus's lurching and terrified cry. Brass, woodwind, and violent off-beat thumps on the bass-drum are added to the rushing and trembling of the strings to create a magnificent sound picture of the Last Judgment. As chorus and orchestra subside into a frightened hush, four trumpets in the orchestra, and another four which Verdi wishes to be distant and invisible, call to one another across, as it seems, the waste land of the world. The idea may have been suggested by the example of Berlioz in his *Messe des Morts*, but Verdi executed it with rather more economic artistry. The trumpet calls rise to a climax in which they are joined by the rest of the orchestra and by the chorus basses in "Tuba mirum". The volume of sound breaks off suddenly, and the solo bass enters pianissimo with "Mors stupebit", accompanied by a repeated march figure in the strings and by a beat in each bar from the bass-drum.

The mezzo's "Liber scriptus" is a passionate solo, eloquently scored, and occasionally punctuated by the chorus's very quiet whisper of "Dies irae". Towards the end of the mezzo solo, the orchestra too begins to threaten with references to the "Dies Irae", and the fierce outburst of the beginning of the movement returns, only to retreat into the middle distance, and then to fade as the mezzo begins the trio, "Quid sum miser tunc dicturus", in which she is joined by soprano and tenor and a plaintive solo bassoon. This delicate trio leads into "Rex tremendae majestatis", which, begun majestically by the chorus basses, quickly moves into the great soaring prayer of "Salva me, fons pietatis", for soloists and chorus. Suffering humanity moved Verdi more than the tremendous majesty of the tribal god. The pleading vocal line is deeply moving, and nowhere more so than in its final mezzoforte utterance [Ex. 113].

Ex. 113

A gentle duet, "Recordare, Jesu pie", for soprano and mezzo, is followed by the tenor's lyrical solo, "Ingemisco tanquam reus". The section beginning "Inter oves", when a solo oboe alternates a peacefully beautiful phrase with the tenor, against divided violins, reaches its climax with the tenor aspiring to be separated from the goats and placed at the right hand of God, on a proud cry rising to a sustained B flat [Ex. 114].

Ex. 114

The bass solo, "Confutatis maledictis", one of the noblest tunes Verdi provided for the bass voice, has barely time to reach its final cadence before the "Dies Irae" returns in all the fury of its complete recapitulation. The movement ends with "Lacrymosa dies illa", a tune similar in feeling to the "Recordare". It is sung first by the solo mezzo, then by the other soloists and the chorus, who add Verdi's tearful figure of rising semitones. The mournful atmosphere is lifted at the very end by the G major "Amen", which falls on the ear like a blessing.

3. Offertorio

This movement for the four soloists and orchestra opens with a warm, lyrical theme first stated by cellos and then developed by the voices. At "Quam olim Abrahae", the style becomes more vigorous, but gives way to the hushed beauty of the tenor's "Hostias" [see Ex. 132], to which the other voices later contribute. This sublime melody is virtually contained within the compass of a major third. A reprise of "Quam olim Abrahae" is followed by a vocal unison restatement of the movement's opening cello theme. In a brief orchestral coda the theme is heard four times, twice played by strings but differently harmonised each time, then by solo clarinet against tremolando strings, and finally by cellos and double basses.

4. Sanctus

Trumpet fanfares introduce this short double fugue, whose choral writing is light and animated, and whose orchestration is quite brilliant.

5. Agnus Dei

A peaceful andante tune in C major is sung by the soprano and mezzo in unaccompanied octaves, and repeated by the chorus. The soloists repeat the tune in C minor, and are answered by the chorus in the major with the last six bars of the tune. The third statement of the tune, by soloists and later by chorus, has the addition of a flowing counterpoint by three flutes.

6. Lux aeterna

Only the three lower soloists are heard in this movement. Verdi allows the soprano a rest in preparation for the "Libera me". The light colours of the mezzo's opening quasi-recitative are answered by the dark chords of the low woodwind underlying the solo bass's "Requiem aeternam". The struggle between "lux" and "requiem" is resolved in a radiantly scored lyrical theme which emerges and which continues to the end of the movement.

7. Libera me

Though this movement utilises material from the "Libera me" which Verdi had already written for the abortive collaborative Mass for

Rossini, the movement is largely re-written. It is not to be thought, for instance, that the "Requiem aeternam" and "Dies Irae" themes, which are reprised in this "Libera me" were written before Manzoni's death and merely taken over by Verdi when composing the earlier movements of the Manzoni Requiem. According to Dyneley Hussey, the only sections of the "Rossini" "Libera me" remaining in the Manzoni Requiem are the introductory recitative and the final fugue. His argument in support of this contention seems to me to be con- clusive.[1]

The movement opens with the soprano's urgent recitative, and the frightened murmuring of the chorus. The soprano's agitated "Tremens factus" is followed suddenly by a full restatement of the beginning of the "Dies irae". The consoling phrases of the opening "Requiem" now return, unaccompanied, for solo soprano and chorus. The soprano rises to a B flat hopefully marked *pppp*. It should, in performance, be the most beautiful moment in the entire score [Ex. 115]. It is also the last

Ex. 115

moment of repose, for the soprano begins the final section with an even more urgent repeat of her "Libera me" and the chorus bursts into a dramatic fugue, above which the soprano's solo line soars. After the climax, soloist and chorus are left repeating their prayer in a frightened whisper. The music ends, poised over the void.

If this is music more suitable for the theatre than the church, then so much the worse for the church. But that particular criticism was never worth answering. If parts of Verdi's Requiem sound theatrical, so, and enjoyably so, does much of the church music of the presumably devout Mozart. Verdi brought his dramatist's art to the Requiem. He had many times in his operas written death scenes, and music in which death is contemplated by one or more of the characters. In the Requiem, he was free to reveal something of his own attitude to death; and, predictably, gentle resignation and joyful anticipation of an after-life were no part of his thoughts. Verdi's Requiem is a Mass not for the dead but for the living. The intensity and the compassion of his tragic view of the human condition are Shakespearian in stature: the prodi- gality of his technique deserves, as I have said elsewhere, to be called Mozartian.

[1] Hussey, Chapter XIV.

XXVI

Otello

Dramatis personae:

Otello, a Moor, General in the Venetian army	(tenor)
Iago, his Ensign	(baritone)
Cassio, Otello's Lieutenant	(tenor)
Roderigo, a Venetian gentleman	(tenor)
Lodovico, Ambassador of the Venetian Republic	(bass)
Montano, Otello's predecessor in Cyprus	(bass)
A Herald	(bass)
Desdemona, Otello's wife	(soprano)
Emilia, Iago's wife	(mezzo-soprano)

LIBRETTO, based on Shakespeare's play *Othello*, by Arrigo Boito

TIME: The end of the fifteenth century
PLACE: Cyprus

FIRST PERFORMED at La Scala, Milan, February 5, 1887, with Romilda Pantaleoni (Desdemona); Ginevra Petrovich (Emilia); Francesco Tamagno (Otello); Victor Maurel (Iago); Francesco Navarrini (Montano); Giovanni Paroli (Cassio)

Otello

I

THE QUESTION WHETHER Verdi and Teresa Stolz, his Milan Aida and soprano soloist in the Requiem, were lovers, has long been a problem for Verdi's biographers. The evidence pro and contra is best assembled in Frank Walker's *The Man Verdi*. Walker plays fair with the known facts, which, on the whole, suggest there was a romantic attachment, though he is reluctant so to interpret them. Whatever the truth of the matter, Stolz, a close friend of the Verdis, spent a great deal of time at Sant' Agata as their guest.

Verdi, in these post-*Aida* years, occasionally travelled, to produce *Aida* in Paris, for instance, or to conduct the Requiem in Cologne. At one time, he quarrelled bitterly with Tito Ricordi, when he discovered that, for a quarter of a century, the firm appeared to have been falsifying the accounts and cheating him out of royalties. He agreed to accept 50,000 lire in compensation, though it was considerably less than the sum involved.

Verdi had no plans for writing another opera, and, when the Countess Maffei tried to shame him into composing, he replied that it was all over, the account was settled. And, for four or five years, it seemed likely that the account would never be reopened. But in 1879, when Verdi and Giuseppina were in Milan where Verdi was to conduct a performance of the Requiem in aid of the victims of the Po Valley floods, they invited Giulio Ricordi and the conductor Franco Faccio to dinner at the Grand Hotel, where they always stayed in Milan. The talk after dinner was about possible operatic subjects, and was brought round to Shakespeare and, in particular, *Othello*. Ricordi said later that, when he first mentioned *Othello*, Verdi's eyes fixed on him with interested suspicion. Ricordi was keen for Verdi to collaborate with Arrigo Boito on an opera. Boito had already provided the libretto for Faccio's Shakespeare opera, *Amleto*, and was eager to work with Verdi. Verdi reluctantly agreed to meet Boito, and Faccio brought him round to the hotel the next day.

Boito (1842–1918) was then in his late thirties. He was well-known as poet, critic, librettist and composer, though his fame as a composer rested on one opera, *Mefistofele* which, a failure when it was first produced in 1868, had been revived with great success in 1875. At the age of twenty-one he had written a poem which referred offensively to Verdi. Called "All' Arte italiana" (To Italian Art), it contained the lines

> Forse già nacque chi sovra l'altare
> Rizzerà l'arte, verecondo e puro,
> Su quel' altar bruttato come un muro
> Di lupanare.

(Perhaps the man is already born who, modest and pure, will restore art to its altar stained like a brothel wall.)[1]

With maturity, wisdom had come to Boito, and he was now one of Verdi's most enthusiastic admirers. Three days after their meeting in Milan, he gave Verdi his scenario for an opera to be based on *Othello*, and Verdi, without committing himself to the project, encouraged him to write a complete libretto. Boito enthusiastically set to work, and Verdi returned to Sant' Agata. Reading the Ricordi magazine, the *Gazzetta Musicale di Milano*, one day, he chanced upon an extract from the memoirs of a sculptor, Giovanni Dupré, who quoted a remark of Rossini's to the effect that Verdi, a composer of dark and tragic calibre, would never be able to write a lighter work like Donizetti's *Linda di Chamounix*, much less an opera buffa like *L'elisir d'amore*. Verdi immediately wrote to Giulio Ricordi:

> I have read in your paper Dupré's words on our meeting, and the sentence pronounced by Jupiter Rossini as Meyerbeer called him. But just a moment: for the last twenty years I've been looking for an opera buffa libretto, and now that I may have found it you print an article that will encourage the public to damn the work before it is even written, thus prejudicing my interests and yours. But have no fear! If by chance, misfortune or destiny, despite the Great Sentence, my evil genius drives me to write this opera buffa, I repeat you need have no fear. I'll ruin some other publisher.[2]

Ricordi was both perturbed and puzzled: perturbed at the thought of losing Verdi to another publisher, and puzzled by his reference to a comic opera when he was supposed to have no operatic project in mind other than, perhaps, *Othello*. The opera buffa idea may have been Molière's *Tartuffe*, one of the subjects Camille Du Locle and Verdi had discussed immediately prior to *Aida*. Verdi had kept a manuscript scenario, in French, which Du Locle had sent him. But nothing more came of it. Ricordi poured all the oil he possessed on the troubled waters of Verdi's paranoia, and suggested that he "and a friend" visit Sant' Agata. The composer's reply was cautious:

[1] The inference was that the music of Verdi was the stain on the altar.
[2] *Copialettere*, pp. 308–9.

A visit from you with a friend, who would of course be Boito, will always be a pleasure. But on this subject let me speak very clearly and frankly. A visit from him would commit me too definitely, and I wish absolutely to avoid committing myself. You know how this "chocolate idea" came into being. You and a few other friends dined with me. We spoke about *Othello*, about Shakespeare and about Boito. The next day, Faccio brought Boito to visit me at the hotel, and three days later Boito brought me his *Otello* scenario which I read and liked. "Write the libretto," I told him. "It will come in handy for yourself, for me, or for someone else." If you come here now with Boito, I shall have to read the finished libretto he will bring with him. If I find it completely satisfactory, then I am somewhat committed to it. If I like it, but suggest modifications which he accepts, then I'm even more committed. If, however good it is, I don't like it, it would be difficult to say so to his face. No, no, you have gone too far, and must stop before there is any gossip or unpleasantness.[1]

Verdi had, in fact, begun to compose again. In the autumn he completed a *Pater Noster* and an *Ave Maria* to texts from Dante (see p. 462), for performance in the following year, 1880, by the new Milan Orchestral Society, whose presidency he had refused to accept. Early in 1880, he went to Paris to supervise the production of *Aida* in French. By this time he had received Boito's libretto and liked it, but kept postponing a decision about the opera. Ricordi became anxious, but Giuseppina advised caution in dealing with Verdi. "Let us allow the stream to find its own way down to the sea," she wrote.[2] To another friend she confided that Verdi had put Boito's libretto "beside Somma's *Re Lear*, which has slept profoundly and without disturbance for thirty years in its portfolio."[3]

Ricordi deviously attempted another scheme to bring Verdi and Boito together. He suggested revising *Simon Boccanegra*, which had hardly ever been performed since its première in 1857. Verdi was interested, and Boito reasonably willing to patch up Piave's libretto, so they set to work, and within six months had produced the revision, which was performed at La Scala on March 24, 1881 (see pp. 296–8). By this time, the two men had discussed the "chocolate idea" on numerous occasions, and gradually it came to be assumed that they were in active collaboration on *Otello*. But Verdi had not set pen to music paper for three years. During that time, he and Boito had continued to correspond. Verdi treated his new librettist with somewhat more respect than his earlier collaborators were wont to receive, but he was, to say the least, an active participant in the creation of the *Otello* libretto, as this letter to Boito in August 1881 clearly reveals:

I am in Milan, and your two letters were sent on to me here from Busseto. The finale is very well done indeed. What a difference between this one and the first!

[1] *Copialettre*, p. 311.   [2] Abbiati, Vol. IV, p. 113.   [3] Walker, p. 476.

I shall add the four lines for Roderigo. Perhaps the other four for Desdemona will not be needed.

It's so true that a silent Otello is grander and more terrible that my opinion would be not to have him speak at all during the whole ensemble. It seems to me that Iago alone can say, and more briefly, everything that must be said for the spectator's understanding, without Otello replying. Iago: Hurry! Time is flying! Concentrate on your task, and on that alone. I'll see to Cassio. I'll pluck out his infamous, guilty soul. I swear it. You shall have news of him at midnight. (Altering the verses, of course.)

After the ensemble, and after the words, "Tutti fuggite Otello", it seems to me that Otello does not speak or cry out enough. He is silent for four lines, and it seems to me that (scenically speaking), after "Che d'ogni senso il priva", Otello ought to bellow one or two lines: "Away! I detest you, myself, the whole world!"

And it seems to me too that a few lines could be spared when Otello and Iago remain together:

Otello: Only I cannot flee from myself. Ah, the serpent.
Iago: Signor!
Otello: To see them together, embracing. Accursed thought. Blood, blood.
    The handkerchief. (He cries, and faints.)
Iago: My poison is working.
Offstage cries: Long live the hero of Cyprus!
Iago: Who can stop me from stamping my heel on that brow?
Offstage cries: Glory to the Lion of Venice!
Iago: Here is the Lion!

A strangled cry on the word "fazzoletto" seems to me more terrible than a commonplace exclamation like "O Satana". The words "svenuto", "immobil" and "muto" somewhat hold up the action. One stops to think, and here it's a case of hurrying on to the end. Let me have your opinion.

I haven't finished. The chorus has little or nothing to do. Could one not find a way of moving it about a bit? For example, after the words, "In Cyprus my successor is to be—Cassio!" Chorus, with four lines not of revolt but of protest: "No, no, we want Otello!"

I know perfectly well that you will reply at once: "Dear Signor Maestro, don't you know that nobody dared to breathe after a decree of the Serenissima, and that sometimes the mere presence of the Messer Grande sufficed to disperse the crowd and subdue the tumult?"

I would dare to rejoin that the action takes place in Cyprus, the Serenissima were far away, and perhaps for that reason the Cypriots were bolder than the Venetians.

If you come to Milan, I hope to see you. I'm not sure, but I think you have all the poetry of the third act.[1]

In 1883 Wagner, Verdi's senior by a few months, died in Venice, and a scrawled note to Ricordi shows how deeply affected Verdi was.

[1] Quoted in Walker, pp. 486-7.

Later that year, he revised and shortened *Don Carlo* (see p. 352) for its production in Vienna. When this production was cancelled, the revised version was produced at La Scala in January 1884. In March, the seventy-year-old Verdi at last began to compose *Otello*. The project almost came to grief when Verdi read a newspaper article in which Boito was quoted as having said that he regretted not being able himself to set *Otello* to music. Verdi, oversensitive and easily depressed, immediately wrote to Boito's friend, the conductor Faccio:

> The worst of it is that by regretting he cannot set it to music himself, Boito creates the impression that he does not expect me to be able to set it in the way he would like. I admit this possibility, and so I ask you, as Boito's oldest and best friend, to tell him when he returns to Milan, not in writing but by word of mouth, that I am ready, without any resentment, to give the manuscript back to him.[1]

Boito had, apparently, been misreported, and hastened to reassure Verdi that he wanted only to collaborate with him: "This theme and my libretto are yours by right of conquest. You alone can set *Otello* to music. All the dramatic creations you have given us proclaim this truth."[2]

Mollified, Verdi resumed work on the opera. He wrote spasmodically, short bouts of intense creativity alternating with periods of neurotic inactivity. By early October of the following year, 1885, he had finished composing, and was ready to begin scoring and revising. This took, on and off, another year. It was December 1886 before he was able to write to Boito that he had just sent off to the firm of Ricordi the last pages of *Otello*. For years, rumours and gossip about Verdi's forthcoming *Iago*, as the newspapers had called it, had been circulating. The French baritone Victor Maurel, on the strength of a remark made to him by Verdi during the rehearsals of the revised *Simon Boccanegra*, had repeatedly announced that the composer was writing Iago for him. As it turned out, Verdi still had him in mind, and he sang Iago at the Scala première, which took place on February 5, 1887, in an atmosphere of excited public anticipation that had been building up for weeks. After all, it was the first new Verdi opera in fifteen years. Verdi and Giuseppina had come to Milan early in January; the coaching of the singers and the first orchestral rehearsals had been directed by Verdi, but the actual performances were conducted by Faccio.

Blanche Roosevelt, an American singer who was in Milan at the time, published in the same year a book on Verdi[3] from which, since

---

[1] *Copialettere*, p. 324.   [2] Nardi, p. 494.
[3] *Verdi: Milan and Otello* (London 1887). The second part of the book is written in the form of letters to the novelist Wilkie Collins, to whom it is dedicated.

it has been unobtainable for many years, I reproduce part of her lively account of the excitement surrounding the first performance of *Otello*.

Otellopolis, February 5th, 1887:

At last, at last the great day has come and gone, and Verdi has added the crown jewel to his diadem of triumphs. I cannot tell you the anxiety felt in the city before nightfall. As early as five a.m. every one was astir, and when Gianetta brought my tea she informed me that she had already been to La Scala: the posters were unchanged, the opera would surely come off, unless—you may imagine I sent her about her business with her "unlesses" —unless the tenor, or the soprano, or the wig-maker, or the some particular hinge of the cast, she explained, "did not 'run ill' before seven p.m." Speaking of wig-makers, she also reminds me that any number of ladies in the hotel were having their hair dressed even at that unearthly hour—not me—eight "and may it please you", making preparations exactly as if the occasion were a State ball or a Royal wedding. These ladies will sit all day with bejewelled and elaborately-dressed pates, and not dare to lie down, or sit back, or lean over, for fear of ruining their puffs, &c.

You may imagine the excitement was not lost on me. I hastily dressed, and before noon was in the streets. Streets? There were no streets—at least, no crossings—visible, and had the blocks of houses not divided the town architecturally, everything would have been run together, like honey, with human beings, human beings, human beings! I never knew how the day passed. Vergil ran up against the La Scala doctor, and actually turned pale as the M.D. went to speak to him. "Don't tell me!" Vergil cried. "All right," laughed Doctor L.; "he is not quite well, but will sing, of course." The "he" meant, naturally, the tenor. I met Madame M. leaning over the piazza. "And to think of it!" she cried; "it is four o'clock. Iago's wig was brought home, and fits so badly that not even *glue* will stick it on to his head. He simply won't sing if—" "Don't," I cried; "I will give him my hair, every inch of it, and sew it on to a pate myself, rather than that." Just then the wigmaker came round a corner. Madame M. gave him one look; I slipped into the Galleria, and was busy staring at photographs. Poor wretch! that look reminded me of legends of Sioux scalping their victims, and the fitful dripping tress that decorates the successful warrior's belt, flashed before my eyes. "The end of this day will be human gore," I muttered; then turned to look again into the square. It was alive. An hour passed; men, women, children, beggars and ballias, hand-organs pealing forth Verdi tunes, Ernani, "Fly with me," and Manrico, "Do not leave me;" pardon the vernacular. Leonardo da Vinci's statue gleamed out of the sea of faces like a white eaglet's plume drifting towards a storm-swept sea. The windows of the tall houses looking out on the quadrangle were a mass of shifting heads: balconies were freighted with excited humanity, and the Italian-terraced roofs, where people were eating and drinking and shouting, were literally black with moving forms. But the exteriors of these old stone palaces was the most curious sight. The panels were a perfect kaleidoscope of light and colour. You know the Italian women are fond of bright raiment. When they have not covered their heads with their pretty black veils, they wear veils in cream-colour studded with artificial flowers; they wear hats which would shame a hot-house for brilliancy, and their necks are hung with gewgaws: their bodices glow like an Oriental chasuble; then, too, these creatures looked so happy, laughing eyes, glittering teeth, bodies swaying to the pantomime of anticipated pleasure: all this made an impression on me I shall not soon forget; and as to the others, their spirits were so contagious that the crowd seemed charged with electricity.

The Piazza della Scala was a sight to see, and the cries of "Viva Verdi! viva Verdi!" were so deafening that I longed for cotton in my ears. Poor Verdi! had he been there, he would certainly have been torn to pieces, as a crowd in its enthusiasm rarely distinguishes between glory and assassination. You will ask what I was doing in the streets at such a time; and I will answer: I don't know; I merely obeyed the common impulse—went where the others did: the truth is, I also wanted to watch the Scala bill-board, to see that no change would be made in the announcements. We all stood staring at the old theatre, just as those idiots on the Paris boulevards on a summer night watch the magic-lantern, to read the different advertisements for enterprising firms: and this, you say, in dead of winter? O, an Italian does not feel the cold on an occasion like this. But to return. In case there had been any change of programme I need not say there would not have been found a person in all Milan courageous enough to have put up the notice. There was death in the eyes of some of those men, waiting like hungry wolves since the night before to be first to crowd into the pit and galleries. Well, at last—after dinner—I didn't dine, I swallowed food—we started to the theatre. The carriage had to be sent off long before we reached the door, the horses could not make their way through the crowd. At best, human beings one by one between a line of police could struggle towards the entrance. I expected my dress would be in rags; however, I managed to get in whole, and once there the sight was indescribable. La Scala has never before held such an audience, and although it was fully an hour before the time to commence, every seat was occupied. The light murmur of expectant voices issuing from three thousand throats, audible, but discreetly indistinct, reminded me of the sounds in an enchanted forest on a summer night. No one was too exalted or too proud on this greatest of all solemnities to jostle the contadina on the doorstep, or the fruit-vendor humming a Verdinian measure under the portico of La Scala: all were frantic to be seated before the curtain rose. Only in Italy could such a scene take place; for here pride of birth, or rank, or position gives way before the homage which a land of song sows in perennial laurel at the feet of her great composers.

From pit to dome, the immense auditorium was one mass of eager faces, sparkling eyes, brilliant toilettes, and splendid jewels. The Italian Court was a rainbow of colours, and Queen Margherita's ladies of honour like a hothouse bouquet of rarest exotics. The first and second tiers of boxes were so packed with the Milanese high-bred women, so covered with dazzling jewels and filmy laces, that the house seemed spanned with a river of light, up, up, up to where the last gallery was lost in a dainty cornice of gold. The gleam of diamond tiara and corsage bouquet shot oblong rays on the black-coated background; while the new electric lights, imprisoned in their dead-white globes, shed so unearthly a radiance over the auditorium that we all looked like spectres uprising from some fantastic dead-and-gone rout. As to the platea or "stalls," it was simply marvellous. I know of no city in the world which could present a spectacle of similar brilliancy. In the first place, it was packed with officers—certainly the handsomest men in the world—gorgeous in the varied and brilliant Italian uniform: staff-officers in full dress, and scarred veterans with their whole record in speaking breast-decorations; and the women—such pretty women as one could see only in Italy; for the Italians are a decorative race when seen in Italy, and picturesque, my dear friend, is the only word possible to describe them. The men look well anywhere; the women may not shine on the Corso, but at the play they will put women of every other nation in the shade. They are a special embellishment, a part of the gorgeousness, the glitter, the performance. They know just how to dress, and just what jewels to wear; how to sit, how to stand, how to listen at the right moment, and to look bored at the right moment; in short, their princely boxes are packed with such a baggage of perfections that the universal playgoing world most unanimously acknowledge their rightful supremacy.

"And the other portions of the house?" you say. That is a just question; for La Scala is not alone in its nobility, its platea and boxes. Besides the celebrities here and there, the romancer who has left his pen, the painter his brush, or the sculptor his chisel, La Scala's real public is in the upper tiers, in pit, or lobbione. Besides the throng of strangers, there were present all the old theatre-goers who never miss a first-night, and those who go but on such occasions were there in full force, conspicuous in their habitual places. They never need programmes, they know the names of every living and working artist; they have heard all the great singers since Catalani and Pasta; have seen all the dancers since Taglioni, father and daughter. They have supped with Bellini after success and failure; and they have seen Verdi[1] on the one occasion when he was at his conductor's place in the orchestra. They know La Scala and everything pertaining to it by heart; nine cases out of ten, they are better musicians than those in the band, better artists than those on the stage. They come to sit in judgment: to applaud or hiss, as they honestly feel; to lend their presence to the event of what is to them the entire world: the annual opening of a new opera, or a first-night at their renowned opera-house; in short, they are a part of it. They have not dined, perhaps not even breakfasted, and their pockets are filled with chestnuts: grave, anxious, preoccupied, they are at the theatre-doors hours before the opening of the doors, waiting their chance to rush pell-mell into the roof-gallery, called the lobbione. There are many amongst them who have not tasted food for a week: the body may be starved, but never the soul. They consider no sacrifice too great to enable them to figure at a first-night at La Scala: no king is prouder than this old and faithful person. Can you not recognise him? No detail of toilette is neglected: hair is pomaded; moustache waxed; linen spotless;

---

[1] Second performance of Verdi's *Requiem Mass* at La Scala, 1874.

cravat tied in perfect knot; habit guiltless of dust; a flower in the button-hole, a rose or garofano; gloves of a sickly white, from having seen the cleaner's too often. Can you not remember him as, opera-glass in hand, his eye roams over the sea of faces, calculating which tier is to have the honour of his first glance? Last night this ancient man stood in his place until he had seen each member of the orchestra come in; then he sat down, unfolded a silk handkerchief, spread it on his knees, and with a friendly wave of his hand saluted his brother fossils right and left, as much as to say:

"You see me; here I am. Do you think *Othello* could go on were I not present?"

When I saw him I knew that the opera was about to begin. The habitué wore the same eager look he has assumed twice or thrice a year for half a century of Carnivals; he has forgotten the hours of waiting at the street-door, the scrimpy dinner, the meagre lunch of polenta, and the long, uneventful year. He is a part of the whole, and believes he is responsible for this night's failure or success.

I saw the ancient man stir, saw the glass move and the handkerchief flutter; saw him reseat and settle himself more comfortably; then I said to myself, "Ah, the opera is about to begin: now for *Othello*."

It is generally supposed that on a first-night Verdi conducts his operas, but the idea is an erroneous one. With very few exceptions, for forty years or more he has not taken his place in the orchestra-leader's chair. On this occasion he would have been too nervous to have attempted such a thing. The present incumbent of the leader's place at La Scala is Franco Faccio, an admirable musician and composer, one who knows his band as a flautist knows his stops, and who for years has directed Verdi's operas under the maestro's own eye and dictation. Faccio's appearance in the conductor's chair, which he has filled so long and so well, was a signal for thunders of applause. The orchestra at once struck up a few glorious chords representing a tempest, which were followed by an instantaneous rise of the curtain.

.   .   .

The scenery, costumes, choruses, and orchestra were nearly perfect; the cast was certainly weak. Victor Maurel is the only real artist in the opera, and he is a Frenchman. In voice, acting, appearance, and dress he is the ideal of what an operatic artist should be, and the ideal of what any operatic Iago could be. He sang as even his best friends never dreamed he could sing, and his acting was the consummate work which we always have at his artistic hands. He entered at once into the fullest sympathies of the audience, and I could not help then and there contrasting the Iagos we have seen in other countries with the Iagos we always see in Italy. Iago even seems a *persona grata* to the public; the qualities which raise a thrill of horror in the righteous Anglo-Saxon are received by this susceptible nation with placid contentment and relief. His vileness, ruses, and perfidy are accepted for their art, not their nature; his ingenious devices arouse heart-felt plaudits, and let me add that never will you hear a gallery god in Italy express any disapprobation with a successful knave. Had Iago not suc-ceeded there is every reason to believe that *Othello* would be left out of the

Italian Shakespearean repertory. On noting his more than prominence in this opera, rendered doubly so by Maurel's sublime creation, I could well understand Boito's and Verdi's inclination to call their work *Iago*, and not *Othello*. Iago is essentially Italian, not in the sense of vice, but of artistic villainy: he reasons from the personal standpoint, and his reasons find a universal echo in the land which gave birth to such a student of human nature as Macchiavelli. Othello, you will see, is an inferior creature, and plays an inferior part.

Maurel will be well remembered as one of the most gifted artists we have ever seen at Covent Garden. His Iago ranks with Nilsson's Ophelia—to my mind the finest lyric creation on the operatic stage. His elegance, grace, subtlety, and exquisite style in Iago find their most perfect expression. I need not refer to his appearance, the beau-ideal of a handsome Venetian, whose years are but "four times seven," and whose graces in this artist's hands are the climax of elegance and histrionic art. But you will see him in London, and I am sure will allow that you have never witnessed or heard anything to equal his impersonation of this part. Tamagno, the tenor, looked and acted Othello, but he did not sing—he bleated. Desdemona has never been a favourite of mine in history, and the present exponent of the role suggested to me all my thousand unavenged wrongs laid at the door of Brabantio's daughter. Madame Pantaleone is an excellent person, but as Desdemona she ought to have been suppressed the night before at her dress rehearsal. Her voice is naturally fine and dramatic, but she has no more knowledge of the pure art of singing than I have of the real science of astronomy. She has a vile emission of tone in the medium open notes; the upper notes are clear, but rarely in tune. The lovely music assigned to Othello's wife must have splendid resisting powers not to have fallen flat in her hands or throat. In appearance Madame Pantaleone is likewise unfortunate: she is short, slightly cross-eyed, and of a physical plainness, which dwarfed the already insignificant Desdemona. She acted very well in the first and third acts, but not so well in the last. Of the other singers, I will add that Petrovitch as Emilia was deservedly hooted; V. Fornari as Roderigo was not important to help or hinder the work; and M. Paroli as Cassio was a really fair second tenor; he, at least, knows how to sing, but Nature evidently never intended him to sing at La Scala.

The ovations to Verdi and Boito reached the climax of enthusiasm. Verdi was presented with a silver album filled with the autographs and cards of every citizen in Milan. He was called out twenty times, and at the last recalls hats and handkerchiefs were waved, and the house rose in a body. The emotion was something indescribable, and many wept. Verdi's carriage was dragged by citizens to the hotel. He was toasted and serenaded; and at five in the morning I had not closed my eyes in sleep for the crowds still singing and shrieking "Viva Verdi! viva Verdi!" Who shall say that this cry will not reëcho all over the world? At seventy-four this second conqueror may well exclaim: *Veni, vidi, vici, Verdi!*

II

It cannot have been an easy task to transform Shakespeare's *Othello* into an opera libretto, but Boito has managed it brilliantly. He stripped the play to its essentials, perhaps even to less than its essentials, knowing that Verdi's music would add another dimension. His adaptation is not only skilful but also remarkably uncluttered. It is also, formally, more attractive than Shakespeare's original, not least because its structure in four uninterrupted acts is more compact than Shakespeare's rambling five-act division into fifteen scenes. Boito dispenses with Shakespeare's Act I, thus allowing his four Acts all to take place on Cyprus. The Venetian Senate is no great loss; more regrettable, perhaps, is the jettisoning of the confrontation of Brabantio and Othello, and Brabantio's parting thrust,

> Look to her, Moor, if thou hast eyes to see:
> She has deceived her father, and may thee!

But Boito has taken what he needs from Shakespeare's Act I: some dialogue for Iago and Roderigo and, most memorably, Othello's lines,

> She lov'd me for the dangers I had pass'd,
> And I lov'd her that she did pity them.

which are worked into the love duet at the end of Verdi's Act I, when Otello addresses them directly to Desdemona, and she echoes them: "E tu m'amavi per le mie sventure, ed io t'amavo per la tua pietà" (And you loved me for my misfortunes, and I loved you for your pity). The "Esultate" which so vigorously and immediately establishes Otello's character as a warrior has no counterpart in Shakespeare. It was, in fact, Verdi's idea. At the end of the act, Boito wanted Iago on stage, watching the love scene and commenting cynically to himself on it. Again it was the composer who insisted that he needed a pure love duet before showing Iago's poison working upon the relationship.

The four acts of the opera follow one another with the relentless dramatic thrust which one of Verdi's earliest librettists, Piave, had achieved in *Rigoletto* and *La traviata*, but which had eluded him in *Macbeth*. To adapt the shape of an Elizabethan drama to that of a nineteenth-century libretto required knowledge, sensitivity and daring, qualities which Boito appears to have possessed in abundance. His verse is elegant, though he can lapse into bombast when he departs from Shakespeare's thought and language. He was, for Verdi, the ideal Shakespeare librettist, and by the same token he was fortunate that in his two important collaborations with Verdi, he had Shakespeare behind him. Boito's libretto for Ponchielli's *La Gioconda*, for instance, is, to put it mildly, not noticeably superior to the work of Solera and Piave.

The greater part of Shakespeare's Act III is contained in Boito's Act II, though Shakespeare's Othello-Desdemona scene of Act III,

Scene 4, in which Othello asks her to produce the handkerchief he had given her, finds its way quite naturally into Boito's Act III. Bianca, hardly more necessary to Shakespeare than to Boito, is dispensed with, and the roles of Cassio and Roderigo are severely, but by no means disastrously, curtailed.

Boito's method of rendering Shakespeare into singable Italian verse can be seen at its most successful in Otello's Act III monologue, "Dio, mi potevi scagliar", which is based on Othello's speech

> Had it pleas'd Heaven
> To try me with affliction; had they rain'd
> All kinds of sores and shames on my bare head;
> Steeped me in poverty to the very lips;
> Given to captivity me and my utmost hopes;
> I should have found in some place of my soul
> A drop of patience: but, alas! to make me
> The fixed figure for the time of scorn
> To point his slow and moving finger at,
> Yet could I bear that too; well, very well:
> But there, where I have garner'd up my heart,
> Where either I must live, or bear no life,
> The fountain from the which my current runs,
> Or else dries up; to be discarded thence,
> Or keep it as a cistern for foul toads
> To knot and gender in! Turn thy complexion there,
> Patience, thou young and rose-lipp'd cherubin;
> Ay, there, look grim as hell!

A comparison of this with Boito's Italian reveals that, though he has neither translated the whole of the speech nor given a line-for-line faithful rendering of those passages he has chosen to parallel, his verse acts as a neutral preserver of Shakespeare's meaning, an objective defender of the poet's faith. Here is Boito, followed by a literal prose translation of his Italian verse:

> Dio! mi potevi scagliar tutti i mali
> Della miseria, della vergogna,
> Far de' miei baldi trofei trionfali
> Una maceria, una menzogna.
> E avrei portato la croce crudel
> D'angoscie e d'onte
> Con calma fronte
> E rassegnato al volere del ciel.
> Ma, o pianto, o duol! m'han rapito il miraggio
> Dov'io, giulivo, l'anima acqueto.
> Spento è quel sol, quel sorriso, quel raggio

Che mi fa vivo, che mi fa lieto!
Tu alfin, Clemenza, pio genio immortal
Dal roseo riso,
Copri il tuo viso
Santo coll' orrida larva infernal!

(God! You could have hurled at me all the evils of misery, of shame.
Made a ruin and a lie of my proud triumphal trophies. And I would
have carried the cruel cross of anguish and shame with a calm brow.
But, o tears, o sorrow, they have stolen from me the deception from
which, rejoicing, I refreshed my spirit. Gone is that sun, that smile,
that ray that made me alive, that made me happy. Finally you,
clemency, pious, immortal spirit of the rosy laughter, cover your
sacred face with the horrible, hellish apparition!)

Boito's ending to the opera, or rather Verdi's, as it was he who was
responsible for the condensation of the final scene, improves upon the
ending of Shakespeare's play by moving more quickly and clearly after
the death of Desdemona. In general, Boito has been faithful to Shakespeare's conception of the characters. He has invented, in the "Credo",
a focal point for Iago who, in Shakespeare, only partially articulates his
creed. In essentials, however, Boito's Iago is Shakespeare's embittered
nihilist. And Boito's Otello, at any rate when clothed in Verdi's violent
and passionate music, is, if anything, an even more real and moving
character than Shakespeare's.

Sixty years before Verdi's, there had been an *Otello* by Rossini. First
produced in Naples in 1816, it held the stage successfully in Italy and
abroad until superseded by the even greater success of Verdi's opera.

The entire action of the opera takes place on the island of Cyprus. The
setting of Act I is described thus in the stage directions: "The exterior
of the castle. A tavern with a pergola. At the back, ramparts and the sea.
It is evening. Thunder, lightning, wind." Cassio, Montano, Iago and
Roderigo are among the crowd of Cypriot citizens and Venetian
soldiers anxiously keeping watch for the arrival of the ship carrying
Otello. By flashes of lightning they can discern the ship battling against
the storm. Finally, it is safely harboured, and Otello disembarks.
Pausing briefly only to announce a victory over the Turkish fleet, he
enters the castle, followed by his lieutenant, Cassio, his predecessor as
Governor of Cyprus, Montano, and the soldiers. Iago and Roderigo
remain on stage. Roderigo has journeyed from Venice because he is in
love with Desdemona, Otello's wife. Iago, the General's ensign, has
promised to help him win Desdemona, and now tells Roderigo that he
hates the Moor for having promoted Cassio. When Cassio returns,
Iago, knowing he cannot hold his liquor, persuades him to drink and

then involves him in a brawl with Roderigo. Cassio draws his sword, Montano attempts to restrain him, other people intervene, and when the fighting is at its height Iago sends Roderigo off to raise a general alarm. The tolling of the alarm bells brings Otello on to the scene, and he demands to know how the quarrel arose. Iago gives a disingenuous account which implies that Cassio is to blame. Aroused by the noise, Desdemona enters. Otello angrily tells Cassio he is no longer his lieutenant. The crowd disperses, and Otello and Desdemona sing a love duet (whose verbal content Boito has assembled from Acts I and II of Shakespeare's *Othello*). They embrace, and enter the castle as the curtain falls.

Act II takes place in a hall on the ground floor of the castle, separated from the garden by a glass-panelled door. Cassio and Iago have been conversing, and Iago assures Cassio that he will soon be restored to his rightful place in Otello's affections. He advises Cassio to ask Desdemona to intercede for him, and tells him he is sure to find her now strolling in the garden with her companion, Iago's wife Emilia. Cassio leaves, and Iago gives voice to his Credo. He believes, he says, in a cruel and vengeful God who has made man in his own image. He believes in his own gratuitous evil. Death is nothingness, and heaven an absurd lie. He looks out into the garden, and sees Cassio greet and talk with Desdemona. Hearing Otello approach, he mutters as though to himself, "That distresses me". He refuses to explain himself, and, when Otello casually asks if that was not Cassio he glimpsed with Desdemona, cunningly replies, "Cassio? Surely not. That man started guiltily when he saw you."

With apparent reluctance, Iago continues to dwell on the subject of Cassio, hinting at an illicit relationship between him and Desdemona. When he sees that Otello is beginning to be disturbed, he warns him to beware of jealousy but to keep a careful watch on his wife. At this moment, Desdemona reappears in the garden, surrounded by women and children, and, according to the libretto, Cypriot and Albanian sailors, who serenade her and present her with flowers. Dismissing her serenaders, Desdemona enters the hall with Emilia. Innocently, but in the circumstances unfortunately, she intercedes with Otello for Cassio. Otello claims to have a headache but, when Desdemona produces a handkerchief to soothe his brow, he throws it on the floor. Emilia picks it up, but Iago surreptitiously seizes it from her: it was a precious gift, given to Desdemona by Otello when they first met, and Iago is certain he can make use of it. Otello dismisses Desdemona and, when she and Emilia have gone, Iago airily advises his master to think no more about what they have been discussing. The miserable Otello turns on him, crying that Iago has already robbed him of his happiness by planting suspicion in his mind. (His outburst, "Ora e per sempre addio, sante memorie", closely follows Shakespeare's

O now for ever,
Farewell the tranquil mind! Farewell content!
Farewell the plumed troops and the big wars
That make ambition virtue! O farewell!
Farewell the neighing steed, trump,
The spirit-stirring drum, the ear-piercing fife,
The royal banner, and all quality,
Pride, pomp, and circumstance of glorious war!)

He demands that Iago produce proof of Desdemona's infidelity, and Iago tells him that one night, sleeping beside Cassio, he overheard him talking in his sleep of Desdemona as though they were lovers. ("Last night I lay with Cassio . . .") But this, he says, was only a dream. He can produce real evidence. Does Otello not remember a certain embroidered handkerchief he once gave Desdemona? Otello can certainly remember it. "È il fazzoletto ch'io le diedi, pegno primo d'amor" (It is the handkerchief I gave her as my first token of love) is the simple and moving reply. Iago assures him he has recently seen this handkerchief in Cassio's possession. Otello is roused to a fury of jealous passion and, kneeling, swears he will be avenged. Iago kneels with him and consecrates himself to Otello's cause.

Act III takes place in the great reception hall of the castle. On the right is a colonnade, beyond which is a smaller room. A balcony runs along the back of the hall. Otello and Iago are talking together when a Herald enters to announce that the galley bringing the Venetian Ambassador has just been sighted. Otello acknowledges this information, and continues his discussion with Iago, who is about to bring Cassio into the hall and encourage him to talk about Desdemona. He advises Otello to conceal himself and observe them. As he goes, Desdemona enters and again tries to persuade Otello to reinstate Cassio in his favour. Claiming to have one of his headaches, Otello asks for the handkerchief he gave Desdemona, and becomes violent when she is unable to produce it. He accuses her of adultery and thrusts her from the room. Alone, he soliloquises on his misery and uncertainty. He retreats as Cassio and Iago enter, and Iago persuades Cassio to engage in ribald talk about his whore Bianca (whose name Iago utters in a whisper, so that Otello shall not hear it). Otello overhears the gist of the loose conversation, believing it to refer to Desdemona. Iago had planted the embroidered handkerchief in Cassio's room, and Cassio now produces it at his instigation. Iago waves it about, making sure that Otello shall recognise it. When a cannon shot announces the arrival of the ship from Venice, Cassio leaves. The distraught Otello re-enters, determined to kill Desdemona, and asks Iago to procure a poison. Iago advises him instead to smother her "there in her bed, there, where she has sinned".

The Venetian dignitaries, Desdemona and Emilia, other ladies and gentlemen and soldiers enter ceremonially. Lodovico, the Venetian

Ambassador, hands Otello a message from the Doge. While he reads it
Otello mutters venomous asides to Desdemona, and ends by striking
her in full and horrified view of the assembled company. He announces
that the Doge has recalled him to Venice and has appointed Cassio as
his successor in Cyprus. Seizing Desdemona, he flings her to the ground.
Under cover of the ensuing ensemble, Iago busies himself. To Otello he
promises to kill Cassio. To Roderigo, who is bewailing Desdemona's
imminent departure for Venice, he suggests that, should anything
happen to Cassio, Otello and Desdemona would be forced to remain in
Cyprus. Otello suddenly dismisses the assembly and, left alone, succumbs to a fit of epilepsy. As voices outside shout, "Long live Otello!
Glory to the Lion of Venice", Iago returns and, pointing triumphantly
to Otello's prostrate form, cries "Ecco il Leone!" (There is the Lion).

The final act takes place in Desdemona's bedroom, which contains
bed, prie-dieu, table, mirror and chairs. A lighted lamp is on the
table. As Emilia helps her undress, Desdemona sadly recalls a dirge her
mother's maid Barbara used to sing, a song of unrequited love. After
saying good night to Emilia, she prays to the Virgin and then goes to
bed. A few moments later, Otello appears. Setting his scimitar down on
the table, he considers for a moment whether or not to extinguish the
lamp. (This stage direction is presumably intended to recall "Put out
the light, and then put out the light.") He kisses the sleeping Desdemona and, when she awakens, advises her to say her prayers, as he is
about to kill her. He accuses her of loving Cassio, and refuses to listen
to her plea that she is innocent. When she asks him to let Cassio speak
for himself, he informs her that Cassio is dead, and smothers her. Immediately, Emilia enters to announce that Cassio and Roderigo have
fought, and that Cassio has killed Roderigo. Desdemona calls faintly
from the bed, and dies. Emilia cries for help, and Ludovico, Cassio and
Iago enter. Otello calls on Iago to support him but, in the presence of
Emilia and Cassio, Iago's villainy is established. When Montano enters
confirming that Roderigo had incriminated Iago with his dying
breath, Iago rushes out and makes his escape. Heart-broken, Otello
draws a dagger and stabs himself, dying as he makes a last attempt to
kiss Desdemona's corpse.

III

Otello begins without preamble. The curtain rises on the opening bars
of Verdi's *allegro agitato*, the most brilliant storm music in all opera
The dynamic level varies as the wind now drops, now rises again, and
the thunder and lightning are intermittent, but the tension remains
high throughout the whole of this opening section, due in no small part
to the deep organ pedal point which is sustained for the first two
hundred and twenty-five bars. The chorus, anxiously narrating the

progress of Otello's ship, adds to the tumult. The sound is positively Beethovenian in its splendour, its aural range and its magnificent instrumentation. The whole of this storm movement is so varied in its detail that any attempt at close description would occupy a disproportionate amount of space. The thunder's nerve-racking fortissimos, the lightning's flute and piccolo arpeggios, the excited and exciting commentary of Cassio, Montano, Roderigo and Iago, the chorus's great prayer, and its relieved E major cry of "È salvo" (He's saved), all lead swiftly and inevitably to Otello's entrance and his twelve splendid bars of arioso, "Esultate!" in which, over sustained horn chords, his phrases punctuated by string arpeggios, Otello boasts of his victory over the Turks. The storm abates, and the crowd rejoices in a brilliantly light, scherzo-like chorus in which the words are merely sprinkled across the surface of the vivid orchestral writing. The brief but eloquently tuneful recitative conversation of Iago and Roderigo is followed by the chorus, "Fuoco di gioia!" at first gay, later wistful, as the crowd gathers around a fire that has been kindled. (This is not in the play, but is justified by the lines of Shakespeare's Herald: "It is Othello's pleasure, our noble and valiant general, that, upon certain tidings now arrived, importing the mere perdition of the Turkish fleet, every man put himself into triumph; some to dance, some to make bonfires, each man to what sport and revels his addiction leads him.") Verdi's orchestra is at its most colourful here. The drinking ensemble, led by Iago with his catchily insinuating "Beva con me", is an intricate yet riotous affair which effectively advances the dramatic action. The vocal writing, for the chorus as well as the principals, is remarkable, paradoxically, for both its freedom and its sheer inevitability. Iago's vocal line requires him lightly to touch the baritone's high A. The fight between Montano and Cassio, Iago's cunning spreading of the alarm, and the sudden entrance of Otello are all portrayed in music which extraordinarily contrives both to serve the drama and to excite by its own beauty and appropriateness. Otello makes his entrance to an arresting fortissimo phrase on all the strings, and the music becomes calmer, more orderly as he assumes command.

The love duet with which the act ends is one of the most beautiful imaginable. Introduced by a lyrical passage of great warmth on four cellos, it opens quietly and simply with Otello's "Già nella notte densa s'estingue ogni clamor" (In the dark night all noise now has ceased). The higher strings usher in Desdemona's opening phrases. This duet, warmly tranquil, passionately calm, is somehow like distilled Wagner: the essence without the long-windedness. Its beauties succeed one another, to reach a climax in the sensuously lovely passage shared between the orchestra and Otello [Ex. 116]. It occurs again, most movingly, at the very end of the opera. More, perhaps, than in any other work by Verdi, one finds oneself noting in *Otello* first the beauty

Ex. 116

and then the skill of the orchestration. The subtly changing colours of Verdi's orchestra are nowhere more stunningly revealed than in this scene. The ending of the duet is of a particularly sumptuous quality. As Otello declaims, "Già la pleiade ardente in mar discende" (Now the glowing Pleiades descends into the sea),[1] slow harp arpeggios and high pianissimi strings, with flute and cor anglais, surround his phrases and Desdemona's response, to rise to a shimmering chord of D flat over which Otello and Desdemona hold their final note. As it dies away, the sound of a pianissimo violin trill and the four solo cellos repeating the opening phrase of the duet follow it into silence.

    The second act begins with Iago's dialogue with Cassio, followed by his "Credo". Verdi introduces a theme [Ex. 117] which he associates

Ex. 117

with Iago, and which he adapts to Iago's varying moods in this scene. It fiercely ushers in the orchestral introduction, which assumes a suavely charming air as Iago exerts his wiles on Cassio. When Cassio leaves, Iago waves him away with a friendly "Vanne" (Go then), but as soon as Cassio is out of earshot, Iago repeats his "Vanne" with a considerably different tone colour, and to a tremendous unison outburst in the orchestra begins his "Credo", an astonishing and disturbing depiction of evil. Largely declamatory, the aria is propelled by its own demonic force and by the whiplash fury of Verdi's orchestra.

    [1] Both words and music are recalled in Britten's *Peter Grimes*, when Peter begins his aria, "Now the Great Bear and Pleiades".

At its conclusion, when Iago deliberates upon death, an unearthly quiet surrounds his whispered, "La morte è il nulla" (Death is nothingness), and a deluge of brass supports his defiant shout, "È vecchia fola il ciel" (Heaven is an old fable).

The scene in which Iago first plants the seed of jealousy in Otello's mind is conducted in Verdi's own melodic dialogue style. The remarkable passage where Iago disingenuously advises Otello to beware of jealousy is underlined by an eloquently sinister orchestra. He and Otello observe Desdemona and her serenaders in the garden. The chorus of women, sailors and children sings a graceful tune to the accompaniment first of bagpipes, then later of mandolines and guitars.[1] In a coda in which the full orchestra joins, Desdemona echoes the final phrase of the chorus, and Otello and Iago add their comments. The quartet for Desdemona, Emilia, Otello and Iago is one of those extraordinary Verdian ensembles in which the conflicting feelings of the various characters both stand out clearly and blend into a homogeneous whole. Desdemona's lyrical top line soars above the more agitated phrases of the others.

From the dramatic dialogue of Otello and Iago which comprises the remainder of the act, three separate numbers emerge, two of them quite superb. Otello's "Ora e per sempre addio, sante memorie" (Now and forever, farewell, sacred memories) releases all his emotion in a magnificent and vigorously martial outburst. Iago's account of Cassio's dream, "Era la notte", is insinuatingly effective. Verdi differentiates orchestrally between Iago's utterance and Cassio's reported speech, and even curiously colours the vocal phrases attributed to Cassio in such a way that the evil spirit of Iago is filtered through them. The difficulty of persuading singers to sing softly is reflected in the *ppppppp* that Verdi writes over a bar of Iago's music. The descending chromatic phrase in which Iago quotes Cassio's ecstatic murmur is graphically slimy, and the healthy ascent into the fresh air, at "E allora il sogno" (And then the dream), is correspondingly a moment of great relief. The level of inspiration from phrase to phrase of this opera is continually astonishing. Immediately after Iago's account of the dream, when he asks Otello about the handkerchief, Otello's reply is set with such a sure instinct, childlike in its simplicity and innocence, that one's heart leaps [Ex. 118].

Ex. 118

È il faz-zo - let - to ch'io le die-di, pe-gno pri-mo d'a-mor.

[1] The libretto stipulates cornamusa and guzla. The cornamusa is an Italian bagpipe; the guzla is described by Verdi as a kind of mandoline, but according to Grove it is "a kind of rebab, a bowed instrument with one string only, used in Illyria and Serbia".

The oath duet that ends the act is certainly exciting, and the situation hardly calls for subtlety of expression. If the vocal writing strikes one as somewhat bombastic, a rereading of Shakespeare's "Arise, black vengeance, from thy hollow cell" is a salutary reminder that Shakespeare was Verdi's equal in this, as in many things. And Verdi's orchestral comment on the oath is masterly.

Act III begins with a short orchestral introduction which is based on the phrase descriptive of jealousy that Iago had sung in the preceding act. After the Herald's announcement and the brief dialogue for Otello and Iago, there follows a scene for Otello and Desdemona in which passages of lyrical beauty, such as her opening line, alternate with spasmodic outbursts of fury from Otello. As his anger mounts and is answered by moving phrases in which Desdemona protests her innocence, Verdi portrays Otello's condition with such compassion that we are already moved to almost greater sympathy for him than for his unjustly accused wife. His cries of "Indietro" (away) are suffused not with fury but with misery. The great soliloquy, "Dio, mi potevi scagliar tutti i mali della miseria, della vergogna" (God, you could have heaped on me all the evils of misery and shame), is begun by Otello in a stifled near-monotone. Eventually his voice broadens into melody and begins to rise, lifting itself, slowly and almost painfully, into the lyrical song of "Ma, o pianto, o duol" (But, oh tears, oh sorrow). His fury returns, but his expression of it is interrupted by Iago. The trio in which Iago and Cassio chatter about the latter's love-life while Otello listens, thinking they are referring to Desdemona, develops into a light, rapid scherzo.

Trumpets and cannon announce the arrival of the Ambassador from Venice. It was at this point in the opera that, for the Paris production of *Otello* in the autumn of 1894, seven years after its première, Verdi inserted the obligatory ballet music, even though he considered the custom "an artistic monstrosity". Although usually, and rightly, omitted from modern performances, this music, which Verdi composed a year after the première of *Falstaff*, is as enjoyable to listen to as his ballet music invariably is.[1] The eighty-one-year-old composer sketched a scenario for the Paris ballet, involving Turkish slaves, Venetian lads and lasses and "beautiful young Greek girls". He timed the music to last five minutes and fifty-nine seconds.[2] The dances are "Arab Song" which is a splendid piece of pastische orientalia, "Invocation to Allah", "Greek Dance", "La Muranese" which means, apparently, not a girl

[1] Some years ago, Charles Mackerras concocted a ballet score, *The Lady and the Fool*, from vocal and instrumental numbers taken from several early Verdi operas. Perhaps he would consider making another ballet out of the music which Verdi intended should be danced to.

[2] Toscanini's recorded performance takes 6 minutes, 5 seconds, which I thought was pretty accurate until I timed Karajan's recording. It takes precisely 5 minutes, 59 seconds! (Serafin takes only 5 minutes, 47 seconds.)

from Murano but a dance from that island, and finally "War Song".

When the ballet is not performed, the trumpet fanfare leads straight into the chorus's acclamation of Otello and the ensemble scene which concludes the third act. The ensemble, begun by Desdemona with one of those Verdian soprano tunes which the old wizard was still able to conjure out of the air whenever he needed them [Ex. 119], is one of

Ex. 119

Verdi's most complex and ingenious, during whose course the plot is busily advanced by Iago. At its climax, the distraught Otello orders the crowd to leave and, turning on Desdemona, curses her with a desperate cry as pathetic as it is terrifying. When the crowd outside is heard shouting Otello's praises, Iago points at the body of the now prostrate Moor and utters his sneer about the Lion of Venice, with a trill which is also heard in the lower strings and woodwind of the orchestra. A final shout by the crowd of "Viva Otello" is ironically commented on by the orchestra as the curtain falls.

The orchestral introduction to Act IV, for wind instruments alone, opens with the poignant phrase which permeates Desdemona's Willow Song, sung after a brief passage of recitative for her and Emilia. The song actually begins with the phrase from the orchestral introduction [Ex. 120]. With its sad repetitions of "Salce" (Willow) to a descending

Ex. 120

minor third, its plangent wind writing, and its rich and imaginative harmonies, the Willow Song contributes to a scene of rare beauty. After Desdemona sings the words, "Buona notte", to Emilia, the orchestra plays four solemnly portentous chords of F sharp major, and then, in a sudden moment of terror, she cries, "Ah, Emilia, Emilia, addio, Emilia, addio!" to an incredibly anguished and moving phrase that seems to be drawn from her without her conscious participation [Ex. 121].

Ex. 121

Desdemona's "Ave Maria", a simple yet affecting prayer accompanied by muted strings, ends quietly on the soprano's high A flat. She goes to bed, and then from the tense silence the sound of muted double basses arises from the lowest depth of their range to accompany Otello's movements. These are a remarkable twenty-six bars of masterly writing for the instruments, and they were insensitively, but perhaps not surprisingly, encored at the first performance. As Otello leans over the sleeping Desdemona to kiss her, the orchestra recalls the most beautiful phrases of the Act I love duet, which accompanied the words, "Un bacio, ancora un bacio" [Ex. 116]. This deeply affecting moment is something the spoken theatre cannot achieve. There is nothing more remarkable in Shakespeare's *Othello*. As Otello kisses her for the third time, Desdemona awakens. In the dialogue preceding the murder, there occur what seem to me the only conventional few bars in the entire score: conventional in the sense that they momentarily but disturbingly recall Verdi's style of some forty years earlier [Ex. 122].

Ex. 122

The murder, the entrance of Emilia, Desdemona's last poignant phrase, the arrival of Lodovico, Cassio and Iago, and the latter's flight when Montano enters and denounces him, are all portrayed with economy of means to splendid and swift theatrical effect. The opera ends with Otello's "Niun me tema" (None need fear me) in which, defeated, heart-broken, dignified, and overcome with disgust for himself and love for Desdemona, he stabs himself. "E tu, come sei pallida, e stanca, e muta, e bella" (And you, how pale you are, and weary, and silent, and beautiful) is set to a phrase of timeless beauty which could be by Monteverdi, Mozart, Britten or Stravinsky [Ex. 123].

Ex.123

To the final, and most overwhelming, repetition of Ex. 116, Otello dies as he attempts to kiss Desdemona's dead body, breathing his last on the word, "bacio", which he fails to finish. So ends Verdi's greatest opera.

His greatest opera? With *Falstaff* yet to be considered? Yes, I think so, though to debate the point would be meaningless at such a level of achievement. There are times when *Don Giovanni* seems to me to be indisputably Mozart's greatest opera, and times when *Così fan tutte* drives it from first place. While I am experiencing it in the theatre, I am usually convinced that *Otello* is the finest of all operas, of all music dramas. What an incredibly fresh, youthfully inspired score for a man in his seventies to create. How Verdi sustains the melodic, harmonic and dramatic level of achievement from the first shattering chord to the final stillness. What psychological acumen the musical characterisation reveals. It is easy to say that *Falstaff* is a considerably greater work of art than *The Merry Wives of Windsor*. Nowadays, after twenty years' acquaintance with *Otello* and a love of Shakespeare which goes back even farther, I find myself seriously contemplating the proposition that *Otello* is superior to *Othello*. The opera's combination of those Elizabethan qualities of tenderness, violence and sensuality never fails to impress and astonish me. And Verdi's musical language and style are really beyond praise: the melody as glorious as in his more youthful days, but now freed from the harmonic constrictions of his earlier period and able to range where it will, the numbers merging skilfully and subtly into one another. What enormous influence the Verdi of *Otello* has had on modern opera. Wagner produced only other Wagnerians before his quasi-symphonic style came to a dead-end, but the voice of late Verdi, the Verdi of *Otello* and *Falstaff*, can still be heard. From the best pages of Puccini, through Strauss's *Intermezzo*, to Britten's *Peter Grimes* and *Billy Budd*, it has continued to exert a strong and living influence. I can even point to passages in Stravinsky's *Oedipus Rex* that have their obvious beginnings in *Aida*: some of Jocasta's music, for instance. But the tracing of influences is a dangerous, and fortunately unnecessary, game to play. *Otello* itself betrays the influence of no other composer. It is the opera that the musical dramatist Verdi had been working his way towards, throughout his long career. Wagner, after all, did not invent music drama any more than Verdi did. Both of them, really, are for many reasons in Mozart's debt. But with *Otello*, that tragic confrontation of life's opposites, and deeply searching study of the heart's reasons, Verdi's part of the debt is repaid.

XXVII

Falstaff

Dramatis personae:

Sir John Falstaff	(baritone)
Ford	(baritone)
Fenton	(tenor)
Doctor Caius	(tenor)
Bardolph, follower of Falstaff	(tenor)
Pistol, follower of Falstaff	(bass)
Alice Ford	(soprano)
Nannetta, daughter of the Fords	(soprano)
Mistress Quickly	(mezzo-soprano)
Mistress Meg Page	(mezzo-soprano)

LIBRETTO by Arrigo Boito, based on Shakespeare's *The Merry Wives of Windsor* and several passages in *Henry IV* concerning Falstaff.

TIME: The reign of Henry IV
PLACE: Windsor

FIRST PERFORMED at La Scala, Milan, February 9, 1893, with Emma Zilli (Alice); Adelina Stehle (Nannetta); Virginia Guerrini (Meg); Giuseppina Pasqua (Quickly); Edoardo Garbin (Fenton); Victor Maurel (Falstaff); Antonio Pini-Corsi (Ford); Giovanni Paroli (Caius); Paolo Pellagalli-Rosetti (Bardolph); Vittorio Arimondi (Pistol)

Falstaff

AFTER THE MIRACLE of *Otello*, Verdi was immediately urged to begin another opera. It was even rumoured that he was already at work on a subject. The directors of La Scala suggested a comic opera based on *Don Quixote*, but Verdi refused to be rushed, and returned to Sant' Agata and the life of a farmer. For the next two years he busied himself with his country affairs; with, among other things, the new hospital he had built at Villanova, near Sant' Agata. He himself was largely responsible for the simple design, carefully supervised the construction of the building, engaged the medical staff, and enlisted the aid of Giuseppina in choosing furniture and linen. The hospital had been badly needed in the district, and after it opened on November 6, 1887, all its beds were quickly filled. Verdi refused to have his name on the façade, which to this day has the single word "Ospedale" imprinted upon it. The hospital still serves the local community.

Verdi's social conscience was not stilled by his provision of a hospital for his people. It was a time of depression, and many country workers were drifting to the towns. In order to combat this in his area, Verdi reduced the rents on his farms, improved the properties themselves, introduced a new irrigation system, and in various other ways produced more employment in the district. There was more than enough to occupy him and, as the year 1889 began, there was plenty to annoy him as well. It was the fiftieth anniversary of his first produced opera *Oberto*, and the newspapers mentioned plans to honour the composer with a series of performances. Verdi wrote irritably to Giulio Ricordi in an attempt to stop anything from being done, but he was unable to prevent La Scala from reviving *Oberto* on the anniversary date, November 17th. He refused, however, to go to Milan, and stayed at home at Sant' Agata, where he was swamped with thousands of congratulatory messages. Already his mind was occupied with something new. In July, Boito had sent him the synopsis of a proposed libretto to be called *Falstaff*, and Verdi was absolutely delighted with it. This was the comedy he had hoped to find ever since *Un giorno di regno* of nearly fifty years earlier. When he received the *Falstaff* synopsis, Verdi wrote immediately to Boito:

Excellent! Excellent!

Before reading your sketch I wanted to re-read the *Merry Wives*, the two parts of *Henry IV* and *Henry V*, and I can only repeat: *Excellent*, for one could not do better than you have done.

A pity that the interest (it's not your fault) does not go on increasing to the end. The culminating point is the finale of the second act; and the appearance of Falstaff's face amid the linen, etc., is a true comic invention.

I'm afraid, too, that the last act, in spite of its touch of fantasy, will be trivial, with all those little pieces, songs, ariettas, etc., etc. You bring back Bardolph—and why not *Pistol* too, both of them, to get up to some prank or other?

You reduce the weddings to two! All the better, for they are only loosely connected with the principal plot.

The two trials by water and fire suffice to punish Falstaff: nevertheless, I should have liked to see him thoroughly well beaten as well.

I am talking for the sake of talking—take no notice. We have now very different matters to discuss, so that this *Falstaff*, or *Merry Wives*, which two days ago was in the world of dreams, now takes shape and becomes reality! When? How? . . . Who knows? I'll write to you tomorrow or the next day.

Greetings from Peppina. Farewell.[1]

The next day Verdi wrote again, expressing one or two doubts about the project. He was conscious of his great age, and was also eager that Boito should finish his own opera *Nerone* (which was still not quite ready for production when Boito died in 1918).

In tackling *Falstaff*, have you ever thought of my enormous weight of years? I know that in replying you will exaggerate the robust state of my health. But even if it is as you say, you must agree that in taking on such a task I may over-tax my strength. What if I could not stand the strain? What if I could not finish the music? Then you would have wasted time and trouble for nothing. For all the money in the world, I would not want that to happen. The idea is insupportable to me, and all the more so if you, in writing *Falstaff*, were to, I won't say abandon, but were to move your energies away from *Nerone*, or delay its production.[2]

But, despite the cautious note he was trying to sound, Verdi's delight could not be suppressed: "What a joy to be able to say to the public, 'HERE WE ARE AGAIN ! ! COME AND SEE US!'"[3]

Boito reassured him:

I don't think you will find writing a comic opera fatiguing. A tragedy makes its composer really suffer. His mind dwells on grief, and his nerves become unhealthily agitated. But the jests and laughter of comedy exhilarate both mind and body. "A smile adds a thread to the web of life." I don't know if I've quoted Foscolo correctly, but the idea is true. You

[1] Walker, p. 495.   [2] *Copialettere*, p. 711.   [3] *Copialettere*, p. 711.

have longed for a good subject for a comic opera all your life, which proves you have a natural aptitude for the noble art of comedy. Instinct is a good guide. There is only one way to end your career more splendidly than with *Otello*, and that is to end it with *Falstaff*.[1]

Verdi needed no further convincing. By return of post, he wrote: "Amen, and so be it! Let us then do *Falstaff*. Let's not think now of the obstacles, my age and illnesses! But I want to keep it the deepest *secret*: a word I underline three times to tell you that no one must know anything of it."[2] And he urged Boito to start on the libretto at once. A few weeks later he wrote to say he hoped Boito was at work, for he, Verdi, had surprised himself by beginning to compose. "I'm amusing myself by writing fugues! Yes, sir, a fugue: and a *comic* fugue which would be suitable for *Falstaff*!"[3]

Boito wrote his libretto, which Verdi accepted almost without alteration, and which he began to set. By the following March he had completed the first act. For months he managed to keep the composition of *Falstaff* a secret: not even Giulio Ricordi knew about it. Eventually, Ricordi had to be told, but even then Verdi refused to discuss the possibility of performance of the opera he was composing with such enjoyment. To Ricordi he wrote:

I am engaged in writing *Falstaff* to pass the time, without any preconceived ideas or plans. I repeat, "to pass the time". Nothing else. All this talk, these proposals, however vague, and this splitting of words, will end by involving me in obligations that I absolutely refuse to assume.[4]

Some months later, he mentioned to Ricordi that he was by no means convinced that *Falstaff* would be seen to its best advantage in a large opera house such as La Scala. "I have written it to please myself, and I believe it ought to be performed at Sant' Agata and not at La Scala."[5]

While Verdi was still at work on *Falstaff*, his old friend and pupil, Emmanuele Muzio, "a sincere and devoted friend for the last half-century", died in Paris. "You can imagine my sorrow," Verdi wrote to the singer Maria Waldmann. "I have little wish to go on with an opera which I have recently begun."[6] But he did go on, though he was nearly eighty, though his moods of depression were frequent, and though in April of 1892 he had to interrupt work and go to Milan to conduct the Scala Orchestra on the hundredth anniversary of the birth of Rossini, the last occasion on which he was to conduct an orchestra in public. He had already completed two and a half acts of *Falstaff*, and broke off composing to put what he had already written into full score, afraid that otherwise he might forget some of the instrumentation he

[1] *Carteggi Verdiani*, II, p. 146.   [2] Abbiati, Vol. IV, p. 387.   [3] Abbiati, Vol. IV, p. 388.   [4] *Copialettere*, p. 712.   [5] *Copialettere*, p. 713.   [6] Abbiati, Vol. IV, p. 408.

had in mind. By September the opera was complete,[1] and Verdi sent off the final act to Ricordi accompanied by a note of affectionate farewell to Falstaff, scribbled on the manuscript score, paraphrasing a passage in Boito's libretto:

> Tutto è finito.
> Va, va vecchio John.
> Cammina per la tua via
> Fin che tu puoi.
> Divertente tipo di briccone
> Eternamente vero sotto
> Maschera diversa in ogni
> Tempo, in ogni luogo.
> Va, va,
> Cammina, cammina,
> Addio.

(It's all finished. Go, go, old John. Go on your way for as long as you can. Amusing rogue, forever true beneath the masks you wear in different times and places. Go, go, on your way. Farewell.)

At the beginning of January 1893, Verdi and Giuseppina arrived in Milan, and Verdi began to rehearse *Falstaff*, sometimes for as long as eight hours a day. His colleagues marvelled at the energy and quick-witted resilience of the composer who, in his eightieth year, seemed younger and livelier than any of them, and as much a perfectionist as ever. As the date of the première approached, the world's musical press began to arrive in Milan, and local excitement mounted. The French baritone Victor Maurel, the Iago of the *Otello* première, was to play Falstaff: Verdi admired him as much for his acting ability as for his singing voice. Franco Faccio, the eminent conductor of Verdi, and Boito's close friend, had died insane while *Falstaff* was being composed. During his friend's final illness, Boito had, for more than a year, taken over his duties as Director of the Conservatorium at Parma to ensure the continued payment of Faccio's salary. The *Falstaff* première was conducted by Edoardo Mascheroni. A few days before the great event, Giuseppina wrote to her sister: "Admirers, bores, friends, enemies, genuine and non-genuine musicians, critics good and bad are swarming in from all over the world. The way people are clamouring for seats, the opera house would need to be as big as a public square."[2]

The occasion itself was, of course, a triumphant success. Verdi, leading Boito on to the stage to share the applause, was recalled time and time again. At length, he, Boito and Giuseppina left La Scala by a

---

[1] Verdi continued, however, to make alterations, up to and even after the Milan première.

[2] Abbiati, Vol. IV, p. 472.

side exit to avoid the crowds flocking around the stage door. But, at the Grand Hotel, another cheering crowd awaited Verdi. Although he managed to fight his way through them to the entrance, he had to appear on his balcony three times before they would finally disperse.

International critical opinion tended, on the whole, to confirm the success of the new work, although the Scala performance was apparently far from being perfect. Most of the critics were struck by the beauty and subtlety of the orchestration. One French critic, after noting that people around him in the first-night audience were talking of the influence of *Die Meistersinger*, expressed his own view that the work derived more from Haydn and Mozart. The English composer Sir Charles Villiers Stanford, who wrote a most perceptive and detailed review for the *Daily Graphic*, discerned a strong Beethovenian element in the score.

II

If Boito had succeeded admirably in adapting *Othello*, he performed a miracle in filleting Shakespeare's ploddingly repetitive pot-boiler, *The Merry Wives of Windsor*, throwing out its poor jokes, turning its bad prose into excellent verse, paring down its clumsily extravagant cast of characters in preparation for Verdi's brilliant musical characterisation of Falstaff, the Fords, Mistress Quickly, and the adolescent love bundle made up of Nannetta and Fenton. Boito's excisions and alterations are, almost without exception, beautifully judged. The telescoping of Sir Hugh Evans, Justice Shallow, Slender and Dr Caius into Caius alone works admirably. Anne Page becomes Nannetta Ford, and her two unwelcome suitors are reduced to one. (In the play, Slender and Dr Caius are married off to boys of nubile age; this, more Elizabethan than *ottocento*, is also, one imagines, more enjoyable than being married to Bardolph, which is the punishment Boito inflicts on Doctor Caius.) The number of episodes in which Falstaff is tricked by the wives is sensibly reduced from three to two: thus one does not, in the opera, see Falstaff disguised as Mother Prat, the fat woman of Brentford. In *The Merry Wives of Windsor*, Mistress Quickly is Doctor Caius's servant. (In *Henry IV* she runs a tavern in Eastcheap, and ends up, in *Henry V*, married to Pistol.) In Boito and Verdi's *Falstaff*, her social position is somewhat ambiguous: she appears to be a friendly neighbour of the other wives.

Boito has taken a few ideas from the Falstaff episodes in *Henry IV*, notably some lines from Act V, Scene 1, which become the basis of the opera's Honour monologue, and part of the chatter about Bardolph's nose in Act III, Scene 3, which he utilises at the beginning of the opera.

Each of the opera's three acts is in two scenes. The first scene of Act I

takes place in a room at the Garter Inn. As the curtain rises, Sir John
Falstaff, seated at a table, is sealing two letters he has just written. Then,
stretching himself comfortably, he begins to drink. His companions,
Bardolph and Pistol and the landlord of the inn, are also present. Dr
Caius enters to complain that Falstaff has broken into his house, beaten
his servants and taken one of his horses, and that Bardolph and Pistol
had got him drunk the previous day and picked his pockets. Falstaff
admits most of this, has Caius thrown out, and then criticises his two
colleagues on aesthetic rather than moral grounds. "Steal politely, and
at the right time," he admonishes them. Examining the landlord's bill
and his own purse, he complains that Bardolph and Pistol are costing
him too much to maintain. Calling them to order, he informs them that
he is certain he has attracted the interest of Alice, the wife of the wealthy
merchant, Mr Ford, and Meg, the wife of one Page, equally wealthy.
Both ladies, he believes, hold the purse-strings of their respective house-
holds. He has written a love-letter to each of them, and offers one to
Bardolph and one to Pistol to deliver. But they refuse to oblige, Bardolph
claiming his honour forbids him.

Falstaff sends the inn's page-boy off with the letters, and then rounds
on his colleagues with a scathing harangue on the subject of honour,
addressing them as "cloache d'ignominia" (sewers of ignominy). The
first part of his tirade is drawn from *The Merry Wives of Windsor*, though
from a later scene in the play:

> You stand upon your honour! Why thou unconfinable baseness, it is as
> much as I can do to keep the terms of my honour precise, I, I, I myself
> sometimes, leaving the fear of God on the left hand, and hiding mine
> honour in my necessity, am fain to shuffle, to hedge and to lurch.

The question and answer of the second part of the monologue, beginning at "Può l'honore riempirvi la pancia? No", is suggested by part
of Falstaff's speech to Prince Henry in Act V, Scene 1, of *Henry IV,
Part I*:

> Can honour set to a leg? No. Or an arm? No. Or take away the grief of a
> wound? No. Honour hath no skill in surgery then? No. What is honour?
> A word.

When he has concluded his vituperative sermon, Falstaff takes up a
broom and chases Bardolph and Pistol out.

The second scene is set in the garden of Ford's house. Mistress Meg
Page and Mistress Quickly meet Mistress Alice Ford and her daughter
Nannetta, who are just leaving their house. Both wives have received
Falstaff's letter, and each is dying to tell the other about it. When they
discover that the letters are identically worded and are both from Fal-

staff, all four women laugh at his absurd presumption, and decide to teach him a lesson. As they leave, Ford, Dr Caius, and a young man called Fenton who is in love with Nannetta, enters with Bardolph and Pistol, who have told Ford of Falstaff's scheme to seduce his wife. The men go off to plot their revenge as the women re-enter. Fenton, however, remains behind to flirt with Nannetta. The women arrange that Mistress Quickly shall visit Falstaff carrying a message of Alice Ford's consent, thus luring him to Ford's house at a time when they will be ready to deal with him. The women leave, and the men re-enter, having hatched their plot, which involves Ford in presenting himself to Falstaff in disguise. The women re-enter as the men are still plotting, and the scene ends with the two separate ensembles heard together.

The first scene of Act II is again the room in the Garter Inn. Falstaff is seated, drinking sherry, when Bardolph and Pistol return, pretending to be repentant. They announce Mistress Quickly, who requests a private word with Falstaff. She tells him that Alice Ford returns his love and that her violently jealous husband is always out between two and three in the afternoon. "Dalle due alle tre." The time Shakespeare recommended was "between ten and eleven" which does not make so euphonious a phrase in Italian. Meg Page, Mistress Quickly continues, also reciprocates Falstaff's affections, but, alas, her husband is very seldom away from home. Falstaff thanks Mistress Quickly and dismisses her. He is congratulating himself on his personal charms when Bardolph enters to announce that a Master Fontana (Fountain, the assumed name of Ford) desires to make his acquaintance and to present him with a demijohn of Cyprus. The disguised Ford enters, accompanied by Pistol carrying the demijohn. Ford offers Falstaff gold if he will help him to win the favours of Mistress Ford. He appeals to Falstaff, as a man of the world, to seduce the virtuous Mistress Ford who, he says, has so far refused to listen to his protestations of love. If Falstaff will first melt her coldness, this will make it easier for him, Fontana. Falstaff accepts the commission, mentioning complacently that he expects to be in Alice's arms in half an hour, as he has received a message from her that her husband is always absent between two and three. He goes off to dress for the assignation. Left alone, Ford gives vent to his jealous rage at what he imagines to be his wife's intended infidelity and determines to catch her and Falstaff in the act. (His outburst is a collation of two speeches in *The Merry Wives of Windsor*, from Act II, Scene 2, and Act III, Scene 5.) Falstaff returns, exquisitely arrayed, and the two men leave together.

The second scene of Act II takes place in a room in Ford's house where the two wives and Nannetta are awaiting Falstaff. Quickly enters to tell of the success of her errand, and to warn them that their victim is already on his way. Nannetta is sad because her father wants her to marry Dr Caius, but her mother tells her not to worry. Two servants

come in, carrying between them a large linen basket, which Mistress
Ford orders them to set down in the room. When she calls them later,
they are to empty the basket into the brook. The other women retire
to keep watch, and Alice Ford seats herself at a table and plays a few
chords on a lute as soon as she hears that Falstaff is approaching the
house. Falstaff arrives, and loses no time in setting about his seduction
of Alice. His little song, "Quand' era paggio", in which he boasts of
having, in his youth, been a slender page-boy to the Duke of Norfolk,
has no direct parallel in *The Merry Wives of Windsor*, but was suggested
to Boito by Falstaff's line in *Henry IV, Part I*, "When I was about thy
years, Hal, I was not an eagle's talon in the waist; I could have crept
into any alderman's thumb-ring." The "alderman's thumb-ring"
image becomes:

> Tant' era smilzo, flessibile e snello
> che sarei guizzato attraverso un anello

(I was so slim, so supple and so agile that I could have slipped
through a ring.)

Before Falstaff can get very far with his wooing, Mistress Quickly
enters, as arranged, to announce the arrival of a distraught Meg Page.
Falstaff hides behind a screen as Meg comes in in a state of agitation.
She tells Alice she has just encountered Ford, who knows his wife has a
lover concealed in the house and is determined to search for him.
Suddenly, Mistress Quickly makes an unrehearsed re-entrance to
warn Alice that it is true: her husband is already advancing across the
garden with a gang of men to help him search. While she is speaking,
the furious voice of Ford can be heard outside, and he enters followed
by Fenton, Caius, Bardolph, Pistol and a number of other men. Alice
angrily confronts her husband, who, suspecting Falstaff to be concealed
in the laundry basket, opens it, flinging dirty linen all over the floor.
He and his followers then rush out to search the rest of the house, while
Meg, Alice and Quickly help the terrified Falstaff to clamber into the
laundry basket, Meg pretending shocked surprise to find Falstaff in
Alice's room as she does so. During the commotion, Nannetta and
Fenton quietly creep behind the screen and make themselves comfortable in each other's arms. Ford and his helpers return and continue
their search of the room. Demented with jealous fury by now, Ford even
opens the drawer of a small table. This is Boito's witty private reference
to the two episodes in Shakespeare's play which are combined here:
after the first, Ford (disguised as Mr Brook) learns from Falstaff that
he had been conveyed out of the house in a laundry basket, and is about
to visit Mistress Ford again. In his second fit of jealousy, Ford exclaims:
"He cannot creep into a halfpenny purse, nor into a pepper-box; but,

lest the devil that guides him should aid him, I will search impossible places."

During a moment of silence, the sound of Fenton kissing Nannetta is heard from behind the screen, and Ford imagines he has caught Falstaff. The screen is overturned, disclosing the young lovers, and the disappointed and irritated Ford orders Fenton out of the house. As the hunt continues, and Ford rushes off to another part of the house, Alice instructs four servants to empty the basket out of the window into the brook "in front of that bunch of washerwomen". She calls her husband to observe, as basket and Falstaff disappear into the water.

The final act opens outside the Garter Inn where, as the sun sets, a cold and disgruntled Falstaff is sitting on a bench, brooding on the world's wickedness. He orders a glass of hot wine, and soliloquises on the outrageous treatment he has received at the hands of the wives. When his wine is brought to him, he drinks and revives somewhat. His appreciative comment on the wine is taken by Boito from a long soliloquy in *Henry IV, Part II* in which Falstaff catalogues the excellent properties of "sherris".

When Mistress Quickly arrives with another message from Alice, Falstaff is soon ready to believe in that lady's innocence and to accept her invitation to meet her at midnight in the Royal Park, underneath Herne's Oak. He is to come disguised as the Black Knight whose ghost is reputed to haunt the spot. Falstaff credulously agrees, and he and Mistress Quickly enter the inn, still talking. Their conversation has been overheard by Alice, Meg, Nannetta, Ford, Caius and Fenton, who now appear, congratulating themselves that Falstaff has fallen into the trap they have this time combined to set. Alice teases Ford about his absurd jealousy, and they begin to plan how they will disguise themselves as fairies, elves and devils to terrify Falstaff. They disperse, but Ford and Caius remain behind to talk just as Mistress Quickly emerges from the inn. She overhears Ford promise Caius that he may marry Nannetta that evening during the revels. Everyone will be disguised, and if Caius in his monk's robes presents himself with Nannetta who will be in white, and veiled, he Ford will bless the union. Mistress Quickly hurries off to warn Alice Ford and Nannetta.

Act III, Scene 2, takes place near Herne's Oak in Windsor Great Park, towards midnight. Fenton enters, singing a love song to Nannetta. Nannetta arrives, and they embrace, but Alice Ford appears with Mistress Quickly, tells Fenton to disguise himself as a monk, and gives him a mask to wear. They all go off, as Falstaff is heard approaching. He enters, wearing two stag horns on his head and wrapped in an enormous cloak. When Alice returns, he attempts to embrace her, but she tells him that Meg is close behind her. The voice of Meg is heard in the distance, calling that she is being pursued by witches. Alice runs off. Nannetta and her group of spirits, including Meg as the Green Nymph,

Pistol as a satyr, and children dressed as imps and fairies, all appear and dance around Falstaff, who has flung himself to the ground, scared out of his senses. They threaten him, and begin to kick and pummel him. During the horseplay, Bardolph loses his mask and Falstaff recognises him. At this, they all reveal themselves, while Quickly takes Bardolph aside to dress him in a woman's gown with a veil.

Falstaff accepts the situation with a rueful good humour, and with an exact translation of Shakespeare's line: "I do begin to perceive that I am made an ass." But he reminds them, and here he quotes *Henry IV, Part II*, that they could not have had all this enjoyment without him: "I am not only witty in myself, but the cause that wit is in other men."

Caius, masked, enters leading the Fairy Queen, who is dressed in white. Alice Ford brings forward another couple whose betrothal she asks Ford to bless at the same time, and Ford agrees to a double ceremony, not realising that the disguised couple are Nannetta and Fenton. Only after Ford has blessed the union of both couples is it revealed to him that he has betrothed Fenton to Nannetta, and Dr Caius to Bardolph. Falstaff ironically asks the stupefied Ford which one is now the dupe. Ford accepts the marriage of his daughter to Fenton, and the opera ends in an ensemble led by Falstaff: "Tutto nel mondo è burla" (Everything in the world is a jest).

III

Since it is still possible to read that *Falstaff*, though a work of enormous skill and technical ingenuity, lacks the sheer melodic fecundity of Verdi's youth, let me say immediately that the most striking aspect of this opera is its melodic prodigality. Verdi scatters tunes about as though he were trying to give them away. It is the very profusion of splendid tunes in *Falstaff* which has occasionally led the casual hearer to suppose that it contains no tunes at all, for Verdi rarely repeats a melody, and is inclined in any case to discard it after a few bars. Also, the general tempo of *Falstaff* is extraordinarily brisk; it is not until the beginning of the final scene that there comes a moment of repose, of lyrical relaxation. There is no time for the listener to remember the tunes as they fly past him. For this reason it is difficult to attempt a description of the opera at any reasonable length: ideally, one needs either to confine oneself to one word or to spread to a hundred thousand.

Each of the opera's three acts is in two scenes, and the six scenes are all fairly short, ranging from fifteen minutes to just under thirty minutes. The curtain rises without prelude as the orchestra sets the first scene with a fortissimo bustle, and Dr Caius begins to inveigh against Falstaff and his companions. Throughout the opera, the orchestra's contribution is both lively and startlingly original. When, in this scene, Falstaff momentarily broods on the alarming possibility of his becoming thin, a gloomy tune in the orchestra is doubled by piccolos and, four octaves lower, cellos. His account of the charms of Alice Ford is accompananied by a delicious four-note figure, while the tuneful phrase to which Bardolph's ardently burning nose ("tuo naso ardentissimo") inspires Verdi, and which is never heard again, would have lasted Puccini (and, I think, did) for at least an entire aria [Ex. 124].

Ex. 124

The various episodes in the scene, and this applies throughout the opera, are all beautifully and individually shaped, yet they interlock to add up to an integral unit, while the six scenes combine to produce the superbly satisfying formal unity of the complete opera. The first scene divides itself into three sections: the opening boisterous *allegro* of the Dr Caius incident, the lighter, more lyrical central passages about the merry wives, and finally Falstaff's solo harangue on the subject of honour. The Honour monologue is recognisably by the hand that wrote Rigoletto's "Pari siamo", a hand that could turn from sardonic drama to equally sardonic comedy. The woodwind writing here is absolutely delicious, and the vocal declamation quite perfect. The monologue arrives at a suitably mock-pompous ending with Falstaff's top G followed by four bars which could almost be Elgar at his tweediest. A more down-to-earth coda in which Falstaff drops his wounded dignity, and chases Bardolph and Pistol with a broom brings the curtain down quickly.

A high-spirited tune for woodwind and horns opens the second scene of Act I, which bubbles along as gaily and quickly as the first. Having given the scene its mood of good humour, this tune disappears until the curtain falls fifteen minutes later. The *allegro vivace* in which the separate male and female groups carry on their scheming slackens to an *andante* only for those brief moments when Nannetta and Fenton find time for a little silken dalliance. As Alice and Meg compare notes, and read passages of Falstaff's letter to each other, Alice quotes one of Falstaff's sillier verbal phrases, "E il viso tuo su me risplenderà, come una stella sull' immensità" (And your face will shine on me like a star in the immense firmament), which she is directed to sing "con caricatura". The tune, however, is one of exquisite beauty. Having noted Verdi's failure here to produce an absurd tune to match the words (did he think he had done so, I wonder?) let us be grateful for [Ex. 125].

Ex. 125

The scurrying little quartet in which the four women express their opinion of Falstaff originally had a *ppp* accompaniment for two oboes and two clarinets. Verdi deleted the accompaniment from his manuscript, presumably having found that the four ladies could keep in tune without it. The parts remain in the printed score, and so are occasionally played, but obviously the quartet should be sung unaccompanied if possible. Verdi stated that he had no objection to the accompaniment being used whenever it seemed useful, provided the audience didn't hear it.

The lovers' lyrical phrases, "sprinkled like sugar on a tart", as Boito described the Nannetta-Fenton episodes, are enchantingly scored. I note that Toye considered their little duet, "Labbra di foco", "richly harmonised à la Wagner", but if Verdi's string writing here calls to my mind any other opera it is *Aida*. Nannetta's sustained A flat at the end of the duet, above muted strings, is a magical sound. During the chattering ensemble in which the two groups combine, Fenton pursues an independently lyrical vocal line, with the aid of four horns in unison. When Alice repeats her glorious Falstaff quotation [Ex. 125], she is joined in its final bars first by Nannetta and then by the other two ladies. The curtain falls on a shorter and faster version of the tune on which it rose.

The first scene of Act II, introduced by another brief but rousing orchestral passage, consists in the main of the two interviews in which Falstaff is duped, first by Mistress Quickly and then by Ford. It is a scene which abounds in memorable melodic fragments: Quickly's absurdly obsequious "Reverenza", for instance; her "Povera donna" whose words and music are a direct and presumably deliberate quote from Violetta's self-pitying recitative in Act I of *La traviata*; the setting of "dalle due alle tre" (from two to three), the hours in which Ford is said to be absent from home [Ex. 126]. The orchestra later makes witty use of these six notes.

Ex. 126

In each of the two sections into which this scene naturally divides, the Quickly interview and the meeting with "caro Signor Fontana", the two-and-fro dialogue eventually culminates in a solo arioso. When Mistress Quickly leaves, the self-satisfied Falstaff congratulates himself in "Va, vecchio John", an endearingly smug aria of self-love, introduced orchestrally with this elated outburst [Ex. 127]. Ford enters, disguised

Ex. 127

as Signor Fontana, and enlists Falstaff's aid. He mentions a well-known madrigal, the word "madrigal" inciting him to a passage of baroque ornament, and Falstaff immediately begins to sing it. Left alone, Ford gives way to his jealousy in an arioso beginning "È sogno? o realtà?", a remarkable number which would not sound out of place if transposed up a tone and sung by Otello. Here Verdi and Boito explore the dramatic ambiguity of Ford's feelings. We know he is serious in his jealousy, but elsewhere we are invited not to take him seriously. Here, as in more than one number in *Così fan tutte*, there is more than a possibility that too strong a feeling has been aroused, and that the composer is not certain he can contain it within the stylistic framework he has erected. The mood changes as a dandified, overdressed Falstaff returns, to a violin accompaniment of immense gracefulness and charm. After an exchange of elaborate courtesies, the two men leave together as the curtain falls to a fortissimo orchestral repetition of the passage that introduced "Va, vecchio John" [Ex. 127].

Act II, Scene 2, also begins without orchestral ceremony, and is comprised of three short sections of a few minutes each: preparation for Falstaff's arrival; Falstaff's wooing of Alice; the search for Falstaff. The first section hardly calls for much comment. Nannetta's soon to be dispelled tears are expressed in one of Verdi's familiar weeping figures, this time for oboe and strings. When the preparations are complete, Alice leads the other three women in a sparkling little ensemble, which begins with her solo, "Gaie comari di Windsor, è l'ora". As Falstaff is seen to approach, she busies herself with her lute, though the off-stage instrument providing the sound is a guitar. Falstaff makes his advances to the most elegant of music. His arietta, "Quand' ero paggio del Duca di Norfolk" (When I was page to the Duke of Norfolk), which lasts less than half a minute, is a spontaneous and captivating tune with the lightest and most delicate of accompaniments [Ex. 128]. The accent

Ex.128

falls wrongly on the second syllable of "Norfolk": Boito was aware of this, but, finding that his choice lay between a good verse with a bad accent, or *vice versa*, chose the sensible course.

The search music of the last part of the scene is hectic except when Nannetta and Fenton manage to come into close-up. The ensemble in which the unsuspecting lovers sing behind their screen while Ford and his followers creep up on them is a masterpiece of concerted writing, and not at all like any of those more orderly ensembles which are a feature of Verdi's operatic style. This one is fragmented, scattered, with spikily exposed scoring, and underlying it all a sense of gaiety which bursts out in the final moments as Falstaff is tipped into the stream. The curtain falls to a splendid C major flourish of trumpets and decisive chords in the orchestra.

The third act is the only one to begin with an instrumental prelude, albeit a brief one, consisting of an urgently repeated rhythmic figure which rises in pitch and dynamics. The curtain goes up to the sound of a violent fortissimo chord and a downward rush of violins, which sounds as though it is meant to portray or to accompany Falstaff scurrying in wet from his ducking.[1] The fat knight's bitter and pessimistic mood is revealed in the *parlante* arioso of his great soliloquy as well as by the dark colours of the wind instruments. Irritably, he recalls the opening phrase of "Va, vecchio John".[2] The ending of his scena, as he drinks

---

[1] I have seen Tito Gobbi begin the scene thus, and most effectively, although the stage directions require Falstaff to be already seated as the curtain rises.

[2] This scene directly influenced, to use a polite word, the scene in Act II of Richard Strauss's *Der Rosenkavalier* where Ochs is brooding after his fight with Oktavian. In a letter to his librettist Hofmannsthal, Strauss, who considered *Falstaff* one of the greatest masterpieces of all time, wrote: "In Verdi's *Falstaff* there is an amusing monologue at the beginning of the last act; it starts with the words 'Mondo ladro'. I picture the scene of the Baron, after Faninal's exit, similarly: the Baron on the sofa, the surgeon attending to him, the mute servants lined up behind the couch, and the Baron talking in snatches, partly to himself and partly to the others, in turn boastful and sorry for himself, always interrupted by orchestral interludes."

the mulled wine and feels his spirits reviving, is one of the most exhilarating sounds in all music. As the wine warms him, a trill begins in the orchestra, at first on a solo flute, then on some of the strings and wind, then on more, until finally the whole orchestra is engaged in an enormous trill as Falstaff sings, "È il trillo invade il mondo" (And the trill invades the world) [Ex. 129].

Ex. 129

An immediate anti-climax is provided by the sudden appearance of Mistress Quickly with her "Reverenza!" which returns Falstaff to his earlier mood of vindictive fury. But he is soon won over. When Quickly begins her ghost story and leads him into the inn, Alice Ford takes up the eerie tale, in a sepulchural tone assumed for the occasion. The end of the scene magically anticipates the mood of the opening of the final scene as the participants in the evening's plot variously depart and the orchestra's dissolving harmonies gently fade.

The final scene opens with a distant, off-stage horn call, punctuated in the orchestra by a woodwind reminiscence of the lovers' duet from Act I, Scene 2. Fenton's aria, "Dal labbro il canto estasiato vola", is a beautifully gentle love song, exquisitely accompanied. The mood of the orchestra becomes ominous with Falstaff's entrance (the twelve bell strokes of midnight are each individually harmonised by the strings), agitated during his interrupted love scene, and quite beautifully magical again with Nannetta's fairy song, "Sul fil d'un soffio etesio", whose vocal line is delicate and whose accompaniment is unusually

In 1895 Strauss wrote to Verdi, addressing him as "illustrious Master":

"From my own experience I know how annoying dedications can be. Nevertheless, I dare to send you, the true master of Italian opera, a copy of my first work in this category, *Guntram*, as a token of my sincere admiration, and with the hope that you will kindly accept it.

"I can find no words to describe the impression made on me by the extraordinary beauty of *Falstaff*. Consider my dedication as thanks for this reawakening of your genius." (Giuseppe Verdi, *Briefe zu seinem Schaffen*, Frankfurt, 1963.)

ravishing. The threatening music of Falstaff's chastisement sounds innocuous to us, as it should, but it continues to terrify Falstaff for some time. The ladies' quasi-religious unison chant of "Domine fallo casto" (Lord make him pure), and Falstaff's punning reply, "Ma salvagli l'addomine" [Ex. 131] (But save his abdomen), are set by

Ex. 131

Verdi to what sounds suspiciously like a gentle caricature of the tenor's "Hostias" from the *Requiem* [Ex. 130].

Ex. 130

When Ford ironically asks Falstaff, "Who wears the horns now?" the others all echo his question, "Chi è?" and the sheer beauty of the repeated cadence softens the hard edge of their wit at Falstaff's expense. Expansive and memorable phrases from Act II are recalled as Fontana-Ford and Mistress Quickly step forward to be identified. Falstaff admits he has been something of an ass, in a phrase which ends in a distinctly ass-like cadence, peace is made, and Ford orders the ceremony of the Fairy Queen's nuptials to begin, which it does to a charming *allegretto* in 3/4 time, played by violins and flutes, while Ford and the others converse in free melodic phrases above it. The tables are quickly turned on Ford, who gives in gracefully, and Falstaff launches into the mercurially scintillating C major fugue, "Tutto nel mondo è burla" [Ex. 132], whose appropriately Shakespearean import, "All the world's

Ex. 132

a stage, and all the men and women merely players", makes a perfect end to the opera.

There is so much to admire in *Falstaff*, a score whose wit and wisdom are equalled only by Mozart's three great Italian operas: scoring of chamber music delicacy allied to a wide, Beethovenian range of orchestral expression, the magical evocation of forest and fancy in the last scene, and the fantastic pace of the entire opera which seems to last no longer than one sudden flash of inspiration. There is no call for surprise that Verdi wrote such a superb comic opera, even if one has forgotten *Un giorno di regno*. It was Shaw who pointed out the humour in *Un ballo in maschera*, *Rigoletto* and *Otello* (he might well have included Melitone in *La forza del destino*), and added: "It is not often that a man's strength is so immense that he can remain an athlete after bartering half of it to old age for experience; but the thing happens occasionally, and need not so greatly surprise us in Verdi's case."[1]

At its première, *Falstaff* escaped being called Wagnerian, yet it is today often spoken of in the same breath as that considerably heavier and longer comedy, *Die Meistersinger*. A more proper comparison would be with *Parsifal*, the last opera of that other genius born in the same year as Verdi. The temperamental contrast is immense: on the one hand, *fin de siècle* sickliness and piety, and sentimental homerotic religious yearning; on the other, the timeless gaiety, silvery coldness and golden warmth of old age, and the ironic laughter. Both *Parsifal* and *Falstaff* are works of genius, but the world could more easily afford to lose the five hours of *Parsifal* than the less than two hours of *Falstaff*.

[1] Shaw: *Music in London*, (London, 1932) Vol. II, pp. 281–2.

XXVIII

Miscellaneous Works and Last Years

Miscellaneous Works and Last Years

I

Unpublished Juvenilia

The early works include *I deliri di Saul* (The madness of Saul) (see p. 18), a cantata in eight movements for baritone and orchestra which, according to Barezzi, Verdi composed at the age of fifteen, overtures such as the one the fifteen-year-old composer provided to precede a Busseto performance of Rossini's *Il barbiere di Siviglia*, concertos for piano and other instruments, marches, solo pieces for piano or organ, songs and choruses. The young Verdi also composed a certain amount of music for the church at Busseto: a Stabat Mater, for instance, and a Mass for four voices and orchestra.

At the age of forty, Verdi recalled his early works in these words:

From my thirteenth to my eighteenth year, the age at which I went to Milan to study counterpoint, I wrote an assortment of pieces: hundreds of marches for brass band, perhaps the same number of little sinfonie for use in the church, five or six concertos and sets of variations for the pianoforte which I played myself at concerts, several serenades, cantatas, arias, duets, lots of trios, and various pieces of church music of which I remember only a Stabat Mater. In the three years I was in Milan, I wrote very few original compositions: two sinfonie which were performed in Milan at a private concert in the Contrada degli Orefici, I can no longer remember in which house, a cantata performed at the house of Count Renato Borromeo, and various pieces, most of them comic, which my teacher made me do as exercises and which were not even scored. Then back in Busseto I began to write marches, sinfonie, vocal pieces and so on, a complete Mass, a complete set of Vespers, three or four settings of Tantum Ergo and other church music that I can't remember. Among the vocal pieces, there were choruses from the tragedies of Manzoni, for three voices, and *Il cinque Maggio* for solo voice. All that is lost, which is just as well, except for some sinfonie that are still played here but which I have never listened to again, and the Manzoni hymns which I have kept.[1]

The cantata Verdi refers to was a wedding cantata, commissioned by Count Renato Borromeo. *Il cinque Maggio* (The fifth of May) is a setting of Manzoni's poem of that name, an ode on the death of Napoleon.

[1] Reproduced in facsimile in *Nel primo centenario di Giuseppe Verdi* (Milan, 1913).

The church music is known to have included a setting of "Domine ad adiuvandum" for tenor, with flute obbligato, and "Le lamentazioni di Geremia" (The Lamentations of Jeremiah) for baritone. In later life Verdi refused to allow any of these pieces to be published. Many remained in the possession of Antonio Barezzi until his death in 1867. When Barezzi's second wife died in 1895, Verdi retrieved the manuscripts and burned them. He gave instructions that any other early manuscripts should be destroyed on his death. One of the settings of "Tantum Ergo" for voice and orchestra has survived, and is in the Scala Museum. A scena for voice and orchestra, "Io la vidi", most likely a student exercise, is privately owned in Milan, and the sketches for four sacred vocal duets with organ accompaniment are in the Library of Congress in Washington D.C. The researches of Hans F. Redlich and Frank Walker have proved these sketches to be the remnants of twenty-eight vocal duets which probably comprised the music for a Good Friday service in Busseto.

One of the pieces written for the Busseto band was used in Visconti's film of Lampedusa's novel *The Leopard*.

Sei Romanze (1838)

This album of six songs with piano accompaniment, Verdi's first published work, came out in Milan in 1838. The songs in general reveal a strong influence of Bellini, and the piano parts are simple and of little interest.

i. *"Non t'accostare all' urna"* (Do not approach the urn). This setting of a self-pityingly melancholy poem by Jacopo Vittorelli (1749–1835), a minor classical poet, is a graceful and attractive *andante*, with an *allegro* middle section. "Do not approach the urn which contains my ashes. The kind earth will respect my sorrow. I detest your grief, and I refuse the hyacinths you offer. Of what use to the dead are two tears and two flowers?" The feeling of both words and music is very similar to that of Beethoven's "In questa tomba oscura", written thirty years earlier.

ii. *"More, Elisa, lo stanco poeta"* (The weary poet is dying, Elisa). A gentle, sad *adagio*. The poem, by Tommaso Bianchi, is in the same vein as the poem of the preceding song.

iii. *"In solitaria stanza"* (In a lonely room). Another poem by Vittorelli. This time, the poet's beloved is dying, and he begs the gods to save her. The song, a plaintive yet ardent *andante mosso*, contains a quite startling anticipation [Ex. 133] of a phrase from Leonora's "Tacea la notte placida" in *Il trovatore* [Ex. 63].

Ex. 133

Sal - va - te,o Dei   pie - to - - si,

iv. *"Nell' orror di notte oscura"* (In the horror of dark night). Less assured and effective, perhaps, than the preceding songs, and more obviously immature, this is still a pleasant little song. The poem is by Carlo Angiolini.

v. *"Perduta ho la pace"* (I have lost my peace). This is a translation of Margarete's lament, "Meine Ruh' ist hin", from Goethe's *Faust*. The translation is by Luigi Balestra (1808–63), Verdi's Busseto friend who is mentioned in his curious *Lord Hamilton* letter of 1871[1] (see p. 19). Verdi's simple and touching setting, though it does not penetrate to the heart of the matter as does Schubert's famous song "Gretchen am Spinnrade", nevertheless reveals a most sensitive response to the poem. There is more than a suggestion in it of Gilda's "Tutte le feste".

vi. *"Deh, pietoso, oh Addolorata"* (Have mercy, Mother of Pity). This, too, is from Goethe's *Faust*. It is Margarete's prayer to the Virgin, "Ach neige, Du Schmerzensreiche", translated by Balestra. Verdi has provided a beautifully limpid vocal line which, as Carlo Gatti points out, calls to mind parts of the Act II finale of *Nabucco*. The resemblance of the song's *andante cantabile* tune to the descending phrase that Saint-Saëns was to use nearly forty years later to begin the refrain of "Mon cœur s'œuvre à ta voix" in *Samson et Dalila*, though distinct, does not obtrude itself in Verdi's context. (There is a splendid Schubert setting of Goethe's beautiful lines. Unfortunately, being incomplete, it is not well known.)

"L'esule" (The Exile)

The first of three songs published separately in 1839, the year in which *Oberto* was produced, "L'esule" is a setting of a poem by Temistocle Solera, the librettist of *Nabucco*, describing the feelings of an exile in a foreign land as the sun sinks to rest. Although this particular exile's longing is not so much for his native land as for death, the subject was one likely to touch the hearts of those many who had relatives or friends in political exile, and it was one which Verdi and Solera were to return to in *Nabucco*. This is the most extended of the early songs, a scena which opens with a piano introduction descriptive of the melancholy of sunset. The voice enters in recitative which leads to an *andante*, and a lengthy and varied concluding *allegro*. The phrase, "Ed il pianto all' infelice" (And the tears of the unhappy man) [Ex. 134], appears again, years later

Ex. 134

Ed il pian - to al - l'in - fe - li - ce

[1] "Neither in *Lord Hamilton* nor in *Oberto* is there a line by Luigi Balestra." Abbiati, Vol. I, p. 326.

to express a similar feeling, in the lines, "Ritorna al suo natio, ti seguira il mio cor" [Ex. 96], which Elizabeth sings to her lady-in-waiting in *Don Carlo*.

"*La seduzione*" (The Seduction)

This, the second of the songs written and published in 1839, is a setting of an original, but rather awful poem by Luigi Balestra, Verdi's Goethe translator. A beautiful virgin is seduced and, of course, dies. No cross, no stone or tree marks her grave. Verdi's song is sweetly sentimental, but hardly memorable.

"*Notturno: Guarda che bianca luna*" (Nocturne: See, the pale moon)

This delicate trio for soprano, tenor and bass, with flute obbligato, is the third of the 1839 publications. The poem is by Jacopo Vittorelli.

"*Chi i bei di m'adduce ancora*" (Who will bring back the beautiful days?)

This song is a translation, probably by Luigi Balestra, of Goethe's lyric "Erster Verlust", which Schubert set so memorably. Verdi copied it into an autograph album for Sophie de Medici, Marquise of Marignano, on May 6, 1842. The album was discovered in a second-hand bookshop in Naples some years ago, and in 1948 Verdi's song was published for the first time. It is considerably more florid in style than his two earlier Goethe songs. Frank Walker[1] has drawn attention to an anticipation of the love theme, "Di quell' amor", from *La traviata* [Ex. 70] in two different phrases, the most striking instance being [Ex. 135].

Ex. 135

Oh i bei di chi mi ri - tor - na,

Sei Romanze (1845)

This second album of six songs, published in 1845, consists entirely of settings of contemporary Italian poets.

i. "*Il tramonto*" (The Sunset). The nostalgic poem by Verdi's friend Andrea Maffei (1798–1885) describes the sun sinking to rest over a quiet sea. The song has a modest charm.

ii. "*La zingara*" (The Gypsy Girl). This rhythmically lively *allegretto* is one of the most attractive of the set. The poem is by S. M. Maggioni who for some years was a translator attached to the Covent Garden opera.

[1] In an article in *The Music Review*, IX, 1948.

iii. *"Ad una stella"* (To a Star). Maffei's poem apostrophises a star. "How shall my oppressed soul burst its chains and fly to you?" Verdi's suitably elegant setting contains three bars which are better known in their later appearance, in the Alvaro-Carlo duet in Act III of *La forza del destino*, to the words "Or muoio tranquillo".

iv. *"Lo spazzacamino"* (The Chimneysweep). Maggioni's poem tells of the little chimneysweep who calls up to the windows, "Ladies, gentlemen, I will save you from fire for a few pennies", and Verdi's three stanzas with their catchy waltz refrain are delicious. They are preceded by an unaccompanied bar consisting of the child's cry of "Lo spazzacamin". The lightness and rhythmical élan of the music put one in mind of Oscar in *Un ballo in maschera*.

v. *"Il mistero"* (The Mystery). Verdi's *andantino* is somewhat more ambitious than the other songs in the album, but not entirely successful. The mystery of the title lies in the contrast between the poet's calm exterior and the violent romantic agitation of his heart. The overwrought verses are by Felice Romani, the famous librettist.

vi. *Brindisi* (Drinking song). The poem is by Maffei. Verdi's autograph copy of this song differs somewhat from the version published. Both are in F major, but the tessitura of the published version is lower, and Verdi's second thoughts in general seem improvements. I cannot claim the song, in either version, to be a very distinguished piece of music. It is, in fact, rather sluggish.

"Il poveretto" (The Beggar)

The hungry ex-soldier begs for money from the passers-by. Once, he he had fought for his country, which has now forgotten him. The poem is by Maggioni. Verdi's *andante*, written in 1847, is gently affecting, and the accompaniment, though simple, is skilful. This is a rather beautiful little song of its kind: the three bars of piano prelude are no mere marking of time, but a real contribution to the whole [Ex. 136].

Ex. 136

"Suona la tromba" (Sound the Trumpet)

It was at the request of the republican leader Mazzini, whom he had met in London in 1847, that Verdi wrote this setting of patriotic verses by the young romantic poet of the Risorgimento, Goffredo Mameli, who was killed during the fighting in Rome in 1849 at the age of twenty-two.

The song, intended to be "sung among the music of the cannon on the plains of Lombardy", was composed in October 1848 while Verdi was also at work on *La battaglia di Legnano*, and is in the popular style of the patriotic music from that opera. Verdi sent the hymn, as he called it, to Mazzini, with a letter expressing his fear that he may have tried to be too popular and facile, and suggesting that Mazzini burn the manuscript if he thought it not good enough. Mazzini had it published, of course, but, since the fighting was over by the time the song arrived, it was not heard on the battlefields of Lombardy. Nor did it ever achieve the popular success of "Fratelli d'Italia", another Mameli song with music by Michele Novaro (1822–1885), which has survived to become the present Italian national anthem.

"*L'Abandonnée*" (The Forsaken Woman)

This song, lost and forgotten for years, came to light again in 1959 when the British Museum acquired a copy.[1] Composed in Paris for Giuseppina Strepponi, at the time when she and Verdi were living together there, it was published by Léon Escudier in 1849, as a supplement to his magazine *La France Musicale*. An *andante* with a somewhat over-decorated vocal line and an uninteresting accompaniment, its text is a rather dull lament by M.L.E. who is probably Marie Escudier, though Frank Walker thought the initials might stand for "Monsieur Léon Escudier" or "Marie et Léon Escudier".

"*Fiorellin che sorge appena*" (The little flower that rises)

This quite charming song, the words of which are by Francesco Maria Piave, was written in Trieste in 1850 while Verdi and Piave were preparing *Stiffelio* for production. It remained unpublished until 1951, when it was reproduced in Giuseppe Stefani's *Verdi e Trieste*.

La preghiera del poeta (The Poet's Prayer)

The poem is by Nicola Sole. The song, previously unpublished, appeared in the *Rivista Musicale Italiana* in 1941. It was written in 1858 at the time when Verdi was working on *Un ballo in maschera*.

Inno delli nazioni (Hymn of the Nations)

Verdi had reluctantly agreed to represent Italy at the London Exhibition of 1862 and to write a march for performance at the opening ceremony. Discovering that Meyerbeer for Germany and Auber for France were both producing orchestral pieces, he decided to compose a short choral work for the occasion, and commissioned a text from Boito. The resultant Hymn of the Nations, for tenor, chorus and orchestra, a

---

[1] The details of the discovery are given by Frank Walker in an article in *Bulletin* No. 2 of the Institute of Verdi Studies, in which the song is reproduced.

work which lasts about fourteen minutes in performance, was rejected by Michael Costa, the musical director of the Exhibition, on the ground that it was not in accordance with the terms of the commission. It is possible that Costa, a Neapolitan conductor and composer who was at that time also director of the Covent Garden opera, was jealous of Verdi. It is also likely that Verdi's Hymn, which incorporated the music of two famous revolutionary songs, "La Marseillaise" and Novaro's "Fratelli d'Italia", was considered to be dangerously republican. At that time, of course, neither tune was the national anthem of its country.

Verdi wrote indignantly to *The Times*, stating that the Queen's Commissioners had informed him that "twenty-five days (sufficient to learn a whole new opera) were not enough to learn this short cantata, and they refused it. I wish this fact to be known," he continued, "not in order to give importance to a matter of such little account, but only in order to correct the error that I did not deliver my composition."[1] He soon regretted having published his letter for, when his address in Regent's Park was revealed, the next day's post brought "a hail of letters saying God-awful things about the Commission and Costa, and also requests for autographs from all sides in a very odd and thoroughly English manner."[2] He attended the opening of the Exhibition, and heard the music of Sterndale Bennett, Meyerbeer and Auber. To Escudier in Paris, he wrote: "What carried the day was the March by Auber, to whom please give my regards, and also my thanks, because without him I would have composed a March which would have been performed, and which would have bored the balls off me and everybody else."[3]

The London newspapers took Verdi's side against the Exhibition Committee. The *Morning Post* (on May 25, 1862) hoped that Signor Verdi realised the profound indignation felt by the London public at the spurning of his cordial and friendly collaboration. It concluded: "[Verdi] probably believed that the Exhibition Committee was gifted by Providence with common sense, and with some ability to appreciate art and the intentions of the artist. We are sorry for Signor Verdi, the most widely esteemed composer in Europe, and for ourselves as Englishmen and compatriots of that anything but gentlemanly Committee, to find that in these two perfectly legitimate hopes he has been entirely deceived."[4]

When a rival impresario, Colonel Mapleson, arranged to have Verdi's Hymn performed at Her Majesty's Theatre, Costa refused to release Enrico Tamberlick, the tenor for whom Verdi had written the solo part, from his Covent Garden obligations. Verdi was obliged to

---

[1] *Bulletin* of the Institute of Verdi Studies, No. 5, p. 722.
[2] Verdi to Arrivabene, *Bulletin* of the Institute of Verdi Studies, No. 5, p. 724.
[3] Op. cit., p. 725.   [4] Op. cit., p. 729.

alter the solo part to suit Madame Tietjens. The first performance on May 24th, Queen Victoria's birthday, was received with great enthusiasm, and Verdi took six curtain calls. The press notices were favourable, though *The Times* had reservations about the propriety of including "The Marseillaise" and also referred to the "somewhat bombastic stanzas of the poetaster" Boito.[1] Four further performances were given during the following week.

Dyneley Hussey dismisses the work as an "extraordinary farrago", and Verdi himself in later years said of it, "I wrote a cantata in 1861 or 62 for an Exhibition in London, and wrote it badly!"[2] In fact, the Hymn to the Nations is by no means bad, though Boito's lines have to make up in impeccable sentiment what they lack in literary merit:

> Oggi non v'ha
> In quel tempio che Umana Fratellanza.
> E a Dio che'l volle alziani di laudi un canto.

(Today in this temple, there is only human brotherhood. And to God who willed it so, let us offer a song of praise.)

Verdi's music occasionally suggests *Aida*, which was still eight years in the future. After several introductory chords to focus attention, and a brief but important-sounding orchestral introduction, an opening chorus rejoices in the peace that has come to the world. This is followed by a recitative for the solo tenor who is called "The Bard". After his recitative, which sounds like the preamble to "Celeste Aida" improbably lengthened, the tenor sings, to harp accompaniment, a broad and appealing, though somewhat square tune, "Signor, che sulla terra rugiarde spargi e fior" (Lord, who scatters dew and flowers upon the earth), which is repeated by the chorus. In the final section of the Hymn, the revolutionary songs of France and Italy, as well as England's "God Save the Queen", are quoted in the orchestra, while the tenor sings the praises of the three countries respectively. Eventually, all three tunes are heard simultaneously, the tenor representing Italy, the orchestra France, and the chorus England. The "Signor, che sulla terra" tune is repeated by the chorus, a resemblance to Act II, Scene 2, of *Aida* becomes more pronounced, and the work ends in brief, noisy orchestral flurry.

"*Il brigidin*" (The Rosette)

This song, written in 1863 to a poem by Dell' Ongaro, was intended for the soprano Isabella Galetti-Gianoli to sing at a concert in Parma, but the lady quarrelled with her impresario and did not appear at the

---

[1] Quoted by Toye, p. 128.   [2] *Copialettere*, p. 399.

concert. The song appeared in an Italian magazine *Scenario* (Rome), in February, 1941.

Stornello: *"Tu dici che non m'ami"* (You say you do not love me)

A stornello is a type of Tuscan folk-poem. Verdi's light-hearted little song was his contribution to an album whose publication he organised in 1869 for the relief of Piave, who had suffered a stroke which completely paralysed him. The five other composers whom Verdi persuaded to write songs for the album were Auber, Cagnoni, Mercadante, Federico Ricci and Thomas.

String Quartet in E minor

In December 1872, Verdi went to Naples for several weeks to supervise productions of *Don Carlo* and *Aida*. When his soprano, Teresa Stolz, became ill shortly after the *Don Carlo* première, thus causing the rehearsals of *Aida* to be postponed, Verdi occupied himself during March by composing a String Quartet. A few days after the first Naples performance of *Aida*, he invited a few friends to his hotel to hear the Quartet performed. They liked it so well that it was immediately played again; but Verdi professed to consider it a work of no importance, and for some years forbade not only publication but also further performances. When the Mayor of Parma asked for permission to have it played at a concert, Verdi replied:

> I have given no further attention to the Quartet I wrote for mere amusement when I was in Naples some years ago. It was performed at my apartment for a few people who were in the habit of dropping in every evening. This is to tell you that I have never attached any importance to this piece, and for the present at least I do not wish to have it brought forward in any way.[1]

Verdi's attempted suppression of his own Quartet seems to have been connected with his feeling that the Italian musical genius was for opera, and that chamber music ought really to be left to the Viennese school. But eventually he was forced by constant requests from professional and amateur music societies to allow Ricordi to publish the Quartet. In 1877 it was performed at public concerts in Paris, Cologne, Vienna and Milan.[2] Someone in London wanted to perform it with a huge string orchestra of eighty, an idea which appealed to Verdi.

The Quartet is in four movements. The first subject of the opening *allegro* [Ex. 137] is clearly related to the figure in *Aida* which denotes

---

[1] *Copialettere*, p. 302.
[2] The Eulenberg miniature score mistakenly gives 1877 as the year of composition.

Ex. 137

Amneris's jealousy [Ex. 102]. The second movement, an *andantino*, directed to be played "con eleganza", has a wistful, slightly Haydnesque melodic charm and a contrasting, rhythmically violent middle section. The third movement, *prestissimo*, is a light, dancing scherzo, whose trio is a gently flowing cello melody with pizzicato accompaniment from the other strings [Ex. 138]. The last movement, called

Ex. 138

Scherzo Fuga, and directed to be played "allegro assai mosso", is a lively, bustling fugue which looks forward to the gossiping ensemble music of *Falstaff*. The entire Quartet is a most enjoyable work, excellently laid out for the four instruments and formally satisfying. In general, the influence it reveals is that of Haydn, Mozart and Beethoven, copies of whose chamber music Verdi kept by his bedside at Sant' Agata. It combines something of Haydn's fluent gracefulness with the vigour of early Beethoven. As Verdi said to his friend Count Opprandino Arrivabene, when professing not to know whether his quartet was good or bad, "I do know it's a Quartet".[1] In other words, it is not vocal music in disguise, but real quartet writing, skilful in technique and remarkably amiable in character.

Pater Noster

Written for unaccompanied five-part chorus (first and second sopranos, contraltos, tenors and basses), this is a setting of an Italian translation by Dante from the Latin ("volgarizzato da Dante", as the score puts it). In style, it anticipates the larger choral pieces Verdi was to compose fifteen years later. It was written, probably in the autumn of 1879, for the Milan Orchestral Society's second concert on April 18, 1880, which was conducted by Franco Faccio.

Ave Maria

This companion piece to the *Pater Noster* was written for, and performed at, the same concert in 1880. Its text is also by Dante. Scored for solo soprano and string orchestra, it is a simple, appealing piece whose beginning, moving from a recitative-like monotone into melody, foreshadows Desdemona's "Ave Maria" in *Otello*. Its beginning and end, both in B minor, enclose a sentimental but effectively broad and soaring cantabile middle section in the major.

Pietà Signor

Verdi's last song, which he and Boito contributed to a publication called *Fata Morgana*, for the benefit of victims of an earthquake in Sicily and Calabria in November 1894. The song, whose text Boito adapted from the "Agnus Dei", is dignified and restrained in style.

Quattro Pezzi Sacri

The four separate works which have come to be known as the "Four Sacred Pieces" and are frequently performed together, were certainly not intended by Verdi to form parts of a whole. They were written over a number of years, and although Verdi allowed them to be published together, he withdrew the "Ave Maria" from the first

---

[1] Alberti: *Verdi intimo*, p. 456.

performances. The "Laudi alla Vergine Maria" and "Ave Maria" were composed in 1888–9, between *Otello* and *Falstaff*; and the two longer pieces, "Stabat Mater" and "Te Deum", between 1895 and 1897. When performed together, the four pieces are usually sung not in the chronological order of their composition but in the following order: "Ave Maria", "Stabat Mater", "Laudi alla Vergine Maria" and "Te Deum".

Ave Maria. This four-part unaccompanied chorus is written on an "enigmatic scale", consisting of C, D flat, E, F sharp, G sharp, A sharp, B; with the F sharp replaced by F natural in its descending form. The scale was mentioned in an article in the *Gazetta Musicale*, and Boito suggested that Verdi should write an "Ave Maria" using it, as a penance for his blasphemous "Credo" in *Otello*. Verdi pointed out that, since Boito had written the words for Iago's creed, he was the greater culprit, and had better compose a four-part Credo *alla* Palestrina, and put it into a certain work he thought he had better not mention by name. (Verdi meant, of course, *Nerone*, which Boito spent the rest of his life trying to compose.)

Verdi, nevertheless, acted on Boito's suggestion, and wrote a curiously haunting piece which is not without echoes of Palestrina. To him, it was merely an exercise in harmony: in refusing to have it performed in Paris with the other three pieces, he referred to the "Ave Maria" as "not real music but a *tour de force* or charade".[1] Charade or not, its virtuosity does not conceal the beauty of its shifting harmonies.

Stabat Mater. This setting for four-part chorus and orchestra of the medieval Latin poem, Verdi's last work, is a dramatic piece of deeply expressive beauty. There is no liturgical repetition of words: the poem is set as a dramatic text, and Verdi's involvement is with the reality of the scene, the weeping mother standing by the Cross on which her son is dying, rather than with mystical religious reflections upon it. At "Cujus animam", Verdi's familiar weeping figure is heard on violins and clarinets, the ascending accompaniment to the baritones' "Quae moerebat" bathes the text in compassionate warmth, and the broken syllables of "Dum emisit spiritum", falling into the void as Christ dies, are remarkable in their effect [Ex. 139]. The serene loveliness of the

Ex. 139

"Tui Nati" section calls to mind Fauré's *Requiem*: the melodic figure heard first on the word "vulnerati" is particularly like Fauré [Ex. 140].

Ex. 140

Verdi's own *Requiem* is startlingly recalled by the muttering of the chorus in "Per te, Virgo" and by the frenzy of the accompaniment to "Christe, cum sit hinc exire". The confident and exultant climb on the last lines of the poem, "Fac ut animae donetur/Paradisi gloria", is splendidly heart-lifting. Excitement subsides, and the work, one of Verdi's very finest, ends on a pianissimo "Amen".

Laudi alla Vergine Maria. The words, in praise of the Virgin Mary, are from the last canto of Dante's "Paradiso". Verdi's setting for four-part female chorus (or for four solo voices, two sopranos and two contraltos) is a gentle, attractive piece containing beautiful passages of imitative counterpoint, as well as sections of ravishing harmonies. At the first performances in Paris and Turin, when it was sung by four soloists, the "Laudi alla Vergine Maria" was the most enthusiastically received of the three sacred pieces.

Te Deum. Before beginning his "Te Deum", Verdi made a study of other composers' settings of this fourth- or fifth-century canticle. In his opinion, the poem was more than simply a shout of praise. "Towards the middle it changes colour and expression," he observed. "*Tu ad liberandum*—it is Christ born of the Virgin who opens to mankind *Regnum collorum*. Mankind believes in the *Judex venturus*, invokes him in *Salvum fac*, and ends with a prayer, *Dignare Domine die isto*, moving, and sad to the point of terror."[1]

Verdi's "Te Deum", like the "Stabat Mater", is one of his finest works. Written for double chorus and large orchestra, it is more ecclesiastical in tone than the overtly dramatic "Stabat Mater", and less extravertly joyous than most other composers' settings of the "Te Deum". The music is based on two themes of liturgical character, the first of which begins the work, chanted, *senza misura*, by the unaccompanied basses [Ex. 141]. Full chorus and orchestra assemble

Ex. 141
Senza misura

quietly and slowly, to combine in the sudden, magnificent outburst of "Sanctus". A beautiful woodwind phrase, derived from the opening chant, ushers in "Te gloriosus Apostolorum chorus". At "Sanctum quoque", the first sopranos turn the basic thematic figure into a sublime and typically Verdian phrase [Ex. 142]. The second liturgical

Ex. 142   *dolcissimo*

San - ctum _ _ _ _ quo - que, _ _ _ _

theme is heard on the trumpets, to introduce "Tu, Rex gloriae" [Ex. 143]. The choral harmonies in the unaccompanied section beginning

Ex. 143
Un poco piu sostenuto

(DAL CANTO LITURGICO)

at "Salvum fac populum tuum" are overwhelmingly beautiful, and at "et laudamus nomen tuum" we hear again the moving phrase of Ex. 140. "Dignare, Domine" strikingly anticipates the mood, and indeed the rhythm, of the "Libera me" section of Fauré's *Requiem*. Its serenity gives way to wonderfully expressed doubt and uncertainty at "Non confundar in aeternum", and the final "In te, Domine, in te speravi" is born of desperation. A solo soprano voice asserts its faith, heralded and then punctuated by the trumpet's E, and rises with the chorus to a fortissimo top B: but it is with six bars of chordal doubt and gloom in the orchestra that this complex and subtly scored masterpiece ends.

II

After the excitement and exhaustion of *Falstaff*, not only in Milan but also in Rome, where Verdi had gone to superintend the production, the octogenarian composer was able to relax again. Everyone hoped, of course, that he and Boito would collaborate on yet another Shakespeare opera, and Boito actually suggested *Antony and Cleopatra*, which he had recently translated for Eleonora Duse. He also planned a *King Lear* libretto, and began to write the opening scene. But Verdi was not to be rushed. In any case, he probably thought *Falstaff* a reasonably satisfactory end to his operatic career, and Giuseppina warned Boito that he was now too old and tired. He composed ballet music for the Paris production of *Otello*, and even travelled to Paris for the première, at which the President of the Republic presented him with the Grand Cross of the Legion of Honour. The official festivities in Paris in honour of

Verdi went on for several days, after which the Verdis returned to Genoa for most of the winter.

Early in 1895, Verdi consulted Camillo Boito, architect and elder brother of Arrigo, on a project he had been considering for some time: the construction in Milan of a rest home for aged musicians. This generous and imaginative idea and its implementation occupied Verdi a great deal in his last years. He had actually bought the land in 1889, but had shelved the project while he worked on *Falstaff*. Now he was free to give it most of his attention. The rest home was planned to be large enough to accommodate a hundred. Boito had drawn up plans, and Verdi, typically and movingly, behaved as though Camille Boito were one of his librettists: he interfered, made suggestions and improvements, insisting, for instance, on private bedrooms instead of dormitories. Soon, work on the building of the Casa di Riposo per Musicisti began. Verdi started composing again, slowly completing the "Te Deum" and "Stabat Mater", which eventually were to be published and performed in 1898. The "Stabat Mater" was to prove his last completed composition.

In the autumn of 1897, Giuseppina was in bed for several weeks with bronchitis. She recovered, but some weeks later became ill again, and within a few days died of pneumonia, on November 14th. She was eighty-two years of age. Verdi, who was with her when she died, felt completely desolate. She had been his companion almost from the beginning. Her will, after listing various bequests, ended: "Now, farewell, my Verdi. As we were united in life, may God join our spirits together again in Heaven".[1]

Verdi returned to his music, and to the building of his Casa di Riposo. Arrigo Boito had made tentative arrangements for the première of the sacred works in Paris during Easter week, 1898, and Verdi agreed to allow three of the four pieces to be performed: the recent "Te Deum" and "Stabat Mater", and the "Laudi alla Vergine Maria" of ten years earlier. He tended now to divide his time among Sant' Agata, Genoa and Milan, staying in Milan at the Grand Hotel, as always, and paying frequent visits to the building site of the Casa di Riposo. He busied himself with the setting up of a Foundation to run the rest home, and with its registration as a charity. To it he bequeathed the building itself, a large amount of money in Treasury bonds, his credit of two hundred thousand lire with the firm of Ricordi, and all Italian and foreign royalties from his operas. The Casa Verdi, as it is locally known, is still in operation today. If one wanders into its courtyard to visit the graves of Verdi and Giuseppina, one sometimes hears the elderly voice of a resident, singing a Verdi aria.

Boito wrote from Paris of the success of the *Pezzi Sacri*, and Italian performances followed. In July 1900, when King Umberto was assassinated, a prayer written by Queen Margherita moved Verdi to attempt

[1] Abbiati, Vol. IV, p. 618.

a musical setting of it. But only a few sketches exist. Verdi spent the Christmas of 1900 in Milan, visiting his forty-year-old adopted daughter Maria Carrara-Verdi (his aunt's granddaughter, whom he had taken into his home when she was an orphan of seven), and also his old friends Boito, Teresa Stolz and Giulio Ricordi. Early in January, he wrote to a friend: "Even though the doctors tell me I am not ill, I feel that everything tires me. I can no longer read or write. I can't see very well, my feeling grows less, and even my legs don't want to carry me any more. I'm not living, I'm vegetating. What am I doing still in this world?"[1]

On January 21, 1901, as he was dressing in his suite at the Grand Hotel, he suffered a stroke. He survived for a few days, during which time anxious crowds waited outside the hotel for news, the hotel draped itself in black, and straw was laid down in the street to deaden the noise of traffic in case it disturbed him. At ten minutes to three on the morning of January 27th, the eighty-seven-year-old Verdi died peacefully. He had asked for a simple funeral, "without music or singing." His wishes were respected as far as possible, though, as he was laid to rest beside Giuseppina in the municipal cemetery, people in the crowd who had followed the funeral began to weep, and someone, soon joined by others, began softly to sing "Va, pensiero, sull' ali dorate . . ."

When, a month later, both coffins were removed to the now completed Casa di Riposo as Verdi had requested, the occasion was made a state ceremony. Two hundred thousand people lined the black-draped streets of Milan, to say farewell to the greatest and most loved Italian of the nineteenth century. Arturo Toscanini conducted a choir of eight hundred, and the Royal family and Italian Parliament were represented in the funeral procession. Wreaths arrived from all over the world, and were conveyed in the procession to the Casa di Riposo.

Two months later, replying to Camille Bellaigue, who wanted him to collaborate on the biography of the composer, Boito wrote this heartfelt epitaph:

> Verdi is dead; he has carried away with him an enormous quantity of light and vital warmth. We had all basked in the sunshine of his Olympian old age. He died magnificently, formidable and silent. The silence of death had fallen on him a week before he died. . . . My dear friend, in the course of my life I have lost those whom I have idolised, and my grief outweighed my resignation. But never have I experienced such a feeling of hatred against death, such contempt for its mysterious, blind, stupid, triumphant, monstrous power. It needed the death of this nonagenarian to arouse those feelings in me.[2]

CHARLES OSBORNE

Battersea, 1 September, 1967–31 August, 1968

[1] Gatti, Vol. II, p. 503.
[2] *Lettere di Arrigo Boito* (ed. De Rensis, Rome, 1932) p. 331. Boito's letter is in French.

Bibliography

(This list is not exhaustive. It does not, for instance, include any of the plays or poems from which most of Verdi's libretti were drawn; nor does it include those volumes not directly concerned with Verdi, to which I turned for an occasional fact and whose details will be found in footnotes in the text.)

ABBIATI, FRANCO: *Giuseppe Verdi* (4 vols., Milan, 1959).

ALBERTI, ANNIBALE (Ed.): *Verdi intimo* (Verona, 1931).

BASEVI, ABRAMO: *Studio sulle opere di Giuseppe Verdi* (Florence, 1859).

BELLAIGUE, CAMILLE: *Verdi* (Paris, 1912).

BOITO, ARRIGO: *Lettere di Arrigo Boito* (Ed. Raffaelle de Rensis. Milan, 1932).

CESARI, GAETANO and LUZIO, ALESSANDRO (Eds.): *I Copialettere di Giuseppe Verdi* (Milan, 1913. Reissued Bologna, 1968).

CHECCHI, EUGENIO: *G. Verdi (1813–1901)*, (Florence, 1901).

CROWEST, FREDERICK J.: *Verdi, Man and Musician* (London, 1897).

DE RENSIS, RAFFAELLE: *Franco Faccio e Verdi* (Milan, 1934).

ESCUDIER, LÉON: *Mes Souvenirs* (Paris, 1863).

GARIBALDI, FRANCO TEMISTÓCLE: *Giuseppe Verdi nella vita e nell' arte* (Florence, 1904).

GARIBALDI, LUIGI AGOSTINO (Ed.): *Giuseppe Verdi nelle lettere di Emanuele Muzio ad Antonio Barezzi* (Milan, 1931).

GATTI, CARLO: *Verdi nelle immagini* (Milan, 1941). (The copy in my possession is of the German translation, *Verdi im Bilde* (Milan, 1941.)

GATTI, CARLO: *Verdi* (2 vols., Milan, 1931. Reissued in one volume, 1951). (An abridged English translation, *Verdi, the Man and His Music*, was published in London, 1955.)

HUSSEY, DYNELEY: *Verdi* (London, 1941: revised edition 1963).

KÜHNER, HANS: *Giuseppe Verdi in Selbstzeugnissen und Bilddokumenten* (Hamburg, 1961).

LUMLEY, BENJAMIN: *Reminiscences of the Opera* (London, 1864).

LUZIO, ALESSANDRO (Ed.): *Carteggi Verdiani* (4 vols., Vols. I and II, Rome, 1935. Vols. III and IV, Rome, 1947).

MARTIN, GEORGE: *Verdi, His Music, Life and Times* (London, 1965).

MONALDI, GINO: *Verdi, 1839–1898* (Turin, 1899. Reissued 1926).

NARDI, PIERO: *Vita di Arrigo Boito* (Milan, 1942).

POUGIN, ARTHUR: *Giuseppe Verdi: Histoire Anecdotique de sa vie et de ses œuvres* (Paris, 1886. An Italian translation had already appeared in Milan, 1881).

ROOSEVELT, BLANCHE: *Verdi: Milan and "Othello"* (London, 1887).

SCHLITZER, FRANCO: *Inediti Verdiani nell archivo dell' Accademia Chigiana* (Siena, 1953).

SHEEHAN, VINCENT: *Orpheus at Eighty* (London, 1959).

SOFFREDINI, ALFREDO: *Le opere di Verdi, studio critico analitico* (Milan, 1901).

TOYE, FRANCIS: *Giuseppe Verdi: his Life and Works* (London, 1931. Reissued 1962).

VALORI, LE PRINCE DE: *Verdi et son oeuvre* (Paris, 1895).

VERDI, GIUSEPPE: *Autobiografia dalle lettere* (Ed. Carlo Graziani, Verona, 1941) ("Carlo Graziani" was the pseudonym of Aldo Oberdorfer. The second edition, in 1951, was published under his real name.)

VISETTI, ALBERT: *Verdi* (London, 1905).

WALKER, FRANK: *The Man Verdi* (London, 1962).

WERFEL, FRANZ: *Verdi: Roman der Oper* (Vienna, 1924. English translation, *Verdi*, published in London, n.d.).

WERFEL, FRANZ and STEFAN, PAUL: *Giuseppe Verdi, Briefe* (Vienna, 1926. English translation, *Verdi, the Man in His Letters* published in New York, 1942).

The Bulletins of the Institute of Verdi Studies (Istituto di Studi Verdiani), Parma, on *Un ballo in maschera* (3 vols. 1960) and *La forza del destino* (3 vols. 1961, 1962, 1965); The notebooks ("quaderni") on *Il corsaro* (1963), *Gerusalemme* (1963) and *Stiffelio* (1968).

Index

Page numbers in italics refer to the principal references to the works in question.

A NOTE ON THE TYPE

THE TEXT of this book was set on the Monotype in a type face called Baskerville, a modern recutting of a type originally designed by John Baskerville (1706–75). Baskerville, a writing master in Birmingham, England, began experimenting about 1750 with type design and punch-cutting. His first book, set throughout in his new types, was a Virgil in royal quarto, published in 1757, and it was followed by other famous editions from his press. Baskerville's types, which are distinctive and elegant in design, were a forerunner of what we know today as the "modern" group of type faces.

Printed and bound by the Haddon Craftsmen, Scranton, Pennsylvania.